# MODERN SHORT BIOGRAPHIES AND AUTOBIOGRAPHIES

*Edited by*

MARSTON BALCH

*Professor of English, Tufts College*

NEW YORK

HARCOURT, BRACE AND COMPANY

PRINTED IN THE UNITED STATES OF AMERICA

*To*
*My Mother*

# PREFACE

A STORY is told about Voltaire, who among his countless achievements was familiar with the pitfalls of biography. A Parisian of some distinction whom he cordially detested had died, and friends of Voltaire insisted that the occasion called for a few words of public condolence. After holding out for a long time, Voltaire consented to issue a statement. "I have just been informed," he wrote, "that Monsieur Blank is dead. He was a sturdy patriot, a gifted writer, a loyal friend, and an affectionate husband and father—provided he is really dead."

The ancient maxim, "Of the dead nothing but good," is here twisted with sly cynicism to read, "Nothing good of people until they are dead." Had either of these precepts prevailed in the twentieth century, this book and the whole body of literature it stands for could never have existed. But candor has in our time appeared the better part of discretion. Just as the discreetly posed daguerreotype has yielded place to the candid camera's fresh and informal angle shots and to the subtler light-and-shadow of a Steichen photograph, so the memoir, the eulogy, and the formal critical essay have developed into the searching biographical portrait. Whether mainly journalistic or historical or psychological, whether projected against the whole social panorama or drawn with deft strokes in the small frame of an intimate, individual study, the modern short biography is more dramatic and more living in its re-creation of the experience and impression of personality. In it the intellectual forces of many of our greatest writers have been mobilized to make the reality of the past and present permanent.

When the first edition of this anthology was published five years ago the swollen wave of modern biography had just turned the crest and plunged swirling over the sands of literature. It was clear then that this was more than an ordinary comber, that it would not merely crash and recede again to be as quickly forgotten. For it came with all the impetus accumulated from its alliance with history, fiction, drama, painting, journalism, psychology, and other sources of power. Moreover, despite resistance in some quarters, it was a welcome invasion; it filled a gap in modern life and letters. Since then the initial surge has subsided, the foam has clarified, the mist evaporated. But the ground won has largely been retained and the position consolidated, and biography has taken its place as an integral form of human expression. It is now possible to study its gains with an impartial mind and to appraise its shortcomings frankly and confidently. More than this, since modern biography's strongest points are its human interest and vitality and its vast range of exploration, there is assured enjoyment in it today for every kind of reader. And nearly all its aspects can be appreciated and enjoyed in the form of the short biographies chosen here from twenty years of writing.

Besides providing an enlarged and up-to-date survey of a special type of life-writing which has attracted biographers both great and small, the present collection extends its scope to autobiography, and in the first eleven pieces shows how the modern writer tackles the problems of self-revelation. The order of progression through these, as through the straight biographies that follow, is in general from the near to the remote in subject matter, from the subjective to the objective in the author's attitude, and from the more conventional to the rarer modes of technique and style. Here and there this procedure is varied slightly to bring together groups of pieces with a common interest, such as college experiences or business or political affairs. Besides being arranged in a comfortable sequence for enjoyment rather than in the accidental order of chronology, the twenty-six pieces are whole and unabridged, with the exception of three—those by Perry, Smith, and Untermeyer—which were slightly abbreviated to form more concise reading units.

This book, like its briefer predecessor, is intended primarily for the college student, both as an introduction to the humanizing literature of biography and as a volume of typical contemporary writing. It aims also to give pleasure and information to the general reader who has perhaps not yet explored this rich and exciting field or who, having done some private reconnoitering, desires to have in one collection representative works of the leading modern biographers. Three specific aids are provided: an introductory essay setting forth the chief historical motives and methods of biographers and their present reach and grasp, with special reference to the forms illustrated in the book; separate prefatory notes acquainting the reader rather fully with the life and work of the individual authors; and a good-sized bibliography to suggest further material for independent study. If here and there the book may stimulate a reader to attempt to put down on paper his reconstruction of a human life he has observed or that one good story everyone is said to have in him—his own—it will also caution the inexperienced confessor or portraitist against the major hazards of life-writing. We may well add that even as these selections have survived the test of public judgment they can in turn serve as an index of the reader's own intellectual curiosity and human sympathy, of his apprehension of the biographer's great task in "weighing souls" and perpetuating lives.

The obligations incurred by the anthologist of modern literature are numerous and frequently personal. The editor is pleased to acknowledge his indebtedness to the following authors and publishers who have courteously permitted the reprinting of these selections:

Louis Adamic, for "After Nineteen Years," from *The Native's Return*, copyright, 1934, by Louis Adamic, published by Harper and Brothers, New York.

D Appleton-Century Company, Inc., for "The Sorrows of the Young Werther," from *Mape: The World of Illusion*, by André Maurois, translated from the French by Eric Sutton, copyright, D. Appleton-Century Company, Inc., 1926.

Coward-McCann, Inc., for "An Adventurer Out of the West," from *Lonely Americans*, by Rollo Walter Brown, copyright, 1929, by Coward-McCann, Inc., New York.

Floyd Dell, for "Christmas," from *Homecoming*, copyright, 1933, by Floyd Dell, published by Farrar and Rinehart, Inc., New York.

John Dos Passos, for "Tin Lizzie," from *U. S. A.*, copyright, 1930, 1932, 1933, 1934, 1935, 1936, 1937, by John Dos Passos, published by Harcourt, Brace and Company, Inc., New York.

E. P. Dutton & Company, Inc., for "Thoreau at Walden," from *The Flowering of New England*, by Van Wyck Brooks, copyright, 1936, by E. P. Dutton & Company, Inc., New York.

Janet Flanner, for "Mr. Ambassador," reprinted by arrangement with the editors of *The New Yorker*.

Wolcott Gibbs, for "Time . . . Fortune . . . Life . . . Luce," reprinted by arrangement with the editors of *The New Yorker*.

Philip Guedalla, for "The Stepfather of the United States: H.M. King George III," from *Fathers of the Revolution*, copyright, 1926, by Philip Guedalla, published by G. P. Putnam's Sons, Inc., New York and London.

John Gunther, for "Generalissimo Chiang Kai-shek," from *Inside Asia*, published by Harper and Brothers, New York. Copyright, 1938, 1939, by John Gunther.

Harcourt, Brace and Company, Inc., for "Going to College," from *The Autobiography of Lincoln Steffens*, copyright, 1931, by Harcourt, Brace and Company, Inc.; for "Storm Center in Brookline," from *From Another World*, by Louis Untermeyer, copyright, 1939, by Harcourt, Brace and Company, Inc.; for "The Council of Four," from *Essays in Biography*, by John Maynard Keynes, copyright, 1933, by Harcourt, Brace and Company, Inc.; for "Florence Nightingale," from *Eminent Victorians*, by Lytton Strachey; for "Miss Ormerod," from *The Common Reader*, by Virginia Woolf, copyright, 1925, by Harcourt, Brace and Company, Inc. Used by permission of the publishers.

Harper and Brothers, for "The Wife of Abraham Lincoln," from *Wives*, by Gamaliel Bradford, copyright, 1926. Reprinted by permission of and arrangement with Harper and Brothers, publishers, New York.

Houghton Mifflin Company, Inc., for "These Crude Young Men," from *And Gladly Teach*, by Bliss Perry, copyright, 1935, by Bliss Perry, published by Houghton Mifflin Company, Inc., Boston, Massachusetts; for "J. D. Marstock," from *Some People*, by Harold Nicolson, copyright, 1936, by Houghton Mifflin Company, Inc., Boston. Reprinted by permission of the publishers.

Alfred A. Knopf, Inc., for "Father Sends Me to the World's Fair," reprinted from *Life with Father*, by Clarence Day, copyright, 1935, by Clarence Day, by permission of and special arrangement with Alfred A. Knopf, Inc., authorized publishers.

Corliss Lamont and Granville Hicks, representing the Harvard Alumni John Reed Committee, for "Almost Thirty," by John Reed, reprinted from *The New Republic*, 1936.

Little, Brown and Company, Inc., for "Knowing Walt Whitman," from

*Unforgotten Years,* by Logan Pearsall Smith. Copyright, 1938. Reprinted by permission of Little, Brown and Company, Inc., Boston.

The Liveright Publishing Corporation, for "P. T. Barnum," from *Strenuous Americans,* by R. F. Dibble, copyright, 1923, by Boni and Liveright, Inc., New York.

Emil Ludwig and Robert M. McBride and Company, for "Mussolini," from *Nine Etched from Life,* copyright, 1934, by Emil Ludwig, published by Robert M. McBride and Company, New York.

The Macmillan Company, for "Woodrow Wilson," from *Masks in a Pageant,* by William Allen White, copyright, 1928, by The Macmillan Company, New York.

Vincent Sheean, for "The Modern Gothic," from *Personal History,* copyright, 1934, 1935, by Vincent Sheean, published by Doubleday, Doran and Company, Inc.

The Viking Press, Inc., for "Vocation," from *A Portrait of the Artist as a Young Man,* by James Joyce, copyright, 1916, by B. W. Huebsch, Inc., New York.

The editor is also deeply grateful to the following authors, who have not only given their consent to reprint their biographies but have through personal interviews or letters supplied valuable information upon their professional methods: Mr. Louis Adamic, Mr. Rollo Walter Brown, Mr. Floyd Dell, Mr. John Dos Passos, Miss Janet Flanner, Mr. Wolcott Gibbs, Mr. Philip Guedalla, Herr Emil Ludwig, M. André Maurois, The Hon. Harold Nicolson, Professor Bliss Perry, and Mrs. Virginia Woolf. He wishes to thank, too, his colleagues, Professor John Holmes, Mr. Donald T. Brodine, and Mr. Paul H. Flint, who assisted him in making the final selection; his students, whose candid criticisms lent their support to the choices; Mrs. Elizabeth Bryant, who lightened the labor on the manuscript; and his wife, Germaine Cornier Balch, who lessened the book's factual and stylistic errors. To others, who are obliged to remain nameless, the editor is indebted for the constant coöperation and advice which made the book possible.

M. B.

*Medford, Massachusetts*
*November 1939*

# CONTENTS

# MODERN SHORT BIOGRAPHIES
## AND AUTOBIOGRAPHIES

# INTRODUCTION

## I. BIOGRAPHY

*The proper study of mankind is man.*
—ALEXANDER POPE

BIOGRAPHY is almost as necessary to human life as life is to biography. The farther back we extend our knowledge of mankind's existence on this planet, the stronger grows the conviction that even to prehistoric man the desire to preserve a record of himself was only second to the desire to preserve himself. Life-writing in all its aspects occupies a considerable portion of the human race today, since without it every branch of man's activity would be crippled and one of his strongest instincts thwarted.

The first biographical work was the rude memorial of a man's existence painted or scratched on a monument of stone. The man lived and died, having distinguished himself from his fellows in some manner that seemed worthy to record in brief but lasting form. Perhaps his patriarchal rank claimed this respect from his family. Perhaps some feat of arms or some personal merit impelled his followers to attempt to defy time with a tablet to his honor. At all events, here, however fragmentary, was the record of an individual life preserved for his survivors. From epitaphs inscribed in stone or bronze to longer and less perishable accounts written or printed in books in later ages this has been the primary aim of biography—to perpetuate a man's memory.

But a secondary aim was soon discovered. It was seen that the simple act of commemoration might readily be turned to account as an example of how other lives should be lived. Fables are vivid teachers of behavior; made to order, they point straight to the inevitable moral. But fables are essentially fiction, and to just that extent less impressive than "the plain undoctored incident that

1

actually occurred," especially when a true story is ready at hand. "So-and-so," remarked the moralist, "was a great man—the best we ever had. What better model for our children than his life? Let us set it down and say to everyone who comes to read: 'Go thou and do likewise.'" So to the commemorative purpose was added the didactic, and the struggle for biographical truth and individuality began.

The didactic purpose has always been very strong, so strong that it has produced most of the biographical writing in the world. It has given us both statues and gargoyles—monumental abstractions, that is, of The Father of His Country, The Captain of Industry, The Empire Builder, The Loving Parent, The Loyal Son, The Patriot, The Saint, all wool and a yard wide; and the less dull but equally far-fetched grotesques of their opposites, The Sinner, The Scoundrel, The Renegade, The Good Man Gone Wrong, The Patriot Off His Pedestal. All this may have been useful in moral teaching but it has contributed little to the literature of biography, whereas the desire to commemorate the worthy has led to the gradual development of the portrayal and interpretation of individuals in all the varieties of their personality.

Why this should be so is clearly implicit in the ancient words of Ecclesiasticus:

Let us now praise famous men, and our fathers that begat us. The Lord manifested in them great glory, even his mighty power from the beginning. Such as did bear rule in their kingdoms, and were men renowned for their power, giving counsel by their understanding, such as have brought tidings in prophecies: leaders of the people by their counsels, and by their wise understanding men of learning for the people; wise were their words in their instruction: such as sought out musical tunes, and set forth verses in writing: rich men furnished with ability, living peaceably in their habitations: all these were honoured in their generations, and were a glory in their days. There be of them, that have left a name behind them, to declare their praises. And some there be, which have no memorial; who are perished as though they had not been born; and their children after them. But these were men of mercy, whose righteous deeds have not been forgotten. With their seed shall remain continually a good inheritance; their children are in their testaments. Their seed standeth fast, and their children for their sakes. Their seed shall remain for ever, and their glory shall not be blotted out. Their bodies were buried in peace, and their name liveth to all generations. Peoples will declare their wisdom, and the congregation telleth out their praise.

The writer who sets out thus to commemorate his hero seeks, if he knows his business, to reveal the singularities of the man, those qualities and acts that made him *different* from other people and therefore memorable. The didactic writer, on the other hand, intent on the lesson he is teaching, is likely to view his subject not as an individual but as a representative, as a model of some virtue or vice; hence he does not favor those elements which are peculiar to his subject alone. More to his purpose are the characteristics which his subject possessed in *common* with all men of his type and which the reader may therefore take straight to heart and either emulate or shun. So strong has been the ethical purpose in biography that probably the greater number of lives have been written under its dictation. Yet had it succeeded in dominating the field, we should not now be interested in biography. For it is essentially the desire to understand rather than to imitate men, to become intimately acquainted with their lives rather than to find edifying formulas in them, that has led biographers to seek more and more skillful and satisfying means of interpretation and portrayal.

This desire to understand men and to distinguish them from all others led to the first conscious separation of biography, the record of an individual, from history, the record of a race or nation. Admirable biographies are to be found in both Testaments of the Bible. The Book of Ruth and the Gospel According to St. Luke, to name but two, afford models which may be profitably compared with the most modern life-writing. Not until Plutarch, however, was it clearly stated how this individualizing is to be done. Plutarch was a philosopher rather than historian; he cared less for politics and the fortunes of states, more for personality and the motives and acts of men. His *Lives of the Noble Greeks and Romans* is not only one of the few classics of biography; it is also the earliest and one of the best of biographical manuals. Although a moralist writing of the great, he recognized the responsibility of the biographer to reveal the subject as he lived, and knew that this was not to be accomplished by panegyric or history or romance, but only by selective portraiture. This he makes amply clear in the opening words of his *Life of Alexander*:

> It being my purpose to write the lives of Alexander the king, and of Caesar . . . , the multitude of their great actions affords so large a field that . . . I have chosen rather to epitomize the most celebrated parts of their story, than to insist on every particular circumstance of it. It must be borne in mind that my design is not to write histories, but lives. And the most glorious exploits do not always furnish us with the clearest discoveries of virtue or vice in men; sometimes a matter of less moment, an expression or a jest, informs us better of their characters and inclinations, than the most famous sieges, the greatest armaments, or the bloodiest battles whatsoever. Therefore as portrait-painters are more exact in the lines and features of the face, in which the character is seen, than in the other parts of the body, so I must be allowed to give my more particular attention to the marks and indications of the souls of men, and while I endeavour by these to portray their lives, may be free to leave more weighty matters and great battles to be treated of by others.

This first master biographer not only realized the major problems of his task; he solved them. Instead of ignoring the trivial acts and awkward inconsistencies of his subjects, Plutarch sought them out for the evidence they afforded of the true motives and underlying individuality of each man; for example, Julius Caesar's attempts to overcome his bodily frailty and disease by coarse diet, hard riding, continuous exercise, and sleeping in chariots or litters. To draw forth the telling contrasts of character he invented the parallel biography. He arranged in pairs, a Greek with a Roman, forty-six notables of the ancient world, and, after narrating their lives with all the vividness and truth which his technique provided, compared them in detail. So authoritative was his precept and so successful his practice that the greatest biographers from then until our own day have acknowledged his leadership.

Centuries later another master biographer, Samuel Johnson, found it necessary to reassert the need for the close-up "domestic" view:

> The business of the biographer is often to pass slightly over those performances and incidents which produce vulgar [*i.e.*, popular] greatness, to lead the thoughts into domestick privacies, and display the minute details of daily life, where exterior appendages are cast aside, and men excel each other only by prudence and by virtue.

Again, in the nineteenth century, the counsel is reaffirmed by the French biographer Sainte-Beuve with even stronger emphasis:

> To get inside of your author, to take possession of him, to reveal him under varied aspects; to make him live, move, and speak as he must have done, to pursue him into his own home and even into his domestic life as far as one can penetrate; to fasten him down on every side to this earth, this real existence, these everyday habits on which great men are as dependent as the rest of us.

And we hear it again and again whenever the modern biographer confides to us the open secrets of his profession. Strachey, Bradford, Maurois, Nicolson, and all the others who have expounded their craft from various angles agree on this point, that, in the words of Emil Ludwig, "the most trivial habit will often suggest the interpretation for some major trait of character."

However, trivial habits—those "matters of less moment" of which Plutarch wrote—will not of themselves guarantee a true biography. It is unfortunately only too easy to bring together a curious eccentricity, a private foible, a single striking aberration, and call the result a portrait. Dr. Johnson may have carried orange peelings in his pocket and touched every lamppost on his walks; George Washington may have occasionally "flown off the handle." To set down Johnson as a mere oddity and Washington as an essentially profane man with an uncontrollable temper is to miss the forest for the trees. Yet ever since Plutarch's contemporary Suetonius, the keyhole columnist of imperial Rome, compiled his scandalous *Lives of the Twelve Caesars* there have been writers willing and even eager to make spicy gossip about the great. If one cannot rise to fame oneself, there is, it would seem, a human satisfaction in pulling down the famous from their pedestals. So biography in all times has had its yellow journalists and its "debunkers." Also it has known writers who, although without malice, were nevertheless ignorant of the proper function of anecdote and would permit single incidents that happened to be amusing or unusual to give the prevailing color to whole portraits. Anecdote is indispensable to biography, for it supplies particulars that render the subject individual and lifelike. But to have any real biographical value, an anecdote must, first of all, reveal a salient characteristic of the man rather than an accidental trivality, and, secondly, it must be untransferable, something characteristic of that particular man only. To find and select the truly character-revealing instances, subordinating all items which are untrue to the man's prevailing tendency and rejecting those which are common to most men of his class or period or profession, is one of the important workshop tasks of every biographer. When anecdotes so scrupulously chosen to reveal fair-mindedly the subject's many-faceted personality are then told with narrative skill, they may be worth more than a dozen descriptive or expository chapters.

The correction of false readings of character can be made, of course, only after a knowledge of the truth, the biographical truth, about the subject; that is, truth to fact and truth to impression. The sources of this truth will be found in whatever materials or memories the subject left behind him. Especially valuable are his autobiography, if he wrote one; his reminiscences of people and events he knew, and the memoirs of persons who knew him; his diary, if he kept one; his personal letters, in which his character should be discernible through several phases of his life; if he was an author or a creator of any sort, his works; all miscellaneous pictures and relics of his past; and finally, the unwritten testimony of his close acquaintances, preferably the biographer himself.

One of the first biographers to attempt any systematic compilation of such material about people of importance was the "shiftless . . . roving and magotie-headed" John Aubrey, a charter member of the Royal Society whose appetite for exact and out-of-the-way facts was a lifelong obsession. Wintering in London and spending the rest of the year on horseback on a round of visits to friends in the shires, he gathered baskets of notes, accurate, lively, and unique. Thus it is to Aubrey that we owe the description of Milton's peculiar way of pronouncing "r," of Sir Francis Bacon's eyes—"he had a delicate hazel eie and Dr. Harvey told me it was like the eie of a viper"—and of the old philosopher Hobbes's daily habit of long hikes and brisk tennis matches and his nightly custom of singing in bed—"not that he had a very good voice, but for his health's sake." After Aubrey in time but far superior in results, James Boswell will always remain the biographer's model of thoroughness in research. Long before Johnson strolled into Thomas Davies's bookshop in Drury Lane on Monday the 16th of May, 1763, and met his future biographer, Boswell had begun training himself to hold intelligent interviews with celebrities, retain the language and tone of long conversations, take copious and accurate notes, verify every source of knowledge, analyze and appraise difficult material, narrate events and depict features tellingly, and instill life and order and movement into the reconstruction of human careers. Although Boswell was actually with Johnson a total of less than twelve months, he gathered and classified every scrap of information about him, followed him everywhere, plied him with incessant queries and jotted down the replies, corresponded with Johnson when absent from London, studied all his writings, and when Johnson died in 1784, set to work amid private wretchedness and public opposition and produced after seven years a *Life* of acknowledged permanence and supremacy.

With the growth of material and the improvement of scholarship, however, a new danger besets biography. In the laudable effort to tell the whole truth arises a strong, often unconquerable temptation to put the stress upon sheer accumulation of factual evidence. To insist upon including every vestige of information bearing in any way on the subject tends to obscure the person and overwhelm the book with quotations and footnotes, producing not a narrative but a document, a static array of "cold roast facts," verified and ticketed but unreadable and for all their accuracy rather inhuman. This is all the more likely if the scholarly biographer is a critic, scientist, historian, or any other sort of specialist dealing with a figure and an epoch in his own vocation —unless, as with Boswell, that vocation is biography. His professional interests, which ought to increase his intimate understanding of the subject's career, too frequently only give occasion for a vast record of contemporaneous events and circumstances or for a compendious, de-personalized treatise on the special field. Hence we get "those two fat volumes" of which Strachey writes so feelingly, "with their ill-digested masses of material, their slip-shod style, their tone of tedious panegyric, their lamentable lack of selection, of detachment, of design." Victorian libraries were full of them. "They are as familiar as the *cortège* of the under-taker, and wear the same air of slow, funereal barbarism." Here we see individuality sacrificed to one kind of biographical truth.

The other kind meanwhile is in just as precarious a position. For whereas it takes scholarship and patient industry to find and organize the truth of fact into a faithful reconstruction of a man's career and an expert estimate of his achievement, it re-quires courage, among other things, to convey the truth of im-pression, to give an equally faithful picture of his manner of life and an unbiased interpretation of his character. And courageous impartiality is not a quality we are born with. To subdue the natural emotional urge to praise the famous or beloved dead—*de mortuis nil nisi bonum*—demands a highly educated sense of the ultimate values of life-writing. This was scarcely known in earlier times, and is, in every age, excessively hard to cultivate. Harold Nicolson, the English writer and student of biography, thinks that in periods of religious and moral stability, like the Victorian, this kind of truth is hardly to be expected, but is in general a manifestation peculiar to eras of doubt and unrest like our own.

However this may be, it is not the whole story. For even with the firmest of critical intentions, the biographer is still but half-armed for his task until he possesses that rarest of all skills, an accurate insight into the sources and motives of character. It is the problem again of understanding man, and not man only but men as individuals. This could never be solved so long as people were content with mere recitals of external deeds and honors or with catalogues and criticisms of works. It could come only with man's growing curiosity about his inner life, his personality. As the biographer needs the factual discipline of the scholar and his-torian, he must have in no less degree the taste and ability of the psychologist to tap the physical, mental, and emotional springs of motive and tell us not only the *what* but also the *why* of human behavior. In the words of Edward H. O'Neill:

Biography is, or should be, the study of personality, and the artistic biographer has the right and duty to use every legitimate device to explain and interpret his subject. If he is to be successful, he must so present the man or woman of whom he is writing that the reader will be able to follow the subject not on the printed page but in his imagination to the point where he actually knows that man and woman better than, or at least as well as, they knew themselves. One of the fascinations of biography is that the reader can know the great, the near-great, the famous, and the notorious of all time when their stories are unfolded by writers who are something more than mere chroniclers.

The most modern contribution to this "something more" has been psychology, the science of the human mind and its workings, normal and abnormal. It is the most valuable tool in the biographer's kit, for with it he can understand and explain completely all the unusual thoughts and manners and deeds of the man whose life he is trying to present. Among the authors included in this book Ludwig, Maurois, and Bradford make continual use of it, while outside this volume, in the works of Carl Sandburg, Katharine Anthony, and others, the drafts levied upon psychological data are enormous.

"As a matter of fact," to quote Mark Longaker, "every good biographer is a good psychologist, but every good psychologist is not necessarily a good potential biographer." In order that the reconstruction of a life shall be not only individual and true but also properly framed by chronology and background, biography requires more than the mere employment of psychological principles. We have seen in the past generation a number of striking miscarriages from the single-minded application to life-writing of psychology, and especially of its derivative science, psychoanalysis—Freudian studies of Poe, of Catherine the Great, of Herman Melville, of Dostoevsky—astonishing and plausible explanations of abnormality but of limited value as records of lives. Psychoanalysis is as yet too much an infant science to be made the mainstay of a biography. When in the hands of a gifted writer it can be combined with biography's other tools, it may in time produce works of a value unguessed today.

Meanwhile one of the most interesting methods of presenting a subject's life has been developed by Emil Ludwig and widely imitated in America. Out of his experience and predilection as a playwright Ludwig, who also brought to biography undoubted gifts of psychological insight and remarkable pictorial powers, saw the careers of his heroes as dramatic plots in three or five acts and centered his attention on the personal struggles that ended in victory or more often in defeat. Provided the imagination is kept well under control, as it usually is with Ludwig, this method is capable of giving tremendous sweep, contrast, climax, and even suspense to the biographies of such men as he chooses to depict— titanic geniuses in whose personal fortunes are wrapped the destinies of movements or of states. With less dramatic subjects and in less able hands, the results have frequently been lamentable.

Another modern development, more in evidence in 1925 than today, is that of bringing to the task of biography the novelist's creative and narrative talents. We should like the reconstruction of a life to be not only individual and true but also permanently expressive. For of what value is a heap of relics, however authentic, if the quickening imagination is lacking to restore their living aspects and significance, and if there is not enough narrative and pictorial skill to communicate these powerfully to the reader? Soon after Ludwig began producing his dramatic biographies, Lytton Strachey and André Maurois showed what could be accomplished when certain methods hitherto monopolized by fiction-writers were used to help re-create incidents and emotions. The chief innovation of Strachey was inference, and the most striking example is the final paragraph of his *Queen Victoria,* in which he describes what he conjectures to have passed through the dying Queen's mind:

> Yet, perhaps, in the secret chambers of her consciousness, she had her thoughts, too. Perhaps her fading mind called up once more the shadows of the past to float before it, and retraced, for the last time, the vanished visions of that long history. . . .

Notice that Strachey is not inventing facts; he is not even pretending to relate them. He is merely throwing out plausible suggestions to explain what no man can know. The word that must not be overlooked amid this enchanting prose is the repeated

"perhaps." Other writers, and sometimes Strachey himself, neglected to include this "perhaps," with the result that the new
biography as a class was brought under suspicion.

While the possibilities of inference were being explored, another method was employed by Maurois to recount the romantic
lives of Shelley, Disraeli, and Byron. Based on factual evidence
but infused with a poet's or novelist's imagination, his sparkling
books provoked a veritable epidemic of "fictional biographies."
Now biographical fiction has long been regarded as a legitimate
form of the novel since it frankly uses historical figures or events
as only anchorages in place and time. Fictional biography, on the
other hand, is not legitimate biography at all, since the first re-
quirement of biography is to be true to fact and the romancer
departs from fact or, at his worst, invents fact in the form of
thoughts or speech or acts in order to fill in or round out the
imperfections of the true portrait. When Maurois himself used
such creative data it was with the authority of the subject's own
talk or letters and it was never a departure from biographical
truth. But the game of invention was so fascinating to many of
his imitators that whole libraries of spurious *biographies ro-
mancées* resulted from his example. Maurois in his *Ariel* and
Strachey in *Elizabeth and Essex* have stretched and at the same
time proved the limits of biography as a creative art. Through
their failures as well as their successes we have gained a surer
comprehension of the biographer's unavoidable obligation to the
element of fact.

Of late years, since the first frantic flood of "new" biographies
swept the world and subsided, we have seen something like a
fusion of all these methods, most notably in the work of Americans. If an example is to be taken from each of the two main
biographical approaches, the subjective and the objective, let the
former be Carl Sandburg's great life of Abraham Lincoln and the
latter, Douglas S. Freeman's *R. E. Lee*. Each of these vast works
is longer than the average Victorian biography, yet each combines, according to its method, its author, and its subject, the
best of all the skills which the art and science of biography have
discovered up to now. A few years ago Bonamy Dobrée said:

"We still await the great biographer who can seize the truth, leave it unromanticized, and yet produce a book which gives us the same sense of completion, of imaginative creation, as a great novel does." Perhaps this is a will-o'-the-wisp; perhaps in gifted writers like these, matched as they are to their themes, we have already seen the fulfillment of the "new" biography. Yet experiment and research will continue to widen the biographer's range, deepen his insight, vary his powers of expression, strengthen his grip on facts, and doubtless also enable him to cope with the new problems of documentation arising in this age when many affairs of personal and international importance are settled by telephone instead of by letter, and when the phonograph, the camera, the newsreel, the radio, and even television are bringing fresh biographical data to every eye and ear. "Biography," Virginia Woolf believes, "will enlarge its scope by hanging up looking glasses at odd corners. And . . . from all this diversity it will bring out, not a riot of confusion, but a richer unity. . . . Biography is only at the beginning of its career; it has a long and active life before it, we may be sure—a life full of difficulty, danger, and hard work." Around the corner may lie an era whose tone and aspect will differ markedly from those of the 1920s and '30s and require all the skills of a still newer biography to portray and interpret its past.

We have at any rate reached an understanding of what biography is and is not. Not a panegyric, or a lesson in ethics, or a sensational tabloid, or a history, or a novel, or a document, or a critique, or a psychoanalysis, or even a memoir—it yet shares the best qualities of all these varieties of writing. Defined according to its motive, it is "the history of the lives of individual men as a branch of literature" (*New English Dictionary*); that is, as Mr. Nicolson explains, "a truthful record of an individual and composed as a work of art." Defined according to its type, it is "the narrative, from birth to death, of one man's life in its outward manifestations and inward workings" (Waldo Dunn). Defined according to its dominant method, it is "that type of writing which reveals, in narrative form, the outer and inner experiences of one personality through another" (J. C. Metcalf). Defined

according to the modern spirit, it is "the study and presentment
of a human character, with its contradictions and its failures, with
its inner conflict of aim and impulse and its outer struggle between circumstance and temperament" (Osbert Burdett). Defined according to its essence, it is "the faithful portrait of a soul
in its adventures through life" (Edmund Gosse).

A true biography is, first of all, *grounded in fact*. It is, as far
as the facts and its plan allow, *complete*, based on the entire
career. It may be *objective*, affording a detached interpretation, or
*subjective*, yielding the inmost thoughts and emotions. It should be
*sympathetic*, for true insight into character can only come when
the author is fundamentally in sympathy with his subject.
("When we are negative to people," as Rollo Walter Brown says,
"we cannot gain full understanding of them. When we are in
sympathy with them, we discover what is really there.") As
much as possible, therefore, it should be *intimate*, showing the
man as he was known to his contemporaries. It is *imaginative*,
for only by a vivid reconstruction of the inner and outer circumstances of life can it arouse the imagination of the reader and
make the past real; yet it must never violate the truth of fact. It
is *progressive*; that is, it tells a story; it moves. Even though it be
composed of a series of pictures or of critical analyses, it should
present as a whole a sweeping climactic impression of the life as
it was experienced and seen in its progress. It is *artistic* in purpose
and in form. Written as a work of literature and not of ethics or
scholarship or something else, it should possess in satisfying degree the attributes of art: order, proportion, unity, style. Finally,
it is *living*. "It must, in a few hundred pages," as Lewis Mumford
says, "create the esthetic equivalent of the subject's life; capture
the changing landscape of its seasons; catch the tempo of its
expression; trace out the relationship between the world within—
chaotic, tumultuous, scarcely accessible—and the world without,
in which it exhibited itself and created an order, a form."

Impossible? Well, adds Strachey, "We do not reflect that it is
perhaps as difficult to write a good life as to live one."

## II. MODERN SHORT BIOGRAPHY

*To preserve . . . a becoming brevity—a brevity which excludes
everything that is redundant and nothing that is significant—that,
surely, is the first duty of the biographer.*

—LYTTON STRACHEY

Up to this point we have considered the essential steps by
which biography, as we understand it, has come into being. We
now focus our attention on one particular development, not because it claims any superior importance of its own but because
it enjoys certain privileges and calls for certain technical treat-
ments peculiar to itself.

All biography was in the beginning short biography. From
Plutarch to Samuel Johnson the customary length of "lives" was
something between two and twenty thousand words, averaging
rather less than ten thousand. We may credit James Boswell
with inventing the single objective "life" in several volumes. Before the *Life of Johnson* these works were brief from sheer
scarcity of material; after that they were long from sheer profusion. The Victorian biographers combined such industry and
minuteness in research that a book was not finished until every
letter was quoted or classified, every source tapped; but few of
them acquired even the rudiments of selection. It was this "lamentable lack of selection" which, as much as any other shortcoming,
provoked the modern rebellion from the nineteenth-century
mode. No one found fault with the Victorian's facts as such; it
was his indiscriminate and sometimes arrogant manner of shovel-
ing all the raw material into his set of volumes and calling it a
"life" which offended Strachey.

Now biography is both a science and an art. In all that makes
for accuracy of interpretation the writer must be something of
an historian, a psychologist, and even, as Ludwig says, a biologist;
he must be able to weigh evidence of the most difficult sort and
evaluate all the different varieties of testimony, from legal documents to hunches. He must have intuitive insight and experience
to apprehend the all-important spirit motivating the act, "to dis-

entangle what a man says from what he thinks . . . , to pierce beneath the protective crust of pride and reserve." He must have the scholar's knowledge of the past that will enable him to see the subject in his own environment. He needs tolerance and a well-tempered understanding to keep his work undistorted by bias or prejudice, by antipathy or favor. In all this he is largely a scientist. But when it comes to arranging and designing and presenting his findings, he has to be an artist. For this he needs sensitiveness to enter into and reveal another's soul. He needs imagination to revive the physical and spiritual features in a convincing semblance of reality. Together with the patience and ability to gather and appraise the infinite morsels of knowledge that make up every reconstruction of the past, he must possess a superior skill in selection, a fine discernment of those truths which will best transmit personality. To re-create bygone scenes and figures, to reanimate with movement, proportion, and climax the stubborn facts of a man's or woman's whole existence requires a dramatic sense equal if not superior to that of the playwright or novelist. To arrest and foreshorten a fluid and dynamic thing like a human life in paragraphs that cover decades and chapters that compress whole careers takes nothing less than the artistry of a gifted and conscientious painter. While to present this life in such form and language that the reading itself will be a beautiful and thrilling experience calls for literary powers of the first order.

Form—that is the crux of his problem as an artist. For the biographer knows that whether his study be as brief as Strachey's or as long as Sandburg's, the *whole* truth is yet to be uttered, and even if it could be uttered it would still need form to be grasped. He is aware that proportion is, after all, more illuminating than masses of detail, that "contradiction is the salt of character," and that the vitality of a portrait depends upon the amount and kind of contrast. He will therefore study the proportion of light and shadow, of strength and weakness in his subject, the proportion of outward behavior and expression to inner feelings and purposes, the proportion of formative development to mature achievement, the proportion of the stable elements of his personality to the impulsive and accidental variations. On the basis of these contrasts and the magnitude of his scope he will plot the curve and tensions of the man's life, determine the point of view from which he can best interpret it, the details of character and background that will give it the correct perspective. From this selection will result the length, design, style, and tone of his work. Thus a half-dozen lives of the same man will shed light on half a dozen different facets of his character or phases of his career. One biography will foreshorten the figure by stressing the youthful and formative period, another by focusing on its maturity, a third by turning the spotlight upon the inner struggle, a fourth by relating the career as a dramatic or romantic adventure or a realistic achievement, a fifth will treat it retrospectively and perhaps venture to convey the past by means of the "stream of consciousness," while a sixth will set forth the life in a short biography.

What we call "short biography" is only less subject to the shaping influences of its material because the degree of selection is usually fixed by a predetermined length. Even here, as will be seen, the range is wide. Some of these brief lives were written primarily as book reviews, others as prefaces to collected works. A good many first appeared as units in groups of biographies representing general movements or periods or points of view. Most of them came out as contributions to weekly or monthly periodicals. Since more than half of them are written by authors of full-length biographies, the opportunities for comparison and contrast are rich indeed.

Like other literary types, the short biography has grown up in response to special practical and artistic demands. First, the writer, like Sainte-Beuve, may desire to treat many figures, instead of the few which would occupy a lifetime if handled on a large scale. Human character being his objective, he wishes to examine and reconstruct it in as many and diverse manifestations as he can. Secondly, like Plutarch, he sees that certain people fall naturally into such homogeneous or contrasting groups as may illustrate a still wider cross-section of humanity. Thirdly, he has learned that interesting results can be obtained by subjecting chosen groups of persons to similar biographical treatment and noting their individual differences. Fourthly, he finds the short piece best for re-creating the lives of obscure persons hardly permitting or meriting an extended work. Finally, being an artist and wishing to escape all conventional limitations, he turns to the short biography to experiment with original or borrowed literary forms.

The result is very far from the standard Victorian essay with its monotonously inartistic separation of narrative from criticism or interpretation, much more akin to the lively, scintillating portraits found in the great French memoirs from Madame de Maintenon to the Duc de Saint-Simon. Although classifiable in many different ways, short biographies illustrate nearly every variety of treatment in the synthesis of narrative, analytical, critical, and descriptive elements. The reader will find it useful to make his own classification, either according to the proportions of the ingredients just mentioned or according to subjective and objective content or according to the author's concern with character as against career or occupation. In general, it may be said that concentration upon the person as an individual has made the modern short biography infinitely more interesting to us than the Macaulayan or Carlylean essay. The application of Sainte-Beuve's ideals of portraiture by letting the subject speak for himself has given this concentration authority. The extension of these ideals by modes adapted from the short-story, the drama, the interview, the letter, the diary, the conversation, the reminiscence, and the unimpeded stream of consciousness, has vastly increased the scope of the short biography and attracted an international gallery of brilliant authors.

It has also, of course, increased the responsibility without lessening the difficulty of the writer's task. No one will suppose that because the short biography is short it is easy to create. While it does not ordinarily, like the full-length work, invite or require much original research, it offers special difficulties on the side of portraiture. A portrait painter is always drawn by two divergent forces: he must catch the likeness of his sitter and yet make his portrait a work of art. This our author must accomplish by the most skillful touches, since in his small space every detail counts. If he draws with photographic fidelity, he will produce a flat, featureless picture. If he intensifies his subject's characteristic qualities, as the painter does, he risks making a caricature. If, like the novelist, he gives a complete and finished image, he may defeat his own ends, "for human characters are obscure and puzzling, and some loose ends convey this oddity best." Too much character analysis will render the picture static; too much incident will make the career seem unnaturally swift and crowded. A true, vivid, and graceful presentment within his narrow frame—this is what is wanted. The sketches that follow illustrate how some modern biographers have met these requirements.

## III. AUTOBIOGRAPHY

*To confess is the desire of many, but it is within the power of few.*

—LYTTON STRACHEY

Autobiography is a branch of biography, as biography is a branch of literature (or history), yet, being so differently motivated, it is usually considered in a separate category. In the present volume, however, several chapters from autobiographies have been included with the unabridged short lives, so it may be well to take another turn about the subject by way of approach.

First of all, how much can we ascertain by definition about this class of writing? To the librarian an autobiography is any book or article which the author or publisher admits to be one. Right away we are in trouble, for we all know of autobiographical works—James Joyce's *Portrait of the Artist* and Harold Nicolson's *Some People*, to name but two at hand—which their authors present under the label of fiction. To fall back upon etymology and say that autobiography is a narrative of a person's past by the person himself, will satisfy only until we have to apply it; for, apart from the virtual absence of story in some autobiographies, the idea that it must be written by the person concerned will have to be abandoned. Many autobiographies are the product of editors, secretaries, ghost-writers working more or less uncontrolled, or on behalf of illiterates, or in the employ of persons too

busy or crippled or otherwise unprepared to write themselves;
others are pieced together after the subject's death by loyal
friends or, as in the case of Joseph Conrad, interested scholars.
Moreover, as E. Stuart Bates points out, anyone's spontaneous
thoughts and acts are "infinitesimal in comparison with the influences, inheritances, circumstances, and personalities that surround
and delimit and inspire and compel: wherefore on any page of
an autobiography one may find oneself confronted with the
query—is this page part of an autobiography or not?" Some of
the autobiographical pieces in this collection—Louis Untermeyer's,
for instance—are quite as objective as the biographies. Finally,
since all that a man writes must either come from or pass through
his conscious experience, a definition of autobiography which will
be at once strict and practical is out of the question.

"Autobiography, in fact, is not so much a species of literature
as an idea," an attitude taken, whether intentionally or otherwise,
by the author towards his writing. Most novels, plays, and poems
are in greater or less degree autobiographical. So are nearly all
travel books, and many apparently objective biographies, like
Maurois's, and doubtless even a few histories. Some writers excel
in their ability to remain entirely aloof from their subjects, reso-
lutely shutting out every jot or hint of personal bias—though even
in doing so they are telling something about themselves; others,
on the contrary, are at their best when completely immersed in
their subjects so that every phrase is colored with their own personality. It is clear that with these opposite classes of writers, as
with most of those in between, autobiography is simply *what
they make it*. We think we can distinguish autobiography from
diaries, by being written considerably later instead of immediately after the events; from memoirs, by being concerned primarily with the writer rather than with other people or with
subjects introduced for their own sake. Nevertheless, some autobiographies are deliberately written in letter, diary, or memoir
form, just as some others masquerade as straight biography or fiction. We cannot tell autobiography by any external appearance;
the secret lies in the author's own point of view.

Again, what may be included in an autobiography? We ask

the biographer to give us all we need in order to visualize, understand, and form a safe judgment about his subject. On the autobiographer we can make no such demands. He is a law unto himself. He may begin where he likes and end where he likes. He may tell much or little. He may employ any literary mode at his disposal. He may uncover the innermost tissues of his soul in stark confession, or he may merely record dispassionate impressions or interesting observations or amusing conversations or random bits of information. He may, like Somerset Maugham in *The Summing Up*, present a thorough account of all he has learned about his craft, or he may rather offer, like Noel Coward in *Present Indicative*, the racy and entertaining story of his career. He may give us, like Bliss Perry, a concentrate of his life's experience in a few shining chapters, or he may prefer the looser scheme of that other popular professor of English, William Lyon Phelps, and dump in everything—letters, diaries, marginal notes, "doodles," banquet menus, animal pictures—any relic or memento of his public or private experience. In short, the contents of autobiographies are as numerous and diverse as the people who write them.

Mr. Bates, examining five different sorts of autobiography, found, however, one constant factor. "What they have in common is that each deals with what is of fundamental significance as regards a self-revealed personality, after thorough reconsideration. It is that factor of reconsideration that is the distinctive characteristic of autobiography. This is apparent in the fact that the best specimens are generally the shorter ones, written late in life; that is, those to which reconsideration of the life in question has been most thoroughly applied. People," he adds, "become ripe for the purpose of recording their past in so far as what has been sub-conscious has penetrated into consciousness." That this is not invariably a matter of years lived but of mental and emotional age is proved by the considerable number of "ripe" autobiographers—Joyce, Sheean, Reed, Adamic, in our collection—among the young, not to mention the countless youths who simply feel the impulse to confide, and act on it.

Obviously, since one may write his autobiography at almost

any age, no prescription can be made of the amount of life to be covered. "Up to Now" would seem to be a general rule and indeed a suitable title for most autobiographies, yet any list of modern books will include several which, like Adamic's or Day's, take in only a portion of the author's career, or, like Logan Pearsall Smith's, include just the events it pleases him to recall in public. The termini are somewhat easier to fix, inasmuch as few persons acquire before the age of four or five any impressions they can later reconsider, and only the rarest autobiography brings the author up to the day of his death. The usual line of demarcation is staked out from a definite milestone which the writer feels to separate his present from his past. With Joyce it was his departure from Dublin for Paris and the Continent; with Sheean, the end of his adventures as special correspondent; with Perry, his retirement from teaching. Any line, however imaginary, which permits the past to be reconsidered with perspective will serve as the end of the book, just as it may give the occasion for its writing.

Of the forms and methods of autobiography either a great deal or a little must be said, and the presence of twelve different specimens in this volume suggests the briefer answer. From the more conventional pattern of Sheean, Steffens, and Perry to the narrative-descriptive-dialogue mode of Adamic or the dramatic mode of Dell; from the episodic scheme of Nicolson to Joyce's complete absence of transitions—even here we have variety. An analysis of the books from which these specimens come would show still more. Thus whereas Joyce and Dell minimize the chapter divisions, most autobiographers use them as time-markers. In Day's book they separate the subject-items; in Nicolson's, the independent portraits. The range, indeed, is infinite.

Finally, why do people write their autobiographies? For the most various reasons: to preserve a record of their own past against the day when they or their friends or their children may forget; to list their achievements; to erect their own monument; to explain and perhaps defend their behavior or deeds; to collect their thoughts; to compose a picture gallery of earlier friends and scenes; to lay the ghosts of the past; to restore self-esteem; to dramatize themselves as in a play or novel; to make a full confession in order to start a new chapter with a clean sheet or to die in peace; to expound a pet theory; to sum up all they have learned—and so on and so on. The logical and acknowledged reasons are counted by the hundred, the psychological and probable reasons, frequently unknown to the authors, by the thousand. Whether the writer is primarily in search of the past or in flight from the past, his motives are not likely to be simple. In fact, if one compares the world's outstanding autobiographies from St. Augustine and Cellini to Rousseau, Mill, Franklin and on to Edmund Gosse, Henry Adams, Mark Twain, and Lincoln Steffens, one will observe the motives growing more and more complex as the authors themselves become increasingly aware of the multiple and conflicting forces impelling them to write. Back of all autobiography, however, just as at the source of biography in general, lies the universal instinct for self-perpetuation. Man will not let his memory die or his name be blotted out if he can prevent it.

# VINCENT SHEEAN

VINCENT SHEEAN'S *Personal History*, of which "The Modern Gothic" is the opening chapter, bears the publisher's subtitle of *Youth and Revolution: The Story of One Person's Relationship to Living History*. And that is exactly what the book is. Mr. Sheean was born in 1899 of Irish parents living in rural Illinois—Pana, Christian County. There he grew up, a bookish lad with an aptitude for languages and an appetite for French and English literature which, together with his attractive manner and appearance (he is six feet two inches tall), stood him in good stead at the University of Chicago. Three and a half years of college life, as related in the following selection, ended abruptly with the death of his mother. For a few weeks he worked on *The Chicago Daily News;* he lost his job and promptly transferred himself to New York, where he spent a year as a tabloid (*Daily News*) reporter. Then, at twenty-two, he went to Paris and began the most spectacular part of his career.

For three years, as foreign correspondent for *The Chicago Tribune*, he covered the Rhineland disturbances, the Ruhr Occupation, the Lausanne Conference, Mussolini's march on Rome, Primo de Rivera's coup d'état, and the principal conferences and crises of Western Europe resulting from the Versailles Treaty. These experiences were all tame compared to his feat during the war between Spain and the Rif tribes of northern Morocco, when with great difficulty and risk he penetrated to the headquarters of Abd El-Krim, interviewed the Rif leader, and emerged to bear the chieftain's peace negotiations in person to the Spanish dictator (*An American Among the Riffi*, 1927). As a special correspondent for the North American Newspaper Alliance he returned to the Rif to cover the new outbreak with France, then went to Persia and out of his observations produced *The New Persia* (1927). The next year he spent in China interviewing war lords, studying the work of the Communists, witnessing the Hankow massacres, visiting remote parts of Manchuria, and winning the confidence of Madame Sun Yat-sen, the "mother of the Chinese Revolution." After a tragic stay in Moscow, he returned to Paris for a short while, then to America to lecture. In 1929, finding himself in Jerusalem when the Arab-Jewish riots broke out, he resumed his role of special correspondent, reporting the whole situation in Palestine. This much of his life is covered by *Personal History* (1935).

Since 1929, Mr. Sheean has devoted himself mainly to literary work. In the midst of his foreign corresponding he had already written a novel of English life, *The Anatomy of Virtue* (1927), and his Russian experience is reflected in *Gog and Magog* (1929). To these he has since added *The Tide* (1933), *San Felice* (1936), *The Pieces of a Fan* (1937), and a work of non-fiction, *Not Peace but a Sword* (1939). He is married to the daughter of the late Shakespearean actor, Sir Johnston Forbes-Robertson.

Although the sensational events of his life as foreign correspondent all come after the years described in "The Modern Gothic," Mr. Sheean makes up in quiet sincerity and particularized depiction for the unavoidable absence of spectacle. He does, in fact, what many college undergraduates (and graduates) are apt to find impossible: he makes his campus experiences interesting to others, communicating to strangers on other campuses and to readers who never trod a campus the sharp, fresh, first-time feeling of personal contact. No wonder, with this skill for reporting the ordinary events, Mr. Sheean was equipped to bring us with the force of direct sensations the unusual incidents of his amazing career.

# THE MODERN GOTHIC

THE ARMISTICE came when I was eighteen. What it meant to the war generation I can only imagine from the stories they tell; to me it meant that we in the University of Chicago, that mountain range of twentieth-century Gothic near the shores of Lake Michigan, went out of uniform and into civilian clothes.

The world has changed so much that it seems downright indecent to tell the truth: I was sorry when the war ended. I fumed with disappointment on the night of the false armistice—the celebrated night when the American newspapers reported the end of the war some days before it happened. We were all patriots then. We knew nothing about that horror and degradation which our elders who had been through the war were to put before us so unremittingly for the next fifteen years. There were millions of us, young Americans between the ages of fifteen or sixteen and eighteen or nineteen, who cursed freely all through the middle weeks of November. We felt cheated. We had been put into uniform with the definite promise that we were to be trained as officers and sent to France. In my case, as in many others, this meant growing up in a hurry, sharing the terrors and excitements of a life so various, free and exalted that it was worth even such hardships as studying trigonometry. So we went into uniform and marched about the place from class to class like students in a military academy; listened to learned professors lecturing about something called "War Aims"; lived in "barracks"; did rifle drill. The rifles were dummies, and the "barracks" were only the old dormitories rechristened, but such details made little difference. We played at being soldiers for a few months with tremendous seriousness, and then the glorious uproar to which we had been preparing our approach suddenly died down. Our part of the war had been a prelude to something that did not take place.

And when demobilization came at last the prospect of returning to the regular life of the University had become repellent to me. I had nobody to persuade but my mother, who was still too thankful for the Armistice to make many objections. Consequently I went job hunting and spent three months as secretary to a millionaire builder and real estate operator in the Chicago financial district. It was there, hanging out a window above the crevasse of LaSalle Street, that I watched the Black Hawk Division come home. Waving flags and the thump of a military march were enough to stir me to any extravagance; we all shouted and waved and winked back the hysterical tears. Those were patriotic days.

My employer was an odious little man who had quarreled with his wife and disinherited his son because the latter wanted to go on the stage. He was a brilliant entrepreneur, the little man: he used to point with pride to the ceilings of the skyscraper in which he had his office, saying, "That ceiling is a good six inches shallower than the law allows. You can always arrange things if you know how. I got eight extra stories into this building by that little detail." When I inquired if the building was likely to fall down he sniffed contemptuously. "Buildings don't fall down," he said. The building did start to fall down some years later, was condemned and demolished. By an unfortunate accident, its builder was not buried under the ruins.

He sent me on one occasion to collect rents from the impoverished tenants of a village he owned in Indiana. It was a horrible experience from which I escaped as quickly as I could, but the thought of it came back to me for years. The tenants of the wretched little Indiana town worked in a coal mine belonging to my employer when they worked at all, but they had not worked for many months. They lived in houses belonging to him (if you could call such hovels houses) and bought their food from stores belonging to him. I was to collect what I could of the back rent owed on the disgraceful shacks in which they were obliged to live. I was a failure at the job, for the sight of the life into which children were there being born disorganized whatever efficiency I possessed as a secretary. That day in the little mining town was my introduction to capitalism at work, and it filled me, even then, with disgust. I blamed the busy little entrepreneur as well as the system of which he was a part, and it was not long before the idea of continuing to work for him became insupportable. "Business" (if this was business) bored, irked and revolted me, and I. determined to do whatever I could to avoid being involved in it again.

In the spring of 1919, therefore, I went back to the University and stayed on throughout the summer to make up for lost time. My education up to then had been a sorry failure. I had never made any headway with science, mathematics or the classical languages. Of the first two I remembered nothing; of the second I remembered just one Greek sentence, *enteuthen exelaunei* ("and the next day he marched onward")—this not because it had any stirring significance for me, but because it marked the welcome end of nearly every chapter in the Anabasis.

I had derived, it was true, considerable pleasure of a low order from some other academic pursuits in my first two years of college. I had come to the University knowing some Italian, German, and French (particularly French), and could easily make a better showing in these subjects than my contemporaries. My favorite trick had been to register for courses in which I was unlikely to encounter anything I did not already know. Such conduct was lazy and dishonest, but you could make out a good case for the theory that young people were all lazy and dishonest when they could be. Certainly what the undergraduates called "snaps" (i.e., courses easy to get through without undue effort) were always crowded in my day at the University. The football players, the social lights, the pretty co-eds, and all the other students who regarded study as an inconvenient detail in college life, rushed to inscribe themselves for "snap" courses. I was in a more advantageous position than some of my fellows for wasting time, since more courses were "snaps" for me. I could go to a series of lectures on Victorian Prose, for example, and be confident of hearing nothing new; similarly, in French, with the novels of Victor Hugo or the plays of Molière. I had read altogether too much in the two languages, thanks to a bookish childhood. There was thus a group of studies open to me at the University in which I could, without working or learning, impress my instructors sufficiently to make a good record.

More than two years of my three and a half at the University of Chicago had already been wasted in this way. It was a kind of confidence game of which the victim was, of course, myself. I did well enough in the subjects I already knew to make up for my failures in the subjects I did not know and was too lazy to study. I was too undisciplined, too indolent, and too dishonest to force myself to learn what did not interest me. And it was not until that summer of 1919 that I began to realize the silliness of such an approach to what ought to be one of the great experiences of a life. The University of Chicago in summer was invaded by hordes of earnest men and women from the smaller colleges and schools of the Middle West, working towards their master's or their doctor's degree. These thin, spectacled myrmidons, humpbacked from carrying armfuls of books up and down academic steps for many years, filled the cool gray corridors and covered the green lawns I had always thought reserved for pretty girls and long-legged youths. The summer school, I discovered, was an altogether different affair from the ordinary academic year. If you tried to talk to a summer student during a lecture, a cold glance through glittering spectacles was the only reply. The brilliant hot sun of a Chicago July threw into merciless relief all the unloveliness of these dank visitors from the provincial colleges of Indiana, Wisconsin, Illinois, Iowa, and Minnesota. Their presence was somehow unbecoming, both to their surroundings and to the general fitness of things. I resented them for two or three weeks, and on the few occasions when I saw my vacationing friends, the undergraduates who had finished their college year in June, we were exceedingly witty about the looks, manners, lives, and minds of the pitiable summer students. There were probably not half a dozen of these bookworms, we calculated, who could dance the fox trot decently.

But as the summer study advanced I became more and more uncomfortable about them. They were not beautiful, but neither were they ignorant. They were always putting me to shame, somehow or other. I was not to remember much about most of the studies of that summer; only one was vivid in retrospect. It was a fairly advanced course in French—the poetry of Victor Hugo, all of it, including every pitiless line of *La Légende des Siècles*. The instructor was a visiting bigwig from one of the Eastern universities, a Frenchman with a German name. He used to conduct the course in an informal fashion, lecturing some of the time, reading occasionally, and starting discussions whenever the spirit moved him. It was assumed that students in such a course as this would be mature and educated enough to know something besides the actual subject matter itself. Comparisons were always popping up, were constantly invited. Most of the students— there may have been twelve or fifteen, men and women—were well past thirty, and probably all of them taught French literature somewhere or other. In that company, through July and August, I first began to be ashamed of my evil ways, and no amount of smug scorn for the bookworms could disguise the fact.

"Vous trouverez ici sans doute que Hugo a beaucoup emprunté à Chateaubriand; n'est-ce pas, Mademoiselle?" the professor would inquire innocently, smiling across his desk at an eager spinster from Indiana. And then off she would go, talking about Hugo and Chateaubriand in a French accent that would have been incomprehensible to either of those gentlemen—but talking, just the same, with information and intelligence. The professor would argue with her; others would join in; and it appalled me that I could not even follow their battle from afar. I had never read a word of Chateaubriand; my interest in Christianity was almost nonexistent; I had no real idea why it had ever seemed intellectually important to Victor Hugo or to anybody else. And I looked at the summer students in amazement. Their excitement over such subjects actually brought color to their wan faces; they could smile, make jokes, go through all the movements of living organisms when their attention was aroused.

My salvation was that the instructor was a Frenchman. If he had been an American or an Englishman he would have seen at once that my glibness in French was a sheer accident, and that I actually understood nothing of the turmoil through which Victor Hugo had lived and written. But, being French, the professor had a natural prejudice in favor of hearing his language pronounced correctly. In spite of all their knowledge and interest, most of the students in this course had abominable accents; it seemed to be a rule among American school teachers. I had learned French so young that all the laziness in the world could never rob me of a fairly good pronunciation. Consequently, when I had occasion to read some of Victor Hugo's detested verses aloud, the professor would lean back in his chair with satisfaction. This, combined with a prudent silence when the discussions were out of my depth, gave the good man the idea that I really knew something of the subject, and I finished the course with an unjustifiably handsome record.

But something important happened to me during the summer of 1919, thanks chiefly to the Hugo poems. I had been realizing with increasing clarity, week after week, the superficial character of my own mind. I was nineteen, and I knew nothing. The fact that I could speak a sort of French had nothing to do with me; what credit there might be for that should have gone to the devout and kindly Irish priest who had tutored me in it for years. Of the actual meaning of French literature I knew far less than the scrubbiest high-school teacher from Iowa. The struggles of men's minds—whether of contemporary minds or of those like Chateaubriand's and Hugo's, long gone to dust—meant nothing to me at all. I had existed without realizing that it seriously mattered to anybody what men believed, or under what form of government, in what structure of society, they lived. The summer's study gave me no love for the poetry of Victor Hugo: on the contrary, the mere thought of *La Légende des Siècles* made me feel slightly uneasy for years to come. But I did derive from it some idea of what the process of literature could be—some hint of the stormy sincerity in which minds like Hugo's sought for the truth. The suggestion, however dim, was sufficient reward for the boredom of reading what then seemed to me an intolerable quantity of pompous, overstuffed verse.

My ideas of what I might get out of the University thereafter submitted to rearrangement. Words could no longer suffice: I understood Hugo's words well enough, the upholstery of his mind, but it was the mind itself that escaped me. If a mind of Hugo's quality was incomprehensible, how could I expect to know anything about the rarer minds that did (even then) seem to me most worth the effort of comprehension: Molière, Racine, Shakespeare? And, even in a world I found tiresome beyond my powers of resistance, the world of the "Victorian Prose Writers," what could I hope to understand by words alone? It was clear, after the Hugo experience, that literature involved something at once more complex and more ordinary, more closely related to the whole life of mankind, than the science of stringing words together in desirable sequences, however fascinating the contemplation of such patterns might seem to a bookish and word-conscious nature.

Nothing could be learned about literature by studying literature: that was what it came to. Courses in literature seldom took on the vitality of that special Hugo course with its special participants. In general, they were either arranged to suit average students with no interest in the subject, or specialists with an interest so minute that it was (in my view) equivalent to no interest at all. I had no desire to count the feminine endings in the lines of the Canterbury Tales. What I wanted to know—in so far as I really wanted to know anything about them—was why the Canterbury Tales were written; what mysterious springs existed in the mind and heart of a man named Geoffrey Chaucer to bring forth such a particular stream of articulated language; what the world was like for which he wrote, in which he lived, and what was his particular struggle with it. Professors did some-

times try to convey this sort of information; but it was obvious
that they had obtained it elsewhere and were passing it on in
capsule form. Where had they obtained it?

History, perhaps, was the answer; philosophy might be part
of it.

That autumn, when the regular academic year began, I
switched from the faculties of English literature and Romance
languages to those of history and philosophy. And perhaps if
this had been the arrangement two years before I might not have
wasted quite so much time.

I am not suggesting that I became a model of industry and
scholarship promptly at nine o'clock on the morning of registra-
tion day in October, 1919. I still frittered away a good three
quarters or four fifths of my time, still registered for an occasional course of lectures that could be treated cavalierly as a
"snap" (History of Venetian Art, for instance). But at least I was
not behaving altogether as if the University were a country club.
Both in history and in philosophy I learned something—not much,
but something. There was a course in Plato that conveyed meaning to me; another, on the German idealists, I found as exciting
as a romantic novel. But perhaps the most interesting of all—the
one to be recalled most often in subsequent life—was a term of
lectures and reading on the Decline of the Ottoman Empire.

This—an "advanced," and therefore a rather small, class—was
in charge of an inspired teacher. I never knew what made the
difference between a good and a bad teacher, but I did know that
Ferdinand Schevill was a superlatively good one. He was a
German, short and rather formidable in appearance, with eye-
glasses and a neatly trimmed Vandyke beard. His university was
Heidelberg or Bonn, I believe, and yet he had none of that ped-
antry which is supposed to be the vice of German scholarship.
When he led us through the immense and complicated story of
the decay that fell upon Suleiman's empire after the seventeenth
century he did not try to treat it microscopically as an isolated
phenomenon. He talked about the Arabs, the Turks, the Balkan
peoples, as if they were alive; and they soon began to come to
life for me. Schevill's system was to allow his students to read at

will through the whole literature of the subject, and therefrom to choose, halfway through the course, a particular aspect for further reading and a final paper. I began to read everything I could find about the Asiatic empire of the Turks. Almost from the first day that side of the Bosphorus seemed to me of greater interest than this. I extended my researches to the files of newspapers and magazines, and when it came time to choose, I took for my term paper the history of the Wahabite movement.

An odder choice for a nineteen-year-old undergraduate at the University of Chicago would be hard to imagine. Ibn es-Sa'ud was then almost unknown to the Western world, and the literature on the Wahabi was scarce indeed. I read everything I could find in English, French, or German, and performed the best piece of honest work I had ever done. For a few weeks, while I was reading in the library, I nearly persuaded myself that I was living in Arabia, and sometimes the vast cloaks and camel turbans of the Bedawin seemed more real than the swishing skirts of the co-eds going by. Later on I obtained permission to go down into the stacks of that huge library—steel stacks with glass floors running among them, layer upon layer. The world's knowledge lay there like a sunken continent swimming in subaqueous light, and through its fields I ranged more or less at will. My interest in Islam, such as it was, began that year, and what I learned in Schevill's course was never wholly forgotten. If other teachers had been like him, other subjects as vivid to me as the distintegration of Turkey became, I might have learned more in my long sojourn under the sham-Gothic towers.

But the social system of the undergraduate world in which I lived was the villain of the piece. No teacher could have compelled full attention from a mind preoccupied with elaborate details of social relationship. The University of Chicago, one of the largest and richest institutions of learning in the world, was partly inhabited by a couple of thousand young nincompoops whose ambition in life was to get into the right fraternity or club, go to the right parties, and get elected to something or other. The frivolous two thousand—the undergraduate body, the "campus"—may have been a minority, for the University contained a great many solitary workers in both the undergraduate and graduate fields; but the minority thought itself a majority, thought itself, in fact, the whole of the University. And it was to the frivolous two thousand that I belonged.

Chicago was by no means the worst American university in this respect—it was supposed, on the contrary, to be one of the best; but even at Chicago "campus activities" were the most serious part of life. Freshmen chose, on the advice of their elders, which of these "activities" to pursue throughout the four years. Some "went out for the *Maroon*" (i.e., worked for the college's daily newspaper), some "for the team" (i.e., football), some for other organized athletics, and some for "class politics." Rare and wonderful freshmen "went out for" everything at once.

There were hierarchies in the *Daily Maroon*, in the Dramatic Club, which made productions every two or three months, and in the Blackfriars. This last was an association of undergraduates interested in producing an operetta (original, more or less) in the spring of every year with men in all the parts. Freshmen were graduated through the successive steps in all these organizations until the survivors, by natural selection and incredibly hard work, stood out in their senior year, immortal: the editor of the *Maroon*, the president of the Dramatic Club, the abbot (and other officials) of Blackfriars. Football and track athletics had their four-year plans as well, but they were not my line of country, and I knew little about them.

Organized "activities," as occupation for the energies of youth, could have done no harm if they had not been supplemented, and o some extent even controlled, by a social life of singular ferocity. The women undergraduates had a number of clubs to which all the "nice" girls were supposed to belong. Four or five of these clubs were "good" and the rest "bad." Their goodness and badness were absolute, past, present and future, and could not be called into question. They had no houses or rooms of their own, but they maintained a rigid solidarity and succeeded in imposing upon the undergraduate society a tone of intricate, overweening snobbery.

The men were grouped in Greek-letter fraternities with houses for residence. Half a dozen of these were "good" and the rest "bad"; but their goodness and badness were not quite so irremediable as the similar qualifications among the women's clubs. The fraternities were national organizations, with chapters in most of the American universities, and it was well known that the same fraternity might be "good" at the University of California and "bad" at Yale. The salutary effect of this consideration was supported by the fact that the men did not seem to have the same high degree of social cruelty as the women. Men often joined a fraternity because their brothers or fathers had belonged to it, because they had friends in it, because they liked some one person in it, or even because its house or its food or its heating system appealed to them. Such homely, sensible reasons weighed little with the women. All of them, true to the great tradition of American womanhood, took the very "best" club to which they could possibly be elected, and the logic of their behavior kept their club system rigid throughout my four years at the University.

My experience with the fraternity system was a weird one. It was in no way typical, but it exhibited some of the cannibalistic character of the institution and the intensity with which its importance was felt among the undergraduates. I entered the University ignorant of even the names of the Greek-letter societies. On my first or second day I was asked to lunch at a fraternity house and went. On the next day I discovered that that godlike creature, the editor of the *Maroon*, was a member of this very fraternity. When, on about the fourth day, I was asked to pledge myself to join it, I accepted at once.

Followed what has since appeared to be a grand tragicomic episode. I moved into the fraternity house, where lived the friends, ready-made, among whom I was supposed to pass four years. My roommate was Alan Le May, a dour, dark and silent freshman with a sharp intelligence. He afterwards took to making vast sums of money by writing about the wild and woolly West, but at the time he was more concerned with such effete Eastern matters as French composition and English literature. There were a number of other brothers-in-the-bond who loomed particularly large. Above them all, in a kind of hazy splendor like that which crowns a high mountain in the sun, there dwelt the supreme god, A. B., the editor of the *Maroon*. He was kind to me, suggested books to read, talked to me about the scraps of verse I used to write. I never saw anybody afterwards who possessed quite his Olympian quality, and two or three kings, with a pope and a president thrown in, could not possibly have awed me so much in later days as he awed me then. In all, I was happy in that life; but it was not prolonged.

On the day of our initiation into the fraternity, three months after the taking of the pledge, a girl asked me to cut my classes and take a long walk with her. She was a pretty girl, a freshman, whom I had met in the office of the *Daily Maroon* and with whom I was conducting a shy and tentative flirtation. It was bitter cold that day; she was wrapped in furs, and I decidedly was not; but we walked for many hours through the snowy streets, down to Jackson Park with its trees hung in ice, and out to the wintry lake. After we had been chattering about ordinary things for ten or fifteen minutes she suddenly opened up on me.

"I've been talking to various people around the *Maroon* about you," she said. "We all think you're a pretty good freshman. You might amount to something if you had any sense. I don't think you know what you're doing. I realize it's none of my business, but I've made up my mind to talk to you about it before it's too late."

This meant nothing to me, and I said so.

"Oh, don't pretend that you don't understand," she said. "It's that damned fraternity. You can't possibly belong to it and make anything at all out of your college life. You'll be miserable in another year, when you know where you are. No girl will go out with you—no nice girl, that is. And you're barred from everything that makes college life what it is. Of course, I know you're not Jewish, but everybody doesn't realize that, and I think it's a terrible shame."

In my entire life I had never heard a more surprising series of statements.

"But what are you talking about, anyway?" I asked. "Why on earth should anybody think I was Jewish?"

"Because you belong to a Jewish fraternity," she said.

Ensued a ludicrous, painful, silly and melancholy conversation. In the course of it I made acquaintance with (a) the social system of the University of Chicago; (b) the Jewish problem; (c) the way of the world; (d) my own colossal ignorance. Incredible though it seemed afterwards, I had never known a Jew in my life and had no idea that there were so many of them growing there under my eyes. I had only the romantic and provincial notions about Jews: thought of them as bearded old gentlemen with magic powers and vast stores of gold. Except for Rebecca in *Ivanhoe*, I had never made the acquaintance of a *young* Jew even in literature. I suppose I must have thought they had sprung full grown into the Middle Ages and thence vanished into the oblivion of eastern Europe. At any rate, the fact was that I had never thought of the Jews as a possibility in the here and now: my contemporaries in America, in Chicago. To Lucy, my pretty little girl-friend—a wise little girl indeed, striding along in her muskrat coat—I must have seemed an imbecile. At first she refused to believe that this was new to me.

"You're sixteen years old," she scolded. "You've got a fair amount of brains. My God, boy, do you mean to tell me you don't know a Jew when you see one? Look at them, idiot; look at them. They have noses, hair, eyes, features, mouths, all different from anybody else. Can you honestly tell me you didn't know that ——— was a Jew?"

And then the melancholy catalogue began. One by one we ran through the list of every member of my fraternity. They were all, it seemed, Jews.[1] So were half the freshmen, male and female, on the *Daily Maroon*. The last name, the one I dreaded to pronounce, was that of the godlike senior, the editor of the *Maroon*. And he too, as Lucy proved by a merciless analysis of his name and appearance, was certainly Jewish.

[1] They weren't, but this was a detail I did not know for years. The undergraduate body called it a "Jewish fraternity" because it contained Jews; and among the supposed Jews were a good many Gentiles.

After this I walked along for a long time in silence. Lucy kept on talking, but I scarcely heard what she said. I was trying to realize that I had been living for nearly three months in a houseful of Jews and had never known it. I was shocked, humiliated, and angry, not because my fraternity brothers were Jewish, but because I had not known about it. The shock would have been the same if they had all turned out to be Swedenborgians, or Spaniards, or vegetarians, or believers in the transmigration of souls. It made them a special caste, a marked and unvariable species, to which I could not possibly belong. To have failed to recognize a quality so singular was also a proof of abysmal ignorance on my part. I was naïf and provincial, of course, but I had never realized to what a degree. In the end I had recourse to the expedient we all come to at one time or another—I refused to believe the truth.

"Well, Lucy," I said combatively, "I don't believe a single thing you say, but let's just suppose for a minute that it's true. Then what? What's the difference? What possible harm can it do me to belong to a Jewish fraternity?"

She began a recital that horrified me. It horrified me more afterwards, as I came to know that the state of affairs described was by no means peculiar to the University of Chicago or to university life. The Jews, it seemed, could not possibly go to the "nice" parties in college. They could not be elected to any class office, or to office in any club, or to any fraternity except the two they had themselves organized; they could not dance with whom they pleased or go out with the girls they wanted to go out with; they could not even walk across the quadrangles with a "nice" girl if she could possibly escape. And so on. The picture was painted with violence, but it was true, as I was to learn before long. Hitler himself could not have invented a more savage and degrading system of anti-Semitism than that worked out by those little monsters, the undergraduates. The system had been operating all around me from the day I entered college, and I had never seen it. As Lucy explained, my position was peculiar. I was a non-Jewish freshman pledged to a Jewish fraternity. My own brothers-in-the-bond would naturally not explain these things to me, said she, and nobody else had the courage to do so.

It took another period of painful argument to convince me that such prejudices and restrictions existed. Having, finally, accepted them as true on Lucy's testimony, I then asked why they should apply to me.

"After all," I argued, "I've got the map of Ireland in my face. Not to speak of my name. How on earth could anybody think I was Jewish?"

"It doesn't make any difference," she said. "You belong to a Jewish fraternity. That's enough. Lots of Jews take Irish names, and lots of Jews don't look especially Jewish. You'll be marked as a Jew, all right, if you go on into the fraternity. Take my word for it: I know."

After hours of explaining, exhorting and laying down the law, Lucy brought forth the suggestion to which all this had been a preparation. It was that I should break my pledge to the fraternity, spend two or three months living in a "dormitory" (i.e., a college hall), and then, in the spring, join one of the better Gentile fraternities.

I repudiated the notion with vehemence. What? Leave the place I liked best in the whole University? Abandon my friends? Desert the roommate who was the only person I knew foolish enough, and amiable enough, to sit up arguing with me until two or three in the morning? Above all, forsake the precincts hallowed by the presence of that saint, that prince of the world, the editor of the *Maroon*? Impossible!

And on that note the afternoon ended. We had walked from early afternoon until dark; we had plowed through snow and shivered on the icy lake front; I had been more thoroughly upset than ever before in my seventeen years. Lucy entered the gates of Foster Hall without knowing whether her effort had been in vain or not, and I went on home to the fraternity house, which seemed to have been invested, between lunch and dinner, with mystery.

It is difficult to make out just what my idea of a Jew was. It seems probable that the word had no significance at all, except the dubious significance given it in the romances I had spent my

childhood reading. But it must have set up some kind of reverberation in my mind, because all my friends began to seem a little
mysterious to me from the moment I thought they were Jewish.
The ideas that Jews are a terrifying people, that they deal in dark
magic, that they belong to an especially gifted and especially
tragic race, are scattered so widely through all the literature of
Christian Europe that we take them in unconsciously, more or
less as we absorb air and moisture, without troubling to notice the
process. Unconscious anti-Semitism was here, as in larger issues,
what made the problem so extraordinarily difficult. I was not
knowingly anti-Jewish; I had never knowingly spoken to a Jew or
thought about the Jewish problem; and yet the accumulated
prejudices of two thousand years had so subtly and insensibly
poisoned my mind that it came as a shock to hear that my particular friends, the most admired of my acquaintance, were Jews.

Such shocks are absorbed by time. Along with other oddments
of superstition, the origins of which we cannot always trace,
there disappears the notion that the Jews are a sinister race, gifted
in the black arts or banded together in sorcery; we learn that
when they are treated like anybody else they do not greatly differ
from anybody else. But to dispel these ancestral fancies, clinging
like vague vapors in the mind, we require the light and air of
experience. And it was precisely experience that was most conspicuously lacking in the equipment of the freshman who plowed
through the snow that night, going home, for the first time in
his life, with a Problem.

"Lemmy!" I said, coming into my room, "I've got to talk to
you. Do you think that A. B. is Jewish?"

"Of course," he said. "What's the matter?"

I told him as much as I could of the afternoon's discoveries,
but there was little time. The dinner bell was ringing, and freshmen could not be late.

"It's all true enough," he said. "I've known it all the time.
Haven't you?"

His glum face was glummer than ever; he frowned intently,
scratched his close-cropped black head.

"After dinner," he said, "we can lock the door and talk it out. Let's eat."

Lemmy completed the education Lucy had begun. After dinner, a nervous meal under the circumstances, we made for our room at once to "study." With the door locked we sat there and talked in the quiet voices of conspirators. He had learned, from his father probably, a great deal about the world we lived in.

Our fraternity, he told me, had been founded to include (and perhaps to reconcile) Jews and non-Jews; it had only succeeded in getting itself labeled as wholly Jewish; and a national convention the year before had restricted its membership in future to Gentiles. (I remember my feeling of relief when I learned that he too was a Gentile; I was never to be sure whether anybody else in the house was or not.)

Like Lucy a few hours earlier, Lemmy found my ignorance hard to believe. He said, patiently enough, that everybody knew these things; that the difference between Jews and Gentiles was as obvious as that between men and women, and that it would never occur to anybody to state it. He further corroborated everything Lucy had told me about the opprobrium, the ridicule, the complicated varieties of discrimination and prejudice, to which any Gentile who belonged to a Jewish fraternity would have to submit throughout four years in college. He had known all this when he was pledged, he said; and he had still taken the pledge because (in his humility) he supposed the "bid" to join a fraternity to be a rare thing, and a Jewish fraternity to be better than none. He agreed that no house could be pleasanter than ours, no friends more satisfactory; but he was convinced that remaining in the fraternity meant accepting a kind of permanent ostracism from the life of the Gentile part of the undergraduate body.

We agreed, in a high state of hysterical agitation, to do "something." But that "something" could not be long delayed. The informal initiation into the fraternity would take place in an hour, and the following day we were to take the solemn, irrevocable oaths of the formal initiation. We were still in turmoil when a solemn knock on our door summoned us to the ordeal.

"Informal initiation" into a fraternity was supposed to be a test for the courage or endurance of the freshman candidate for membership. The candidate was stripped naked and led, blindfolded, into a room where the elders of the fraternity exercised their strength and wits in an attempt to try his nerve. Actually no candidate, however poltroonishly he behaved during the tests, was ever refused admission to the brotherhood, and the "informal initiation" was therefore merely an excuse for some rather rudimentary fun. The ordeal by fire, the ordeal by water, and a dozen other curious relics of savagery were brought into play, ostensibly to prove that a boy of sixteen or seventeen was made of the right stuff to be a brother in the bond.

I went into the initiation in a state of nerves that might have made the simplest trial difficult for me. Fortunately it worked the opposite way. No matter what the brothers had done I doubt if I should have cried out or betrayed my mortal terror. The only thing I can remember saying is a sudden and involuntary "What's that?" when the brand of the fraternity's initial letter was put on my arm and I felt the searing of the flesh. That brand remained ever afterwards, faint but quite clear, to remind me of the fantastic episode of which it was a part.

My initiation was short and easy. In five minutes it was all over and I heard A. B.'s kindly voice saying, "All right, Jim, you can go back to your room." Trembling with relief, I raced down the corridor to my own place and got into my clothes. Lemmy was already there, dressing. The house was quiet with our door closed, but occasionally the loud laughter of the upper classmen came through from the continuing initiation. Lemmy sat on the edge of the bed and looked glum.

"We can pack a bag," he said, "and go to Aurora after everybody is asleep. We'll have to jump out the window. But that is only if you've made up your mind. You've got to make up your mind. If you want to do it, I'll stick."

We agreed on the plan of escape. We both felt that it would be impossible to face the assembled brethren, headed by A. B., and tell them our decision. They could easily overwhelm us with arguments; and tomorrow, after the formal oaths of allegiance, it would be too late.

It was most unpleasant, after this, to receive congratulations on having passed through the horseplay initiation "successfully." I suppose we both felt like the lowest of traitors; I know I did. But the congratulations were over in half an hour; the whole house went to sleep; at some time after midnight, with the precautions and terrors of an elopement, we dropped a bag out the window and jumped after it. From the narrow garden side of the house it was a quick scramble to the street, to a taxicab, to the train. We arrived in the middle of the night at the house of Lemmy's astonished parents in Aurora and remained there for the next two days. It was Lemmy who wrote to the fraternity to explain what we had done.

On the following afternoon A. B. arrived to talk to us. In that painful interview, all the arguments were brought forth in their unrelieved ugliness. Lemmy and A. B. did most of the talking. In the end A. B. said that since our decision was not to be changed, he would accept it, and that it would make no difference to either of us on the *Daily Maroon*. In a state of suicidal gloom, all three of us then returned on the afternoon train to Chicago and to the University.

A. B. seemed to me, then and afterwards, the most admirable person I knew in Chicago. He could not have been more than twenty, but he was invested (in my eyes at least) with the wisdom of the ages. He had apparently founded great hopes for the fraternity on both of us, and our desertion was a blow to him; but he had a sense of justice. He could see that there was something to be said on our side, and having accepted the monstrous situation he made the best of it. During the rest of the year A. B. seemed to be little changed, and in the spring, when the freshmen were weeded out for the next step in the *Daily Maroon's* hierarchy, it was A. B. who made me night editor for the following year. I never took the job; my exploits in the democratic army, followed by three months out of college, kept me from going on in the scheme that was to lead (in A. B.'s plan) to the editorship-in-chief. But anybody who knows the fierce antagonisms and merciless injustice of the fraternity system can see that in treating a renegade so fairly A. B. was showing a character rare among undergraduates. There may have been other fraternity men with enough maturity of mind to rise above the system, but I never knew one.

The next three months were, for Lemmy and me, a taste of thoroughgoing ostracism from the normal "campus." In the fraternity system the offense of "pledge stealing" (i.e., inducing a freshman pledged to one fraternity to break his pledge in order to join another) was rigidly condemned. Consequently nobody in any other fraternity would talk to us. The offense of "pledge breaking" was regarded as equally heinous by our former brothers in the bond, and not one of them except A. B. ever spoke to us again. It was a curious and painful experience to pass them on the campus, as we did a dozen times every morning. After a few experiences we learned to look the other way, but the effort was not pleasant. We were, for the winter term, "barbs" (i.e., "barbarians," since "all who are not Greeks are barbarians"). But we were in a far worse position than other "barbs," because they, for the most part, cared nothing about the ordinary undergraduates, led their own lives, and had their own friends. We had none.

"Barbarians" included most of the Jewish students, who were a majority of the total enrolled; the "grinds" and "Christers" among the Christian students; and a few notably "queer" ones who were too violently unlike the average to be desirable recruits to the campus life. Glenway Wescott, descending upon the University from a Wisconsin farm, frightened most of his classmates with his waving yellow hair and his floating black cape and his weirdly literary manner of speech. Elizabeth Roberts, austere and diligent, serious with a terrifying concentration, never showed the slightest interest in the frivolities of the ordinary undergraduates. These and other eccentrics came to be almost my only acquaintances in the University during that term of ostracism from the gaieties of the campus. They were (God save us all!) the "Poetry Club."

The Poetry Club had been formed early in the winter of my freshman year by professorial advocates of an intellectual life for undergraduates. It had started as a prize competition for student poetry. The prize was the sum of $25. I had sent in two bits of verse, neither of them much good, and had thereafter concealed my temerity from everybody, even from A. B. The prize was awarded to a senior whose name I forget, a medical student; but it was explained in the *Daily Maroon* that this had required two ballots, since on the first it was found that three undergraduates had tied for first place. The three were the aforesaid medical student, Glenway Wescott, and myself. The medical student got the $25 and we got the Poetry Club.

We used to meet solemnly in little padded drawing rooms in Ida Noyes Hall and discuss the productions of our colleagues. Glenway always had a sheaf of immortal poetry somewhere about him, which he was ready to read out at the drop of a hat. His poetry was exceedingly "modern," without rhyme or meter or capital letters or punctuation, and very often (to my untutored ear) without sense either. But I was conscious enough of my shortcomings to realize that this was probably my fault, not his; and I sat through many a long reading of which I could make neither head nor tail. His modern verse was eclipsed in modernity and incomprehensibility by that of a senior who was president of the Poetry Club. Indeed, the whole club was excessively modern, and it would have taken more courage than I possessed to affront its contemporary ears with such a deplorable throwback as a sonnet. And since, at that time, I was writing sonnets by the dozen, my contribution to the poetic feast was nil.

We used to enjoy, in our first year, a flattering amount of attention from literary personages not in the University. We were thought, for some reason, to be "promising," and consequently Miss Harriet Monroe, Mr. Carl Sandburg, and other notables from the Chicago *cénacle,* condescended to visit us and read us their own verse. Thus I formed the belief that all poets loved reading aloud and traveled about with reams of unpublished poetry in their pockets.

The solemnity of our gatherings at the Poetry Club would have stunned T. S. Eliot himself. It was sometimes difficult for me to keep from snickering, particularly when the young poets were carried away by the excitement of reading their own productions. More than once the president had to reprove me for undue levity in comment. No doubt the whole thing was funny, but not perhaps so uproariously funny as it seemed to me at seventeen. The whole fraternity-and-campus-collegiate side of me crinkled with hostile, unreasoning laughter at the sight of Glenway declaiming his impassioned verses, his yellow mane thrown back and his childish face uplifted. His later development into a sincere and sensitive artist would have seemed incredible to me then, if anybody had been so rash as to predict it.

The barbarians, the grinds, and the highbrows learned much more than I did at the University. Scornful of the "campus life" that preoccupied the rest of us, they grew into intellectual maturity more rapidly than their fellows, and their interest in general ideas was aroused before most of us knew what an idea was. They knew nothing of the fraternities or clubs, went to no "parties," and ignored the existence of football. It might have been a good thing if I had remained one of them. But I was afflicted by a dichotomy that has never left me: I could not avoid trying to make the best of two worlds. The term of ostracism to which Lemmy and I had been submitted by interfraternity rules came to an end in the spring, and I soon forgot all about the Poetry Club in the excitement of readmission to the other, the average, world of the undergraduates.

No freshman who had broken his pledge to one fraternity could be "rushed" for another for three months. But when the period of suspension ended, at Easter, a change came over the complexion of things. People who had avoided me like the plague all through the winter suddenly started asking me to lunch. In two or three weeks after the ending of the ban I had been pledged again to another fraternity—this time to a Gentile one, which I believe had been exceedingly "good" and was afterwards "good" again. At the precise moment of my admission it was not one of the most brilliant of the undergraduate houses, but it did contain two or three freshmen who were to be among my best and most lasting friends in Chicago. Lemmy—who was off to the wars that summer—joined me in it the following year.

But I was never what is called a "good fraternity man." After the bizarre introduction I had had to the system, it was impossible for me to take it with the literal seriousness it required of its adherents. The adolescent sentimentality that was supposed to be lavished upon the fraternity and the brothers in the bond had been pretty well burned out by my unorthodox experience. It was hard to get up enthusiasm for songs, rituals, and ceremonies when I knew they were being gone through in a couple of dozen other fraternity houses at the same time and by almost exactly the same people. Uniformity—the true uniformity of the good American undergraduate, who talked the same language and wore the same clothes and did exactly the same things as every other undergraduate—was not really accessible to me. It fascinated me for a long time, and I attempted for two years to achieve it; but the effort was useless and soon began to appear uninteresting as well. After about a year in the house (the new house) I moved away from it, to a college hall, and for the rest of my time in the University I lived alone, like a "barb," with the single difference that I did have a fraternity to go to when I pleased. The brothers did not like this attitude and said so more than once, but by the time I had been two years in the college I knew that the heavens would not fall if I went my own way, and their protests did not disturb me.

Christmas of 1920 was my last in the University. My mother was very ill; early in January, 1921, she died. The disaster would probably have made college life unbearable in any case, but there was also the question of money. There had been little enough before; there was none now. January passed in unrelieved gloom. I returned to Chicago lonely and helpless. There was a job for me (thanks to a friend) as a reporter on the Chicago *Daily News*, but I must have been phenomenally stupid at it, for I lasted only two or three weeks. When I received my congé I did, almost without thinking, something that had probably been floating about in the undergrowth of my mind for weeks or months. I walked out of the *Daily News* office, down to the old Dearborn Street station, and onto a train for New York—without luggage and with very little money. For hour after hour I sat at a train window and stared out through tears and dirt. It was a fairly typical departure, to be worked out during the next ten years into a system of going away. *Fuir, là-bas fuir,* could serve as a kind of epigraph for my youth, for it was spent in flight.

I was not to see Chicago again except on two short visits years later, in a world altogether different from that of the University. Those brief visits were sufficient to show me, in retrospect, how narrow my experience had been. For example, there were in Chicago some of the finest collections of modern pictures in the world: I never saw one of them while I was in the University. The Chicago Symphony Orchestra had a long season of concerts and was one of the best ensembles to be found in the United States: but the only concerts I heard in college were a few of the few (four or five a year) given in the University chapel. There were buildings, clubs, interiors, examples of modern art and architecture, and a thousand varieties of life to be seen in the lusty, sprawling, vulgar and vigorous town: I had seen only one. For the whole of my three years and a half beside Lake Michigan I was walled up in a world self-contained, self-governing and self-sufficient, the world of the college undergraduates. Ten years later I could not even remember my way about Chicago, and had to walk all the way to the lake front every time I wanted to distinguish north from south. So much for the people who believed that a university could not lead its own life in a great cry! Youth, at least my variety of ignorant youth, built its own walls very high, and no city was powerful enough to batter them down.

Within those walls what, after all, had I learned? What did I take away from the pseudo-Gothic sanctuary of my pseudo-education? Not much. I had some vague idea of history and philosophy, a bowing acquaintance with English and French literature. I had learned a good deal about snobbery, cruelty, prejudice, injustice and stupidity. I had acquired half a dozen friends—perhaps. I had learned how to dance the fox trot.

It is stupefying to remember how little else I carried from Chicago with me. I spent the next ten years learning the course of events in the world from 1917 to 1921, approaching them as one approaches the course of events in the Renaissance or the Middle Ages. I was a freshman when the Bolshevik Revolution took place, and I am certain that I did not even read the accounts of it that appeared in the Chicago newspapers. The Treaty of Versailles, the defeat and collapse of Woodrow Wilson, the crash of monarchies all through Europe, the revolution in Turkey and the whole bestirring of assorted nationalisms, Wilson's legacy to the world, were duly recorded in history while I went to class dances and wrote songs for Blackfriars. The bourgeois system insulated all its children as much as possible from a knowledge of the processes of human development, and in my case it succeeded admirably in its purpose. Few Hottentots or South Sea Islanders could be less prepared for life in the great world than I was at twenty-one. As I sat in that filthy day coach on the train to New York (filthy with a concentrated filth known only to American day coaches) I was the least respectable of passengers: my ticket went one way only, and I had no baggage of any kind.

# LINCOLN STEFFENS

"WHAT I want," Lincoln Steffens says in one of his letters, "is to gain a deeper insight into the heart of my day." The search for this ideal began early in his youth with certain clear notions regarding the practical means of attaining it. Born in San Francisco in 1866, he grew up in and around the then small capital at Sacramento under the wisely liberal guidance of parents who knew how much was enough of responsibility, direction, and means to permit their resourceful son his maximum self-development. Before he went to college, he knew what he wanted, what he did not want. "He did not want merely to make money," writes Ella Winter; "he did not want to find out things solely to satisfy his own curiosity. He wanted power, but not for personal ends. He wanted to write; but he could not be only 'a writer.' He wanted to discover how men behaved." Beginning at the University of California, he went to five great centers of learning—Berlin, Heidelberg, Leipzig, and the Sorbonne—to work out a system of ethics, a philosophy of life that would set the world of men and women in some orderly relation to his own existence. The quest enriched his mind, enlarged his experience, but, failing to give him his answer, disillusioned him deeply as to the realistic worth of higher education. "Damn these universities, all of them," he wrote late in life to a sister. "They have made my life one of *unlearning* literally, and all my discoveries are of well-known, well-kept secrets."

No armchair philosopher, Steffens returned from his studies abroad and plunged into active newspaper work in New York, first as a reporter and assistant city editor of the *Evening Post* (1892-98), then as city editor of the *Commercial Advertiser* (1898-1902). There he struck his stride. As Ella Winter describes it, " 'Men of affairs' soon observed his peculiar gift for interviewing, his capacity for getting their story. He had humor and intelligence; his interest, his understanding, his integrity inspired their trust and endeared him even to people he was attacking. Business men told him 'shocking' things about their business conduct. . . . They remarked on his courtesy (Steffens was called 'the gentleman reporter'). . . . Steffens could listen. He made it easy to talk. . . . He could meet on equal terms the successful industrialist and the social outcast; make friends with, and explain to themselves, businessmen and bankers, teachers, politicians, reformers, and revolutionists, unhappy wives, crooks, scientists, artists. He saw the connection between things, and could adapt his experience from one field to another." These powers he put to use in the practical ordering of a portion of that world about which the schools had had nothing valid to say. He began by boldly exposing the corruption in the New York police headquarters. He became a gadfly to the big bosses, political and financial, but won the confidence of men like Theodore Roosevelt and Jacob Riis who shared his ideals of American government and refused to accept the alliance between the City Hall and the underworld as a necessary civic evil. Becoming magazine editor of *McClure's* in 1902, Steffens extended his salutary muckraking to St. Louis, Minneapolis, Philadelphia, and Chicago (where he happened upon "an example of reform"), publishing his findings fearlessly in a series of articles called *The Shame of the Cities* (1904). Graft in several state capitals he uncovered in *The Struggle for Self-Government* (1906). In the same year he became associate editor of *The American Magazine* and *Everybody's* (1906-11), from which posts he could give effect to his next articles, *Upbuilders* (1907), a series of studies of Theodore Roosevelt, William Howard Taft, the elder La Follette, and other new political leaders and reformers. Month after month he made himself heard throughout the nation, attacking business evils, upholding free speech, staunchly praising men whom his previous public writings and direct persuasion had brought round to even partial support of his ideals, until a whole generation of Americans in all sorts of places and positions had felt his bracing influence.

Not only those he wrote about but also younger men and women of liberal leanings came into his orbit: Max Eastman, John Reed, Carl Sandburg, Robinson Jeffers, the sculptor Jo Davidson, Ella Winter (who became his second wife), Upton Sinclair; newer writers like Granville Hicks, John Steinbeck, and Robert Cantwell; dozens of newspapermen whom he had inspired to quit their professional cynicism and "care like hell" about the actual conditions of American life. After 1919, when Steffens went with the Bullitt mission to Russia, he spent a good deal of his time living (and observing affairs) in France and Italy in a state as near to retirement as it was in him to achieve. But he was frequently in America, too, at his home in Mount Carmel, California, or lecturing to public audiences and groups of liberal students in the universities, keeping up a wide and steady correspondence with public figures and private friends everywhere, and still seeking that "deeper insight" which had been his early ideal.

As he entered his sixties, Steffens began to gather up the strands of his own life, and five years before his death he published his remarkable *Autobiography* (1931), one of the most readable and stimulating works of life-writing every produced by an American. The reader could find the true Steffens note of fearless, militant honesty in any section of the book. Since a choice had to be made, two chapters are offered here from Steffens's first adventures among intellectuals.

## GOING TO COLLEGE

### *Preparing for College*

T HE YEAR 1884-85 was a period of great adventure for me. When I came up to Berkeley for the entrance examinations at the University of California I failed in Greek, Latin, and enough other subjects to be put off for a year. My father was alarmed. I was eighteen years old, and he thought, I think, that my failure was his fault; he had chosen the wrong school for me. He had, but the right school for me and my kind did not exist. There were schools that put boys into the colleges, east and west, and at a younger age than mine. I came to know those boys well. They are the boys (and they become the men) that the schools, colleges, and the world are made for. Often I have envied them; more often I have been glad that I was not of them.

The elect were, for the most part, boys who had been brought up to do their duty. They memorized whatever their teachers told them to learn. Whether they wanted to know it, whether they understood it or no, they could remember and recite it. Their own driving motives were, so far as I could make out, not curiosity; they rarely talked about our studies, and if I spoke of the implications of something we had read or heard, they looked dazed or indifferent. Their own motives were foreign to me: to beat the other fellows, stand high, represent the honor of the school.

My parents did not bring me up. They sent me to school, they gave me teachers of music, drawing; they offered me every opportunity in their reach. But also they gave me liberty and the tools of quite another life: horses, guns, dogs, and the range of an open country. As I have shown, the people, the businesses, and the dreams of this life interested me, and I learned well whatever interested me. School subjects which happened to bear on my outside interests I studied in school and out; I read more than was required, and I read for keeps, too. I know these subjects to this day, just as I remember and love still the men and women, the boys and girls, who let me be friends with them then and so revealed to me some of the depths and the limitations of human nature. On the other hand I can remember few of my teachers and little of the subjects which seemed to me irrelevant to my life.

These other subjects are interesting, and they might have been made interesting to me. No one tried to interest me in them; they were put before me as things that I had to have to get into college. The teachers of them did not appeal to my curious, active mind. The result was that I did not really work at them and so got only what stuck by dint of repetition: the barest rudiments of a school education. When I knocked at the college gates, I was prepared for a college education in some branches; my mind was hungry enough for the answers to some profound questions to have made me work and develop myself, especially on lines which I know now had no ready answers, only more and ever more questions: science, metaphysics, etc. I was not in the least curious about Greek, Latin, mathematics, and the other "knowledge" required by the standardization of that day.

My father discovered and put me into the best private school in San Francisco as a special student to be crammed for Berkeley— and he retained one of the teachers there, Mr. Evelyn Nixon, to tutor me on the side. Characteristically, too, my father gave me liberty: a room to sleep and work in, with no one to watch over and care for me. I could go and come as I pleased. And I came and went. I went exploring and dreaming alone around that city as I had the country around Sacramento, and the place I liked best was the ocean shore; there I lived over the lives of the Greek heroes and the Roman generals and all the poets of all the ages, sometimes with ecstasy, but never, as in my boyhood, with myself as the hero. A change had come over me.

Evelyn Nixon formed it. He was the first teacher I ever had who interested me in what I had to learn—not in myself, but in the world outside, the world of conscious culture. He was a fanatic of poetry, especially of the classic poets. When he read or recited Greek verse the Greeks came to life; romance and language sang songs to me, and I was inspired to be, like him, not a hero nor even a poet, but a Greek scholar, and thus an instrument on which beautiful words might play. Life filled with meaning, and purpose, and joy. It was too great and too various for me to personify with my boyish imitations and heroism. I wrote verses, but only to learn the technique and so feel poetry more perfectly. I wanted to read, not to write; I wanted to know, not to do and be, great things—Mr. Nixon expressed it.

"I'm nobody," he used to say. "I'm nothing but one of the unknown beings Homer and Dante, Shakespeare, Caesar, and the popes and the generals and statesmen have sung and fought and worked for. I'm the appreciator of all good words and deeds."

A new, a noble rôle, and Evelyn Nixon was a fine example of it: the receiver, not the giver, of beautiful inventions. He was an Englishman; he took a double first at Oxford, I heard, and came for his health to San Francisco. There was a group of such men, most of them with one story. They were athletes, as well as scholars at Oxford and Cambridge; they developed muscles and a lung capacity which they did not need and could not keep up in the sedentary occupations their scholarship put them into. Lung troubles exiled them.

"Keep out of college athletics," they advised. "Don't work up any more brawn there than you can use every day afterward."

Nixon taught me Greek, Latin, and English at school, and at his house he opened up the beauty and the meaning of the other subjects I had to cram up for entrance. I worked for him; I worked more, much more, for myself. He saw this, he saw my craving for the answers to questions, and he laughed.

"I will answer no questions of yours," he shouted. "Men know no answers to the natural questions of a boy, of a child. We can only underline your questions, make you mad yourself to answer them, and add ours to whip, to lash you on to find out yourself —one or two; and tell us! That is what youth is for: to answer the questions maturity can't answer." And when I looked disappointed and balked, he would roar at me like a demon.

"Go to, boy. The world is yours. Nothing is done, nothing is known. The greatest poem isn't written, the best railroad isn't built yet, the perfect state hasn't been thought of. Everything remains to be done—right, everything."

This said, he said it again and again, and finally, to drive me, he set our private hour from seven till eight o'clock Saturday evenings, so that I could stay on into the night with his group of friends, a maddening lot of cultivated, conflicting minds. There were from four to ten of them, all Englishmen, all Oxford and Cambridge men, all exiles and all interested in any and all subjects, which they discussed with knowledge, with the precise information of scholarship, but with no common opinions on anything apparently. There were Tories among them and liberals and one red: William Owen, a grandson, I think, certainly a descendant, of Robert Owen, the first of the early English socialists. There was at least one Roman Catholic, who showed me so that I never forgot it the Christianity of that church; his favorite thesis was that the Protestant churches were Old Testament, righteous sects and knew nothing really of Christ's teachings of love and forgiveness. And there were Protestants there, all schooled in church history, and when a debate came to a clinch, they could quote their authorities with a sureness which withstood reference to the books. I remember one hot dispute of the Catholic's reference to some certain papal bull. Challenged, he quoted it verbatim in the original Latin. What they knew was amazing to me, and how they knew it, but what they did not know struck me harder still. They could not among them agree on anything but a fact. With all their knowledge they knew no essential truth.

It was conversation I was hearing, the free, passionate, witty exchanges of studied minds as polished as fine tools. They were always courteous; no two ever spoke together; there were no asides; they all talked to the question before the house, and while they were on the job of exposition anyone, regardless of his side, would contribute his quota of facts, or his remembrance of some philosopher's opinion or some poet's perfect phrase for the elucidation or the beautification of the theme. When the differences rose the urbanity persisted. They drank their Californian wine with a relish, they smoked the room thick, and they pressed their views with vigor and sincerity and eloquence; but their good temper never failed them. It was conversation. I had never heard conversation before; I have heard conversation sometimes since, but rarely, and never like my remembrance of those wonderful Sat-

urday nights in San Francisco—which were my preparation for
college.

For those conversations, so brilliant, so scholarly, and so consciously unknowing, seemed to me, silent in the background, to
reveal the truth that even college graduates did not know anything, really. Evidences they had, all the testimony of all the wise
men in the historical world on everything, but no decisions. None.
I must myself go to college to find out more, and I wanted to.
It seemed as if I had to go soon. My head, busy with questions
before, was filled with holes that were aching voids as hungry, as
painful, as an empty stomach. And my questions were explicit; it
was as if I were not only hungry; I was hungry for certain foods.
My curiosity was no longer vague.

When on Sundays I would take the gatherings I had made out
of the talk of the night before down to the Cliff House with me
and sit there on the rocks and think, I formed my ignorance into
a system. I was getting a cultivated ignorance, a survey not of the
solved but of the unsolved problems in every science from astronomy to economics, from history to the next tricks in versification.
I thought of them; I thought, rejoicing, that there were things
to do for everybody in every science, every art, every business.
Why, men did not know even how to love, not technically, not
beautifully! I learned of the damage done me by having my sex
feelings separated from love and poetry, and as for astronomy,
government, conversation, play and work, men were just crawling
on their hands and knees out of their caves.

But the best that I got out of it all was objectivity. Those men
never mentioned themselves; apparently they never thought of
themselves. Their interest was in the world outside of themselves.
I caught that. No more play-acting for me. No more dreaming I
was Napoleon or a trapper, a knight, a statesman, or the younger
son of a lord. It is possible that I was outgrowing this stage of a
boy's growth; the very intensity of my life in subjective imagination may have carried me through it, but whether I would have
come out clearly impersonal or no by myself, I don't know. All I
am sure of is that their conversations, the attitude and the interest
of those picked Englishmen, helped and, I think, established in

me the realization that the world was more interesting than I was. Not much to see? No, but I have met men since, statesmen, scholars, business men, workers, and poets, who have never made that discovery. It is the scientific attitude, and some scientists have it—not all; and some others, too.

When I went up for my examination this time in Berkeley I passed, not well in all subjects, but I was admitted to the University, and that fall I entered the University of California with a set of examination questions for the faculty, for the professors, to answer.

## I Become a Student

It is possible to get an education at a university. It has been done; not often, but the fact that a proportion, however small, of college students do get a start in interested, methodical study, proves my thesis, and the two personal experiences I have to offer illustrate it and show how to circumvent the faculty, the other students, and the whole college system of mind-fixing. My method might lose a boy his degree, but a degree is not worth so much as the capacity and the drive to learn, and the undergraduate desire for an empty baccalaureate is one of the holds the educational system has on students. Wise students some day will refuse to take degrees, as the best men (in England, for instance) give, but do not themselves accept, titles.

My method was hit on by accident and some instinct. I specialized. With several courses prescribed, I concentrated on the one or two that interested me most, and letting the others go, I worked intensively on my favorites. In my first two years, for example, I worked at English and political economy and read philosophy. At the beginning of my junior year I had several cinches in history. Now I liked history; I had neglected it partly because I rebelled at the way it was taught, as positive knowledge unrelated to politics, art, life, or anything else. The professors gave us chapters out of a few books to read, con, and be quizzed on. Blessed as I was with a "bad memory," I could not commit to it anything that I did not understand and intellectually need. The bare record of the story of man, with names, dates, and irrelative events, bored me. But I had discovered in my readings of literature, philosophy, and political economy that history had light to throw upon unhistorical questions. So I proposed in my junior and senior years to specialize in history, taking all the courses required and those also that I had flunked in. With this in mind I listened attentively to the first introductory talk of Professor William Cary Jones on American constitutional history. He was a dull lecturer, but I noticed that, after telling us what pages of what books we must be prepared in, he mumbled off some other references "for those that may care to dig deeper."

When the rest of the class rushed out into the sunshine, I went up to the professor and, to his surprise, asked for this memorandum. He gave it me. Up in the library I ran through the required chapters in the two different books, and they differed on several points. Turning to the other authorities, I saw that they disagreed on the same facts and also on others. The librarian, appealed to, helped me search the book-shelves till the library closed, and then I called on Professor Jones for more references. He was astonished, invited me in, and began to approve my industry, which astonished me. I was not trying to be a good boy; I was better than that: I was a curious boy. He lent me a couple of his books, and I went off to my club to read them. They only deepened the mystery, clearing up the historical question, but leaving the answer to be dug for and written.

The historians did not know! History was not a science, but a field for research, a field for me, for any young man, to explore, to make discoveries in and write a scientific report about. I was fascinated. As I went on from chapter to chapter, day after day, finding frequently essential differences of opinion and of fact, I saw more and more work to do. In this course, American constitutional history, I hunted far enough to suspect that the Fathers of the Republic who wrote our sacred Constitution of the United States not only did not, but did not want to, establish a democratic government, and I dreamed for a while—as I used as a child to play I was Napoleon or a trapper—I promised myself to write a true history of the making of the American Constitution. I did not do it; that chapter has been done or well begun since by two men: Smith of the University of Washington and Beard (then) of Columbia (afterward forced out, perhaps for this very work). I found other events, men, and epochs waiting for students. In all my other courses, in ancient, in European, and in modern history, the disagreeing authorities carried me back to the need of a fresh search for (or of) the original documents or other clinching testimony. Of course I did well in my classes. The history professors soon knew me as a student and seldom put a question to me except when the class had flunked it. Then Professor Jones would say, "Well, Steffens, tell them about it."

Fine. But vanity wasn't my ruling passion then. What I had was a quickening sense that I was learning a method of studying history and that every chapter of it, from the beginning of the world to the end, is crying out to be rewritten. There was something for Youth to do; these superior old men had not done anything, finally.

Years afterward I came out of the graft prosecution office in San Francisco with Rudolph Spreckels, the banker and backer of the investigation. We were to go somewhere, quick, in his car, and we couldn't. The chauffeur was trying to repair something wrong. Mr. Spreckels smiled; he looked closely at the defective part, and to my silent, wondering inquiry he answered: "Always, when I see something badly done or not done at all, I see an opportunity to make a fortune. I never kick at bad work by my class: there's lots of it and we suffer from it. But our failures and neglects are chances for the young fellows coming along and looking for work."

Nothing is done. Everything in the world remains to be done or done over. "The greatest picture is not yet painted, the greatest play isn't written (not even by Shakespeare), the greatest poem is unsung. There isn't in all the world a perfect railroad, nor a good government, nor a sound law." Physics, mathematics, and especially the most advanced and exact of the sciences, are being fundamentally revised. Chemistry is just becoming a science; psychology, economics and sociology are awaiting a Darwin, whose work in turn is awaiting an Einstein. If the rah-rah boys in our colleges could be told this, they might not all be such specialists in football, petting parties, and unearned degrees. They are not told it, however; they are told to learn what is known. This is nothing, philosophically speaking.

Somehow or other in my later years at Berkeley, two professors, Moses and Howison, representing opposite schools of thought, got into a controversy, probably about their classes. They brought together in the house of one of them a few of their picked students, with the evident intention of letting us show in conversation how much or how little we had understood of their respective teachings. I don't remember just what the subject was that they threw into the ring, but we wrestled with it till the professors could stand it no longer. Then they broke in, and while we sat silent and highly entertained, they went at each other hard and fast and long. It was after midnight when, the debate over, we went home. I asked the other fellows what they had got out of it, and their answers showed that they had seen nothing but a fine, fair fight. When I laughed, they asked me what I, the D.S., had seen that was so much more profound.

I said that I had seen two highly-trained, well-educated Masters of Arts and Doctors of Philosophy disagreeing upon every essential point of thought and knowledge. They had all there was of the sciences; and yet they could not find any knowledge upon which they could base an acceptable conclusion. They had no test of knowledge; they didn't know what is and what is not. And they have no test of right and wrong; they have no basis for even an ethics.

Well, and what of it? They asked me that, and that I did not answer. I was stunned by the discovery that it was philosophically true, in a most literal sense, that nothing is known; that it is precisely the foundation that is lacking for science; that all we call knowledge rested upon assumptions which the scientists did not all accept; and that, likewise, there is no scientific reason for saying, for example, that stealing is wrong. In brief: there was no scientific basis for an ethics. No wonder men said one thing and did another; no wonder they could settle nothing either in life or in the academies.

I could hardly believe this. Maybe these professors, whom I

greatly respected, did not know it all. I read the books over again with a fresh eye, with a real interest, and I could see that, as in history, so in other branches of knowledge, everything was in the air. And I was glad of it. Rebel though I was, I had got the religion of scholarship and science; I was in awe of the authorities in the academic world. It was a release to feel my worship cool and pass. But I could not be sure. I must go elsewhere, see and hear other professors, men these California professors quoted and looked up to as their high priests. I decided to go as a student to Europe when I was through Berkeley, and I would start with the German universities.

My father listened to my plan, and he was disappointed. He had hoped I would succeed him in his business; it was for that that he was staying in it. When I said that, whatever I might do, I would never go into business, he said, rather sadly, that he would sell out his interest and retire. And he did soon after our talk. But he wanted me to stay home and, to keep me, offered to buy an interest in a certain San Francisco daily paper. He had evidently had this in mind for some time. I had always done some writing, verse at the poetical age of puberty, then a novel which my mother alone treasured. Journalism was the business for a boy who liked to write, he thought, and he said I had often spoken of a newspaper as my ambition. No doubt I had in the intervals between my campaigns as Napoleon. But no more. I was now going to be a scientist, a philosopher. He sighed; he thought it over, and with the approval of my mother, who was for every sort of education, he gave his consent.

# BLISS PERRY

LET the author of "These Crude Young Men" speak for himself:

"I have had a long and exceptionally happy career as a teacher at Williams, Princeton, and Harvard. It began before I was twenty-one, and ended at seventy, for I did not wish to have it said of me, as was once remarked of a venerable Oxford don who refused to retire, that he had all the Christian virtues except resignation.

"This term of service was occasionally broken: by two years of graduate study in Germany, one year of lecturing in various universities of France, and ten years devoted to editing the *Atlantic Monthly*—although in the first of these ten years, and the last two, I was carrying college work at the same time. I have never traveled very far from the beaten paths in America and Europe—except on an occasional fishing trip—but I have had the good fortune to know many interesting persons, in and out of my own profession. I have written many books. They might be better, but they were as good as I knew how to make them."

Does not the reader already feel in these words the inbred modesty and genial warmth of Bliss Perry? For his virtues of honest, fearless, fair-minded judgment, of quick and generous sympathy, of quiet charm, let the reader but look further into this book of his life with the apt Chaucerian title, *And Gladly Teach* (1935)—"And gladly wolde he lerne, and gladly teche"—or into his essays, *The Amateur Spirit* (1904), *Park Street Papers* (1909), *The Praise of Folly* (1923), *Pools and Ripples* (1927), and he cannot fail to experience some of the cheering glow of his personality.

Bliss Perry was born in 1860 and grew up at Williamstown, Massachusetts, the son of Professor Arthur Latham Perry of Williams College. "There is," he admits, ". . . a good deal of the schoolmaster in the Perry blood"; and there continued to be a good deal in his own generation, with (besides himself) his youngest brother Lewis first succeeding to Bliss Perry's professorship of English at Williams and then becoming the present headmaster of Phillips Exeter Academy and another of the five boys becoming a prominent clergyman. There was also a great deal of Williams and Williamstown and the Berkshire Hills, if not in their blood, at least in their spirit. After graduating from college in 1881, Bliss Perry stayed and taught English for two years, taking his A.M. in 1883; then he followed the then popular scholar's trail abroad and studied at the universities of Heidelberg, Berlin, and Strassburg, making a "grand tour" of Western Europe before returning to his *alma mater* as professor. He married Annie L. Bliss of New Haven, "daughter of those old friends of Father and

61

Mother after whom I had been named." From 1893 to 1900, under the exciting administration of Woodrow Wilson, he taught at Princeton, but before his stay there ended, his teaching and writing and reputation as literary critic caused him to be invited to take the editorship of the *Atlantic Monthly*, an office he filled with great distinction and continued in until 1909. Meanwhile, in 1907, President Eliot of Harvard called him to a famous professorship previously held by Ticknor, Longfellow, and James Russell Lowell. For twenty-three years, the most fruitful of his life, he walked with his green bag and his pipe to the College Yard, where he lectured to invariably large classes of delighted undergraduates and shared with eager graduate students his mellow understanding and good-natured advice, diffusing in that "cockpit of learning" the love and appreciation of the humanities.

During these years, too, he produced frequent books, adding to his earlier works on Whittier, Whitman, and prose fiction several ripe studies from his scholarship and observations: *The American Mind* (1912), *Carlyle* (1915), *The American Spirit in Literature* (1918), *The Study of Poetry* (1920), *The Life and Letters of Henry Lee Higginson* (1921), and *The Heart of Emerson's Journal* (1926). Since his retirement in 1930, he has written also *Emerson Today* and a life of Richard Henry Dana (1933). As a result of his year (1909-10) spent in Paris as exchange professor at the Sorbonne, Mr. Perry was made a Chevalier of the Legion of Honor. He is the recipient of many honorary degrees, a Fellow of the American Academy of Arts and Letters and of the Royal Society of Literature.

The following chapter on his Williams days differs from the other college reminiscences in this collection in the ease and freedom with which the author makes one a member of his intimate circle. Fellow students and teachers are introduced by name and personalized by sharp depiction or humorous anecdote. If a biographer's business is to recapture the past, surely this picture of Williams in the seventies and eighties is biography of a high order.

## THESE CRUDE YOUNG MEN

*Ah! that life that I have known! How hard it is to remember
what is most memorable.
We remember how we itched, not how our hearts beat.*
                                                —THOREAU, *Journal*

HALF the advantage of going to college lies in going away to college. Your mother packs your trunk, your father gives you his blessing and some money, and you are off, like the hero of a picaresque novel, to make your own way in the world. To my sister Grace, who left for Wellesley just as I was entering Williams, college was a romantic adventure. "Pioneers, O Pioneers!"

For me it meant loading a little furniture into the lumber wagon and driving across the field where the Thompson Laboratories now stand to the south entry of West College, on whose fourth floor I was to room for the next four years, taking my meals at home. It was the only sensible thing to do, for an old law of Williams allowed free tuition to the sons of professors. Father, with five boys to educate, and Professor Safford, with four, were the most obvious beneficiaries of this ancient statute. I admired Father's pioneering energy in seeking out Mark Hopkins's college for himself, instead of following his own father's example and going to Harvard. I still like to meet men who tell me that they went to Amherst because Garman taught there, or to Bowdoin for Hyde, or to Yale for "Billy" Sumner, or Stanford for David Starr Jordan. It makes education seem real. In my student days in Germany, men were constantly migrating from one university to another in order to get the benefit of some particular course offered that year by a famous scholar. For men mature enough to know what they want, all this is admirable; but it is fairly certain that not one out of ten American freshmen knows what he wants or where he can find it.

So all the Perry and Safford boys, aware that the paternal salary never exceeded twenty-five hundred dollars, went cheerfully to Williams; and there was one period of fourteen years when either a Safford or a Perry, or both, ornamented the college nine. But we could scarcely feel that romantic glamour about Williams which many of our classmates experienced. We had been born and bred in that briar bush. Still, we thought it as good as any other, and indeed it was, for most of us; though we were informed occasionally that a gifted and ambitious boy might be better off at Harvard, where the youthful President Eliot was introducing some very radical ideas. . . .

The studies of our freshman year . . . were the immemorial Latin, Greek, and mathematics. The fifty or more boys in our class recited in each of these subjects every day. There were no sections; good, bad, and indifferent students had precisely the same assignments and were called up in turn. We were doing, literally, what our fathers had done before us. My first Latin lesson, in the preface to Livy, was, as I discovered later in Father's diary, exactly the same assignment which he had had in 1848; and it was also precisely what my son had at Williams as a freshman in 1916. For sixty-eight years at least, and probably much longer, it was the same squirrel in the same cage! One would think that some Professor of Latin, at some time, in an access of emotional insanity might have altered the assignment, even if he kept the dreadful secret to himself.

The theory was, of course, that what freshmen needed was grammatical drill, and that certain Latin and Greek texts were convenient, not to say hallowed implements for this purpose. The irony of the situation was that some of us actually liked Latin and Greek, loved to turn those splendid periods into the best English which we could command, and were ready to be interested in whatever the Greeks and Romans had to say. But we fared less well in the classroom than some boy with an accurate verbal memory for the list of rules and exceptions as set down in the grammars of Goodwin and Allen and Greenough. I had been captivated in school by the poetry of Virgil. That meant to me the six books of the *Aeneid* that were then required, but I cannot recall that any teacher informed me that Virgil had ever written anything but those six books. What Virgil's real place was in Roman literature and in world literature was never mentioned.

I liked to read Horace, and a knowledge of the scansion certainly increased my sense of his cleverness, but in the college classroom his wit and wisdom seemed to evaporate, and there was only the grammar and scansion left. The extracts which we read from Thucydides and Herodotus were interesting, but we were warned never to use "ponies," and no one hinted to us that we would do well to read in an English translation the entire work of these or any other Greek authors. Professor Fernald was an admirable drillmaster in the rudiments of the Greek language, but his conscientious interpretation of his duty as a teacher left him no time to initiate us into the wonders of Greek literature— even in an English dress.

I obeyed strictly that rule forbidding the use of translations. When we came to read Cicero's *Letters*—for which no "pony" was available—many of my friends were in sore trouble. I have lived long enough to hear Cicero described today as a "stuffed shirt," but I found his *Letters* amusing and eloquent, and I wish that as an undergraduate I could have had Gaston Boissier's *Cicéron et ses Amis*, which I remember reading with my children one winter in Rome. But I had four classmates who could not read a sentence of the *Letters* without a translation, though they knew their Latin grammar well enough. We were then reciting to Professor E. H. Griffin at five in the afternoon. I used to come up from baseball practice about four, and having then a knack for fluent though somewhat inaccurate reading of Latin at sight, I would translate Cicero's *Letters* to my four grammatical classmates. I do not doubt that my Latinity was much like David Garrick's. "He has not Latin enough," declared Samuel Johnson, who had once taught "Davy." "He finds out the Latin by the meaning rather than the meaning by the Latin." At any rate, that was what Professor Griffin evidently thought of me, for at the end of the term all of my four friends received a better grade in Latin than I did. . . .

Enough, however, of Greek and Latin! Our third subject was mathematics, in which we were instructed, in a gloomy basement room of the old gymnasium, by Professor Dodd. "In his younger days," as I have written elsewhere,[1] "he had been a Latinist, until the loss, by fire, of his manuscript Latin grammar disheartened him, and he accepted a chair of elementary mathematics, which he kept till his death. He fulfilled his duties as instructor with perfect gravity and fidelity, but cared wholly for other things: for his collections of Phaedrus and black-letter Chaucers; for Scott's novels, which he used to read through once each year; for the elder dramatists; for Montaigne and Lamb. Weather permitting, he drove from twenty to forty miles a day in his rusty, mud-covered buggy; he knew every wild flower, every lovely or bold view, within reach of Williamstown. To be his companion upon one of these drives was to touch the very essence of fine, whimsical, irresponsible scholarship."

But to us freshmen he appeared to be simply a taskmaster. The system by which, irrespective of our training and aptitudes, we were all herded together in one classroom, was not of his devising. He was himself performing an uncongenial duty, and he did not see why we should not perform ours. We had a few brilliant mathematicians who used to annoy him purposely by substituting original demonstrations in place of those given in Loomis. We had one man, at least, who had no conception whatever of the meaning of geometry, but whose verbal memory was so remarkable that he could recite every proposition by heart. Dodd gave him a high mark and he ultimately became a bishop.

Yet one adventure of my own in his classroom may serve to illustrate Professor Dodd's wisdom and patience in handling a sulky boy. I disliked mathematics intensely, and aimed to do just enough work to secure a passing grade. One day, in our study of trigonometry, he told us to be ready to box the compass. It did not involve ten minutes of work, but I balked at it, holding that boxing the compass was a sheer mechanical exercise, beneath the dignity of a college classroom. Dodd called us up by lot—or at least pretended to do so—for we were never certain that the name written on a piece of paper and drawn from his pasteboard box was the name which he actually announced. At any rate, "Perry"

[1] *The Amateur Spirit*, p. 98.

was the first name called to box the compass. I rose decorously, shook my head firmly, and sat down. It meant a "zero." For six days running, this little ceremony was repeated, to the delight of the class. Then I consulted the oracle of the coal-closet, for on the inside of that closet door in No. 32 West College I kept a careful record of my "zeros" and "x's" under Dodd. Those six "zeros" in a row looked as big as the national debt, and a very few minutes of applied mathematics proved to me that I could not afford to take another one if I wished to pass the course. Accordingly on the seventh day, when the Professor began the hour by inquiring mildly, in his queer throaty voice: "Perry, are you ready to box the compass for us today?" I boxed it, amid great applause. Dodd twinkled, but said nothing; he knew all along that he held the winning card.

Our life in West College, as in the other dormitories of that period, was primitive enough to have satisfied Rousseau. In fact, we may almost be said to have lived like the beasts that perish. There was no water except what we carried up in pitchers from an outside pump. It may be imagined that we carried as little as possible. Even in the gymnasium, which I frequented for four winters to keep in training for baseball, there were only three or four hand-basins for washing. "Showers" had not been invented, and there was neither water nor money for tubs. We had to provide ourselves with coal stoves, as no dormitory was heated. There was no service of any kind, except that ash-cans and slop-pails were placed in the hallway of each floor, to be emptied whenever the college janitor got around to it. If we chose to sweep our rooms occasionally and make up our beds, we did so; but this was a matter of individual taste rather than prescription. Carpets were a rare luxury: I had an oilcloth to cover the middle of the room, a table with a kerosene "student-lamp," two or three chairs, a bookcase, and a few prints.

But happiness, as many an unwashed philosopher has pointed out, does not depend upon furnishings. We had youth and health and high spirits. I fear we kicked too many ash-cans and pails downstairs; and since our fathers were charged two dollars a term for any windows we might break and we considered this charge an economic outrage, we took pains to smash, each term, two dollars' worth of glass, very roughly calculated. Carpenter Clark, in deep gloom, described a student as "a window-breaking animal." That was also the opinion of Dr. Chadbourne, who lived in the beautiful President's House opposite West College. The favorite sport of the denizens of the north entry of West College was to smash a few panes of glass, start the ash-cans rolling, blow a tin horn, and yell "Chad!" Instantly, at any hour of the day or night, the President would jump out of his front door like a "jack-in-the-box," gold-headed cane in hand, his eyes blazing behind his gold-rimmed glasses, and his beard and coat-tails flying all abroad. If he caught a student he would expel him on the spot, though he usually took him back, with the kindliest admonitions, the next morning. I used to wonder that it never seemed to occur to so bright a man that, if he simply stayed in his study, our whole game would be spoiled. He thought himself, however, a masterful disciplinarian, and that the secret of discipline was in threats. He was the first President of Williams to take any interest in the beauty of the college grounds, but his method of persuading undergraduates to share his desire for better lawns was simply to post notices: "Keep off the Grass." We had never heard of such a thing, and those words became, alas, the unofficial motto of his administration! Professors were expected to act as policemen. A few years later, at Princeton, when the same question arose of protecting the lawns against the ball-playing and short-cut propensities of undergraduates, I heard President Patton drawl out indolently but with finality: "Are not pleasant relations between students and faculty more important than a little grass?"

It was fortunate that most of our surplus energy went into athletics rather than mischief. Williams had given up intercollegiate rowing, and organized football was still a thing of the future, but everyone played baseball after a fashion, and it is impossible to convey to a present-day undergraduate the enthusiasm which we felt for it. The annual "horn-game" between freshmen and sophomores, when tin horns and monstrous "devil's fiddles"

were used by each class to rattle the opposing team, was the chief
athletic event of the year—more important, in fact, than the "college" nine's games with Amherst. I happened to be captain of our
class team, and caught. The mask, invented by Thayer of Harvard, was just coming into use, but the first models had brittle
wire and were likely to be broken by a foul tip. Otherwise the
catcher had no protection whatever: neither chest pad nor shin-
guards nor even a regulation glove, though many catchers bought
a pair of farmers' buckskin gloves, cutting off the fingers of the
left-hand glove, and padding the palm with a handkerchief. This
helped a little, but not much. Fielders' gloves were unknown, and
most of us carried bone-bruises from one end of the season to
the other. Pitchers were beginning to work the curve ball, though
still compelled to throw underhand, at a distance of only forty-
five feet from the plate. There was no coaching except what the
captain ventured to offer, and he had to be tactful about that;
and there was no medical or other supervision. If we were hurt,
we were hurt. I still carry the scar of a left finger badly broken
by a foul tip; I remember pushing the bone back under the skin,
wrapping a handkerchief around it and playing the game out,
since we had no other catcher. It was boyish folly, of course, but
any one of us would have preferred to lose a finger rather than
lose a ball game.

We formed our own social groups with entire freedom. There
was of course, among the freshmen, a "West College crowd," a
"South College crowd," and so on; but these associations were
spontaneous and flexible. The Greek letter fraternities, which
since our time have assumed great prominence in the social life
of Williams, were then a minor matter. There was no organized
"rushing season," and though a few freshmen were pledged in
advance, not more than a third of each class—and those mainly
the wealthier men—joined the fraternities. The rest of us were
called "neutrals," and though we indulged in occasional satire
upon what we considered the snobbishness of awarding a claim
for social distinction upon a cash basis, there was little heart-
burning over it, and no apparent effect upon class politics or

individual popularity. The question of remaining a "neutral" was
simplified for me by Father's attitude. As an undergraduate he
had been a charter member of Alpha Delta Phi, but twenty-five
years of observation had convinced him, rightly or wrongly, that
the fraternities did more harm than good, and he directed his sons
not to accept an invitation. By the time his youngest boy entered
college, Father had retired from teaching and relaxed his rule; so
that Lewis, who had already been excused from learning to milk
(the only real blot upon his career, in the opinion of his older
brothers!), was allowed the additional indulgence of joining a
fraternity.

There were, however, two other undergraduate organizations
(both of them now extinct) which I joined early and greatly
enjoyed: the Lyceum of Natural History, and the Philologian
Literary Society. The "L.N.H." had had an honorable history,
had sent out the first scientific expedition ever attempted by an
American college, and had helped to train many distinguished
naturalists. . . . As Professor Tenney's chair had not been filled,
we were obliged to work without any supervision, but we had
rooms in Jackson Hall, and free access to zoological collections.
We organized our own field work, wrote reports, and tried our
hand at dissections. I spent a good deal of time trying to learn to
mount birds, but I had no real instruction in that art, and finally,
after removing the skin from a great blue heron—a rank feeder
on frogs and fish, and quite too "high" when it was brought in—
I abandoned the effort in disgust.

The rivalry between the Philologian and Philotechnian literary
societies had once been intense, and freshmen had been pledged
to one or the other before entering college. I "went" Philologian,
like my father. Each society had pleasant rooms in South College, with excellent libraries, which were then more used by
undergraduates than the college library. At the weekly meetings
there were essays, orations, and debates. We elected an undergraduate "critic," who was usually merciless. I debated with zeal
throughout my college course, and was thought by my classmates to have uncanny luck in being on the winning side. As a
matter of fact I had a "system," whose secret I guarded as closely

as I had once guarded old Hadsell's "side-holt." It was very simple. In a small college you knew rather accurately the mental habits of each of your opponents in debate. If the other boy was likely to spend two hours in preparation, I spent four; if he spent ten, I would spend twenty. It worked. Not long ago, I explained this "system" to a group of Harvard intercollegiate debaters, but it did not seem to impress them. They had hoped I would talk about the "strategy" and "tactics" of debating—which are indeed interesting enough; but if you have mastered a particular subject twice as well as the other fellow, you may not need any strategy in order to smash him. Alas, how fluent and cocksure I was in those old debating days, and when we Philologians man-handled the Philotechnians in joint debates—the smiling Mark Hopkins acting as judge, as he did in my father's time—how ineffably proud we were! It seemed almost as important, though perhaps not quite, as banging out a base-hit when a hit was needed.

At the end of freshman year, I was promoted to the "college" or varsity nine, and usually played third base thereafter. Bowdoin, Union, and Amherst were about the only colleges we played, though some of our keenest games were with semi-professional teams from manufacturing towns near-by, like Hoosac Falls, Blackinton, North Adams, and Renfrew. We had both a spring and a fall season, and toward the end of my senior year I discovered that baseball was taking a great deal of time. For four years I had scarcely gone trout-fishing or mountain-climbing except in vacations, and now I had developed a sudden passion for archery. I explained this to Captain Fred Fox at the close of a Saturday game, and resigned from the team. The Amherst game was only two or three weeks away. Fox was a taciturn fellow, and one of my best friends, but when I mentioned the claims of archery, he found plenty of words for once, and on Monday I was the first man to report for practice. I think I have wanted few things in life more ardently than to make a hit the last time I came to bat in college. I got it—and then an extra game was scheduled, and I had to get it all over again. Even now, after more than half a century, I have vivid dreams of those old strains and chances and mischances of the game. When the Boston Symphony Orchestra played *Til Eulenspiegel* for the first time in Cambridge, a very musical lady declared that there were only two men in Sanders Theatre who smiled at the right moments, Professor Münsterberg and myself. I did not dare to confess to her that I was really one hundred and forty miles distant from the music, playing over again a ball game against Renfrew, where I came in very fast from third base to field a bunt and missed it altogether! What Münsterberg may have been thinking of, I cannot say.

Our classroom work in the sophomore and junior years gained somewhat in interest and variety. The elective system had not then been introduced, except that a few choices were offered, as for instance between French and German. . . .

I chose German rather than French. Professor Gilson, a lame man with a dark, silky beard, was a Romantic by temperament and had been confirmed in it by long sojourns in Germany. He was an intimate in our household, and had given me as a small boy Kingsley's *Water Babies,* a book full of the strangest natural history, and containing what I thought was a wonderful sentence spoken by Mother Carey ("natura naturans") in her Peacepool: "I am not going to trouble myself to make things. I sit here and make them make themselves." That seemed to me to explain Darwinism. I tried hard to please Gilson now, and he was a patient and enthusiastic teacher. I can never read the wonderful quatrain of the Harper's song in *Wilhelm Meister,* beginning

Wer nie sein Brod mit Thränen ass

—lines that reveal the very essence of Gilson's own personality— without remembering how he asked us once to bring an English translation of that quatrain to the next recitation. I toiled all the evening over a metrical translation, quite unaware that thousands of men had attemped that task without much success. As we were going into the classroom the next day, I was accosted by "Fatty" Smith, the best poker-player in our class, but notably weak in German. "Bliss," he said, "lend me your translation. Gilson called you up yesterday, and he won't call you today; but he is sure to call me!" It seemed priggish to refuse, for "Fatty" was in a tight place; and I parted with my carefully wrought jewel. Smith was the first man called, and obediently wrote that translation upon the blackboard. Gilson read it, looked quizzically at "Fatty" Smith, and then his eye roamed over the class and rested upon me. "Perry," he said blandly, "will you write *your* translation upon the blackboard?" I had to think fast, but by dint of using phrases which I had rejected the night before, I managed to produce a second version. Gilson shook his head as if in deep depression. "Bliss," he remarked sadly, addressing me by my first name, "your poetical style reminds me of Ossian." I suppose none of us knew who Ossian was, but I found Macpherson's poems in the college library that afternoon, and decided that Professor Gilson had not intended to compliment me. Charming, lonely, sorrow-stricken Gilson, with his inner life so completely hidden from that group of happy-go-lucky boys!

> Wer nie sein Brod mit Thränen ass,
> Wer nie die Kummervollen Nächte
> Auf seinem Bette weinend sass,
> Der Kennt euch nicht, ihr himmlischen Mächte!

Under the system of required courses then in vogue, we all studied three subjects under my father: the Constitution of the United States, English history, and political economy. His public reputation, then at its height, had been won in the latter field,[1] but it often happens that a teacher with wide-ranging intellectual interests is known to the academic public mainly by one of his courses, while his best teaching may actually be done in courses that do not catch the public eye. I think that my father's lectures on the Constitution were admirable, although we were not mature enough to grasp all of their implications. We could not appreciate, for instance, the significance of many of those Supreme Court decisions which he analyzed with such zest. As Grandfather Smedley once said of John Bascom's sermons in a little church in Pownal, "He put the fodder too high for the calves." On the other hand, his course in the history of England has been criti-

[1] See Carroll Perry, *A Professor of Life* (1923), and the sketch by Broadus Mitchell in the *Dictionary of American Biography*.

cized as being too elementary—"practically a memoriter exercise."
I cannot agree with this verdict. It is true that we were required
to familiarize ourselves, for each recitation, with a few pages of
J. R. Green's *Short History of the English People*, then a new
and—to me at least—a fascinating book. But this was only the beginning: we had to rise and state the substance of each of Green's
paragraphs in our own words, and then discuss the facts and
judgments involved, amid constant questioning and illustrations
offered by the Professor and the class. To me it was an immensely
stimulating course, and in view of my subsequent studies, quite
the most valuable one which I had at Williams, although there
were some moments in Mark Hopkins's recitation room which
made a deeper impression upon me at the time.

In the famous course on political economy I was self-conscious,
and often alarmed lest Father, in the intensity of his convictions,
should become too excited. He had just turned fifty in our junior
year, and seemed in robust health and splendid vitality; but he
had toiled and thought and felt too passionately, and ten years
later he was a broken man. On many aspects of his subject he
was content with clear and dispassionate exposition. Production
and exchange, labor and capital, land and currency and credit,
he could discuss with scientific precision and poise. But when he
came to foreign trade and American tariffs, he smelled the battle
like a war-horse. His very bones cried out against "Protection,
falsely so called." I had heard all this at home since I had heard
anything, and I had no doubt that Father, like his friends W. G.
Sumner and David A. Wells, was on the right side of the tariff
reform argument. I think so still. But I hated to have my classmates egg him on, by their questions, to more and more dogmatic
and extravagant utterance. There was no help for it. His absolute
frankness, his devotion to truth as he saw it, his ethical conviction that tariffs drawn in favor of privileged groups were simply
a question of Right and Wrong, made him a formidable advo-
cate, and his wit and humor were weapons that often made the
class howl with delight, even though these weapons were turned
against their own arguments. "Peri's" classroom was alive—everyone admitted that; but I wondered whether it were not too con-

troversial, too much of a spectacle. A generation later, at Harvard, one might have seen much the same intermittent intolerance in a very different man, Irving Babbitt. Babbitt had naturally a finely critical intelligence, but when he touched Rousseau and Romanticism he threw dispassionate criticism to the winds and became a stark, uncompromising dogmatist, a Peter the Hermit, leading a Crusade. A delightful passage in Logan Pearsall Smith's *More Trivia* may serve to illustrate the point:

"I expressed my conviction briefly; but the time-honored word I made use of seemed unfamiliar to [these youngsters];—they looked at each other and began whispering together. Then one of them asked in a hushed voice, 'It's *what*, did you say?'

"I repeated my monosyllable loudly. Again they whispered together, and again their spokesman came forward.

" 'Do you mind telling us how you spell it?'

" 'I spell it, I spell it with a *W!*' I shouted. 'W-R-O-N-G— *Wrong!*' "

Arthur Latham Perry and Irving Babbitt had scarcely a trait in common except this: they respected the unfashionable word "Wrong" and were not afraid to shout it.

In view of my undergraduate interest in speaking, writing, and miscellaneous reading, it is curious that I can recall so little about our class work in English. I remember that we studied D. J. Hill's *Rhetoric* and were informed that the distinction between "synecdoche" and "metonymy" was important. We had a *Manual of English Literature*, and must, I suppose, have recited from it. My brother Carroll, whose class also used a *Manual*, avers that he learned just one thing about English literature in college, namely, that "The lyrics of Edmund Waller can never die." I did not carry away from the classroom even as much as that.

We were obliged to write and deliver "orations" once or twice a year under the supervision of the Professor of Rhetoric, Llewellyn Pratt. He was a courteous, cultivated gentleman, and a master of public speech; and no doubt he gave our productions as much attention as they deserved. It was very little. We had also, during part of each year, the services of a friendly and enthusiastic Professor of Oratory, George L. Raymond, author of many volumes of verse and a series of books on Esthetics. We used his *Orator's Manual*, containing an ingenious and elaborate system of voice-production, stress, gesticulation, posture, etc. We called him "Bulldozer," because he was nervous in the classroom and easily overawed; his nickname when he taught at Princeton was "Mary" —for the same reason. But no one could be kinder to me, or more encouraging. Up to my senior year, the "gloomy shine" of my oratorical efforts had not impressed the judges of our contests, but now, under "Bulldozer's" direction, I toiled away, in the big empty Museum room of Jackson Hall, at his "vocal exercises," and learned the trick of deep-breathing and the proper "placing" of the voice. Even the moth-eaten stuffed moose behind the glass cases must have thought the performances of this young Demosthenes absurd, and I let no one, except Raymond, know what I was doing. But I was bent, grimly and ferociously, upon mastering every secret of *The Orator's Manual*, in order to win the Graves Prize speaking contest at Commencement. And there was really more than that at stake, though I did not then suspect it.

Whatever the defects of the curriculum were in our day, we had the inestimable advantage of plenty of time to ourselves. In our senior year, for example, we recited in ethics or philosophy, at nine in the morning and five in the afternoon. Dr. Chadbourne and Dr. Hopkins were supposed to divide these courses, but Dr. Chadbourne spent the fall term stumping the country for Garfield, and as he was retiring from office at the end of the year (and was also trying to run two cotton mills!) he left most of the senior instruction to Dr. Hopkins. We had textbook assignments, but a half-hour of preparation was all that most of us gave. The theory was that seniors should have ample time for reading, writing, and general reflection upon man's place in the universe! This suited me exactly and the winter nights in Williamstown were long.

I had been elected an editor of the college paper, *The Athenaeum*, in my sophomore year, and was greatly flattered until I discovered that the youngest editor was expected to read all the proof and write whatever verses were needed for "fillers." I kept at it, however, and learned to write my share of those smart and caustic editorials which long have been the curse of Williams journalism. I wrote about new books, hailing Swinburne's latest volume, for instance, with all the rapture with which undergraduates of today have welcomed D. H. Lawrence and Ernest Hemingway. Robert Louis Stevenson was just beginning to print short stories. Any day might bring a new book by Browning or Tennyson, Darwin or Huxley, Hardy or Arnold. Emerson and Carlyle were living, though they had ceased to write. But Whitman, Whittier, Holmes, Longfellow, and Lowell were still productive. Melville was alive, though we did not know it, and Mark Twain was very much alive indeed. And so were Victor Hugo and Ibsen, Turgeniev and Tolstoi and Karl Marx.

"Here is God's plenty," and enough to turn any boy's head. No one was aware of the deep and subtle change about to take place in the spirit of English literature. We had already had the best that the Victorians could offer, and after 1880 there was to be less of that "quality of nobleness" which had been the distinctive trait of English writing since 1830. But we boys in a rural New England college knew nothing about literary tendencies or literary labels: it never occurred to us that we were "Victorians" or "Puritans" or even New Englanders. There were the books if we wanted to read them, and whether the authors were American or English, Romantics or Realists, mattered little to us.

I read without any plan or purpose except to gratify an appetite for books. Unluckily, none of us, I think, read in college any Latin and Greek except what was required. That was the tragedy of the system: we broke with the classics just when they might have served us most. I read no French as an undergraduate and only a little more German than was demanded. I was still reading Emerson, and began now to dip into some of the authors whom he praised, like Montaigne and Rabelais and old Burton of the *Anatomy of Melancholy*. I had read Milton and Wordsworth and Whittier since childhood, and can no more recall my first reading of *The Scarlet Letter* than my first reading of *Hamlet*. But now I began to make some discoveries: Keats and Byron (though neither Shelley nor Coleridge as yet), Carlyle (to whom

I was introduced by a "village atheist," a Welsh cobbler who trained his dog to bark whenever the Methodist Church bell rang!) and Browning and Walt Whitman. What happiness in picking such "finds" as these from the upper shelves of the college library, and carrying them off to 32 West College! I was warned that Mark Hopkins had declared that *he* could not understand Browning, but secretly I believed that the old gentleman had not made much of an effort. I was sure that there was "gold in them hills," and I mined them for a score of years. There was no one to share my enthusiasm for Browning and Whitman, but Fred Bard and I used to wander over the hills spouting Swinburne and *The Earthly Paradise* and *Sigurd the Volsung* to each other, and when Fred reported that his barber in New York (or it may have been a barkeeper) could declaim more pages of *Sigurd the Volsung* than either of us, our cup of delight was full.

Yet I think that for the majority of our class the chief intellectual adventure of the senior year was the morning or evening hour with Mark Hopkins. He was then seventy-eight, but his powerful frame and noble features showed little or no trace of the burden of years, and there was never, up to the time of his death at eighty-five, any apparent diminution of his mental vigor. This exceptional endowment played its part in the spell which he cast upon his contemporaries. No one can furnish an adequate definition of greatness, but Mark Hopkins, like Gladstone and Bismarck, gave the beholder the instant impression of being in the presence of a great man. He had already become in his lifetime a legend, a symbol of teaching power: "Mark Hopkins on one end of a log, and a student on the other." [1]

Four of his pupils and colleagues, Professors Bascom, A. L. Perry, Carter, and Spring, have made painstaking analyses of the Doctor's personality and methods. They all agree that he was not,

---

[1] As a matter of fact, this famous phrase, as originally uttered by General Garfield at a Williams dinner at Delmonico's in 1872, did not contain the word "log." Washington Gladden, who heard the speech, reported that Garfield's actual words were: "A pine bench with Mark Hopkins at one end of it and me at the other is a good enough college for me." *Life and Letters of James Abram Garfield,* by Theodore C. Smith, New York, 1925, vol. II, p. 812.

in the strict academic sense, a "scholar"; the source of his power was not in his knowledge of books. But that is an old story in the history of the world: "He taught them as one having authority, and not as the scribes." Any teacher can study books, but books do not necessarily bring wisdom, nor that human insight essential to consummate teaching skill. I think that the peculiar gift of Mark Hopkins has rarely been better described than by a single phrase from my old friend Professor Dodd. I was driving with him over Mason's Hill, a year or two after my graduation, and I was telling him about attending the brilliant lectures on the history of philosophy which Stanley Hall was then giving to Williams seniors.

"After all," I said—captivated by the new horizons which Stanley Hall was opening for us—"Dr. Hopkins taught us nothing about the history of philosophy." "No," said Dodd slowly, "he taught you nothing *about* philosophy, but he taught you *to philosophize*." This is essentially what my father wrote, in pointing out that the Doctor's favorite question—"What do *you* think about it?"—was the key to his success as a teacher. After beginning by asking the pupil what the textbook stated upon this and that topic, the Doctor would almost invariably inquire: "*What do you think about it?*" "It stole the hearts of crude young men to hear such a man as he was plumping down upon them from his desk, as if it were a matter of much importance, such a question as that! It suddenly increased their own self-respect."

To discover that you had a mind—narrow, commonplace, or ill-trained, perhaps, but a mind of your own, was a thrilling experience. You rose when your name was called, and sometimes the Doctor's initial questions, like those of Socrates, seemed remote from the matter in hand. The fascination lay partly in the effort to guess what the Doctor was driving at. He knew, and we did not, but the game gradually revealed itself as one bland question succeeded another. He always had an objective and sometimes the class perceived it more quickly than the boy who was on his feet, trying to keep his wits and to avoid foolish answers. But often the objective was remote: we were like a party of mountain-climbers, conscious that we were well above the timber-line, but ignorant of the particular peak for which the guide was headed. We were having a good climb and were made to feel that we could keep up the pace and get some grand views, even though the Doctor did not seem to care whether we reached any particular hut by nightfall. To some men in each class, no doubt, he seemed a philosopher without a system, a moralist indifferent to definitions. He was in truth a builder of character who could lay a stone wall without ever looking at a blue-print.

All of us recognized his immense latent power. "Half his strength he put not forth." Yet this apparently indolent wrestler with ideas—never dogmatic, never over-earnest, never seeming to desire converts to any creed or platform—was ceaselessly active in studying the members of each class and in directing, however subtly, the questions by which he sought to develop and test their individual capacity. "Also he knew men at once," it was said of Cosimo de' Medici, "when he looked into their eyes."

I must limit myself to a single illustration of this wise handling of one of his "crude young men." In our senior year the mutterings of the famous Andover controversy in theology began to be heard throughout New England. Was "everlasting" punishment the same thing as "eternal" punishment? What was really at issue was not the exact meaning of some Greek words, but the whole Calvinistic conception of the actuality of a fire and brimstone hell. I had been brought up in a very liberal and deeply religious household, and I knew that on this question of a material hell my father and his friend John Bascom thought very differently from Grandfather Smedley. Being now twenty and fond of debating, I was wholly on the side of the "new theology," as it was then called. Nobody knew where Dr. Hopkins really stood, although he was supposed to be a pillar of Orthodoxy. He was an old man and a wise one, and refused to be drawn into controversy.

One Saturday morning, in reviewing some passage from a textbook, he called me up and put this question: "Perry, do you think that the fear of future punishment is a proper motive for human action?" I fear the light of battle gleamed in my eyes, for I saw the whole of the New Theology at stake in the Doctor's apparently abstract and innocent inquiry. And the textbook had said "Yes"; which was only an additional reason why a self-confident youth should take the other side. So I straightened my shoulders and answered "No, sir."

The Doctor looked me over. "I will repeat the question," he said slowly. "Do you think that the fear of future punishment is a proper motive for human action?"

"No, sir, I do not." I was ready to debate against a whole Bench of Bishops; *Athanasius contra mundum;* Luther at the Diet of Worms, etc., etc.

To my disappointment, the Doctor straightway called up "Turk" Parsons, a missionary's son, who recited the textbook position with fluent precision. But by that time the Doctor seemed to have lost all interest in the question, and went on to something else. The fight was evidently off, and I sulked for the rest of the hour. When the class was dismissed, I had to pass directly in front of the Doctor's desk. He leaned over toward me, bowing his magnificent shoulders and superb head. It was as if an old lion had turned in his cage to look at you, only that all the bars were magically down.

"Bliss," he said gravely, "did I understand you to say that you thought the fear of future punishment was not a proper motive for human action?"

I was still obstinate, "Yes, sir, that is what I think."

The leonine features relaxed into a captivating smile. "Well, now, Bliss," he remarked confidentially, as if to a very intimate friend; *"a great many young men have felt about that question exactly as you do."*

All the anger and conceit went out of me. I saw myself, not as a lonely rebel, but as one of the great company of the immature. With one sentence Mark Hopkins had put me in my place, and had nevertheless managed to let me feel that he liked me. I hope I had manners enough to thank him, for no teacher had ever rendered me a greater service.

The class of 1881 was the last to be graduated under President Chadbourne. We represented, although we were not aware of it, the end of an era. President Carter's administration was to

bring in new professors, new methods of instruction, new buildings and endowments, and a large increase in the number of
undergraduates. The rural isolation of Williamstown began to be
less marked, though it was still to be a score of years before tele-
phones and motor cars began to herald vaster changes still. I do
not pretend to hold a brief for the old order of things, either at
Williams or at the other Eastern colleges of our time, but before
the old order is quite forgotten, it is fair to say that with all of its
obvious defects, it bred some very good men. William Howard
Taft (Yale, 1878), Woodrow Wilson (Princeton, 1879), and
Theodore Roosevelt (Harvard, 1880) all belonged to our undergraduate generation. Their children, and now their grandchildren, have enjoyed far richer academic opportunities than those
three men. Whether the second and third generations have
worked as hard or felt as keen a prompting of ambition for leadership is perhaps an idle question; but the educational conditions
that obtained in the late eighteen-seventies were not quite so un-
fruitful as they may easily be made to appear.

At Williams, at least, it must be admitted that during the eighteen-seventies there were more teachers of national reputation,
in proportion to the total number of the faculty, than there have
been in any subsequent period. The multiplication of courses and
instructors, made necessary by the sudden increase of students,
has resulted, as probably in all American colleges, in a lowering
of the proportion of teachers of exceptional ability. There is less
extreme poverty, and no physical hardships whatever, for Williams undergraduates today; but whether luxurious surroundings
are really any stimulus to scholarship—even in the "houses" of
Harvard and the "colleges" of Yale—remains to be proved.

Our social life, like our esthetic life, was undeniably barren.
We had practically no contact with our professors outside of the
classroom, and it did not occur to us that this might be desirable.
When one thinks of the tutors and preceptors and advisers and
deans of today, it is curious to remember that we had no one to
"hold our hand" in time of trouble, and that—precisely like the
university students of France and Germany both then and now—
we had not the slightest desire to have our hands held. We

wanted to be let alone. We chafed very little over the rigid requirements of attendance: chapel twice a day, and no allowance
whatever of classroom "cuts" except for illness. Discipline, swift
and simple, was administered by the professors who served as
"class officers," for deans had not been invented.

About half the men in our class confessed to taking an occasional drink, although I do not remember seeing a single drunken
undergraduate in the four years. Nevertheless, of the ten men
who were photographed for the varsity nine in our senior year,
four were hopelessly ruined by drink before they reached middle
life. My own impression is that at Williams, Princeton, and Harvard—the colleges that I have known best—there has been a fairly
steady improvement in undergraduate morals for the past fifty
years. (My son says that I know nothing about it!) There is certainly less attention given to formal religious exercises, such as the
class and college prayer meetings of half a century ago, and the
rôle of religious leadership of the college, once taken by such
professors as Albert Hopkins, is now left to chaplains and pastors.
It is probably true that the informal and inevitable ethical discussions by undergraduates avoid just now the unfashionable words
"right" and "wrong." The boys use other synonyms in their restless search for originality in expression. But to affirm that they
are no longer interested in what was once called right and wrong
seems to me a complete misunderstanding of the undergraduate
mind. "Not interested in right and wrong?" said one of my ablest
colleagues once, as we were walking home from a lecture on
Goethe's *Faust;* "why, at bottom, young fellows aren't interested
in anything else!"

Whatever the gains or losses which the subsequent years have
brought to American colleges, our undergraduate days were now
over. Trained or untrained, wise or foolish, we had had our
chance. Our Commencement was saddened by the assassination
of President Garfield, just as he was leaving Washington on the
way to his twenty-fifth reunion at Williamstown. He was one of
the most popular of the alumni, and his election to the Presidency
had been one of the excitements of our senior year. Only a few

hours after the tragic news reached us (Saturday, July 2) came the first of the Commencement festivities: the Graves Prize contest in the public delivery of the six best essays written by seniors. No one pays much attention to such contests now, but in our day crowds attended them. I remember how "Bulldozer" Raymond rushed up to us six boys—who were quite excited enough already—to tell us that all subsequent Commencement exercises would probably be canceled, as Garfield's death was momentarily expected; and that we must do our best before the great audience that had gathered. My speech was on Russian Nihilism, and I had toiled as hard over it as the Boy Orator of the Platte did upon his "cross of gold" masterpiece. And I doubt if even Bryan ever declaimed with a fiercer conviction that he was right! For once my "gloomy shine" seemed to dazzle the eyes of the judges, and I had my reward for all of the lonely months of practice in the cold and empty Jackson Hall.

On Sunday President Chadbourne preached his last Baccalaureate. The news from Washington seemed more encouraging. On Monday we beat Amherst in baseball. In the evening we listened to Senator J. J. Ingalls's oration before the Adelphic Union of the literary societies. I had to preside, but recall the orator's eloquence less vividly than my own struggle to decide whether I ought to wear my new (and first) swallow-tail or a blue suit. Luckily I put on the latter, for the famous Senator from Kansas strolled down to the church ten minutes late, smoking a long cigar, and clad in a checked suit of very loud pattern. He explained that the trunk containing his evening clothes had been lost in New York. Privately I believed that that trunk was, as the Senator once said of purity in politics, "an iridescent dream." On Tuesday I read a long and solemn Class Poem inspired by George Eliot; Mr. T. B. Aldrich showed me a great kindness in rejecting it for the *Atlantic Monthly*. In the blazing noonday of Wednesday, clad now like most of my classmates in a swallow-tail, I delivered a graduating oration on "The People's Poet"; probably a plea for more men like Burns. But I remember nothing whatever about it except Professor Pratt's candid remark upon the manuscript: "Page after page, Bliss, you seem just on the point of saying something, but you never quite reach that point!" However, I forgave this undoubtedly just criticism, for I collected the Van Vechten Prize for extemporaneous speaking, and had more money in my pocket than I had ever had in my life.

Of course, in those final days I was trying to do too many things. Even now, and many times each year, I have a recurrent dream that I am about to be summoned to the platform to deliver a graduating speech; but alas, it is unwritten, and there are only a few minutes left. Oddly enough, there is always a double consciousness about this dream, for I invariably say to myself, in my distress: "You have been making all kinds of addresses, for half a century. You could easily make a better speech than these youthful classmates of yours, if only there were five minutes in which to collect your thoughts." But there are no five minutes:—that is the agony of this hallucination. There is not even one minute! And then I wake up, roll over, and thank Heaven that I have retired and need never make another speech.

# CLARENCE DAY

CLARENCE DAY, whose *Life with Father* became first a best seller and then the source of a delightful play, was born in New York City in 1874. His father, Clarence Day, senior, was a partner in the Wall Street firm of Gwynne and Day. His grandfather was Benjamin Henry Day, founder of *The New York Sun*, and his uncle, Ben Day, invented the engraving process which now bears his name. New York was both his background and his foreground, something always there but something which during his lifetime changed so radically that his descriptions of the brownstone house in mid-town Madison Avenue where he grew up remind one of backdrops from a Boucicault melodrama. In summer the scene shifted to New London, Connecticut, where Clarence and his three younger brothers enjoyed the usual seaside pleasures of the sons of well-to-do parents. He attended St. Paul's School at Concord, New Hampshire, and went to Yale. His father's graduation present, in 1896, consisted of a seat on the New York Stock Exchange and a partnership in his brokerage business. Both of these Clarence soon rashly rejected to enlist in the navy.

This abrupt change in his life was soon followed by another when, in 1899, while stationed on a training ship in New York harbor, he was suddenly stricken with arthritis, never again to enjoy more than partial use of his limbs. He bought a ranch in Colorado and managed to ride ponies every day, keeping his general health as robust as he could. Back home in New York, unable except infrequently to leave the house (his father's), he took to writing. He conducted the book department for *The Metropolitan Magazine*. Publishers took his short humorous poems, his financial articles, his first book, *This Simian World*. The book, like its successor, *The Crow's Nest*, brought him wide notice, at thirty-six, but did not overcome parental disapproval of his needlessly free-lance life. Quite as strong-willed as his father, Clarence took an apartment by himself, where he grew a red beard, managed a glove business from his bedroom, and speculated (for a while successfully) in stocks and bonds only to lose all his money in 1929. The year before this happened he married Katharine Briggs Dodge, a young New England girl.

Irrevocably committed now to a literary career and almost totally bedridden, Day wrote several volumes of essays and poems, humorously illustrating them with his own pen-drawings, and in 1932 produced a small and little-known book called *God and My Father*. Here, in the shape of informal and conversational boyhood recollections of his father's attitude toward the Episcopal Church, was a penetrating analysis of the relation

86

of natural man to his Maker, classic in its simplicity and finish. Three years later, in his sixty-first year, appeared *Life with Father*, developing the same infinitely witty fancy, but reconstructing the whole background of his parental home with his father cast as the "heavy" and himself as the male juvenile lead. Such was the book's immediate success that it was inevitably followed by the essays that were collected posthumously in *Life with Mother* (1937), equally enchanting and alive.

When in 1935 Clarence died, he had, it would seem, most generously repaid his filial debts, leaving behind not only portraits of Father and Mother Day—all of them—but also a wise interpretation of human life. For the books are more than acts of piety; with unsweetened affection and gusto, with kind, unflinching eyes, and with the thoughtful laughter of high comedy Clarence Day has looked back at the figures of his youth and made them live again. It is a final merit of his books that they are written for the ear, that they sound like the best talk, as his own talk was.

## FATHER SENDS ME TO THE WORLD'S FAIR

FATHER and Mother and my brothers went out to the World's Fair in Chicago in 1893. I was finishing my freshman year at Yale, and by the time I got home they had gone. Father had written me that I had better follow on and join them, but I couldn't. I had spent all my allowance. There would be no more money coming to me until college opened again in September. In the meantime I didn't even have carfare or money enough for tobacco. It wasn't this that bothered me, however, or not going out to Chicago. It was the fact that for the first time in my life I had got deep in debt.

I owed Warner Hall forty-two dollars for seven weeks' board, I owed Dole for a heavy turtle-neck sweater, and De Bussy, Manwaring & Co. for ascot ties and shirts and a pair of pointed-toed shoes. I owed Heublein's for the rounds of drinks I had signed for, on what had once seemed jolly nights. I was in debt to Stoddard the tobacconist for sixty or seventy dollars for all sorts of fancy pipes—one of them was a meerschaum head of a bull with large amber horns. The total due to these and other tradesmen was nearly three hundred dollars, and I didn't see how I could have been so reckless, or when I could ever pay up. Worst of all, my creditors too had become pessimistic.

I borrowed a nickel for carfare from old Margaret, after she had cooked me my breakfast, put a sandwich and a banana in my pocket, and went downtown at once to Father's office to ask for a job. They didn't have any work for me down there and didn't want me around, but it was lucky I went, because while I was eating my sandwich one of my creditors entered. He had come down to New York with a bundle of overdue bills to see whether he could collect any of them by calling upon his customers' parents.

I was appalled. It had never occurred to me that anyone would come to Father's office like this. It seemed to me most underhanded. If Father had been there and I hadn't, I'd have been in serious trouble, for Father had warned me repeatedly to keep out of debt. I was thoroughly frightened, and I attempted to frighten that creditor. I said in a loud, shaky voice that if he was going to behave in this manner, I would never buy anything more from him as long as I lived.

He said he was sorry to hear it. But he didn't sound very sorry. Times were bad, he explained, and he had to have money. I didn't believe him. Looking back, I realize that the long depression of the nineties had started and banks were beginning to close, but I knew nothing about this at that time. I was preoccupied with my own troubles. These looked blacker than ever to me when my creditor said, as he left, that since my father was out, he would have to call on him again the next time he came to New York.

I didn't know what to do. But one thing was clear. I saw I must stick around Father's office for the rest of that summer. So as soon as he got back from the Fair, I begged him to give me a job. I didn't need any vacation, I told him, and I would be getting a lot of valuable experience if he would let me go to work.

After thinking it over, he said that perhaps I could make myself useful as an office boy while his clerks were taking turns going on their vacations. I started the very next day at four dollars a week.

I might have got slightly better wages elsewhere, but I couldn't have made enough anyway to pay much on my bills, and the most important thing was not to make a few dollars extra but to stand on guard at the door of Father's office to keep my creditors out. When I was sent out on an errand, I ran all the way there and back. When I was in the office, turning the big iron wheel on the letter press, I always kept one eye on the grated window where the cashier sat at his counter, to make sure that no old buzzards from New Haven were coming in to see Father.

But late in the summer I got into trouble. The cashier told Father that I had taken hold better than he had expected, and that although I was not very accurate I was punctual and quick and seemed to be especially interested in getting down early. Father was so pleased that he sent for me to come into his inner office and told me that he had decided I had earned a vacation.

I said that honestly and truly a vacation was the last thing I wanted.

He smiled at the immense pleasure I seemed to be taking in sealing envelopes and filling inkwells, but he explained that he wanted me to have some rest and recreation before college opened, and he added that he would advise me to go to Chicago and see the World's Fair.

I said I didn't care about seeing the Fair.

Father didn't quite like this. "I have just told you, Clarence," he said, "that I would advise you to go." I saw that he would regard it as disrespectful of me if I refused.

I uncomfortably made a partial confession. I said I couldn't afford to go to Chicago. I didn't have any money.

Father was surprised. "What about your allowance?" he asked.

"I'm sorry to say I've spent it all, Father."

"That was very imprudent of you," he observed.

I said in a low voice that I knew it.

Father said that he hoped this would be a lesson to me to be more careful in future. By failing to exercise even the most ordinary prudence, he explained in his firm, friendly way, I had deprived myself of seeing a sight that might never come again in my lifetime. He said he felt badly about it.

I didn't, however. I went back to working the letter press. I liked to turn the big, painted iron wheel and tighten the plates. We didn't use carbons. Instead, after writing letters by hand in copying ink or else on the typewriter, we pressed them down hard on damp tissue paper to make copies to file. It took a good deal of practice to do this correctly. If the tissue was too dry, the copy was so faint it could hardly be read, and if I got it too wet, it made the ink run and smudged the whole letter.

The next day, Father interrupted me at this interesting occupation again. He had had a long talk with Mother, it seemed, and, as all the rest of the family had seen the Fair, they wanted me to go, too. He said that he would therefore help me out this once and give me some money, and he asked how much I had saved from my wages.

I had saved nearly all of them, as a matter of fact. I had spent less than a dollar a week. Margaret had wrapped up little lunches for me, and my only other needs had been a haircut and carfares and a new pair of cuffs. But as I had been using all I saved to pay small installments to those men in New Haven, I had only forty-eight cents on hand.

"Well, the devil!" Father laughed disappointedly. "You have attended to your duties here faithfully enough, I suppose, but I see you have a damn lot to learn."

I thought to myself that he little knew how much I was learning.

He lit a cigar and looked at me reflectively. "Clarence," he said, "I think I should reproach myself afterward if I allowed you to miss seeing this Fair. It is a great educational opportunity that may never recur. So I will make you a present of one hundred dollars to enable you to go to Chicago."

"Thank you very much, Father," I said, as he shook hands with me, "but if you wouldn't mind, I'd rather have the money, sir."

Father frowned.

I stood beside his desk, waiting. A hundred dollars would be a magnificent windfall for me and my creditors.

His reply killed my hopes. "I see no point in giving you a

hundred dollars to fritter away as you have done with your other funds," he said. "If you don't choose to avail yourself of this educational—"

"Oh, I do, sir," I said. If the only way to get that hundred dollars was to go to Chicago and back, I saw that of course I'd better go. I felt sure I could save at least some of it to use in paying my bills.

I went to the cashier and begged him to keep an eye out for my creditors and not let any of them in, in my absence. He said he would do all he could, but he wouldn't like to be caught surreptitiously keeping out callers. I argued that these people would annoy Father if they saw him, and that they ought to be treated like book-agents; but he said Father might regard their disclosures as important, however unwelcome, and that he couldn't keep anyone out who came on legitimate business.

I almost gave up going, at this. But Father and Mother were so eager to give me a treat that I couldn't. I had to pretend to be eager myself, with my heart in my boots.

I wrote to my creditors that I would begin paying my bills very soon and that I hoped they would wait.

Father asked me what road I was getting a ticket on. He said the Lake Shore was the best. I made some vague answer to that. I didn't like to tell him, after he had been so generous to me, that I had bought a cut-rate ticket to Chicago and back, for eleven dollars, on an Erie Special Excursion. The Erie was so awful in those days that it was a joke. It didn't go nearly as far as Chicago, of course, but it had arranged for trackage rights over a number of other one-horse railroads for its Special Excursions.

It took that train three days and two nights, if I remember correctly, to get to Chicago. We stopped at every small station. We waited for hours on sidings. Most of the time I had very little idea where we were. The Excursion wandered around here and there, in various parts of this country and Canada, trying to pick up extra passengers. Of course, the train had no sleeping cars or diner—only day coaches. There was quite a crowd of us in them—men, women, and children. In the seat back of mine was a woman with two babies. I had my seat pretty much to myself, however, because the old man who sat with me spent most of his time in the smoker. I didn't go to the smoker myself. I had nothing to smoke.

All the windows were open, it was so hot. We were coated with coal dust. The washroom got out of order and had to be locked. The little drinking tank was soon emptied. Most of us had nothing to eat, and we slept sitting up. But it was fun. Nearly everybody but the overworked trainmen was good-natured and friendly. At every stop we'd all pile out of the cars and bolt for the washroom in the station, or try to buy pie and sandwiches and stand in line at the water-cooler, and those of us who went dry at one stop would try again at the next. At one little place where the station was locked and there was no other building in sight, we had the best luck of all, because there was a pond near the tracks, rather yellow, but with plenty of water for everybody. I was rinsing my undershirt in it when the whistle blew, and I only just managed to scramble aboard the train as it started. The day before that, at a little place where the eating was good, several passengers who didn't run fast enough had been left behind.

At Chicago, I hunted up a boarding house. As those near the Fair Grounds were expensive, I went to the outskirts, where I found an old boarding house near the railroad which was clean and decent. I sent off a postcard to Mother saying that the Fair was simply fine, and got a good bath and sleep.

I went to the Fair the next day. My boarding house was so far out that I had to go by train, but the fare was low and the station was handy. And when I walked into the Fair Grounds, I was deeply impressed. They were a wonderful sight. The vast buildings weren't solid stone, of course, and they wouldn't be there a hundred years hence, but in the meanwhile they provided a vision of grandeur, at least for innocent eyes. The eyes, for example, of persons who had come on the Erie.

I sat in the Court of Honor, I walked admiringly around the artificial lagoon, I sauntered through one or two of the exhibition halls, and went back to my boarding house.

On my next visit, I explored the grounds more thoroughly

and I was upset to find that all the places which I wanted to see most cost money. This was particularly true of the Midway Plaisance, a broad promenade lined with sideshows. There were Bedouins, a Ferris Wheel, a fearsome (canvas) Hawaiian volcano, a wonderful captive balloon, and a "Congress of Beauty." And there was also a real Dahomey village of genuine savages. I could reach out and touch them as they stalked about, scowling; and whenever I did I could hear them muttering things to themselves. They occasionally danced in a threatening manner uttering genuine war-cries; and the guide-book said, "They also sell products of their mechanical skill." And, what had excited the most talk of all in the newspapers, there were dancing girls with bare stomachs, who wriggled in what clergymen said was a most abandoned way, right before everybody.

I had heard so much about these girls that I forgot all my vows to economize and went into their tent. They didn't come up to my hopes. I had already noticed in New Haven that such things never did.

That night in my boarding house, I counted my money, and I saw that if I had good times on the Midway, I'd have a bad time with creditors. My creditors won and I didn't go to the Midway again.

There was a great deal else to see, however, and I saw nearly all of it, because it was free. But as Father had said, it was educational. I spent hours and hours roaming through the principal exhibits which were supposed to be good for the mind. They were interesting but monotonous. It was like visiting a hundred museums at once. A few of these palaces fascinated me when I came to them fresh; the Krupp guns were better than anything on the Midway. But the showmanship wasn't. Herr Krupp had announced, by the way, that he was presenting the biggest gun of all to America, "for the defense of the great port of Chicago."

These free exhibits increased my expenses, some days; they made me so hungry. I had a hard time trying to be economical at the White Horse Inn, I remember. This was a reproduction of an old English inn, swollen to an extraordinary size, and the big chops at the next table looked juicy and the steaks smelled delicious. And every time I went to the Transportation Building and got in a coma, I had to revive myself on beer and cheese afterward in a place called Old Vienna.

Father had especially enjoined upon me the duty of studying the Transportation Exhibits, because he was an officer or director of several small railroads, and he hoped that by and by I might be too. It was quite an assignment. That building had eighteen acres of floor-space. It was built in the form of several large train sheds. The guide-book explained that "in style it is somewhat Romanesque," and it added that "the ornamental color designs, in thirty different shades, of its exterior, produce an effect almost as fine as embroidery."

On rainy days I didn't go to the Fair Grounds. I sat in my boarding house and saved money. But this was dull and I felt lonely, so I bought a chameleon for company. He wasn't much company. On the other hand, as the end of his tail had been broken off, he only cost twenty cents. He wore a chain with a little brass collar at one end and a pin at the other, and I stuck the pin in the window curtain to tether him, and fed him live flies.

I wanted to go home after a week of this, but I figured that I'd better not. Father might think I had been too lavish with his money if it only lasted a week. So I stayed on for over a fortnight to inspire him with confidence in me, and make him see that I wasn't always a spendthrift in spite of my bad freshman record.

When I wasn't at the Fair, I wandered around Chicago. There was something about Chicago I liked. It seemed bigger and busier to me than New York, and much fatter, much more spread-out and roomy.

At last, when I thought Father must surely be feeling that I had used up that hundred dollars, I packed my suitcase, pinned the chameleon to the lapel of my coat, and embarked again on the Erie. The chameleon had a miserable time on the train and the rest of his tail got joggled off, but even so he was luckier than he knew, for we made much better time going east than we had made going west.

I had gone away worried and alarmed, but I came home in

triumph. No creditors had gone to the office, I learned, and I had saved fifty-two dollars to send to New Haven. I hadn't brought home any presents for the family, but I presented the chameleon to Mother.

Father and I had a little talk about what I had liked. "Did you see the Midway?" he asked.

"I saw a little of it," I said cautiously. "Did you see it, Father?"

"Yes," he said, "I was interested in those filthy Hottentots. How people can live in that disgusting manner I don't understand. I didn't know it was allowed."

He was pleased when he found I had gone only once to the Midway and had apparently spent all the rest of my time in the right places.

"Well," he finally said in approval, "I gather, then, that you found it was an educational experience for you."

"Yes, Father," I told him, "I did."

# JOHN REED

THE author of "Almost Thirty" is best introduced by his friend and biographer, Granville Hicks, who wrote the preface reprinted below to accompany the article on its first publication in 1936 in *The New Republic*. There remains but to enlarge the record of Reed's brief career and to set the main events in order.

Jack Reed, as he was always known, was born in Portland, Oregon, in 1887 into a family of wealth and high social standing. (His father was a United States Marshal.) His public schooling was topped off with two exciting years at Morristown School, New Jersey, where "his tremendous explosive energy" made itself felt and remembered both in sports and in student publications. In 1906 he went to Harvard, filled with lighthearted ambition to achieve new triumphs in a place overflowing with romantic associations and enjoying the liberal dispensation of President Eliot. Reed soon "made" the swimming team, the Dramatic Club, the *Lampoon*, the *Monthly*, though he failed of election to the *Crimson* board and was considered socially ineligible to the "final" clubs. Along with Walter Lippmann, Hans von Kaltenborn, Robert Edmond Jones, Lee Simonson, and other contemporaries, he allied himself with serious undergraduate causes, while keeping the appearance and reputation of a "playboy" and "activity man." He wrote a football song and a play produced by the Hasty Pudding Club, became Harvard's most inspired cheer-leader, and in his senior year (1910) was Ivy Orator and Class Day Poet.

Two weeks after graduating he shipped on a cattle-boat for Europe, saw everything he could abroad, and came back when his money ran out. In quick succession he then joined the staff of *The American Magazine*, published his first poems, was roused by Lincoln Steffens and Ida Tarbell to a serious interest in social problems, joined forces with Max Eastman, Louis Untermeyer, and others on *The Masses*, experienced the first of his many arrests for speaking on behalf of the strikers in the Paterson, New Jersey, silk mills, and three weeks later staged a mammoth pageant of the strike in Madison Square Garden. Next he spent four months with Pancho Villa's army as war correspondent for *The Metropolitan Magazine*, publishing his complete account in *Insurgent Mexico* (1914); then, on the outbreak of the World War, he was sent to cover events in Germany, Serbia, Bulgaria, Rumania, and Russia (*The War in Eastern Europe*, 1916). Back in America, incapacitated for military service by a surgical operation, he brought out his *Tamburlaine and Other Poems*. Early in 1917 he married Louise Bryant, a journalist (later the wife of Ambassador Bullitt), and sailed in August for Russia in time to witness the October Revolution in Petrograd. He became a confidant of Lenin, produced with the same zest he had shown in college much of the Bolshevist propaganda dropped over the German lines, and in January 1918 made an important speech at the All-Russian Soviet Convention. Out of his study and observation of the events there he wrote *Red Russia* and *Ten Days That Shook the World*.

In Moscow he was a hero; back in America his speeches and articles brought *The Masses* into Federal court and Reed and his wife before a Senate investigating committee. Expelled from the National Socialist Convention for his extreme views, he formed the Communist Labor Party, wrote its manifesto and platform, and edited its paper, *The Voice of Labor*. In 1919, under indictment for sedition, he escaped from the United States by a forged passport and worked his way to Finland as a stoker, only to be thrown into prison there, while still being sought at home. Three months later he gained his release to Russia on an exchange of prisoners and spent the bitter winter of 1919-20 hard at work speaking, writing, and conferring with Soviet leaders as the representative of the revolutionary workers of America. Still the tall, handsome, gay-hearted enthusiast, he baffled his American friends who could not understand how a young man of his background could be so engaged. The next summer his wife managed to join him in Moscow, making the last part of her voyage disguised as a sailor, and Reed eagerly began to show her the new Russia. At the height of his career, in October 1920, he was stricken with typhus and died, aged thirty-three. He was buried with highest honors in the Kremlin.

Since then John Reed Clubs have been formed in nearly all the large cities of the United States to keep alive the spirit of this most extraordinary youth, and the literature about him has multiplied.

The reader may be interested in following his brief autobiographical essay with John Dos Passos's portrait, "Playboy," in *U.S.A.* and with Mr. Hicks's full-length biography.

# ALMOST THIRTY

In the spring of 1917, when he wrote the following essay, John Reed felt little of the self-confidence that had carried him so buoyantly through the preceding decade. A serious operation—the removal of his left kidney —had been followed by the termination of his three years' employment by *The Metropolitan Magazine*, with whose editors he had quarreled over their war policy. The eminent position he had created for himself by his articles on Mexico, the World War and American labor struggles was crumbling. And at the same time the thing he had dreaded ever since

August, 1914, had happened: the United States had been drawn into the War. All this gave him the sense, so strongly revealed in the essay, that an era of his life had ended, and led him to attempt the task of personal understanding and evaluation.

Precisely why the essay was not published I do not know. It remained with Reed's papers, until these were turned over by Louise Bryant to the Harvard Alumni John Reed Committee, by whose permission it is now printed. If it had appeared when it was written, what would chiefly have surprised one group of readers, those who still thought of him as a play-boy, was Reed's seriousness. What would have surprised another group was the note of uncertainty, almost of despair. The truth is that Reed, on the one hand, had always been more reflective and somewhat less sure of himself than his conduct indicated, and, on the other, was even at this time by no means so inhibited in action by his doubts as a reader of the essay might be led to suppose, for all his energies were engaged in the struggle to prevent the declaration of war and, later, to mitigate the effects of militarism.

Yet Reed's skepticism was real enough, and its focal point is apparent: as a result of the collapse of the revolutionary movement in the War, he had lost his confidence in the working class. This is important, because, soon after "Almost Thirty" was finished, Reed went to Russia. No reader of *Ten Days That Shook the World* can doubt that the triumph of the revolution had overwhelming personal significance for Reed. Why this was so, "Almost Thirty" makes clear.

—GRANVILLE HICKS

I AM twenty-nine years old, and I know that this is the end of a part of my life, the end of youth. Sometimes it seems to me the end of the world's youth too; certainly the Great War has done something to us all. But it is also the beginning of a new phase of life; and the world we live in is so full of swift change and color and meaning that I can hardly keep from imagining the splendid and terrible possibilities of the time to come. The last ten years I've gone up and down the earth drinking in experience, fighting and loving, seeing and hearing and testing things. I've traveled all over Europe, and to the borders of the East, and down in Mexico, having adventures; seeing men killed and broken, victorious and laughing, men with visions and men with a sense of humor. I've watched civilization change and broaden and sweeten in my lifetime; and I've watched it wither and crumble in the red blast of war. And war I have seen, too, in the trenches, with the armies. I'm not quite sick of seeing yet, but soon I will be—I know that. My future life will not be what it has been. And so I want to stop a minute, and look back, and get my bearings.

A great deal of my boyhood was illness and physical weakness, and I was never really well until my sixteenth year. The beginning of my remembered life was a turmoil of imaginings—formless perceptions of beauty, which broke forth in voluminous verses, sensations of fear, of tenderness, of pain. Then came a period of intense emotion, in which I endowed certain girls with the attributes of Guinevere, and had a vision of Galahad and the Sangraal in the sky over the school football field; a furious energy drove me to all kinds of bodily and mental exercise, without any particular direction—except that I felt sure I was going to be a great poet and novelist. After that I was increasingly active and restless, more ambitious of place and power, less exalted, scattering myself in a hundred different directions; life became a beloved moving picture, thought about only in brilliant flashes, conceived as emotion and sensation. And now, almost thirty, some of that old superabundant vitality is gone, and with it the all-sufficient joy of mere living. A good many of my beliefs have got twisted by the Great War. I am weakened by a serious operation. Some things I think I have settled, but in other ways I am back where I started—a turmoil of imaginings.

I must find myself again. Some men seem to get their direction early, to grow naturally and with little change to the thing they are to be. I have no idea what I shall be or do one month from now. Whenever I have tried to become some one thing, I have failed; it is only by drifting with the wind that I have found myself, and plunged joyously into a new role. I have discovered that I am only happy when I'm working hard at something I like. I never stuck long at anything I didn't like, and now I couldn't if I wanted to; on the other hand, there are very few things I don't get some fun out of, if only the novelty of experience. I love people, except the well-fed smug, and am interested in all new things and all the beautiful old things they do. I love beauty and chance and change, but less now in the external world and more in my mind. I suppose I'll always be a Romanticist.

From the very beginning my excitable imagination fed on fantasy. I still remember my grandfather's house, where I was born—a lordly gray mansion modeled on a French château, with its immense park, its formal gardens, lawns, stables, greenhouses and glass grape-arbor, the tame deer among the trees. All that remains to me of my grandfather is his majestic height, his long slim fingers and the polished courtesy of his manners. He had come around the Horn in a sailing ship when the West Coast was the wild frontier, made his pile and lived with Russian lavishness. Portland was less than thirty years old, a little town carved out of the Oregon forests, with streets deep in mud and the wilderness coming down close around it. Through this my grandfather drove his blooded horses to his smart carriages, imported from the East—and from Europe—with liveried coachmen and footmen on the box. The lawn terrace below the house was surrounded on three sides by great fir trees, up whose sides ran gas-pipes grown over with bark; on summer evenings canvas was laid on the turf, and people danced, illuminated by flaming jets of gas which seemed to spout from the trees. There was something fantastic in all that.

Then we were poor, living in a little house down in the town, with a crowd of gay young people around my gay young father and mother. My head was full of fairy stories and tales of giants, witches and dragons, and I invented a monster called Hormuz, who lived in the woods behind the town and devoured little children—with which I terrified the small boys and girls of the neighborhood and incidentally myself. Almost all the servants in those days were Chinese, who stayed for years, at last getting to be almost members of the family. They brought ghosts and superstitions into the house, and the tang of bloody feuds among themselves, idols and foods and drinks, strange customs and ceremonies; half-affectionate, half-contemptuous, wholly independent, and withal outlandish, they have left me a memory of pigtails and gongs and fluttering red paper. And there was my uncle, a romantic figure who played at coffee-planting in Central America, mixed in revolutions, and sometimes blew in, tanned and bearded and speaking "spigotty" like a *mestizo*. Once the tale ran that he had helped to lead a revolution that captured Guatemala for a few brief days, and was made Secretary of State; the first thing he did was to appropriate the funds of the National Treasury to give a grand state ball, and then he declared war on the German Empire—because he had flunked his German course in college. Later he went out to the Philippines as a volunteer in the Spanish War—and the tale of how he was made King of Guam is still told with shouts of mirth by the veterans of the Second Oregon.

My mother, who has always encouraged me in the things I wanted to do, taught me to read. I don't know when that was, but I remember the orgy of books I plunged into. History was my passion, kings strutting about and the armored ranks of men-at-arms clashing forward in close ranks against a hail of cloth-yard shafts; but I was equally enamored of Mark Twain, and Bill Nye, and Blackmore's *Lorna Doone*, and Webster's Unabridged Dictionary, and *The Arabian Nights*, and the *Tales of the Round Table*. What I didn't understand, my imagination interpreted. At the age of nine I began to write a Comic History of the United States—after Bill Nye—and I think it was then I made up my mind to be a writer.

About that time we moved to an apartment hotel, and I went to school. Those first few years of school stimulated my ambition to learn; but since then the curricula of schools and colleges have meant little to me. I've always been an indifferent student, to say the least, except when some subject like elementary chemistry, or English poetry, or composition caught my imagination—or the personality of some great teacher, like Professor Copeland of Harvard. Why should I have been interested in the stupid education of our time? We take young soaring imaginations, consumed with curiosity about the life they see all around, and feed them with dead technique: the flawless purity of Washington, Lincoln's humdrum chivalry, our dull and virtuous history and England's honest glory; Addison's graceful style as an essayist,

Goldsmith celebrating the rural clergy of the eighteenth century, Dr. Johnson at his most vapid, and George Eliot's *Silas Marner;* Macaulay, and the sonorous oratings of Edmund Burke; and in Latin, Caesar's Gallic guide-book, and Cicero's mouthings about Roman politics. And the teachers! Men and women—usually women—whose chief qualification is that they can plow steadily through a dull round of dates, acts, half-truths and rules for style, without questioning, without interpreting and without seeing how ridiculously unlike the world their teachings are. I have forgotten most of it, forced on me before I was ready; what I do know came mostly from books I had the curiosity to read outside school hours. And many fine things I have had to force myself to explore again, because school once spoiled them for me.

But in going to school I first entered the world of my fellows, and the social experience meant more and more to me until it almost crowded out the study side altogether. I can still see the school playground full of running and shouting and clamoring boys, and feel as I felt then when they stopped here and there to look at me, a new boy, with curious and insolent eyes. I was small though, and not very well, and at the beginning I didn't mix much with them. . . . But after school was out there were great doings, which were too exciting to keep out of. The town was divided into districts, ruled over by gangs of boys in a constant state of fierce warfare. I belonged to the Fourteenth Street gang, whose chief was a tall, curly-headed Irish boy who lived across the street—he is now a policeman. My best friend could make sounds like a bugle, and he was trumpeter. Standing in the middle of the street he would blow, and in a minute boys would come swarming to him, tearing up lawns and making mud-balls as they came. Then we'd go running and shouting up the hill to give battle to the Montgomery Street gang, or beat off their attack. . . . And there were the wooded hills behind the town, where Indians and bears and outlaws might be lurking to be trailed by our scouts and Robin Hoods.

Both my mother's parents and my father came from upper New York State, and when I was ten years old my mother and my brother and I went East to visit them. We spent a summer month at Plymouth, Massachusetts, visited New York (I still remember the awful summer heat, the vermin in our boarding-house and the steam-engines on the Elevated), and were in Washington when the *Maine* blew up and the first volunteers left for the Spanish War.

Then I was back in Portland, in a new house, settling into the life of school and play. We had a theatre in our attic, where we acted our own plays, and we built scenic railways in the yard, and log cabins in the woods back of town. I had a number of highly colored schemes for getting adventure and wealth at the same time. For instance, I once began to dig a tunnel from our house to school, about a mile away; we were going to steal two sheep and hide them in the tunnel, and these two sheep were going to have children, and so on, until a large flock had gathered—then we'd sell them. My brother and I had a pony, and we went on camping trips back in the woods, and sailing and swimming and camping up the Willamette River. I began to write poetry, too, and read voraciously everything I could get hold of, from Edwin Arnold's *Light of Asia* and Marie Corelli, to Scott and Stevenson and Sir Thomas Malory.

But with all this I wasn't entirely happy. I was often ill. Outside of a few friends, I wasn't a success with the boys. I hadn't strength or fight enough to be good at athletics—except swimming, which I have always loved; and I was a good deal of a physical coward. I would sneak out over the back fence to avoid boys who were "laying" for me, or who I thought were "laying" for me. Sometimes I fought, when I couldn't help myself, and sometimes even won; but I preferred to be called a coward than fight. I hated pain. My imagination conjured up horrible things that would happen to me, and I simply ran away. One time, when I was on the editorial board of the school paper, a boy I was afraid of warned me not to publish a joking paragraph I had written about him—and I didn't. . . . My way to school lay through a sort of slum district, called Goose Hollow, peopled with brutal Irish boys, many of whom grew up to be prizefighters and baseball stars. I was literally frightened out of my senses when I went through Goose Hollow. Once a Goose Hollowite made me promise to give him a nickel if he didn't hit me, and walked up to my house with me while I got it for him. . . . The strange thing was that when I was cornered, and fought, even a licking wasn't a hundredth as bad as I thought it would be; but I never learned anything from that—the next time I ran away just the same, and suffered the most ghastly pangs of fear.

I wasn't much good at the things other boys were, and their codes of honor and conduct didn't hold me. They felt it, too, and had a sort of good-natured contempt for me. I was neither one thing nor the other, neither altogether coward nor brave, neither manly nor sissified, neither ashamed nor unashamed. I think that is why my impression of my boyhood is an unhappy one, and why I have so few close friends in Portland, and why I don't want ever again to live there.

It must have disappointed my father that I was like that, though he never said much about it. He was a great fighter, one of the first of the little band of political insurgents who were after-wards, as the Progressive Party, to give expression to the new social conscience of the American middle class. His terrible slash-ing wit, his fine scorn of stupidity and cowardice and littleness, made him many enemies, who never dared attack him to his face, but fought him secretly, and were glad when he died. As United States Marshal under Roosevelt, it was he who, with Francis J. Heney and Lincoln Steffens, smashed the Oregon Land Fraud Ring; which was a brave thing to do in Oregon then. I remem-ber him and Heney in the Marshal's office guying William J. Burns, the detective on the case, for his Hawkshaw make-up and his ridiculous melodramatics. In 1910 a man came around to browbeat my father into contributing to the Republican cam-paign fund, and he kicked the collector down the courthouse stairs—and was removed from the marshalship by President Taft. Afterward he ran for Congress, but lost out by a slim margin, mainly because he came East to see me graduate from college instead of stumping the state.

When I was sixteen I went East to a New Jersey boarding

school, and then to Harvard College, and afterward to Europe for a year's travel; and my brother followed me through college. We never knew until later how much our mother and father denied themselves that we might go, and how he poured out his life that we might live like rich men's sons. He and mother always gave us more than we asked, in freedom and understanding as well as material things. And on the day my brother graduated from college, he broke under the terrible effort, and died a few weeks later. It has always seemed to me bitter irony that he couldn't have lived to see my little success. He was always more like a wise, kind friend than a father.

Boarding school, I think, meant more to me than anything in my boyhood. Among these strange boys I came as a stranger, and I soon found out that they were willing to accept me at my own value. I was in fine health. The ordered life of the community interested me; I was impressed by its traditional customs and dignities, school patriotism, and the sense of a long settled and established civilization, so different from the raw, pretentious West. My stories and verses were published in the school paper; I played football, and ran the quarter-mile, with very good average success; I had a fight or two, and stuck it out. There were perilous adventures, too, when a few of us stole down the fire escapes at night and went to country dances, slipping back to bed in the dormitory at dawn. With the school social butterflies, I "fussed" girls in the town, and was not laughed at. Busy, happy, with lots of friends, I expanded into self-confidence. So without trying I found myself; and since then I have never been very much afraid of men.

In 1906 I went up to Harvard almost alone, knowing hardly a soul in the University. My college class entered over seven hundred strong, and for the first three months it seemed to me, going around to lectures and meetings, as if every one of the seven hundred had friends but me. I was thrilled with the immensity of Harvard, its infinite opportunities, its august history and traditions—but desperately lonely. I didn't know which way to turn, how to meet people. Fellows passed me in the Yard,

shouting gaily to one another; I saw parties off to Boston Saturday night, whooping and yelling on the back platform of the
street car, and they passed hilariously singing under my window
in the early dawn. Athletes and musicians and writers and statesmen were emerging from the ranks of the class. The freshman
clubs were forming.

And I was out of it all. I "went out" for the college papers,
and tried to make the freshman crew, even staying in Cambridge
vacations to go down to the empty boat-house and plug away at
the machines—and was the last man kicked off the squad before
they went to New London. I got to know many fellows to nod
to, and a very few intimately; but most of my friends were
whirled off and up into prominence, and came to see me no more.
One of them said he'd room with me sophomore year—but he
was tipped off that I wasn't "the right sort" and openly drew
away from me. And I, too, hurt a boy who was my friend. He
was a Jew, a shy, rather melancholy person. We were always
together, we two outsiders. I became irritated and morbid about
it—it seemed I would never be part of the rich splendor of college
life with him around—so I drew away from him. . . . It hurt
him very much, and it taught me better. Since then he has forgiven it, and done wonderful things for me, and we are friends.

My second year was better. I was elected an editor of two of
the papers, and knew more fellows. The fortunate and splendid
youths, the aristocrats who filled the clubs and dominated college
society, didn't seem so attractive. In two open contests, the trial
for editor of the college daily paper and that for assistant manager of the varsity crew, I qualified easily for election; but the
aristocrats blackballed me. However, that mattered less. During
my freshman year I used to *pray* to be liked, to have friends, to
be popular with the crowd. Now I had friends, plenty of them;
and I have found that when I am working hard at something I
love, friends come without my trying, and stay; and fear goes,
and that sense of being lost which is so horrible.

From that time on I never felt out of it. I was never popular
with the aristocrats; I was never elected to any clubs but one, and
that one largely because of a dearth of members who could write

lyrics for the annual show. But I was on the papers, was elected
president of the Cosmopolitan Club, where forty-three nationali-
ties met, became manager of the Musical Clubs, captain of the
water-polo team, and an officer in many undergraduate activities.
As song-leader of the cheering section, I had the supreme blissful
sensation of swaying two thousand voices in great crashing
choruses during the big football games. The more I met the college aristocrats, the more their cold, cruel stupidity repelled me.
I began to pity them for their lack of imagination, and the
narrowness of their glittering lives—clubs, athletics, society. College is like the world; outside there is the same class of people,
dull and sated and blind.

Harvard University under President Eliot was unique. Individ-
ualism was carried to the point where a man who came for a good
time could get through and graduate without having learned anything; but on the other hand, anyone could find there anything
he wanted from all the world's store of learning. The undergraduates were practically free from control; they could live
pretty much where they pleased, and do as they pleased—so long
as they attended lectures. There was no attempt made by the
authorities to weld the student body together, or to enforce any
kind of uniformity. Some men came with allowances of fifteen
thousand dollars a year pocket money, with automobiles and
servants, living in gorgeous suites in palatial apartment houses;
others in the same class starved in attic bedrooms.

All sorts of strange characters, of every race and mind, poets,
philosophers, cranks of every twist, were in our class. The very
hugeness of it prevented any one man from knowing more than
a few of his classmates, though I managed to make the acquaintance of about five hundred of them. The aristocrats controlled
the places of pride and power, except when a democratic revolution, such as occurred in my senior year, swept them off their
feet; but they were so exclusive that most of the real life went
on outside their ranks—and all the intellectual life of the student
body. So many fine men were outside the charmed circle that,
unlike most colleges, there was no disgrace in not being a "club

man." What is known as "college spirit" was not very powerful;
no odium attached to those who didn't go to football games and
cheer. There was talk of the world, and daring thought, and intellectual insurgency; heresy has always been a Harvard and a
New England tradition. Students themselves criticized the faculty
for not educating them, attacked the sacred institution of intercollegiate athletics, sneered at undergraduate clubs so holy that no
one dared mention their names. No matter what you were or
what you did—at Harvard you could find your kind. It wasn't a
breeder for masses of mediocrely educated young men equipped
with "business" psychology; out of each class came a few creative minds, a few scholars, a few "gentlemen" with insolent manners, and a ruck of nobodies. . . . Things have changed now.
I liked Harvard better then.

   Toward the end of my college course two influences came
into my life, which had a good deal to do with shaping me. One
was contact with Professor Copeland, who, under the pretense
of teaching English composition, has stimulated generations of
men to find color and strength and beauty in books and in the
world, and to express it again. The other was what I call, for lack
of a better name, the manifestation of the modern spirit. Some
men, notably Walter Lippmann, had been reading and thinking
and talking about politics and economics, not as dry theoretical
studies, but as live forces acting on the world, on the University
even. They formed the Socialist Club, to study and discuss all
modern social and economic theories, and began to experiment
with the community in which they lived.
   Under their stimulus the college political clubs, which had
formerly been quadrennial mushroom growths for the purpose
of drinking beer, parading and burning red fire, took on a new
significance. The Club drew up a platform for the Socialist Party
in the city elections. It had social legislation introduced into the
Massachusetts Legislature. Its members wrote articles in the college papers challenging undergraduate ideals, and muckraked the
University for not paying its servants living wages, and so forth.
Out of the agitation sprang the Harvard Men's League for

Women's Suffrage, the Single Tax Club, an Anarchist group. The faculty was petitioned for a course in socialism. Prominent radicals were invited to Cambridge to lecture. An open forum was started, to debate college matters and the issues of the day. The result of this movement upon the undergraduate world was potent. All over the place radicals sprang up, in music, painting, poetry, the theatre. The more serious college papers took a socialistic, or at least progressive tinge. Of course all this made no ostensible difference in the look of Harvard society, and probably the clubmen and the athletes, who represented us to the world, never even heard of it. But it made me, and many others, realize that there was something going on in the dull outside world more thrilling than college activities, and turned our attention to the writings of men like H. G. Wells and Graham Wallas, wrenching us away from the Oscar Wildean dilettantism that had possessed undergraduate littérateurs for generations.

After college Waldo Peirce and I went abroad as "bull-pushers" on a cattle-boat, for a year's happy-go-lucky wandering. Waldo rebelled at the smells and the ship's company, and jumped overboard off Boston Light, swimming back to shore and later taking the *Lusitania* to Liverpool; meanwhile, I was arrested for his murder, clapped in irons and brought before an Admiralty court at Manchester, where Waldo turned up in the nick of time. I tramped down across England alone, working on farms and sleeping in haymows, meeting Peirce in London again. Then we hoofed it to Dover and tried to stow away on a Channel steamer for France—and got arrested in Calais, of course. Separating, we went through northern France on foot, to Rouen and Paris, and started on a wild automobile trip through Touraine to the Spanish border, and across; and I proceeded into Spain alone, having adventures. I spent the winter in Paris, with excursions around the country, letting it soak in. Then I came home to America to settle down and make my living.

Lincoln Steffens recommended me for a job on *The American Magazine*, where I stayed three years, reading manuscripts and writing stories and verses. More than any other man Lincoln

Steffens has influenced my mind. I met him first while I was at Harvard, where he came loving youth, full of understanding, with the breath of the world clinging to him. I was afraid of him then—afraid of his wisdom, his seriousness, and we didn't talk. But when I came back from France I told him what I had seen and done, and he asked me what I wanted to do. I said I didn't know, except that I wanted to write. Steffens looked at me with that lovely smile: "You can do anything you want to," he said; and I believed him. Since then I have gone to him with my difficulties and troubles, and he has always listened while I solved them myself in the warmth of his understanding. Being with Steffens is to me like flashes of clear light; it is as if I see him, and myself, and the world, with new eyes. I tell him what I see and think, and it comes back to me beautiful, full of meaning. He does not judge or advise—he simply makes everything clear. There are two men who give me confidence in myself, who make me want to work, and to do nothing unworthy—Copeland and Steffens.

New York was an enchanted city to me. It was on an infinitely grander scale than Harvard. Everything was to be found there— it satisfied me utterly. I wandered about the streets, from the soaring imperial towers of down-town, along the East River docks, smelling of spices and the clipper ships of the past, through the swarming East Side—alien towns within towns—where the smoky flare of miles of clamorous pushcarts made a splendor of shabby streets; coming upon sudden shrill markets, dripping blood and fish-scales in the light of torches, the big Jewish women bawling their wares under the roaring great bridges; thrilling to the ebb and flow of human tides sweeping to work and back, west and east, south and north. I knew Chinatown, and Little Italy, and the quarter of the Syrians; the marionette theatre, Sharkey's and McSorley's saloons, the Bowery lodging houses and the places where the tramps gathered in winter; the Haymarket, the German Village, and all the dives of the Tenderloin. I spent all one summer night on top of a pier of the Williamsburg Bridge; I slept another night in a basket of squid in the Fulton Market, where the red and green and gold sea things glisten in the blue light of the sputtering arcs. The girls that walk the streets were friends of mine, and the drunken sailors off ships new-come from the world's end, and the Spanish longshoremen down on West Street.

I found wonderful obscure restaurants, where the foods of the whole world could be found. I knew how to get dope; where to go to hire a man to kill an enemy; what to do to get into gambling rooms, and secret dance halls. I knew well the parks, and the streets of palaces, the theatres and hotels; the ugly growth of the city spreading like a disease, the decrepit places whence life was ebbing, and the squares and streets where an old, beautiful leisurely existence was drowned in the mounting roar of the slums. I knew Washington Square, and the artists and writers, the near-Bohemians, the radicals. I went to gangsters' balls at Tammany Hall, on excursions of the Tim Sullivan Association, to Coney Island on hot summer nights. . . . Within a block of my house was all the adventure of the world; within a mile was every foreign country.

In New York I first loved, and I first wrote of the things I saw, with a fierce joy of creation—and knew at last that I could write. There I got my first perceptions of the life of my time. The city and its people were an open book to me; everything had its story, dramatic, full of ironic tragedy and terrible humor. There I first saw that reality transcended all the fine poetic inventions of fastidiousness and medievalism. I was not happy or well long away from New York . . . I am not now, for that matter; but I cannot live continually in its heart any more. In the city I have no time for much but sensation and experience; but now I want some time of quiet, and leisure for thought, so I can extract from the richness of my life something beautiful and strong. I am living now in the country, within an hour of town, so I can go down occasionally and plunge into the sea of people, the roaring and the lights—and then come back here to write of it, in the quiet hills, in sunshine and clean wind.

During this time I read a good deal of radical literature, attended meetings of all sorts, met socialists, anarchists, single-taxers, labor-leaders, and besides, all the hair-splitting Utopians and petty doctrine-mongers who cling to skirts of Change. They interested me, so many different human types; and the livingness of theories which could dominate men and women captivated my imagination. On the whole, ideas alone didn't mean much to me. I had to see. In my rambles about the city I couldn't help but observe the ugliness of poverty and all its train of evil, the cruel inequality between rich people who had too many motor cars and poor people who didn't have enough to eat. It didn't come to me from books that the workers produced all the wealth of the world, which went to those who did not earn it.

The Lawrence strike of the textile workers had just ended, and the I.W.W. dominated the social and industrial horizon like a portent of the rising of the oppressed. That strike brought home to me hard the knowledge that the manufacturers get all they can out of labor, pay as little as they must, and permit the existence of great masses of the miserable unemployed in order to keep wages down; that the forces of the State are on the side of property against the propertyless. Our Socialist Party seemed to me duller than religion, and almost as little in touch with labor. The Paterson strike broke out. I met Bill Haywood, Gurley Flynn, Tresca and the other leaders; they attracted me. I liked their understanding of the workers, their revolutionary thought, the boldness of their dream, the way immense crowds of people took fire and came alive under their leadership. Here was drama, change, democracy on the march made visible—a war of the people. I went to Paterson to watch it, was mistaken for a striker while walking the public street, beaten by the police and jailed without any charge. In the jail I talked with exultant men who had blithely defied the lawless brutality of the city government and gone to prison laughing and singing. There were horrors in that jail too; men and boys shut up for months without trial, men going mad and dying, bestial cruelty and disease and filth— and all for the poor. When I came out I helped to organize the Pageant of the Paterson Strike, in Madison Square Garden, New York, drilling a thousand men and women in Paterson and bringing them across New Jersey to act out, before an immensely moved audience of twenty thousand people, the wretchedness of their lives and the glory of their revolt.

Since then I have seen and reported many strikes, most of them desperate struggles for the bare necessities of life; and all I have witnessed only confirms my first idea of the class struggle and its inevitability. I wish with all my heart that the proletariat would rise and take their rights—I don't see how else they will get them. Political relief is so slow to come, and year by year the opportunities of peaceful protest and lawful action are curtailed. But I am not sure any more that the working class is capable of revolution, peaceful or otherwise; the workers are so divided and bitterly hostile to each other, so badly led, so blind to their class interest. The War has been a terrible shatterer of faith in economic and political idealism. And yet I cannot give up the idea that out of democracy will be born the new world—richer, braver, freer, more beautiful. As for me, I don't know what I can do to help—I don't know yet. All I know is that my happiness is built on the misery of other people, that I eat because others go hungry, that I am clothed when other people go almost naked through the frozen cities in winter; and that fact poisons me, disturbs my serenity, makes me write propaganda when I would rather play—though not so much as it once did.

I quit my job to work on the Pageant, and when it was all over I went to pieces nervously, and friends took me abroad for the summer. The strike was starved and lost, the men went back to work dispirited and disillusioned, and the leaders, too, broke down under the long strain of the fight. The I.W.W. itself seemed smashed—indeed it has never recovered its old prestige. I got diphtheria in Italy, and came back to New York weak and despondent. For six months I did almost nothing. And then, through the interest of Lincoln Steffens, *The Metropolitan Magazine* asked me to go to Mexico as war correspondent, and I knew that I must do it.

Villa had just captured Chihuahua when I got to the border, and was getting ready to move on Torreon. I made straight for Chihuahua, and there got a chance to accompany an American mining man down into the mountains of Durango. Hearing that an old half-bandit, half-general was moving to the front, I cut loose and joined him, riding with a wild troop of Mexican cavalry two weeks across the desert, seeing battle at close range, in which my companions were defeated and killed, and fleeing for my life across the desert. I joined Villa then in his march on Torreon, and was in at the fall of that stronghold.

Altogether I was four months with the Constitutionalist armies in Mexico. When I first crossed the border deadliest fear gripped me. I was afraid of death, of mutilation, of a strange land and strange people whose speech and thought I did not know. But a terrible curiosity urged me on; I felt I *had to know* how I would act under fire, how I would get along with these primitive folks at war. And I discovered that bullets are not very terrifying, that the fear of death is not such a great thing, and that the Mexicans are wonderfully congenial. That four months of riding hundreds of miles across the blazing plains, sleeping on the ground with the *hombres*, dancing and carousing in looted haciendas all night after an all-day ride, being with them intimately in play, in battle, was perhaps the most satisfactory period of my life. I made good with these wild fighting men, and with myself. I loved them and I loved the life. I found myself again. I wrote better than I have ever written.

Then came the European War, to which I went as correspondent, spending a year and a half traveling in all the belligerent countries and on the front of five nations in battle. In Europe I found none of the spontaneity, none of the idealism of the Mexican revolution. It was a war of the workshops, and the trenches were factories turning out ruin—ruin of the spirit as well as of the body, the real and only death. Everything had halted but the engines of hate and destruction. European life, that flashed so many vital facets, ran in one channel, and runs in it now. There seems to me little to choose between the sides; both are horrible to me. The whole Great War is to me just a stoppage of the life and ferment of human evolution. I am waiting, waiting for it all to end, for life to resume so I can find my work.

In thinking it over, I find little in my thirty years that I can hold to. I haven't any God and don't want one; faith is only another word for finding oneself. In my life as in most lives, I guess, love plays a tremendous part. I've had love affairs, passionate happiness, wretched maladjustments; hurt deeply and been deeply hurt. But at last I have found my friend and lover, thrilling and satisfying, closer to me than anyone has ever been. And now I don't care what comes.

# LOUIS ADAMIC

LOUIS ADAMIC'S origins and early life are sufficiently indicated in our selection from *The Native's Return*, published in 1934. Coming in 1913 from Carniola, Austria (now Yugoslavia), to New York, a boy of fourteen, he found his first job as an assistant to the mailer on a Slovenian newspaper and began almost at once to describe his new experiences in little sketches, some of which found their way into the paper. At the same time his natural curiosity about his adopted country led him to read, with the aid of a Slovenian-English dictionary, all sorts of printed matter indiscriminately until, after three years, he was able to translate ordinary American news articles into his native language and to take on the duties of editor's assistant. "My advancement," he says, "enabled me to wear better clothes and eat more substantial lunches, and tended to lessen the bitterness about America that had seized me upon reading Upton Sinclair's *The Jungle*. My curiosity about the country increased."

But the paper failed, and at seventeen he had to face alone the disillusioning realities of joblessness. After two months he found work in a Paterson, New Jersey, silk mill, but dropped it to enlist in the U. S. Army upon our declaration of war in the spring of 1917. His unit was sent to the Panama Canal Zone, then to France, taking part in the actions and inactions of the Meuse-Argonne front. Discharged late in 1920 after three years of soldiering, "almost twenty-one years old and a very serious young man," he set out from New York with three hundred dollars to get a better look at the land he had fought for. Through that winter he visited Washington, Chicago, St. Louis, Kansas City, piecing out his dwindling savings with laboring jobs when he could get them. Back East again and unable to find other work, he went to sea, and during the next ten months sailed on five different ships to ports in Europe and South America. Then, leaving the sea, he worked in restaurants, cabinet-shops, shoe-factories, and textile mills in several eastern cities; went to Los Angeles, where, after taking various laboring jobs, he became a newspaper reporter; quit several months later (June 1923) because his duties left him no time for reading, and with fifteen dollars in his pocket moved to San Pedro, where he was occupied for the next five years as a stevedore, while he continued to read and to commit his daily observations and experiences to writing.

At length, in 1928, one of these pieces was accepted by H. L. Mencken for publication in *The American Mercury* and was soon followed by other articles in other magazines. In 1929 appeared his biographical portrait of Robinson Jeffers, the poet, and in 1931, his first full-length book, *Dynamite: The Story of Class Violence in America*. The same year he married Stella Sanders of New York. His immigrant experiences found their first expression in *Laughing in the Jungle* (1932) which led to his award of a Guggenheim Fellowship, enabling him to spend a year in Europe with his wife and to revisit his family in Carniola, as he describes in the following selection. With *The Native's Return*, Mr. Adamic became, at thirty-five, a figure in the American literary scene, and he has remained one ever since, continuing to draw deeply from his own life the unusual material which has gone into *Grandsons: A Story of American Lives* (1935), *Cradle of Life* (1936), *The House in Antiqua* (1937), and *My America* (1938), and expanding his audience by frequent magazine articles and lectures all over the country.

"After Nineteen Years," the opening portion of the section called "Home Again in Carniola," shows Louis Adamic at his best. It reflects his characteristic optimism and sympathy and modesty, his gift for revealing significant details, his ability to tell a story so that emotions as well as ideas and facts are firmly communicated.

# AFTER NINETEEN YEARS

EARLY in the spring of 1932, when I received a Guggenheim Fellowship requiring me to go to Europe for a year, I was thirty-three and had been in the United States nineteen years. At fourteen—a son of peasants, with a touch of formal "city education"—I had emigrated to the United States from Carniola, then a tiny Slovene province of Austria, now an even tinier part of a *banovina* in the new Yugoslav state.

In those nineteen years I had become an American; indeed, I had often thought I was more American than were most of the native citizens of my acquaintance. I was ceaselessly, almost fanatically, interested in the American scene; in ideas and forces operating in America's national life, in movements, tendencies and personalities, in technical advances, in social, economic, and political problems, and generally in the tremendous drama of the New World.

Events and things outside of America interested me but incidentally: only in so far as they were related to, or as they affected, the United States. I spoke, wrote, and read only in

English. For sixteen years I had had practically no close contact with immigrants of my native nationality. For three years I had been a soldier in the American army. After the war I had roamed over a good half of the United States and had been to Hawaii, Philippines, Central and South America. In the last few years I had become an American writer, writing on American subjects for American readers. And I had married an American girl.

To Stella I had told but a few main facts about my childhood and early boyhood in the old country; and what little I had told her of my parents, and the village and house in which I was born, had seemed to her "like a story." She scarcely believed me. To her I was an American from toes to scalp.

Now, because of my Guggenheim Fellowship, we were going to Europe.

One day early in April, Stella said, "We'll visit your folks in Carniola, of course." She evidently thought that would be the natural thing to do.

"Of course," I said. "Of course," I repeated inaudibly to myself, then added aloud, "Just a short visit, though—for an afternoon, perhaps."

She said, "I suddenly realized that you told me you have people over there—in Carniola (I like the sound of the name)—and now I'm curious about them—what they're like."

"So am I," I said, though actually, I think, I wasn't; not in any deep, vital sense, at any rate.

None the less, I wrote to my family in the old country that my wife, who was an American and spoke no Slovenian, and I should, in all probability, visit them on Sunday afternoon, May 15th. The ship that we decided to sail on was scheduled to arrive in Trieste on the 14th, and I figured that we might as well get the visit over with the first thing; then we should immediately find a place in the mountains somewhere in Italy or Austria and I should begin to work on my new book dealing with America.

## II

Three weeks later, in mid-Atlantic, I said to Stella, "I'm a bit scared of this visit home."

"I thought something was bothering you," she said. "Why?"

"Well," I began to explain, "although in a way it seems like the day before yesterday, it's a long time since I left home. I was very young and I think I've changed a great deal—fundamentally —since then. All my emotional and intellectual life now seems to be rooted in America. I belong in America. My old country, somehow, is a million miles away—on another planet—and my old country includes my people."

Stella listened sympathetically.

"Of course," I went on, "I remember my parents as they were before I left home, but now my memory of them is seriously blurred by the idea which abruptly intrudes itself upon my mind, that in these nineteen years, which have been a drastic, turbulent period for everybody in Europe, they, too, must have changed— not merely grown older, but changed, probably, in their characters. This adds to the distance between them and me.

"I have four brothers and five sisters in Carniola. Seven of them were already in the world nineteen years ago. Of the two born since then, I have, of course, no notion, except that their names are Yozhé and Anica, and their ages seventeen and fifteen, respectively. The other seven I remember but dimly as they were in 1913. I was the oldest (three children before me had died). My oldest sister, Tonchka, was thirteen. My oldest brother, Stan, was ten. My youngest brother, Francé, was a little over a year. Now he is nearly twenty-one. Tonchka is thirty-two, married, and has two children. Stan is twenty-nine. Another sister, Mimi, was four when I left. Now she is twenty-three, a nun in a hospital, and her name is Manuela. Why she became a nun is more than I know. Then there is my brother Anté and my sisters Paula and Poldka—barely more than names to me. In fact, I have to strain my memory to tell you their names. And now I'm going to visit them because that, somehow, seems the proper thing to do."

"It'll probably be very interesting," said Stella.

"Probably very awkward," said I. "During the last fifteen years my contact with home has been exceedingly thin. For two years after America's entry into the war I could not write to my people because I was in the American army and they were in Austria. We were 'enemies.' For two or three years after the war my circumstances were nothing to write about to anybody; so I didn't. In the last eight or nine years I wrote home, as a rule, once in six months—a card or a short note, to the effect that I was well and hoped they were all well, too. I could not write much more. For one thing, I could not begin to tell them about America and myself; how I felt about America, what a wonderful and terrible place it was, how it fascinated and thrilled me. They might misunderstand something; something I'd say might disturb them; then I'd have to explain, and so on; there would be no end to writing—to what purpose? At the end they would really know nothing or very little about America or me. One has to live in the United States a long time to even begin to know it. Besides, if I got them interested in America, some of my brothers and sisters might want to come over—and I did not want that. I had troubles enough of my own. And they were possibly as well off in Carniola as they would be in America. . . . Another thing: of late years I could express only the most ordinary things in my native tongue. I could not write in Slovenian of involved matters, such as my life in America.

"At home, of course, they did not understand me, what I was up to in America, why I wrote so little; and they, with their peasant patience and pride (which, as I recall, does not break down even before members of their own family)—they, in turn, asked me for no explanations, and their letters to me were almost as brief as mine to them. They—mother or one of my sisters or brothers—usually answered that they were well, too, thank you. Occasionally they added some such information as that Tonchka had married or had had a child, or that Stan or Anté had had to go into military service, or that Mimi had become a nun—bare facts, nothing else.

"So I don't know what I'll find. I have no idea how they stand economically. When I left for America my father was a' well-to-do peasant in the village. Now, if one is to believe American newspapers, all of Europe is in a bad way, and I don't know what's happened to my people lately. Then, too, you must remember that I'm coming from America, and when one returns from America one is supposed to bring with him a pot of money and help those who have stayed at home—while all I have is a Guggenheim Fellowship, barely enough to keep you and me in Europe for a year!"

Stella was optimistic. "Chances are it won't be so bad as you think. Perhaps your people are as scared of you, what America has done to you, and the kind of girl you married, as you are of them and what the nineteen years have done to them."

"Maybe," I said. I felt a little better, not much, and not for long.

## III

Our ship stopped for a few hours each at Lisbon, Gibraltar, Cannes, Naples, and Palermo. Save in Cannes, everywhere, on getting ashore, we were mobbed by ragged youngsters, crying, "Gimme! Gimme!" and making signs that they were famished and wanted to eat. In the streets (especially in Lisbon) women with children in their arms approached us and made signs that their babies were hungry. Most of these, no doubt, were professionals, dressed and trained for begging; but even so it was depressing.

"In Yugoslavia it may be even worse," I said.

On the morning of May 13th we began to sail along the coast of Dalmatia, once also a province of Austria, now a part of Yugoslavia. We passed tiny islands and bright little towns along the shore line, and gradually I began to feel better. I scarcely know why. Perhaps because the hills ashore looked so much like the hills from San Pedro to San Diego in southern California where I lived for years. Perhaps also because the Adriatic Sea, with the sun on it, was even bluer, lovelier than the Mediterranean.

But even so, I was hardly prepared for Dubrovnik, or Ragusa. From the ship, as we approached it, it appeared unreal. "Like a stage set for a play," Stella remarked. And another American, leaning next to her on the rail, said, "One expects a bunch of actors to appear out there at any moment and begin to sing, 'We are the merry villagers. . . .'"

The boat stopped for three hours and we went ashore. Here we were not mobbed by beggars. Some of the young boys on the pier were almost as ragged as those in Lisbon and in Palermo, but they looked anything but starved or sick. Their grins reached from ear to ear. Their white, strong teeth flashed in the sun. Their faces were brown. Locks of straggly dark hair hung over their blue eyes.

To one of the ragamuffins Stella offered a coin. He looked at her, startled. "*Zashto?* (What for?)" he asked. I explained to the youngster in Croatian (which, to my surprise, I suddenly began to speak with very little difficulty) that my wife wanted to make him a present of the coin. He scowled: "*Hvala liepa!* (Thank you!) No alms!" Then, as if something just occurred to him, his sun-tanned young features lit up. "If you and the lady wish to be friendly and generous," he grinned, "please offer me an American cigarette if you have one and see if I'll take it."

He got several cigarettes; then his mouth and eyes—his whole face—broke into a smile that I cannot describe "*Hvala liepa!*" he shouted, and dashed off. Several other boys, all shouting, followed him.

I felt grand. "My people!" I said to myself. "'No alms!'" I could have run after the urchin and hugged him. "My people!" I said, aloud.

Stella laughed. We both laughed.

We walked through the ancient, sun-flooded, and shadowy streets of Dubrovnik, whose history reaches back to the fifth century. Many of the streets were not streets at all, but twisty stairways running from the main thoroughfares up the steep grades. Some of the people we saw were obviously foreigners—visitors or tourists from Austria, Czechoslovakia, Germany, France, and England—but the majority were native Dalmatians of all ages, many in colorful homespun costumes, and Serbo-Moslem laborers from near-by Bosnia and Herzegovina, wearing *opanke*, Serb sandals, with upturned toes and baggy Turkish breeches, close-fitting jackets, and red fezes. On one street we saw two veiled Mohammedan women walking on one side; on the other side were two Catholic nuns. In the doorways sat mothers, giving their breasts to infants. There were swarms of children everywhere.

"Such faces!" exclaimed Stella every few minutes. "Even the homely ones are beautiful, they're so healthy and brown."

In Dubrovnik—unlike in Lisbon, Gibraltar, Naples, and Palermo —no one forced himself upon us to sell us something. Here no guides were offering their services; there were no shifty-eyed peddlers of obscene photographs. In the little bazaars, where business evidently was poor, the men and women in charge of the stores seemingly did not care whether the passers-by stopped to look at and buy their handmade peasant embroidery, jewelry, and earthenware or not. They talked and laughed among themselves, or sat still and dozed in the warm sun.

On the way back to the pier, going down a steep stair-street, we came upon a tall, splendidly proportioned girl, dark-haired and blue-eyed, clad in an agreeably colorful medley of several south-Dalmatian costumes, among which the local Ragusan dress predominated. On her head she balanced a great basket of something or other; perhaps of wash for one of the modern houses above the old town. The basket seemed a part of her. She walked and swayed from her hips. Her arms were bare and firm. One of them she held akimbo. In the other hand she carried a bunch of golden-rain blossoms. She slowed her pace to look at us; possibly Stella's American dress interested her.

I said, "*Dobar dan!* (Good day!)"

"*Dobar dan!*" she returned, smiled—again one of those smiles to which words cannot do justice—and stopped. "Are you *nashki?* (of our nationality?)"

"I was born in Slovenia," I said, "but went to America as a young boy. My wife is American."

"So!" said the girl, eagerly. "An uncle of mine is in America. He is a fisherman in Louisiana, where the great river Mees-sees-seep-pee," she syllabicated, "falls into the ocean." She smiled all the while.

"She is beautiful," said Stella. "What a body!"

I translated, "My wife says you are beautiful and you have a fine body."

The girl's smile widened and deepened, and her face and neck colored. "*Hvala liepa!*" she said. "Please tell your American wife that *she* is beautiful."

I told Stella what the girl had said. Then from the bunch she carried the girl handed her several twigs of golden-rain and, without saying anything, went on up the stairs.

"That is what I call nice," said Stella, looking after the girl. "Such a simple, sincere gesture."

I had a sudden feeling that I would like Yugoslavia, her people; that, perhaps, even my visit home would be more a pleasure than an ordeal.

## IV

Fifteen hours later—Saturday forenoon—the ship docked in Trieste.

Before we got off, there came aboard a Slovene gentleman, overwhelming in his eager politeness and courtesy. He bowed, shook my hand, bowed again and kissed Stella's hand. Then he proceeded to inform me, in most precise, formal, and yet not unbeautiful words, that he was the personal representative of the *ban* (governor) of Dravska Banovina (now the official government designation for Slovenia), and that his special duties were to officially welcome us to my old country, to see that at the Italo-Yugoslav border the Yugoslav customs and immigration people would not disturb our luggage or cause us any other annoyance, and generally to see, so far as was within his power, that our stay in the *banovina* would be the essence of comfort and delight. He was at our command—and he bowed again. Thereupon he bowed once more and said that Slovenia—indeed, entire Yugo-slavia—was honored and overjoyed by my homecoming.

All this I tried to take matter-of-factly and thanked the gentle-man in as good Slovenian as, in my embarrassment, I could command after not having spoken it for sixteen years Then I told Stella what it was all about.

Wide-eyed, she said after a moment: "But why? Because you're a writer?"

"I suppose so," I said.

"The boy who went into the big world and made good comes home!"

We laughed and the Slovene, who understood no English, politely joined in our laughter. Of course, I did not explain to him why the thing was funny to us. I did not tell him, for in-stance, that the two books I had published in the United States, while praised by the critics and reviewers throughout the coun-try, had had tragically unsatisfactory sales; that in America I was a nobody—one of many young scribblers living in eternal dread of the rejection slip; that in America no writer draws much water; that for the government to officially honor an author was almost inconceivable in the United States.

Out of his briefcase the gentleman then produced a batch of Slovene and other Yugoslav newspapers of recent date. Here were long articles about my "wide fame" and "great achieve-ments" in America, containing translated quotations from favor-able reviews of my books. In addition, some of them carried brief editorials which ended: "To our distinguished countryman and visitor: WELCOME HOME!"—in capital letters.

"As you see, sir," said the man, "the whole country is agog. The newspaper men in Lublyana"—the capital of the *banovina*—"are extremely eager to interview you, but since the first thing you doubtless wish to do is rest after the trip and visit your peo-ple, I have warned them not to disturb you, say, until Monday or early next week, when and if it shall please you to talk to them."

"Oh, thank you very much! It was very nice of you." . . .

Interview me! On what? I had never been interviewed in my life.

At first I could not understand how all this publicity had broken loose on the eve of my return. I recalled that I had sent copies of my books to my parents, but surely they had not engineered the ballyhoo. I recalled, too, that now and then my people had inclosed in their letters one or two little clippings about me from the Lublyana papers, but that could not be the genesis of all this.

Then it occurred to me that a week before we sailed a man had telephoned to me who said he was the American correspondent for several journals in Yugoslavia, and that he had read in New York papers about my getting a Guggenheim Fellowship and my forthcoming trip to Europe, which he hoped would include Yugoslavia. Would it? I said that it would. What ship was I going on?—and a few other such questions, which I had answered. Then he said that he had followed my "career in America for years" and, now that I was going home, he would write "a little article" about me. And these columns of stuff in a dozen papers printed in Lublyana, Zagreb, Belgrade, Split, Sarajevo and one or two other cities of Yugoslavia were the "little article."

But the real reason and significance of all this, which had little to do with me, I learned much later.

## V

The short train ride from Trieste to Lublyana was a delightful experience, especially after we crossed the Italian border, when I was in my old country at last.

It was a perfect midspring afternoon, and most of my misgivings of the week before had vanished. Carniola, to all seeming, had not changed a whit. Here was the same river Sava with the same tributaries; the same little lakes and waterfalls; the same thickly wooded hills and mountains, with the snow-capped peaks above them; the same fields and meadows; the same villages and little churches, with crude frescoes of saints painted by peasant artists on the outer walls; and the same people, toiling in the same old way—slowly, patiently, somewhat inefficiently (to my American eyes) with semi-primitive tools and implements, on the same fertile black soil. The World War (although some of the worst battles were fought within hearing distance of Carniola) and the drastic political change, in 1918, from Austria to Yugoslavia had had no effect upon its essential aspects, its exquisite and wholesome beauty.

I do not mean to say that the regions of Carniola by themselves, with all their congestion of lovely valleys, lakes, rivers, hills, woods, and mountains, are more beautiful than other regions I have seen elsewhere in the world. I know of vastly grander places in the United States, but houses and towns in America, a new country, often spoil a natural scene. If not houses and towns, then outdoor advertisements and heaps of tin cans and discarded machinery. In Carniola, however, the simple peasant architecture of the small villages seems to enhance the beauty of the countryside. The houses and villages *belong*. They appear to have grown out of the soil. They belong exactly where they are, both esthetically and economically. Most of them have been where they are for five, six, seven hundred years. They are harmonious with the woods, the fields, the lakes. They are in the pattern of the country as a whole, an elemental and sympathetic feature thereof.

The same goes for the people. The peasants driving the oxen on the dirt roads; the women, young and old, in their colorful working-clothes, weeding or hoeing in the fields and now pausing in their work to smile and wave to us in the train; the girls by the riverside, with their up-drawn petticoats, washing the heavy homespun linen by slapping it on big smooth rocks; the woodsmen floating freshly felled logs down the river; the barefoot, sturdy children playing before the houses—they all seemed to me inextricably and eternally an important, indigenous part of the scenery, the beauty-pattern, the deep harmony of Carniola.

I was glad to be back. My reaction to the beauty of Carniola, of course, was enhanced by the fact that it was my native land. I felt like shouting greetings to the peasants in the fields along the railroad.

There was another general impression that I got on the train.

Carniola seemed so very, very small. I remembered, for instance, that in my boyhood a trip from Lublyana to Trieste was considered a long journey, an event in anybody's life to make it. And here Stella and I were coming from Trieste to Lublyana in a couple of hours by a slow train, humorously called an express, and we thought it was a short trip. The train stopped every few minutes in villages and small towns, which I suddenly recalled at least by names. With my consciousness of distances in the United States, and with the tens of thousands of miles that stretched behind me over the American continent and over two oceans, the distances in Carniola now seemed scarcely one-tenth of what I had thought them to be nineteen years before. Carniola had shrunk from an Austrian province to hardly more than a big Western ranch or a small national park in America.

When, toward evening, we arrived in Lublyana, which once upon a time I had considered a large city, it, too—with its 75,-ooo inhabitants—impressed me as a very small place; for I had behind me New York, Los Angeles, Kansas City, Chicago.

I had an impulse to go from Lublyana right on to my native village, not far from the city, but since I had written to my people that we would not come till Sunday afternoon, we let the *ban's* representative put us up for the night at one of the hotels.

After dinner, Stella went to bed, but I couldn't.

I went out and walked in the dimly-lit, quiet, almost deserted streets till past midnight, and discovered, to my great satisfaction, that, like the rest of Carniola, Lublyana, too, had not changed in its essentials; indeed, hardly even in its superficial aspects. The World War and the change from Austria to Yugoslavia did not touch it.

The old Roman wall seemed a little more crumbled than I remembered it, and in the middle of the city a twelve-story *nebotichnik* (skytoucher) was being built. But there were the same bridges over the River Lublyanica; the same nine-hundred-year-old fort and castle on the hill, now lit up at night; the same five-hundred-year-old City Hall, except that in place of the statue of the Emperor Francis Joseph in front of it there was now a new statue of the late King Peter of Serbia. There were the same old

churches and monuments to writers, grammarians, musicians, orators, and poets; the same old stores, with the same old signs over
the doors. Here, I remembered, I used to buy paper and pencils
while attending the Gymnasium in my early teens. And here I
used to buy rolls and apples for my midday lunch; here, my
occasional piece of cake or chocolate; here, in this two-hundred-
year-old bookshop, my books; and here my mother used to come
shopping for drygoods once in a fortnight. ("She probably still
does," I said to myself.) And here was the school I had gone to;
here the house I had roomed in for two years; and here the
theatre where I had seen my first Shakespearean performance.
Everything came back to me, and once more Lublyana was an
important, vital part of my life.

Here were street-sweepers, old men with long birch brooms,
sweeping the streets at night in the same old way. Here was a
lamplighter with his tall pole, now, toward midnight, putting
out some of the lights. Here I almost bumped into a black little
fellow, a chimneysweep! and, amused at myself, I swiftly grabbed
a button on my coat, for in my boyhood I had shared the folk
superstition that to hold onto a button when meeting a chimneysweep meant good luck.

Here glowed the curtained windows of an old coffee-house.
I entered and ordered a coffee, just to make sure its tables were
occupied by the same types of men as nineteen years before,
reading newspapers, playing chess and dominoes, talking, talking, talking in low tones so as not to disturb those who read or
played chess. . . . Here was stability; or so it seemed.

I returned to the hotel tired, inwardly excited, deeply content.

## VI

Tired as I was, I didn't fall asleep till after daylight. A tense-
ness, not unpleasant, from which I could not relax, held my body,
and my mind throbbed with new impressions, newly stirred
memories, thoughts of tomorrow. . . . My mother—how did she
look? This, suddenly, was very important. When I had left, she
was still on the sunny side of middle life, "rather tall," as I de-

scribed her in my autobiographical narrative *Laughing in the Jungle*, "with a full bust and large hips; long arms and big, capable hands; a broad, sun-browned, wind-creased Slavic face; large, wide-spaced hazel eyes, mild and luminous with simple mirth; and wavy auburn hair which stuck in little gold-bleached wisps from under her colored kerchief, tied below her chin." That was how I remembered her. Now she was in her late fifties; she had borne thirteen children, raised ten, and worked hard without pause all her life. . . . My father? He was over eighty. . . . Our house? It was over six hundred years old, but with the possible exception of a new roof it probably was unchanged since I last saw it. . . .

On coming down the next morning, Stella and I saw two tall young men in the middle of the otherwise deserted hotel lobby. They did not see us immediately. One of them nervously paced up and down. The other was furiously smoking a cigarette.

"They must be your brothers!" breathed Stella. We stopped on the stairs. "They resemble you terribly," she added; "only they're handsome—Lord, they're handsome!"

Then the boys saw us, too. They recognized me, and their broad, bronzed faces split into big white-toothed grins. They rushed toward me, I rushed down, and we collided at the foot of the stairs. Shaking hands, we began to laugh, all three of us at once. Then Stella joined us, too. We didn't say a word for minutes; we just laughed.

They were Francé and Yozhé, my two kid brothers, Gymnasium students; only, unlike myself in my time, they did not room and board in Lublyana, but came in daily by train. Basically, however, beneath the thin crust of city polish they were young peasants, strong and healthy, exuding vitality, each with a pair of enormous hands. Looking at them, I had a weird-happy feeling. It was as if I looked in a magic mirror and saw myself at once twelve and sixteen years younger. Stella and I could not take our eyes off them. They spoke a little German and some French, and Stella could exchange a few words with them. But at first they could hardly talk at all, due to excitement only partly under control.

By and by they explained to me that mother had sent them to Lublyana on the early-morning train with orders to find us in the city and fetch us home on the first afternoon train without fail.

Francé said, "The whole village—the whole valley, in fact—is excited as it never was before. For a week now nobody in the seventeen villages of our county has talked of anything but your homecoming, and the talk has already spread to other counties. In our valley the circulation of city newspapers has increased a hundredfold. Everybody has read about you. Everybody wants to see you. The girls and women want to know what sort of girl you married. You're the first from our valley to marry an *Amerikanka*. It's a sensation. . . . At home, in our house, of course, they are all beside themselves. None of us have had a decent night's sleep for a week. Mother, Paula, and Poldka—they sleep in the same room—scarcely closed their eyes for three or four nights, talking, speculating. Last night they spoke of killing our newest bull-calf to celebrate the return of the prodigal, but the calf, poor thing, is only two weeks old and as yet not particularly 'fatted'—so they decided to wait a week or two, till it gets a little closer to the scriptural weight."

We laughed for several minutes. I was unable to translate Francé's words to Stella till later.

I began to realize that during these nineteen years I, in America, had meant much more to my people than they, remaining in the old country, had meant to me. In the excitement of my life in America, I had lost nearly all feeling for them and for the old country in general. To them, on the other hand, I had been their own intrepid Marco Polo who had ventured from tiny Carniola into the big world at the age of fourteen. Now, after long years, I was coming home! And according to the newspapers, I had become a great man in the big world. I had become "famous," and thereby I had brought renown to their hitherto unknown, microscopic Carniola!

In the afternoon, going home in the train, Stella and I talked about this.

"It's very funny!" she said.

"Of a sudden," I said, "I'm a big frog in a tiny pond!"

At the little country railroad station, which is in the village next to ours and which seemed ten times smaller than I recalled it, stood a crowd of people—elderly peasants, women, young men, girls, children, all in their Sunday best, some of the men in coat-sleeves, some of the girls in costumes of the region.

They stood in silence, save that some of the girls giggled. I didn't know any of them; only a few faces seemed faintly familiar.

It was a grand, sweet, painful moment.

Here and there, as we walked from the train, one of the young men stuck out his paw to me and said, "*Pozdravlyen!* (Greetings!) Remember me? I'm So-and-so."

I remembered him, then we laughed, and there was a loud murmur in the crowd.

Then two young men who looked very much alike and resembled Francé, Yozhé, and myself stepped out of the crowd. My two other brothers, a little older than Francé and Yozhé, and even a little taller. One of them was better-looking than all the other three put together. Stella let out a little shriek of delight. We shook hands.

"I am Stan," said the older one, grinning. He had a tremendous hand, but his grip and the look in his eyes with which he greeted me had the gentleness of a truly strong person.

"I am Anté," said the other, also grinning. He was the handsomest, but, like Stan, a young peasant without city education or polish.

Then all five of us brothers and Stella laughed for all we were worth, and the crowd joined in.

"Where are mother and father and the girls?" I asked.

"At home, all of them," said Stan.

And, I don't know why, but we all laughed again, and we walked home through the fields and meadows, with a mob of young boys and many dogs behind us. The valley seemed very, very small to me, and very beautiful. Spring was late and things were just beginning to grow. In the bright green of the meadows were big splashes of yellow buttercups and purple clover ahum

with bees. Along the ditches grew forget-me-nots in great abundance, and in the shade of a row of hazel bushes I noticed more
lilies-of-the-valley in one spot than I had seen during all my nineteen years in America.

For a minute everything threatened to go soft in me and
I barely managed to hold back my tears.

In Blato, our village, was another, smaller crowd. I recognized
a few faces. There were two or three uncles, and as many aunts
and scores of cousins, some of whom had come from other villages, but no one said anything. With deep innate tact, they let
me hurry on to our house.

## VII

The sight of my mother, who waited for me (as I recalled in
that instant) on the same spot in the courtyard of our home
where I had said good-by to her in 1913, gave me a sharp sting.
She had aged and her body had shrunk; her hair was gray and
thin, her eyes and cheeks were sunken, but her hug told me she
was still hale and strong.

Suddenly I was sorry that I hadn't written to her oftener.
I wanted to say something, but what was there to say? What
could anyone say in a moment like this? She herself said nothing. She smiled a little and, holding my hands stiffly in front of
her, her body swayed a little, right and left, in sheer, unword-
able happiness.

My father, also gray and shrunken, offered me a trembling,
wrinkled hand, but on the whole, despite his age, was well and in
full possession of his faculties. He smiled and said, "You have
come at last. We greet you, son."

And there were the girls. Four of them stood against the wall
of the house.

"I am Tonchka," said my oldest, married sister, who had come
from Belgrade to be home when I arrived. She looked like a
young matron.

"I am Paula,"—my next-to-the-oldest sister. Great coils of
brown hair were wound around her head. A tragic love-affair, of

which I learned subsequently, had etched into her face, which was lovely before, a beauty that now causes a crisis in my vocabulary.

"I am Poldka,"—my third sister, a vivacious, open-faced human being in national costume. Two thick light-brown braids hung down her face. She was the only one who gave way to emotion and cried a little. "I'm *so* glad!"

"I am Anica,"—my youngest sister, the baby of the family, a reticent, shy young girl whom, like Yozhé, I had never seen before.

Finally, a nun appeared in the doorway above the stairs—my sister Mimi, now called Manuela. This was her first visit home since her ordination a year before. A victim of confused feelings, I ran up to her. She said nothing; she smiled; a young Madonna face, if a face was ever entitled to be called that. We shook hands. I had been told a moment before that because she was a nun I could not embrace or kiss her. I could shake hands with her only because I was her brother. I looked at her—at the oval, smooth, serene face, with its lively blue eyes and glowing red cheeks, under the broad starched white headgear of her order—and couldn't (and can't yet) understand why she became a nun.

After a while we all trooped into the house, in which all ten of us had been born, and before us our father and grandfather and our ancestors for I don't know how many generations back. But for some improvements here and there, the house had not changed; only, of course, with my consciousness of the Empire State Building and the interior of the Grand Central in New York City, it seemed much smaller to me than I had thought it was.

I noticed that mother and sisters used the same sort of utensils in the kitchen as were used in 1913. There were the same old tile stoves downstairs and upstairs; the same beds, tables, chairs, benches, and chests; the same pictures and ornaments on the walls. Upon the window-sills were flower-pots with flowers just beginning to bud. Throughout the house new curtains, bedspreads, and tablecovers had been spread and hung for my homecoming. They were my sisters' handwork—lace and embroidery,

exquisite designs and color combinations. . . . (Later I learned
that my sisters were members of the Yugoslav Peasant Handi-
craft Institute, which sold the products of their hands to Belgian
lace merchants and English curio-dealers in Egypt, who then
sold them to American importers and foreign tourists as Belgian
or Egyptian native handwork. One of my sisters showed me lace
she was making with sphinx and pyramid designs. She said,
"Some American lady will probably buy this in Alexandria or
Cairo next year!"—and we all laughed.)

In the large-room, the big table was set with a great bowl of
forget-me-nots in the center. There was food and wine for all
of us, and we sat down and tried to eat and drink, but, to mother's
dismay, none of us was very successful. We were all too excited
and happy, too full of emotions for which we had no expression.

In the middle of the meal, apropos of nothing in particular,
my sister Paula, her sad face all in a big smile, silently pinned a
few lilies-of-the-valley on Stella's jacket and a few on my coat
lapel.

"They're lovely," said Stella, which I translated to Paula.

"Yes," said Paula; "there are so many of them this year that
one could take a scythe and mow them like grass or clover." She
smiled again, "I guess it's all in your honor, and your wife's."

Stella, understanding almost nothing of what was said, found
herself in an awkward position. I translated some of the conversation to her. Everybody looked at her and tried to please her.
I was discreetly questioned as to her family. Of course, unable
to speak her language, it was as awkward for them as for her.
But after a while she and they developed a system of hands-and-
eyes language with which they managed to communicate some
of their simpler thoughts to one another without my aid.

Essentially a simple, straightforward person, Stella won my
people from the start. My sister Poldka said to me, "You have no
idea, we were all so scared that you—a famous writer—would
come home with some stiff, haughty foreign dame, and now, I
guess, you can imagine how relieved we all are. How I wish I
could talk with her!"

And Stella said to me, "It's almost unbelievable, this family of yours—the sort of family one could write a saga about. . . . I thought that, having let you go to America at fourteen, they were and would be indifferent to you. But now I see they love you without being possessive. I suppose that, peasant-like, they accepted your going to America the same way as they accept any other trick of fate, without changing their basic affection for you; when you didn't write for a long time, that was another trick of fate for them to accept; but it really made no difference so far as caring for you was concerned. I think it's wonderful to be that way. . . . Please tell them I love them all."

I told them.

"*Hvala liepa*," said mother and Poldka. The others said nothing. They grinned and lowered their eyes. Poldka, who, as I say, is the most free-spoken in the family, said, "Tell her for us that we love her, too. We could just hug her, even though we have no practice in hugging."

I translated this to Stella. We all laughed again.

# VIII

In the courtyard and in the apple orchard people began to gather—people of our own village and of near-by communities, neighbors, relatives, friends of the family's. "I guess they want to see you," said mother, "and since we can't ask them all into the house, you will have to go out."

So out we went, Stella, a few of my brothers and sisters, and I. Then there was much sincere handshaking. "*Pozdravlyen!* . . . *Pozdravlyen!* Welcome home!" The men made some reticent remarks, asked a few hesitant questions. "I remember well when you went to America. . . . After all these years, how does the old village look to you, eh?" Some acted embarrassed, as they thought peasants should act in the presence of a man who was written up in the newspapers, but after a while this manner broke down, whereupon there was a lot of good, simple talk, punctuated by bursts of honest mirth.

I became acquainted with a young peasant, now married and the father of five children, who claimed that he had once whipped me in a fight over the possession of a whistle, and now that he mentioned it I seemed to recall the occasion.

Another young fellow, now also married and the father of several kids (one of whom was wrapped around his leg), admitted I had beaten him up several times and recalled to my mind the causes of our frequent battles.

One old peasant woman insisted I come to her house, a stone's-throw from ours, and there she showed me something I had scrawled on a wall about another boy in the village when I was ten or eleven years old.

I talked with Uncle Mikha, my favorite uncle, who is in his seventies, slightly bent and shrunken but still hale, with a hard peasant intelligence. Till lately, he had been mayor of our county. He and I had been good friends in my early boyhood. First we exchanged a few conventional remarks, then he drew me aside, cleared his throat, shifted the weight of his body from one leg onto the other, and said, "You may be a big man in the world, as the newspapers have it, but I am going to give you a piece of my mind anyhow. I think it wasn't at all nice not to write to your mother oftener than you did. She talked to me about you when you didn't write for a long time. She worried. At night she couldn't sleep, thinking maybe you were in trouble or dead. I am telling you this because I have liked you ever since you were knee-high and because your mother herself won't say anything about it to you—and when you go back to America I want you to write to her oftener."

"I will, Uncle Mikha," I said.

"But don't feel bad about what I said," said Mikha. "Now that you've come home, she's forgotten all about it."

Then there were the several *Amerikanci*—men who had been laborers in America for a few years and had returned home to stay. They each knew a few words of English and tried to parade their knowledge before their fellow villagers. They asked me about America. Was the *kriza* (the economic crisis) really as bad there as the papers said? Were there really so many people out of work? Was the depression hard on the Slovenian and other Yugoslav immigrants?

Other questions: Were the buildings in America really so tall? Was it true that there was a tree in California so thick that they had bored a tunnel through it for an automobile road? How did the American farmers till their soil? Was it true that most of the work on the land was done by machinery?—that New York had a population of seven million?—that there were ranches in the West bigger than entire Carniola?—that there were underground railroads in New York?—that there was a tunnel under a river in New York?—that Henry Ford was worth a billion dollars?—and how much was a billion dollars, anyhow, in Yugoslav dinars? And this man Seenclair Levees (Sinclair Lewis)—was he the biggest writer in America? Did I know him personally? Were these books *Arovsmeet* and *Babeet,* which have been translated into the Yugoslav, his best? . . .

Stella went walking with my brothers through the village, and the women, especially my cousins and aunts, commenced to ask me about her, at first discreetly, hesitantly, then more boldly: How old was she? How long were we married? Were her people well-to-do? How much dowry had she brought me? Had she sisters and brothers? Did she make her own clothes? . . . Which led to questions about American women in general: Did they all buy their clothes in stores? Did any of them bake their own bread, do their own wash, do fine needlework? Were houses in America very different from houses in Carniola? . . .

No end of questions, naïve, foolish, and sensible, which I found pleasure in answering, nevertheless. But I was glad, too, when, toward dusk, mother came and said I should come in to eat and drink something. "You must be starved and tired, talking all afternoon," she said. "And where is Styelah?" . . . I loved the way she pronounced her name. . . .

In the house mother said to me: "Yesterday I had a million questions to ask you, too, but now I forget them all. It doesn't matter. You are back and have a nice wife. Why ask questions? . . . Come now, eat something."

We sat down.

"Mother," I asked, "how do you all manage? I mean, what do you use for money?"

She laughed a little. "There's this *kriza*, of course, which does us no good, but now and then we sell a little of what we produce, so we can buy some of the things we need and can't produce at home. Ours is a big family, but Poldka and Paula make the clothes for all of us, and the clothes they make are better made than those one can buy in the city. Anté is handy with tools and he can make or repair almost anything. He can build a wall. Last year he and Stan put a cement bridge over the creek; you'll see it. The year before they dug the new water well, which you saw. Stan is a plowman second to none hereabouts. They are all healthy and capable, thank God. We don't need to employ help even at harvest time. . . . We manage, more or less."

That night, after a supper of home-cured ham and mildly spiced cooked wine which came from one of our relatives' vineyard in Bela Krayina, I slept, between sheets of rough home-made linen, in the bed in which I and all my brothers and sisters had let out our first wails.

## IX

Stella and I wanted to stay in Blato a couple of weeks (and my people wanted us to stay forever), but that soon became impossible.

The Sunday papers had reported my arrival, and on Monday morning reporters from Lublyana and other cities came to the village. Would I tell them my impressions of the old country and about "the social, economic, political, and literary life in the United States." On Tuesday the newspapers carried columns reporting my impressions of Carniola, my views of America, and the fact that Stella, who was also delighted with Carniola, already knew a dozen Slovenian words.

The same day there began to come to Blato letters and telegrams by the handful. I was welcomed to my native land by literary and cultural clubs. One magazine writer requested "a comprehensive interview about America." There were invitations to house parties in Lublyana and elsewhere, to picnics and "evenings," to excursions into the mountains and the lake region of Upper Carniola.

To accept at least some of the invitations, we moved back to the hotel in Lublyana.

We no sooner re-registered than the gentleman who had met us in Trieste appeared, in semi-panic. Breathless and wiping his brow, he spoke about some hammering that was going on in the house next to the hotel and begged us to let him transfer us to another hotel where he was certain no noise would discomfit us. We laughed and told him that, used to the din and tumult of New York, we hadn't even noticed the hammering next door!

## X

We were taken to Bled Lake by a group of young journalists, most of whom were also poets. All afternoon we drifted around the little island in the middle of the lake in a huge rowboat, which, besides us, contained several paper bags of sausages, loaves of black bread, containers of thick sour milk, flagons of red and white wine, an accordion, and two or three stringed instruments. By the end of the picnic my head whirled in consequence of our hosts' insatiable curiosity about America which, in my lame Slovenian, I tried to satisfy with such information as I had.

On Thursday was our first "evening," at the home of Slovenia's leading living novelist, who is also a Gymnasium professor, an editor and publisher, and a grand person. It was like two subsequent "evenings"—one at the home of Slovenia's foremost living poet and the other in the house of the editor of Slovenia's oldest literary review.

There gathered a dozen or more of Slovenia's literary and cultural lights and their wives. Fortunately some of them spoke or understood English and helped me with my Slovenian when I tried to answer a thousand and one questions about Upton Sinclair, Sinclair Lewis, Theodore Dreiser, Dos Passos, Edna St. Vincent Millay, Robert Frost, Countee Cullen, Langston Hughes, Hart Crane, Robinson Jeffers, James Stevens, Walter Winchell, and the new trends in American literature; about the depression, racketeering and Al Capone, the labor movement, the race problem, Henry Ford, the new woman in America, and the future of the United States.

Stella sat between a minor poet and a promising young novelist comprehending not a word, except my occasional bursts of English when I could not express myself in Slovenian. I answered questions from nine in the evening till three the next morning.

Then, according to custom, the host, the hostess, and all the other guests—some thirty people—walked Stella and me to the corner nearest to our hotel. Before we said good-night to all of them, dawn was breaking over the mountains.

There were ten days of this sort of thing, and opera, theatrical performances, and concerts, for all of which tickets were sent to us.

# XI

Gradually, I realized what I had dimly known in my boyhood, that, next to agriculture, Slovenia's leading industry was Culture. It was an intrinsic part of the place. In Lublyana were seven large bookshops (as large as most of the hardware, drygoods, and drug stores in town), two of them more than a hundred years old.

Every year, I learned, bookseller-publishers and the book clubs, of which there were eleven, published hundreds of books, few of which failed to pay for themselves. A "failure" was a book which sold less than 1,000 copies! Besides, each bookstore carried a selection of the latest German, French, Czech, Serbo-Croat, and a few English and Italian books. The publishers did almost no advertising, for in Slovenia nearly everybody—merchants, peasants, priests, teachers, students—bought books anyhow, or subscribed to book clubs. One book club had over 40,000 subscribers, another nearly 30,000, two over 20,000, and the rest had between 2,000 and 15,000. One juvenile book club distributed nearly 100,000 books every year among 23,000 children between the ages of ten and fourteen. And it must be remembered that there are only 1,100,000 Slovenians in Yugoslavia, with about 300,000 more in Italy and some 250,000 scattered as immigrants in the United States, various South American countries, and else-where; and over half of those in Slovenia live in villages with less than 500 population.

In two years, I was informed, there had been forty-eight per-formances of *Hamlet* in Lublyana. Most of the city's streets are named after poets, essayists, novelists, dramatists, grammarians. The largest monument in town is to a poet, Francé Presheren, who was at his height about a hundred years ago. When students take hikes into the country, their destinations usually are the graves and birthplaces of poets, dramatists, and other writers.

The year before I returned home there had been a hundredth-anniversary celebration of the birth of a writer, Francé Levstik, in the town of his birth, Velike Lasche, not far from Blato. It was the greatest event in Slovenia that year. Nearly 100,000 people attended the festival.

Shortly after I came back I happened to see a piece in a Lubly-ana newspaper that the village of X (the name now escapes me), somewhere in the mountains, twenty kilometers from the near-est railway, was about to unveil a modest monument to one of its sons, the late So-and-so, who a century ago had had a hand in the working out of certain rules of Slovenian grammar. The committee in charge of the occasion was frank in announcing that the village was very poor and the people would be unable to entertain the guests in suitable style; the peasants, however, would provide all visitors with such transportation from the rail-way to the village as they had, namely hay-wagons; and cherries, due to ripen by then, would be free to all comers.

In 1928, as I was told some time after my homecoming, Slo-venia's foremost living poet—Oton Zupanchich—celebrated his fiftieth anniversary, and on that occasion, which was a special holiday for the entire province, nearly one hundred delegations from all parts of the country called on him. Most of them were peasant delegations, some from remote mountain villages and counties. All of them brought him gifts. Women came with exquisite national handwork. Some presented him with bags of potatoes, hams, sausages, and other peasant products. Nearly all of them brought him money which had been appropriated by their respective county or village councils. Singing societies came from country districts to sing under his window. Student quartettes from Lublyana schools sang his poems set to music.

Most larger villages and all towns have public libraries, reading-rooms, and little theatre groups. My brother Anté and sister Poldka belong to one of the latter, in the town of Grosuplye, which is near Blato. Most homes, city and village alike, have bookshelves with books on them.

In the coffee-houses most of the talk I heard was about plays, paintings, sculpture, architecture, books and music, and social and economic ideas. Most of the questions I was asked about America had to do with cultural and social problems, and among the people who asked them were a young priest, an army officer, the wife of a bookbinder, and a veterinary whom I met casually. Their interest, evidently, was not of a dilettante nature. It was definitely an intimate part of their lives, of Lublyana, of the country.

The fact that I had written a few things in America, and received some recognition there, impressed my native countrymen much more than if I had come back, say, a millionaire industrialist or a champion wrestler or pugilist. Hence all this publicity, this whirl of hospitality.

There were other reasons for the ballyhoo and excitement.

One was political. Slovenes, as I have stated, are a tiny nation; if I am not mistaken, the smallest in Europe; and for nearly a thousand years they have not had any sort of independent political or economic life. In recent centuries they have been a minority group under Bavaria, then under Austria, and now, inevitably, are a minority group in the new Yugoslav state. Economically, they are almost utterly dependent on Belgrade (as they formerly were on Vienna) and, as I discovered after a while, none too happy about it. All these centuries they have had but two things which they felt were completely their own and which gave them the status of a nationality—namely, their language (which is similar to the Serbo-Croat) and their culture. And of these two things, along with their lovely country, they are immeasurably proud. They are immensely patriotic, but not offensively so.

Therefore, whenever one of "Slovenia's sons" achieves anything, either at home or in the outside world, they make a noise about it. If he achieves something in a cultural way, they are naturally impelled to make their noise even louder. They exert their utmost to make the Serbs and Croats take notice of him. This happened in my case.

Another reason was emotional—or perhaps I should say politico-emotional. Here I cannot begin to explain it in detail and in all its ramifications. The details, I think, will gradually appear in this book. Here I shall merely state that when I arrived in Yugoslavia, the country had been for over three years under the ruthless military dictatorship of King Alexander, which I knew but vaguely before I came there. I did not know what that really meant. I was not interested. I did not fully realize till months later that dictatorship meant that thousands of people were in prisons because they believed in such socio-political concepts as democracy, liberty, and economic justice, and dared to talk and act accordingly; that every city swarmed with secret agents; that newspaper, magazine, and book editors and publishers were under strict censorship; that public meetings, except those or-ganized by henchmen of the dictatorial regime, were forbidden; and so on.

Anyhow, that, roughly, very roughly, was the political situa-tion in Slovenia, in the whole of Yugoslavia, when I came there, although I did not see it at once. For three years and longer nearly everyone there had been living under an oppressive and suppressive government. I met people who whispered most of the time. Afraid to talk aloud in restaurants and coffee-houses or in the streets, they had been whispering ever since the dicta-torship was established; now they whispered even when they asked me what kind of trip I had had or how I liked spring weather in Slovenia. At first I did not know what was the matter with them.

But to them, as it occurred to me later when I began to under-stand them, I was a rare and exceedingly welcome apparition. Here I came, by origin one of them, from distant America, from the great, free world across the sea, from beyond the horizon, where I lived a free man, a free citizen in a democracy; where I said what I pleased and no one put me in jail; where, in fact, I was paid money for writing what I wanted to write. And they clustered about me, scores and scores of them, full of "unemployed emotions," as George Bernard Shaw called them; full of eager questions about everything under the sun, semi-vicariously experiencing through me, by having contact with me, liberty, democracy, and everything else they were denied in Yugoslavia.

The papers were "playing" me up because the censor would not let them print anything else that was interesting. To make me interesting, they exaggerated my "success" and importance" in America.

After I became better acquainted with some of my new friends in Lublyana, I tried to tell them that they had an exaggerated notion of me, but by then it was too late. Some of them accused me of modesty.

## XII

Off and on, during the first ten days of glory, Stella and I managed to run to Blato for a few hours in the afternoon. We became better acquainted with my family, our relatives, and the other villagers. My brothers Francé and Yozhé taught Stella to say whole phrases and long sentences in Slovenian, which gave our family and the village much satisfaction and cause for merriment.

We were all very happy. We laughed a great deal. The spring was beautiful. Momentarily, somehow, it did not seem important whether Yugoslavia was under a dictatorship or not.

The young calf in our barn was gaining weight, and the family council at home decided that the feast of the fatted calf would occur on the second Sunday after the prodigal's return. My father sent for wine. My sisters and mother schemed for a week as to the sort of cakes they would bake. My brothers Stan and Anté took some lumber and improvised tables and benches under the apple trees, just then coming to full bloom. All our relatives and family friends were invited.

Then it occurred to me to invite all my new friends, the literati and their wives. The idea startled my whole family. But would they come? For a son of our family to invite to Blato the foremost living poet, the leading living novelist, the editor of the oldest literary review in Slovenia, and other writers potentially as great, was as though a farmer's son in Pennsylvania got the notion to invite to a Sunday dinner such people as Henry Ford, Will Rogers, Calvin Coolidge, Al Smith, John Barrymore, and Gene Tunney. It must be remembered that literati are the biggest people in Carniola, especially to peasant folk.

But I invited them, in my father's name, and they came with their wives—so many of them that Stan and Anté were required to hurriedly build another table.

It was a bright, warm Sunday afternoon, with a light mountain breeze blowing through the valley. The literati mixed with the villagers, praised the village, exclaimed over the beauty of the fields and the meadows, and raved about the prodigal's sisters and brothers.

The foremost poet was pleased to the verge of tears when a little peasant girl, urged by my sister Poldka, stepped before him and recited his most famous poem. Pleased, too, was the leading novelist when a peasant woman brought him a copy of one of his books and asked him to "write something in it with your own hand."

My sister Paula and mother were in the kitchen, both happy beyond utterance. Francé and Yozhé, coatless and beaproned, brought out the plates (borrowed from the whole village) and platters heaped with pieces of the fatted calf. ("Poor thing!" said Stella, who, three days before had seen it alive in the barn.) Stan and Anté poured the wine. Poldka pinned forget-me-nots and lilies-of-the-valley on the garments of the guests. My youngest sister, Anica, brought on the bread and the cakes. Tonchka and Manuela had had to return to Belgrade.

The feast lasted all afternoon. The mountain breeze shook the apple blossoms upon the tables and the heads of the guests. There was much light, irresponsible talk and laughter around the tables. No whispering. Dictatorship or no: it did not matter that Sunday afternoon. By and by, the villagers and the literati began to sing Slovenian national songs about love, wine, and beautiful regions.

Stella exclaimed: "I wish my mother were here! And my brother, and Seren and Meta"—the whole crew of her girl friends in America.

"And Ben and Kyle and Carey . . ." I began to emumerate my friends back in the United States.

During a lull in the singing, the poet rose, glass in hand, and everyone became silent to hear him. He spoke awhile of the fine afternoon, the breeze from the mountains, the apple blossoms, the fatted calf, the wine in his glass, into which the petal of an apple blossom had fluttered as he talked. He eulogized the village, its people, and especially my mother and father, and referred to the fields and meadows around the village in words of sheer poetry. Finally he came to "the prodigal" and spoke of his departure for America and his return. It is not possible for me to give his words. It was all I could do to hold back my tears.

The poet ended, "Let us drain our glasses!"

The glasses were drained and someone began another song.

# FLOYD DELL

SHYNESS and mettle, "a valiant gentleness, a robust sensitiveness," unite in the temperament of this poet-editor-novelist, whom Sinclair Lewis described as "a faun at the barricades." And the little piece that follows throws some light upon the origin of these elements.

Floyd Dell was born at Barry, Illinois, in 1887, and began early to make his independent way in a world that has never ceased to be difficult. His family had declined, as Ben Ray Redman puts it, "from the lower fringe of American mid-western 'respectability' to the contiguous fringe of the laboring class wherein the father is often jobless and no hero by his own hearth." A factory-hand at sixteen, deprived of a high-school education, he nevertheless felt irrepressible promptings to write, and snatched at the first opportunity that promised a living. It happened to be newspaper reporting, in Davenport and Chicago. In 1909, when Francis Hackett became editor of the Friday Literary Review of *The Chicago Evening Post*, Dell was chosen as his assistant. Two years later, at twenty-three, still looking a mere boy, tall, slender, shy, Dell himself became literary editor, and in three years' time brought the book section of his paper up to a par with the best in the country.

In 1914 he went to New York, where he was associate editor, first, of *The Masses*, then, of *The Liberator*, sharing with Louis Untermeyer, Max Eastman, John Reed, and other young radicals of their Greenwich Village group the tempestuous fortunes of those spirited and unpopular periodicals. He also married, had several of his plays produced, and wrote a fine autobiographical novel, *Mooncalf* (1920), in which both he and his generation found themselves strikingly epitomized. Since then his books have been both numerous and varied—poetry, fiction, drama, essay, criticism, biography, and other kinds—but through them run strains of gusty humor, delicate feeling, and the high seriousness of a courageous intellectual and cultural vision. To single out a few representative works, one may mention his novels *Janet March* (1923) and *Diana Stair* (1932), his *Intellectual Vagabondage—An Apology for the Intelligentsia* (1926), his biography, *Upton Sinclair—A Study in Social Protest* (1927), his Broadway comedy hit, *The Little Accident* (1928), and his dauntless modern commentary, *Love in the Machine Age* (1930).

Having already painted himself in *Mooncalf* under an imaginary name, Floyd Dell undertook in *Homecoming* (1933) the harder but, for him, unavoidable task of undisguised self-portraiture. It meant, for this sensitive romantic, looking himself straight in the eye and delivering a candid and

148

unsentimental report of his findings. How (also how well) he succeeds in recapturing the slight but significant events and the interwoven states of mind throughout forty-six years of slow maturing and self-fulfillment the reader may judge from the following selection. At the end, let the reader ask himself whether, had such an incident occurred in *his* childhood, he could now write of it with Dell's freedom from affectation and self-pity, and whether, in addition, he could relate it so dramatically.


## CHRISTMAS

Memories of childhood are strange things. The obscurity of the past opens upon a little lighted space—a scene, unconnected with anything else. One must figure out when it happened. There may be anomalies in the scene, which need explanation. Sometimes the scenes are tiny fragments only. Again they are long dramas. Having once been remembered, they can be lived through again in every moment, with a detailed experiencing of movement and sensation and thought. One can start the scene in one's mind and see it all through again. Exactly so it was— clearer in memory than something that happened yesterday, though it was forty years ago. And, oddly enough, if there is some detail skipped over, lost out of the memory picture, no repetition of the remembering process will supply it—the gap is always there.

THAT fall, before it was discovered that the soles of both my shoes were worn clear through, I still went to Sunday school. And one time the Sunday-school superintendent made a speech to all the classes. He said that these were hard times, and that many poor children weren't getting enough to eat. It was the first time that I had heard about it. He asked everybody to bring some food for the poor children next Sunday. I felt very sorry for the poor children.

Also, little envelopes were distributed to all the classes. Each little boy and girl was to bring money for the poor, next Sunday. The pretty Sunday-school teacher explained that we were to write our names, or have our parents write them, up in the left-hand corner of the little envelopes. . . . I told my mother all about it when I came home. And my mother gave me, the next Sunday, a small bag of potatoes to carry to Sunday school. I supposed the poor children's mothers would make potato soup out of them. . . . Potato soup was good. My father, who was quite a joker, would always say, as if he were surprised, "Ah! I see we have some nourishing potato soup today!" It was so good that we had it every day. My father was at home all day long and every day, now; and I liked that, even if he was grumpy as he sat reading Grant's *Memoirs*. I had my parents all to my-self, too; the others were away. My oldest brother was in Quincy, and memory does not reveal where the others were: perhaps with relatives in the country.

Taking my small bag of potatoes to Sunday school, I looked around for the poor children; I was disappointed not to see them. I had heard about poor children in stories. But I was told just to put my contribution with the others on the big table in the side room.

I had brought with me the little yellow envelope, with some money in it and sealed it up. My mother wouldn't tell me how much money she had put in it, but it felt like several dimes. Only she wouldn't let me write my name on the envelope. I had learned to write my name, and I was proud of being able to do it. But my mother said firmly, *no*, I must *not* write my name on the envelope; she didn't tell me why. On the way to Sunday school I had pressed the envelope against the coins until I could tell what they were; they weren't dimes but pennies.

When I handed in my envelope, my Sunday-school teacher noticed that my name wasn't on it, and she gave me a pencil; I could write my own name, she said. So I did. But I was confused because my mother had said not to; and when I came home, I con-fessed what I had done. She looked distressed. "I told you not to!" she said. But she didn't explain why. . . .

I didn't go back to school that fall. My mother said it was be-cause I was sick. I did have a cold the week that school opened; I had been playing in the gutters and had got my feet wet, be-cause there were holes in my shoes. My father cut insoles out of cardboard, and I wore those in my shoes. As long as I had to stay in the house anyway, they were all right.

I stayed cooped up in the house, without any companionship. We didn't take a Sunday paper any more, but the *Barry Adage* came every week in the mails; and though I did not read small print, I could see the Santa Clauses and holly wreaths in the advertisements.

There was a calendar in the kitchen. The red days were Sundays and holidays; and that red 25 was Christmas. (It was on a Monday, and the two red figures would come right together in 1893; but this represents research in the *World Almanac*, not memory.) I knew when Sunday was, because I could look out of the window and see the neighbor's children, all dressed up, going to Sunday school. I knew just when Christmas was going to be.

But there was something queer! My father and mother didn't say a word about Christmas. And once, when I spoke of it, there was a strange silence; so I didn't say anything more about it. But I wondered, and was troubled. Why didn't they say anything about it? Was what I had said I wanted (memory refuses to supply that detail) too expensive?

I wasn't arrogant and talkative now. I was silent and frightened. What was the matter? Why didn't my father and mother say anything about Christmas? As the day approached, my chest grew tighter with anxiety.

Now it was the day before Christmas. I couldn't be mistaken. But not a word about it from my father and mother. I waited in painful bewilderment all day. I had supper with them, and was allowed to sit up for an hour. I was waiting for them to say something. "It's time for you to go to bed," my mother said gently. I *had* to say something.

"This is Christmas Eve, isn't it?" I asked, as if I didn't know.

My father and mother looked at one another. Then my mother looked away. Her face was pale and stony. My father cleared his throat, and his face took on a joking look. He pretended he hadn't known it was Christmas Eve, because he hadn't been reading the papers. He said he would go downtown and find out.

My mother got up and walked out of the room. I didn't want my father to have to keep on being funny about it, so I got up and went to bed. I went by myself without having a light. I undressed in the dark and crawled into bed.

I was numb. As if I had been hit by something. It was hard to breathe. I ached all through. I was stunned—with finding out the truth.

My body knew before my mind quite did. In a minute, when I could think, my mind would know. And as the pain in my body ebbed, the pain in my mind began. I *knew*. I couldn't put it into words yet. But I knew why I had taken only a little bag of potatoes to Sunday school that fall. I knew why there had been only pennies in my little yellow envelope. I knew why I hadn't gone to school that fall—why I hadn't any new shoes—why we had been living on potato soup all winter. All these things, and others, many others, fitted themselves together in my mind, and meant something.

Then the words came into my mind and I whispered them into the darkness:

*"We're Poor!"*

That was it. I was one of those poor children I had been sorry for, when I heard about them in Sunday school. My mother hadn't told me. My father was out of work, and we hadn't any money. That was why there wasn't going to be any Christmas at our house.

Then I remembered something that made me squirm with shame—a boast. (Memory will not yield this up. Had I said to some Nice little boy, "I'm going to be President of the United States"? Or to a Nice little girl: "I'll marry you when I grow up"? It was some boast as horribly shameful to remember.)

*"We're poor."* There in bed in the dark, I whispered it over and over to myself. I was making myself get used to it. (Or—just torturing myself, as one pressed the tongue against a sore tooth? No, memory says not like that—but to keep myself from ever being such a fool again: suffering now, to keep this awful thing from ever happening again. Memory is clear on that; it was more like pulling the tooth, to get it over with—never mind the pain, this will be the end!)

It wasn't so bad, now that I knew. *I just hadn't known!* I had thought all sorts of foolish things: that I was going to Ann Arbor —going to be a lawyer—going to make speeches in the Square, going to be President. Now I knew better.

I had wanted (something) for Christmas. I didn't want it, now.
I didn't want anything.

I lay there in the dark, feeling the cold emotion of renuncia-
tion. (The tendrils of desire unfold their clasp on the outer world
of objects, withdraw, shrivel up. Wishes shrivel up, turn black,
die. It is like that.)

It hurt. But nothing would ever hurt again. I would never let
myself want anything again.

I lay there stretched out straight and stiff in the dark, my fists
clenched hard upon Nothing. . . .

In the morning it had been like a nightmare that is not clearly
remembered—that one wishes to forget. Though I hadn't hung up
any stocking, there was one hanging at the foot of my bed. A
bag of popcorn, and a lead pencil, for me. They had done the
best they could, now they realized that I knew about Christmas.
But they needn't have thought they had to. I didn't want anything.

# *JAMES JOYCE*

IF I were determined (let the reader ask himself) to tell the story of my youth from infancy to the age of twenty and, dissatisfied with the divers imperfections of all the *tried* methods of autobiography, I were to set myself the task of communicating not the external happenings but rather my inmost states of mind, the very flight of fancies and emotions as they passed across my consciousness and merged into memory—how could I do it? How could I do it so that the inner, spiritual realities of my twenty years' existence on this planet would be arrested and held there on paper, a true, sequential record of my emergence out of childhood into adolescence, out of adolescence into early manhood? How could I do it, moreover, so that others, reading it, would unmistakably catch the thought-drifts and feel the compulsions which I myself experienced, the thousand tensions and releases of my inner dynamism, and would know that they know me? I should of course have first to deal with the practical necessity of limiting my record to the principal crises of my youth, since even a day's experience, faithfully and accurately tabulated, would yield volumes, and I have years to cover. I should also have to give some picture of each significant environment through which I passed and of the boys and girls, the men and women, who peopled it; but they must be shown as I successively saw them and they became a part of me. And then, for reasons of modesty, not perhaps about my frankness so much as over my apparent presumption in making such bold though tacit claims to self-revelation, it would be well to tell the story objectively or even present it as a novel and give myself a fictitious name.

This, in brief—though there is of course more to it than is here indicated—is the autobiographical mode which James Joyce invented and used in *A Portrait of the Artist as a Young Man,* first published in New York in 1916. He was working toward it already in a group of brilliant short stories known as *Dubliners* (1914), re-creations of people he had known in his native city and of events he had witnessed. Not until the *Portrait,* however, was he to subordinate the visible world and concentrate upon his own spiritual self, recording, as Robert Sage puts it, "the *de profundis* of a sensitive boy's turbulent passage through the sexual and spiritual crises of adolescence." Later, in *Ulysses* (1922), he went further, and, actually setting forth his "stream of consciousness" through a single day, displayed "a Joyce who had advanced from the spiritual conflicts of youth to the more complex ones of maturity." And later yet, in *Finnegans Wake* (1939), he has carried his vision of Dublin to a cosmic level, universalized

154

his characters, and attempted by the invention of an extremely complex style to reproduce the states of half-consciousness in a unique spiritual and intellectual autobiography.

James Joyce was born in 1882 into a large, shabby-genteel family of Dubliners. His father (the "Simon Dedalus" of his books) gave him a good Catholic education at the Jesuit "colleges" of Clongowes Wood and Belvedere, where the boy showed marked intellectuality and independence of mind. At seventeen he wrote an essay for *The Fortnightly Review* on Ibsen, whom he wanted so much to understand that he learned Norwegian in order to read him in the original, just as he was later to read Aristotle in Greek, St. Thomas Aquinas in Latin, Dante in Italian, and to master for his own scholarly and literary purposes Sanscrit, Arabic, and a dozen other ancient and modern tongues. Padraic Colum, Gogarty, and other companions of his student days at the Royal University, Dublin, testify to Joyce's singularity of mind, talk, and appearance—"tall and slender, with a Dantesque face and steely blue eyes," wearing "a peaked cap and tennis shoes more or less white" and swinging along the street "carrying an ashplant in his hand for a cane." After taking his B.A. degree at twenty-one, Joyce went to Paris and began the study of medicine. Lacking funds and confidence for the pursuit of this vocation, he began to train his fine tenor voice (inherited from his father and reputed to be the chief rival of John McCormack's in Ireland) for the concert stage. His mother's death the following year called him back to Dublin, where he married, wrote his first stories and some of the verses that went into *Chamber Music* (1907), and started work on the *Portrait*. He and his wife soon returned to the Continent, living in Trieste, Zurich, Rome, and Paris, finally settling permanently in the French capital in a familiar quarter near the Odéon. There his later books have been published and there, though handicapped by near-blindness, he still delights his intimates with the songs and stories and hearty laughter that reflect a personality drawn deeply from his native soil yet rich in learning and in life.

In the *Portrait* the narrative opens in the babbling language and from the irrational point of view of a small child. As the child grows older the language and point of view become imperceptibly riper in proportion, until toward the end of the book the story takes the form of the entries which Stephen Dedalus (Joyce) makes in his diary to unburden his soul tortured by the revolt of adolescence. The passage given below reconstructs the crisis resulting from the Jesuit retreat at which Stephen was required to declare his intentions, whether to become a priest or not. It opens with the director's charge and takes the youth through the events of the afternoon and night immediately following, in the course of which Stephen decides he is unsuited for the priesthood and gropingly but ecstatically envisions the creative vocation of a poet and singer. Nothing outside of Stephen's own consciousness is included, nor is there a phrase which does not contribute directly to the development of the theme. Of particular note here is Joyce's preoccupation with words, especially in the limpid passage depicting his emotional response to the view from the North Bull Bridge—"A day of dappled seaborne clouds. . . ." Stephen is here reacting, as one critic says, "to the occult power of words as another might react to caresses or blows. His 'soul frets,' in their presence, they 'fill him with fear.' This is not an affectation; it is as vital a part of Joyce as his Irish birth or his Catholic training. Perhaps his weakness of eyesight has sensitized his appreciation of the images that may be built from words." Unusual as Joyce's writing admittedly is, this remarkable self-portrait can scarcely fail to reward the reader with a new and vivid experience.

## VOCATION

—I will offer up my mass tomorrow morning, said the director, that Almighty God may reveal to you His holy will. And let you, Stephen, make a novena to your holy patron saint, the first martyr, who is very powerful with God, that God may enlighten your mind. But you must be quite sure, Stephen, that you have a vocation because it would be terrible if you found afterwards that you had none. Once a priest always a priest, remember. Your catechism tells you that the sacrament of Holy Orders is one of those which can be received only once because it imprints on the soul an indelible spiritual mark which can never be effaced. It is before you must weigh well, not after. It is a solemn question, Stephen, because on it may depend the salvation of your eternal soul. But we will pray to God together.—

He held open the heavy halldoor and gave his hand as if already to a companion in the spiritual life. Stephen passed out on to the wide platform above the steps and was conscious of the caress of mild evening air. Towards Findlater's church a quartette of young men were striding along with linked arms, swaying their heads and stepping to the agile melody of their leader's concertina. The music passed in an instant, as the first bars of sudden music always did, over the fantastic fabrics of his mind, dissolving them painlessly and noiselessly as a sudden wave dissolves the sandbuilt turrets of children. Smiling at the trivial air he raised his eyes to the priest's face and, seeing in it a mirthless reflection of the sunken day, detached his hand slowly which had acquiesced faintly in that companionship.

As he descended the steps the impression which effaced his troubled selfcommunion was that of a mirthless mask reflecting a sunken day from the threshold of the college. The shadow, then, of the life of the college passed gravely over his consciousness. It was a grave and ordered and passionless life that awaited him, a life without material cares. He wondered how he would pass the first night in the novitiate and with what dismay he would wake the first morning in the dormitory. The troubling odour of the long corridors of Clongowes came back to him and he heard the discreet murmur of the burning gasflames. At once from every part of his being unrest began to irradiate. A feverish quickening of his pulses followed and a din of meaningless words drove his reasoned thoughts hither and thither confusedly. His lungs dilated and sank as if he were inhaling a warm moist unsustaining air, and he smelt again the moist warm air which hung in the bath in Clongowes above the sluggish turfcoloured water.

Some instinct, waking at these memories, stronger than education or piety, quickened within him at every near approach to that life, an instinct subtle and hostile, and armed him against acquiescence. The chill and order of the life repelled him. He saw himself rising in the cold of the morning and filing down with the others to early mass and trying vainly to struggle with his prayers against the fainting sickness of his stomach. He saw himself sitting at dinner with the community of a college. What, then, had become of that deeprooted shyness of his which had made him loth to eat or drink under a strange roof? What had come of the pride of his spirit which had always made him conceive himself as a being apart in every order?

The Reverend Stephen Dedalus, S. J.

His name in that new life leaped into characters before his eyes and to it there followed a mental sensation of an undefined face or colour of a face. The colour faded and became strong like a changing glow of pallid brick red. Was it the raw reddish glow he had so often seen on wintry mornings on the shaven gills of the priests? The face was eyeless and sourfavoured and devout, shot with pink tinges of suffocated anger. Was it not a mental specter of the face of one of the jesuits whom some of the boys called Lantern Jaws and others Foxy Campbell?

He was passing at that moment before the jesuit house in Gardiner Street, and wondered vaguely which window would be his if he ever joined the order. Then he wondered at the vagueness of his wonder, at the remoteness of his own soul from what he had hitherto imagined her sanctuary, at the frail hold which so many years of order and obedience had of him when once a definite and irrevocable act of his threatened to end for ever, in time and in eternity, his freedom. The voice of the director urging upon him the proud claims of the church and the mystery and power of the priestly office repeated itself idly in his memory. His soul was not there to hear and greet it and he knew now that the exhortation he had listened to had already fallen into an idle formal tale. He would never swing the thurible before the tabernacle as priest. His destiny was to be elusive of social or religious orders. The wisdom of the priest's appeal did not touch him to the quick. He was destined to learn his own wisdom apart from others or to learn the wisdom of others himself wandering among the snares of the world.

The snares of the world were its ways of sin. He would fall. He had not yet fallen but he would fall silently, in an instant. Not to fall was too hard, too hard: and he felt the silent lapse of his soul, as it would be at some instant to come, falling, falling, but not yet fallen, still unfallen, but about to fall.

He crossed the bridge over the stream of the Tolka, and turned his eyes coldly for an instant towards the faded blue shrine of the Blessed Virgin which stood fowlwise on a pole in the middle of a hamshaped encampment of poor cottages. Then, bending to the left, he followed the lane which led up to his house. The faint sour stink of rotted cabbages came towards him from the kitchen gardens on the rising ground above the river. He smiled to think that it was this disorder, the misrule and confusion of his father's house and the stagnation of vegetable life, which was to win the day in his soul. Then a short laugh broke from his lips as he thought of that solitary farmhand in the kitchen gardens behind their house whom they had nicknamed The Man with the Hat. A second laugh, taking rise from the first after a pause, broke from him involuntarily as he thought of how The Man with the Hat worked, considering in turn the four points of the sky and then regretfully plunging his spade in the earth.

He pushed open the latchless door of the porch and passed through the naked hallway into the kitchen. A group of his brothers and sisters was sitting round the table. Tea was nearly over and only the last of the second watered tea remained in the bottoms of the small glass jars and jampots which did service for teacups. Discarded crusts and lumps of sugared bread, turned brown by the tea which had been poured over them, lay scattered on the table. Little wells of tea lay here and there on the board and a knife with a broken ivory handle was stuck through the pith of a ravaged turnover.

The sad quiet greyblue glow of the dying day came through the window and the open door, covering over and allaying quietly a sudden instinct of remorse in Stephen's heart. All that had been denied them had been freely given to him, the eldest: but the quiet glow of evening showed him in their faces no sign of rancor.

He sat near them at the table and asked where his father and mother were. One answered:

—Goneboro toboro lookboro atboro aboro houseboro.—

Still another removal! A boy named Fallon, in Belvedere, had often asked him with a silly laugh why they moved so often. A frown of scorn darkened quickly his forehead as he heard again the silly laugh of the questioner.

He asked:

—Why are we on the move again, if it's a fair question?—

—Becauseboro theboro landboro lordboro willboro putboro usboro outboro.—

The voice of his youngest brother from the farther side of the fireplace began to sing the air *Oft in the Stilly Night*. One by one the others took up the air until a full choir of voices was singing. They would sing so for hours, melody after melody, glee after glee, till the last pale light died down on the horizon, till the first dark nightclouds came forth and night fell.

He waited for some moments, listening, before he too took up the air with them. He was listening with pain of spirit to the overtone of weariness behind their frail fresh innocent voices. Even before they set out on life's journey they seemed weary already of the way.

He heard the choir of voices in the kitchen echoed and multiplied through an endless reverberation of the choirs of endless generations of children: and heard in all the echoes an echo also of the recurring note of weariness and pain. All seemed weary of life even before entering upon it. And he remembered that Newman had heard this note also in the broken lines of Virgil "giving utterance, like the voice of Nature herself, to that pain and weariness yet hope of better things which has been the experience of her children in every time."

He could wait no longer.

From the door of Byron's publichouse to the gate of Clontarf Chapel, from the gate of Clontarf Chapel to the door of Byron's publichouse, and then back again to the chapel and then back again to the publichouse he had paced slowly at first, planting his steps scrupulously in the spaces of the patchwork of the footpath, then timing their fall to the fall of verses. A full hour had passed since his father had gone in with Dan Crosby, the tutor, to find out for him something about the university. For a full hour he had paced up and down, waiting: but he could wait no longer.

He set off abruptly for the Bull, walking rapidly lest his father's shrill whistle might call him back; and in a few moments he had rounded the curve at the police barrack and was safe.

Yes, his mother was hostile to the idea, as he had read from her listless silence. Yet her mistrust pricked him more keenly than his father's pride and he thought coldly how he had watched the faith which was fading down in his soul ageing and strengthening in her eyes. A dim antagonism gathered force within him and darkened his mind as a cloud against her disloyalty: and when it passed, cloudlike, leaving his mind serene and dutiful towards her again, he was made aware dimly and without regret of a first noiseless sundering of their lives.

The university! So he had passed beyond the challenge of the sentries who had stood as guardians of his boyhood and had sought to keep him among them that he might be subject to them and serve their ends. Pride after satisfaction uplifted him like long slow waves. The end he had been born to serve yet did not see had led him to escape by an unseen path: and now it beckoned to him once more and a new adventure was about to be opened to him. It seemed to him that he heard notes of fitful music leaping upwards a tone and downwards a diminished fourth, upwards a tone and downwards a major third, like triple-branching flames leaping fitfully, flame after flame, out of a midnight wood. It was an elfin prelude, endless and formless; and, as it grew wilder and faster, the flames leaping out of time, he seemed to hear from under the boughs and grasses wild creatures racing, their feet pattering like rain upon the leaves. Their feet passed in pattering tumult over his mind, the feet of hares and rabbits, the feet of harts and hinds and antelopes, until he heard them no more and remembered only a proud cadence from Newman:

—Whose feet are as the feet of harts and underneath the everlasting arms.—

The pride of that dim image brought back to his mind the dignity of the office he had refused. All through his boyhood he had mused upon that which he had so often thought to be his destiny and when the moment had come for him to obey the call he had turned aside, obeying a wayward instinct. Now time lay between: the oils of ordination would never anoint his body. He had refused. Why?

He turned seaward from the road at Dollymount and as he passed on to the thin wooden bridge he felt the planks shaking with the tramp of heavily shod feet. A squad of Christian Brothers was on its way back from the Bull and had begun to pass, two by two, across the bridge. Soon the whole bridge was trembling and resounding. The uncouth faces passed him two by two, stained yellow or red or livid by the sea, and as he strove to look at them with ease and indifference, a faint stain of personal shame and commiseration rose to his own face. Angry with himself he tried to hide his face from their eyes by gazing down sideways into the shallow swirling water under the bridge but he still saw a reflection therein of their topheavy silk hats and humble tapelike collars and loosely hanging clerical clothes.

—Brother Hickey.
Brother Quaid.
Brother MacArdle.
Brother Keogh.—

Their piety would be like their names, like their faces, like their clothes; and it was idle for him to tell himself that their humble and contrite hearts, it might be, paid a far richer tribute of devotion than his had ever been, a gift tenfold more acceptable than his elaborate adoration. It was idle for him to move himself to be generous towards them, to tell himself that if he ever came to their gates, stripped of his pride, beaten and in beggar's weeds, that they would be generous towards him, loving him as themselves. Idle and embittering, finally, to argue, against his own dispassionate certitude, that the commandment of love bade us not to love our neighbors as ourselves with the same amount and intensity of love but to love him as ourselves with the same kind of love.

He drew forth a phrase from his treasure and spoke it softly to himself:

—A day of dappled seaborne clouds.—

The phrase and the day and the scene harmonised in a chord. Words. Was it their colours? He allowed them to glow and fade, hue after hue: sunrise gold, the russet and green of apple orchards, azure of waves, the greyfringed fleece of clouds. No, it was not their colours: it was the poise and balance of the period itself. Did he then love the rhythmic rise and fall of words better than their associations of legend and colour? Or was it that, being as weak of sight as he was shy of mind, he drew less pleasure from the reflection of the glowing sensible world through the prism of a language manycoloured and richly storied than from the contemplation of an inner world of individual emotions mirrored perfectly in a lucid supple periodic prose?

He passed from the trembling bridge on to firm land again. At that instant, as it seemed to him, the air was chilled; and looking askance towards the water he saw a flying squall darkening and crisping suddenly the tide. A faint click at his heart, a faint throb in his throat told him once more of how his flesh dreaded the cold infrahuman odour of the sea: yet he did not strike across the downs on his left but held straight on along the spine of rocks that pointed against the river's mouth.

A veiled sunlight lit up faintly the grey sheet of water where the river was embayed. In the distance along the course of the slowflowing Liffey slender masts flecked the sky and, more distant still, the dim fabric of the city lay prone in haze. Like a scene on some vague arras, old as man's weariness, the image of the seventh city of christendom was visible to him across the timeless air, no older nor more weary nor less patient of subjection than in the days of the thingmote.

Disheartened, he raised his eyes towards the slowdrifting clouds, dappled and seaborne. They were voyaging across the deserts of the sky, a host of nomads on the march, voyaging high over Ireland, westward bound. The Europe they had come from lay out there beyond the Irish Sea, Europe of strange tongues and valleyed and woodbegirt and citadeled and of entrenched and marshalled races. He heard a confused music within him as of memories and names which he was almost conscious of but could not capture even for an instant; then the music seemed to recede, to recede, to recede: and from each receding trail of nebulous music there fell aways one longdrawn calling note, piercing like a star the dusk of silence. Again! Again! Again! A voice from beyond the world was calling.

—Hello, Stephanos!—

—Here comes The Dedalus!—

—Ao! . . . Eh, give it over, Dwyer, I'm telling you or I'll give you a stuff in the kisser for yourself. . . . Ao!—

—Good man, Towser! Duck him!—

—Come along, Dedalus! Bous Stephanoumenos! Bous Stephane-foros!—

—Duck him! Guzzle him now, Towser!—

—Help! Help! . . . Ao!—

He recognised their speech collectively before he distinguished their faces. The mere sight of that medley of wet nakedness chilled him to the bone. Their bodies, corpsewhite or suffused with a pallid golden light or rawly tanned by the suns, gleamed with the wet of the sea. Their divingstone, poised on its rude supports and rocking under their plunges, and the roughhewn stones of the sloping breakwater over which they scrambled in their horseplay, gleamed with cold wet luster. The towels with which they smacked their bodies were heavy with cold seawater: and drenched with cold brine was their matted hair.

He stood still in deference to their calls and parried their banter with easy words. How characterless they looked: Shuley without his deep unbuttoned collar, Ennis without his scarlet belt with the snaky clasp, and Connolly without his Norfolk coat with the flapless sidepockets! It was a pain to see them and a swordlike pain to see the signs of adolescence that made repellent their piti-able nakedness. Perhaps they had taken refuge in number and noise from the secret dread in their souls. But he, apart from them and in silence, remembered in what dread he stood of the mystery of his own body.

—Stephanos Dedalos! Bous Stephanoumenos! Bous Stephane-foros!—

Their banter was not new to him and now it flattered his mild proud sovereignty. Now, as never before, his strange name seemed to him a prophecy. So timeless seemed the grey warm air, so fluid and impersonal his own mood, that all ages were as one to him. A moment before the ghost of the ancient kingdom of the Danes had looked forth through the vesture of the haze-wrapped city. Now, at the name of the fabulous artificer, he seemed to hear the noise of dim waves and to see a winged form flying above the waves and slowly climbing the air. What did it mean? Was it a quaint device opening a page of some medieval book of prophecies and symbols, a hawklike man flying sunward above the sea, a prophecy of the end he had been born to serve and had been following through the mists of childhood and boyhood, a symbol of the artist forging anew in his workshop out of the sluggish matter of the earth a new soaring impalpable imperishable being?

His heart trembled; his breath came faster and a wild spirit passed over his limbs as though he were soaring sunward. His heart trembled in an ecstasy of fear and his soul was in flight. His soul was soaring in an air beyond the world and the body he knew was purified in a breath and delivered of incertitude and made radiant and commingled with the element of the spirit. An ecstasy of flight made radiant his eyes and wild his breath and tremulous and wild and radiant his windswept limbs.

—One! Two! . . . Look out!—
—O, Cripes, I'm drownded!—
—One! Two! Three and away!—
—The next! The next!—
—One! . . . Uk!—
—Stephaneforos!—

His throat ached with a desire to cry aloud, the cry of a hawk or eagle on high, to cry piercingly of his deliverance to the winds. This was the call of life to his soul not the dull gross voice of the world of duties and despair, not the inhuman voice that had called him to the pale service of the altar. An instant of wild flight had delivered him and the cry of triumph which his lips withheld cleft his brain.

—Stephaneforos!—

What were they now but the cerements shaken from the body of death—the fear he had walked in night and day, the incertitude that had ringed him round, the shame that had abased him within and without—cerements, the linens of the grave?

His soul had arisen from the grave of boyhood, spurning her graveclothes. Yes! Yes! Yes! He would create proudly out of the freedom and power of his soul, as the great artificer whose name he bore, a living thing, new and soaring and beautiful, impalpable, imperishable.

He started up nervously from the stoneblock for he could no

longer quench the flame in his blood. He felt his cheeks aflame and his throat throbbing with song. There was a lust of wandering in his feet that burned to set out for the ends of the earth. On! On! his heart seemed to cry. Evening would deepen above the sea, night fall upon the plains, dawn glimmer before the wanderer and show him strange fields and hills and faces. Where?

He looked northward towards Howth. The sea had fallen below the line of seawrack on the shallow side of the breakwater and already the tide was running out fast along the foreshore. Already one long oval bank of sand lay warm and dry amid the wavelets. Here and there warm isles of sand gleamed above the shallow tide: and about the isles and around the long bank and amid the shallow currents of the beach were lightclad figures, wading and delving.

In a few moments he was barefoot, his stockings folded in his pockets, and his canvas shoes dangling by their knotted laces over his shoulders: and, picking a pointed salteaten stick out of the jetsam among the rocks, he clambered down the slope of the breakwater.

There was a long rivulet in the strand: and, as he waded slowly up its course, he wondered at the endless drift of seaweed. Emerald and black and russet and olive, it moved beneath the current, swaying and turning. The water of the rivulet was dark with endless drift and mirrored the highdrifting clouds. The clouds were drifting above him silently and silently the seatangle was drifting below him; and the gray warm air was still: and a new wild life was singing in his veins.

Where was his boyhood now? Where was the soul that had hung back from her destiny, to brood alone upon the shame of her wounds and in her house of squalor and subterfuge to queen it in faded cerements and in wreaths that withered at the touch? Or, where was he?

He was alone. He was unheeded, happy, and near to the wild heart of life. He was alone and young and willful and wildhearted, alone amid a waste of wild air and brackish waters and the seaharvest of shells and tangle and veiled gray sunlight and gayclad lightclad figures of children and girls and voices childish and girlish in the air.

A girl stood before him in midstream: alone and still, gazing out to sea. She seemed like one whom magic had changed into the likeness of a strange and beautiful seabird. Her long slender bare legs were delicate as a crane's and pure save where an emerald trail of seaweed had fashioned itself as a sign upon the flesh. Her thighs, fuller and softhued as ivory, were bared almost to the hips where the white fringes of her drawers were like feathering of soft white down. Her slateblue skirts were kilted boldly about her waist and dovetailed behind her. Her bosom was as a bird's, soft and slight, slight and soft as the breast of some darkplumaged dove. But her long fair hair was girlish: and girlish, and touched with the wonder of mortal beauty, her face.

She was alone and still, gazing out to sea; and when she felt his presence and the worship of his eyes her eyes turned to him in quiet sufferance of his gaze, without shame or wantonness. Long, long she suffered his gaze and then quietly withdrew her eyes from his and bent them towards the stream, gently stirring the water with her foot hither and thither. The first faint noise of gently moving water broke the silence, low and faint and whispering, faint as the bells of sleep; hither and thither, hither and thither: and a faint flame trembled on her cheek.

—Heavenly God! cried Stephen's soul, in an outburst of profane joy.—

He turned away from her suddenly and set off across the strand. His cheeks were aflame; his body was aglow; his limbs were trembling. On and on and on and on he strode, far out over the sands, singing wildly to the sea, crying to greet the advent of the life that had cried to him.

Her image had passed into his soul for ever and no word had broken the holy silence of his ecstasy. Her eyes had called him and his soul had leaped at the call. To live, to err, to fall, to triumph, to recreate life out of life! A wild angel had appeared to him, the angel of mortal youth and beauty, an envoy from the fair courts of life, to throw open before him in an instant of ecstasy the gates of all the ways of error and glory. On and on and on and on!

He halted suddenly and heard his heart in the silence. How far had he walked? What hour was it?

There was no human figure near him nor any sound borne to him over the air. But the tide was near the turn and already the day was on the wane. He turned landward and ran towards the shore and, running up the sloping beach, reckless of the sharp shingle, found a sandy nook amid a ring of tufted sandknolls and lay down there that the peace and silence of the evening might still the riot of his blood.

He felt above him the vast indifferent dome and the calm processes of the heavenly bodies: and the earth beneath him, the earth that had borne him, had taken him to her breast.

He closed his eyes in the languor of sleep. His eyelids trembled as if they felt the vast cyclic movement of the earth and her watchers, trembled as if they felt the strange light of some new world. His soul was swooning into some new world, fantastic, dim, uncertain as under sea, traversed by cloudy shapes and beings. A world, a glimmer, or a flower? Glimmering and trembling, trembling and unfolding, a breaking light, an opening flower, it spread in endless succession to itself, breaking in full crimson and unfolding and fading to palest rose, leaf by leaf and wave of light by wave of light, flooding all the heavens with its soft flushes, every flush deeper than other.

Evening had fallen when he woke and the sand and arid grasses of his bed glowed no longer. He rose slowly and, recalling the rapture of his sleep, sighed at its joy.

He climbed to the crest of the sandhill and gazed about him. Evening had fallen. A rim of the young moon cleft the pale waste of skyline, the rim of a silver hoop embedded in grey sand: and the tide was flowing in fast to the land with a low whisper of her waves, islanding a few last figures in distant pools.

# LOGAN PEARSALL SMITH

LOGAN PEARSALL SMITH, who was born in Philadelphia in 1865, has been a familiar figure in English and American letters longer than any other writer in this book. Probably he is best known for his sensitive and charming miniature essays published in *Trivia* (1918) and *More Trivia* (1921), but many years before these he had struck his characteristic vein in *The Youth of Parnassus* (1895) and *The English Language* (1912), and had reached out in other directions in *The Life and Letters of Sir Henry Wotton* (1907) and in *Songs and Sonnets* (1909). His art is essentially a delicate flower, making little appeal to the general public but delighting all those whose lives are not too filled with *doing* for them to pause at quiet moments to enjoy the pleasures of *seeing* and *reflecting*. The most recurrent objects of his notice are words—the elements of human communication, not merely as etymological phenomena in the history of linguistics, but also as living and changing symptoms of human experience and thinking, as subtle organisms with their private lives and public reputations. Fine perceptions set forth with ripe wisdom and gentle humor are to be found in *Words and Idioms* (1925); and in the little books, *On Reading Shakespeare* (1933) and *Reperusals and Re-collections* (1936), lies much sound and mellow thought.

The fragmentary passage depicting his youthful acquaintance with Walt Whitman is from Mr. Smith's brief autobiography, *Unforgotten Years,* published in 1938. Short and interrupted as the selection is, it nevertheless reports what must certainly have been a rare if not unique relationship with "the Good Grey Poet." It takes us back to Mr. Smith's Haverford College days when he was still a "local boy," before Harvard had removed him permanently from Philadelphia, and before Oxford and the great Jowett had made him an Englishman.

## KNOWING WALT WHITMAN

IN 1882, returning home again for the Easter holidays, I was told important news by my sister, when she too arrived for her holidays from Smith College, for the ban on college education for girls was now removed. There was a poet, she informed me and the rest of our family, a great American poet and prophet,—though most Americans were not at all aware of his greatness,—now living in poverty and neglect among us in America, living actually not far from our neighborhood, and it was her purpose, she informed us, to go without delay and offer him a due tribute of praise and admiration. How had she heard of this poet, her anxious and perturbed relatives inquired. A lady lecturer, she replied, had come from Boston to Smith College, and had praised his works, which she herself had immediately ordered from Boston, and which had revealed to her a message of tremendous import, and the purpose of her intended visit was to discuss this message. Consternation fell upon us all, and my father at once forbade it. He vaguely knew the name of the poet, which was by no means a name of good repute in Philadelphia; the district in which he lived was a district not visited by people who respected their own position. No daughter of his, my father declared, should, while she lived under his roof, be allowed to take so unseemly a step.

My father's refusal to permit this indecorum, though impressive as the poor man could make it, had no effect whatsoever upon my sister. She thought of going, she said, on the following Thursday; and my father, being in his heart well aware of the powerlessness of American parents in their dealings with their daughters, and convinced, as he was, that if my sister meant to go on Thursday, on Thursday she would go, wisely, if unheroically, decided that the best thing under the circumstances was for him to accompany her and thus lend an air of propriety to this visit. I was invited to join the party, and so off on Thursday afternoon we started from our home in Germantown, behind the pair of my father's fine horses. We flashed along through Fairmount Park, we drove across Philadelphia, we embarked in the ferry and crossed the Delaware, and dashed up before the little two-story wooden house in Camden to which we had been directed. The poet's elderly sister, who answered the doorbell, ushered us into a little parlor, and shouted upstairs, "Walt, here's some carriage folk come to see you." We heard a stirring above us as of a slow and unwieldy person, and soon through the open door we saw two large feet in carpet slippers slowly descending the stairs, and then the bulky form of the old man appeared before us. Walt Whitman greeted us with friendly simplicity; he had no notion who we were, and we had no introduction to him, but the unannounced appearance of these "carriage folk" from across the river—this portly and opulent-looking gentleman with his tall son and beautiful tall daughter—did not seem to surprise him in the least. My sister informed him that our name was Smith, that she had read his *Leaves of Grass*, and had come to express her immense admiration for that volume, and this explanation was received with great complacency; we were all invited to follow him upstairs to his den, where we sat down on what chairs could be hastily provided, and were soon engaged in lively talk.

My father, who at first held himself aloof in the most disapproving manner, soon, to the surprise of my sister and myself, began to join in this friendly conversation, and we were still more surprised, when we got up to take our departure, to hear our impulsive parent invite the object of his grave disapprobation to drive back with us to Germantown and spend the night. The afternoon was, he urged, a fine one, the drive across the Park would be pleasant, and it would be a pity to bring to a premature end so agreeable a confabulation. "No, Mr. Smith, I think I won't come," the poet answered; but when he had hobbled to the window and seen, waiting in the street outside, my father's equipage, he said that he thought he might as well come after all, and, hastily putting a nightshirt and a few other objects in a little bag, he hobbled downstairs and we all drove off together. It was, as my father had said, a pleasant afternoon; we crossed again the ferry, we drove through Philadelphia and through the Park to our home in Germantown, where Walt Whitman remained with us for a month, and whither he would often afterward return. He became indeed a familiar and friendly inmate of the house, whose genial presence, even when we did not see him, could hardly pass unnoticed, for he had the habit of singing "Old Jim Crow" when not occupied in conversation, and his loud and cheerful voice could be heard echoing every morning from the bathroom. His arrivals were always unannounced; he would appear when he liked, stay as long as he liked; and then one morning we would find at breakfast a penciled note to say that he had departed early, having had for the present enough of our society.

The reputation which the author of the *Leaves of Grass* had acquired by that daring and not decent publication was but a dubious one in America at that time; this reputation had reached our Quaker suburb, and our neighbors and relations would avoid our house and forbid their children to visit it when it was known that Walt Whitman was staying with us. Our friendship with him shocked them gravely; but no one who met him could retain this prejudice for long. His manners were grand and primeval, like those of old patriarchs or bards; he treated all human beings with the same politeness, and only on one occasion did we notice in him any sense of times and occasions and the demands of social etiquette. He had arrived on a visit in a knitted jacket, and, when told that a number of people were coming that evening to dinner, the thought occurred to him that probably he ought to put on a coat for the occasion, and after some meditation he appeared at dinner-time a consummate man of the world in his overcoat, thus sacrificing his comfort, for the night was hot, to the demands of the occasion.

Almost every afternoon my father would take Walt Whitman driving in the Park; it was an unfailing interest to them to drive as close as they could behind buggies in which pairs of lovers were seated, and observe the degree of slope towards each other, or "buggy-angle," as they called it, of these couples; and if ever they saw this angle of approximation narrowed to an embrace, my father and Walt Whitman, who had ever honored that joy-giving power of nature which the pagans symbolized under the name of Venus, would return home with happy hearts.

My acquaintanceship with this great and famous poet,—for Walt Whitman had already become famous in England, and his glory had flashed back across the Atlantic to Boston, and thence, as I have described, to where we sat in Germantown in darkness,— the familiar presence of this poet in our house, must have had an influence upon me which was much greater than anything that I was aware of at the time. He was, as John Burroughs has well described him, "large and picturesque of figure, slow of movement, tolerant, receptive, democratic and full of charity and good will towards all. His life was a poet's life from first to last—free, unworldly, unhurried, unconventional, unselfish, and was contentedly and joyously lived." He was already old and half-paralyzed when we made his acquaintance, but of the disabilities of age he never spoke, although their shadows are not absent from his poems of this period. In one of these, for instance, "Queries to My Seventieth Year," which was written just when we came to know him, he thus addresses the oncoming year:

> Approaching, nearing curious,
> Thou dim, uncertain specter—bring'st thou life or death?
> Strength, weakness, blindness, more paralysis and heavier?
> Or placid skies and sun? Wilt stir the waters yet?
> Or haply cut me short for good? Or leave me here as now,
> Dull, parrot-like and old, with crack'd voice harping, screeching?

It was, however, the calm serenity of age, its placid skies and sun, which diffused about him that atmosphere of peace and leisure which made his companionship so genial, and our endless conversations with him so great a pleasure. He was fond of talking with young people, and would listen with the utmost good nature to our crude notions; and when he was not with us, my sisters and I would often visit him in Camden, where on summer days we would find him seated at his window, fanning himself with a large palm-leaf fan, and gazing out on the lazy sunshine that filled his little street. Not infrequently during our visits he would recognize some workingman of his acquaintance as he passed, and call out, "Come in, Bill, and meet some friends of mine," and the workingman would come in, or the passing postman, or the driver of an express wagon, and we would all share an improvised meal together.

The floor of the room upstairs in which he lived was covered to the depth of a foot or so with a sea of papers, and now and then he would stir this pool with his stick and fish up a letter from an English admirer—Tennyson perhaps, or Symonds, or Edward Dowden, or some newspaper article about "the Good

Grey Poet." Walt Whitman, who had been himself so long a newspaper writer, was curiously fond of newspaper publicity; his floor was strewn with press cuttings in which his name was mentioned, and he would even, I believe, now and then, write anonymous articles about himself for insertion in the local papers. Otherwise he was quite free from literary vanity, and never spoke of his writings unless we questioned him. Then, however, he would answer with great simplicity and frankness. . . .

I remember once speaking to Walt Whitman about his poem, "With husky haughty Lips O Sea," which had just been published, and he told me, sitting one summer evening on our porch in Germantown, of the way he had come to write it; how always, from the days of his boyhood on the Long Island coasts, he had tried and tried again to seize the meaning which the voice of the ocean was always whispering in his ears; how often by day, and more often by night, he had sat or lain amid the sandhills on its margin, listening in a kind of torment of attention to that great voice—some voice—in what words could he best describe it?

Some voice, in huge monotonous rage, of freedom-lover pent,
Some vast heart, like a planet's, chain'd and chaffing in those breakers.

This notion of receptivity to experience, and of a complete surrender to it, combined with a patient effort to grasp its deepest meaning and to embody that meaning in significant and reverberating words—this account of the old man's poetic method, as he told it one summer evening, was deeply impressive to his boyish listener, although that listener had then no thought of attempting to coin his own experience into enduring metal. To melt material sand into salable glass bottles—this, he believed, was to be his destiny; and the idea that all such massy unmetaphorical gold might be gladly bartered, as Walt Whitman would gladly have bartered it, for the ability to embody in words some one of Nature's aspects,—the sea's voice, for instance, or the breath of its salt fragrance, or even, as he himself had said, "the undulation of one wave,"—the idea of so mad a preference would have seemed to his youthful listener at that date fantastic indeed.

✦

Thus I listened to the impressive talk of the old poet, and though I had no notion of following his example, the effect upon me of his poems, as I read and reread that strange volume, the *Leaves of Grass*—how can I adequately describe it? There are books which come to us as revelations, which, as Emerson says, "take rank in our lives with parents, lovers and passionate experiences," and to come on such a book to which one can yield oneself in absolute surrender—there is no intellectual enjoyment, I believe, no joy of the mind greater in youth than this. Books of this kind, for their most passionate acceptance, should be contemporary books, written by the living for the living; and should present us with a picture of life as we ourselves know it and feel it. And they should above all reveal us to ourselves, should hold up a looking glass before our eyes in which we see our own faces. Much that was suppressed in the young people of my generation found a frank avowal in the *Leaves of Grass;* feelings and affection for each other, which we had been ashamed of, thoughts which we had hidden as unutterable, we found printed in its pages, discovering that they were not, as we had believed, the thoughts and feelings of young, guilty, half-crazy goblins, but portions of the Kingdom of Truth and the sane experience of mankind.

It was above all Walt Whitman's rejoicing in his flesh and blood,—"there is so much of me," he sang, "and all so luscious,"—his delight in his own body and the bodies of his friends, which seemed a revelation and gave the *Leaves of Grass* so strong a hold upon a generation born of puritans who had ignored, or treated as shameful, those habitations of the spirit. Then, too, Walt Whitman's affection for his fellow human beings,—for he was one of those rare spirits who really love the human race,—his feeling that all men and women, of whatever race or class and in whatever state of degradation, were all of them not worthless and of no account, but lovable and mysterious and divine—this seemed to fill for us the many-peopled world with innumerable creatures all dear and infinitely precious to us. These were the streams of life which flowed from that fountain; and catching also from its pages the fervor of his exultant pride in Democracy, in America and the age we lived in, and moved also by the splendid passages here and there of great poetry, we came to regard as a sacred book the vast printed chaos of the *Leaves of Grass*. It gave us ears, it gave us eyes, it revealed to us the miracle of our own existence, and for me, at least, with my meager ideals of borrowed culture, it seemed to open a great shining window in my narrow house of life.

# HAROLD NICOLSON

HAROLD GEORGE NICOLSON came by birth and tradition to diplomacy, by marriage and taste to writing. Born in 1886 at Tehran, Persia, where his father, Sir Arthur Nicolson, 1st Baron Carnock, was British *chargé d'affaires*, he lived at Constantinople, Budapest, and Tangier before beginning his education in England. From Wellington College (scene of the sketch of "J. D. Marstock") he went to Balliol, Oxford (M.A.), then entered the Foreign Office and the Diplomatic Service, in which alternately he was engaged, in various capitals, from 1909 to 1929. He was the Balkan expert of the British Delegation at the Paris Peace Conference, a prominent member of the League of Nations, head of the British Legation at Tehran (1925), and Counselor of the British Embassy at Berlin (1927). Resigning from the Diplomatic Service in 1929 to devote himself to writing, he joined the editorial staff of the London *Evening Standard*. Since 1935 he has been the National Labour Member of Parliament for West Leicestershire. Besides holding several academic and courtly honors, Mr. Nicolson, through his marriage to the novelist and poet Victoria Sackville-West, is connected with one of the most famous families of English history. They reside at Sissinghurst Castle, Kent. Notwithstanding these distinctions, he has won an independent reputation as a writer, notable in his light essays for a bright and fanciful touch and in his articles on current affairs for an authoritative liberalism.

Harold Nicolson's main literary pursuit has been biography, to which, as a compeer of Lytton Strachey, he has made important contributions. First came his four sound and entertaining lives of poets: *Verlaine* (1921), *Tennyson* (1923), *Byron, The Last Journey* (1924), and *Swinburne* (English Men of Letters Series, 1925)—no mere conventional rehashing of familiar facts, and no "debunkery" either, but products of fresh research and original treatment. In 1927, with a concise little manual called *The Development of English Biography*, he put all modern students of that subject in his debt and, though somewhat pessimistic about the future of "pure" biography, did "that ungentle art" a service in separating its province from the conflicting claims of history, fiction, journalism, and science. In 1929 appeared Mr. Nicolson's *Portrait of a Diplomatist*, a study, through a life of his father, of pre-war European affairs. This was followed by *Peacemaking, 1919* (1933), the author's personal recollections of the Peace Conference with a summary of its achievements and mistakes. As the third part of this political trilogy, *Lord Curzon, The Last Phase, 1919-25* (1934) describes the author's chief as he knew him and studied his methods and

177

work. His *Dwight Morrow* (1935) is in the nature of an "official" life, while his *People and Things* and *Public Faces* are light and amusing excursions along the fringe of biography.

Meanwhile, in a small volume entitled *Some People* (1926), Mr. Nicolson experimented with a new sort of life-writing, whereby he managed to compose a modest autobiographical record under the guise of nine objective portraits drawn more or less directly from life. While several of the subjects' names are fictitious, the figures and events are authentic; the following sketch of "J. D. Marstock" comes, as the reader will perceive, directly from Mr. Nicolson's Wellington school-days and subsequent years. This short piece, in addition to giving a progressive biographical sketch (*cf.* Virginia Woolf's "Miss Ormerod") of the rise and fall of a typical Big Man on the Campus, provides an intimate self-portrait, also progressive, of the author as a youth.

Enlarging this original mode of "indirect autobiography," Mr. Nicolson has now begun a series of longer volumes under the general title "In Search of the Past," each volume to center on some interesting figure whom he has known personally and whose character and career he will treat partly in narrative form, partly in terms of his own memory and states of mind. By this method he hopes to be able to record the transitions in social, political, and ethical conditions from the period of his childhood in the closing years of Queen Victoria until the present day. *Helen's Tower* (1937), first of these ingenious lives, amplifies through its account of his uncle Lord Dufferin's life the author's own 1892-1902 phase, and thus affords the reader a parallel with which to judge the subjective and objective portraiture in the early chapters of *Some People*.

# J. D. MARSTOCK

I AM not of those who thoroughly disbelieve in British education. I have seen so much of the foreign product that I have come to feel that our school system, if placed on a wider basis, may yet prove best adapted to our national temperament. It is true, of course, that it standardises character and suppresses originality: that it somewhat ruthlessly subordinates the musical to the gymnastic. I am not convinced, however, that this is a bad thing. It provides society with a mass of standardised entities who, although unintelligent, yet do in fact possess τὸ βουλευτικόν: [1] upon the individual the effect is only rarely disastrous. The physi-

[1] The capacity for making decisions.—Ed.

cally gifted enjoy for a short space of years a prominence of which it would be ungracious to deprive them: nor do I think it unfitting that during the same period the intellectuals should very frequently and brutally be snubbed. True originality will by such measures merely be pruned to greater florescence; and sham originality will, thank God, be suppressed.

I admit, however, that my own mental development was checked by my education for a period of some years. But the circumstances were exceptional. My home life was so unusually exciting, my school life so unusually dull, that a gulf was formed between myself and my education which it took me a decade to bridge. On the one hand was Morocco, disturbing and aromatic, with wide nights beside the campfire, the smell of gumcistus, the rootling of wild boar in the swamp behind the hill, the boom of a warmed Atlantic on a distant beach. And on the other were "The Grange" (Folkestone) and subsequently Wellington College; the smell of varnished wood and Sunlight soap, the smell of linseed oil in the pavilion, the white light of acetylene gas upon a Latin grammar. Between these two, sundering them by four days of seasickness, came "the journey"; the heavy P. & O. seething past the light of Ushant and out into the cold wet loneliness beyond. Thirty-six times during those years did I either cross or recross the Bay of Biscay, and thirty-six times did I lie for three days in my cabin while my brothers tried to revive me with exhortations and cheap Médoc and little bits of cake.

I think also that both my private and my public school were exceptionally rigid and restrictive. At the Grange we were cold and underfed: we were incessantly being bothered to live up to our moral tone, which, so they assured us, was higher than that of any school in England. Mr. Hussey, the Head Master, would speak to us of "high endeavour" and kick us if we made the slightest noise. I was puzzled by all this and spent my time dreaming about things to eat, dreaming about warm rooms, dreaming constantly about Morocco. Mr. Moore, the Latin master, had a pair of skis in his sitting-room; Mr. Harrison, the man who taught sums, had only four fingers on his left hand; Mr. Reece one summer gave me a nectarine. I was not in the least unhappy, only absent-minded: they cursed me for being untidy, for laughing in form, for drawing pictures. And the impression arose in me that neither the games nor the lessons nor the high moral tone were things in which, somehow, the masters expected me to share.

At Wellington it was different: one ceased so completely to be individual, to have any but a corporate identity, that the question scarcely arose whether one might or might not be odd. One was just a name, or rather a number, on the list. The authorities in their desire to deprive us of all occasion for illicit intercourse deprived us of all occasion for any intercourse at all. We were not allowed to consort with boys not in our own house: a house consisted of thirty boys, of whom ten at least were too old and ten too young for friendship; and thus during those four years my training in human relationships was confined to the ten boys who happened more or less to be my contemporaries. In addition, one was deprived of all initiative of action or occupation. The masters took a pride in feeling that not only did they know what any given boy should be doing at that particular moment, but that they knew exactly what the said boy would be doing at 3.30 P.M. six weeks hence. We had thus no privacy and no leisure, there was never open to us the choice between two possible alternatives. I entered Wellington as a puzzled baby and left it as a puzzled child. And the vices which this system was supposed to repress flourished incessantly and universally, losing in their furtive squalor any educative value which they might otherwise have possessed.

I repeat that I was not unhappy. I took everything for granted: I even took for granted the legend that we were all passionately devoted to the school. It seemed natural to me (it still seems natural to me) that being bad at games I should, although head of the house in work, be debarred from all exceptional privileges. I was not, I think, unpopular: I was on excellent terms with all the other boys: at football even I finally evolved a certain prowess by being able, at crucial moments, unerringly to tumble down. I would drop like a shot rabbit in front of an approaching on-slaught: "Well played!" Marstock would shout at me: I would rise and rub myself,—κύδεϊ γαίων—all aglow. But until I came into direct contact with Doctor Pollock I learnt nothing serious from Wellington; and even then my enlightenment was blurred by the vestiges of my admiration for J. D. Marstock.

## 2

How fortuitous and yet how formative are the admirations which our school life thrusts upon us! With no man have I had less in common than with J. D. Marstock, and yet for years he exercised upon me an influence which, though negative, was intense. How clean he was, how straight, how manly! How proud we were of him, how modest he was about himself! And then those eyes—those frank and honest eyes! "One can see," my tutor said, "that Marstock has never had a mean or nasty thought." It took me six years to realise that Marstock, although stuffed with opinions, had never had a thought at all.

I can visualise him best as he appeared when head of the school, when captain of football. A tall figure, he seemed, in his black and orange jersey striped as a wasp. Upon his carefully oiled hair was stuck a little velvet cap with a gold tassel: he would walk away from the field, his large red hands pendant, a little mud upon his large red knees. He would pause for a moment and speak to a group of lower boys. "Yes, Marstock,—no, Marstock," they would answer, and then he would smile democratically, and walk on—a slight lilt in his gait betraying that he was not unconscious of how much he was observed. Those wide open eyes that looked life straight, if unseeingly, in the face were fixed in front of him upon that distant clump of wellingtonias, upon the two red towers of the college emerging behind. His cheeks, a little purple in the cold, showed traces of that eczema which so often accompanies adolescent youth. But it was not an ugly face. A large and slightly fleshy nose: a thin mouth: a well-formed chin: a younger and a plumper Viscount Grey.

Under the great gate he went and across the quadrangle. He must first look in upon the Sixth form room, a room reserved apparently for prefects who were seldom in the Sixth. He sank into a deck chair by the fire. The other prefects spoke to him about conditions in the Blucher dormitory, and the date of the pancake run. Yes, he would have to tell the Master about the Blucher, and there was no reason why they should not have the run on Tuesday. And then out under the great gate again and across through pine trees to Mr. Kempthorne's house. There on the floor would be his basin ready for him and a can of hot water beside it. And he had ordered that seed-cake. The smell of cocoa met him as he entered the passage. Seed-cake, and cocoa, and Pears soap, and the soft hum of a kettle on the gas: then work for two hours and then prayers. He would read the roll-call himself that evening. Oh, yes! and afterwards there was a boy to be caned. The basket-work of his armchair creaked as he leant forward for the towel.

### 3

When I arrived at Wellington, Marstock, who was my senior by some eighteen months, was already prominent. He took particular pains with me since, as he informed me later, I reminded him of a little cousin who had died of scarlet fever. This painful coincidence earned me his protective affection; and I for my part was awed and flattered. He thought me a good little boy with a healthy influence among my fellows: it was his lack of observation, I suppose, or his inference from the little cousin, which placed him under this misapprehension. My behaviour, however, as distinct from my basic morals, caused him many hours of puzzled anguish. He ascertained one day that I knew the names of only eight members of the school XV. He made me write them all out a hundred times, and repeat them to him after lunch. I had forgotten to put in their initials, and had to do it again. And then next summer he discovered that I was equally weak on the subject of the XI. My incapacity for games, or "exercise" as they were called at Wellington, filled him with pained dismay. I liked games, and it was obvious that I tried: I used to flounder about and get in the way and shout very hard to the forwards. There was a system called "passing the ball": it meant that one kicked it to someone in front, warning him by shouting out his name: "Hamilton!" I would yell—but no ball would follow. It would have wriggled off sideways somewhere, and I would pick myself up slowly, conscious that once again I was in disgrace. "But you're absolutely rotten," Marstock would say in saddened protest. A lowering grey sky above the white goal-posts and behind them a bank of wellingtonias. "You're *hopeless*, you simply can't be taught." And then the goal-post and the wellingtonias would swim together in a mist of suppressed tears.

Nor was it games alone which showed Marstock that as a pupil I was unsatisfactory. I see myself in retrospect as the most re-signed and normal of little boys, and yet I can recollect his chid-ing me for being mad. The particular occasion for this outburst, the actual manifestation on my part of paranoia, was an ink-pot shaped in the semblance of the Temple of Vesta at Rome. We were not, and with justice, allowed fountain pens: for some strange reason, ink was not provided in the classrooms: at the beginning of each term we were given a portable safety ink-pot, a red or blue little affair, with a double lid which pressed hard upon the aperture by dint of a round rubber pad and spring. I used to lose my ink-pots. I used to lose them at the very moment when it was time to rush to school. I had had particular trouble on this score with Mr. Elton, who taught me algebra. He told me that if I forgot again I should be whipped. So that morning when I lost my ink-pot I realised how needful it was to replace it by another.

The boy who had the cubicle next to mine was called Juniper. His real name, I think, was McEuan, but he lived at Juniper House, Guildford. I therefore darted into his room to look for an ink-pot. There was none to be found, but on his table was a small brass model of the Temple of Vesta, which opened at the top. It was an ink-stand rather than an ink-pot, it was clearly liable to slop or spill, but it would do. I proceeded with it up to college, gingerly and yet hurriedly as a man wheeling a barrow on a tight-rope. It served its purpose well enough; it was only on my return, my very inky but equally gingerly return, that I was stopped by Marstock. "What on earth," he said, "are you doing with that?" "It's an ink-stand, Marstock." I held out the Temple of Vesta, down the columns of which the ink had poured in shining runnels. "An ink-stand!" he snorted, "who but you would take an ink-stand up to college? And a model of St. Paul's, too! Oh, why, *oh*, *why* will you persist in being different to other people? I give you up; you simply *refuse* to be the same." He paused and looked at me with real perplexity in those open eyes. "*I think you must be mad*," he concluded solemnly.

I went to my room determined, at whatever cost, not to surrender to this creeping dementia: I must pull myself together: it was only a question of being careful: if one was terribly careful one could succeed in being exactly the same. My whole energy during the terms that followed was concentrated on achieving uniformity.

## 4

The terms passed. Marstock became head of the house, then captain of the XV, then school-prefect and then head of the school. I also had crept upwards and was in the Lower Sixth. But this my own prowess was of no avail to me: I was not even a dormitory prefect: I had not yet attained the privilege of leaving my house-cap in the ante-Chapel: I was contented but obscure. And I still feel that all this was very fitting: I have had my fun since: they haven't. Marstock at this stage was, in spite of his glory, very gracious to me: he had given me up as an athlete, but he felt that none the less the school, the spirit which he had infused into Kempthorne's house, had done me worlds of good. He would come into my room sometimes for tea: he would talk about our prospects against Marlborough: I showed a sycophantic but not an unintelligent interest. "Good God!" he would say, "you *are* a freak, but you're less of a freak than you were." And then during his last term there occurred that awful incident which finally shattered in him all belief that I had come to possess, at bottom, some of the right stuff.

The great event of the summer was the match against Charterhouse. Some years we went to Charterhouse, and some years they came to us. That year it was our turn to receive and combat the visiting team. The afternoon, I remember, was hot but overcast: the warm grey clouds spread widely over the wide playing fields —a sheet of shadowed green below, a sheet above of shadowed grey: and against this background clustered little dots of white—

five hundred straw hats, white cricket pads, flannels, the scoring board, the staring face of the pavilion clock, the masters' wives and daughters;—some parents, over there under the trees. Reggie Cooper and I had brought a paper bag of cherries and we sat on the grass together—watching carefully lest the other should exceed his share. Reggie then as now was the most stimulating of companions, and it was for me a stroke of fortune that had brought him to Kempthorne's. We had become inseparable; but at least once a week we ceased for a while to be on speaking terms, for several consecutive hours each would avoid the other with averted eyes. The Charterhouse match, the bag of cherries, coincided with one of our moments of reconciliation: we had not spoken to each other for at least twelve hours: we had therefore a great deal to say. The match dragged on around us as we talked: the little white figures on the wide expanse of green would cross and recross slowly, or make sudden galvanic motions with their arms and thighs: a great silence brooded over earth and sky, broken at intervals by the dry tock of ball on bat, by some sharp and distant voice calling directions, by a sudden rattling wave of clapping and applause. Reggie and I joined in the applause with abstracted fervour: we had no idea in reality of what was happening: we clapped our hands when the others clapped, and when the others cheered, we cheered: the bag was getting emptier and emptier; we had already had two arguments which threatened to be of a heated nature, and finally we embarked on the third.

We had scarcely become immersed in this discussion when we observed a ripple passing up the fringe of boys who lined the field. They were standing up and taking off their hats and then sitting down again. Behind them, causing this jagged and rippling edge in the flat line of recumbent figures, slowly walked a group of five people. There was the Duke of Connaught in a grey top-hat, the Master in his robes, the senior tutor, an equerry, and the Head of the School. Marstock, who was not in the eleven, walked behind talking to the equerry, giving him doubtless the name and initials of the boy who was bowling, of that boy over there who had so miraculously caught the ball. Reggie and I were lying at the extreme edge of the field, the edge nearest the college. We stood up as they passed us and took off our hats. We watched them enter the Master's Lodge. "That means," said Reggie, "that it's nearly over. They have gone to have tea." We sat down again and continued our discussion. The college clock struck half-past five—surely the beastly match would soon be finished.

Reggie was describing the most exciting day he had ever had. I had already described to him my own most exciting day, giving a slightly coloured version of an attack by Shereefian troops upon a village in the lower Anjera. We had watched from a neighbouring hill: the bullets, in my story, had sung above our heads "like this, sizzz . . ."; the smoke of the burning village had for a moment obscured our vision of the attacking forces: then suddenly it had blown to the west again and the meadow below was dotted with little writhing figures of the wounded and dying. Reggie had been rather bored by my story, supposing, and unjustly, that it was wholly untrue; impatient also to embark on his own. "It was," he began, "the most beautiful morning that I have ever seen. The sea was absolutely blue, and the snow on the distant Alps glittered in the sun. As our yacht steamed into Nice there was first the excitement of seeing whether we were the largest in the harbor. We landed about eleven. . . ." I was rather impressed by Reggie's story, regretting somewhat that my father for his part should have failed to be tremendously rich. Reggie's most exciting day, I remember, ended with a visit to the opera. "It was Tannhauser," said Reggie. "Not Tannhauser," I remarked, "Tannhäuser. I thought everyone knew that."

"No, it's Tannhauser."

"It isn't Tannhauser. It's Tannhäuser. There's a di . . . there are two dots over the 'a' which makes it 'oi.'"

"You're wrong, as usual. It's Tannhauser. After all you don't do German, and I do."

"But, you silly ass, whoever heard it called Tannhauser? Besides, I know German far better than you do. I learnt it as a kid in Buda Pesth."

"You didn't."

"I did. . . ."

There was a wild burst of cheering from the field in which we joined. People were waving their hats, the little white figures of the players trooped suddenly towards the Pavilion. "It's over," said Reggie, "let's do a bunk." We turned and started to run towards the college. As we approached the Master's Lodge we saw a figure running towards us down the drive. It was Marstock. "Well," he panted when he reached us, "what did they score?" I looked at Reggie: Reggie looked at me. "Well, at least," said Marstock impatiently, "they can't have beaten our 278?" I looked at Reggie: Reggie looked at me. "Well, at least we won?" Marstock shouted. We both got very red. "I think we must have, Marstock, everybody seemed very pleased." He snorted and left us. And that evening we both descended to the boot-room and were caned.

I bear no resentment towards Marstock for exacting this reparation. We had committed an enormity, and it was right that the traditions of the college should be maintained. And then it was so obvious that he was deeply and sincerely distressed. He came to my room after the operation and sat upon the settee. "I can't make it out," he said. "I *wish* I knew what to do." He scarcely spoke to me during the weeks that followed. Speech-day came and he received, as was inevitable, the King's medal. We all cheered wildly: he stood there with his back to us, while Princess Henry of Battenberg handed him his badge of honour. I had a lump in my throat: my admiration for him welled up and stung my eyes. And at the end of the term he called me into his room to say good-bye. He put his hand on my shoulder. "You promise," he said to me, "that during the next year you will *try*." I said I would, Marstock, yes, I really would. I left his room hurriedly and on the verge of tears.

## 5

The next term I was moved into the Upper Sixth. This meant a small but somewhat glorified class-room; the desks were of a different shape, there was actually a carpet, there were photographs around the room of the Niké Apteros and of Mycenae, there was a large plaster cast above the mantelpiece of a Centaur struggling with one of the Lapithae; there was above all constant and continuous contact with Dr. Pollock. The Master hitherto had been for me a remote and rather alarming mystery; my feelings in regard to him were a mixture of fearful curiosity and religious awe: there was something emotionally magnificent about him, something theocratic. His tall slim figure billowed in a silken gown as he glided rapidly through the cloisters, leaving behind a faint but pleasant smell of hair-wash, an impression of something rich and luxurious and mundane: a striking contrast to the drab penury of our existence: a touch of the great coloured world beyond. The other masters cowered visibly at his approach: they seemed, when standing beside him, to become moth-eaten and affable and unimportant: the boys, as he spoke to them in his quick and gentle voice, were somehow more natural and less afraid. My worship for him had hitherto been uncoloured by the richer tone of personal intimacy: the Upper Sixth became for me a large excitement, a rapid intellectual and above all emotional fermentation. To a large extent, of course, this expansion was due to the adjustments of puberty, but its development was hastened and controlled by the subtlety and sympathy of Dr. Pollock. He was so intelligent, he was so human, he was so gently amused: gradually it dawned upon me that what had hitherto been merely lessons, were in fact *my* lessons, bore a distinct personal relation to myself. The school, my house, the games, my efforts to become "the same" remained, as before, inevitable and detached: but the work, the Master, the class-room of the Upper Sixth, became gradually a part of my central consciousness, fused gradually with such secret feelings as my people, and the yearning for Morocco, and the novels of Mr. Anthony Hope, and the smell of pines on summer evenings.

I realise, on looking back, that his methods, for all their subtlety, were perfectly calculated and deliberate. He knew that the system of the school had scored upon our brains a few deep grooves of habit which were in danger of becoming rigid: he set himself to render these grooves more flexible, to create new channels and associations in our minds. For the purposes of scholarship, for the needs, that is, of examinations, the Upper Sixth were entrusted to Mr. Perkins, most exact of hellenists, most meticulous of scholiasts. Dr. Pollock, for his part, appeared to devote his energies to destroying all the educational convictions which we had hitherto absorbed: he taught us that the mere avoidance of howlers was a means only and not an end: he taught us that the greater proportion of classical literature as it figured in the school curriculum was not only dull but silly: that the really jolly bits were yet to come: he taught us that life was more than scholarship, and literature more than books: he taught us to feel, and even to think, for ourselves. The greed with which I absorbed these lessons was voracious: whatever projects I may have had of becoming an exact scholar were destroyed for ever in the space of a few gay weeks; but if I have since understood in any way the meaning and the purposes of culture, my understanding is due entirely and absolutely to Dr. Pollock. And I render thanks.

For him indeed the classic letters were more human. He dislocated even the setting in which instruction had been conveyed. We would sprawl on pine-needles in his garden, we would lounge beside the fire on his floor. He would give us coffee, strong and redolent, and granulated sugar and little cakes: the two footmen would appear with the Georgian silver and the Wedgwood cups: the contrast with the scrubbed boards and chipped enamel of our school life spread a sense of Olympic ease and privilege; and in his gentle voice he would read to us some lines from Lucretius, a page of Shelley, a passage in Walter Pater, an article even by Max Beerbohm in the *Saturday Review*.

## 6

The conflict between my admiration of the Master and my admiration of J. D. Marstock was still unrealised. The latter, although now at Magdalen, continued by his remembered example to inspire and direct my daily life at school. I was now a dormitory prefect, and I would give to the younger boys such advice and counsel as Marstock in his time had given to me. I taught them with firm but not ungentle insistence that they must all strive to be alike.

It was only in my last term that a slight doubt assailed me regarding the efficacy and necessity of Marstock's ideals. The flash which then illumined my lowering sky was evoked, indirectly, by Dr. Pollock. The contrast between my two allegiances became a conflict and culminated in an explosion.

It was a Saturday evening, and we were sitting under the pine trees reading the Journey to Brundisium. The Master had pointed out to us how indelicate this story was, how gross, in fact, were the sensibilities of the poet: how, in fact, with acquired success, the fingers of Horace had all become thumbs. It was a stimulating theory, and in the middle of it the footman appeared leading a young man in a brown suit across the lawn. I did not recognise Marstock at first, he seemed to have lost something both in height and colour: the eczema was very bad indeed. The Master greeted him warmly and made him join us. We had gone back to that passage about Virgil refusing to play tennis because he had sore eyes. The Master closed the book and began to talk of Virgil, of his gawky nervousness, of his shy provincialism, of how much he had disliked being made to write the *Aeneid*. Marstock watched him with straight but puzzled eyes. "I *loathe* the *Aeneid*," I remarked with sudden conviction. Marstock turned his eyes in my direction: they were not only puzzled but disapproving. "But you're wrong," said Dr. Pollock, and then, in that soft and rapid voice, he began to intone:—

"Tum pater Anchises, lacrimis ingressus obortis . . ."

The warm July sun was slanting through the pine trees. The soft and solemn hexameters rolled onwards.

"manibus date lilia plenis . . .
His saltem accumulem donis et fungar inani
Munere. . . ."

The Master stopped intoning and leant down towards me. "As a punishment for a pert and unsolicited remark you will learn that passage by heart. Whenever in after life we meet again, I shall ask you to repeat it." I glanced at Marstock: his face wore a contented but reserved expression, such as a guest's face should wear when a spoilt, an intolerable, child receives at last the merited rebuke. I looked up at the Master. He smiled back at me with friendly humour; there was a touch of unusual meaning in his smile and he gave just the slightest side-glance at Marstock. I felt my cheeks flaming as from a sudden emotional shock: was it possible, was it conceivable, that the Master could have had an eye-meet with me behind Marstock's back? Was it possible that Dr. Pollock should have found Marstock, even for a moment, even in a little thing, absurd? I walked back under the stars buoyant with some strange delight of liberation. I did not fully comprehend the nature of this winged exultancy: I thought it came merely from the pleasure of that evening, the warm pine-needles, the coffee-sugar, the beauty of those resonant lines. The rows of windows in Kempthorne's house were ablaze between the wellingtonias: I paused in the shadow of the rhododendrons. Three weeks more and I should be free. It was mere humbug to pretend regret. I should be free, free, free. . . . I looked up at the house which for four years had been my prison. The figure of Marstock seemed to rise from it, to assume gigantic shape, to quiver for a moment and then to fall a crumbling idol among the pines. "Poor old Marstock," I murmured, as I climbed the dark and smelling stairs.

## 7

On leaving Wellington I spent nearly a year in Germany. When I reached Oxford Dr. Pollock had been appointed Bishop of Norwich, and Marstock was already preparing for his final schools. He had failed somehow to be given his football blue and had therefore concentrated his whole energies on obtaining a first. No one has ever worked as Marstock worked, and in the process his straight and open eyes became emptied of all but a forlorn bewilderment. When the examination approached, he funked it. He would stay on at Oxford and work another year: he would make it a certainty. "You see," he explained, "people never know afterwards whether one gets a good second or a bad first. They merely say—'he got a first at Oxford,' or 'at Oxford he only got a second.' " So for another year Marstock slaved in his rooms in Beaumont Street and succeeded in obtaining a very creditable third. He then decided to enter the Foreign Office. But here again he thought it wiser to take his time. And thus when I also on leaving Balliol devoted two years to acquiring foreign tongues, I would find Marstock working away in the various pensions which we frequented. I went to Jeanne de Hénaut—Marstock was there: at Hanover, Marstock: at Pisa, Marstock again. His mind, in all those years, had become a trifle rigid; but his affection, the memory of the little cousin who had died of scarlet fever, was wholly to be depended upon. It was solid and all of a piece: it was like Portland cement: it was exceedingly difficult either to evade it or to push it aside. He would come for walks with me among the Tuscan hills and wonder what had happened to J. L. Wallace of the Hopetown, or R. B. Brinsmead of Toyes. I remember in particular a summer evening in Paris: we had walked across the river and looked for books under the arcades of the Odéon: I had shown him the hotel where Wilde had died, and we had emerged on the Quay at a moment when every window in Paris and Montmartre was flaming back at a low red sun. We leant over the parapet and looked at the purple river swirling below us. The hum of life reached us in the hot air; behind us was the Quartier Latin, in front those myriad flaming windows. I showed him the two sphinxes at the end of the bridge and told him how Wilde in those last shambling years would tell how that sphinx there on the right was the only person who returned his smile. "But why," said Marstock, "the one on the right? They're both exactly the same!" I was silent at this, looking into the river and thinking vaguely of mighty poets in their misery dead. "Do you remember," said Marstock, "how after footer one would come back to the house and one would brew and read a book?" I said that I remembered very well.

It was only when Marstock had failed for the third time in the Foreign Office examination that he passed definitely out of my life. Fifteen years went by before I saw him again. The occasion was a public luncheon given in honour of the Byron centenary. I was late for the luncheon and found my place with difficulty. When it was over we crowded into the ante-room. I suddenly felt my arm seized from behind.

"Well, I'm blowed," said Marstock, "fancy meeting *you* here!" I did not myself feel that my attendance at that luncheon was in any way a startling coincidence, but I forbore to say so. I was pleased to see Marstock again, pleased to notice how slightly he had changed. There was a touch of grey about the carefully combed hair, he was a little thinner, and his eyes had given up being merely open and had become just blank. But it was the same good old Marstock in his brown suit and old Wellingtonian tie.

I asked him what he was doing now. He said that he was an underwriter at Lloyd's. I asked him whether he was married. He laughed a little shyly. "No," he said; "you see it's the wimskies." I put on a serious and condoling expression, imagining that he had mentioned some obscure disease. "The wimskies?" I inquired considerately. "The women, you know—I always call them that. They're all so fascinating, I can't make up my mind." I assured him that, to my mind also, women were delightful and perplexing little things.

I have not seen Marstock since, except once on the Embankment when I passed him in a taxi. But that Byron luncheon is memorable to me for yet another and far more emotional encounter. The crowd had parted suddenly, and in front of me, sitting on a sofa, I saw the Bishop of Norwich. My pulses raced suddenly with a return of the old excitement. I went up to him. "Do you remember me?" I said. He looked up and smiled. He remembered me perfectly. He remembered—ah, yes—"Tum pater Anchises" . . . would I please continue? I hesitated and flushed: not a week had passed during the long years since that evening at Wellington without my repeating to myself those lines, preparing for such an encounter. I knew them perfectly. But for the moment they wouldn't come.

"I am afraid," I stammered, "that I have forgotten."

# LOUIS UNTERMEYER

"The three worlds I have lived in were as dissimilar as imaginable. There was the world of security and some serenity, of creative excitement, serious play, and happy conflict; a world that ended in 1917. This was followed by the world of distorted rumor and daily nightmare, of the World War and the false peace. And there is the world in which we are now living, the world of undeclared wars and methodical violence, of political aggression and moral disintegration, a world of fear which has exchanged the forces of security for the security of force."

SO wrote Louis Untermeyer in 1939 on dedicating to his three young sons his autobiography, *From Another World*. Because the aspects of his "worlds" do appear so dissimilar and because he felt no desire to make a confession of his "inner" self, the book is really, as he declares, not so much an autobiography as a history of a period, reviewing with deliberate objectivity the chief persons, causes, and events with which he has been concerned. "Storm Center in Brookline" is consequently both a portrait of Amy Lowell and a study of the Imagist school of poetry—at least of its beginnings—viewed over the author's shoulder.

Mr. Untermeyer, who is still a major figure in American poetry, was born in New York City in 1885. On his father's side he is descended from Bavarian Jews who reached New York only after a generation's stopover in the "Down-East" environment of Waldoboro, Maine. To this already complex background was added the glamour of his mother's Southern parentage, both elements exerting a lifelong influence on this particular son. "It was decided," he writes, "long before I was ten, what was to become of me. To be on the safe (Untermeyer) side, I was to be a businessman; to uphold the cultural (Michael) strain I was to be an accomplished musician." From his thirteenth birthday, when he wrote his first poem, however, he had something to say about it himself; and though when he grew up he usually kept an anchor to windward in the family jewelry business, he managed to take a prominent part in the literary upsurge that synchronized with his own coming of age. He was associated with Floyd Dell, John Reed, Art Young, Max Eastman, and other "flaming youths" on *The Masses* and *The Liberator*. With Waldo Frank, James Oppenheim, Randolph Bourne, Van Wyck Brooks, and others he edited and wrote for *The Seven Arts*, "one of the best, if shortest-lived, literary magazines that the country has known." He was thrice married: to Jean

Starr (Untermeyer), to Virginia Moore—both poets—and to Esther Antin. He was in, as has already been mentioned, at the birth of Imagism; he effectively encouraged Vachel Lindsay and Sara Teasdale; waged literary battles with Harriet Monroe, editor of *Poetry* magazine; joined forces with H. L. Mencken ("The Bad Boy of Baltimore") as poetry editor of *The American Mercury*; refereed the long, friendly rivalry between Robert Frost and Edwin Arlington Robinson; proclaimed the genius of Elinor Wylie; and observed at an interested and critical close-range the rise, the triumph, and sometimes the fall of innumerable "prodigies and fugitives" on the cultural stage of America.

His own writing has been mainly of four kinds: poetry, parodies, translations, and critical prose, to which must be added the successful anthologies of verse known to most readers, his biography of Heinrich Heine (1935), and now his book of recollections, *From Another World*.

Despite the immense prestige enjoyed by Amy Lowell during her flourishing years and the legends that were quick to gather about her contradictory existence, few persons knew her intimately. Mr. Untermeyer was one of these. If the following sketch gives off a satirical ring, it also portrays beneath the outward eccentricities the true creative stature of the woman herself. The well-narrated anecdotes, out of the thousands he might have used, show the author's gift for biography and his shrewd (though perhaps not unbiased) critical appraisal of her character and her work.

## STORM CENTER IN BROOKLINE

THAT was a strange evening the first time I visited Amy Lowell. It was strange that I should have been there at all. A year or two before this I had reviewed her first book, and reviewed it most unfavorably. It had come to my desk with several other pleasantly competent volumes, from which it differed in no distinguishable way. It seemed the conventional "slender sheaf" full of apostrophes to dead romantic poets, second-rate imitations of Robert Louis Stevenson, and a lengthy tribute to the Boston Athenaeum whose spirit dominated the book; everything about it was familiar except the author's name. Not being a Bostonian, and unaware of any august relationship, I had pictured the author as a young female Laocoön struggling, not too strenuously, in the coils of poetic stereotype. I had resolved to read her a lesson. My review must have been insuffer-

LOUIS UNTERMEYER

ably patronizing—she told me later it was one of the few reviews that had ever made her weep—and I remember that I concluded the offensive paragraph by saying that the only good line in the book was the title, *A Dome of Many-Colored Glass*, and that was taken from Shelley. Less than two years after I had disposed of the sentimental disciple of Tennyson and Keats, I had to change my tune. Another Amy Lowell had confronted me with *Sword Blades and Poppy Seed*. It was an experimental and far more belligerent poet who exhibited a new individuality and range, who expressed herself with equal determination in precise cameos of verse and roughhewn masses of polyphonic prose. I was astonished at the transmogrification, and I said so in print.

And now I was waiting for her to descend the great staircase of the famous house, which, according to rumor, was occupied only by herself, a companion, and a retinue of servants—a house fronted by its own park and backed by a fabulous garden, a house where the mirrors were always draped in black, whose every door-knob was of sterling, and in which the owner lived in a kind of shrouded battlement on the top floor of her castle. I had even heard that, like the legendary princess, she slept on a bed made of eighteen pillows because ordinary sheets were too coarse for her. Like Caesar, she was reputed to keep two secretaries continually at work. She ignored the clock, and her world waited until she woke and the sleeping palace accommodatingly came to life.

I waited. I had been summoned to appear at seven in the evening. I learned later that all new guests, obviously on probation, were put through an ordeal not of fire but of patience. I did not know it then—so I waited. Sometime between thirty minutes and an hour after my arrival Miss Lowell appeared. It was easy for her. Her routine was the opposite of everyone's. A wealthy woman, she could indulge herself not only in her fancies but in her hours. She slept all day and worked all night, claiming that in this way she was free from the telephone, the importunities of friends and tradesmen, and all the countless interruptions of the day. She awoke about three in the afternoon, planned the details for the following day with her housekeeper over a four o'clock breakfast, and came down to dinner, her first real meal of the day, at eight. After dinner there were friends, concerts or other diversions. This lasted until midnight. Then she began to work, to write new poems and revise old ones. At five in the morning she sustained herself with a light lunch, arranged the manuscripts for the secretaries, and so to bed. Nothing could interrupt, no one could intrude upon her. It was a system much to be recommended—for those who could afford it.

Miss Lowell came down the stairs. She waved no plumes and rattled no sabers, but she seemed to be advancing at the head of a victorious army. There was gunfire in the air; I thought I heard bugles. She endeavored to put me, a stranger, at my ease. She offered me a cigarette, pulling out a drawer which seemed to contain the contents of the United Cigar Stores, Incorporated.

"No, thank you," I said, "I do not smoke."

"I hope you don't mind that I do," said she, taking up a rich-looking cigar. "My doctor tells me the paper in cigarettes is injurious. Besides, I prefer tobacco wrapped in its own leaf."

The shock was only for a moment. I had heard of Hungarian duchesses who smoked cigars imperturbably and, years later, I was to know a Viennese grand dame who cherished a meerschaum pipe. But I was unprepared to watch a Lowell, the sister of Harvard University, knocking the ash from a colorado claro. (She had a supply of ten thousand.) The apparition seemed the more grotesque because of Miss Lowell's size. I do not know what she weighed at the time, but, although she was forty, it must have been well over two hundred pounds. To make the effect still more incongruous, she preferred high-collared dresses sprinkled with beads and lavishly trimmed with passementerie. Some glandular defect made the heavy body seem more swollen and the short frame more stunted than it really was. ("Lord," she would say, "I'm a walking side-show.") Yet the rakish cigar and the abnormal stoutness were forgotten five minutes after she had seated herself. One noticed only the marvelous neatness, the fine hands and delicate ankles, the small mobile mouth, the coolly modulated voice, the quick-appraising but not unkind eyes, the fine features and almost transparent skin. One saw a woman who was not only intelligent but—there is no other word for it—pretty. The most implacable adversary, more masculine than most males, she could also be the most charming feminine persuader. I capitulated. I think I apologized for not smoking. Then we went in to dinner.

It was a good, even a grand, dinner. But I was not comfortable. There were six or eight celebrities at the table; but it was not the guests or the service that undid me. It was the dogs. They were English sheepdogs, immense longhaired creatures, and there seemed to be a ferocious flock of them. They sat around the dining-room in a semicircle, their mouths dribbling with hungry anticipation. As the meal progressed their eyes grew larger and larger, like the magic dogs in Hans Christian Andersen's tale, and I felt more and more like a frightened bone.

Dinner over, the guests, led by Ada Dwyer Russell, who served as Amy Lowell's companion, confessor, wailing wall and buffer state, trailed into the imposing library. I had barely begun to examine the famous collection of volumes with Keats's own annotations when I was motioned to a chair. The other guests were seated; they knew the ritual which was to ensue. We were grouped about a fireplace large enough to roast an ox or a critic. One maid entered with the coffee. Another followed with a huge pile of bath towels.

"Thank you very much," I said, trying to cover my bewilderment with a poor facetiousness, "but I had my bath this morning, and I rarely spill the coffee."

"Don't be absurd," Miss Lowell replied. "It's for the dogs."

"Surely, you're not going to bathe them here?"

"Nonsense." She made a moue. "The darlings don't need a bath, either. But they are so companionable, and their hair is so long, and they *do* dribble after food, and they like to put their heads in your lap."

So there we sat with towels across our knees, while the seven dogs—there seemed to be seventeen—alternately guzzled their food and nuzzled us, and the conversation grew increasingly animated.

But my contretemps with Amy Lowell's pet monsters was nothing compared to the misadventure suffered by another poet.

Maxwell Bodenheim was expected to arrive at about seven one evening. Amy sent her huge Pierce Arrow (with tires deflated for luxurious driving) for the more important guests; the others arrived by the blue Chestnut Hill street car. Bodenheim was not one of the favored; he was intransigent and his clothes were shabby. He got off at Heath Street and walked up the curving driveway to the entrance of Sevenels. There was a sign: "Motors be careful not to run over the dogs." Ordinarily the dogs were put in their kennels before strange visitors arrived; but Bodenheim, fearful of being late, arrived much too early. The seven oversize dogs spied him. They wanted to play. Barking, they sprang about—and on—him. Bodenheim misunderstood their motives. He dodged behind a tree.

"Aha!" thought the dogs. "Here is a new diversion. Here is a bone that runs." Immediately a thousand pounds of dog leaped to the chase. Bodenheim zigzagged desperately, trying to throw them off the scent. But they surrounded him, barking all the more furiously. He reached the house, spent and bespattered, guided but not helped by the stone statue of Flora which stood, apathetically, above the doorway. He had just strength enough to ring the bell. A maid, incongruously small, appeared.

"Shoo!" she cried. Bodenheim did not know whether to be grateful or offended. Then he realized she was talking to the dogs.

"Shoo!" she said a second time, stamping her little foot. The monstrous seven, the worst watch-dogs in the world, dropped their tails and fell over each other in an awkward rush to escape.

A similar mishap occurred to Randolph Bourne. Bourne . . . was a hunchback, physically weak and easily frightened. He was sure that the dogs had viciously attacked him, and he was so terrified that he could not rise to his hostess's sallies during dinner. Amy, in turn, despised the "weakling." Her repulsion extended even to his writing; in a talk with James Oppenheim and me she insisted that his deformity showed itself in his "tortured style and twisted mentality." Oppenheim told me she returned to the false charge at another session with him.

"Everything he writes," she repeated, "shows he is a cripple."

Intending nothing more than a sentencious generality Oppen-heim said, "Aren't we all cripples?"

Amy's aggressiveness fell away from her. "Yes," she said, sur-veying her enormous girth. "Look at me. I'm nothing but a dis-ease."

## I I

At the time I knew little about Amy Lowell's militancy. It was not until later that I heard (and saw) how she invaded editorial offices, bore down upon the heads of magazines and publishing offices, treated editors as if they were office boys, and brought every kind of armament into play—wealth, charm, po-litical astuteness, family background, good-fellowship, and dic-tatorial commands—to forward her powerful offensive. Every new book was a new campaign, and never has there been a more determined general. "I am as bad as Napoleon," she wrote un-ashamedly to the editor of *The New York Tribune*. "I believe in my star."

I remember one of her sorties into what she considered enemy territory. She descended upon New York, accompanied by the faithful Mrs. Russell, and put up at the Hotel St. Regis, from which she sent out her summonses. I shall never forget that "re-ceiving room." As in her own home, the mirrors were concealed behind black cloths. One table held a dozen pitchers of ice-water; another table was precariously balanced with scores of the latest books; a third table was a litter of clippings, letters, telegrams, memoranda. During dinner, which was served in her rooms, Amy discharged a battery of dicta; gave orders over the tele-phone to obviously cowed listeners; alternately blandished and bullied the waiters—"Here! put all my vegetables on one plate. I don't want them sitting around in little bird-baths"—and kept her guests in a state of amusement and apprehension. Joyce Kil-mer told me she had "made" him interview her on the subject of the new poetry. What is more (such was her power) she got him to send her his manuscript and permitted him to print it in *The New York Times* only after she had approved it.

Later she attempted to bring a weightier influence to bear upon the newspapers. "You advertise so much in the *Times*," she wrote to her publishers, "that you ought to force them into a somewhat less hostile attitude." She believed in controversy, not only for its own sake but for its advertising value. I mocked her once by saying, "Sweet are the uses of publicity," and she did not resent it. She wrote to Ezra Pound, "I consider you an uncommonly fine poet. You ought to have an impresario—your knowledge of how to 'get yourself over,' as we say in this little country, is *nil*."

It was Ezra Pound who told me how Amy had "captured" the Imagist movement. . . . In London in 1912 Pound and one or two others, chiefly T. E. Hulme, revolted against the current "morbid romantic attitude and outworn false generalities." Seeking, most of all, a cure for the stock allusions and general vagueness, they hit upon the *image* as a clear and definite objective. To express this definiteness Pound and his coadjutors, organizing themselves into a group, drew up a manifesto which declared for "the hard, definite word. Each word," they continued, "must be an image seen, not a counter or cliché. Images in verse are not mere decorations, but the very essence of an intuitive language." Endeavoring to use no word that did not contribute to the presentation of the image, the group was led by Pound to challenge the critics with *Imagisme*. Pound says he invented the term "to avoid vain gabble as to the nature of poetry." He wrote me during the brief period following my Italian sojourn when we seemed to be friends, "I have no objection to the pleasure others have had in exploiting the label and offering cheap imitations, but I regret the loss of critical distinction between poetry which uses no word which does not contribute to the presentation—and verbosity (more or less rhythmic)." Pound attracted and repelled disciples; one of them, Hilda Doolittle, born in Bethlehem, Pennsylvania, began signing her Tanagra-like poems "H. D., Imagiste." While the movement was gaining momentum, Amy Lowell arrived in London with a letter of introduction to Pound. The two, born doctrinaires and dictators, met head on. A few months later Amy returned to America at the head of an Imagist movement of her own. Her group consisted of three Englishmen: D. H. Lawrence, Richard Aldington, and F. S. Flint; and three Americans:

H. D., John Gould Fletcher, and herself. Pound's anthology, *Des Imagistes*, was published in 1914; Amy's collections, *Some Imagist Poets*, appeared in 1915, 1916, and 1917. Pound repudiated any connection with the American wing which he always referred to as "the Amygist movement."

Pound made light of the defection when he told me about it as we sat in the *Giardino Pubblico* looking toward Sestri. But there must have been a day when he threatened suit, for, in November, 1914, Amy wrote to him, "So far as I know you have not copyrighted the name 'Imagiste.' I never heard of a school of poetry being copyrighted; I doubt if it could be done. But if you should feel inclined to sue, I should be exceedingly delighted, as then they would put new jackets on the book, which I should greatly prefer. Also, it would be a good advertisement." Imperturbable and magnificent Amy! Anything for "a good advertisement." Lowell or no, she would have made an independent fortune as a promoter of bond issues or the head of a public relations firm.

Never has there been a leadership like Amy's. She used every form of persuasion, every kind of weapon. She fought alone and with badgered recruits; she stormed every battlement of convention. As a determined Imagist she not only laid siege to Poetry, she invaded it. Since much of the work was written in unrhymed lines with "cadence" instead of a regular rhythm, Imagism became (falsely) synonymous with free verse, that contradiction in terms. The emancipated champions of *vers libre* were maliciously ticketed as "vers-libertines." Free verse, more challengingly than free love, became a fighting phrase, and Amy exulted in the conflict. "By Jove!" she ended one of her letters to me in the midst of the controversy. "We are pushing the Philistines to the wall!"

Pound could never have done it; Pound, she wrote in one of the first letters I received from her, "would have ruined the movement, important though it was, as he has ruined everything he has touched. You are quite right in implying that bitterness has upset his brain. The only thing I object to in your article is your saying that it was under his leadership 'that the Imagists became not only a group, but a fighting protest.' It was not. The Imagists during the year and a half in which he headed the movement were unknown and jeered at, when they were not absolutely ignored. It was not until *I* entered the arena, and Ezra dropped out, that Imagism began to be considered seriously. I feel sure that if I had not done all I did and worked hard to prove the value of the movement, the thing would never have achieved the recognition it now has. . . . The name is his; the idea was wide-spread; but changing the whole public attitude from derision to consideration came from my work." This was Amy *in excelsis*.

At this time her letters were variations on the theme. She evidently kept carbon copies of every letter she wrote, for I read excerpts in Foster Damon's comprehensive biography, quoting from letters whose originals I must have destroyed. Yet in 1916 alone I find more than twenty epistles, all on the chaste and businesslike letterhead: "Miss A. Lowell, Heath Street, Brookline, Mass." Her very first communication was a reproach for not being sufficiently enthusiastic about the new gospel. After thanking me for a *causerie* in which I praised her, she wrote, "I think perhaps you are a little hard on the Imagists. Don't you think you are reading into them characteristics which perhaps they have not got? One of the things which they represent to my mind, is the ascendancy of the purely imaginative impulse. It is this quality of imagination which has seemed so hard to get America to fitly understand. It frightens them, worries them, repels them."

It was the form, rather than the imagination itself, which worried the critics. Amy herself continually violated the Imagist manifesto and extended her work far beyond its tenets; but she, too, confused the form with the substance. It was not until much later that she was able to separate the true "inwardness" of the poem from the outer technique. She was (at least in the flush of her Imagist triumph) so convinced that *vers libre* was the only possible contemporary form that she extended her prejudice into the past. She intimated that even translations of the classics should be "cadenced"; in the midst of a highly complimentary review of my Heine versions she wrote, "Why, O why, has Mr. Untermeyer chosen to follow Heine in his tight little rhythms and mathematically cut stanzas?" At about this time Keith Preston, then writing a lively column in Chicago, sent me a paraphrase of his much-quoted quatrain:

A toast to Amy Lowell,
That most incredible She,
And all the little magazines
That died to make verse free.

Amy would have relished it. She enjoyed the quick thrust and parry; she did not disdain puns. (Referring to my Michigan lectures at Ann Arbor she hoped I had been pleasantly entertained by the "Ann Arborigines.") It was only in (and about) her work that she lacked a sense of humor. I remember once, when we were discussing the Imagist credo, she insisted that words could render not only the exact nuances of music but record the most minute differences of color. "But," she added, "it takes an unusually trained vision to apprehend and register the shades of difference. For example, you must have noticed how the color of a country road is changed when seen through the spokes of a fast-moving car. What color would you say it was?"

"Well," I hazarded, trying to play the game, "earth-color. Or dull brown. Or dusty tan. Or . . ."

"Cinnamon!" she shouted triumphantly. "Use your eyes!"

Although she herself was not precious as a person, she pushed theory into preciosity. She claimed so much for her pet project that she rated Emily Dickinson as a precursor of the Imagists. ("It is an odd story," she wrote, "this history of Imagism, and perhaps the oddest and saddest moment in it is comprised in the struggle of this one brave, fearful, and unflinching woman.") She went further; she insisted that Emily Dickinson would have been a better poet had she written in *vers libre;* "a knowledge of the principles of unitary verse (that is, verse based upon a unit of time instead of a unit of accent) would have liberated Emily Dickinson from the bonds against which she chafed." She pushed her theory so far in this instance that she completely misread and misunderstood the poet to whom she was paying tribute. "She

(Emily Dickinson) made use of what I have called elsewhere the 'unrelated' method; that is, the describing of a thing *by its appearance only.*" Misapprehension can go no further than the italicized phrase (the italics are mine), for no poet dealt less with "appearance only" than Emily Dickinson. Her descriptions, startlingly vivid and exact though they were, were backgrounds for the play of the restless mind; the outer and inner world surpassed appearance to form "the landscape of the soul."

## III

The effect of the new poetry was explosive, and Amy laid much of the dynamite. Although her illness was aggravated by an umbilical hernia that necessitated four operations within three years, she stormed about the country, horrified the pedants, made enemies in order to fight them, and shocked her audiences into feverish debate. She was continually traveling "for the cause," although train trips were a torture to her, for her blood pressure compelled her to sit at open windows no matter how much other passengers complained. Once she broke a glass pane in a sleeping-car to get air. The hotels rarely had the accommodations she required; she was never satisfied with a suite of less than four rooms —a whole floor in the smaller hotels—clocks had to be stopped, mirrors covered, meals served in the middle of the night. The lecture halls were never right; the lecterns had the wrong slant, and the lights were such that she always carried her own reading lamp with her. This led to a curious mishap at the University of Michigan. When her lamp was plugged in, it blew a fuse and the hall was in a dark confusion while chairmen and the heads of various departments fumbled for the janitor who was groping for them. Wherever she went she astounded the naïve and sophisticates alike; a storm center in Brookline and a cyclone on the warpath. She was not merely a lecturer, she was an event, a national phenomenon, a freak of nature, a dynamo on the loose.

In personal relationships she was the kindest of friends and the warmest of defenders. She fought until the experiments of John Gould Fletcher were acknowledged and H. D. was established.

Yet her most admiring friends could not help but resent her assumption of power, even when it was exercised in their behalf.
Upon my first return from Europe, H. D. wrote me from
Switzerland, "Do let me know how Amy is now. I expect you
to give her tactful messages from me, for I do wish the best in
the world for her. My only objection is: she will NOT leave other
people alone." Fletcher had less cause to complain; he realized
she was "chiefly responsible for the furor caused in academic
circles by the new poetry." But he, too, was indignant at her
high-handedness, yet had not the temerity to gainsay her. . . .

## I V

It was Amy's own delight in parody and masquerade that
made her publish *A Critical Fable* anonymously. But she did
more than that. To insure secrecy she misled almost everyone
concerned in the publication. Even if a literary detective had had
access to her publisher's files, he would have found that the author
was William Williams John—who happened to be the husband
of one of her secretaries. The work itself was a heterogeneous
picture-gallery of the leading living American poets, somewhat
in the manner of her distant dead relative, James Russell Lowell.
To increase the confusion Amy subtly and mendaciously spread
reports that various poets were responsible. She wrote blandly to
John Farrar, then editor of *The Bookman*, "Have you seen *A
Critical Fable?* I must say I find it immensely amusing in spite
of not particularly enjoying the part about myself. . . . I wonder who wrote it? Louis Untermeyer guessed me, and I guessed
him; and then we agreed to cry quits on the strength of each
other's denial and find a third person. Sara Teasdale says it is
Gamaliel Bradford; Gamaliel Bradford says it is Leonard Bacon;
who Leonard Bacon says I do not know. . . ."

From the beginning I was certain that Amy was the author,
partly because the critical estimates generally agreed with those
she had so often expressed, partly because of the hit-and-miss
rhythms and the wretched rhymes. I was not at all complimented
when Amy insisted that she recognized my touch throughout.

Purist that I was in the matter of rhyme, my teeth were continually set on edge by such awkward pairings as "grand-aren't," "absurdities-acerbities," "Piano-and so," "clearly-really," "Olympus-impasse," "goddess-progress," "parley-finale." Yet I could not help but be flattered by the pleasant pages she devoted to me in the volume, and her letter of disclaimer was as disarming as it was disingenuous. She wrote in part:

My dear Louis, You are mad if you think I wrote it; I wish to God I had. And permit me to offer my congratulations on your excellent *bluff!* From the first moment I opened the book, I said to myself: Louis is the *only* person who would have been likely to write this book—and now you hastily forestall me by suggesting that I have done it, which is one of the neatest little side-steppings I have ever seen. Oh, Louis, Louis! So you were not going to do that sort of thing again, weren't you. *Heavens* was to be your last skit! And all the time you had this up your sleeve. All I can say is I envy you in the way you have got us all off and the neatness of your versification. [*Sic! L. U.*] Oh, but don't I recognize that neatness: I chuckled again when I read your "Roast Leviathan." How anybody, after reading that poem, can think it was not written by the same man who wrote *A Critical Fable* I do not see. I think it is a bully book, and you have hit the people off wonderfully. If nothing else gave it away, your remarks about my "thunderous" quality would have done it.

By the time I had finished the letter and had received other congratulations (prompted by Amy) I was almost ready to believe that I *had* written the book. I was beginning to see new virtues in it; in another month I would have convinced myself that the rhymes were as daring as Emily Dickinson's. However, it never came to that. Amy could never keep a secret from her public; she enjoyed herself—and her public—too much.

I will never forget the pleasure she took in one of the most curious public functions I have ever attended. It was a Civic Forum dinner given at the Hotel Astor for a group of poets. Ten of us were guests of honor—three English and seven American poets—and its chief reason was a hail-and-farewell to John Masefield, who had been in America as "an ambassador of good will." I was seated at the speaker's table between Amy and a tall southerner whose name I had not caught.

"But we have met," he said. "Not in the flesh, but in the newspaper columns—in one of your reviews."

"That's gratifying," I smiled. "I hope I said something more than ordinarily pleasant."

"On the contrary," he replied without a smile. "You were extraordinarily *un*pleasant. You began your attack with the title of your review and ended it with a gratuitous insult. You quoted my worst lines, including the typographical errors, and you turned my most serious phrases into shoddy flippancies. You ridiculed my tragedies; you—"

"There is only one living poet I ever treated like that," I interrupted, still trying to hold a smile. "And that was—years ago —Cale Young Rice."

"I," he echoed grimly, "am Cale Young Rice."

Since, at that time, the Hotel Astor did not offer alcoholic comfort, I spent the rest of the dinner talking to Amy Lowell. At the end of it she said, "Louis, I've never heard you talk so much and so badly. I haven't the faintest idea what you've been saying— and I don't think you have either."

It was not only my discomfiture she enjoyed, but her eminence. Each of the guests of honor read, spoke, or mumbled. Next to Masefield, Amy received the most applause. But she raised her hand and asked them to stop. "Just to make me feel at home," she said, "please add a few hisses. I'm not used to speaking without them." Later, when she attacked some of the enshrined poets of the past, the hissing was renewed—and this time the audience meant it.

(A newspaper cut is before me as I write. There we are: "American Poets Gathered at Farewell Dinner." Amy is in the center, seated on a Louis Quinze couch much too frail for her. She is clad in a magnificently unbecoming dress with half-length sleeves and a yoke calculated to increase her width, strewn with a maze of gold beadwork. She is clutching a purse and a program, her head cocked, daring the world to come to blows. Seated next to her is the only other woman; birdlike, bright-eyed Josephine Dodge Daskam Bacon, with the smile of a canary that has just swallowed the cat. The rest of us are grouped about Amy. Reading from the traditional left to right, they are Laurence Housman, brother of A. E. Housman, bearded, dark-browed, staring into eternity like a bashful, even a benevolent, Mephistopheles; Witter Bynner, tall, immaculate, and aloof; Percy MacKaye, his arm about Bynner's shoulder, smiling archly at the camera; Edwin Markham, looking like a slightly blurred composite photograph of four Hebrew prophets and all the New England poets; Cale Young Rice, trying to forget he was the husband of *Mrs. Wiggs of the Cabbage Patch;* I, a cross between a frightened rabbit and a complacent anteater; Vachel Lindsay, his head tilted back dangerously as though he were about to explode in a chant; Alfred Noyes, doggedly facing his inquisitors and desperately clutching one of his own books; and John Masefield, quizzical and vague, like a benign but slightly befuddled leprechaun.)

## V

In 1920 . . . I was living in Vienna, and Amy was deep in her Keats biography: "Keats is nearly killing me. I have completed six hundred and thirty pages and have three hundred and seventy left to do. I think I shall never want to undertake so long a job again."

The last sentence was prophetic. If Keats was killed by the critics, Amy, by the same exaggeration, was killed by Keats. She had been a sick woman for more than ten years; her first letter to me in 1915 ends: "Do try and get here as early as possible before they have quite minced me to pieces and swept me up in the dustpan." Her labors on the Keats material, of which she owned one of the largest collections in existence, and the almost vituperative English reviews, aggravated her ailment. She was as unaffectedly in love with Keats as Elinor Wylie was with Shelley; and when such presumably friendly critics as J. C. Squire and Robert Lynd questioned her conclusions, they seemed to be suddenly striking at her and exposing a wound so vulnerable as to be vital. For Keats she spent interminable nights puzzling over his manuscripts, tracking down his annotations, and retracing the worn pencil-scrawls; for Keats she suffered uncounted pains in head and groin and ruptured the small blood-vessels of her eyes. Into the dead poet she poured her life-blood, and after the transfusion she died.

Perhaps this is not altogether exact. She also poured her life-blood into her poetry; her vivacity invigorated it, her gusty personality gave it color and warmth. After her death the blood went out of it. The color seemed superficially applied, the warmth simulated; with the exception of some seven or eight poems the verse was suddenly lifeless. Robert Frost once said that she never touched the deep emotions because she did not know where to look for them, and D. H. Lawrence wrote, "If it doesn't come out of your own heart, real Amy Lowell, it is no good, however many colors it may have. . . . How much nicer, finer, bigger you are, intrinsically, than your poetry is."

This much seems apparent: Amy too often wrote to fit a theory, to mold her work in the fashion of the moment; she cast herself in the rôle of public poet. Instead of being urged by the quiet subconscious self, she continually prodded the conscious will. She sacrificed a slow searching for quick brilliance, and exchanged a broad understanding for narrow contemporaneousness. Her amazing range of subject and variety of techniques—the adaptations of Indian folklore, extensions of Peruvian myths, translations from the French, melodramas in New England dialect, verbal imitations of Stravinsky, Japanese lacquer prints, Chinese legends, exotic impressionism, homespun couplets —no longer hide the central poverty. She had energy, enthusiasm, power, skill, "everything," as one poet, paraphrasing Goethe, said of her, "everything except genius." It might be truer to say that she had genius—genius for everything except the thing she wanted most: permanence as a poet. Yet how could she have attained it? She had many pleasures, few ecstasies; she wept because of little griefs, never touched by immedicable woes. "It is hard," Malcolm Cowley wrote, "to write true poems when one is rich, blanketed with four-percent debentures and rocked to sleep in a cradle of sound common stocks."

She died an isolated patrician, antagonistic to radicals, suspicious of liberals, and scornful of "the ignorant proletariat." It sometimes seems a pity she determined to be a poet at all; she would have been so much happier as the Senator from Massachusetts.

Her poems, shrunk to a repeated few, still find their way into the anthologies. But her memorial is the collection she bequeathed to the Widener Library at Harvard. The Poetry Room contains not only her invaluable Keats letters, rare manuscripts, first drafts and first editions, but holograph manuscripts and volumes by almost every modern poet, a record of private influence and public accomplishment. Here is Amy's great mausoleum, a library, once the setting for what seemed the controversial battles of the century.

Several years after her death I stood there, in the Poetry Room of the Harvard College Library, waiting for her ghost. Except for the pale young custodian and myself, the room was empty. It remained unvisited during the time I rummaged about the unresponsive shelves and investigated the sacred vault. Not a sound penetrated, not a specter raised its reminiscent head. After an hour of silent loneliness I thought I detected a murmur. I was not wrong. The murmur grew to a hum, a rumble, a roar. The undergraduates were now underneath the window, loudly returning from the stadium. They went by, and the room was quieter than ever. The shadows did not stir. Even the past refused to speak.

# ROLLO WALTER BROWN

IT is no slight achievement for an American writer to have stood firmly and unsentimentally for dignity, good taste, and honest workmanship in life and in art amid the chaotic standards and indifferent rewards of our century. Yet this is one of the distinctions of Rollo Walter Brown, both as teacher, lecturer, and writer. Born the son of a potter in the hill-town of Crooksville, Ohio, in 1880, he went to Ohio Northern and Harvard Universities, became Professor of Rhetoric and Composition at Wabash College (1905-20) and Carleton College (1920-23), then Lecturer in English at Harvard (1923-24), where he did his last formal teaching. Meanwhile, by his books, *The Art of Writing English* (1913), *How the French Boy Learns to Write* (1915), and *The Writer's Art* (1921), he carried his sound instruction far afield.

Confident that he could employ his talents to greater advantage outside the classroom, Mr. Brown resigned his post and wrote a series of influential magazine articles later collected in *The Creative Spirit, An Inquiry into American Life* (1925). The next year he published his first biography, *Dean Briggs,* a full-length portrait of a famous and beloved teacher. (*On Writing the Biography of a Modest Man* describes the amusing difficulties in its preparation.) As a summer resident in the MacDowell Colony at Peterborough, New Hampshire, Brown formed an intimate friendship with Edwin Arlington Robinson, illuminatingly reported in a small volume called *Next Door to a Poet.* Besides a sequence of four novels dealing with the struggle of the creative spirit for expression in America, a book of penetrating observations entitled *I Travel by Train* (1939) further attests his deep understanding of this country.

*Lonely Americans* (1929), from which the following sketch is taken, supplies varied examples of the integral man at work. "It isolates one anywhere to think beyond a certain point," quotes Mr. Brown for his text. In a nation where democracy has too often exerted a leveling effect upon culture, this isolation has never been popular. The eight "individualists" singled out in this book—C. W. Eliot, Whistler, Edward MacDowell, George Bellows, C. E. Norton, Raphael Pumpelly, Emily Dickinson, Lincoln—all extended the reach of culture at the cost of living intellectually alone. All these lives show the strain of that "dynamic tension" which Mr. Brown looks for in selecting his subjects, and with all of them he has found himself in that "fundamental sympathy" without which the biographer's reactions can be only negative and his real findings correspondingly meager.

In the sketch of George Bellows (1882-1925) Mr. Brown characteristically combines portraiture and narrative. Unlike Gamaliel Bradford, who keeps his "victim" suspended in time while he examines him from all angles, producing a static portrait so far as chronology is concerned, Rollo Walter Brown tries to keep walking round and round the subject as he moves forward through his life. In structure the piece is well-proportioned, natural, and dynamic. In tone and style it is sympathetic without idolatry, realistic without irony, graphic without a play to the gallery. Nothing would have been easier than to throw sensational lights and shadows upon the figure of this painter who himself saw life in dramatic terms. Mr. Brown, in sincere and readable prose, makes us see the steady, purposeful artist as the public and even his friends rarely saw him. One of the first Americans outside the profession to recognize the importance of George Bellows's work, he was also the first to inquire deeply into the hidden springs of his power. The author's appreciation suffuses the whole sketch; his wide research lies artfully concealed.

# AN ADVENTURER OUT OF THE WEST

GEORGE BELLOWS's short life was a joyous, unaccompanied pursuit. He looked about on the face of the earth and said: "Not so bad—as raw material. I wonder what it would all mean if you could get it straightened out so you could see it. And I wonder what it could be made to look like to anybody else." Before the bright terrestrial flash should pass he meant to explore as far as possible. There was not much to guide one. Why not inform oneself and act as one's own guide? Why not? He had all the capacities of a "lone wolf."

In trying to understand what he was about, his family, his friends, and the public were always a step or two behind; in trying to anticipate the direction of his next move, they were always wrong. His mother early dreamed that her slender, light-haired son would become a bishop. Every Sunday morning he was hauled to church in the high-wheeled surrey in the hope that his pushing young spirit would be impressed with the solemnity of mortal existence. Charley, a boy indentured by the family, had been so tremendously impressed that he decided to become an undertaker. In the back yard, in Columbus, Ohio, he fenced off a miniature cemetery and began with great enthusiasm to conduct funerals and inter remains. But George Bellows was interested only aesthetically: he made the designs for the tombstones that Charley erected. And as for the bishopric, the nearest he ever came to it was singing in a church choir—which is not necessarily a close approach. His father saw, evidently, that the bishopric was too far a reach. He proposed that his son become a banker. It would afford him an infinite peace in his last years to see this exploring son intrenched in an occupation of such solid respectability. But George said: "I don't want to be a banker. I'm going to Ohio State. I believe I can 'make' the baseball team."

In college he was a sprawling young barbarian very much concerned with finding something to do. When he reported for baseball and the coaches and fans said, "He looks like an outfielder," he replied: "Oh, no; I'm a shortstop." And, despite the fact that shortstops are usually not six feet two inches tall, he went daily with a team-mate and practiced throwing to first base from every position on his side of the infield until he was accepted generally as the greatest shortstop that had ever played on an Ohio State team. He played basket-ball too, and he sang in the glee club. Still there was energy left. So when his fellows had played or sung until they were exhausted and begged for sleep, he devised ingenious means of keeping them awake. But still there was energy left. So he made cartoons of his professors.

The newspapers were full of comment on this boisterous, good-natured athlete. Fellow collegians and fellow townsmen said he was good enough for the big leagues. "Of course you will go into professional baseball." But he amazed them by replying: "Hu-uh! I'm going to be an artist."

"Whew!" was all they could say; and they said that under their breath.

It had never occurred to him that there might be any doubt about his qualifications as an artist. He had begun the fundamentals early. In the rigid Methodist days of his childhood he had been permitted two activities on Sunday—reading and drawing. Since his mother always delighted in reading to him, he could draw undisturbed while he listened! That meant that he drew all the time on Sunday afternoons. This experience—and he always thought it had much to do in determining his career— enabled him to draw better than any of his fellow pupils in school. He was known as "the artist." In college he illustrated undergraduate publications. Professor "Joey" Taylor, sympathetic confessor for all brave spirits at Ohio State, encouraged him to believe that his ability was important. But in New York he encountered people who were not so sure. He came from way out in Columbus, Ohio, did he not, or some other unheard-of place? What did anybody know about art out there?

He met one teacher, however, who immediately supported his confidence in himself—Robert Henri. Henri had come from the Middle West himself, and he liked this stalwart chap with the intent face and the healthy will. A pupil who was always gay, always full of deviltry, yet always serious about the business of painting, was not to be found in the New York School of Art every day. From every word his original-minded teacher uttered, from every movement he made, from every criticism he offered, Bellows learned with white-hot mind. Henri never criticized anyone else so severely. He knew Bellows could stand what would crush others. But he also encouraged him. "You will succeed," he assured him; "some degree of success is certain. The quality of your success will depend upon the personal development you make." So, after all, maybe he might paint just as good a picture as anybody!

His fellow students looked upon him with inquiring, amused eyes. He was so little acquainted with the life of New York that the only social organization he knew when he arrived was the Y.M.C.A. It maintained a swimming-pool and a basket-ball floor, and he knew how to use both. In appearance nothing marked him as a devotee of the aesthetic. He was self-conscious in the presence of so many artistic strangers; he sprawled—there was so much of him that it was difficult to be graceful except when standing up; and he laughed with such untrammeled heartiness that everyone turned and stared at him whenever anything set him going. But how much did he care? Perhaps, if he only knew the truth, they were all just as raw as he was. Maybe they didn't know half as much about painting! Certainly they didn't know one-tenth as much about it as he meant to know some day.

No one could deny that he was interesting. His fellow students soon became busy in trying to make him out. His clumsy externals could not prevent them from seeing his essential good nature, his essential dignity of spirit, and his sound emotional and intellectual power. They liked especially his glowing vigor. When the school had its first dance of the year he took a very beautiful Scandinavian girl—from Minnesota. His friends stood in wonder at the magnificence of this light-haired couple. "Wouldn't they make a prize-winning bride and groom?" everyone asked. But when the whisperings came to Bellows he exclaimed: "Oh, no! You are absolutely wrong! I'm going to marry that dark-haired girl from Upper Montclair!"

This girl from Upper Montclair, Miss Emma Louise Story, out of sheer pity for an overgrown boy who was spending his long Christmas vacation away from home, invited him to come to her father's house for a meal. "The steak," she assured her mother, "must be the biggest one you can find; for I never saw such an eater as he is." But George was so nervous he could not handle the silverware, much less eat. His embarrassment was increased, too, by the young lady's father. He did not care much for male artists. He had known one, a man who could paint a feather so perfectly that you couldn't tell it from the real thing; but, apart from being able to do that, he did not count for much. This feeling against artists was accentuated, too, when George Bellows began to appear on the landscape with a degree of regularity. But George was ready to contest with the father as well as with the hesitant daughter. What does a little matter of waiting around for six years amount to?

All the while he was painting, painting with unequaled persistence. "No time to waste! No time to waste!" One day John W. Alexander went home from his duties as a juror in the National Academy's annual exhibit and said to his wife: "There's a picture over there, by a young fellow named Bellows, from out West somewhere—'Forty-Two Kids' he calls it—that you must see. There's genius in it." Others saw it and were startled. "But," some of them asked, "is it an artistic subject? Do such things as boys in swimming lend themselves to artistic treatment?" "Why not?" Bellows asked in reply, and went on painting. He painted the river front, the prize-ring, the crowd in the steaming street, the city cliff-dwellers, the circus, the stevedores on the docks. All the things possessing everyday dignity and significance but long treated with disdain, all the unglorified struggle of his kind, cried to him for expression. The uncomprehending dismissed it as wild art, decadent art, drab art! They declared that Billy Sunday had broken into the aesthetic world. Those who were more sympathetic said: "Now we are getting him. He believes in painting the red-blooded American life. He is the painter with the punch!"

So he was hailed as the artist who made things anybody would understand; so, too, was he as completely misunderstood as ever. For if he was the painter of the vigorous, the physically dramatic, he was to be even more the painter of the subtle and the intimate. If he could produce "Sharkey's," he could also produce "Spring, Gramercy Park"; "Blue Snow, the Battery"; "Crehaven"; "Aunt Fanny"; "Portrait of My Mother"; "Emma in Purple Dress"; "Anne in White"; "Lady Jean"; "Portrait of Katherine Rosen"; "Eleanor, Jean, and Anna."

His diversity had kept the public guessing, yet he did not find enough in the entire range of painting to keep his own mind busy. It is not so easy to paint in New York in the dead of winter. Inasmuch as he liked black and white and enjoyed working on stone, he took up lithography. "But what are you doing that for?" his admirers asked. "Who cares anything about lithography in these days? If you want to work in black and white you ought to etch."

"But I can't etch," he insisted, "and I can make lithographs."

"But don't you wish to sell your work?" dealers protested. "There is no demand for lithographs."

"Then," he replied with characteristic braggadocio, "we'll put lithographs on the map!"

And he did. The first prints attracted favorable attention. One of his intimates counseled him: "You had better slip one or two proofs of each stone away and keep them awhile. The price

might go up; you might make some money." He took the advice
and he and his wife had much amusement over the fund they
were going to develop for the college education of Anne and
Jean. They never dreamed that the day would come when some
of these prints would sell for a thousand or twelve hundred dollars apiece.

In lithography he found just the right opportunity to round
out his record of America's emotional life. The stone served perfectly for many brief chapters that did not readily admit of treatment in color: "Village Prayer-Meeting"; "Initiation in the Frat";
"Benediction in Georgia"; "The Shower-Bath"; "Dance in a
Mad-House"; "Old Billiard-Player"; "The Law Is Too Slow";
"Billy Sunday"; "Sixteen East Gay Street"; "Dempsey and
Firpo"; "Business Men's Class, Y.M.C.A."; "Electrocution." In
lithography, too, he could laugh as much as he liked. His "Re-
ducing," the representation of a meek-looking husband calmly
asleep in bed, and his very stout wife flat on her back on the floor
doing some very energetic exercises, will be amusing as long as
there are fat women of social importance in the world. A very
stout woman, one day after Bellows had become somewhat the
vogue among those who interest themselves in art socially, entered a museum and asked what there was new to be seen. She
was told that yonder was a new lithograph by George Bellows.
"Oh, how lovely!" she exclaimed, bringing her lorgnette to bear
upon it as she moved nearer. "What is it, a shell?" When she
saw, she was scandalized, and turned away with disgust that could
be expressed only in a violent crescendo of "Pooh! Pooh!!
Pooh!!!"

"Now we have him at last," the public said, after his lithographs had become current. "He gives us life just as he sees it.
He has ability—great ability perhaps—but he lacks the imagination
to make anything wholly new from simple elements. He cannot
express himself in the symbolic." Then he produced "Edith
Cavell," and later "Allan Donn Puts to Sea"; "The Return to
Life"; "Amour"; "Punchinello in the House of Death"; and "The
Crucifixion." In truth, he began to reveal so much interest in
such subjects that some of his contemporaries were disturbed.

Joseph Pennell, known for his ability in combat as well as for his ability as an artist, on one occasion at the National Arts Club enlarged upon the dangers of painting when one has not the object before one at the time. "George Bellows," he went on to say, "would have made a better painting of Edith Cavell if he had been on the spot and seen with his own eyes. He was not there, certainly." When he had finished, Bellows was asked to discuss the point. In proceeding he said: "No, I was not present at the execution of Edith Cavell. I had just as good a chance to get a ticket as Leonardo had to get one for the Last Supper!"

## II

When a man of such capacity to go his own way emerges from surroundings where he might little be expected to appear, he soon becomes a legend. Everybody wants to know about him. Few had learned about the personal George Bellows. He had not been seen much either in high places or in Bohemia; he had been too busy. But when people did see him, unless they came to know him intimately, they were as much mystified as ever. He did not conform to their notions of a great artist. He was only one of those typical Americans whom Americans are always talking about but rarely see. When they do see one, they have difficulty in believing their own eyes; he seems too good to be true.

Most of those magnified American qualities whose names have been outworn, but whose essences have not, he possessed. For instance, he was full of the American's gusto. He was unafraid to like things. Wherever he went everything was interesting and moving. Life was full of emotions to which he would give organized expression, architectonic integrity. The spectacle of New York—the Hudson, the East Side, the Battery, the parks—filled him with such enthusiasm that he confessed great difficulty in stopping long enough to paint what he saw. Columbus, Ohio, was just as interesting; people back there were bully, even if he did sometimes laugh in their faces. The spectacle that men make for themselves was fascinating, too. When he went to the theater—and he went often—he laughed with such unrestrained and honest joy that he heartened not only the audience but the actors. "Can't you see anything interesting?" he asked somewhat impatiently. The soporific "pure art" that the disillusioned and the burnt-out produce in an effort to "escape" something or other did not concern him. His times were overwhelming in their possibilities. He had fun in finding what seemed most significant, and he had greater, agonizing fun in struggling to expression. When one of his most brilliant portraits had been placed on exhibition with a note in the catalogue implying that it had been painted as a commission, he corrected the error by writing: "Painted for fun." He liked the world. He liked his friends. He liked himself pretty well, thank you, and his own work. And he liked good work done by others. No one ever joined the procession of honor with more enthusiasm than he did when he discovered genius in the work of somebody else.

American, too, was his zeal as a crusader. He was always fighting for causes. "I am a patriot for beauty. I would enlist in an army to make the world more beautiful. I would go to war for an ideal—far more easily than I could for a country." *The Masses*, a journal which Bellows had hoped might do something for the people to whom it was addressed, slowly deteriorated, and he drew up a complete program for its rejuvenation—and supported his contentions vigorously. Convinced that the jury system employed by the National Academy for selecting pictures for the annual exhibit was unfair to the young variants who did work of marked individuality, he waged war—a long and hot war—against the majority system of selection. "The iconoclasts among us, and I count myself one," had many changes to propose that would give the unlabeled man a better chance to have his work seen. And he was interested in international good will. Despite the fact that from the beginning to the end of his life he never left his own shores to visit another country, he dreamed of universal friendship. Especially did he wish to have his own country and France understand each other. One of the great enthusiasms of his life was the promotion of an American exhibition for the Luxembourg at the time of the World War.

There were, too, less agreeable matters that called for the crusader. The editor of an art journal undertook to have artists pay for his news notes about them and for the space that he proposed to devote to reproductions of their work. George Bellows wrote to the editor that he had always supposed news notes and reproductions were published because they were of public interest, and not because they were paid for as advertising. He would not lend himself to any such graft. The editor attempted to justify himself by saying that since every artist would buy space, there would be in the end a right comparative representation. Bellows asked what was going to happen to the good artist who chanced not to have money with which to buy news about himself, and proceeded to wage the most extensive war possible upon the editor and his practices. There was always something to fight for —or against!

He had the crusader's faith, too. Things might be bad enough— he sometimes declared that conditions were "rotten"—but they could be made better. "It is not because America has great wealth, great opportunities," he said, "and what is blandly termed 'great educational facilities' that she has any claim to the attention of the world's culture. It must some day be because of the fact that, among the vast sum of her population, there appears now and then a man who can create things of wonder and beauty." To this end something might be done. He did not, he protested, expect Mayor Hylan to proclaim a holiday when Glackens produced such a masterpiece as his "Portrait of Walter Hampden." Yet why should not an artist's neighbors in general be led to see their own need of art with such burning clearness that they would be moved to provide the artist with a normal, legitimate, economic support? "A great artist," he was accustomed to say, "can exist in a country which buys bad art; his situation is more difficult in a country which buys none." Nor need the public fear to buy the work of American artists. When the citizens of our own country free themselves from traditional prejudices and are able to exercise their own sense of delight, their own judgment, they will see how distinguished much American painting is. "It is not necessarily ridiculous to have faith. It is, however, very important to have it. Among some of our artists some time the great genius of America will arise. Some of him is probably here now. Look!"

American also was his feeling that he was just as good as the other fellow—at least. He never felt inferior; in fact, he liked the center of the stage. He was a brother to a certain manner of American soldier, who boasts before a battle that he will do thus and so, and then makes good his boast. He was not awed by sophistication; he could always match it with homely wisdom. He would pit himself against the most skillful, the most argumentative, and enjoy the experience. From the Catskills he wrote: "I have called it a summer, taken stock, showed the work to everybody, and am ready to pack up, go to New York, and start arguing with Pennell." And his feeling of equality or better he maintained in the presence of the most experienced, most "authoritative" art critics. Instead of waging a defensive war, as Whistler so often did, or suffering unspeakable agony, as Edward MacDowell did when assailed by the unintelligent, Bellows smoked the matter over a little, took his sturdy pen in hand, invited the critic to draw and paint awhile in order to discover how much he did not know, and told him to go to hell. "So that's that. I've got to paint."

In keeping with the great American legend, too, he was a family man. He gave the best of himself—his ability, his good humor, his boyish fun, his profound affection—to his kin. His father, an "Amen Methodist," was fifty-five years old when George was born. He was unapproachable on many matters close to a boy's heart. Yet George loved him while he stood in awe of him. "By charging less than he was worth," he once wrote of his father, an architect and builder, "and by investing in worthy causes, his fortune remained reasonably easy to calculate. He planned for me to become president of a bank. He had, however, the greatest respect for Michael Angelo, holding him second to no man with the exception of Moses. His main feeling seemed to be sorrow for the hard life I would be forced to lead as an artist in this generation. In this, owing greatly to his own support, he guessed wrong."

With his father it was not easy to be whimsical. But he could be with his mother. With her he could play the clown and the

tease as much as he liked. He never ceased to chide her about his
poor bringing-up, to make pseudo-sacrilegious remarks about the
things she held sacred, to enlarge upon her son's financial plight,
or to be shocked by the great range of vices that her Methodism
permitted.

> "*Dear Ma:*
>     '*The melancholy days are come,*
>     *The saddest of the year,*'
>     *When the sluice gates of the pocketbook*
>     *Are opened from the rear.*"

Or:

    "And what is the name of the new pastor?
    "And does he Chew?"
    "Now, now, now, don't be angry. Don't you remember Dr.
Smith?
    "Have you been flinching from Dominoes or dominoing from
Flinch?
    "Answer yes or no."

And who ever had such a wife and such daughters? Emma,
whom he had won after six years of the most studious persistence! With all of his uproarious nonsense, he could never be
wholly nonsensical about Emma. He loved her too passionately,
too profoundly. And there were "the kids—Anne the slim and
Jean the bean." He romped with them; he devised and wore the
most astounding costumes to startle and delight them; he gave
them the liberty of the studio while he worked; he wrote them
letters in verse—good enough to be published; he dreamed of
them; and he painted them in the best pictures he ever made.

And when the lean years were over and he seemed to have a
long stretch of full ones ahead, he began to express his affection
for his kin in new ways. To Aunt Fanny—the Aunt Fanny of the
portrait, and the Eleanor of the "Eleanor, Jean and Anna"—he
always felt especially attracted. She had helped to look after him
when he was very small, and had kept him immaculately combed
up and clean; and she had experienced the great romance of refus-

ing twice to marry the man who loved her, and then accepting him the third time! But her possessions were few and her pride great. So when he once invited her to come to the Catskills for a visit, and received no reply, he suspected the reason. In the course of a shrewdly tactful letter, he wrote:

"I am aware, my dear Aunt Fanny, that you have not been blessed with the best of luck. I have. Therefore, I think it would be a nice idea to try and strike something like a mean proportion.

"I have what I think is a well-grounded belief that both you and your daughter Laura would welcome a vacation from the same scene—if you are anything like me. I must change around a bit.

"Further than this, I want to feel that you are not needing to worry about the future. As the chances are that it would not be a very available plan to leave you something in my will, I think I will leave you something right away. My mother is going to do exactly what I am proposing for myself, and between us you are to have a regular income of a thousand a year, which added to what income you have of your own, should make the days comfortable."

Then, after a description of his country place, and the information that the round-trip tickets and money for incidentals were on the way, he added the clinching postscript that he had chosen his picture of her to represent him in "the great exhibition in the Luxembourg, Paris."

He met the requirements of the national legend, finally, by combining a homely exterior with an essential refinement. He was tall, he was ungainly in some of his movements, and early he became bald. In addition, he was a believer in the informal. As a result, he looked much of the time like a plumber. Always he was making something at his work-bench on the mezzanine floor of his studio. He must have at hand every conceivable kind of nail and screw and bolt. For these he went to a neighboring hardware-store, where the salesmen liked him so much that they proudly kept the newspaper reproductions of pictures made by this customer who knew the names and sizes of nails as if he might be a person of solid character. In the country he plunged into every kind of manual labor. When his new house was ready for the roof he went to work on it. "Why don't you hire a man to do it?" his wife protested. "Can't ask anybody else to do what I'm afraid to do myself." But sitting on an unroofed house in the summer sun is not the easiest of chores. His untoughened body became so sore that he could scarcely proceed. But he stuffed a pillow into his overalls and worked valiantly, painfully on, until he had driven the last nail in the last shingle.

In general, strangers gained the impression that he was uncouth. When he was not sprawling, he was rocking. He brought from the Middle West the rocking-chair state of mind. So, whenever there was nothing else to do, he rocked—energetically, obliviously. Sometimes one of his intimates, who confessed that he loved the man more than a brother, would command: "You stop that rocking!" He would stop for a time. But as soon as the conversation or the meditation became absorbing again he fell into his rolling, swaying pace.

Yet in all matters of the spirit he was one of the most sensitive of men. He could not endure any music short of the best; he refused to listen to it even when played by Emma! He read not only great books, but books which require unusual refinement of intellect and feeling in the reader. Plays, too, must have quality. And his friends had to come up to the same requirements as his plays and books and music. When someone criticized him for having only friends of intellectual or artistic brilliance, he retorted: "What do you suppose I have friends for—to be bored by them?" His handwriting was that of a crude country boy, and he did not always spell according to the dictionary; yet he possessed a startling sense of fitness in words, a feeling for the rhythmical power in a sentence, and a perfect intuition for the total effect that a paragraph or a letter would produce.

### III

Now a man with such an array of traditional American qualities would excite wonder—if not skepticism—wherever he chanced to appear. But the wonder was almost inexpressibly great when he chanced to appear in the world of art. Questioned concerning the peculiar artistic circumstances in which he arose, he replied jovially: "I arose surrounded by Methodists and Republicans!" And what he humorously implied was literally true: almost everything surrounding his early life, viewed in the obvious manner, was non-artistic.

Yet it is just because his individuality came from such an environment that he was able to make his greatest contribution to art. The tendency of art when it is wholly in the hands of organizations devoted to its perpetuation is to become ascetic, over-refined, "arty." American art schools for some decades have been filled, in the main, with young ladies who develop a technique for doing nothing in particular with great skill. If art is not to become drivel, there must constantly be injected into it some of the life of the soil, something that corresponds to the uncultivated health of a robust body. It requires a cross-fertilization of sanity from "the provinces." Somebody must occasionally give to it a strain of life comparable to what Abraham Lincoln gave to politics. It was this fresh life, this instinctive feeling for a healthy relation, that Bellows brought to art. He was unalterably a lone wolf. If somebody who professed to be very wise said in patronizing fashion, "Now that is the way artists do that," Bellows was certain to reply: "Well, hold on! Let's take a look. I don't know whether it is or not!" Not that he had any closed system of his own! "He was the readiest man in the world to have you prove that you were right," said the person who was the greatest single influence in his life as a painter; "but you had to prove it. He always brought himself to his work." This habit of bringing himself to his work was what led many to call him a revolutionist. "If I am," he said, "I don't know it. First of all, I am a painter, and a painter gets hold of life—gets hold of something real, of many real things. That makes him think, and if he thinks out loud he is called a revolutionist. I guess that is about the size of the matter." The reasonable thing to do, he contended, was to "watch all good art and accept none as a standard for yourself. Think with all the world and work alone."

Many, in attempting to evaluate his contribution, have compared him with Kipling, with Jack London, with Whitman. In each comparison there is a certain soundness. But he had more warmth, more fluidity, than Kipling; and he was more comprehensive in his sympathies, more healthy in his vigor, than Jack London. The parallel with Whitman is closest. Both were impatient with outworn forms and outworn subjects; both felt the energy of American life and were able to express it; both believed in the sacredness of the individual and hesitated not to take pride in themselves; and both believed that the artist should celebrate all life, whether "beautiful" or not, that reveals significance.

But Bellows was a more complete person than Whitman, a more representative person. Whitman was, with all of his democracy, an exotic democrat. He was an exotic American. He was not himself representative; he only wrote about representative things. He was, moreover, in his sympathies a remote pagan, and George Bellows was close and warm and reverential. Bellows might easily have painted something comparable to "The City Dead House," "By the Bivouac's Fitful Flame," "O Captain, My Captain," or "With Husky Haughty Lips, O Sea," but if Whitman had tried for a lifetime, he never would have written anything having the emotional tone of "Aunt Fanny," "Emma and Her Children," or "Lady Jean."

But any attempt to compare Bellows with somebody else must always be for convenience of discussion merely. The comparisons always turn out to be contrasts. He was made in his own proportions of vigor, understanding, dramatic power, humor, intimacy; and he had his own methods of supplanting the malarial sentimentality of American art with a robust sentiment.

# I V

Nothing in anybody's effort to "place" him in the world of art, nothing in the solid fame that yearly became more solid, ever lured him away from the great pursuit. He meant to attain a perfection that Columbus, Ohio, and New York City had little dreamed about. He wanted to learn just because he wanted to learn. He was ready, too, to learn from anybody—from the ancient masters, from the most youthful of his artistic contemporaries, from the philosopher, from the fool. If he discovered some day that he was securing an effect as Tintoretto had secured it, he must write to his friends about the whole matter with boyish delight. If a new exhibition, a new school, or a new process was announced, he had to look into it at once to see if there were not something to learn. Such a possibility he approached with sublime expectancy. After he had gone through a new exhibition with alertness, he would say, "Nothing here I have not already learned"; or, "I mean to work until I can finish a canvas as perfectly as that myself." He was enthusiastic over the appearance of Jay Hambidge's *Dynamic Symmetry*, and later made frequent acknowledgment of his indebtedness to the volume. He was just as enthusiastic over new possibilities in color. If he applied himself to his painting until he grew stale and was unable to make progress, he did not try to sink into a restful stupor, but went to Brentano's, bought an armload of good solid reading, and buried himself from the world until he felt restored. "Can't paint if I don't feed my mind!"

By the time he had carried on his pursuit until he was forty, he had become the enriched person that must go into the making of a great artist. He was a philosopher, wise in his own increasing humility. "Try it in every possible way," he once told some art students. "Be deliberate—and spontaneous. Be thoughtful and painstaking. Be abandoned and impulsive. Learn your own possibilities. There is no impetus I have not followed, no method of technique I am unwilling to try. There is nothing I do not want to know that has to do with life or art." He was no longer—if he ever had been—a good-natured barbarian who had hit upon good painting and good lithography, but a man who had some coherent notions of the ways of men and artists. "Art isn't made in Bohemia, neither is it not made in Bohemia. It is wherever life exists and expresses dignity, humor, humanity, kindness, order." He quoted with approbation the words of Robert Henri: "To hold the spirit of greatness is in my mind what the world was created for—and art is great as it translates and embodies that spirit."

More and more he became impatient of mere formalities. "The Independent show this year is a hummer," he wrote in a letter. "The only stalling was on this damned dance which none of us want to go to. *And will not!*" What he wanted was a day that would give him a chance to work his head off, sometimes on a new canvas, often enough on one that he had kept about for months or years. In 1920 he wrote to a friend: "Have three fine portraits of Anne, Jean, and Emma, with no heads on any." Three years later the satisfying head was still not on Emma. After repeated attempts at it, he had her sit for him again one morning in the country. "Can't do it! Give it up! Go on!" he cried. But before she got away he called: "Come back here! Let me try just once more!" And in an hour the head that has been so widely praised for just the right reflective attitude was completed.

When he had worked himself to exhaustion he would call up one of his friends: "Hello! Is this Frans Hals?"

"Why, yes, Michael Angelo!"

"Well, how about a game of pool?" Or, if possible, baseball or tennis; he was not enough of a loafer to master pool.

Then dinner and music, or the theater, or some hours over a new lithograph, if he chanced to be in the city. Sometimes he worked on his lithographs till two in the morning, up on the mezzanine floor of his studio. That was the life!

There was ever a little crusading to do, too. Less than a year before the brief, agonizing days in the hospital that brought all to an end, the editor of a journal cut shamefully an illustration that Bellows had made under contract. "Result," he wrote, "the most awful botch imaginable. Emma has ordered me to war. I have gone. After two letters, very well done, not a glimmer of guilt from the editor. So I have started a legal attack—I expect to lose money, but I hope to line up the art world and get some kind of protection against the arbitrary changing of artists' work."

But nothing could permanently ruffle him. He was still the boisterous adventurer. The night before he was stricken with appendicitis—and he was only forty-two—Robert Henri had a number of friends in for the evening. They were the group that Bellows called "The Society of Perfect Wives and Husbands." As usual, he was much in the center of the stage. He found some old clothes and made himself up as Queen Victoria. Either because his friends were in special need of amusement or because he was in very high spirits, he never seemed such a perfect clown. The evening lasted until one or two o'clock. When the guests departed they descended from the studio—on the third floor—together. In the quiet that followed, the host stood by the window looking reflectively out. Below in the street there was a burst of laughter—genuine, honest, infectious laughter. It was George Bellows moving off into the night.

# GAMALIEL BRADFORD

THE success that some men without genius win from long, continual, systematic, and indomitable effort in one spot on a single, well-defined task could not be better exemplified than by Gamaliel Bradford. He was born in Boston in 1863 of a well-to-do family and of strong New England literary and historical antecedents. He attended the public schools, fell very early in love with books, and enjoyed as a boy many rich intellectual contacts with the elder generation of scholars and philosophers of that "Athens of America." At fifteen, threatened by tuberculosis, he spent a year in Europe. The sojourn did not restore his health, but it stimulated a lifelong devotion to languages that opened up to him a familiar converse with the Greek and Latin classics and with the great minds of France, Germany, Spain, and other countries. When, at nineteen, in his first weeks at Harvard College, he was compelled by an illness that proved permanent to live at home in Wellesley Hills, he adopted letters as a profession. He also began recording in the utmost detail, by way of practice and memoranda, his daily reflections on books and his own private thoughts. Mr. Van Wyck Brooks has edited in a large volume (1933) about one-seventh of this immense *Journal*. In this and in Bradford's score of books is the story of his struggle through the next fifty years to win fame as a writer.

Books were the substance of his life and Bradford wanted, above all else, to be a poet and novelist. Failing there, he tried plays, the most unsuitable of all forms for a man so isolated; then novels again, and poems. With a sickly man's will to achieve, he apportioned his day's work according to a most productive routine. For years he groped for the right medium. In 1895 he published a book of essays called *Types of American Character* that now seems to foreshadow his true *métier*. But not until the immediate success of his first psychological biography, *Lee the American* (1912), when he was already fifty, was the subsequent course of his life work clearly set. Then, through twenty years, came that long series of portraits—*Confederate Portraits* (1914), *Union Portraits* (1916), *Portraits of Women* (1916), *A Naturalist of Souls* (1917), *Portraits of American Women* (1919), *American Portraits, 1875-1900* (1922), *Damaged Souls* (1923), *Bare Souls* (1924), *Wives* (1925), *As God Made Them* (1929), *Daughters of Eve* (1930), *The Quick and the Dead* (1931), *Saints and Sinners* (1932), *Biography and the Human Heart* (posthumous, 1932)—the one hundred and fifteen "psychographs," by which Gamaliel Bradford will be longest remembered. With these came three more full-length lives—*The Soul of Samuel Pepys*

231

(1924), *Darwin* (1926), *D. L. Moody: A Worker in Souls* (1927)—also a play, two books of verse, and, right up to his death in 1932, a steady succession of articles and prefaces elaborating his special biographical aims.

What permanent artistic success he attained it is too soon to say. Insulated from the world as few men can be—though his wife and family and home made him an ideal environment—he had nothing whatever in common with contemporary movements or schools; and the loose talk in this country about his being an American Lytton Strachey was never more sharply denied than by himself. The two writers were not alike in aims, methods, temperaments, or capacities; and beyond saying that Bradford the plodder, who began earlier, discerned the weak points in the genius's work and admired to desperation the virtues, there is no comparison. Bradford produced no single outstanding book of psychographs. Yet the uniform standard of character analysis which he perfected and which he applied throughout the one hundred and fifteen portraits and the four longer studies may prove to have given, if not great literature, at least an extremely valuable instrument for biographers to come.

Bradford did not like the name "portrait" for his own studies. Though it had, he admitted, the excellent authority of his master Sainte-Beuve and others, and looked better on his books, it designated too strictly a face and figure seen only at one particular moment, rather than a picture of the sum of many particular moments. He preferred "psychograph," a term not coined by him but independently arrived at. For there is a basic difference between the two. "Biography," he said, "is bound to present an elaborate sequence of dates, events, and circumstances, of which some are vital to the analysis of the individual subject, but many are merely required to make the narrative complete." Psychography, being "the condensed, essential, artistic presentation of character, . . . swings clear from this chronological sequence altogether. . . . Out of the perpetual flux of actions and circumstances that constitutes a man's whole life, it seeks to extract what is essential, what is permanent and so vitally characteristic." It differs, on the other hand, from psychology in dealing primarily with individuals.

In analyzing character into its component elements, Bradford discerned certain universal qualities and forces—love, ambition, money, religion, etc.—by which every man and woman can be tested. His method was to master all the available printed evidence on his subject and then to walk round and round him, filling out, as it were, a set of personal questionnaires on each of these general qualities and on any others peculiar to that individual. In order quickly to orient his reader, Bradford invariably prefixed a brief chronology, while to support his deductions he always appended a bibliography and full reference notes. He finished in eight thousand words. This dry, schematic procedure, as Bradford feared, is apt in the long run to tire the reader. But the rigidity is somewhat softened by the author's profound interest in his "victim," by his shrewd and fresh perceptions, and by his clear, even, and flexible style.

"More and more," he confessed, "as I study the lives of men of prominence, or of any men, for that matter, do I feel the curiosity of studying their wives." With Mary Todd Lincoln (*Wives*), accordingly, Bradford is at the top of his bent, eagerly testing this oddest of First Ladies by his well-known formula and enjoying meanwhile all the delights and miseries of a detective. He himself considered *Bare Souls* to contain his best psychographs, because with Voltaire, Cowper, Gray, Horace Walpole, and the other great letter-writers he found unlimited evidence of their characters. The present study is valuable for just the opposite reason. Here was an exceptional dearth and contradiction of material. This very handicap, added to the special challenge of the subject, brings out some of Gamaliel Bradford's finest workmanship as a "weigher of souls."

# THE WIFE OF ABRAHAM LINCOLN

## CHRONOLOGY

Mary Todd Lincoln.
Born, Lexington, Kentucky, December 13, 1818.
Educated in Kentucky and lived there till 1839.
Married Lincoln, November 4, 1842.
Son Willie died, 1862.
Lincoln assassinated, April 14, 1865.
Son Tad died, 1871.
Died, July 16, 1882.

KINGS and princes are in the habit of selecting their wives, or having them selected, with a view to the exalted station they are destined to occupy. Presidents of the United States usually marry young, like other men, and do not arrive at the White House until they are old, and sometimes they bring with them partners not wholly adapted to such a conspicuous career. The complication in Lincoln's case is peculiar. A brilliant but uncouth and almost grotesque lawyer and politician from the backwoods, with no inherited social position or distinction, marries a showy, popular belle, who considers herself an aristocrat in the limited circle which is all she knows, and feels that she is condescending vastly in accepting the husband whose only asset is an extremely nebulous future. Then the husband shows an unexampled capacity for growth and development, intellectual and spiritual, if not social, and the wife, remaining to the end the narrow rural aristocrat she was in the beginning, is decidedly left behind. The strange destiny which made the man who was to save the future of American democracy a typical American and a typical democrat was hardly equal to making him also an ideal husband, at any rate an ideal husband for such a wife. Mrs. Lincoln married Lincoln with condescension and hope that he might rise to her level, or even above it. He did, and so far as to be altogether beyond her limited power of ascent. She made a useful helpmate for a practical, aggressive lawyer in Springfield, Illinois. As the wife of the great, dreaming, smiling, creating democratic statesman of the modern world, she was just a trifle over-parted.

The difficulty of getting at the actual Mrs. Lincoln is extraordinary and exasperating. The cloud of anecdote and hearsay and gossip which envelops Lincoln himself, hangs even more impenetrably about her, because we have not the solid substance of her own words, as to a considerable extent we have his. There are but a few of her letters in print, and those few are not very significant. Many people have written about her, but they contradict one another, and misrepresent, according to their own prejudices and the strange passion for exalting Lincoln by either elevating or debasing everybody about him. How unsatisfactory the materials are may be judged from the fact that the most illuminating document, on the whole, is the record of Mrs. Keckley, the colored seamstress at the White House. Mrs. Keckley was an intelligent observer, devoted to Mrs. Lincoln, and admitted to many intimate scenes and experiences. But I suppose few women would care to have their lives filtered to posterity through such a record. In short, I cannot ask my readers to give implicit belief to anything I say about Mrs. Lincoln, for I believe very little of it myself. Yet the difficulty of investigating her adds to the fascination. One sighs at times for such superb self-presentment as one gets in the letters of Sarah Butler or Harriet

Blaine. But there is a peculiar pleasure in finding little hints and threads of suggestion and following them out patiently, even when they seem to lead nowhere.

The bare indisputable facts in the life of Mary Todd Lincoln are few and simple. She was born of a good Kentucky family, in 1818, ten years after her husband. In 1839 she came to live with her sister, Mrs. Edwards, in Springfield. After a stormy courtship Lincoln married her in 1842. Her life then led her through Illinois law and politics to the White House, and the war, and the culmination of triumphant peace. All the triumph and hope were blasted by the assassination of her husband, and her remaining years, in spite of a brief sojourn in Europe, were darkened by sorrow and misfortune till a temperament, always impulsive and intense, was unbalanced to a point of oddity approaching and at times reaching actual derangement. She died in 1882.

In studying Mrs. Lincoln, one must admit that, while it is possible to get more or less reliable accounts of her external interests and activity, her inner life is almost hopelessly obscure. She had apparently a very good education, as educations went in Southern girls' schools in the middle of the nineteenth century. Mr. Rankin tells us that "while a resident of Springfield before and after her marriage, she impressed all who were acquainted with her with the excellent and accurate literary taste she had acquired by education and general reading, especially in history, poetry, and fiction." But this was in a country town in 1840, and it must be remembered here, as elsewhere, that we are dealing with Mr. Rankin's kindly after-dinner memory. Education of a sort Mrs. Lincoln certainly had, education superior to that of many about her, and at any rate far superior to her husband's. She had also a nimble gift of words, and wrote with ease when she wished. Her natural intelligence was unquestionably shrewd, quick, and keen. Within her limits she saw into the nature of things and the motives of men, and she had a notable faculty of making observations upon them, often with a turn of wit and sarcasm which did not add to her popularity. That she had a trace of the larger humorous attitude seems unlikely, and it is still more unlikely that she ever grasped or enjoyed that attitude in the subtle, pervading, dissolving form in which it was constantly manifest in her husband. The element of Touchstone, of Charles Lamb, the instinct of remoteness, of detachment, even in the midst of vast tragic passions, perhaps most precisely in the midst of such, of illuminating them with the strange glory of laughter, which was so haunting and so fascinating in Lincoln, evidently annoyed and perplexed her, as it has many other excellent people.

If she read, we should like to know a little more definitely what she read. Mr. Rankin enlarges on her familiarity with French, as a matter of both reading and speaking, and assures us that she read the latest French literature. I wonder if Sainte-Beuve was included in the list. I doubt it. Victor Hugo she did read, which perhaps is all one could expect. She read current novels, since Lincoln writes to a friend in regard to one, "I am not much of a reader of this sort of literature; but my wife got hold of the volume I took home, read it half through last night, and is greatly interested in it." She liked to read aloud; but what I should be glad to know is whether she was one of the two or three to whom Lincoln enjoyed reading aloud in quiet evenings; yet no one tells us. And in the middle of an agitated night he used to traverse the White House corridors to read the trifles of Tom Hood to his sleepy secretaries; but I do not hear that he read them to her.

Again, we have little light as to other amusements of an intellectual order. There is no sign of any considerable aesthetic interest. Lincoln liked music, of a rather rudimentary type, but it does not appear that she played it to him. She does not seem to have cared for natural objects. Her husband enjoyed the pet goats who played about the White House. They bored her. She liked to give away the flowers from the conservatory, but I do not read that she had a passion for them, any more than had Lincoln, who complained that he had "no taste natural or acquired for such things." One pleasure they shared, that of the theater, and in Washington they were able to indulge this till it culminated in the performance that was ruinous for both.

As to Mrs. Lincoln's religion, there is a good deal to be said on the practical side. She was generous and kindly, ready to help and to give. Stoddard's account of her hospital visitation during the war is very attractive. She made no display, sought no publicity whatever, but just went and gave and sympathized. In regard to the higher elements of spiritual life she was probably rather conventional, though she was a faithful member of the Episcopal, and then of the Presbyterian, Church, and Doctor Barton thinks that after her boy Willie's death she had some profounder religious experience. It may seem a trifling matter to note, but Mrs. Keckley's record of the ejaculation, "God, no!" as habitual seems to me singularly indicative of the woman.

I cannot think that there was much spiritual sympathy between her and her husband. We have, to be sure, Whitney's delightful sentence, "They were *en rapport* in all the higher objects of being." I do not believe that anybody was really *"en rapport"* with Lincoln in such matters, and I certainly do not believe his wife was. They both had, indeed, a superstitious turn of mind, and when the husband had dreams of horror and foreboding, the wife was ready to accept and interpret them. But, in Mr. Stephenson's admirable phrase, Mrs. Lincoln's soul "inhabited the obvious." The remote, gloomy, spiritual regions haunted by him, whether he was smiling or praying, were hardly likely to be visited by her. Thousands of pages have been written about Lincoln's religion; but he still smiles and remains impenetrable. He practiced with God the same superb, shrewd opportunism by which, as contrasted with the dogmatic idealism of Jefferson Davis, he saved the American Union. With him, if ever with anyone, it seems a case for remembering Lamb's remark, which Lincoln would have thoroughly enjoyed, that he was determined his children should "be brought up in their father's religion—if they can find out what it is." Yet it is curious that, after all, the practical, unmystical wife should have given us what is perhaps the very best summary on this point (italics mine): "Mr. Lincoln had no faith and no hope in the usual acceptation of those words. He never joined a church; but still, as I believe, he was a religious man by nature. . . . But it was *a kind of poetry in his nature,* and he was never a technical Christian." Excellent example of the keen common sense of the woman who understands even where she is wholly unable to appreciate. And we come across this with Mrs. Lincoln at every turn.

## II

In dealing with Mrs. Lincoln's external life we are on somewhat surer ground, though not much, for still the cloud of intangible gossip is likely to mislead us. Socially it is evident that she was ambitious and eager for success. On the whole, it cannot be said that she achieved it. Her appearance was by no means against her. Her face, in the photographs, is to me totally without charm. It is a positive, aggressive face, without a ray of sensitiveness in it. But, even in the heaviness of later years, she had a certain formal beauty and dignity, both of face and figure, and could bear herself well. It would seem that she dressed with taste, though at times too ostentatiously, and Lincoln objected to her extreme low necks. As regards this matter of clothes I cannot resist quoting one passage, both because it is one of the few touches of real self-revelation that we have from her own pen and because it is so thoroughly human. Three years after her husband's death she writes to Mrs. Keckley: "I am positively dying with a broken heart, and the probability is that I shall be living but a *very* short time. May we all meet in a better world, where *such grief* is unknown. Write me all about yourself. I should like you to have about four black widow's caps, just such as I had made in the fall in New York, sent to me. . . . The probability is that I shall need few more clothes; my rest, I am inclined to believe, *is near at hand*."

There are pleasant accounts of the Lincoln hospitality in Springfield. As to what happened in the White House observers differ. But it must be remembered that few hostesses have been subjected to such cruel criticism as Mrs. Lincoln had to meet. Those who watched her impartially, like W. H. Russell, Bancroft, and Laugel, report in the main favorably, though it is noticeable that they are inclined to speak of her as better than they expected. The truth is, her ardent and impulsive temper made her tactless and uncertain. People could not count upon her, and it is said that she changed her intimates and social advisers too frequently. The basis of her social zeal was rather an intense ambition than a broad human sympathy, and for the widest popularity and success the latter is indispensable. Then it must always be remembered that she had the strange, incalculable, most undomestic and unparlorable figure of Lincoln to carry with her, which would have been a terrible handicap to any woman. His dress was strange, his manners were strange, his talk was strange. And there was always that flood of homely stories, reeking with the unexpected. He would not lay himself out to be agreeable to his wife's callers. Not that he was untidy. This is always justly denied. But he was magnificently inappropriate, disconcerting. One must not think of him as Dominie Sampson, but rather as if one were to attempt to introduce Charles Lamb or Shelley into a complicated conventional social life. So, if the poor lady failed, it must be admitted that she had her difficulties.

In her housekeeping and domestic arrangements she seems to have been excellent. Her table is highly spoken of and she was an exact and careful manager as to neatness and punctuality. Here again her husband was far from being a help to her. He was quite indifferent to what he ate and it was impossible to make him systematic about meals or hours generally. The remote world in which he lived was but imperfectly accessible to the tinkle of the dinner bell.

As regards the most essential element of domestic tranquillity, money, he was unsystematic also. In his legal business he could not be kept to exact accounting, had no commercial or speculative instinct whatever. Also, he was largely generous and more anxious to win his client's cause than to get his money. But he was no spender, had few needs and no costly tastes, and above all he abhorred debt, though circumstances sometimes forced him into it. How simple his financial ideas were appears in his reported remark shortly before his election as President: "I have a cottage at Springfield and about eight thousand dollars in money. . . . I hope I shall be able to increase it to twenty thousand, and that is as much as any man ought to want." As a matter of fact, his estate was much larger than this at the time of his death.

Mrs. Lincoln no doubt did her best. In the early days she made her own dresses and she had always moments of violent economy. Her first remark to Mrs. Keckley was: "We are just from the West, and are poor. . . . If you will work cheap, you shall have plenty to do." But her tastes in the matter of outlay were far different from her husband's. She liked to give, and did give. She liked the pleasant things of life, especially the kind that cost money. We have her own written words—and it is such a comfort when we do have them—on this subject: "When I saw the large steamers at the New York landing ready for the European voyage, I felt in my heart inclined to sigh that poverty was my portion. I often laugh and tell Mr. Lincoln that I am determined my next husband shall be rich." Which of course was agreeable for him. But the most pitiable exhibition in regard to Mrs. Lincoln's finances is Mrs. Keckley's story of the debts incurred from real or imagined necessities of dress to keep up the presidential dignity. The maddening pressure of these debts doubled the wife's anxiety as to the chances of her husband's second election in 1864. It must not be supposed that Mrs. Keckley's record of conversations that took place is verbally exact, but it is surely close to reality in its general tone. She says to Mrs. Lincoln, "And Mr. Lincoln does not even suspect how much you owe?" And the answer is, " 'God, no!' This was a favorite expression of hers. 'And I would not have him suspect. If he knew that his wife was involved to the extent that she is, the knowledge would drive him mad. He is so sincere and straightforward himself, that he is shocked by the duplicity of others. He does not know a thing about my debts, and I value his happiness, not to speak of my own, too much to allow him to know anything. This is what troubles me so much. If he is re-elected, I can keep him in ignorance of my affairs; but if he is defeated, then the bills will be sent in and he will know all.' " Such are the domestic tragedies of money.

In her dealings with those about her in subordinate positions

Mrs. Lincoln's uncertain temper is said to have caused her a good deal of difficulty. Herndon declares very definitely that "on account of her peculiar nature she could not long retain a servant in her employ." But it is evident that she was much attached to Mrs. Keckley, who served her faithfully for a number of years. And the testimony of the White House secretary, Stoddard, is exceedingly friendly and favorable. She was considerate, he says, and did not burden you with unreasonable demands. Probably, like many people of quick temper, she regretted her outbursts and did her best to make amends for them.

It is with her children that Mrs. Lincoln is most attractive. Both she and Lincoln were devoted to them, he in his gentle, humorous, abstracted fashion, she with no doubt erratic but effusive and genuine demonstrations of tenderness. She was interested in their education, in their health, in their mental and moral development. But fate was as cruel to her in the maternal as in the conjugal relation, and she lived to bury three of her four sons. The eldest died in the early days in Springfield. The youngest, Tad, who was her chief consolation after her husband's death, so that she wrote, "Only my darling Taddie prevents my taking my life," was snatched away in 1871. But the death of Willie, in the midst of the at once anguished and triumphant days in the White House, was the bitterest blow of all. The mother was inconsolable, and her grief led her into strange and fantastic ecstasies of passion, till the crisis came in the scene so vividly related by Mrs. Keckley, when Lincoln took his wife by the arm and led her to the window. "With a stately, solemn gesture, he pointed to the lunatic asylum, 'Mother, do you see that large white building on the hill yonder? Try to control your grief or it will drive you mad, and we may have to send you there.'"

Yet, with the curious perversity of fortune which attended so much of Mrs. Lincoln's life, even her mother's sorrow, which would seem as if it ought to have won her public respect and doubtless did so, was turned by her inborn tactlessness into an element of unpopularity. The military band had been in the habit of playing in the square near the White House. But Mrs. Lincoln's reminiscent grief could not endure the music, and she insisted upon its being stopped for months, till the people became so indignant that Lincoln was forced to overrule her. Truly, one cannot but sympathize with Mrs. Keckley's exclamation, even if it is a little exaggerated: "I never in my life saw a more peculiarly constituted woman. Search the world over, and you will not find her counterpart." And she was married to a man as strange as herself, and as strangely different.

### III

Now, having established Mrs. Lincoln's general character, as far as it is possible to do so, we come to the profoundly curious and interesting study of her relation with her husband, and this should begin with the history of their marriage.

In early life Lincoln seems to have had a susceptible imagination with regard to women, the more susceptible, perhaps, because he had so little to do with them. His profound affection in his twenties for Ann Rutledge, which has been embroidered by so many story-tellers, and her melancholy death, almost unhinged him for the time, and Herndon insists that he never really loved anyone afterward. But a varied list of feminine names appears. There is the robust Mary Owens, with whom his courtship seems mainly to have consisted in endeavors to persuade her that she would do better not to marry him. There is a more shadowy Sarah Rickard. And there is Matilda Edwards, sister-in-law of the lady with whom her own sister, Mary Todd, was also staying. But the substantial charms of Mary and her decided habit of getting what she wanted, in the end fixed the rather wandering lover, and in 1840 they were definitely engaged.

Here we strike one of the most debated points in Mrs. Lincoln's life, and in dealing with the course of this engagement we are at once confronted with the question of the veracity of Herndon. It seems to me that his essential tone and attitude must be regarded as satisfactory. He ventured a prophetic protest against the drift of a silly legendary atmosphere tending to envelop Lincoln as it enveloped Washington. Such a tendency evinces much more the timidity of the worshiper than the greatness of the idol, for if he is really great, nothing will make him more so than to prove that he was really human. At the same time, after the industrious researches of Miss Tarbell, it is difficult to accept in detail Herndon's account of the stormy progress of Lincoln's love-affair. According to Herndon, the day for the wedding was actually fixed, the supper was ordered, the bride arrayed, the parson present—and the bridegroom failed to appear, tormented by doubts and hesitations approaching mental derangement. The disturbance was so great that Lincoln's friends for a time feared suicide.

Without pronouncing positively on the more highly colored details of this narrative, we may regard the indisputable facts as curious enough. It is certain that the engagement was broken, certain that Lincoln a year later referred to the "fatal first of January, 1841," the day which, according to Herndon, was set for the wedding. Also, we have the remarkable series of letters to Speed, a near friend who was wooing and marrying at the same time, in which Lincoln uncovers his tormented soul, a soul clearly well versed in all the tortures of self-analysis, self-criticism, and self-reproach. Long before this crisis he had written to Mary Owens: "Whatever woman may cast her lot with mine, should anyone ever do so, it is my intention to do all in my power to make her happy and contented, and there is nothing I can imagine that would make me more unhappy than to fail in the effort." In March, 1842, he writes to Speed that, since the breaking of his engagement he "should have been entirely happy but for the never-absent idea that there is one still unhappy whom I have contributed to make so. That kills my soul. I cannot but reproach myself for even wishing to be happy while she is otherwise."

Then Speed is married and likes it, which impresses Lincoln, and somehow or other Mary regains her control, and on the 4th of November, 1842, the two are married very simply and quietly. In a letter of Lincoln's only recently published there is this admirable phrase, turned with a delicate significance which Lamb or Touchstone might have envied, "Nothing new here, except my marrying, which to me is a matter of profound wonder."

It is matter of profound wonder to most of us, and we endeavor, without much success, to find out how it happened. To begin with, what was Mary's motive, why did a woman so proud as she seek to retain a lover who appeared so obviously reluctant? Herndon's theory is fantastic. He asserts that Mary's pride was so bitterly wounded that she married Lincoln to make his life miserable, purely for revenge. Even put in more rational fashion, with the idea that she was a person who persisted relentlessly in getting what she had once wanted, the explanation is scanty. There is also the theory that Mary was ambitious and that she foresaw Lincoln's future, even preferring him in this regard to so promising a candidate as Douglas. Something there may be in this: she was a keen-sighted woman, and she is said to have prognosticated her husband's success from the start. But I think we must add that she loved him, felt instinctively the charm that so many men felt, the almost inexplicable charm which went with that strange, ungainly, physical make-up of which an early friend could say, "he was the *ungodliest* figure I ever saw."

In the same way I feel that probably something in her fascinated Lincoln. His conscience forced him, say some; her family forced him, say others. Both may have contributed. He was morbidly sensitive. He was indolent and in some ways easily led. Yet I have no doubt he loved her, and that quick, narrow, masterful spirit gained and kept a hold over his vaguer and more fluid one.

I imagine that the love on both sides persisted to the end. Herndon insists that there was no love at all. To Mr. Rankin the whole affair apparently seems a sweet idyl of uninterrupted bliss. It was probably just an average earthly marriage, with an increasing bond of association overcoming all sorts of wear and tear and pulling and hauling. Lincoln could never have been a comfortable husband for any wife. His casual ways, his irregular habits, his utter disregard of the conventions and small proprieties would have worn on a far more tranquil temper than Mary Todd's. And her temper was not tranquil at all; in fact, patience was the least of her distinguishing qualities. Her violent outbursts on small occasions are matter of record, and it is impossible to put aside altogether the scenes of furious, disgraceful public jealousy described by Badeau and confirmed by General Sherman. Lincoln took it all quietly, though it must have wrung his heart, patted her on the shoulder, called her his child-wife, and she was ashamed of herself—and did it again.

It was an every-day marriage, with some rather dark spots in it, but hardly so bad as has been represented. They loved their children and called each other "father" and "mother," in the old homely way, and their hearts grew more and more bound up in each other, and they just took life as it came. There is the cruel saying of La Rochefoucauld, "there are comfortable marriages, but no delicious ones," which simply means that life, as we go on with it, with all its trials, may at its best be comfortable, but can rarely be delicious. There is the other saying of the French comic writer, "in marriage, when love exists, familiarity kills it; when it does not exist, it gives it birth." Both have a certain significance in connection with the marriage of the Lincolns.

But what has afforded infinite entertainment to the inquiring biographer, and what I think must be equally entertaining to the judicious reader, is the violent contrast with which the same simple facts may be stated according to the prejudice of the person who states them. Take the two extremes, Herndon and Mr. Rankin: their analysis of Lincoln's married life cannot but be instructive as well as diverting.

First, there is Lincoln's absence from home. He left on every excuse, Herndon says. He lived in his office. Where other lawyers returned from their work to the comfortable fireside, he lingered in the country store or anywhere, rather than face the nagging that daily tormented him. All a mistake, says Mr. Rankin. He was a great deal from home, attending to more or less important business, and why? Because he had such a competent, careful, devoted wife that his presence at home was entirely unnecessary.

Take clothing. Mrs. Lincoln was always fussing about her husband's dress. Again, explains the unfailing Mr. Rankin, this was all a matter of health. He was threatened with consumption and her loving care in seeing that he was properly clothed may have saved his life. It was the same with food and regularity at meals. Innumerable stories are told of her sending arbitrarily at the most inconvenient times to insist upon his attendance, and even appearing herself, with some indulgence of shrewish tongue. Wrong, wrong, urges Mr. Rankin. She may have spoken quickly, but affectionate anxiety about his health was at the bottom of it all.

The best is the story of the ring. Herndon enlarges, with rather fiendish satisfaction, upon Lincoln's reluctance when even the *bona fide* wedding day arrived. Speed's little boy, says Herndon, seeing the bridegroom so finely dressed, inquired where he was going. "To hell, I suppose," was the gloomy answer. Oh, cries Mr. Rankin, cruel, cruel, even to imagine that he could have uttered such a word! There was the wedding ring. Did not Lincoln have engraved in it the tender sentiment, "Love is eternal"? Innocent Mr. Rankin! he apparently does not remember Jaques's remark to Orlando: "You are full of pretty answers. Have you not been acquainted with goldsmiths' wives and conned them out of rings?" I will not suggest that the sentiment may have emanated from Mary herself, though there have been such instances. But, alas! we know how many rings with similar mottoes are clasping unloved and loveless fingers all about the world. And always, to sum the whole, there is the cynical, cruel, profound, significant sentence of Dumas *fils:* "*Dans le mariage, quand l'amour existe, l'habitude le tue; quand il n'existe pas, il le fait naître.*"

## I V

Having thus analyzed, with delightful inconclusiveness, the conjugal affection of the Lincolns, we may consider with equal inconclusiveness, the important question of Mrs. Lincoln's influence over her husband. It is clear that she was a person who naturally tended to dominate those about her. Could she dominate him? In little things he was no doubt yielding enough, to her and to others, as appears from his jocose remark that it was fortunate he was not a woman, since he never could say no. When it came to great matters, especially moral, he may not have bothered to say no, but he did what he thought right, without the slightest regard to the demands of others. Hear what Mrs. Lincoln says herself: "Mr. Lincoln was mild in his manners, but he was a terribly firm man when he set his foot down. None of us, no man or woman, could rule him after he had once fully made up his mind." Can you not read the outcome of many fruitless battles here? Mrs. Edwards gives a pretty picture of the wooer's absorbed attention during their courtship, how Mary talked and Lincoln listened. No doubt he listened all his life. Sometimes he heeded.

Mrs. Lincoln's chief wrestle was with her husband's social peculiarities. Here she was obviously in part successful and it cannot be questioned that her experience and knowledge of the world were of great benefit. As Newton puts it, she "taught him particularly that there was such a thing as society, which observed a man's boots as well as his principles." At the same time, from his boots to his hat, and through all the long six feet between, the man was thoroughly unconventional and nothing could make him otherwise. In the early married days in Springfield he would open the door himself in his shirt sleeves and assure august visitors that his wife would be down as soon as she could get her trotting harness on. Such things torment any well-constituted woman. Mary resented them. Yet she was sweetly contrite afterward. When a friend said to her, "Mary, if I had a husband with such a mind as yours has, I wouldn't care what he did," she answered, "It is foolish—it is a small thing to complain of." The oddities may have been toned down a little in Washington; but they were never got rid of. You could believe in the man, you could admire him, you could scold him; but you could not domesticate him.

On broader matters, less naturally within her sphere, even on the conduct of the war, Mrs. Lincoln evidently had her word. What wife would not? And sometimes it was the apt and poignant one. How characteristic is her retort to Stanton, who proposed to have her painted as she appeared at Fort Stevens, when she had come under fire: "That is very well, and I can assure you of one thing, Mr. Secretary, if I had had a few *ladies* with me, the rebels would not have been permitted to get away as they did." Large military policy was perhaps beyond her, but she gave her sharp, quick judgment of military commanders, bearing out, to some extent, her husband's admission that she had quicker insight into character than he. The words, as reported by Mrs. Keckley, can hardly be relied upon; but the general drift of them must be accurate. Of McClellan she said: "He is a humbug. . . . He talks so much and does so little. If I had the power, I would very soon take off his head and put some energetic man in his place." As to Grant, she is equally severe: "He is a butcher and is not fit to be the head of an army. . . . He has no management, no regard for life. . . . I could fight an army as well myself." How perfect is Lincoln's quiet answer to all this: "Well, mother, supposing that we give you command of the army. No doubt you would do much better than any general that has been tried."

With politics Mrs. Lincoln was of course more interested and more at home than in military details. She watched her husband's career from the time of her earliest acquaintance with him and followed every step of it with the intensest ardor. Lincoln's appreciation of this shows most charmingly in his remark, on first hearing the result of the presidential nomination in 1860, that there was "a little short woman at our house who is probably more interested in this dispatch than I am; and if you will excuse me, gentlemen, I will take it up and let her see it." [1] Abstract political principles may not have appealed to her much. Before the war her sympathies were more or less Southern, and this brought her criticism and added to the unpopularity which she was not able to overcome. But there can be no question about her entire loyalty to her husband's cause, which was in every sense her own. And whenever there was a personal point

[1] It is profitable to compare this remark, as thus reported by Lamon, with the refined, genteel version given by Mr. Rankin (*Personal Recollections of Abraham Lincoln*, page 190), "There is a lady, over yonder on Eighth Street, who is deeply interested in this news; I will carry it to her." Very likely neither version represents what Lincoln actually said; but the Rankin method is always the same.

to be decided, her judgment was always quick and sometimes sure. It is only just to say that I have not found one single case of her attempting to exert influence for the benefit of her friends or family, no soliciting of offices or commissions where they were not deserved. But she did interfere when her husband's, and her own, interests seemed to be involved. It was she who prevented Lincoln from accepting the governorship of Oregon in 1849, from political foresight, say Lamon and Mr. Rankin, because she did not want to go off into the woods, say Nicolay and Hay. And in other cases she exerted a pressure which was strong and perhaps effective.

As in army matters, so in politics, it was the human side which interested her, and she criticized Seward and Chase just as savagely as she criticized Grant. Also, she was much inclined to work on human agents where it was possible. Russell complains that she was accessible to flattery and filled her parlors with "men who would not be received in any respectable private house in New York." Her own explanation of this proceeding, in the dialogue with Mrs. Keckley, bearing on the election of 1864, is profoundly interesting: "In a political canvass it is policy to cultivate every element of strength. These men have influence, and we require influence to re-elect Mr. Lincoln. I will be clever to them until after the election, and then, if we remain at the White House, I will, drop every one of them, and let them know very plainly that I only made tools of them. They are an unprincipled set, and I don't mind a little double-dealing with them." When Mrs. Keckley inquires if Mr. Lincoln knows, the answer is: "God, no! he would never sanction such a proceeding, so I keep him in the dark and will not tell him till all is over." Somehow in all these political concerns Mrs. Lincoln reminds one at times of Mr. Strachey's Victoria. There is the same dignified, yet dumpy figure, the same round, hard, positive, dominating face. And one cannot but think of the remark of an Englishman to Mrs. Fields, which Mr. Strachey would enjoy. "We call her 'Her *Un*gracious Majesty.'"

It is clear enough that back of Mrs. Lincoln's political interest and indeed back of all her life there was a tremendous driving force of ambition. There is much debate whether she had more ambition or he. They were different in this, as in everything. His ambition was vague, dreamy, fitful, mystical. Hers was narrower, more concrete, but it never rested, and went straight at its ends. How much we are to believe of the apparently well-authenticated stories of her aiming at the White House almost from girlhood, is a question. Any girl may aim at the White House, I suppose. No doubt a good many do who never get there. Perhaps the most impressive anecdote on the subject is Lamon's account of his first talk with her, in 1847. "Yes," she said, of her husband, "he is a great favorite everywhere. He is to be President of the United States some day; if I had not thought so, I never would have married him, for you can see he is not pretty. But look at him! Doesn't he look as if he would make a magnificent President?" That a woman should speak thus in her first interview with a stranger is extraordinarily suggestive, if you can believe it. And Lamon's emphatic insistence upon her use of the word "magnificent" makes the story somewhat more credible.

At any rate, she got to the White House and reigned there through four of the greatest years in the history of the country. I wish I had a little more authority for the seemingly sane and not unfavorable account of her White House career given by Mr. Willis Steell, the immense effort for popularity and social success and supremacy, ending in satiety and disappointment: "The 'court' she set up had turned into a mock bubble, shining in iridescent colors only in her imagination; created from sordid materials, and wholly empty." Then the triumphant election of 1864 set the crown upon it all, if crown there was. In April, 1865, the war was over. On the afternoon of the 14th Mr. and Mrs. Lincoln drove out alone together and Lincoln seemed singularly happy, so much so that Mary's ill-divining soul presaged the woe to come. He talked to her of well-earned rest, of peaceful plans and projects for the future. In the evening they went to Ford's Theater. And still his mind was rather on the coming dreamy years than on the play. We will go to Europe, he said to her, go to the Holy Land, go to the city I have always wanted to see, Jerusalem— While he was busy with such thought, the pistol of Wilkes Booth shattered the world of Mary Todd Lincoln into diminutive fragments, which no man ever again could piece together.

## V

As this portrait is mainly made up of questions that cannot be answered, we might as well conclude with the most unanswerable of all: would Lincoln's career have been different, for better or worse, if he had married a different wife? Here again a variety of speculations present themselves, each urged with partisan eagerness. It would perhaps be possible to work out some such theory as Mr. Van Wyck Brooks cleverly applied to the case of Mark Twain—that is, that the constant conventionalizing pressure of a prosaic wife chilled and deadened, to some extent, the quick burst of spontaneous genius; but we should always have to remember that Mark was passionately devoted to Livy from beginning to end. There is, on the whole, a singular unanimity of biographers in the view that Mrs. Lincoln was helpful to her husband; but there is an astonishing difference as to the way she helped. Herndon, always critical, admits the helpfulness, in fact emphasizes it. Lincoln, he says, was naturally indolent, contented, stay-at-home (though elsewhere he calls him ambitious). If home had been delightful, he would have enjoyed it and would not have been so eager to make a mark in the world. Mary made home hideous, and by so doing made her husband great. Mr. Rankin does his best to involve this cynical explanation in the rosy mist of his amiable memory, and goes to the other extreme. According to him Mary was a sort of protecting angel, who advised, cautioned, impelled, always at the right time. "Without Mary Todd for his wife, Abraham Lincoln would never have been President. Without Abraham Lincoln for her husband, Mary Todd would, probably, never have been a President's wife." This beatific solution may be correct; but if it is so, I find it difficult to explain the fact that, though Nicolay and Hay were intimately present in the White House, in all the ten volumes of their *History* Mrs. Lincoln gets only a few lines here and there, and in the close daily record of Hay's *Diary* her name is hardly mentioned.

Surely a guardian, ministering angel would deserve and receive a little more than this. For myself, I find Mr. Stephenson's moderate statement very satisfying: "She had certain qualities that her husband lacked. . . . She had that intuition for the main chance which shallow people confound with practical judgment. Her soul inhabited the obvious." Lincoln's natural danger was the world of dreams and going astray in it, said Mr. Stephenson: "That this never occurred may be fairly credited, or at least very plausibly credited, to the firm-willed, the utterly matter-of-fact little person he had married."

The problem of Lincoln's melancholy brings the question of his life with Mary to a point: that haunting, brooding sadness, which rarely left him, though he shot the dark cloud through with constant fantastic sallies of laughter, that sadness which Herndon expressed with such extraordinary power when he said that "melancholy dripped from him as he walked," and which Lincoln himself described as so terrible that "if what I feel were equally distributed to the whole human family, there would not be one cheerful face on the earth." Did Mary cause this grief or did she alleviate it? Herndon by no means affirms the former, but he evidently thinks that the misery of home surroundings much augmented a constitutional tendency. Then along comes Mr. Rankin, from whom a mellow optimism is constantly dripping, and assures us that, on the contrary, so far from causing the melancholy, Mary was the one who could cure it. When the spells grew acute, "she . . . was the only one who had the skill and tact to shorten their duration. . . . I revere her memory for this most gracious service." Again Mr. Rankin may be correct; but when I think of that concise, hard, unsympathetic face, I wonder.

Among the varied possibilities connected with Lincoln's other early loves, the suggestion of melancholy brings up most of all the image of Ann Rutledge. It has even been suggested that the melancholy had its origin in the loss of her of whom he said, the thought of "the snows and rains falling upon her grave filled him with indescribable grief." If he had married Ann, would it all have been different? We know so little of her that we cannot conjecture further than that a devoted, self-forgetful passion such as he hardly felt for Mary Todd might have changed his world. As for the substantial, hearty Mary Owens, it is not likely that his experience with her would have been very different from his experience with the other Mary.

And then one thinks of a woman of real genius, of large capacity, of sweet human comprehension, a woman like Theodosia Burr or Sarah Butler. With a wife like this would Lincoln have done, perhaps not greater things, but done them with an ampler serenity and spiritual peace?

I doubt it. Lincoln was not in any way a woman's man, in spite of the early loves. Mary Owens thought him "deficient in those little links which make up the chain of woman's happiness." Lincoln himself, much later, wrote, in his dry way, "The truth is, I have never corresponded much with ladies; and hence I postpone writing letters to them, as a business I do not understand." He may have been a master of men; for dealing with women he was at once too self-contained and too sincere. I am sure the words of the *Imitation* would have pleased him: "Be not a friend to any one woman in particular, but commend all good women in general to God."

More than that, he lived in a solitude which neither man nor woman ever perfectly penetrated. No doubt we all live in such a solitude. The difference is that nine hundred and ninety-nine out of a thousand rarely think of it. Lincoln thought of it all the time. He ruled over millions of men and women who loved him; yet he was enormously alone, because he felt himself to be so. In this one point there is a curious resemblance between him and the greatest of all his contemporaries, a man who differed from him in so many other respects, Robert E. Lee. Lee was lonely as Lincoln was. Yet Lee had a most exquisite, devoted, sympathizing wife and children whose affection was constant and complete. The loneliness, with him, as with Lincoln, was that isolation of the human soul which the yearning of the deepest love merely accentuates. Lincoln's own words to Speed convey it with clarifying intensity, "I have no doubt it is the peculiar misfortune of both you and me to dream dreams of Elysium far exceeding all that anything earthly can realize." When there was such an ideal as this to compete with, neither the perfection of wit, nor of beauty, nor of sacrifice, would have been any more satisfying than poor Mary Todd.

# VAN WYCK BROOKS

IT has remained for one not a New Englander by birth or early environment to become New England's cultural biographer. Van Wyck Brooks's Pulitzer Prize work, *The Flowering of New England, 1815-1865* (1936), is not a history; political and social changes form only a background to its great central theme. It is not a collection of essays, even of biographical essays; its characterizations are subordinate and tributary to the main flow of intellectual achievement. It is the portrait of a period, but for the individual portraits of its leading figures one must refer to several different places in the book. It has been called "essentially a highly documented historical novel"; but the characters and events, numerous and interacting, are no part of fiction, and the period itself—its values, qualities, and significance—rises more important than any of the men who made it. The following selection, taken from two chapters of the book, forms a composite sketch of Henry Thoreau (1817-62) during the most interesting phase of his life. It is not all Mr. Brooks has to say about Thoreau, yet it is a rounded portrait studded with concrete details assembled with a scholar's thoroughness and an artist's precision, a portrait that *lives* by reason of its fine and even-tempered writing, its memorable images, its masterly story-telling, its quiet humor.

*The Flowering of New England* is by no means the first of its author's books about this period or about New England. All his life he has been delving beneath the surface of American culture to explore its hidden sources, the origins of its power and the causes of its direction and occasional drying up. He was born in Plainfield, New Jersey, in 1886, and, after receiving his schooling there, went to Harvard as a member of the class of 1907. Already leaning to literary criticism and editorial work, he joined the staff of Doubleday, Page and Company, publishers, remaining until 1909. In that year appeared his first book, *The Wine of the Puritans,* examining American civilization from the point of view of two expatriated citizens, a study so brilliant for a man of twenty-two that it led to his appointment as lecturer and instructor at Leland Stanford University (1911-13). There in California he met and married Miss Eleanor Kenyon. In quick succession came other literary studies: *The Malady of the Ideal* (1913), *John Addington Symonds* (1914), *The World of H. G. Wells* (1915), and a timely treatise on our national culture, *America's Coming of Age* (1915). By this time, still in his thirties, Mr. Brooks was beginning to be regarded as a major intellectual prophet (though he himself has been cautious of prophecy) and a trusty guide in the field of letters. From

1915 to 1918 he was on the editorial staff of The Century Company; from 1920 to 1924 associate editor of *The Freeman;* and in 1927 editor, with Alfred Kreymborg, Lewis Mumford, and Paul Rosenfeld, of *The American Caravan,* resigning from the board after the first edition because of poor health. Meanwhile he has published several books that gained national prominence, including *The Ordeal of Mark Twain* (1920, revised in 1933) and *The Pilgrimage of Henry James* (1925), and he went on to produce a *Life of Emerson* and two collections of critical essays before coming to the volume from which "Thoreau at Walden" is taken.

Mr. Brooks's manner, both personal and literary, is quiet, urbane, persuasive. His public addresses sound like books, while his writing reads like the dignified, well-considered talk of a man who keeps the highways and bridges of his mind in good repair. Henry Thoreau, one feels, is a peculiarly sympathetic subject for his pen. Quite different from the "skulker" misunderstood by Stevenson (*Familiar Studies*), we see instead the sensible Yankee depicted at full length in the admirable life (1939) by Henry Seidel Canby, except that in the present sketch he is viewed not alone but as a character in the drama of our national culture.

# THOREAU AT WALDEN

IN EMERSON's white house on the Boston turnpike, Henry Thoreau had taken up his quarters. He occupied the room at the head of the stairs, a little room, but he was a little man: his nose and his thoughts were the biggest things about him. Emerson, and especially Emerson's children, had formed a warm affection for their difficult Henry, difficult, that is, for the rest of Concord but a treasure for the household of a sage. He was short, lean, frail, although nobody guessed it, he was so tough and muscular, with a meagre chest, long arms falling from the collar-bone, a workman's hands and feet, a huge Emersonian beak, rather like Julius Caesar's, bright blue eyes and flaxen hair. He walked with the swinging stride of an old campaigner. His manners were of the homespun sort, different indeed from Emerson's. But, after the first encounter, one perceived that, if Henry Thoreau was a thorn-bush, he was the kind that bears the fragrant flowers.

He was the son of the pencil-maker, who had his little house and shop on Main Street: "J. Thoreau and Sons." The Thoreaus were a mercantile family of small pretensions who had seen better days. They were well-connected in the Channel Islands, where the French Thoreaus were prosperous wine-merchants. Their forbears in Maine, the Scottish Dunbars, had taken the royalist side in the Revolution. As a barefoot village boy, Henry had driven the turkeys and the cow to pasture, and Emerson had vaguely heard of him as a poor student at Harvard. He had written to President Quincy, suggesting Henry's name for a scholarship. Later, Henry walked in to Boston, eighteen miles from Concord, to hear Emerson speak, and walked home again after the lecture. Emerson, touched by this, was still more touched when, after one of his Concord lectures, his sister-in-law, who was boarding with Mrs. Thoreau, said to him, "Henry Thoreau has a thought very like that in his journal." A friendship had soon sprung up between them, and when, one day, the Emersons went on a picnic, to the Cliffs on the Concord river, they asked Henry to join them and bring his flute. The village people looked askance at him because he was so pugnacious. He had queer ideas about teaching school, refusing to use the ferule; for with children and simple folk he was always gentle. With others, he was obstinate and harsh. He liked to administer doses of moral quinine, and he never thought of sugaring his pills. He had withdrawn from Dr. Ripley's church with a thesis more defiant than Martin Luther's. He liked to speak of a cold spot as "sultry," and he had a way of calling the woods "domestic." But at boating and camping he was a master-woodsman, skilled as Ulysses, shrewd as any fox. The redskins had forgotten the arts he knew. Arrowheads and Indian fireplaces sprang from the ground when he touched it. He charmed the snakes and fishes. Wild birds perched on his shoulder. His fingers seemed to have more wisdom in them than many a scholar's head.

This young Briareus of the hundred hands was something more than Emerson's factotum. There was nothing he could not do in the matter of painting and papering, building walls, repairing chicken-houses, pruning and grafting fruit-trees, surveying, tinkering, gardening. But these were trifles in his bag of tricks, useful to pay his way in the world and justify his creed of self-reliance.

He was a master of other arts that Emerson also knew, and a scholar of unusual distinction; and he wished to be a philosopher, not a mere thinker of subtle thoughts but one who, loving wisdom, lived a life that was simple, magnanimous, free. In fact, he recalled those ancient sages who, when an enemy took the town, walked out of the gate empty-handed, without a care for the morrow. Why should one be burdened with impedimenta? Henry liked the soldier's life, always on the stretch and always ready for a battle. Each of his mornings brought its strenuous sortie. He lived "for to admire and for to see." He had spoken his mind in his college themes about the "blind and unmanly love of wealth" that actuated most of his fellow-beings. The order of things, he said, should be reversed. The seventh should be man's day of toil, wherein to earn his living by the sweat of his brow; he should keep the rest of the week for his joy and wonder.

These views delighted Emerson. In fact, the two agreed on so many subjects, always with an edge of difference, that one might well have supposed the relation between them was that of master and pupil. Emerson was fourteen years the elder; and it was true that Henry had acquired some of his traits and mannerisms: his handwriting, his voice, even his nose seemed to have gone to school to Emerson. There was something contagious in Emerson's aura; everyone was affected by it, nobody seemed able to resist it. Alcott was more than a little Emersonized; and as for Ellery Channing, what did the lady say who heard him lecture?— that his gait, his inflections, the very turn of his eyebrow were Emerson to the life. Henry Thoreau had felt this influence, as he had felt the influence of Carlyle. He had his own form, none the less. Emerson and he had grown in Concord, as two flowers grow in a common bed, one of them larger and more luxuriant, the other with a much more pungent odour; but they stood in different corners of the bed, with an ample space between them, so that the breeze could blow upon each of them freely. They were different enough in temperament, as in their personalities; and Henry phrased their common points of view with a sort of acidulous accent that was never heard on Emerson's lips.

They were of one mind in a dozen matters, not least in regard to the reformers. "As for these communities," said Henry, expressing their joint opinion, "I had rather keep bachelor's hall in hell than go to board in heaven." Much as he liked Alcott, the "best-natured man" he had ever met,—"the rats and mice make their nests in him,"—he turned up his nose at Fruitlands as well as at Brook Farm. He meant to bake his own bread in heaven, and wash his own clothes there. And suppose, he said, these grievances do exist? So do you and I. And the universal soul prefers the man who sets his own house in order first. A foul thing, this "doing good," observed the contemptuous Henry, instead of looking after one's own life, which ought to be one's business, taking care to flourish, and taste and smell sweet, refreshing all mankind. He had had encounters with reformers that filled him with abhorrence. They would not keep their distance. They tried to cover him with a slimy kindness that fairly took the starch out of his clothes. These "lovers" of their kind were almost more injurious to their kind than the feeble souls that met in drawing-rooms, fabulating and paddling in the social slush, and going to their beds unashamed, to take on a new layer of sloth.

Henry had plenty of acid in his composition. He had taken a few suggestions from Zeno the Stoic,—for one, that he had two ears and a single mouth, in order to hear more and speak less,—as Alcott had followed Pythagoras and Emerson, largely, Plato. Emerson, older and riper, with a fund of sunny benevolence, the fruit of a happier culture and a fortunate bringing-up,—Emerson deplored this hedgehog's posture, the spikes, the spines, the quills that made his Henry a John Quincy Adams of the village. But time would certainly soothe and rectify him. Meanwhile, he was a living illustration of all his own ideas, endowed with hands and feet. Henry described himself, or his hope for himself,—"stuttering, blundering clodhopper" that he said he was,—in words that seemed to have their truth already. He was prepared for a glorious life; he had laid out an avenue through his head, eight rods wide; he had got the world,—much more, the flesh and the devil, —as it were by the nape of the neck, and held it under the tide of its own events, and let it go down stream like a dead dog, till he heard the hollow chambers of silence stretching away on every side and his own soul expanded and filled them. He could not help taunting his fellow-Yankees. Seek first the kingdom of heaven! Lay not up for yourselves treasures on earth! What does it profit a man! Think of this, Yankees, think twice, ye who drone these words on the Sabbath day and spend the other six denying them! "Doing a good business!"—words more profane than any oath, words of death and sin. The children should not be allowed to hear them. If most of the merchants had not failed, and most of the banks as well, Henry's faith in the laws of the world would have been sadly staggered; for what was the sweetest sight his eyes could see but a man who was really fulfilling the ends of his being?—maintaining himself, as he could, if he wished to do so, paying the price in terms of simplification, by a few hours a day at manual labour. Was he a little impatient and a little narrow? If there was anything wrong with his angle of vision, there would always be plenty of others to correct it. For himself, he wished to live deep. He wished to suck out all the marrow of life, to cut a broad swath and shave close, to put to rout all that was not living. If the days and the nights were such that he greeted them with joy, if life emitted a fragrance like herbs and flowers, if it was more elastic and more starry, that was his success and all he asked for. . . .

Henry Thoreau had built a hut at Walden. In March, 1845, he had borrowed Alcott's ax,—which he took pains to return with a sharper edge,—and cut down some tall, arrowy pines for the timbers, studs and rafters. For the boards he bought a shanty from one of the Irish labourers on the railroad. The hut was ten feet by fifteen, shingled and plastered, with a garret and closet, a trap-door below, a brick fireplace, windows at the sides and a door facing the cove. The cost, all told, was $28.12½,—less than the annual rent of a student's room in Cambridge. There was a bean-field, close by, with a patch of potatoes, corn, peas and turnips. As a quasi-Pythagorean, Thoreau seldom indulged in beans. He exchanged his crop for rice in the village. Rice was the proper diet for one who loved so well the writings of the Oriental sages.

He had long cherished the notion of a forest-life. Ellery Channing had built himself a hut on the prairie in Illinois, and Henry's college class-mate, Stearns Wheeler, who had just died in Leipzig, had also built a rough woodland cabin, over at Flint's Pond, where he had lived for a year to save money, to buy Greek books and pay his way to Germany to study. Henry had spent six weeks in Wheeler's cabin, sharing one of his bunks of straw. There was nothing new in his own adventure, and he could not understand why his friends thought it was so peculiar. Some of them spoke as if he had gone to the woods in order to starve or freeze. Emerson had bought land on both sides of the pond, intending to build a summer-house, and Henry had carried out the project. Alcott, who liked to tinker at rustic architecture, helped him with his saw and hammer, along with the young Brook Farmer, George William Curtis of New York, who was boarding at Edmund Hosmer's in the village and working as a farm-hand. Henry felt at home in his sylvan dwelling. It made him think of some of those mountain-houses he had seen on his inland excursions, high-placed, airy, fragrant, with a fresh, auroral atmosphere about them. It was quiet, clean and cool, fit to entertain a travelling god. For company, birds flitted through his chamber, red squirrels raced over the roof, chickadees perched on the armfuls of wood he carried. There were moles living in the cellar. He had occasional visits from a hare. As he sat at his door in the evening, he remembered that he was descended from the Greeks of old. He was a wanderer, too, one of the crew of Ulysses. The shore of the cove was another Ithaca.

There was nothing about his "experiment," as his friends liked to call it, to arouse such curiosity and contempt. It was a common-sensible undertaking, and only a slight departure from Henry's usual mode of living. His average weekly outlay, for necessaries he could not supply himself, was twenty-seven cents. A few days at manual labour, building a boat or a fence, planting, grafting or surveying,—six weeks of work out of the year, when he had grown extravagant and had to have a microscope,—gave him an ample surplus. Why should anyone live by the sweat of his brow and bore his fellow-men by talking about it? Why should not everyone live with an ample margin?—as anyone could do, provided he followed the path of simplification, logically and ruthlessly enough. The mass of men led lives of quiet desperation. Why, if not to maintain a "standard of living" that every law of the universe controverted? Did they not know that the wisest had always lived, with respect to comforts and luxuries, a life more simple and meagre than the poor? Had all the philosophers, Hindu, Greek and Persian, lived and taught in vain? Had anyone measured man's capacities? Was it fair to judge by precedents, when so very little had been attempted? Who could say that if a man advanced, boldly, in the direction of his dreams, endeavouring to live the life he had imagined, he would not meet with a success that he had never expected in common hours? Henry believed, and wished to piove, that the more one simplified one's life the less complex the laws of life would seem. Why all this pother about possessions? He liked to think of the ancient Mexicans, who burned all their goods every fifty years. Hawthorne, in one of his stories, had pictured a similar holocaust; and this was the kind of reform that Henry thought was worth considering. He meant to have his furniture, actual and symbolic, as simple as an Indian's or an Arab's. There were three bits of limestone on his table. They had to be dusted every day, while the furniture of his mind was still undusted. Out of the window, quick!

If he had had the wealth of Croesus, Henry's mode of living would not have been different. Space, air, time, a few tools, a note-book, a pen, a copy of Homer, what could he wish more than these? A bath in the pond at sunrise, a little Spartan sweeping and cleaning, then a bath for the intellect, perhaps in the Bhagavad-Gita, the pure water of Walden mingling in his mind with the sacred water of the Ganges. The day was his, for any wild adventure. Sometimes, on a summer morning, he would sit for hours in his sunny doorway, amid the pines and hickories and sumachs, in undisturbed solitude and stillness. The birds flitted noiselessly about him. He could feel himself growing like the corn. He knew what the Orientals meant by contemplation and the forsaking of works. He was a Yogi, too, a forest-seer, who might have composed the Upanishads. His Reality was also

Brahma, not the actualities of the world, but its potentialities. What did he care for temporal interests? It was his vocation to discover God. His days were no longer days of the week, bearing the names of pagan deities, nor were they minced into hours or fretted by the ticking of a clock. He felt like a Puri Indian or a Mexican. If you had put a watch in his hand and asked him what the hour was, he might have looked at the dial and said, "Quién sabe?" The sounds of the railway rose and died in his ears like the distant drumming of a partridge.

His life here seemed to flow in its proper channels. It followed its own fresh currents, and he felt himself lurking in crystalline thought as the trout lurked under the verdurous banks. Not so much as a bubble rose to the surface. At sunset, he jumped into his boat and paddled to the middle of the pond. There he played on his flute, while the charmed perch hovered about the stern, and the moon travelled over the floor of the pond, strewn with the wrecks of the forest. The wildest imagination could not conceive the manner of life he was living, for the Concord nights were as strange as Arabian nights. He struck the side of the boat with his paddle, filling the woods with a circle of sound. What a pleasant mission it would be to go about the country in search of echoes! He knew where to find the prophetic places, the vocal, resounding, sonorous, hollow places, where oracles might be established, sites for oracles, sacred ears of Nature.

What could he say to a man who feared the woods, who shuddered at their solitude and darkness? What salvation was there for such a man? Did he not know that God was mysterious and silent? Henry could never have wearied of the woods, as long as he could visit a nighthawk on her nest. He could hardly believe his eyes when he stood within seven feet of her. There she was, sitting on her eggs, so sphinx-like, so Saturnian, so one with the earth, a relic of the reign of Saturn that Jupiter had failed to destroy, a riddle that might cause a man to go and dash his head against a stone. No living creature, surely, far less a wingéd creature of the air. A figure in stone or bronze, like a gryphon or a phoenix. With its flat, greyish, weather-beaten crown, its eyes were all but closed with stony cunning; and yet all the time this sculptured image, motionless as the earth, was watching with intense anxiety, through those narrow slits in its eyelids. Wonderful creature, sitting on its eggs, on the bare, exposed hill, through pelting storms of rain or hail, as if it were a part of the earth itself, the outside of the globe, with its eyes shut and its wings folded. It was enough to fill a man with awe. Henry thought for a moment that he had strayed into the Caucasus, and that around the hill, on the other slope, he would find Prometheus chained to the rock.

Round and round the pond, Henry followed the footpath worn by the feet of Indian hunters, old as the race of men in Massachusetts. The critics and poets were always complaining that there were no American antiquities, no ruins to remind one of the past, yet the wind could hardly blow away the surface anywhere, exposing the spotless sand, but one found the fragments of some Indian pot or the little chips of flint left by some aboriginal arrow-maker. When winter came, and the scent of the gale wafted over the naked ground, Henry tramped through the snow a dozen miles to keep an appointment with a beech-tree, or a yellow birch perhaps, or some old acquaintance among the pines. He ranged like a grey moose, winding his way through the shrub-oak patches, bending the twigs aside, guiding himself by the sun, over hills and plains and valleys, resting in the clear grassy spaces. He liked the wholesome colour of the shrub-oak leaves, well-tanned, seasoned by the sun, the colour of the cow and the deer, silvery-downy underneath, over the bleached and russet fields. He loved the shrub-oak, with its scanty raiment, rising above the snow, lowly whispering to him, akin to winter, the covert which the hare and the partridge sought. It was one of his own cousins, rigid as iron, clean as the atmosphere, hardy as all virtue, tenacious of its leaves, leaves that did not shrivel but kept their wintry life, firm shields, painted in fast colours. It loved the earth, which it over-spread, tough to support the snow, indigenous, robust. The squirrel and the rabbit knew it well, and Henry could understand why the deer-mouse had its hole in the snow by the shrub-oak's stem. Winter was his own chosen season. When, for all variety in his walks, he had only a rustling oak-leaf or the faint metallic cheep of a tree-sparrow, his life felt continent and sweet as the kernel of a nut. Alone in the distant woods or fields, in the unpretending sprout-lands or pastures tracked by rabbits, on a bleak and, to most, a cheerless day, when a villager would be thinking of his fire, he came to himself and felt himself grandly related. Cold and solitude were his dearest friends. Better a single shrub-oak leaf at the end of a wintry glade, rustling a welcome at his approach, than a ship-load of stars and garters from the kings of the earth. By poverty, if one chose to use the word, monotony, simplicity, he felt solidified and crystallized, as water and vapour are crystallized by cold.

All praise to winter, then, was Henry's feeling. Let others have their sultry luxuries. How full of creative genius was the air in which these snow-crystals were generated. He could hardly have marvelled more if real stars had fallen and lodged on his coat. What a world to live in, where myriads of these little discs, so beautiful to the most prying eye, were whirled down on every traveller's coat, on the restless squirrel's fur and on the far-stretching fields and forests, the wooded dells and mountain-tops,—these glorious spangles, the sweepings of heaven's floor. He watched the men cutting the ice on the pond. Some of this ice, stowed in the holds of ships, was going over to India; and many a seeker of Brahma in Calcutta was destined to drink from his own Walden well. If winter drove one in-doors, all the better. It compelled one to try new fields and resources. Days of merry snowstorms and cheerful winter evenings by the fire. Evenings for books of natural history, Audubon, for one. It was pleasant to read about the Florida Keys, the flowering magnolia, the warm spice-breezes, while the wind beat the snow against one's window. Days to sit at home over one's journal, in one's own nest, perhaps on a single egg, though it might prove to be an egg of chalk.

These were the days for writing, days to speak like a man in a waking moment to others in their waking moments. For Henry was hard at work. He was writing articles, which Horace Greeley placed for him. He had begun to write a book, and he wished to pay his tribute to Carlyle, who had liberated the English language, cutting away the fetters imposed upon it by the pedantic writers of the British reviews. The frigid *North American* was even worse, a venerable cobweb that had escaped the broom. He liked to think of Carlyle, on his vacations, riding on his horse "Yankee," bought from the American sale of his books. His own book, rewritten from his journal, was the *Week on the Concord and Merrimac Rivers*, the story of the journey with his brother, never to be forgotten, when they had doubled so many capes and run before the wind and brought back news of far-away men. He did not propose to crowd his day with work, even if the book had to be written. A writer, he thought, should saunter to his task surrounded by a halo of ease and leisure, and the labour of his hands should remove from his style all trace of sentimentality and palaver. One did not dance idly at one's writing when one had wood to cut and cord. As the strokes rang cheerily through the wood, so the stroke of the pen should ring on the reader's ear. Was the voyage an old story, eight or nine years old, and only a week at that? It represented a lifetime's memories. No boy who had grown up on the Mississippi recalled those floating enchantments, the river-boats, and the fabulous river-men, with more of a thrill than Henry felt, remembering the canal-boats of his childhood. The news had spread through Concord that one of these boats was stealing through the meadows, silent as a cloud, with its crew of "foreigners" from New Hampshire, and all the village boys had flocked to see it. Henry wished to write a book that would be saturated with his thought and reading, yet one that would not smell so much of the study, even the poet's cabin, as of the fields and woods. He dreamed of an unroofed book, lying open under the ether, a book that could hardly be forced to lie on a shelf.

He was not by nature a hermit. He might have frequented the bar-rooms, he thought, if he had had any business that called him thither. Almost every day he walked to the village, to trade his beans for rice, to get a boot repaired, to collect the news of the family. Sometimes he returned late at night, with a bag of rye or Indian meal, sailing back under the moon to his harbor in the

woods. It was only that he was wary of gossip. He did not wish
to lumber his mind with the rubbish that most men seemed to
rejoice in, the details, for example, of some case in court. One
day he was arrested in the village for refusing to pay his poll-tax.
He felt as Alcott felt. The government supported slavery, the
government was backing the Mexican War; well, he would not
support the government. He did not wish to trace the course of
his dollar until it bought a man, or bought a gun to shoot a
Mexican. He spent the night in jail,—a fruitful night. It inspired
his essay on *Civil Disobedience*. He wished to establish a principle, that one man locked up in jail for refusing to countenance
slavery would be the end of slavery, or, to express it on a broader
basis, "If the alternative is to keep all just men in prison, or give
up war and slavery, the State will not hesitate which to choose."
A foolish notion, many people thought, but some of them
changed their minds, in later years, when one of Henry's Hindu
readers, Gandhi, acting on the principle, disturbed the British
Empire for several months. The next morning, Henry, released
from jail, gathered some of the boys and girls for a huckleberry
party, on a hill, whence the State was nowhere to be seen. He
never fastened his door at Walden, though sometimes, in his
absence, he had unwelcome visitors. How did Mrs. X happen
to know that his sheets were not as clean as hers? But nothing
was ever stolen, except his copy of Homer. One had to keep
one's eye on bookish people.

He had other guests, especially in April, when all the world
seemed to be on the move. A runaway slave appeared, then Alek
Therien, the French-Canadian woodchopper, a true Homeric
peasant who had learned a little Greek from his priest in the
north, then Hugh Quoil, an Irish soldier, who had fought at the
Battle of Waterloo. Old Quoil, with his wife and his jug, was
patiently waiting for death in a hut in the woods. The shanty-
Irish folk along the railroad sometimes came to see him. Henry
thought them shiftless enough, with their women washing under
the trees and the pigs poking about among the tubs. He eyed
them with a vague hostility. as the red men had eyed the first

settlers, and with as much reason; for were they not the first
wave of the sea that was to sweep away so many landmarks?
Among the little ragamuffins that swarmed about these cabins,
there were some in whom the prophetic eye might have seen the
masters of the future, the lords of Greater Boston, mayors, governors, captains of police, even, perhaps, a cardinal. Henry had
one good friend among them, little Johnny Riordan, with his
quaint "old worthy" face, behind the sober visor of his cap, plodding to school through the snow in his next-to-nothing, facing
and routing it like a Persian army. A great sight, Johnny, in his
rags, beside the well-fed villagers, waddling about in their furs
and finery. Emerson also came, of course. Henry read aloud to
him some pages from his book, while they sat under an oak beside the pond. Alcott arrived one night, struggling through the
snow. Ellery Channing spent a fortnight with him. When the
poets and sages came, he was glad that his dwelling was so spa-
cious. As the conversation assumed a grander and loftier tone,
they shoved their chairs further and further apart, until they
touched the walls in opposite corners. This left plenty of neutral
ground for their sentences to deploy in martial order.

Once Henry left his house for a fortnight's excursion. He had
cousins in Bangor, Maine, one of them in the lumber-trade, a
good excuse to visit the northern woods. He wished to study the
Indians in their forest wilderness, and he wished to climb Mount
Ktaadn. He never travelled without prayer and fasting, for he did
not wish to dissipate his mind. With all the industry of a busy
life, how could one hope to know, really know, an area more
than six miles square? Isaac Hecker had asked him to go to Rome,
the two of them together, Hecker to pay the expenses, for
Hecker, who had tried Brook Farm and Fruitlands, was boarding
with Mrs. Thoreau for a taste of Concord. He hoped to carry
Henry over to Rome, in more than one fashion. Later, another
friend, an Englishman, invited him for a visit in England. In both
cases, Henry said, No. If Europe was much in his mind, and became more and more to him, Concord might become less and less;
and what sort of bargain would that be? He did not wish his life
to lose its homely savour. If the fields and streams and woods that

he loved so well, and the simple occupations of his townsmen, ever ceased to interest and surprise him, what culture or wealth could ever atone for the loss? He did not wish to go to Europe, nor did he wish to go—like the farmers—west. What could he think of this foolish American habit, going east or west to a "better land," without lifting an honest finger to till and redeem one's own New England soil? As for the rush to California, it was a disgrace to humankind,—digging gold, the merest lottery, a kind of toil, if it deserved the name, in no sense beneficial to the world. A startling development, this, of the ethics of trade and all the modes of getting a living. It filled Henry with a cold scorn. For the rest, he had his own western horizon, towards which he was always moving, pitching his tent each day nearer the Golden Gate. But the really fertile soils and luxuriant prairies lay on one's own side of the Alleghanies, wherever a man minded his own business. Were not all the essentials of life to be found in Concord, ten times found if one properly valued them?—which a man could only do if he stood his ground. Henry had something to say to the men in the covered wagons, who were running away from something besides the rocks. If the men in the covered wagons had no ears for Henry, he would be glad to wait for a few generations. The great-great-grandsons of the covered wagons would be ready to listen to him.

Nobody knew the riches of Concord. As for natural history, he had found some of the Arctic phenomena there, red snow and one or two Labrador plants. Still, a little travel now and then was not so bad to give one's mind an airing, especially if it offered him a chance to observe the ways of the Indians. For the Indians had a special charm for Henry; they suggested a simpler mode of life and a greater nearness to the earth. Were there not two eternities, one behind him, which the Indians represented, as well as one before? Wherever he went, he trod in their tracks, yet only a few poets remembered them. Here and there, one saw their lonely wigwams, on the banks of some quiet stream, like the cabins of the muskrats in the meadows,—an old squaw, perhaps, living in her solitary hut, with her dog, her only companion, making baskets and picking berries, insulted by the village boys and girls.

Henry dreamed of writing a book about them;[1] for their memory seemed to him to harmonize with the russet hue of autumn that he loved. A race that had exhausted the secrets of nature, a race tanned with age, while the young, fair Anglo-Saxon slip, on whom the sun had shone for so short a time, was only just beginning its career. As sportsmen went in pursuit of ducks, and scholars of rare books, and all men went in pursuit of money, Henry went in search of arrow-heads, when the proper season came round again. He often spent whole afternoons, especially in the spring, when the rains had washed the ground bare, pacing back and forth over a sandy field, looking for these relics. It might have rained arrow-heads. They lay all over the surface of the country, sometimes mingled with arrow-headiferous soil, ash-coloured, left by Indian fires. They were like so many fossil thoughts to Henry, forever recalling the far-away mind that shaped them.

To Maine, then!—where the Indians grew with the moose. A fortnight in the forest, the home of the bear and the caribou, the wolf, the beaver and the Penobscot redskins, where the wild fir flourished and the spruce-tops, seen from an elevation, were like the odour of cake in a schoolboy's nostrils. Hemlocks and cedars, silver and yellow birches, watery maples, damp and moss-grown rocks, real woods, these, wild and bearded. One caught the whistle of ducks on solitary streams, the flicker of the darting chickadee, the loon's desolate laugh. Sometimes, through the moss-clad aisles, one heard a dull, dry, rustling sound, as if smothered under the fungus-covered forest, the falling of a tree, like the shutting of a door in some distant entry of the dark and shaggy wilderness. There one could feel at home, shooting the rapids in one's birch canoe, like a bait bobbing for some river monster, darting from side to side of the stream, then gliding swift and smoothly. This was the place to sing the "Canadian boat-song," or to play on one's flute, at night, under the stars, while the wolves howled about, in the darkness of the continent. Henry watched Joe Polis, the Indian guide, glued to the bank on

---

[1] Thoreau left eleven manuscript volumes, about 3000 pages, filled with notes about the Indians for the book he had hoped to write.

his stomach, talking to the muskrats in their sylvan language. Sometimes, by the fireside, Joe Polis also sang, a mild and simple nasal chant, like the dawn of civilization over the woods. The white man's brow was clear and distinct, but over the brow of the Indian lingered a haze or mist. For the Indian, the white man's noon was four o'clock in the morning.

A journey like this was only a foretaste, too rewarding not to be repeated. Henry was writing about his travels, and one of the magazines was glad to print his essay on Ktaadn. Later, on two occasions, he went to Maine again. He wished to visit Chesuncook, the Allegash and the East Branch. He was in his element in the woods, as Richard Henry Dana on the sea, as an old French-Canadian *coureur de bois*. Was he not a Frenchman as well as a Yankee, who might have run wild with Du Lhut and harried the woods for beavers? In the meantime, he had left his Walden cabin. Why? For as good a reason as he had gone there. He had other lives to live, and he had no more time to spare for this one. He wanted a change, he did not wish to stagnate. About two o'clock in the afternoon, he had felt the world's axle creaking a little, as if it needed greasing, as if the oxen laboured with the wain and could hardly get their load over the ridge of the day. Who would accept heaven on terms like this?—and a ticket for heaven had to include, for Henry, tickets for hell and purgatory also. Walden was only a bivouac in his campaign. He had other journeys in mind, to Cape Cod, for instance, with Ellery Channing, and later a jaunt to Canada, Quebec and Montreal. (Total expense, two guide-books included, $12.75.) Ellery was not a man for camping out,—that was an art one had to acquire slowly; but he shared Henry's taste for a simple equipment. And Henry would no more have thought of dressing,—dressing for a journey!—than he would have blacked his boots for fishing. Honest travelling was dirty work. A pair of overalls was the proper costume, a gray sack, corduroys perhaps; and as for this blacking of boots, he despised it on all occasions. In this, he was like some of the Harvard professors, who, as Mrs. Story was shocked to note, on one of her visits from Italy, did not have their boots blacked even for Commencement. Henry, who always carried a piece of tallow, in order to keep the water out of the leather, looked like a woodchuck or a musquash. This was his desire, at least,—the more like a quadruped the better, tawny, russet, yellow-brown, the colour of the sands. Vermont grey was not so bad; and once he had had the perfect suit, a skillful mixture of browns, with light and dark cleverly proportioned, and a few threads of green. He had looked like a corner of a pasture, with patches of sweet-fern and lechea. He had been able to glide over the fields, as unperceived from the farmer's windows as a painted cruiser through a spyglass. The wild animals thought he was one of them. Ellery, who was not so systematic, shared Henry's feeling in the matter of hats. His own hat was old and weather-beaten and had plenty of holes around the brim. It was as rare and high as a good Stilton cheese. As for the rest of Henry's outfit, a handkerchief served for a bag, or a firm, stout sheet of brown paper, well tied up. What else? An umbrella, of course, a knapsack, with partitions for books and papers, a music-book for pressing flowers, a field-glass and a measuring-tape. A fish-line, spoon and dipper, a little salt and sugar, tea, Indian meal and a slice of fruit-cake. If anyone asked him along the way to do a little tinkering, that was a tribute to his common sense.

So Henry tramped to Provincetown. Having seen the woods, he wished to see the ocean, and Cape Cod was surely the place to see it. There, on the stretches of sand blown clean by the wind, he could forget the towns, where he felt so unspeakably mean and disgraced. He could forget the bar-rooms of Massachusetts, where the full-grown were not weaned from their savage and filthy habits, sucking cigars and guzzling whiskey-punch. On the Cape, one saw wholesome faces, well preserved by the salty air, faces bleached like old sails, hanging cliffs of weather-beaten flesh. The Cape Cod boys leaped from their leading-strings into the shrouds; it was only a bound from their mother's laps to the masthead. They boxed the compass in their infant day-dreams. They could hand, reef and steer by the time they flew a kite. This was a country almost as thrilling as Maine. Henry had three books more or less on the stocks: *The Maine Woods*, full of the scents of the forest, *Cape Cod*, redolent of the sea, even *A Yankee in Canada.* The well-known publishers, Time & Co., could be trusted to see that they were safely printed. One of his neighbours wrote about Human Culture. Why should he not write about Cape Cod, another name for the same thing, and hardly a sandier phase of it? Or Canada, for that matter? He wrote an opening paragraph, with both hands clenched: "Read my book if you dare!"

# R. F. DIBBLE

ROY FLOYD DIBBLE has been classified, perhaps permanently, as an imitator of Lytton Strachey and a minor American biographer of the nineteen-twenties. He was born and lived his youth in obscurity on a farm near Lake Erie in the westernmost corner of New York State, Chautauqua County. But a creative instinct which set him composing amidst the domestic routine a long sonnet-sequence impelled him at twenty-one to seek a higher education. He took his A.B. degree at Clark University in 1912. After a year of school-teaching, he began his connection with Columbia University which proved a bulwark in his brief, unsteady life. Graduate student, University Fellow, Instructor in English (1916), he climbed the academic ladder; then—it is his friend and colleague, Mark Van Doren, telling us in the *Dictionary of American Biography*—with a surgical operation came the sudden news that he had but three more years to live. This sentence "dulled his ambition" for a time and "confirmed him in a 'quietism' inspired by Thoreau's *Walden*." Yet he did not die. Gradually aroused by radical reactions to America's entrance into the World War, he summoned energy to write a thesis and take the degree of Doctor of Philosophy in 1921. His thesis, as it happened, was a biographical and critical sketch of an obscure politician and novelist of the post-Civil-War days, Albion W. Tourgée; and, though the subject was unimportant, the biographical experience prepared Dibble for a new influence.

He soon found himself caught up into a strong sympathy with the new books of Lytton Strachey, and set out to fashion an American book that might compare not too unworthily with *Eminent Victorians*. *Strenuous Americans* (1923), dedicated with unconcealed admiration "To the Greatest Living Biographer," did not of course reveal a second Strachey. It did indeed bring Dibble enough encouragement for him to resign his post at Columbia and give himself entirely to biography. But only two more works followed. The first of these, *John L. Sullivan: An Intimate Biography*, was a vivid and entertaining life of the celebrated heavyweight champion, another "strenuous" American. Given average ability, any biographer of "the Strong Boy of Boston" could probably have produced a popular success in 1925; Dibble wrote with journalistic color and enthusiasm. When he next turned to popularizing the founder of a world religion in *Mohammed* (1926), however, he was clearly beyond his depth; and a third long biography, of Martin Luther, failed to find a publisher. Thereupon Dibble returned to teaching. He was serving as Associate Professor of English at Hunter College when disease, aggravated by the economic depression, ended his career in 1929 at the age of forty-two.

The imitators of Strachey have been the target of some heavy attacks, many of them exaggerated. In his obituary on Strachey, J. C. Squire regretted that though his books will be read, "his influence was not good, because his imitators lack his taste and skill." Especially true is this in America, he says, where there is a plethora of "books by authors who think they are doing something when they call Emerson 'Ralph' and Longfellow 'Harry'; books in which 'imaginative reconstruction' runs to seed." He may well have had Dibble in mind, for was not *Strenuous Americans* inspired in title and ironical manner by *Eminent Victorians*, and does not Dibble treat his subjects—Jesse James, Brigham Young, James J. Hill, P. T. Barnum, Frances E. Willard, Mark Hanna—with a joyous irreverence? Yet, as Dibble probably realized, neither were his own gifts particularly Stracheyan nor were his characters veiled in that nimbus of sanctity which would draw a biographer's subtle play of wit or paradox. So in the following sketch, realizing that even caustic satire never fazed America's most flamboyant showman, the author writes with a heartiness rare in the books of his master.

As for his method, Dibble explains: "I have tried, so to speak, to view each one as though he were seated on some height; then I have paced round and round that height, in order to study him from every angle. At times I have stepped back for a considerable distance, at other times I have approached within arm's length, so that my viewpoint might be neither too distant nor too near. . . . In tracing their lives, I have strenuously endeavored to maintain a precise exposition, a scrupulous interpretation, a controlled but generous enthusiasm, and a cool-headed but warm-hearted detachment." The reader will find it valuable to compare this sketch of Barnum with the longer one by Constance M. Rourke in *Trumpets of Jubilee* and with the full-length life by M. R. Werner.

# P. T. BARNUM

ON JUNE 25, 1874, the most influential citizens of Bridgeport, Connecticut, gave a banquet in honor of their leading townsman, P. T. Barnum. It was, as successive speakers carefully reiterated, a very poor and inadequate way of showing the gratitude which was due him because of the enormous favors he had so generously conferred upon the city; but at least it was better than nothing at all. An unstinted abundance of good food, good liquor, and good fellowship, together with an absolute faith that Bridgeport was unquestionably the finest of the many fine spots in God's own country, made the occasion uncommonly felicitous. At its end, the participants were actually almost ready to agree with the sentiment expressed by a clergyman, who, as was fitting, made the concluding speech—in which, as was even more fitting, he temporarily directed the thoughts of his audience toward higher things. "What a spiritual showman he would have made!" the good man exclaimed; "how he would have exhibited the menagerie of the heart, in which ferocious beasts, in the form of fiery passions, play upon the soul!" Nor had poetry failed to grace the event in the form of a spirited recitative of Barnum's many-sided accomplishments. A member of the bench, doffing his judicial dignity, had poured out his admiration in these capering lines:

> Of all demnition wonderments that swell his fame and pelf,
> There never was a demder one than Barnum is himself!
>
> One day in Bridgeport staking out new streets across his farm,
> The next, in Windsor Castle, with Victoria on his arm;
> One day upon the prairies, looking out for freaks of nature,
> The next in Hartford, speech-making before the legislature;
> One day the Bearded Woman; next, the Mermaid with her comb;
> And now the Hippopotamus and now the Hippodrome.
>
> And finally—

But Barnum himself had been the chief speaker of the evening; and, since his public remarks were apt to be over-humble and less frank and engaging than his actual life had been, it may be well to take a rapid but inclusive glance at that life before the last stanza of the judge's poem is given.

The patriotic din of July 4, 1810, had barely died away when Phineas Taylor Barnum came bouncing into the world—or, in his own words, "made my *début*." The stage was the little town of Bethel, Connecticut, where for some twenty years the youthful actor played his part in episodes that fitted him excellently for his eventual place—the "prince of showmen." He was "born and reared in an atmosphere of merriment," which did not exclude a fair amount of religion, a great deal of close-fisted stinginess, and not a little downright knavery. His father, "a tailor, a farmer, and sometimes a tavern-keeper," had been granted a large share of all these attributes; so had his mother, although in her case religion and penuriousness dominated. More important than either of the parents, in the estimation of the son, was his maternal grandfather, Phineas Taylor, in whose honor he had been named: a voluble old fellow with a Thackerayan profile, who was a Universalist, a justice of the peace, a great practical joker, an astute inventor of profitable lotteries, and a lover of snuff. His paternal grandfather, however, was distinguished only by the fact that he had been a captain in the Revolutionary War. Practically all of these traits, together with many that were even more transcendent, were inherited by the youth himself, and he always gloried in his lineage.

While still at a tender age, he began to demonstrate his kinship in various ways. In school he was a quick scholar, particularly in arithmetic; but farm work he hated. "I always disliked work," he confessed at middle age. "Head-work I was excessively fond of . . . but hand-work was decidedly not in my line." He thoroughly learnt the value of money before he had outgrown babyhood; for Grandfather Taylor's pride in his little namesake occasionally impelled him, against his better judgment, to give the youngster pennies with which to buy raisins and candies, "which he always instructed me to solicit from the store-keeper at the 'lowest cash price.'" Grandfather Taylor's casual generosity was strictly a family matter. Little Phineas, guided by such an excellent teacher, soon began to branch out on various speculative lines of his own in order to increase his pile. When his schoolmates were skylarking about in the holiday seasons, he would purchase a gallon of molasses, boil it down, work it into candy, sell it to the neighbors, and ultimately gain a dollar by the transaction. Soon his stock in trade increased until it included ginger-bread cookies, sugar candies and cherry rum; the last article sold particularly well to the soldiers who gathered at Bethel on military training days. By the time he was ten years old, therefore, he had so much money that his father "considerately allowed me to purchase my own clothing." Nevertheless, he continued to look out "for the main chance" so shrewdly that at twelve he felt himself to be a man of substance. But at this time he had an experience which taught him very forcibly that there were other people in the world as shrewd as he—an experience destined to be repeated on a far greater scale at a later day. He obtained permission to help a neighbor drive a herd of cattle to New York; and, upon arriving, he began to spend his solitary dollar in a prodigal way. Before long, a shopkeeper short-changed him; in addition to this tragedy, he soon fell into the pit he had so often dug for others. Some molasses candy tempted him so strongly that he bought chunk after chunk. In the end, he bartered the pocket knife with its two blades, its gimlet, and its corkscrew, the top, and the glittering breast-pin (all of which he had just bought), for more candy. Still he was not appeased; two handkerchiefs and an extra pair of stockings met the same disaster that had befallen the toys. As hungry as ever, but more or less resigned to his fate, he then trudged home. His mother, discovering the loss of the handkerchiefs and stockings, immediately whipped him and sent him to bed, much to the delight of his brothers and sisters, who were envious of his good fortune in visiting the city and angry at the gluttony which had made him entirely forget that they were gluttonous too.

But these were week-day occurrences; Sundays were another matter. Even before he could read, little Phineas had trotted regularly to Sunday School in the single church that the village boasted; for differences in creed were rarely discussed in the little town—the people generally had more important matters to argue about. Faithfully, every Sunday, he was there, shivering in the winter months—for stoves in village churches were then unknown—as he chattered satisfactory responses to searching inquiries as to the condition of his spiritual state here and hereafter. But it seems almost certain that more distinctly tangible rewards were partially responsible for making him so punctual. Each Sunday's attendance won a little red ticket worth one mill; thus, one hundred tickets meant a prize in the form of a book. It was true that, at this rate, it would take two years to win the prize; but did not the prize mean, in a general way, something for nothing? "Infinitesimal as was this recompense," he once remarked, "it was sufficient to spur me to intense diligence."

When the boy was no longer a boy—when he had crossed that vague boundary which separates boyhood from youth—he had attained the distinction of being known as the laziest young fellow in town, "probably because I was always busy at head-work to evade the sentence of gaining bread by the sweat of the brow." The father, despairing of making anything better of his shiftless son, decided to put him to work as clerk in a store, which was bought as a possible corrective of the son's leading propensity. The choice was wise and big with portent of the future; for, since it was a "cash, credit and barter store," Phineas soon forgot his indolence in the opportunities that came for outwitting his neighbors in exchanging tenpenny nails, starch, saleratus and rum for butter, eggs, beeswax, feathers and rags. The only drawback attached to the position was that he had to rise early in order to sweep the floor, take down the shutters, and make the fire; but blissful balm came when he condescended to talk with common fellows who had to work with their hands for a living. A still greater pleasure came when he purposefully kept the store open until eleven o'clock or later, so that the chronic story-tellers of the town would be tempted to stay and divert him with anecdotes that were not less boisterous than clean.

The death of his father in 1825 forced him to slide down the family tree and depend entirely upon himself. For a year or two, he still clerked in various stores; he spent nearly a year in a Brooklyn grocery, where he was compelled to rise so early that he was in perpetual danger of losing his position until a native ingenuity came to his aid. For two shillings a week, he hired a watchman to pull a string which, attached to his great toe, hung out of his chamber window. But he was not satisfied to work on a regular salary, great or small: "My disposition is, and ever was, of a speculative character," he wrote at a later day. Accordingly, in 1828 he seized an opportunity to open a store of his own in Bethel, in which, as a public announcement stated, he sold "all kinds of dry goods, groceries, crockery, etc., etc., 25 per cent cheaper than any of his neighbors." Furthermore, it furnished a very convenient medium for conducting lotteries—a practice by which he had already been sharpening his wits for some years. He pondered briefly over the morality of the business, but it was forunately unnecessary to ponder long. "One of our neighbors, a pillar in the church, permitted his son to indulge in that line . . . and the morality of the thing being thus established, I became a lottery manager and proprietor." In distinct contrast to the present time, indeed, lotteries were then commonly patronized by both church and state; and Barnum, who tickled millions of people with thousands of amusingly quaint devices during his life, always took an infinitude of pains in selecting allurements that bore the badge of moral approval. He worked several gambling schemes of this sort to the great benefit of his purse, and some twenty years later explained how they had been engineered, for the sake of any foolish mortals who might be tempted to squander their money upon similar frauds. "If this *expose* shall have the effect of curing their ruinous infatuation," he commented, "I, for one, shall not be sorry." It is a little difficult, in fact, to see why he should have been greatly distressed at imparting information which had long since served his own special purposes.

Games of chance were now becoming a matter of course with him; accordingly, in 1829, when he was only nineteen, he married a seamstress, "an industrious, excellent, sensible, and well-behaved girl," and managed to scrape along for two years more with the help of his wife, his store and his gambling tickets. Then he started a weekly newspaper whose modest purpose was to "oppose all combinations against the liberties of our country"; but the excess vigor of youth soon impelled him to take undue liberties with his own townsmen. Eventually he was prosecuted three times for libel; twice he escaped penalty, but the third time was sentenced to pay a $100 fine and spend sixty days in the Danbury jail. But he did not take the affair seriously, and proceeded, after the manner of Leigh Hunt in a similar situation, to have a highly diverting time. Before he entered jail, the cell was papered and carpeted; he was constantly visited by his friends, edited his paper regularly, and was rewarded by receiving several hundred new subscriptions during his imprisonment. His release was a gala occasion. Forty horsemen and a marshal bearing the national flag preceded the coach, drawn by six horses, in which he and a band were carried; and behind this coach came a vehicle which bore the orator of the day, followed by sixty other carriages full of citizens. The roar of cannon attended the march of the procession from Danbury to Bethel, while the band continuously played national airs, concluding with "Home, Sweet Home" when the little town came into view. Apparently, Barnum did not believe that the liberties of his country might conceivably be imperiled by those who took its laws too lightly; however, the notoriety that was aroused by this episode enabled him to keep his store and his paper running for a little more than a year. Then he decided that he was not in his proper element ("I was not in my natural sphere. I wanted to do business faster than ordinary mercantile transactions would admit . . ."), and in the winter of 1834-5 moved his family to New York, where he at once began to look around for opportunities to indulge in extraordinary mercantile transactions.

Such opportunities soon came. For several months, to be sure, he found nothing in which his "faculties and energies could have full play, and where the amount of profits should depend entirely upon the amount of tact, perseverance and energy which I contributed to the business." But in July, 1835, sunny fortune began to smile upon him, and not often thereafter did the fickle dame frown. In that month he heard of an amazing Negro woman, Joice Heth, who swore with positive conviction that she was one hundred and sixty-one years old. But extreme age was a minor attraction; her chief hold upon public credulity lay in the equally positive claim that she had been the nurse of George Washington. As a public entertainer, she showed remarkable garrulity in relating anecdotes about "dear little George," and in expressing, both in verse and prose, her firm faith in the theology of the Baptist church. It was therefore apparent that her exhibition was certain to be extremely interesting and remunerative, and Barnum's sharp nose at once sniffed out this fact. Her "story seemed plausible, and the 'bill of sale' had every appearance of antiquity"; and so he sold out his small business interests, borrowed $500, and bought the "animated mummy" for $1,000.

Thus began his extraordinary career as a public showman. From the beginning to the end, that career was dominated by one idea: "I can fool all of the people all of the time." Like his countrymen, he was democratic and sentimental in everything except in matters of business; in that field he was as thoroughly autocratic and cold-blooded as were all other good Americans in his generation—but, as everyone knows, that time has long since passed away. In his initial experiment, Barnum did not fail to employ some of the devices that led in the end to his undisputed, unrivaled and unparalleled eminence as the "prince of humbugs." More than anyone else of his time, he was "aware of the great power of the public press" and the immense possibilities of advertising. It is, indeed, impossible to over-emphasize the significance of the fact that he was the first American to appreciate the enormous financial rewards that were to be won by extravagant advertisements. And he was also aware of another important fact. To an inquirer who once asked him to state the indispensable qualifications of a good showman, he confidentially replied that the first qualification was "a thorough knowledge of human nature, which of course included the faculty of judiciously applying *soft soap*," which, he explained, was "the faculty to please and flatter the public so judiciously as not to have them suspect your intention." The second qualification, however, he did not state—for the excellent reason that there was none.

Perhaps it was fitting that the most practical and efficient of American humorists should have gained his tremendous fortune principally by employing the leading element in American humor—hyperbole, in countless forms and fashions; but, whether fitting or not, it is true. New York soon began to be flooded with handbills which tugged at two of humanity's strongest instincts: curiosity and patriotism. Joice Heth was set forth as "unquestionably the most astonishing and interesting curiosity in the world," and as the slave of Washington's father; but her most compelling attraction lay in the fact that she "was the first person *who put clothes on the unconscious infant* who was destined in after days to lead our heroic fathers to glory, to victory, and to freedom." Flesh and blood could not withstand such a combination of irresistible enticements; and Barnum was soon clearing a neat $1,500 a week. The loathsome old wench played her part to perfection. An absolute invalid, unable to move any part of her body except her right arm, totally blind, toothless, the nails on her helpless left hand four inches long and those on her toes a quarter of an inch thick, she lay hunched up on her couch day after day, spouting a steady torrent of affecting stories about "dear little George," occasionally varying these tales with edifying hymns to which she beat accompaniment with her withered but still mobile right arm. When at length audiences began to fall off, Barnum was ready. He printed an anonymous notice to the effect that Joice was not a living person at all, but merely an automaton ingeniously constructed of whalebone, rubber and numerous springs, which talked with the aid of a ventriloquist. Thousands who had already seen her came tumbling back immediately to discover whether they had actually been cheated on their first visit, and they departed no wiser than before.

In his autobiography, Barnum candidly answers the question as to whether Joice was an impostor. "*I do not know. I taught her none of these things.*" His private reflections, at the time when she was being displayed, were even more candid: "I do not know—and neither do I care . . . so long as the cash keeps rolling in."

Whatever she may have been, Joice was not immortal; and in February, 1836, she went on exhibition elsewhere. An autopsy was performed; and the doctor who supervised the operation was agreeably delighted when he did not (as he had feared he would) spoil "half a dozen knives in severing the ossification in the arteries around the region of the heart and chest," for there was no ossification at all. Newspaper controversy now waxed hot about the question of her antiquity; and since there was no way in which the matter could be settled, it was natural that the discussion should grow hotter and hotter. Meanwhile Barnum sat by, watching the row and chuckling as he reflected that all this clamor "served my purpose as 'a showman' by keeping my name before the public." "I will only add," he concluded, "that the remains of Joice were removed to Bethel, and buried respectably."

Barnum was now fairly started on the road to fame and fortune, although for the next five years he failed to find any lure so bewitching as "Aunt Joice" had been. As an itinerant showman he traveled over the eastern United States, meeting with varying success, with amusing experiences, and occasionally with danger. It seems probable, in fact, that he was the originator of the variety theatrical program, which has developed to such complex and enormous proportions. His principal performer was Signor Antonio, a juggler who had been in England and Canada for some years; but Barnum wisely decided that such a title was not sufficiently foreign, and therefore changed it to "Signor Vivalla," the "eminent Italian artist," who had "just arrived from Italy." Barnum himself rarely took part in the different programs that he offered, although his mobile face with its versatility of expression, and his moderate skill in legerdemain and ventriloquism, occasionally helped to swell the receipts. Once, when his leading Negro singer suddenly deserted, he blacked himself thoroughly and succeeded so well that "in two of the songs I was encored!" Then something unanticipated happened. Hearing a disturbance outside his tent, he rushed out and found a Southerner disputing with the members of his company. Having completely forgotten his blackened face, he began to "speak my mind very freely" to the Southerner, who instantly drew a pistol and shouted, "You black scoundrel!" meanwhile cocking the weapon. In a trice Barnum took in the situation and rolled up his shirtsleeves with a "presence of mind which never yet deserted me." His threatening opponent saw the white arms, and, struck with consternation at the nearly fatal mistake he had made, dropped the pistol. For this providential escape, "I cannot but realize that I am deeply indebted to the mercy of God," Barnum reflected. The mercy of God, moreover, regularly occupied his thoughts every Sunday, when no business could be done. Often, on that sacred day, he would gather the members of his company and read the Bible and printed sermons to them, pausing frequently to point out the general correctness of the Biblical doctrine of wretchedness in vice and happiness in virtue. Yet it was sadly apparent that his words carried very little weight for some members of the company—particularly for several women with whom the vigorous showman was somewhat better acquainted than with the troupe in general. After four years, it had become evident that, in spite of everything—tact, perseverance, energy, advertisements and the mercy of God—the business was not thriving; and in April, 1841, he came home "re-resolved that I would never again be an itinerant showman."

Nevertheless, he at once began to look around for some new scheme to mend his fortune; and such an opportunity soon appeared in the form of a collection of oddities for sale in New York. Lacking the funds necessary to effect an outright purchase, he cajoled the owners into selling the outfit to him upon a promise to pay $12,000 in seven annual installments. He had no such sum; but he offered as security five acres of absolutely worthless swamp land near Bethel, which Grandfather Taylor, in an expansive moment, had once given his little namesake as a witness of his generosity. The owners accepted this as a satisfactory security, without taking the trouble to visit the place; but Barnum at least more than kept his word, for the enterprise was so successful that all the indebtedness had been paid off before the end of the first year. Curiosity and patriotism were again the supreme inducements that were offered to the public, although curiosity, which almost invariably took the shape of abnormality and deformity, tended to dominate: "Industrious fleas, educated dogs, jugglers, automatons, ventriloquists, living statuary, tableaux, gypsies, albinoes, fat boys, giants, dwarfs, rope-dancers, . . . instrumental music, singing and dancing in great variety (including Ethiopians), etc. . . . mechanical figures, fancy glass-blowing, knitting machines and other triumphs in the mechanical arts, dissolving views, American Indians, including their warlike and religious ceremonies enacted on the stage, etc., etc." It was no wonder that Barnum's chief demonstrator, after pointing out to the sightseers the staggering attractions of this unheard-of array, was accustomed to close his lecture by advising his audience to go home and "ponder over the marvels that a beneficent Creator and a liberal management placed before us for the low sum of 25 cents."

Nor is it to be doubted that such an aggregation of monstrosities was, indeed, "abundantly worth the uniform charge of admission," and that a little clap-trap occasionally, "in the way of transparencies, flags, exaggerated pictures, and puffing advertisements," was more than offset by "a wilderness of wonderful, instructive, and amusing realities." "Indeed," he continued, "I cannot doubt that the sort of 'clap-trap' here referred to is allowable, and that the public like a little of it. . . ." The public got a great deal. Many people who, tempted by the seductive bait: "THE GREAT MODEL OF NIAGARA FALLS, REAL WATER," entered and found that a single barrel of water, churned by a small pump, served as a representation of the huge cataract, felt a bit disappointed at first; but "they had the whole Museum to fall back upon for 25 cents, and no fault was found." "I confess I felt somewhat ashamed of this myself," Barnum tells us, "yet it made a good line in the bill."

The most notorious of the many hoaxes introduced into the American Museum was undoubtedly the "Fejee Mermaid." Having been informed that he could buy "a preserved specimen of a veritable mermaid," Barnum investigated and found that it was an ingenious contraption with the head, arms and breast of a female monkey and the tail of a fish, about three feet long, apparently the handwork of some tireless and unscrupulous Japanese. This was excellent; and when he noted that its "mouth was open, its tail turned over, and its arms thrown up, giving it the appearance of having died in great agony," he was firmly assured that it would be a worthy successor to Joice Heth. In order to "modify general incredulity in the existence of mermaids," he carefully worked up a series of newspaper articles which stated that Professor Griffin, a high authority on anatomy, had found this particular specimen, had become thoroughly convinced that it was genuine, and was bringing it to New York for exhibition. He then manufactured a number of woodcuts which showed schools of mermaids sporting around in the ocean in all their classic beauty. Furthermore, he managed to have an article "proving the authenticity of mermaids" published in the New York Sunday papers on the same date, by insinuating to their respective editors that each one would be able to score a "scoop" on the others. Since the "mermaid fever was now getting pretty well up," he engaged a special hall, hired a bogus "Professor Griffin," and began exhibitions for "the small sum of 25 cents." The huge throngs that came scrambling and pushing their way in assured Barnum that he had found a gold-mine; and one week later a notice appeared stating that the curio was henceforth to be seen at the Museum "without extra charge." In a month's time it had increased the total receipts of the building by nearly $2,000, and for some years thereafter continued abundantly to prove the truth of its owner's sagacious dictum: "The American people love to be humbugged."

Once in a while, to be sure, Barnum failed to get, for his incredible collection, certain ensnaring decoys over whose money-making possibilities he had long gloated. His laudable endeavor to bring Shakespeare's birthplace, in separate sections, to America fell through on account of British pride, which, Barnum was amazed to discover, would not even consider such a transaction. Indeed, his relatively few failures generally came as a result of some obstacle which was intrinsically insuperable—something which no amount of money whatever could buy, and which for that very reason appealed irresistibly to an imagination that ever loved to sport with impossibilities. One failure of this sort came when he projected a scheme to tow an enormous iceberg from the Arctic Ocean to New York, put a floating fence around it, charge the usual twenty-five cents for admission, and regale those who were admitted upon sherry cobbler made from the iceberg itself; but icebergs, he was much chagrined to find, ordinarily have a most unpleasant habit of disappearing entirely before they even come in sight of New York. He once remarked to a visitor that, if the Sultan of Turkey could only be persuaded to permit excavations in the traditional Cave of Machpelah, great results might follow. "If we could only get the remains of Abraham and bring them to New York!" he exclaimed, rubbing his hands with delight at his own ingenious conception. "What do you think of Spurgeon for a show?" he asked the same visitor a moment later. "Could he be got over here?" Apparently he could not; for it seems that the famous English preacher's own personal exhibition was occupying all of his time.

But it was not long before the public began to realize that the greatest drawing card in the Museum was Barnum himself. One fact, indeed, seems to indicate that he had anticipated and worked for this very end. His office in the Museum was at the head of a stair near the entrance, so situated that each visitor had to pass it as he entered the building; and, while "Mr. Barnum—Private" was inscribed on the door, it invariably stood a little ajar. One day a man who had just bought a ticket inquired, "Is Barnum in the Museum?" "That is Mr. Barnum," replied the ticket-seller, pointing toward the place where the showman was sitting, absorbed in a newspaper. "Is this Mr. Barnum?" he was asked. "It is," was the answer. For a moment the man stared fixedly at him; then, throwing down his ticket, he exclaimed, "It's all right. I've got the worth of my money," and departed without paying the least attention to any of the other prodigies. *Hamlet* without Hamlet would not be more impossible than the Museum would have been without Barnum. Once seen, he was never forgotten, for he bulked large in every particular: the tall, portly figure, the massive head with its great face surrounded by wavy, patriarchal locks, the ears, nose, mouth, chin and eyes were all large—bulkiness was the one word that described everything. It pleased the better class of his contemporaries to believe that he closely resembled Daniel Webster; but among the lower ranks of society it was widely whispered that, even more closely, he resembled Jack Falstaff (or at least his spiritual descendants), both in his general appearance and in his general attitude toward life. Wherever he went, in the Museum or in the city, he saw peering eyes and pointing fingers, and frequently overheard people saying, "There's Barnum! That's old Barnum!"

Soon there came the first of those successive events which gave him an international reputation. Toward the end of 1842, he gained possession of Charles S. Stratton, a five-year-old dwarf, a native of Bridgeport, barely two feet in height and weighing less than sixteen pounds, but perfectly healthy and symmetrically formed. The manikin's natural attractions would doubtless have made him a sufficiently lucrative investment for anyone except P. T. Barnum; but he was taking no chances, and besides, the habit of exaggeration had now become easy and natural. So it happened that Museum handbills heralded the triumphant entrance to the shores of America of "General Tom Thumb, a dwarf eleven years of age, just arrived from England." Within a year's time, the precocious elf had made Barnum lose all direct interest in the Museum—except in the monthly receipts—and had inspired him to go abroad. In January, 1844, he sailed for England with little Tom, who was accompanied by his doting parents and his French tutor, and who was to receive $50 a week together with all expenses.

Then an unanticipated obstacle arose. At first it almost seemed as though British stolidity would not relax—as though dwarfs were either too common or too insignificant to arouse such phlegmatic people out of their steadfast impassivity. The perturbed showman almost believed for a time that he had met the most marvelous of all curiosities—a nation that could not be humbugged; but he was happily disappointed. Perceiving that the usual Yankee methods would not serve in this frigid environment, he began to meet the enemy on their own grounds. He sent letters of invitation to editors and several nobles, politely requesting them to come and see the General; and little by little they began to respond. Word of all this was soon passed around; and before long certain uninvited parties began to drive in crested carriages to Barnum's apartments—"*and were not admitted.*" Barnum's servant, dressed in good English style, had been instructed to deny admission, in a dignified way, to all who did not present cards of invitation. This sort of thing was naturally noised about, although it was noised quietly; and it was not long before Barnum received an invitation to dine with Edward Everett, the American Minister, and with Baroness Rothschild also. "I felt that the golden shower was beginning to fall," he commented; nor was he at all remiss in hastening the deluge. He whispered in the ear of Mr. Everett that the Queen's children would surely like to see little Tommy. Barnum, in fact, in all his multitudinous endeavors, had always been careful to select attractions that would appeal to children—whose "voices are the echo of heavenly music," as he was wont to say. His keen brain fully appreciated the fact that, if children could be tempted into using their voices for purely mundane things—into making clamorous appeals to go and see his various marvels—most parents would succumb to the inevitable and not only permit their little ones to go and see, but would also go along. Indeed, his portraits, with which America was by this time liberally flooded, rarely had his signature appended because it was not necessary; but underneath each one was written "The Children's Friend." So it happened that, in a few days, a note came "conveying the Queen's invitation to General Tom Thumb and his guardian, Mr. Barnum, to appear in Buckingham Palace on the evening specified." Tom had already begun to appear publicly in Piccadilly; and his crafty master, before starting for the royal residence, posted this notice on the door of the exhibition hall: "Closed this evening, General Tom Thumb being at Buckingham Palace by command of Her Majesty."

At the Palace, the Lord in Waiting drilled Barnum with great care in the etiquette of royalty; he was in no event to speak directly to the Queen, and in taking leave he was to back out of the room, always keeping his face turned toward Her Majesty. When these preliminaries were over, the visitors entered the imposing *salon* where the Queen, Prince Albert, the Duchess of Kent, and some thirty of the nobility were waiting—for it seems that the royal children, after the fashion of all good Victorian youngsters, had scrupulously obeyed their mother in the matter of going early to bed. Everybody showed much surprise and delight when it was seen that Tom was even a more diminutive mite than had been expected. The General, perfectly at his ease, advanced with a firm tread until he was within hailing distance, when he bowed gracefully and shouted, "Good evening, ladies and gentlemen!" All the nobility shook with laughter; and the Queen then took Tom by the hand, showed him around the gallery, and inquired how he liked the pictures. "First-rate," he answered; and then, after singing and dancing a bit, he talked with the Prince Consort. Barnum now had his opportunity. With the Lord in Waiting acting as interpreter, he entered into conversation with Victoria; but, after two or three passages of this sort, he boldly started a direct conversation, while the miserable Lord in Waiting looked as aghast as his impassive and thickly powdered face would permit. Barnum was pleased to note that the Queen appeared to enjoy the informality of the proceeding, but he did not fail to make his exit according to the prescribed formula. However, the gallery was long and the General, finding that he was being out-distanced, started to run. The Queen's favorite poodle, properly resenting this breach of royal etiquette, instantly chased after him; the General, equally angry, attacked it with his cane, and the two combatants were so nearly matched in size that the distinguished company once more gave way to loud merriment.

General Thumb, in fact, was just as free and easy in the presence of royalty as he had been among the common people in the Museum. Again accompanied by Barnum, he paid two more visits to the Queen. On the second occasion, he was ushered into the magnificent Yellow Drawing Room, where he remarked to his hostess that he "had seen her before." Her Majesty then said she hoped he was well. "Yes, ma'am," he replied, "I am first-rate." "General," she said, "this is the Prince of Wales." "How are you, Prince?" Tom inquired; then, standing by the side of the future King Edward VII he coolly measured their respective heights, and piped up, "The Prince is taller than I am, but I *feel* as big as anybody," at which everybody roared. One day a celebrated and lovely countess visited Tom, "kissed and caressed him over and over again; lavished upon him the most endearing epithets; and laughingly regretted that she was married"—for, said she, "I should like you for a husband." The General "made a complimentary reply, as he sat upon the lady's arm and leaned luxuriously against her voluptuous bust." In truth, according to his employer, "his morals in all respects" were unobjectionable and his "disposition most amiable." The Duke of Wellington was a not infrequent caller upon the two American celebrities, and on one occasion, when Tom was impersonating Napoleon, asked him what was occupying his thoughts. "I was thinking of the loss of the battle of Waterloo," came the instant response. This brilliant reply was "chronicled through the country, and was of itself worth thousands of pounds to the exhibition," wrote Barnum; but he failed to say whether or no the *bon mot* had been previously suggested.

For three years the European tour progressed, until in 1847 the wanderers returned to America. But Barnum was naturally unable to resist the temptation of capitalizing Tom's now worldwide reputation; and for nearly a year more they reaped rich harvests from many American cities. In May, 1848, arrangements were made whereby the General's tour could be carried on without Barnum's assistance, and he then returned to his home in Bridgeport. "I had now been a straggler from home most of the time for thirteen years," the modern Sinbad wrote, "and I cannot describe the feelings of gratitude with which I reflected that . . . I should henceforth spend my days in the bosom of my family." Nevertheless, like Sinbad, Barnum was wrong; for in less than a year and a half, the "Swedish Nightingale" drove all thoughts of home, and even of Tom Thumb, from his mind.

By October, 1849, he had become infatuated with the idea of bringing Jenny Lind to America. In this undertaking he was not, it is true, very deeply concerned about elevating the standards of artistic taste in his native land. "I had never heard her sing," he admitted. "Her reputation, however, was sufficient for me." After pondering very seriously over the matter, he reached two conclusions, and their order is significant. First—"The chances were greatly in favor of immense pecuniary success"; second—"Inasmuch as my name has long been associated with 'humbug,' and the American public suspect that my capacities do not extend beyond the power to exhibit a stuffed monkey-skin or a dead mermaid, I can afford to lose $50,000 in such an enterprise as bringing to this country . . . the greatest musical wonder in the world. . . ." In an even better fashion, a contemporary satirist expounded Barnum's real motive, as well as his low opinion of his countrymen's mentality, in these lines:

> They'll welcome you with speeches, and serenades, and rockets,
> And you will touch their hearts, and I will tap their pockets,
> And if between us both the public isn't skinned,
> Why, my name isn't Barnum, nor your name Jenny Lind!

It soon became known that Barnum intended to enter into negotiations with Miss Lind; and several theatrical managers, who had an eye on her themselves, hastened to warn her not to make any engagement with that notorious liar and cheat, P. T. Barnum, assuring her that he would not hesitate to coop her up in a box and tote her around throughout the country for exhibition at 25 cents a head. But at length she was persuaded that he was not quite such an ogre as he had been represented to be; and a contract was drawn up, by the terms of which he was to place $187,500 in the care of London bankers—an amount sufficient to cover all deficits in the event of failure. Notwithstanding the immense profits that had come through Tom Thumb's unique personality, he found it very difficult to collect such a large sum; appeals to New York bankers convinced him that it was "useless in Wall Street to offer the Nightingale in exchange for gold-finches"; but in the end he won out. There remained the even more important task of preparing the public for the advent of the singer; and in this case it is a pleasure to note that the plain truth was so extraordinary that he conscientiously dispensed with his customary embellishments. But he played safe and played well. The press responded nobly to the urge of his purse; but "little did the public see of the hand that indirectly pulled their heart-strings preparatory to a relaxation of their purse-strings" he confessed at a safely remote day. When Miss Lind stepped upon the wharf at Canal Street, New York, she found herself in a bower of green trees decorated with blazing flags, together with two triumphal arches which bore the American eagle and the gaudy inscriptions "Welcome, Jenny Lind!" and "Welcome to America!"

What followed is a matter of musical history. During her first concert at Castle Garden, 5,000 people were wrought up to such a pitch of delirious enthusiasm that they entirely forgot the exorbitant prices that had been charged for tickets. At the close of the concert, she was encored again and again by the audience, which also vociferously shrieked for "Barnum! Barnum!" until he "responded reluctantly to their demand." Numbers of doubting financial Thomases, now entirely converted, besought Barnum to sell out his contract with Miss Lind; but these baits only made him more certain that the quantity of purse-strings destined to be relaxed would exceed his fondest hopes. Also, they warned him that he would have to look sharply to his laurels in order that the singer herself might not choose to search for more attractive bargains. Accordingly, even before her first concert, when it had become evident that the public demand to hear her was to be tremendous, he had considerably increased the figure that he had previously offered her—not so much from generosity as from the realization that it would be "a stroke of policy to prevent the possibility of such an occurrence." Miss Lind's tour of American cities during the following months was a series of successes never before paralleled by any domestic or foreign artist. Two concerts in Washington were attended by the President, his family, and all the Cabinet members. On the morning after one of these concerts, she was visited by Mr. Clay and Mr. Webster; and the renowned New England orator "signified his approval by rising, drawing himself up to his full height, and making a profound bow." She found recreation in playing at games of India-rubber ball with her manager; and when he was completely tired out, she would make good-natured fun of him, saying, "Oh, Mr. Barnum, you are too fat and too large; you cannot stand it to play ball with me!"

In the end it turned out that she herself could not stand it to sing for him, when she was given the chance of accepting a better contract. Notwithstanding her "character for extraordinary benevolence and generosity," which, as Barnum had sagely calculated, proved to be an attraction of incalculable force in loosing the purse-strings of a sentimental public, the singer began to listen to seductive offers. One unkind parodist had already

shocked her unnumbered admirers with a blasphemous rendition
of the closing lines of *Thanatopsis:*

> Sustained by an unfaltering trust in coin,
>   Dealt from thy hand, O thou illustrious man,
> Gladly I heard the summons come to join
>   Myself the innumerable caravan.

Visits to her employer's Museum, it seems, together with stories
of his exploitations of such freaks as the Fejee Mermaid and the
Woolly Horse—a most delicate monster, "extremely complex—
made up of the Elephant, Deer, Horse, Buffalo, Camel, and
Sheep"—eventually outraged her sense of artistic propriety. Was
she herself to be remembered, in after years, as merely one of the
most important freaks of that innumerable caravan? Not if she
could help it! By June, 1851, Barnum saw how the wind was
blowing, and, having tired once more of incessant travel, offered
to release her from the contract on condition that she should pay
a forfeit already stipulated in case such a contingency should
arise—a forfeit of $32,000. She accepted the offer; but—so we are
told—she continued to be as "polite and friendly as ever." But
Barnum felt much satisfaction at a later day when, having met
him by chance, she told him that she was being atrociously
cheated and swindled by employers who lacked his scrupulous
honesty. At all events, scrupulous honesty had paid him very
well: his gross receipts from all the concerts, after Miss Lind
had been paid in full, amounted to more than $535,000.

Although barely of middle age, Barnum was now a very
wealthy man. Jenny Lind and Tom Thumb, in spite of their outstanding eminence, had been only two of the irons he had held
in the fire. The Museum had continued to prosper, models of it
were springing up, under his management, in other cities, and in
1849 he had projected the first of those huge traveling entertainments with which, more than anything else, posterity associates
his name. In that year "Barnum's Great Asiatic Caravan, Museum
and Menagerie" began to tour the country; within four years
its profits were nearly $1,000,000, one-third of which went to its
director. Competition arose, of course; but the man who was unquestionably one of the most astute financiers of his generation

crushed his competitors with little effort. When "side-shows," enticed by the vast popularity of his own spectacle, started to operate near by, he fitted out a circus company that performed at the same time and place with his main entertainment; then, if opposition of any sort threatened, he combined both of his companies at a single price of admission, and competition thus became impossible. Naturally enough, therefore, at the close of his engagement with Miss Lind, he had decided that it was high time for him to rest from his labors in order to cultivate life's amenities.

In pursuit of this ideal, he erected a palatial house near Bridgeport at a cost of $150,000, which, modeled after the Pavilion of King George IV, was the only specimen of Oriental architecture in America. "In deciding upon the kind of house to be erected," he remarked, "I determined, first and foremost, to consult convenience and comfort." Nevertheless, while convenience and comfort were not entirely wanting, he had chosen to build Iranistan—for that was its name—because of its distinct novelty, which "might indirectly serve as an advertisement of my various enterprises"; and the structure was also erected within plain view of a much-traveled railroad. Then he bought an elephant, which was used to plow the fields near the house; and it was observed that the huge beast was particularly industrious when trains were passing, and very lazy when no trains were within sight.

But Barnum himself could not rest, even beneath the inviting domes of his bizarre mansion; and he soon engaged in an activity which contrasted pleasantly with the daily occupation of reckoning up his gains of the preceding day. Few things—there were a few, however—pleased him more than to be regarded as a public benefactor. The public, to be sure, he had beguiled in almost every conceivable way; but it might still be possible to entertain and interest it by preaching the virtue of temperance. In the past, he had been, on somewhat rare occasions, a moderate drinker, and, as a youthful store-clerk, he had "drawn and bottled more rum than would be necessary to float a ship"; but now, after listening to a strong temperance lecture, he spent a sleepless night. Next morning he carried all his champagne bottles out of doors, knocked off their heads, and poured their contents on the ground. He then signed a teetotaler's pledge, and was much astonished to see his wife burst into joyful tears when he told her of his new resolve; and she then informed him that she had often wept all night long through fear that wine-bibbing was leading him straight to destruction. Moreover, he also abandoned another cherished practice—the smoking of from ten to fifteen Havanas every day—for he now felt that he "had a great duty to perform. I had been groping in darkness, was rescued, and I knew it was my duty to try and save others." Accordingly, he spent the winter of 1851-2 "traveling at my own expense" in Connecticut, speaking to thousands concerning the dire necessity of turning from the error of their ways. Already, while with Miss Lind, he had often spoken for temperance on evenings when she did not sing; and the crowds which heard him sometimes outnumbered those which heard the singer—his performance was free of charge. His audiences, while very large, were composed principally of two classes of people: those who wished to see P. T. Barnum in the flesh for the first time, and those who wished to see him a second or even third time in order to find out what new enormity he was showing off. Anyhow, his altruism was rewarded; many hundreds who listened to his free lecture felt that it would be unfair not to repay him by hearing Miss Lind; but the lectures themselves do not appear to have produced any very concrete results. At any rate, it is not known that Frances Willard ever included his name among her bountiful lists of temperance reformers.

Meanwhile, Barnum had also been busily engaged in penning his first autobiography, which, as the preface carefully points out, contained nothing that would "shock the feelings of the most fastidious." As a matter of fact, outside of a few racy episodes, the book as a whole is rather dull, even though it was written "in the confessional mood." Furthermore, despite its occasional extraordinary candor, the book is chiefly remarkable for its curious mingling of pious exhortation with an absolutely naïve conceit, and an equally naïve nescience of any vital distinction between brazenly shameless exploitation and genuine altruism. Some thirty years later, in fact, Barnum confessed to having written it for a purpose that might have shocked fastidious people—"for the purpose, principally, of advancing my interests as proprietor of the American Museum." The announcement of the forthcoming volume set the public crazy with excitement, and many publishers offered fortunes for the copyright; for Barnum had announced that he was ready to receive bids from responsible publishers. All of them, except the most generous one, were naturally disappointed; and, as it turned out, they had good reason to be, for 160,000 copies were sold. The book was dedicated to "The Universal Yankee Nation"—a less provincial and far shrewder phrase than it appears to be on first thought. A different type of autobiography—a lecture on the "Philosophy of Humbug"—was also occupying a part of his time. He covered the topic with satisfactory thoroughness, except that he exercised much discretion in talking about his most notorious and most profitable tricks. The ticket-seller, watching the mobs that fought their way in to hear the lecture, once felt moved to pour out his wrathful contempt upon them. "Old Barnum always draws a crowd," he snorted; ". . . the people *will* go to see old Barnum. First he humbugs them, and then they pay to hear him tell how he did it!"

But now, when everything seemed to be going so well—when he was "at home, in the bosom of my family," which, as the closing lines of his autobiography states, are "the highest and most expressive symbols of the kingdom of heaven"—his earthly kingdom was suddenly swept away. In 1851 he had bought a large tract of land, which eventually developed into East Bridgeport, as an enterprise in "profitable philanthropy." In carrying out this scheme, he endorsed the notes of the Jerome Clock Company, a firm in New Haven, to the extent of over $500,000; for he believed that this company would attract other industrial enterprises. A favorite business maxim of his, which had been included in his "Golden Rules for Money-Making," was "Don't indorse without Security," and he had believed upon investigation that this particular firm was amply secure. But it turned out that he had been duped. The company's directors had shown him falsified figures; and they immediately applied his money to the payment of some long-standing notes, meanwhile entirely neglecting to transfer their business to East Bridgeport.

So it came about that, in 1855, Barnum was a temporarily ruined man. When this became known, there was an immense newspaper sensation; and, even in his despair, he could not help rejoicing because he was once more so conspicuously in the public eye. His house, his family, his leisure, even his temperance activities, now had to be abandoned. He closed Iranistan, moved his family to a modest residence in New York, and once more sallied forth to retrieve his loss. The Museum was still working for him day and night, although in comparison with his other speculations its profits were small; Jenny Lind had sunk into the pleasant obscurity of matrimony; but Tom Thumb was still available, and just as satisfactorily Lilliputian in size as ever. In 1857 Barnum again went to Europe with Tom and "little Eva," a diminutive actress, where multitudes of the General's old friends came to see him again, and Barnum himself gave a lecture—no longer free of charge—on "The Art of Money-Getting," which thus became a fine practical illustration of that art. And he did not fail to call on the friends of his prosperous days. When Thackeray came to America in 1852 to lecture on "The English Humorists of the Eighteenth Century," he had wisely decided that the most competent American to advise him in regard to managing his lectures would be P. T. Barnum. The two had met repeatedly at that time; and four years later Thackeray had again sought Barnum's advice before speaking on "The Four Georges." It was not strange that the writer, who had himself posed as a showman pointing out the curious puppets in *Vanity Fair*, should have been irresistibly attracted to the greatest living showman. Barnum therefore called on Thackeray in London and told him the story of his own misfortunes. "Mr. Barnum, I admire you more than ever," said the novelist, who then inquired whether any financial assistance was needed. After refusing to accept any aid, Barnum told his host something that very few people knew: he was not so badly crippled financially as was supposed, for he had transferred nearly $200,000 worth of property to his wife, in whose name it was of course safe from legal confiscation.

By August, 1857, he was home again, with his fortunes considerably bettered; but in December of that year Iranistan, which had been put in shape for reoccupancy, was burned to the ground. Undaunted by this disaster, he still struggled on, and by 1860 his debts were nearly paid. The Museum was now his principal source of income; it had grown to be so deservedly famous that, when the Prince of Wales toured America in 1860, stirred perhaps by memories of the funny man and the wonderful dwarf to whom his indulgent mother had once introduced him, he visited the famous building. It "was the only place of amusement the Prince attended in the country," Barnum proudly remarked; but his knowledge concerning the youthful amusements of the distinguished visitor was a little vague. A new phenomenon had now appeared at the Museum in the form of white whales. Some mean persons, to be sure, insisted that they were only porpoises, but Barnum induced Agassiz to certify that they were actual whales, "and this endorsement I published far and wide." At first, he tried to keep them alive by the simple expedient of hiring an attendant, whose duty it was to moisten their mouths and blow-holes with a sponge dipped in a barrel of salt water; but in spite of this kindness, the whales ungratefully died. He then piped water, from New York's harbor, into a tank large enough for new specimens to swim in, and thus they were coaxed to live a bit longer than the others.

With the return of prosperity, his interest in the moral values of life also revived. The "Lecture Room" in the Museum, where "industrious fleas," etc., had thus far reigned supreme, now became a shelter for strictly moral dramas, from which, as playbills devoutly announced, all "indecent allusions or gestures" were rigidly excluded. The gestures and allusions in "Uncle Tom's Cabin" and "The Drunkard," however, were undeniably decent; and inasmuch as some church members, and other people who were almost as respectable, looked askance upon the typical theatrical shows of the day, it was very fortunate that they could be properly entertained and edified by such excellent performances. Perhaps the greatest of these instructive dramas was the "Christian Martyrs," which positively reeked with morality. It portrayed the sufferings of the Christians in the worst days of pagan Rome, and included a series of scenes in which gorgeous costumes, martyrs cast up to the lions, and superbly pious rant were happily blended. In the final tableau, Constantine's cross appeared in the sky, and the Roman Empire was converted wholesale amidst bursts of reverent applause; then the curtain fell—a curtain covered with tawdry advertisements that revealed the virtues of "Horse Liniment," "Yahoo Bitters," and similar indispensable family drugs. And all this could be seen for only thirty cents.

But there were also other ways of furnishing clean and instructive entertainment; for example, dwarfs of both sexes still persisted in being born at intervals nicely timed to fit Barnum's needs. Tom Thumb, who by this time had "increased considerably in rotundity," was waddling around the world as his own master; but his successor, Commodore Nutt, was almost as microscopic and wholly as moral as the General. In 1862 Lincoln asked Barnum to bring the Commodore to the White House. When they arrived, the President was busy in a special Cabinet meeting, but "had left word if I called to be shown in to him with the Commodore." So they were admitted, and Lincoln genially introduced his distinguished visitors to the Members of the Cabinet. A general conversation followed; then, bending his long body, the President took Nutt's hand and said: "Commodore, permit me to give you a parting word of advice. When you are in command of your fleet, if you find yourself in danger of being taken prisoner, I advise you to wade ashore." The Commodore allowed his eyes to travel up the tall form by his side, and responded, "I guess, Mr. President, you could do that better than I could," and the President was immensely tickled by the unusually brilliant repartee. Earlier in the same year, Barnum had bought a dwarf girl for his Museum, one Lavinia Warren, with whom General Thumb promptly proceeded to fall in love; but unfortunately Commodore Nutt was also deeply smitten with her many charms. For a time, all their friends feared that there would be a serious physical encounter between them, for Nutt had a very peppery temper; but Tom continued to be just as amiable as ever, and reason eventually prevailed. Much to the despair of the Commodore, Lavinia finally decided that the superior military rank of the General made him the more desirable husband; and the announcement of their forthcoming marriage tremendously increased the crowds that visited the Museum. Barnum offered to give $15,000 to the amorous pigmies if they would postpone the wedding for only one month, but their mutual passion was too ardent, and the bribe was therefore refused. The ceremony took place in Grace Church, where admittance could be gained only by a special card, and among the guests were several Governors and Members of Congress, together with a few generals of the army, who attended as a mark of respect for the proprieties of military etiquette. The happy couple retired to a very private life for some months, but the attractions of public life proved to be stronger than the pleasures of domesticity, and so they encircled the globe. When, after the fashion of other business men, Tom finally gave up an active career, he could comfort his declining days with the reflection that more than twenty millions of people had bought tickets to see him.

By 1865 there were very few democratic institutions that Barnum had not, in some way, touched and elevated with his diversified talents; however, for one thing, he had not yet played any part in the political game. In that year the voters of his district decided that he was by far the citizen best qualified to lead the fight against the monopolizing tactics of the state railroad companies; and so they elected to the State Legislature the man who had shown himself to be by all odds the most successful and merciless monopolist of public entertainments who flourished in the century. During the Civil War his Museum had been particularly successful, for he had pulled the strings of patriotism in every conceivable way; and, while a few disgruntled reformers might now claim that his election to office had been possible only because of the debased attitude toward individual and civic responsibility that prevailed after the war, ordinary people knew better. And still, although he thundered mightily against the usurping and criminal tactics of the railroads, it was observed that, for some strange reason, their directors and defendants did not seem to be much disturbed.

One day in July, 1865, when he was speaking in the legislative hall with his usual vehemence, a dispatch stating that his Museum had been destroyed by fire was placed in his hand. He read it through, and then went on with his speech as though nothing had happened. The destruction had been complete; nothing was left of all those marvelous rarities that he had obtained by twenty years of unstinted labor and money. Among other things, the wax figures of once renowned Americans had sunk away in the flames even more completely than they had already disappeared in the popular imagination. He worked prodigiously; agents all over the world again strained every nerve to ferret out fascinatingly gruesome mishaps of nature, and in November of that year the Museum was once more displaying its dazzling glories to the public. But in March, 1868, it was again destroyed by fire. Barnum felt that this sort of thing was getting to be a little too common; therefore the "American Phoenix," who had twice demonstrated his ability to make new buildings rise from the ashes of those that had perished, retired permanently from the museum business and settled down at home. Lindencroft, his second Bridgeport mansion, was succeeded in 1869 by Waldemere which adjoined Seaside Park—one of the many benefactions by which he had advertised both his generosity and his business endeavors at the same time. Such uncommon altruism, his townsmen rightly felt, should not go unrewarded; so they staunchly supported all of his undertakings, advised many others to do likewise, and, as a final proof of their reverential admiration, elected him to the office of Mayor in 1875. During these years he had spent several months each season with his family in an elegant residence at Fifth Avenue and Thirty-Ninth Street, New York. Here, for weeks at a time, he found pleasure in entertaining his jolliest crony, Horace Greeley; and the great editor repaid the geniality of his host by using the influential columns of the New York *Tribune* to support him in his political ambitions.

Barnum's *magnum opus* was organized in 1870. This, the most stupendous of all his spectacular achievements, was then known as the "Great Traveling World's Fair." In April, 1871, it made its first appearance in Brooklyn, where the towering tents covered nearly three acres of ground; but in spite of its size thousands of spectators were unable to gain admission to the entertainment. By 1872 it had grown so large that from sixty to seventy freight cars and six passenger coaches were needed to carry its live stock, both animal and human, throughout the land, and its receipts for each six months of activity averaged nearly $1,000,000. Wherever and whenever it appeared, nearly all other forms of business were temporarily demoralized. A certain factory once expressed the feelings of all sensible people with conclusive force when it posted this notice: "Closed on account of the greatest interference on earth." Who, indeed, except a few perverse moralists, could resist its infinite appeal? Certainly, no American may properly be called educated unless he has seen its magnificent splendors from beginning to end: the enormous, flaunting posters announcing its coming, the unloading of its special trains in the romantic duskiness of early dawn, the erection of the huge, flapping tents, and finally the gorgeously complex parade—the steam calliope screeching out its barbaric toots; the Oriental princesses lolling inside of lurching howdahs on the backs of gayly caparisoned elephants; the ungainly camels; the graceful prancing zebras; the strong, iron-barred cages incarcerating an uncanny mixture of sullen, yawning lions, snarling tigers, slinking leopards, and hideously grinning hyenas; the cavorting clowns and tumbling acrobats engaged in back-breaking contortions; the bewigged and powdered women in their highly suggestive flesh-colored tights. And then—the performance itself!

Perhaps the most superb attraction that the great organization ever boasted, among its countless superb attractions, was the monstrous elephant Jumbo. For many years that unwieldy creature had seen all England at his feet, which occupied an alarmingly large part of the ground in the Royal Zoological Gardens in London. English children without number had shrieked with joyous fright from the top of Jumbo's broad back, and among those who had shrieked loudest were the children and grandchildren of the Queen. So it happened that, when in February, 1882, the announcement was made that Jumbo had been sold to the awful, the unspeakably utilitarian American, P. T. Barnum, all England went into mourning and made frantic attempts to have the sale rescinded. Stories and poems celebrating Jumbo's extraordinary virtues appeared in the greatest profusion; Jumbo hats, collars, neckties, cigars, polkas, fans, and so on, were to be seen everywhere. Nevertheless, the hard-hearted American remained adamant. He replied to those who offered a much larger sum for repurchasing Jumbo than the original sale price had been, that he would not part with him now, after all this widely advertised consternation, for any consideration—not even for twenty times what he had paid. But when the attempt was made to lead Jumbo away for embarkation, he became embarrassingly obdurate. Loudly trumpeting his alarm, his homesickness, and his loyalty to British traditions, he flopped himself down in the middle of a much-traveled street and refused to budge; and, in view of his formidable proportions, it was rather difficult to see how he could be made to budge except of his own free-will. Barnum's distracted agent immediately sent this cablegram to his employer: "Jumbo has laid down in the street and won't get up. What shall we do." The delighted employer at once cabled back: "Let him lie there a week if he wants to. It is the best advertisement in the world."

At length, after many difficulties, the now world-famous monster reached America, where for more than three years he delighted untold numbers with his unparalleled accomplishments. During these years a part of his regular daily diet was a keg of beer; and when Barnum was told of Jumbo's solitary vice, he winked jocosely, in utter forgetfulness of his strong temperance principles. Doubtless it was fitting that the weak and erring elephant eventually went to a drunkard's grave. In September, 1885, while stumbling in a drunken stupor across a railroad in Ontario, he was struck by a locomotive. Since an irresistible force had met an immovable mass, there could be but one result: the engine, derailed and shattered, died at once, and Jumbo, whose skull had been fractured, gave up his great ghost in a few minutes. Barnum later presented his stuffed skin, together with other benefactions, to Tufts College; and from that time until the present, Jumbo has held the same place in the hearts of all loyal Tufts students that the bulldog holds for Yale and the tiger for Princeton.

As the busy years passed, many competitors matched their strength against Barnum's circus; but they found it utterly impossible to compete successfully with such a masterly organization, and so almost all of them failed—with one notable exception. That was the "London Circus," headed by Mr. Bailey; and Barnum was unable to breathe easily until he had bought out his only dangerous rival. This he did in 1880, although not until 1887 was the twin spectacle called "Barnum and Bailey's Circus"—those magical words that have meant more to the average American of the last three decades than any others, with but a few exceptions such as home, country, God and business. When the ponderous three-ring circus was exhibited in London in 1889, it was witnessed by the entire royal family, together with many of the nobility; and the general British public forgot its rage over the Jumbo episode in the presence of the colossal entertainment. The Members of Parliament also attended in a quorum greater than that which commonly foregathered on those dull occasions when ordinary affairs of state were discussed; and Gladstone himself came to boom his respects into Barnum's ear during a brief interval when all the other lions happened to be quiet.

The illustrious showman was now very old; and old age found him on a pinnacle of peculiar eminence. The trite saying, "His name is a household word," was perhaps as nearly true of him as of any person then living. In his eightieth year he could write, without too much modesty, "I think I can, without egotism, say that I have amused and instructed more persons than any other manager that ever lived." He was known not merely in America and Europe, for his agents had carried his fame into almost every section of the uncivilized earth; and when an unknown person in a remote corner of Asia mailed a letter to "Mr. Barnum, America," it reached him without any trouble whatever. After ex-President Grant had girdled the globe, Barnum visited him and assured him that, as the dominant military figure of his time, he

was the most famous person alive. "No, sir," Grant replied.
"Your name is familiar to multitudes who never heard of me.
Wherever I went, among the most distant nations, the fact that
I was an American led to constant inquiries whether I knew
Barnum." The good fortune which, barring a few disastrous occurrences, had steadily favored him was as abounding as ever.
His wife, to be sure, had died in 1873 while he was in Germany,
but prayer had mitigated his anguish. "I implored our dear Father
to give them [his children] strength to bear their loss and to
sanctify her death to the benefit of us all." In his own case, at
least, the supplication seems to have been answered very
promptly; for less than a year later he remarried. The doors of
Waldemere continued to remain hospitably open to all comers,
although it was noticed that they swung a little wider for persons
of social or literary rank than for others. Particularly welcome
were those who could play a good hand at euchre, or amuse
their host with distinctly masculine stories and reminiscences.
Bayard Taylor, Elias Howe and Greeley were constantly coming in; and Mark Twain often ran down from Hartford to spend
the day, although his refusal to write something in the nature
of a humorous send-off for "The Greatest Show On Earth" was a
continual disappointment to Barnum. Matthew Arnold found
time, in an interval when he was not lecturing uncouth Americans on their complete lack of culture and incontinent faith in
democracy, to be Barnum's guest for some days; but the polished
English critic, somehow or other, would never tell whether he
had assigned his odd entertainer any definite place in his own
famous tripartite classification of society.

Happy and contented in this life and certain, as he was, of
endless bliss in the next, Barnum nevertheless neglected nothing
that might help to strengthen his already firm grasp upon earthly
fame. Death—the greatest curiosity of all—was not going to catch
him napping; he would cheat the grim monster of at least a part
of his prey! Accordingly, he brought his autobiography up to
date in 1869; but the price—from $3.50 to $5.00—charged by his
publishers turned out to be prohibitive; in 1878, therefore, he
bought the plates and printed a "new and independent" edition

which was sold for only $1.50 a copy, "besides which I present a fifty-cent ticket to my Great Show to each purchaser." Who could resist such an appeal as that? Apparently not many people could, for he was soon printing editions of 50,000 copies. Again, in 1889, his life's history appeared, once more brought up to date and "including his Golden Rules for Money-Making."

But the time was approaching when the last page of that history was to be written by the hand of a far greater showman than Barnum himself. His religious faith had grown to be so sincere that, during his last years, he read daily from the Bible and from two volumes, *Manna* and *Strength for Daily Needs*, which contained a medley of excerpts from notorious writers whose profound wisdom, he sagely commented, seemed to sum up "the whole philosophy of life." The venerable man had been endowed with such amazing physical vitality that, until his eighty-first year, he had enjoyed almost unbroken health; but by November, 1880, the muscles of his heart began to degenerate. The man who had so often gambled with chance was too sly to gamble with death, and in 1883 he had made a will which in many ways gave proof of his foresight. Its most important stipulation had been that a large part of his immense fortune—it was then ten millions—should be devoted to the support of the circus which, he well knew, was to be his living monument. It was furthermore specified that $8,000 should be expended upon the erection of his statue in Bridgeport, where it may be seen today —a great bronze effigy, on the water-edge of Seaside Park, sitting at ease and gazing benignantly southward across the waters of Long Island Sound. He had several legitimate daughters, but no legitimate son; his one grandson, therefore, was to be given $25,000 as a consideration for retaining only the initial letter of his first name and changing his middle name to Barnum. The remainder of his estate was to be parceled out among his descendants, or given to various forms of charity.

With all his earthly interests thus provided for, he made ready for the end. He, who had always taken great pride in his ability to manage all manner of public spectacles, showed the same pride in planning the final spectacle. None knew better than Barnum that his funeral would occasion a tremendous public outpouring, and he set about arranging for it with all his old-time skill. But in two very important particulars it was to differ sharply from the others. The designer, in all probability, would not be able to witness the triumph of his design—although, as usual, he would be the chief center of attraction—and the customary fee of twenty-five cents would not be charged for admission. And yet, in imagination, he could see what it would be like: the multitudes of mourners, the whole city draped in mourning, the flags at half-mast, the display of his photograph in nearly every public window, the half-holiday granted to the school children, and last of all—the crowning triumph!—a sign posted at Madison Square Garden in New York, where his show was then running, "Closed on account of the death of P. T. Barnum." Several days before the end, he embarrassed his Universalist minister very much by choosing, as a text for his funeral sermon, "Not my will but Thine be done"—words which were also engraved on his head-stone. Even the imminence of death, it appears, did not seriously interfere with his life-long habit of employing highly question-able advertisements. In another way, also, his innocent vanity showed itself. His illness, which was prolonged for nearly five months, had emaciated him to a shocking degree; the great face, with its look of corpulent good-humor, its carnal complacency, its callous and furtive sagacity, its ponderous worldliness, had shrunken into an expression of pinched and wizened resignation. Fully determined to be remembered as he was when in the hey-day of strength, he directed that none but near relatives should be permitted to view his body. After all, it was perhaps natural enough that he should not have desired to emulate the leading attraction of the Fejee Mermaid.

Until the last, his buoyant spirits rarely failed. Three days before his departure, he spoke suddenly in his high-pitched voice to his secretary who was standing by the bedside: "Ben, I'm going to die this time." After the secretary had expressed a pious hope that he was wrong, Barnum again repeated, "No, Ben, I'm going to die." A moment's painful silence followed; then, in a matter-of-fact tone, he remarked, "I say, Ben, you'd better see the contractor about putting up some houses on those shore lots. I've got too much money in the bank, Ben, too much money in the bank." "Why, Mr. Barnum," the surprised secretary exclaimed, "you said you were going to die!" "Yes, Ben, yes," he answered, as his dark eyes twinkled with fun, "but I ain't dead yet, Ben, am I?" As death drew near, he suffered much pain and often swallowed sedatives; but his belief in temperance remained strong until the last. At four o'clock on the morning of April 7, 1891, he was asked if he would like a drink of water. "Yes," he replied, and shortly afterwards became semi-unconscious. Thus he lingered all day. In the evening, as the April sun was setting, the uniquely original, the extraordinarily creative, the peerlessly fertile and resourceful old showman . . .

The concluding lines of the judge's poem ran thus:

> And finally, discovering the brink of Hades' crater,
> He'll put out the conflagration with his Fire Annihilator;
> Exorcise from the neighborhood the cussed imp of evil,
> Nor rest, till he has raised, reformed, and then—ENGAGED—the Devil!

# WOLCOTT GIBBS

"YOUNG people should not forget that literature is something that is *still going on*," said an eminent publisher to the editor of this anthology. "They are likely to stumble on it almost anywhere. They *might* even produce it themselves!" This counsel will scarcely be needed by those who are already acquainted with the Profiles of that brisk weekly, *The New Yorker*. These engaging portraits contributed by young, sophisticated journalists, some from the editorial staff, are written to no definite formula except that which governs the whole magazine—they must be fresh, interesting, objective, and readable. Although one may usually detect signs of "the *New Yorker* style"—a strictly modern flavor compounded of a shrug and a smile, of suave but wicked satire and guarded admiration, of well-mannered doubt and wild surmise, of a lively sense of the humor and wonder of daily incongruity checked by understatement and anticlimax—this varies greatly with the writers. In length, these Profiles range from 3,000 to 16,000 words and, regardless of length, from little more than expanded interviews to carefully documented biographies. Their subjects, as befits a democracy, include all sorts and conditions of people, from queens to window-washers. Most of the sketches make no pretense to be full or, still less, final, but aim to depict, as their name implies, the salient features of interesting contemporaries. Some are essentially topical, others of more general and lasting value. Though their biographical quality also varies, they have offered during the past fifteen years a standing challenge to young writers and, through their example as adopted by other magazines, have measurably extended the reach and the reward of that literature which is "still going on."

The following Profile is something of a *tour de force* in biography. As the title implies, it is the portrait not so much of a man as of a business, and not so much of the business itself as of its familiar products. It is, in fact, a *pastiche* made up of all sorts of characteristic statements, lists, footnotes, casual comments, advertising "plugs," specific facts and figures, wishful thoughts and public boasts—the inside story of the founding and promotion of the magazine *Time* and its fellows—racily parodying all the literary and typographical affectations of "Timestyle." It is a satirical sketch of Mr. Luce and his high-pressure publications, but it is also a satire on the great American theme of "strive and succeed," with success typically translated by speed and size. It was first published on November 28, 1936.

The author, Wolcott Gibbs, is known to readers of *The New Yorker* for his equally brilliant and satirical (though more regular) Profiles of

311

Lucius Beebe and Alexander Woollcott and for his frequent dramatic reviews. He was born in New York City in 1902 and "went to practically every prep school in the East, but not to college (because I could never understand any math course after algebra)." He "spent four years monkeying around the freight yards of the Long Island Railroad, then worked on a chain of Long Island papers, not because I wanted to be a writer but because my cousin owned them." From there, in 1926, he went to *The New Yorker*, "starting as a proof-reader and winding up as an associate editor." Now he "does the Theatre" when Robert Benchley is away, writes Notes and Comment, Profiles, fiction, "and anything else that turns up." This is "all right," he admits, "but if I had my choice I would just lie on the beach at Fire Island and watch the boats."


## TIME . . . FORTUNE . . . LIFE . . . LUCE

SAD-EYED last month was nimble, middle-sized *Life*-President Clair Maxwell as he told newshawks of the sale of the fifty-three-year-old gagmag to *Time*. For celebrated name alone, price: $85,000.

Said he: "*Life* . . . introduced to the world the drawings . . . of such men as Charles Dana Gibson, the verses of . . . James Whitcomb Riley and Oliver Herford, such writers as John Kendrick Bangs. . . . Beginning next month the magazine *Life* will embark on a new venture entirely unrelated to the old."

How unrelated to the world of the Gibson Girl is this new venture might have been gathered at the time from a prospectus issued by enormous, Apollo-faced C. D. Jackson, of Time, Inc.

"*Life*," wrote he, "will show us the Man-of-the-Week . . . his body clothed and, if possible, nude." It will expose "the loves, scandals, and personal affairs of the plain and fancy citizen . . . and write around them a light, good-tempered 'colyumnist' review of these once-private lives."

29,000 die-hard subscribers to *Life*,* long accustomed to he-she jokes, many ignorant of King of England's once-private life (*Time*, July 25 *et seq.*), will be comforted for the balance of their subscription periods by familiar, innocent jocosities of *Judge*. First issue of new publication went out last week to 250,-

---

* Peak of *Life* circulation (1921): 250,000.

ooo readers, carried advertisements suggesting an annual revenue of $1,500,000, pictured Russian peasants in the nude, the love life of the Black Widow spider, referred inevitably to Mrs. Ernest Simpson.

Behind this latest, most incomprehensible Timenterprise looms, as usual, ambitious, gimlet-eyed, Baby Tycoon Henry Robinson Luce, co-founder of *Time*, promulgator of *Fortune*, potent in associated radio & cinema ventures.

## *"High-Buttoned . . . Brilliant"*

Headman Luce was born in Tengchowfu, China, on April 3, 1898, the son of Henry Winters & Elizabeth Middleton Luce, Presbyterian missionaries. Very unlike the novels of Pearl Buck were his early days. Under brows too beetling for a baby, young Luce grew up inside the compound, played with his two sisters, lisped first Chinese, dreamed much of the Occident. At 14, weary of poverty, already respecting wealth & power, he sailed alone for England, entered school at St. Albans. Restless again, he came to the United States, enrolled at Hotchkiss, met up & coming young Brooklynite Briton Hadden. Both even then were troubled with an itch to harass the public. Intoned Luce years later: "We reached the conclusion that most people were not well informed & that something should be done. . . ."

First publication to inform fellowman was *Hotchkiss Weekly Record;* next *Yale Daily News*, which they turned into a tabloid; fought to double hours of military training, fought alumni who wished to change tune of Yale song from *Die Wacht am Rhein.* Traditionally unshaven, wearing high-buttoned Brooks jackets, soft white collars, cordovan shoes, no garters, Luce & Hadden were Big Men on a campus then depleted of other, older Big Men by the war. Luce, pale, intense, nervous, was Skull & Bones, Alpha Delta Phi, Phi Beta Kappa, member of the Student Council, editor of the *News;* wrote sad poems, read the *New Republic,* studied political philosophy. As successful, less earnest, more convival, Hadden collected china dogs, made jokes.* In

* Once, watching Luce going past, laden with cares & responsibilities, Hadden chuckled, upspoke: "Look out, Harry. You'll drop the college."

1920 the senior class voted Hadden Most Likely to Succeed, Luce Most Brilliant. Most Brilliant he, Luce sloped off to Christ Church, Oxford, there to study European conditions, take field trips into the churning Balkans.

### *"Best Advice: Don't"*

Twenty months after commencement, in the city room of Paperkiller Frank Munsey's *Baltimore News*, met again Luce, Hadden. Newshawks by day, at night they wrangled over policies of the magazine they had been planning since Hotchkiss. Boasted the final prospectus: *"Time* will be free from cheap sensationalism . . . windy bias."

In May, 1922, began the long struggle to raise money to start *Time*. Skeptical at the outset proved Newton D. Baker, Nicholas Murray Butler, Herbert Bayard Swope, William Lyon Phelps. Pooh-poohed *Review of Reviews* Owner Charles Lanier: "My best advice . . . don't do it." From studious, pint-sized Henry Seidel Canby, later editor of Lamont-backed *Saturday Review of Literature*, came only encouraging voice in this threnody.

Undismayed Luce & Hadden took the first of many offices in an old brownstone house at 9 East 17th Street, furnished it with a filing cabinet, four second-hand desks, a big brass bowl for cigarette stubs, sought backers.*

---

* In return for $50 cash, original investors were given two shares 6% Preferred Stock with a par value of $25, one share Class A Common Stock without par value. 3,440 Preferred, 1,720 Class A Common were so sold.

170 shares of Class A Common, 8,000 shares of Class B Common, also without par value, not entitled to dividends until Preferred Shares had been retired, were issued to Briton Hadden, Henry R. Luce, who gave one-third to associates, divided remainder equally.

In 1925, authorized capital of Time, Inc., was increased to 19,000 shares; of which 8,000 were Preferred, 3,000 Class A; as before, 8,000 Class B.

In June, 1930 (if you are still following this), the Preferred Stock was retired in full & dividends were initiated for both Common Stocks. Corporation at this time had 2,400 shares Class A, 7,900 Class B outstanding.

By the spring of 1931 *Time* had begun to march, shares were nominally quoted at $1,000. Best financial minds advised splitting stock on basis of twenty shares for one. Outstanding after clever maneuver: 206,400 shares Common.

In 1933, outlook still gorgeous, each share of stock was reclassified into

JPMorganapoleon H. P. Davison, Yale classmate of Luce, Hadden, great & good friend of both, in June contributed $4,-000. Next to succumb: Mrs. David S. Ingalls, sister of Classmate William Hale Harkness; amount, $10,000. From Brother Bill, $5,000. Biggest early angel, Mrs. William Hale Harkness, mother of Brother Bill & Mrs. Ingalls, invested $20,000. Other original stockholders: Robert A. Chambers, Ward Cheney, F. Trubee Davison, E. Roland Harriman, Dwight W. Morrow, Harvey S. Firestone, Jr., Seymour H. Knox, William V. Griffin. By November Luce & Hadden had raised $86,000, decided to go to work on fellowman.

## "Snaggle-Toothed . . . Pig-Faced"

Puny in spite of these preparations, prosy in spite of the contributions of Yale poets Archibald MacLeish & John Farrar, was the first issue of *Time* on March 3, 1923. Magazine went to 9,000 subscribers; readers learned that Uncle Joe Cannon had retired at 86, that there was a famine in Russia, that Thornton Wilder friend Tunney had defeated Greb.

Yet to suggest itself as a rational method of communication, of infuriating readers into buying the magazine, was strange inverted Timestyle. It was months before Hadden's impish contempt for his readers,* his impatience with the English language, crystallized into gibberish. By the end of the first year, however, Timeditors were calling people able, potent, nimble; "Tycoon," most successful Timepithet, had been coined by Editor Laird Shields

----

⅒th share of $6.50 Dividend Cumulative Convertible Preferred Stock ($6.50 div. cum. con. pfd. stk.) and one share of New Common Stock. New div. cum. con. pfd. stk. was convertible into a share and a half of New Common Stock, then selling around $40 a share, now quoted at over $200.

Present number of shares outstanding, 238,000; paper value of shares, $47,000,000; conservative estimate of Luce holding, 102,300 shares; paper value, $20,460,000; conservative estimate of Luce income from *Time* stock (shares earned $9.74 in 1935, paid so far in 1936, $6.50; anticipated dividend for full year, $8), $818,400; reported Luce income from other investments, $100,000; reported Luce bagatelle as editor of Time, Inc., $45,000; reported total Lucemolument, $963,400.

Boy!

* Still framed at *Time* is Hadden's scrawled dictum: "Let Subscriber Goodkind mend his ways!"

Goldsborough; so fascinated Hadden with "beady-eyed" that for months nobody was anything else. Timeworthy were deemed such designations as "Tom-tom" Heflin, "Body-lover" Macfadden.

"Great word! Great word!" would crow Hadden, coming upon "snaggle-toothed," "pig-faced." Appearing already were such maddening coagulations as "cinemaddict," "radiorator." Appearing also were first gratuitous invasions of privacy. Always mentioned as William Randolph Hearst's "great & good friend" was Cinemactress Marion Davies, stressed was the bastardy of Ramsay MacDonald, the "cozy hospitality" of Mae West. Backward ran sentences until reeled the mind.

By March, 1924, the circulation had doubled, has risen since then 40,000 a year, reaches now the gratifying peak of 640,000, is still growing. From four meager pages in first issue, *Time* advertising has now come to eclipse that in *Satevepost*. Published *Time* in first six months of 1936, 1,590 pages; *Satevepost*, 1,480.

### No Slugabed, He . . .

Strongly contrasted from the outset of their venture were Hadden, Luce. Hadden, handsome, black-haired, eccentric, irritated his partner by playing baseball with the office boys, by making jokes, by lack of respect for autocratic business. Conformist Luce disapproved of heavy drinking, played hard, sensible game of tennis, said once: "I have no use for a man who lies in bed after nine o'clock in the morning," walked to work every morning, reproved a writer who asked for a desk for lack of "log-cabin spirit."

In 1925, when *Time* moved its offices to Cleveland, bored, rebellious was Editor Hadden; Luce, busy & social, lunched with local bigwigs, addressed Chamber of Commerce, subscribed to Symphony Orchestra, had neat house in the suburbs. Dismayed was Luce when Hadden met him on return from Europe with premature plans to move the magazine back to New York. In 1929, dying of a streptococcus infection, Hadden still opposed certain details of success-formula of *Fortune*, new, beloved Lucenterprise.

*Oats, Hogs, Cheese . . .*

In January, 1930, first issue of *Fortune* was mailed to 30,000 subscribers, cost as now $1 a copy, contained articles on branch banking, hogs, glass-blowing, how to live in Chicago on $25,000 a year. Latest issue (Nov., 1936) went to 130,000 subscribers, contained articles on bacon, tires, the New Deal, weighed as much as a good-sized flounder.*

Although in 1935 *Fortune* made a net profit of $500,000, vaguely dissatisfied was Editor Luce. Anxious to find & express "the technological significance of industry," he has been handicapped by the fact that his writers are often hostile to Big Business, prone to insert sneers, slithering insults. In an article on Bernard Baruch, the banker was described as calling President Hoover "old cheese-face." Protested Tycoon Baruch that he had said no such thing. Shotup of this was that Luce, embarrassed, printed a retraction; now often removes too-vivid phrasing from writers' copy.

❡ Typical perhaps of Luce methods is *Fortune* system of getting material. Writers in first draft put down wild gossip, any figures that occur to them. This is sent to victim, who indignantly corrects the errors, inadvertently supplies facts he might otherwise have withheld.

❡ *March of Time* in approximately its present form was first broadcast on March 6, 1931, paid the Columbia System for privilege, dropped from the air in February, 1932, with Luce attacking radio's "blatant claim to be a medium of education." Said he: "Should *Time* or any other business feel obliged to be the philanthropist of the air; to continue to pay for radio advertising it doesn't want in order to provide radio with something worthwhile?" So popular, so valuable to the studio was *March of Time* that it was restored in September of the same year, with Columbia donating its time & facilities. Since then *March of Time* has been sponsored by Remington-Rand typewriter company, by Wrigley's gum, by its own cinema *March of Time*, has made

* Two pounds, nine ounces.

400 broadcasts.* Apparently reconciled to philanthropy is Luce, because time for latest version will be bought & paid for by his organization.

❨ No active connection now has Luce with the moving-picture edition of *March of Time*, which was first shown on February 1, 1935, appears thirteen times a year in over 6,000 theatres, has so far failed to make money, to repay $900,000 investment. Even less connection has he with *Time's* only other unprofitable venture. Fifty-year-old *Architectural Forum*, acquired in 1932, loses still between $30,000 and $50,000 a year, circulates to 31,000.

❨ *Letters*, five-cent fortnightly collection of *Time's* correspondence with its indefatigable readers, was started in 1931, goes to 30,000, makes a little money.

❨ For a time, Luce was on Board of Directors of Paramount Pictures. Hoped to learn something of cinema, heard nothing discussed but banking, resigned sadly.

*Fascinating Facts . . . Dreamy Figures . . .*

Net profits of Time, Inc., for the past nine years:

| | |
|---|---|
| 1927 | 3,860 |
| 1928 | 125,787 |
| 1929 | 325,412 |
| 1930 | 818,936 |
| 1931 | 847,447 |
| 1932 | 613,727 † |
| 1933 | 1,009,628 |
| 1934 | 1,773,094 |
| 1935 | $2,249,823 ‡ |

In 1935 gross revenue of *Time-Fortune* was $8,621,170, of which the newsmagazine brought in approximately $6,000,000. Outside investments netted $562,295. For rent, salaries, production & distribution, other expenses went $6,594,076. Other de-

---

* By some devious necromancy, statisticians have calculated that *March of Time* ranks just behind *Amos & Andy* as most popular of all radio programs; reaches between 8,000,000 and 9,000,000 newshungry addicts.
† Hmm.
‡ Exceeded only by Curtis Publishing Co. (*Satevepost*): $5,329,900; Crowell Publishing Co. (*Collier's*): $2,399,600.

ductions: $41,397. Allowance for federal income tax: $298,169.

*Time's* books, according to Chicago Statisticians Gerwig & Gerwig, show total assets of $6,755,451. Liabilities, $3,101,584. These figures, conventionally allowing $1 for name, prestige of *Time*, come far from reflecting actual prosperity of Luce, his enterprises. Sitting pretty are the boys.

## Luce . . . Marches On!

Transmogrified by this success are the offices, personnel of *Time-Fortune*. Last reliable report: *Time*, 308 employees; *Fortune*, 103; Cinemarch, 58; Radiomarch, 10; *Architectural Forum*, 40; *Life*, 47. In New York; total, 566. In Chicago, mailing, editorial, mechanical employees, 216. Grand total Timemployees on God's earth, 782. Average weekly recompense for informing fellowman, $45.67802.

From first single office, Timen have come to bulge to bursting six floors of spiked, shiny Chrysler Building, occupy 150 rooms, eat daily, many at famed Cloud Club, over 1,000 eggs, 500 cups of coffee, much bicarbonate of soda. Other offices: Cinemarch, 10th Avenue at 54th Street; Radiomarch, Columbia Broadcasting Building.

Ornamented with Yale, Harvard, Princeton diplomas, stuffed fish, terrestrial globes are offices of Luce & other headmen; bleak, uncarpeted the writer's dingy lair.

( Heir apparent to mantle of Luce is dapper, tennis-playing, $35,-000-a-year Roy Larsen, nimble in Radio- & Cinemarch, vice-president & second largest stockholder in Time, Inc. Stock income: $120,000.

( Looming behind him is burly, able, tumbledown Yaleman Ralph McAllister Ingersoll, former Fortuneditor, now general manager of all Timenterprises, descendant of 400-famed Ward McAllister. Littered his desk with pills, unguents, Kleenex, Socialite Ingersoll is *Time's* No. 1 hypochondriac, introduced ant palaces for study & emulation of employees, writes copious memoranda about filing systems, other trivia, seldom misses a Yale football game. His salary: $30,000; income from stock: $40,000.

( Early in life Timeditor John Stuart Martin lost his left arm in an accident. Unhandicapped he, resentful of sympathy, Martin played par golf at Princeton, is a crack shot with a rifle or shotgun, holds a telephone with no hands, using shoulder & chin, chews paperclips. First cousin of Cofounder Hadden, joined in second marriage to daughter of Cunard Tycoon Sir Ashley Sparks, Timartin is managing editor of newsmagazine, has been nimble in Cinemarch, other Timenterprises, makes $25,000 a year salary, gets from stock $60,000.

¶ $20,000 salary, $20,000 from stock gets shyest, least-known of all Timeditors, Harvardman John S. Billings, Jr., now under Luce in charge of revamped *Life*, once Washington correspondent for the Brooklyn *Eagle*, once National Affairs Editor for *Time*. Yclept "most important man in shop" by Colleague Martin, Billings, brother of famed muralist Henry Billings, is naïve, solemn, absent-minded, once printed same story twice, wanted to print, as news, story of van Gogh's self-mutilation, drives to office in car with liveried chauffeur, likes Jones Beach.

¶ Fortuneditor Eric Hodgins is thin-haired, orbicular, no Big Three graduate. Formerly on *Redbook*, boy & girl informing *Youth's Companion*, Hodgins inherited Pill-Swallower Ingersoll's editorial job two years ago when latter was called to greater glory, higher usefulness, still writes much of content of magazine, is paid $15,000; from stock only $8,000.

¶ Doomed to strict anonymity are *Time-Fortune* staff writers, but generally known in spite of this are former *Times* bookritic John Chamberlain, Meistersinger Archibald MacLeish. Both out of sympathy with domineering business, both irked by stylistic restrictions, thorns to Luce as well as jewels they. Reward for lack of fame: Chamberlain, $10,000; MacLeish, $15,000; each, two months' vacation.

Brisk beyond belief are carryings-on these days in Luce's chromium tower. *Time*, marching on more militantly than ever, is a shambles on Sundays & Mondays, when week's news is teletyped to Chicago printing plant; *Fortune*, energetic, dignified, its offices smelling comfortably of cookies, is ever astir with such stupefying projects as sending the entire staff to Japan; new whoopsheet *Life* so deep in organization that staff breakfasts are held to choose from 6,000 submitted photographs the Nude of the Week; so harried perpetually all editors that even interoffice memoranda are couched in familiar Timestyle,* that an appointment to lunch with Editor Luce must be made three weeks in advance.

Caught up also in the whirlwind of progress are *Time, Fortune's* 19 maiden checkers. Bryn Mawr, Wellesley, Vassar graduates they, each is assigned to a staff writer, checks every word he writes, works hard & late, is barred by magazine's anti-feminine policy from editorial advancement.

*Cold, Baggy, Temperate . . .*

At work today, Luce is efficient, humorless, revered by colleagues; arrives always at 9:15, leaves at 6, carrying armfuls of work, talks jerkily, carefully, avoiding visitor's eye; stutters in conversation, never in speechmaking. In early days kept standing at Luce desk like butlers were writers while he praised or blamed; now most business is done by time-saving memoranda called "Luce's bulls." Prone he to wave aside pleasantries, social preliminaries, to get at once to the matter in hand. Once to interviewer who said, "I hope I'm not disturbing you," snapped Luce, "Well, you are." To ladies full of gentle misinformation he is brusque, contradictory, hostile; says that his only hobby is "conversing with somebody who knows something," argues still that "names make news," that he would not hesitate to print a scandal involving his best friend.

Because of his Chinese birth, constantly besieged is Luce by visiting Orientals; he is polite, forbearing, seethes secretly. Lunch, usually in a private room at the Cloud Club, is eaten quickly, little attention paid to the food, much to business. He drinks not at all at midday, sparingly at all times, takes sometimes champagne at dinner, an occasional cocktail at parties. Embarrassed perhaps by reputation for unusual abstemiousness, he confesses proudly that he smokes too much.

Serious, ambitious Yale standards are still reflected in much of

---

* Sample Luce memorandum: "Let *Time's* editors next week put thought on the Japanese beetle. H. R. L."

his conduct; in indiscriminate admiration for bustling success, in strong regard for conventional morality, in honest passion for accuracy; physically, in conservative, baggy clothes, white shirts with buttoned-down collars, solid-color ties. A budding joiner, in New York, Luce belongs to the Yale, Coffee House, Racquet & Tennis, Union, & Cloud Clubs; owns a box at the Metropolitan; is listed in *Who's Who* & *Social Register*.

Colder, more certain, more dignified than in the early days of the magazine, his prose style has grown less ebullient, resembles pontifical *Fortune* rather than chattering *Time*. Before some important body he makes now at least one speech a year, partly as a form of self-discipline, partly because he feels that his position as head of a national institution demands it. His interests wider, he likes to travel, meet & observe the Great. Five or six times in Europe, he has observed many Great & Near Great. Of a twenty-minute conversation with King Edward, then Prince of Wales, says only "Very interesting." Returning from such trips, he always provides staff members with 10 & 12-page memoranda carefully explaining conditions.

Orated recently of conditions in this country: "Without the aristocratic principle no society can endure. . . . What slowly deadened our aristocratic sense was the expanding frontier, but more the expanding machine. . . . But the aristocratic principle persisted in the United States in our fetish of comparative success. . . . We got a plutocracy without any common sense of dignity and obligation. Money became more and more the only mark of success, but still we insisted that the rich man was no better than the poor man—and the rich man accepted the verdict. And so let me make it plain, the triumph of the mass mind is nowhere more apparent than in the frustration of the upper classes." Also remarked in conversation: "Trouble is—great anti-social development—is the automobile trailer. Greatest failure of this country is that it hasn't provided good homes for its people. Trailer shows that."

*Milestones*

Good-naturedly amused by Luce tycoon ambitions was Lila Hotz, of Chicago, whom he married there on Dec. 22, 1923. In

1935, the father of two boys, Luce was divorced by her in Reno on Oct. 5. Married in Old Greenwich, Conn., without attendants, on Nov. 23, 1935, were Luce, Novelist-Playwright Clare Boothe Brokaw, described once by Anglo-aesthete Cecil Beaton as "most drenchingly beautiful," former wife of elderly Pantycoon George Tuttle Brokaw.

Two days before ceremony, "Abide with Me," by new, beautiful Mrs. Luce, was produced at the Ritz Theatre. Play dealt with young woman married to sadistic drunkard, was unfavorably reviewed by all newspaper critics.*

In a quandary was Bridegroom Luce when *Time's* own critic submitted a review suggesting play had some merit. Said he: "Show isn't that good. . . . Go back. . . . Write what you thought." Seven times, however, struggled the writer before achieving an acceptable compromise between criticism, tact.

## A Million Rooms, a Thousand Baths . . .

Long accustomed to being entertained, entertaining, is Mrs. Luce, intimate of Mr. & Mrs. A. Coster Schermerhorn, Bernard M. Baruch, Jock Whitney, glistening stage & literary stars. Many were invited last summer to 30-acre estate in Stamford to play tennis, croquet, swim; many more will be when Mrs. Luce has finished her new play, "The Women," † when *Life's* problems, budding policies have been settled by Luce.

Many, too, will come to 7,000-acre, $100,000 Luce plantation, near Charleston, S. C.; will sleep there in four streamlined, prefabricated guest cottages. Given to first Mrs. Luce in divorce settlement, along with $500,000 in cash & securities, was French Manoir at Gladstone, N. J., where Luce once planned to raise Black Angus cows, to become gentleman farmer.

---

* Of it said Richard Watts, blue-shirted, moon-faced *Tribune* dramappraiser:

"One almost forgave 'Abide with Me' its faults when its lovely playwright, who must have been crouched in the wings for a sprinter's start as the final curtain mercifully descended, heard a cry of 'author,' which was not audible in my vicinity, and arrived onstage to accept the audience's applause just as the actors, who had a head-start on her, were properly lined up and smoothed out to receive their customary adulation."

† Among backers are sad, ramshackle George S. Kaufman, high-domed fur-bearing Moss Hart.

Described too modestly by him to Newyorkereporter as "smallest apartment in River House," * Luce duplex at 435 East 52nd Street contains 15 rooms, 5 baths, a lavatory; was leased furnished from Mrs. Bodrero Macy for $7,300 annually, contains many valuable French, English, Italian antiques, looks north and east on the river. In décor, Mrs. Luce prefers the modern; evasive is Luce. Says he: "Just like things convenient & sensible." Says also: "Whatever furniture or houses we buy in the future will be my wife's buying, not mine."

## Whither, Whither?

Accused by many of Fascist leanings, of soaring journalistic ambition, much & conflicting is the evidence on Luce political faith, future plans. By tradition a Tory, in 1928 he voted for Alfred E. Smith, in 1932 for Herbert Hoover, this year for Alfred M. Landon. Long at outs with William Randolph Hearst, it was rumored that a visit last spring to California included a truce with ruthless, shifting publisher. Close friend for years of Thomas Lamont, Henry P. Davison, the late Dwight Morrow, it has been hinted that an official connection with the House of Morgan in the future is not impossible. Vehemently denies this Luce, denies any personal political ambition, admits only that he would like eventually to own a daily newspaper in New York.

Most persistent, most fantastic rumor, however, declares that Yaleman Luce already has a wistful eye on the White House. Reported this recently Chicago's *Ringmaster*, added: "A legally-minded friend . . . told him that his Chinese birth made him ineligible. Luce dashed to another lawyer to check. Relief! He was born of American parents and properly registered at the Consulate."

Whatever the facts in that matter, indicative of Luce consciousness of budding greatness, of responsibility to whole nation, was his report to *Time's* Board of Directors on March 19, 1936. Declaimed he: "The expansion of your company has brought it

* Smallest apartment in River House has six rooms, one bath.

to a point beyond which it will cease to be even a big Small Business and become a small Big Business. . . . The problem of public relations also arises. *Time*, the Weekly Newsmagazine, has been, and still is, its own adequate apologist. Ditto, *Fortune*. But with a motion-picture journal, a nightly radio broadcast, and with four magazines, the public interpretation of your company's alleged viewpoint or viewpoints must be taken with great seriousness." Certainly to be taken with seriousness is Luce at thirty-eight, his fellowman already informed up to his ears, the shadow of his enterprises long across the land, his future plans impossible to imagine, staggering to contemplate. Where it all will end, knows God!

# JOHN DOS PASSOS

*U. S. A.,* the fat, blue, three-part volume which contains the following portrait of Henry Ford, has been more than once termed the answer to the perennial demand for The Great American Novel. It may be. Fortunately this issue need not be argued here; what does concern us is the part played in that extraordinary volume by this and the other twenty-six biographical portraits, the quality and effect of their most unusual style. To understand these let us first consider the man who made them.

John Chamberlain describes Dos Passos being questioned by a group of admiring young Soviet actors in 1928: "Scrupulously polite, given to deprecatory gestures, he starts up like a flushed partridge, his baldish head bobbing, his near-sighted eyes soft with pleased surprise"—but unready, as he has since remained, to declare himself their comrade. This is the John Roderigo Dos Passos whose grandfather, a Portuguese immigrant, settled as a shoemaker in Philadelphia, and whose father served as a drummer boy in the Civil War until invalided out of the Army of the Potomac at fourteen, married a woman of old Virginia and Maryland stock, and became a corporation lawyer in Chicago, where John was born in 1896. This is the Dos Passos whose early education was a composite of experiences gathered in Mexico, England, Belgium, tidewater Virginia, Washington, D. C., and a Connecticut boarding school; who was a contemporary at Harvard of the writers Robert Nathan, Robert Littell, Gilbert Seldes, and E. E. Cummings, and, graduating in 1916, sailed for Spain with notions of studying architecture but spent three years in the ambulance service in France and Italy, and emerged to write one of the great novels of the World War. This is the Dos Passos whose "instinctive, all-pervasive sympathy for the underdog has caused Communists to hail him, at various times, as Number One Literary Fellow-Traveler," but whose answer is: "You're wrong. I'm merely an old-fashioned believer in Liberty, Equality, Fraternity"; and who sustains this reply by a series of books more genuinely American in tone and fiber than any work of either the esthetes or the flag-wavers.

Soon after being mustered out of the army in July 1919, John Dos Passos began to turn his war experiences into writing; first, in *One Man's Initiation,* published in that year, then in his famous *Three Soldiers* (1921), which brought him national attention for the realistic frankness and biting force of his honest revelations. The next year appeared two books, one of essays entitled *Rosinante to the Road Again,* and one of verse, *A Pushcart at the Curb.* With *Manhattan Transfer* (1925), which has been called the "*Rapsody in Blue* of contemporary American fiction," he made his first important use of the transitionless technique of the movie with its flashes, its cutbacks, its speed, giving, as Sinclair Lewis describes it, "the panorama, the sense, the smell, the sound, the soul, of New York." After that he produced the first of his plays and travel-diaries.

Then came the three books which comprise *U. S. A.: The 42nd Parallel* (1930), *Nineteen Nineteen* (1931), and *The Big Money* (1936)—a composite portrait of this country as Dos Passos sees it. And how does he see it? Let his own words tell:

"U. S. A. is the slice of a continent. U. S. A. is a group of holding companies, some aggregations of trade unions, a set of laws bound in calf, a radio network, a chain of moving picture theatres, a column of stock-quotations rubbed out and written in by a Western Union boy on a blackboard, a publiclibrary full of old newspapers and dogeared history-books with protests scrawled on the margins in pencil. U. S. A. is the world's greatest rivervalley fringed with mountains and hills, U. S. A. is a set of bigmouthed officials with too many bankaccounts. U. S. A. is a lot of men buried in their uniforms in Arlington Cemetery. U. S. A. is the letters at the end of an address when you are away from home. But mostly U. S. A. is the speech of the people."

The book is written in several different styles on several different planes of observation. First, there are the more or less autobiographical parts showing the industrial democracy as seen by the child growing up in it. These are numbered sections labeled "The Camera Eye." Then there are behavioristic studies of ordinary individuals named and presented fictionally as they move through thirty years of American social history. Interspersed among these come fragmentary "Newsreel" sections made up of contemporaneous headlines, slang expressions, and snatches of popular songs. Finally, we have an interrupted series of twenty-seven brief biographies of persons who at one time or another during these decades figured prominently on the American scene: Eugene V. Debs, Luther Burbank, Edison, Steinmetz, "Meester Veelson," Isadora Duncan, the Wright brothers, Thorstein Veblen, Hearst, Insull, and so on.

These sketches are the best part of the book, showing greater depth and solidity than the fictional characterizations and being of altogether greater consequence to the total effect than either the Newsreels or The Camera Eye. Tense with dynamic contradictions and shot out to the reader with a terse, powerful utterance, they not only portray their subjects in their many-sided conflicts but also characterize them through the impact of these people upon our whole social structure. That the author never "pulls his punches" in these narrative-critical-interpretative portraits is self-evident at first glance. What is more remarkable is the skill of selection whereby he has pared away all that is not relevant to his purpose and has singled out all the telling items, running them together in a swift, Joycean flow of racy language. When Dos Passos wants to be sarcastic or ironical he can be so with devastating finality, as in the sketch of Rudolph Valentino, where, having pictured the fantastic idolatry shown by the throngs in the Manhattan funeral chapel, he ends: "The funeral train arrived in Hollywood on page 23 of the New York *Times*." He will show no kindess, indeed, to Henry Ford, instinctively regarding the powerful industrialist with the sentiments of a man on the assembly line though with the historical perspective of an informed student of our era.

## TIN LIZZIE

"*Mr. Ford the automobileer,*" the featurewriter wrote in 1900,

"*Mr. Ford the automobileer began by giving his steed three or four sharp jerks with the lever at the righthand side of the seat; that is, he pulled the lever up and down sharply in order, as he said, to mix air with gasoline and drive the charge into the exploding cylinder. . . . Mr. Ford slipped a small electric switch handle and there followed a puff, puff, puff. . . . The puffing of the machine assumed a higher key. She was flying along about eight miles an hour. The ruts in the road were deep, but the machine certainly went with a dreamlike smoothness. There was none of the bumping common even to a streetcar. . . . By this time the boulevard had been reached, and the automobileer, letting a lever fall a little, let her out. Whiz! She picked up speed with infinite rapidity. As she ran on there was a clattering behind, the new noise of the automobile.*

For twenty years or more,

ever since he'd left his father's farm when he was sixteen to get a job in a Detroit machineshop, Henry Ford had been nuts about machinery. First it was watches, then he designed a steamtractor, then he built a horseless carriage with an engine adapted from the Otto gasengine he'd read about in *The World of Science*, then a mechanical buggy with a onecylinder fourcycle motor, that would run forward but not back;

at last, in ninetyeight, he felt he was far enough along to

risk throwing up his job with the Detroit Edison Company, where he'd worked his way up from night fireman to chief engineer, to put all his time into working on a new gasoline engine,

(in the late eighties he'd met Edison at a meeting of electric-light employees in Atlantic City. He'd gone up to Edison after Edison had delivered an address and asked him if he thought gasoline was practical as a motor fuel. Edison had said yes. If Edison said it, it was true. Edison was the great admiration of Henry Ford's life);

and in driving his mechanical buggy, sitting there at the lever jauntily dressed in a tightbuttoned jacket and a high collar and a derby hat, back and forth over the level illpaved streets of Detroit,

scaring the big brewery horses and the skinny trotting horses and the sleekrumped pacers with the motor's loud explosions,

looking for men scatterbrained enough to invest money in a factory for building automobiles.

He was the eldest son of an Irish immigrant who during the Civil War had married the daughter of a prosperous Pennsylvania Dutch farmer and settled down to farming near Dearborn in Wayne County, Michigan;

like plenty of other Americans, young Henry grew up hating the endless sogging through the mud about the chores, the hauling and pitching manure, the kerosene lamps to clean, the irk and sweat and solitude of the farm.


He was a slender, active youngster, a good skater, clever with his hands; what he liked was to tend the machinery and let the others do the heavy work. His mother had told him not to drink, smoke, gamble or go into debt, and he never did.

When he was in his early twenties his father tried to get him back from Detroit, where he was working as mechanic and repairman for the Drydock Engine Company that built engines for steamboats, by giving him forty acres of land.

Young Henry built himself an uptodate square white dwellinghouse with a false mansard roof and married and settled down on the farm,

but he let the hired men do the farming;

he bought himself a buzzsaw and rented a stationary engine and cut the timber off the woodlots.

He was a thrifty young man who never drank or smoked or gambled or coveted his neighbor's wife, but he couldn't stand living on the farm.

He moved to Detroit, and in the brick barn behind his house tinkered for years in his spare time with a mechanical buggy that would be light enough to run over the clayey wagonroads of Wayne County, Michigan.

By 1900 he had a practicable car to promote.

He was forty years old before the Ford Motor Company was started and production began to move.

Speed was the first thing the early automobile manufacturers went after. Races advertised the makes of cars.

Henry Ford himself hung up several records at the track at Grosse Pointe and on the ice on Lake St. Clair. In his 999 he did the mile in thirtynine and fourfifths seconds.

But it had always been his custom to hire others to do the heavy work. The speed he was busy with was speed in production, the records records in efficient output. He hired Barney Oldfield, a stunt bicyclerider from Salt Lake City, to do the racing for him.

Henry Ford had ideas about other things than the designing of motors, carburetors, magnetos, jigs and fixtures, punches and dies; he had ideas about sales,

that the big money was in economical quantity production, quick turnover, cheap interchangeable easilyreplaced standardized parts;

it wasn't until 1909, after years of arguing with his partners, that Ford put out the first Model T.

✦

Henry Ford was right.

That season he sold more than ten thousand tin lizzies, ten years later he was selling almost a million a year.

In these years the Taylor Plan was stirring up plantmanagers and manufacturers all over the country. Efficiency was the word. The same ingenuity that went into improving the performance of a machine could go into improving the performance of the workmen producing the machine.

In 1913 they established the assemblyline at Ford's. That season the profits were something like twentyfive million dollars, but they had trouble in keeping the men on the job, machinists didn't seem to like it at Ford's.

Henry Ford had ideas about other things than production. He was the largest automobile manufacturer in the world; he paid high wages; maybe if the steady workers thought they were getting a cut (a very small cut) in the profits, it would give trained men an inducement to stick to their jobs,

wellpaid workers might save enough money to buy a tin lizzie; the first day Ford's announced that cleancut properlymar-ried American workers who wanted jobs had a chance to make five bucks a day (of course it turned out that there were strings to it; always there were strings to it)

such an enormous crowd waited outside the Highland Park plant

all through the zero January night

that there was a riot when the gates were opened; cops broke heads, jobhunters threw bricks; property, Henry Ford's own property, was destroyed. The company dicks had to turn on the firehose to beat back the crowd.

The American Plan; automotive prosperity seeping down from above; it turned out there were strings to it.

But that five dollars a day
paid to good, clean American workmen
who didn't drink or smoke cigarettes or read or think,
and who didn't commit adultery
and whose wives didn't take in boarders,
made America once more the Yukon of the sweated workers
of the world;
made all the tin lizzies and the automotive age, and incidentally,
made Henry Ford the automobileer, the admirer of Edison,
the birdlover,
the great American of his time.

But Henry Ford had ideas about other things besides as-
semblylines and the livinghabits of his employees. He was full of
ideas. Instead of going to the city to make his fortune, here was
a country boy who'd made his fortune by bringing the city out
to the farm. The precepts he'd learned out of McGuffey's
Reader, his mother's prejudices and preconceptions, he had preserved clean and unworn as freshprinted bills in the safe in a bank.

He wanted people to know about his ideas, so he bought the
*Dearborn Independent* and started a campaign against cigarette-
smoking.

When war broke out in Europe, he had ideas about that too.
(Suspicion of armymen and soldiering were part of the midwest
farm tradition, like thrift, stickativeness, temperance and sharp
practice in money matters.) Any intelligent American mechanic
could see that if the Europeans hadn't been a lot of ignorant
underpaid foreigners who drank, smoked, were loose about
women and wasteful in their methods of production, the war
could never have happened.

When Rosika Schwimmer broke through the stockade of
secretaries and servicemen who surrounded Henry Ford and suggested to him that he could stop the war,
he said sure they'd hire a ship and go over and get the boys
out of the trenches by Christmas.

✦

He hired a steamboat, the *Oscar II*, and filled it up with pacifists and socialworkers,
> to go over to explain to the princelings of Europe
> that what they were doing was vicious and silly.

It wasn't his fault that Poor Richard's commonsense no longer rules the world and that most of the pacifists were nuts,
> goofy with headlines.

When William Jennings Bryan went over to Hoboken to see him off, somebody handed William Jennings Bryan a squirrel in a cage; William Jennings Bryan made a speech with the squirrel under his arm. Henry Ford threw American Beauty roses to the crowd. The band played *I Didn't Raise My Boy to Be a Soldier*. Practical jokers let loose more squirrels. An eloping couple was married by a platoon of ministers in the saloon, and Mr. Zero, the flophouse humanitarian, who reached the dock too late to sail,
> dove into the North River and swam after the boat.

The *Oscar II* was described as a floating Chautauqua; Henry Ford said it felt like a middlewestern village, but by the time they reached Christiansand in Norway, the reporters had kidded him so that he had gotten cold feet and gone to bed. The world was too crazy outside of Wayne County, Michigan. Mrs. Ford and the management sent an Episcopal dean after him who brought him home under wraps,
> and the pacifists had to speechify without him.


Two years later Ford's was manufacturing munitions, Eagle boats; Henry Ford was planning oneman tanks, and oneman submarines like the one tried out in the Revolutionary War. He announced to the press that he'd turn over his war profits to the government,
> but there's no record that he ever did.


One thing he brought back from his trip
was the Protocols of the Elders of Zion.

He started a campaign to enlighten the world in the *Dearborn Independent;* the Jews were why the world wasn't like Wayne County, Michigan, in the old horse and buggy days;

the Jews had started the war, Bolshevism, Darwinism, Marxism, Nietzsche, short skirts and lipstick. They were behind Wall Street and the international bankers, and the whiteslave traffic and the movies and the Supreme Court and ragtime and the illegal liquor business.

Henry Ford denounced the Jews and ran for senator and sued the *Chicago Tribune* for libel,

and was the laughingstock of the kept metropolitan press;

but when the metropolitan bankers tried to horn in on his business

he thoroughly outsmarted them.

In 1918 he had borrowed on notes to buy out his minority stockholders for the picayune sum of seventyfive million dollars.

In February, 1920, he needed cash to pay off some of these notes that were coming due. A banker is supposed to have called on him and offered him every facility if the bankers' representative could be made a member of the board of directors. Henry Ford handed the banker his hat,

and went about raising the money in his own way:

he shipped every car and part he had in his plant to his dealers and demanded immediate cash payment. Let the other fellow do the borrowing had always been a cardinal principle. He shut down production and canceled all orders from the supplyfirms. Many dealers were ruined, many supplyfirms failed, but when he reopened his plant,

he owned it absolutely,

the way a man owns an unmortgaged farm with the taxes paid up.

In 1922 there started the Ford boom for President (high wages, waterpower, industry scattered to the small towns) that was skillfully pricked behind the scenes

by another crackerbarrel philosopher,

Calvin Coolidge;

but in 1922 Henry Ford sold one million three hundred and thirtytwo thousand two hundred and nine tin lizzies; he was the richest man in the world.

Good roads had followed the narrow ruts made in the mud by the Model T. The great automotive boom was on. At Ford's production was improving all the time; less waste, more spotters, strawbosses, stoolpigeons (fifteen minutes for lunch, three minutes to go to the toilet, the Taylorized speedup everywhere, reach under, adjust washer, screw down bolt, shove in cotterpin, reachunder adjustwasher, screwdown bolt, reachunderadjust-screwdownreachunderadjust until every ounce of life was sucked off into production and at night the workmen went home gray shaking husks).

Ford owned every detail of the process from the ore in the hills until the car rolled off the end of the assemblyline under its own power, the plants were rationalized to the last tenthousandth of an inch as measured by the Johansen scale;

in 1926 the production cycle was reduced to eightyone hours from the ore in the mine to the finished salable car proceeding under its own power,

but the Model T was obsolete.


New Era prosperity and the American Plan
(there were strings to it, always there were strings to it)
had killed Tin Lizzie.
Ford's was just one of many automobile plants.


When the stockmarket bubble burst,
Mr. Ford the crackerbarrel philosopher said jubilantly,
"I told you so.
Serves you right for gambling and getting in debt.
The country is sound."
But when the country on cracked shoes, in frayed trousers,
belts tightened over hollow bellies,

idle hands cracked and chapped with the cold of that coldest March day of 1932,

started marching from Detroit to Dearborn, asking for work and the American Plan, all they could think of at Ford's was machineguns.

The country was sound, but they mowed the marchers down.

They shot four of them dead.


Henry Ford as an old man
is a passionate antiquarian,
(lives besieged on his father's farm embedded in an estate of thousands of millionaire acres, protected by an army of serv-icemen, secretaries, secret agents, dicks under orders of an Eng-lish exprizefighter,

always afraid of the feet in broken shoes on the roads, afraid the gangs will kidnap his grandchildren,

that a crank will shoot him,

that Change and the idle hands out of work will break through the gates and the high fences;

protected by a private army against

the new America of starved children and hollow bellies and cracked shoes stamping on souplines,

that has swallowed up the old thrifty farmlands
of Wayne County, Michigan,
as if they had never been).
Henry Ford as an old man
is a passionate antiquarian.

He rebuilt his father's farmhouse and put it back exactly in the state he remembered it in as a boy. He built a village of museums for buggies, sleighs, coaches, old plows, waterwheels, obsolete models of motorcars. He scoured the country for fid-dlers to play old-fashioned squaredances.

Even old taverns he bought and put back into their original shape, as well as Thomas Edison's early laboratories.

When he bought the Wayside Inn near Sudbury, Massachu-

setts, he had the new highway where the newmodel cars roared
and slithered and hissed oilily past (*the new noise of the automobile*),

> moved away from the door,
> put back the old bad road,
> so that everything might be
> the way it used to be,
> in the days of horses and buggies.

# JANET FLANNER

"MR. AMBASSADOR" was written and first published as a Profile in *The New Yorker* (December 10 and 17, 1938), and it is against the background of those ostensibly fugitive pieces that it should be read and considered. Yet in the degree to which its facts and impressions were patiently gathered and scrupulously sifted it is probably exceptional, and in the opinion of the present editor it is one of the finest Profiles ever printed in that magazine.

Its author, Janet Flanner was born and educated in Indiana, spent a *Wanderjahr* in Germany with her parents before the World War, and became a student at the University of Chicago, where she unconventionally took the same courses over and over with Professors Robert Morss Lovett and Robert Herrick. "They taught writing, big and little," she relates, "and they and their remarkable courses were what I wanted; at the end of two years I had to leave the institution because I hadn't taken anything but Herrick and Lovett and my credits were out of balance. After the war I went to France and have lived in Paris ever since. When I first settled there I wrote what I thought was a novel, but after it was printed I realized it was only a very long character sketch and that I had no talent for fiction; public events in Europe, on which I have reported for *The New Yorker* [over the signature of Genêt] for the past fourteen years, have supplied me and the world with plot enough." Among her other successful Profiles, collected in a new volume under the title of *An American in Paris,* are those of Queen Mary, Elsa Maxwell, Mme. Hanau, Igor Stravinsky, Adolf Hitler, and Pablo Picasso.

An element of her consistent objectivity—distinguishing hers from most *New Yorker* writing—is Miss Flanner's unusual freedom from satire, bitter or mischievous. The explanation of this seems to lie in her thorough and ingenious working methods. "Because I hate interviewing a subject, because I do it badly, and because he (or she) usually knows himself less clearly than do his friends and enemies, I interview the friends and enemies. I use them exactly as if they were documents in a library which I consulted and from which I took notes. This way I get a more general report on the man than I could give myself; I use enemies as correctives, as the givers of shadow without which no portrait has even approximate dimension. (I say 'enemies'; few people possess them; I should properly say 'dislikers.') Most of the Profiles I have done, I did without ever having spoken to the subjects, though I have occasionally arranged to be in a room when they were to be present so that I might hear their voice (an informing organ) or watch them walk or note their physical manifestations." By this "rather slow and eclectic system" Miss Flanner proceeds to her ultimate goal, "getting the whole reflection of the man in, with its shadows and the bright lights on buttons, brains, foibles, and the whole silhouette"—all the time preserving an "uncomposed" informality.

How this method worked in the preparation of the following sketch may be guessed when we know that Miss Flanner is acquainted not only with the subject but with members of his ambassadorial family (secretaries and wives), with former colleagues and Russians who knew him during his Moscow years, with former fellow journalists, and with observers of his war work in Washington—from many of whom, of course, came information and character details. But this was not all: "I also naturally used the U. S. Senate Foreign Relations Committee report on Bullitt's Russian mission; I used English and American newspapers of 1919-20, *The Nation*, the *Times* (New York and London); I used Lloyd George's *Memoirs*, etc., etc. I did two or three weeks of reading to get the climate of post-war Europe, the Wilson quarrel, and Bullitt's notion of peace." Doubtless the reader will feel this to be putting a great amount of effort, time, and expense into the writing of a sketch for a weekly magazine; but, doubtless also, he will realize that in no other way could he be enabled to enjoy such a vivid and fair-minded portrait of this important contemporary. Additional pleasure and interest are here to be gained by topical reference to the sketches by Mr. Keynes and Mr. White.

## MR. AMBASSADOR

WILLIAM CHRISTIAN BULLITT, our Ambassador to France, was born with a set of ancestors ideal for anyone who was to grow up to make a career of representing the United States in Europe. Many of his forebears were Early American historical figures, and two more recent progenitors have become city statues. The Ambassador is descended from the father of George Washington, the sister of Patrick Henry, and from Pocahontas herself. He is still further related to the First Families of the Old Dominion through the intermarriages of his forebears with the Langhornes, Dandridges, and Harrisons. Of the two statues, one is that of the Ambassador's paternal grandfather, John Christian Bullitt, a leading citizen in his day, which is placed before the Philadelphia City Hall. His maternal great-grandfather, Dr. Samuel Gross, because he did so much to advance and standardize the practice of medicine in America, is honored by a statue which stands in front of the Smithsonian Institution in Washington. The first Bullitts came to this country as Huguenot refugees from Provence, and in 1937 Mr. Bullitt, in his capacity as Ambassador, was made an honorary citizen of the town of Nîmes, from which the ancestral Monsieur Boulet fled in 1637. Bullitt feels as close to the French today as if those three hundred years were no more than a week, and is still as cool to England as if 1776 were only yesterday. Fortified by history books, his family blood, patriotism, and a passion for international affairs, he treats the twentieth century as if it were the eighteenth, and comes to the same anti-monarchical, democratic conclusions, and feels the same affections, affiliations, and fears, that his Revolutionary ancestors did. For him, General Lafayette is always at his right hand and George III is still lurking around the corner.

More than most Americans' lives, Mr. Bullitt's was from the beginning an accumulation of things past. A few minutes after he was born forty-seven years ago in Locust Street, Philadelphia, he was laid on an armchair, where his great-aunt, Lady Osler, wife of the noted Canadian physician, Sir William Osler, accidentally sat on the child. Thus immediately began operating on him the mixed advantages and drawbacks of his position as a member of a stylized, sedate, well-upholstered bourgeoisie, rich in fortune, education, and appreciation of the early Colonial democracy—and caste. It was from his antecedents' traditional pride in themselves and the United States, which they had once fought to help create and later thoroughly enjoyed, that he drew his possessive patriotism, and it was from their eminent satisfaction in the way the American Revolution turned out that he probably developed his instinct for rebellion generations after rebellion had gone out of style in his family. From the age of six months, when he was trundled from Philadelphia to Rome to be shown to his aunt, the Duchess d'Assergio, he was annually taken on summer trips to Europe; as a boy, in winter he was sent to the De Lancey private day school, then the best in Philadelphia. At school or at home, the atmosphere he breathed was that emanated by Rittenhouse Square, with more exciting whiffs brought by the grown-ups from the clubs and the select terpsichorean Assemblies of Philadelphia. Through the days of his youth, young Bullitt was persistently educated and photographed; he worked away at sciences and foreign languages, learning his German in Munich and his French at the family luncheon table, where his mother, a good linguist, made French the noon rule; he was posed for the family album from his Fauntleroy period to that of the plastered forelock and high collar proper for prewar Eastern collegiates. At considerable expense he was sent to Yale for his undergraduate work and to Harvard for law. As Mr. Bullitt's late friend, Charles Sweeney of the Philadelphia *Public Ledger*, was the first to say, Bullitt rose from the rich.

For fourteen years of his adult life he has been among the unemployed. In the years when he had jobs, they were good ones. Though he started as a ten-dollar-a-week reporter for the Philadelphia *Ledger*, he soon became a featured World War correspondent for that paper, and later in the war was in charge of the State Department's secret and confidential reports on the Central Powers. Thereafter he served variously as attaché to President Wilson's Paris Peace Commission, special assistant to the Secretary of State, executive officer of the American Delegation to the London Economic Conference; once he was almost a farmer and twice he has been an ambassador. When he resigned from Wilson's peace staff in 1919, in what was considered a scandalous underling's uprising against the Treaty of Versailles, Bullitt said he knew he would be put on the political shelf for fifteen years. His prophecy erred by a twelve-month, for in 1933 Roosevelt brought him out of retirement by naming him Ambassador to Russia. Doing nothing for those fourteen years was the hardest job Bullitt ever tackled, because he has always suffered from, and enjoyed, abnormal energy. His energy drives people either to admiring or detesting him. In human relations he never tastes the peace of indifference; some of the harshest things are said about him by his friends, some of the kindest by his enemies. He is eclectic, enthusiastic, adrenal—in conversation turns scarlet with displeasure or delight—is hospitable, sociable, hot-tempered, and over-punctual. He has an uproarious sense of humor and loves to laugh out loud at his or other people's jokes. He is an inveterate reader and a lively raconteur.

Headstrong, spoiled, spectacular, something of a nabob, and a good showman, he has complicated ambitions which are a compound of his devotion to his own notions of idealism, his interest in his career, and his faith in the ultimate fate of the human race. Two things he can't abide are shilly-shally and criticism. He works best at top speed and surrounded by admiration. He is the first United States Ambassador to France in thirty years who speaks fluent French, and is a better judge of foreigners than of Americans. He is refractory, partisan, and always a fighter, an unembarrassed patriot, and an explosive romantic. He has a shrewd talent for contacts, a remarkable memory, an emotional respect for history, and a serious sense of the value of documentation. He earnestly tries never to be fooled in a trade and in a big issue is indiscreetly unafraid to shoot the works. He is prematurely bald; is blue-eyed, pink-skinned; has heavy shoulders and, though an excellent judge of wines, the blood pressure of a man of twenty-one. For years he slept only four hours a night and regularly had breakfast at five A.M.

In the past an American ambassador's chief duties were to wear a top hat and keep us out of foreign entanglements. But European politics and international trade being what they are today, an ambassador's primary activities now include those of a trade expert who wears a pencil behind his ear and whose main job is to prevent the foreigners from entangling themselves in a bankrupting war. In one month last year Mr. Bullitt gave sixty hours to increasing the quota of American apples allowed to be sold in France and the rest of his time to writing analyses to Washington of what looked like the dangerous political horse trades of the rising and falling French Cabinets. Ever since the epoch of the Venetian ambassadors, secret correspondence has been the great unpublished work of European diplomacy. In the past the United States did less of this, but today our ambassadors are no longer supposed to stare like simple Americans, but instead to get our government its money's worth by keeping their eyes peeled, by edging in on contemporary information, and, above all, by taking notes. Bullitt's confidential reports are considered the amplest in the foreign service because he likes what he calls "keeping in touch with the general situation," and in Europe today the general situation can be anything and anywhere. Since he was once an A-1 newspaperman, his reports are a kind of extraordinary private European gazette; what interests him is the news behind the news, and he thinks yesterday's events less important than today's—and tomorrow's. Because he is a diplomat, this leads him into written prophecy dangerous for any mortal, but he's too interested to be nervous. The last and least duty of an ambassador nowadays, according to Bullitt, is representing his country in a top hat.

However, when there is top-hat work to be done, Bullitt polishes it off handsomely. The daily dark-red carnation he wears in his buttonhole tickles the French. He likes lots of good London-made clothes, has a correct and varied wardrobe of thirty suits, which he wears with dash. The homespun tradition, when manifested by the richest country in the world, has never appealed to Europeans, who expect us to live up to the big money we invariably mention—in the years when we can. Bullitt is able to talk crops as competently as the next politician, but he also makes the required grand drawing-room bow. As the French say, he acts like, looks like, even smells like an ambassador. Certainly to the maintenance of an elegant ambassadorial standard he has given a lot—about $62,000 a year. The late Ambassador Straus annually spent about $75,000. Bullitt, being familiar with France, gets more for his money. He has no housekeeper, has a finger in all the menus, and runs the Embassy himself with the abrupt, expensive efficiency of a man who has no woman to guide him. For a big dinner party of thirty or more, he doubles the staff of Embassy footmen so food may be served the only way he likes it—hot and punctually. He's been known to cut a guest dead who arrived for dinner half an hour late. He is a gourmet with a good digestion, and his food and drink rank so high in European diplomatic circles that King Zog, before his marriage, wrote Bullitt as man to man to ask whether, for his wedding breakfast and state feasts, he could please borrow Bullitt's cook, the former chef of the Hungarian Regent Horthy—the one cook in Europe, the King had heard, competent to meet the approaching gastronomic crisis with style. Bullitt was happy to be of service and the loan turned out fine for all concerned: it gave Bullitt a new story to tell at his dinner table, it gave the King complete satisfaction, it gave the chef not only a grand trip but also the famous Albanian Ordre de Besa, conferred by the grateful monarch.

The wines Bullitt serves are exceptional even in France. For his burgundies he usually goes down to the district and does his tasting and selecting himself. Once, in the famous wine cellars of Horcher's restaurant in Berlin, he spent an afternoon tasting eleven of their finest white wines, a compliment young Horcher offered gratis to a customer who knew wine almost as well as a restaurateur. Bullitt's rarer Embassy vintages he sensibly serves only to small, serious dinner parties that will appreciate them. They include a Château Haut-Brion 1906, a Cheval Blanc 1906 which can't be purchased any more, a Château Margaux 1899, and a Château d'Yquem of 1901. His finest German wine is a 1915 Johannisberg, his favored brandy a Monnet, *très vieille*. The scarcest of his French *crus* are a few bottles of Château Mouton-Rothschild 1858, from Foyot's cellars. He also had some *rarissime* Pontet-Canet 1864, but Herriot, President of the Chamber and France's heartiest political winebibber, polished that off. Bullitt never skimps on his big affairs. At an Embassy ball for six hundred guests, including the Duke and Duchess of Windsor, Bullitt served four hundred and ninety bottles of his favorite champagne, Pommery 1928, a worthy Pouilly-Fumé, and the best proprietary whiskeys and brandies, besides fruit juices, cakes, and the like, and, at one-thirty in the morning, draft Munich beer with baked beans and frankfurters. For the first time in the Embassy there was dancing to a jazz band. The party ended at five A.M. Last summer he gave a ball for three hundred midshipmen and officers from our fleet. That party nearly never ended at all.

Bullitt maintains two establishments, of which his town house, or the Embassy, on the Avenue d'Iéna near the Trocadéro is fortunately rent-free. It was a gift to the American government by the late Ambassador Herrick and was formerly the *hôtel particulier* of the French President Grévy. The Grévy regime having tended decoratively toward gray cupids and rose petals, Mr. Bullitt redid the mansion impressively and comfortably in French *haute-époque* style, with exotic touches provided by some rich Chinese portraits, porcelains, and specially woven Indo-Chinese rugs; he added duck-egg-green walls, grisailles over the salon doors, enormous needlepoint chairs, and plenty of bookcases. He knew exactly what he wanted and told the decorators so.

His country place, which he rents, is the little eighteenth-century château of St. Firmin, in the private woods and on the borders of the fountained lake of the great château of Chantilly, which was originally the estate of the Ducs de Condé and later was owned by the Duc d'Aumale. The Duc willed his unentailed property, which included his fine library of books and the château of St. Firmin, to the Institut de France. Since the Institut consists of the two hundred and twenty-six most illustrious intellectual figures of France, Bullitt has two hundred and twenty-six brainy landlords. What Bullitt likes best about the place is that the two great French horse races, the Chantilly Prix de Diane and the Prix du Jockey Club, are practically run in his back yard. Though he is crazy about all sports, especially tennis, he is craziest about racing, and the first thing he reads at breakfast is the racing page of the London *Times*. Ex-Premier Chautemps liked St. Firmin so well that he turned somersaults down the lawn to show his approval. Bullitt keeps his and his daughter's riding horses in the estate's vast old stables.

Like her father, Anne Bullitt admires horseflesh. She is now fourteen and has been attending the Foxcroft School in Virginia. On her last birthday her doting father, who calls her Duck, telephoned her long distance from Paris and sent an elaborate cablegram that included messages from her favorite dog. Since her mother is dead, the relationship between Anne and her father—who thinks the sun rises and sets by her—is very special. Because she is not of an age to act as her father's hostess at the Embassy, the Ambassador, as is customary when the incumbent has no wife, chooses his presiding hostess for his formal affairs from among the wives of his diplomatic staff.

Being a liberal entertainer is part of being an ambassador, since ninety per cent of the entertainment is done for the government. Most nations grant their ambassadors a handsome allowance for representation. To the British Ambassador in Washington, for example, His Majesty's Government gives an entertainment fund of $70,000 a year. Toward its Ambassador's entertaining in Paris, the United States donates annually $4,800, which sum can also be drawn on in the Ambassador's absence by the Chargé d'Affaires. Bullitt's salary is $17,500 a year, his personal income around $45,000; his global expenses, personal and official, are somewhere above $75,000. No one except ambassadors knows how or why ambassadors manage.

Bullitt's income derives from his share of what is left of the fortune of his grandfather, John Christian Bullitt, who in 1890 was ranked as one of the ten wealthiest men in the country and was reputed to be worth between ten and fifteen million in real estate, Norfolk & Western Railroad shares, and West Virginia coal mines. But the eighteen-nineties also had their recessions; when he died in 1902, his estate had started to fall. It sank to about a million dollars, but later, before 1929, came back to around eighteen million. John Christian Bullitt was born a Kentuckian, married Therese Langhorne of Virginia, and came to live in Philadelphia, where he built up one of the biggest law practices of his time and wrote Philadelphia's new City Charter. The statue of him which stands before the City Hall was a posthumous tribute, and a rare one from Philadelphia to an outsider. In Kentucky, John Christian's great-great-uncle, the lawyer Thomas Bullitt, had staked out the city of Louisville and acquired the thousand-acre family estate of Oxmoor, now owned by another lawyer, former Solicitor General William Marshall Bullitt. Ambassador Bullitt's father, William Christian Bullitt, Sr., besides being a lawyer, was a member of the Pennsylvania State Legislature, at one time vice-president of the Norfolk & Western, and also a member of the firm of Castner, Curran & Bullitt, which controlled the Pocahontas coal mines that formerly furnished coal to most of the major navies of the world. The family coal mines were so named as a sentimental tribute to the Indian maid who had become Mrs. John Rolfe, and one of whose descendants had eventually married into the Bullitt tribe. On his death Mr. Bullitt left his coal business to his employees; he said his children—the Ambassador and his younger brother, Orville H., now a Philadelphia banker—had enough to live on.

The Bullitts have been American lawyers for three hundred years, or ever since they settled at Port Tobacco, on a tributary of the Potomac, but on his mother's side the Ambassador's forebears have a little more professional and ethnological variety. His mother, Louisa Gross Horwitz, was of Pennsylvania Dutch Palatinate stock, with an admixture of German Jewish blood; her grandfather, out from the Old Country, settled in Baltimore as a chemist, but his son, Bullitt's grandfather, Orville Horwitz, who married the daughter of the famous Dr. Gross, became another of those nineteenth-century successful American lawyers. He was so successful that his fine town house in Baltimore is now preserved as the Walters Art Gallery; his country place, Cloud Capped, is today Maryland's Memorial to its war dead.

During Bullitt's four years at Yale, where he was in the class of 1912, he studiously strove to evade becoming a lawyer; he majored in psychology and his professors advised him to become a research psychologist. He was, however, already interested in foreign affairs and was a member of Professor (now President) Charles Seymour's first class in Modern History and Diplomatic Relations. Bullitt was Phi Beta Kappa, Psi Upsilon, Scroll and Key, editor of the Yale *Daily News*, and president of the Dramatic Association. (In a production of Beaumont and Fletcher's "Knight of the Burning Pestle," he wore a suit of full armor while mounted on an unreliable white horse borrowed from the New Haven Fire Department.) He founded a short-lived organization known as the Minced Pie Club, two of whose members were Cole Porter and Chauncey Tinker, who is now Professor Tinker, the eminent Boswell and Johnson authority. All these things availed Bullitt nothing, for when he was graduated from Yale it was to go to Harvard Law School. After he had been there one year, his studies were brought to an end by his father's death and an ensuing chance voyage to Russia, then an untouristed, remote, Czarist land.

Three times in Bullitt's life Russia has shaped him. His first visit to Moscow decided his career, his second visit temporarily ruined it, and his third visit was a three-year sentimental stalemate which did neither him nor Russia any good.

William Bullitt began deciding what his career would be when on an August night in 1914 he was awakened in Moscow by crowds shouting "War! Down with the Austrians!" A few days later in Berlin he heard crowds shouting "Down with the French!", in London they were crying "Down with the Germans!", and in Paris the French cried down with many peoples, including the Turks. Bullitt concluded that in war each nation thought its cause holy, that war was thus illogical folly which a new generation of wiser diplomats must in future avert. To be just such a wise diplomat was the career which, by now, Bullitt had decided on; he and his ideals were then twenty-three years of age. His grandmother just having died at Dinard, leaving her jewels locked in a safe in her Champs-Elysées flat, Bullitt, when he found no locksmiths available in Paris because of the panic during the Battle of the Marne, borrowed a police-escorted safe-breaker from prison, rescued the jewels, and buried them in a garden. Then he sailed for home and confidently offered himself to the Philadelphia *Public Ledger* as an expert on the European situation. He was given a cub job reporting South Philadelphia. However, his subsequent work as correspondent aboard the Ford Peace Ship was so good that he was sent to Europe for eight months in 1916 as a featured war correspondent. He covered Germany, Austria, Hungary, Poland, Belgium, and the battle fronts, and, because of his fluent German, made personal contacts with the leaders of the Central Empires.

After America entered the war, Bullitt, because of his languages and recent experiences, was asked by the War Department's Secret Service to take charge of the Political Section's confidential reports on the Central Powers, which meant compiling dope on the enemy. His officer's boots were already bought when the State Department hooked him for similar work, and he never entered the army. From then on till his career crashed, Bullitt was built up at Washington as State Department expert on enemy and subversive movements. His data on the Central Powers' political and economic status were used by Woodrow Wilson in his speeches on foreign affairs; at the President's request, Bullitt was made his special informer on the new revolutionary movement then rising in Russia and Asia. A future President, Franklin Roosevelt, had at this period, as Assistant Secretary of the Navy, an office three doors away from Bullitt's in the old State, War, and Navy Building, and here the two minor men's friendship began. After the armistice, Bullitt went to Paris as a handy-man attaché to Wilson and his Commission to Negotiate Peace and soon was promoted to Chief of the Division of Current Intelligence. In this capacity he had to tell the American Commissioners each morning what had happened in Europe the day before. The job brought him into illuminating personal contact with the big guns: Asquith, Lloyd George, Orlando, Clemenceau, Paderewski, the present Lord Lothian, Sir Maurice Hankey, Venizelos, Briand, and others. He was still being used as a Leftist documentator and emissary, too, and Wilson sent him to Berne to the Second International, at which the President hoped the Socialists would accept his peace program as a part of their platform.

Then, after the breakup of the Prinkipo proposal in February, 1919, Bullitt was sent to Moscow. It is difficult now to get at the truth of this strange, jumbled slice of history, since of the three major figures concerned, two—Wilson and Lenin—are dead and cannot speak for themselves, and the third, Lloyd George, is still too lively a politician to have his word relied on. However, the facts seem to be that, behind Clemenceau's back, Bullitt was secretly dispatched by Wilson and Lloyd George on a mission to Russia, where he was to do two things: first, compile a truthful, detailed report on how the Soviet Union was really getting along, even if it was getting along better than Wilson and Lloyd George hoped, and, second, discover on what terms Lenin would make peace. Though Bullitt's lengthy report that the Soviets were a going political concern, at least emotionally, which would eventually have to be recognized certainly seemed strange in 1919, Lenin's peace terms appear even more fantastic today. After interviewing Lenin, Litvinoff, and Chicherin, Bullitt was given a document (still little known, though it was mentioned in the United States Senate reports of its hearings on the treaty of peace) in which Lenin agreed to leave Siberia, the Urals, the Caucasus, three-fourths of the Ukraine, Archangel, Murmansk, and North Russia to their *de-facto* governments, thus confining the Soviet influence to Moscow, Leningrad, and their surroundings. This offer the Allied peacemakers, who clearly had no notion of how bad the map of Europe could become once it got into motion, apparently thought not good enough, for the Bullitt mission was concluded at one of those windy moments when straws make history. In London, Lord Northcliffe's *Daily Mail's* influential campaign against the Red Menace was molding an English die-hard public opinion which prevented Lloyd George from being what he called "sensible about Russia." In Paris and New York, White Kolchak's brief advance was hailed with relief as settling the Bolshevik nonsense forever. What really finally killed recognition of Soviet Russia, though (and recognition was what the Bullitt report had been aimed at), was, he says, a Paris breakfast date. On the advice of Colonel House, Bullitt, on his return from Moscow and before he had seen President Wilson, who had a headache, accepted an invitation to breakfast with Lloyd George and three British experts, and, over the tea, the Lenin proposal was pronounced by the Welshman to be "of the greatest importance." By lunch time, Wilson, apparently in a moment of pique such as only worried idealists can know, refused to see his Russian reporter at all because Bullitt had seen Lloyd George first. The Bullitt report was suppressed by Wilson and Lenin's peace proposal was allowed to lapse. Later in the House of Commons, when heckled by Labour leader Clynes, Lloyd George first denied there had been any peace bid at all, then said it could have had no value, since Wilson never brought it before the Peace Conference.

As spring came to Paris, dissatisfaction and disappointment in the Covenant of the League of Nations and in what the Europeans had left of the President's Fourteen Points had, as Secretary of State Lansing later revealed, spread to five of Wilson's American peace experts; in addition, he said, one official was "in a quandary" and one adviser "most bitter." Bullitt resigned from the Commission in May in a letter to Wilson in which he respectfully stated that the Versailles Peace Treaty would lead to new wars; that the League of Nations would be powerless to prevent these wars; that the United States should refuse to enter the League; that Russia, Wilson's favorite "acid test of good will," had been ignored; that Wilson could have won his fight for his "new international order" had he fought in the open rather than behind closed doors. Bullitt also wrote his once beloved leader, "I am sorry that you did not fight our fight to a finish and that you had so little faith in the millions of men like myself in every nation who had faith in you." In a characteristic intimate confidence made to the entire world's press, Bullitt gave the papers copies of his letter of resignation plus his announcement that he was going to lie on the sands of the Riviera and watch the world go to hell. The scandalized New York *Times*, in a nippy editorial, squashed him like a political sand flea.

Later that summer Bullitt returned to America and went to Maine for a fishing trip. When he emerged from the woods, he was met by a sheriff with a summons calling him as a witness before the Senate's Committee on Foreign Relations. Bullitt's testimony covered 138 pages; he submitted twenty-six documents on the League, Russia, the Versailles Treaty, and included private conversations, gentlemen's chats, etc. His testimony, more than any other single individual's, was considered to have brought the greatest weight against America's joining the League. Both the testimony and the documents were revelatory of what had been going on behind the stormy Paris scenes.

Today, attacking the League and admitting that the Soviets exist are conservative American practices, but in 1919 Bullitt was given a rough time. Being Left was not intellectually the mode. By the rich he was treated as a traitor to his class, by Democratic and Republican pro-Leaguers as a renegade; by the press and the bureaucrats he was almost universally tagged as a tattletale for letting cats out of the bag which were familiar to every diplomat in Europe but news to the common man. The London *Post* birched him for not playing the game, the New York *Times* called his revelations treacherous and indiscreet. Oswald Garrison Villard's *Nation*, which was anti-League, backed him as a champion of open diplomacy openly arrived at and was alone in printing *in toto* his important Russian report. He had turned down the post of Minister to the then newly resuscitated State of Poland in order to resign and tell all. Being twenty-eight, he relished equally the battle, the martyrdom, and his share in the victory. America repudiated the League, Wilson became a broken, ill old gentleman, and the young Philadelphian stepped into limbo.

Bullitt's next fourteen years were largely those of a bookworm, rolling stone, and domestic man. In 1916 he had married Ernesta Drinker of Philadelphia. In the seven years of their marriage they lived in Washington, in Europe (where she was with him during the Peace Conference, dazzling the international great with her beauty and her Paris gowns), in New Hampshire, Gramercy Park, and finally Ashfield, Massachusetts. In 1923 the marriage was dissolved by divorce. Bullitt's second marriage, to Louise Bryant, widow of the famous revolutionary John Reed, took place soon after in Paris. The handsome, adventurous Louise Bryant was a public figure in her own right, an established journalist, author of *Six Months in Red Russia*. Reed had had a lasting influence on her and, it is possible, had a posthumous temporary influence on Bullitt. The Bullitts lived in Turkey for a year, returned to Paris in 1924, where their daughter Anne was born, and lived variously in France, Vienna, Philadelphia, and New York until 1930, when they were divorced. After a long and tragic illness, Louise Bullitt died in Paris in 1936.

In the period following his political eclipse, Bullitt's appetite for books and documents was concentrated on the unpublished archives of the war. He was given the run of the invaluable private papers of the former German Chancellor, Prince Max of Baden, at Schloss Salem, Colonel House's papers, and many others.

Wherever Bullitt was, his habit of sleeping only a few hours a night made him a voracious nocturnal reader of biographies, diaries, memoirs, state and court papers—anything on the government of man. His favorite period, French and American, was and remains the eighteenth century, with its twin dawns of democracy. The Civil War has never interested him. Among the Colonials, Thomas Jefferson and Patrick Henry were then, as now, his idols; to their rarified company he has added Franklin Roosevelt. During what he called his exile, Bullitt wrote a lot, mostly interpretations of history, which he's never put in shape to publish. He also wrote a novel, *It's Not Done*. It was not a very good novel, but it had a sale of a hundred and fifty thousand copies and was translated into German and the Scandinavian languages. Philadelphia society thought his book a *roman à clef* about itself and his first marriage and liked his report on neither. The novel was written during Bullitt's year in Turkey, when he lived in a manner suited to the exotic streak in his nature: he dwelt in a golden villa in Anatol Hissar called Yali-Kuprullu, formerly the family residence of four Kuprullu Grand Viziers and noted as one of the loveliest of the Bosporus houses. In an effort to approximate his name, the natives called him Bulut Pasha, which in Turkish means Cloud General. He liked that fine. In his Austrian sojourns, Bullitt twice studied with Dr. Sigmund Freud, though he denies that he was ever psychoanalyzed. Bullitt's bookseller still has a standing order to send him the newest publications on psychoanalysis. After the Anschluss, when Dr. Freud was permitted to depart for London, Bullitt was waiting to greet his old friend at the railway station in Paris as he passed through.

In 1931, Bullitt, because of his admiration for Roosevelt and their close friendship, began to emerge again. In the pre-nomination period he helped shape Democratic foreign policy. He campaigned in 1932, and when the New Deal came in was appointed to the State Department as an assistant to Secretary Hull. Following his participation in the London Economic Conference of 1933, Bullitt, after fourteen years of waiting, was finally responsible, at the President's request, for arranging the details of that recognition of the Russian Soviets which, because he had advocated it in 1919, had caused his downfall.

In November, 1933, he was sent as the first Ambassador of the United States to the U.S.S.R. His three years in Moscow have become legendary. As the old American friend of New Russia, he was received with fantastic acclaim. When he rode in the streets he was cheered, at the Opera the Muscovites rose to shout his name, the Ballet basked in his favor, government circles beamed on him; he moved in an atmosphere of hysterical Slavic emotion which produced a superficial state of the most delightful and confused optimism in all concerned. He was the first ambassador of any country to be presented to Stalin; he taught a Red Army regiment to play polo, taught factory workers to play baseball. A contingent of the American Marines helped him move into Spasso House, a magnificent palace built for a prewar millionaire. Here Bullitt's entertaining was in the millionaire manner. His sumptuous dinner parties were rivaled only by those given by Litvinoff and featured even choicer viands, since Bullitt, in his official capacity, could obtain superior supplies from the world outside. Bullitt's routs became the talk of the Arctic Circle. For one of his balls he borrowed animals and birds from the zoo for decorations. There were cockerels and pigeons crowing and cooing in glass cages, baby bears and mountain goats in pens, and a seal which served guests champagne from a glass balanced on its nose. It was during this spectacular period that a witty Russian lady tartly remarked that Bullitt hadn't made up his mind whether being an ambassador was a job or a charade, and that politically he was aspiring to do with charm what even Talleyrand wouldn't have attempted except with cash, intrigue, or an army.

Once the initial frenzy of acclaim and mutual hospitality was over, Bullitt's ill-concealed curiosity as to how everything was going, in a country which even then was getting ready for tragic Party purges, became increasingly embarrassing to officials to whom an uninterested capitalist ambassador would have been less upsetting. Bullitt spoke his mind about religious freedom, for which he was thanked by the Pope; he became nosy about doctrinal paradoxes, for which nobody thanked him; he asked too many questions, ignored all hints, and talked too freely. In his three years in Russia, Bullitt apparently came to practical conclusions about a regime he had been emotionally interested in, once, at a distance. He had made friends with certain of the most powerful men in the Communist Party, but when he finally judged that the Roosevelt-Litvinoff Agreement had been broken by the Comintern's revision of its American activities and spoke his mind to the Narkomindel, or Soviet Foreign Office, Russian-American affections chilled. Bullitt's big parties ceased; so did his sources of information. He sat in Spasso House, high and dry. At the time, local American journalists said—though they did not write it for their papers—that Bullitt had three ample reasons for resigning: the Comintern had flouted its commitments; he had guilelessly supposed the Russians would play ball; he had a better job waiting for him elsewhere. European diplomats were of the opinion that he did not so much fail at his official task as arrive inopportunely, at a moment in Russian counter-revolutionary xenophobian history when it was unlikely that any enthusiastic, democratic foreigner could have succeeded. Bullitt had been criticized for being pro-Soviet in 1919, when Bolshevism was anathema; he was accused of "turning yellow" on Russia in 1933, when Communism was becoming intellectually stylish. His sense of timing seems to satisfy no one but himself. At the end of his third visit, Bullitt left Russia quoting Thomas Jefferson.

Today, as Ambassador to France, Bullitt says he stands politically just where Roosevelt does, and, like the President, should be called Left or Right according to whether the observer is himself Right or Left. In Paris, Bullitt was *persona grata* with the Front Populaire government and especially with Léon Blum. However, today French extremists regard Bullitt only as a liberal, alert member of his class. Until the New Deal got into rough waters, certain of Bullitt's friends considered he had Presidential possibilities, since they believed there was a chance of Roosevelt's choosing him to be his successor. As Andrew Jackson had appointed Van Buren and Theodore Roosevelt had appointed Taft to be their heirs, so Franklin Delano Roosevelt, it was hoped, would appoint and anoint Bullitt.

It's known that before he became Ambassador, at Roosevelt's request Bullitt made an off-the-record investigation of the Foreign Service with a view to reform. It's also known that he has Roosevelt's ear, hitherto untuned to Foreign Service problems. Part of the Service, especially the underpaid, underpromoted foreign clerks, consider Bullitt the white hope of the Department; part, principally the upper bureaucracy, are his severest critics. In Moscow and Paris he has used consular and diplomatic officers interchangeably and has made as little distinction as possible between officers and clerks, thus outlawing snobbery. Bullitt's reforms would include the Department's adopting the best of the French elastic and the British rigid Service policies. From the French he would borrow the system of promotion on merit, by which common consular men can be moved up into the chic diplomatic corps; from the British he would take their high educational and linguistic requirements and amplify them with special studies in economics, since he thinks expert commercial advice should be one of the Service's returns to the taxpayer. Bullitt was responsible for pressing the much-discussed executive order forbidding men in the United States Foreign Service to marry foreigners without permission from the Secretary of State. He makes no bones about stressing patriotism, devotion to American principles, high standards of personal honor, a respectable private life, and a willingness to swot hard on little pay from Uncle Sam as qualifications for a reformed Service personnel. Briefly, he thinks that because the American Foreign Service isn't given money with which to bribe, as the representatives of other nations are, it has to be more brainy.

Ambassador Bullitt's Paris Chancellery was organized on his ideal functional basis, comprising four units—politics, French and foreign finance, economics, and administration. His system avoids a duplication of effort by the comparatively new Commerce Department and the traditional State Department, and may eventually be used as a model for other American embassies. Because Bullitt's Paris staff is handpicked, he's accused of factionalism;

it's known that through his friendship with Roosevelt he can obtain the best of the Department's brains—and wear them out, critics say. A furious worker himself, he drives his people hard. When he went to Russia as Ambassador, he immediately exhausted two secretaries and cabled Washington, "Please send a secretary who can stand Moscow and me." The new Paris Chancellery, completed in 1933, fronts on the Place de la Concorde and is the finest of any of our government's buildings abroad. The elegant white stone façade follows the original plans of Gabriel, Louis XV's architect, who had conceived the unit as a pendant to the pavilion behind the Ministry of Marine which, with the Hotel Crillon, was to form the grandiose architectural scheme which the Chancellery now completes. Inside, the Chancellery is modern, practical, luxurious, with elevators, a marble staircase, elegant architectonic features, suites of offices, and waiting rooms. Owing to its size, the Chancellery houses all the government's services—the Army, Navy, the Department of Commerce, and consular activities as well as the State Department.

In the United States Foreign Service today, sixty per cent of the ambassadors and seventy per cent of the ministers are career men. By foreign diplomats, Bullitt is considered to be the only non-career man who understands the diplomatic game as it's really played, who knows the moves and the traditional values, and is aware that small things can be big and big things may be zero. While he's praised for being interested in the game, he's also criticized for becoming too interested in his opponent; he's inclined to personality enthusiasms. Though he is not a businessman by training, nobody can steal his suspenders as a trade-treaty maker. He would have been crazy about international politics even if he had been born not a millionaire's son but a bootblack.

In the [1938] European crisis, in which France, England, and Germany eventually came to terms about Czechoslovakia and the Sudetens, Bullitt of Paris and Joseph Kennedy of London were called the key ambassadors. In case of a European war, Bullitt, geographically, would be President Roosevelt's No. 1 informer. In a recent statement about France and America, Bullitt said he hadn't said the two countries would be together in war as in peace; all he would say in the end was that he had been misquoted. He enjoys making tantalizing professional remarks. Last spring some remark he made about "foreign entanglements" excited the French until they discovered Bullitt was quoting from Washington's Farewell Address of 1796.

Those who love him think he merits all he has received from life; those who do not love him think he's a trick done with mirrors.

He is an old-fashioned character in that time and experience have not changed his original mold. He was born with a passion for public, not private, life. He has matured around his one important emotional dominant—an unplatonic, possessive patriotism. As a little boy taught to sing "My country, 'tis of thee," he accepted ownership and honestly thought it was his own wonderful United States of America that he and everybody else were singing about.

# WILLIAM ALLEN WHITE

"THE SAGE OF EMPORIA," as William Allen White is internationally known, is a man whose opinion on matters political is always news. Throughout a long lifetime, beginning in 1868, Emporia, Kansas, has been his home, and since 1895 *The Emporia Daily and Weekly Gazette* has been his organ. Both owe their celebrity to him and, though he has traveled widely, the world has frequently beaten paths to his plain and paper-littered sanctum. He attended the University of Kansas, but at least seven colleges and universities, including Columbia, Harvard, and Northwestern, have honored him with degrees. He has consistently voiced the opinions of a mid-western progressive, but parties and presidents of all political complexions have listened when he spoke and there was no dissenting word when he was awarded the Gold Medal for Citizenship. He served in France during the World War as an observer for the American Red Cross, was our delegate to the Russian conference of 1919, is a member of the Institute of Pacific Relations and of the National Institute of Arts and Letters; yet the address has remained, as always: Emporia, Kansas.

Of Mr. White's many books, not all have been on public affairs; some are of homely, small-town things. But most of them have the blended points of view of the townsman and the citizen of the world. This is as true of his latest volumes, *A Puritan in Babylon* (1938) and *The Changing West* (1939), as of his first ones. The Emporian note was struck rather early in his career in *Stratagems and Spoils* (1901) and continued to sound in *A Certain Rich Man* (1909), *The Old Order Changeth* (1910), and *God's Puppets* (1916). In 1924 and 1925 came his biographies of Woodrow Wilson and Calvin Coolidge. Three years later, in 1928, he published *Masks in a Pageant*, a collection of articles originally written for their news value ("a reporter's notes elaborated"), gathering up into a series of short biographies his observations of American political figures over forty years. Of the eight presidents described in this book, Mr. White's favorite was Theodore Roosevelt, but he knew them all both publicly and privately and he writes with the knowledge and sympathy (even when disapproving) of one who has watched their struggles at close hand. The sketch of Wilson, following so soon after the author's publication of the full-length life, comes with special authority. The piece is notable for its fair-mindedness, a quality on which, in connection with an article about President Taft, Theodore Roosevelt once chided Mr. White, exclaiming, "Don't hold the knife edge of your balance so perfectly poised in this piece that your readers won't see your bias!" If there is evidence here of

359

bias, it is bias restrained by the sportsmanship of a fellow mortal and by the good nature and sincerity of an old newspaperman.

The reader will notice the opportunities offered here for cross references with Mr. Keynes's and Miss Flanner's pieces. In addition to the many books on Wilson, there are interesting short sketches by Emil Ludwig (*Genius and Character*), William Bolitho (*Twelve Against the Gods*), and John Dos Passos (*U. S. A.*)

# WOODROW WILSON

## *Our First Folk Myth*

AMERICA, being a young country, has contributed to the world few folk tales. One of the few is the story of the Aztec youth who was chosen for human sacrifice. As the tale runs, the fairest youth of the Aztec realm was chosen to be worshiped as a god. For a year after he was taken to the temple, every wish was gratified. Every sense of his physical body was satisfied. Every yearning in his heart was answered. No wish was denied him. He lived surrounded by love, nurtured by adulation, lifted to the pinnacle of fame and joy— for he was to become a god—powerful beyond the ambition of men, happy as humanity could make one of its kind. And then, at the end of a year, leading a great procession of his adoring people into a mountain, he ascended an altar and laid him down to have his heart ripped out by the high priests while he still lived and breathed. Perhaps in another age—in the Golden Age men dream of—they will tell the story of Woodrow Wilson in terms like these when he shall live as the mythical god of the first world peace.

Thomas Woodrow Wilson, the twenty-eight President of the United States, was the first Southern gentleman to walk into the White House after James K. Polk left it. Zachary Taylor was Southern, but he was the symbol of more or less Jacksonian boots and whiskers in the White House. Andrew Johnson was Southern, but of the poor whites of Tennessee, an illiterate until after his marriage. Wilson, born in Virginia of a fine large Irish father and a sweet, quiet, aloof lady whose father came from the Scotch border—Wilson, in whose blood ran no American soldier stock except that of his Irish father, who was a chaplain in the Confederate Army—Wilson came from the upper middle class in the South at a time when there was no higher social estate; when the Southern aristocracy of the first half of the nineteenth century had been reduced to penury and shame by the Civil War and by the reconstruction days in which humiliation followed, even more poignant than defeat. Woodrow Wilson, whose parents were born in Ohio, in some way was marked indelibly by the South. It was, of course, only the environment of the South that marked him. Yet during his youth as a preacher's son—the son of the Reverend Joseph Wilson, an orator and a leader of the Presbyterian Church in his day—young Wilson was a migratory boy. He moved with the preacher's family from town to town—from Virginia to Augusta, Georgia; to Wilmington, North Carolina; from North Carolina to Columbia, South Carolina. And because he was not set in the matrix of one town's tradition the legends of his boyhood are slight. Yet the remembrance men have of him in each town is the same—that of a spindle-shanked, awkward, rangy, milk-eyed, freckled boy, with auburn hair and a long solemn face; a boy who carried the handicap of spectacles when he was eight years old and until he was mature. At Augusta, at Wilmington, at Columbia, they recalled him—studious, aloof, mischievous but never naughty, wistfully watching "the young barbarians at play" who romped through woods, swam the creeks, fished in the brooks, and fought in the fields of the South in the days of the sixties and seventies. The royal blood that was in Woodrow Wilson was surely Celtic. His paternal grandfather, a newspaper man, legislator and state senator in eastern Ohio and his paternal grandmother came from the north of Ireland. They were Protestant Irish. His maternal grandfather, a Scotch Presbyterian preacher of renown in Columbus, Ohio, and Chillicothe, and his maternal grandmother came from the north of England on the Scotch border, and were accounted Scotch by their neighbors. Both branches of his family were Calvinists. Wilson himself, to the last—though he lies in an Episcopal cathedral—was an uncompromising denominational Presbyterian by way of creed, and a Calvinist in philosophy. The Joseph Wilsons were a neighborly, expansive, contentious lot. The Woodrows, his mother's people, were reserved, scholarly, meticulous in the performance of their duties, prouder than Punch and conscientious to their own hurt. Wilson's father, a Princeton man, a pulpit orator, a good fellow in every town and an effective money-raiser in every church, smoked his pipe, took his nip, loved society, was a national church leader, helped to organize the Southern Presbyterian Church, and was a figure in his world. Wilson's mother was not a good preacher's wife. She was standoffish. She paid her full and exact obligations to life consistently, but without much joy; was governed by her sense of duty and given to her moods. She made few friends and lost them easily. Out of this blood and environment came Wilson's heredity. As a boy who grew up in three towns he had no lifelong friend; no friend who went with him to the end. He was frail and never ganged with his fellows. It is important to consider the boyhood of this preacher's son, the first boy born to middle-aged parents and the adored idol of two elder sisters who shielded him, coddled him, and of course pampered and hampered him when he should have run wild, a young beast of the field, releasing his energy, trying his fists, his arms, his feet, and his brain in a thousand contests with his fellows; contests that would teach him to give and take, fight or fly, stand or run, and pay for his bad judgment of his fellows with his hide, after the ancient manner of boys in the vast man factory of their youth.

In the small Southern college where he went for part of a year he tried to play baseball, but his glasses bothered him. His eyes failed. He went home and studied with his erudite Princeton father, went in his own turn to Princeton in the middle seventies, and there, in his adolescence, for the first time he found his gang! But his qualities of leadership never moved men or boys of brawn. His leadership was purely intellectual. In college he was business manager of the baseball club, but did not play. He led the glee club and sang well. His singing was an outlet for his emotional nature, which was never well coördinated. Leaving Princeton with an A.B. degree and Johns Hopkins with a Master's, having a year in a law school, he first taught English in a women's college, but rejected teaching women and went to one of the small but first-rate New England colleges, Wesleyan at Middletown, Connecticut, where he made an impression on the faculty and was a favorite with the students. He coached the football team and took an interest in athletics—vicariously—as a promoter. He returned to Princeton as a teacher in 1887, a handsome young man in his late twenties, with a sensitive, refined face, smooth shaven, well set up, spick and span in his tailoring and toilet; a married man who was none the less popular at teas; but who, tradition says, in Princeton refused to be the life of the company after or when other men came to the party; that kind. He taught the social sciences—history, economics, sociology, political science; wrote books about history and political science—books that became textbooks in other colleges; good books of their kind, academic but prepared with pains and understanding, adducing and defending theories of political thought that were popular in American colleges in the eighties and nineties. These political theories he was compelled to abandon in practical politics; chiefly because the world had moved and changed its theories between the eighteen nineties and 1912. New facts had come into American civilization—indeed, into the new civilization of Christendom; facts which disturbed the old theories. And it is no discredit to Wilson that he changed with the times. At Princeton he became a popular professor. His classrooms were crowded. His lectures were most illuminating. He delivered himself in a fine, clear, happy voice in carefully selected language, with here and there a dash of humor indicated by the asterisks of twinkling eyes. For those years were the happiest years of his career. Ellen Axson, his young wife, also Southern, also Presbyterian, was bearing him lovely children. The students liked to lounge in his study. He was the idol of the tutors and instructors. He gathered about him in the college a Wilson cult. His class of '79 was proud of him and, returning on high days and holidays to Princeton, delighted to honor him. The fine Irish smile which illuminated a rather sober countenance, a smile composed somewhat by flexing thin lips and gathering gay wrinkles around hazel gray eyes, a muscu-

lar smile withal, was on his face frequently in those years of the
eighties and nineties. He was one of the demigods of the American academic world even before he took the next upward step
in his career. His books about books concerned with history
and political science, written largely for textbooks, were bringing
him fame in American colleges. He became an authority when
he still was a teacher, an authority on the science of government
as it is taught, not—alas!—as it is practiced. He was a contributor
to magazines of the better sort; always in demand as a speaker of
the occasion at academic, dedicatory services, and inaugurations;
also, he was a figure at those pleasant unions of business and college politics centering about alumni meetings of Princeton and
the other first rate colleges of the East. He wore a silk hat well,
and graced state ocacsions in the cloistered academic circles
where good breeding and a certain air of distinction and refinement are required. Among the ten thousand who ruled America
in the nineties, Professor Wilson was a Distinct Somebody. Then
he took an upward step, became president of Princeton, and was
Somebody Rather Important. For America makes education a
religion, and her educational leaders become ex-officio high
priests. In making public sentiment, and so, ultimately, in ruling
America, the president of any one of the first ten American
colleges—if he take his place in public life without any further
official distinction than his academic rôle—has as much power
and authority as a senator, and if, in addition to that, he has the
knack of leadership, he is as important as a Cabinet officer in the
American system, all without bothering with elections or the
leadership of a national cause. Dr. Woodrow Wilson, president
of Princeton, in this list of ten educational high priests, moved
in the first five, possibly the first two or three, as the century
closed.

In his inaugural address as president of Princeton he attacked
the tendency in American education to follow the materialism
of the German universities and stood for the humanities. Thus
he challenged an evil, and took the leadership of a national cause.
So Woodrow Wilson became, after a fashion, a pundit with
spiritual powers.

### Fate Smiles at Our Hero

But by a curious irony of fate Wilson's talents led him into a channel where he functioned badly. The presidency of Princeton was his first executive enterprise. There he encountered opposition. There pride, which he had released so joyously as an intellectual leader, had to be curbed with tact if he hoped to succeed. There he had to meet and master men. There, if he stood up as an academic leader, he had also to function as an administrator. And there he failed; not miserably, for he had intellectual vigor; not cravenly, for he staged his failure about a noble ideal—the ideals of a changing world. To give practical expression to his democratic ideal, he began a fight for the democratization of Princeton. He was in a way becoming a hero. Princeton, in the first decade of the new century, was, as nearly as an institution might be, the embodiment of the old aristocracy. It was Calvinistic in philosophy, set in its ways, proud of its past, unashamed of its wealth, the harbor of a decent, if sometimes arrogant, conservatism. A well-housed college was Princeton, beautifully conceived architecturally. Its outward phase reflected the dignity of its inner aspirations, a rather tough and gnarly stem upon which to graft the tender buds of the new democracy not yet respectabilized by Theodore Roosevelt.

Explicitly, Wilson's point of attack upon the aristocracy of Princeton was through its fraternity dormitories. Wilson desired to buy the luxurious fraternity houses which had sheltered the gilded youths of Princeton for a century, and use these houses as residences for student groups which should live with faculty preceptors to guide their work. Being thus grouped, the aristocracy of the fraternities would be undermined. Also other issues arose. A graduate school was proposed, and Wilson would have merged this school into the university. Those who opposed him desired the graduate school to assemble in its own buildings and with its own faculty, rather a separate faculty, but not, of course, independent of the university. This division would make the leveling-up process of the undergraduates—the Wilson ideal— more and more difficult. He staged his fight well, and in it he had two weapons. First of all a coördinated brain; then a felicitous faith in himself, and some needed spark of joyous resilience which inspired confidence in others. It was more than charm; it was more even than Irish blarney galvanized with wisdom. It was as though his guardian angel at birth had picked for him the spiritual pulchritude of Apollo, Hyperion, Adonis and Narcissus. But—alas!—in a mischievous gesture of irony his angel soured his birth brew with a drop of the blood of a moody Scot. The spiritual comeliness was always there, the nimble wit, the merry heart; but always, in the wings of Wilson's drama, squatted the Scotch Caliban waiting to wreck the scene.

Wilson, in the first decade of the glowing new century, was moving with the current of his times. Roosevelt, the most considerable Liberal leader of the world, was in the White House preaching economic democracy. In a score of gubernatorial mansions minor Roosevelts were preaching political democracy. The initiative, the referendum, the primary, the recall were coming into American life generally, all to the exaltation of the average man. The gimp of arrogance was being dampened in the top dog of the social contest. So the world saw this Wilson reflecting a gay heart in a merry countenance, battling against the privileges of wealth in Princeton, and hailed him as a new knight and contender for righteousness. But—woe was he!—the bruises that came from the bludgeons of the strong men on the Princeton Board of Trustees and in the Princeton faculty, men whom Wilson had antagonized with his democratic program, these bruises hurt; the Caliban in his heart howled in wounded vanity.

The aristocracy of Princeton was by no means decadent. Grover Cleveland, a director on the Princeton Board, backed by a strong Wall Street coterie of Princeton alumni, faced Wilson in his contest for academic democracy. Wilson—with all his intellectual strength, with all his spiritual felicity—could wave no scepter that would hold back foes when they were men of Cleveland's caste and kind. Moreover, Wilson's life had not prepared him to meet and defeat such enemies. He tried intrigue—and they discovered him. His personal dignity behind the fluttering banners of his gracious Celtic decorum was deeply affronted; seriously wounded. In all his life as a lonely pampered child, unganged in boyhood, a frail student, a youth seeking paths of least resistance, he had no background, no guide of experience to show him how to meet the opposition of brutal, direct, determined men. He preached the righteousness of his cause with smiling serenity, but that did not suffice to heal his inner wounds.

So the battle raged in Princeton. The rich alumni piled up millions in largess for buildings and endowments to establish the graduate school and overthrow the causes which Wilson defended. It was in those battle days that the Wilson of the ebullient, happy professorial period became a man of moods, of good days when he was very, very good, and of bad days when he was horrid. His nerves were strained. He took long rests, and came back from each of his vacations a little less restored than he should have been. In 1910 he was going steadily, inexorably, to a rather splendid failure as president of Princeton. And then, before final failure came, because Woodrow Wilson was a darling of the gods, Opportunity began tapping gently on his door, and when he opened the door he saw politics coming from afar. Politics approached deviously and abashed, but quickly, hat in hand, all but dropping curtsies. The New Jersey Democratic machine, which had been more or less financed from Wall Street, where Wilson's enemies did most congregate, asked Wilson to run for Governor of New Jersey. He accepted their suggestion, being at the end of his academic rope for the moment, also being broken in pride and corroded in vanity. He could not, being what he was, take entire comfort in the righteousness of his academic cause. He could talk bravely about the triumphs of defeat. That was an intellectual conviction. But that defeat was personal with Wilson; defeat always was personal, with him.

Woodrow Wilson was elected Governor of New Jersey in 1910, when the insurgents were getting ready to impale President Taft's head on their pike, and when the waves of political Liberalism were running strong and mounting high. Wilson's cause was politically a restatement of his democratic theory in education.

The measures which he championed in New Jersey had been in the program of Liberal governors of both parties in America for half a decade. They looked to one thing—the exaltation of the common man: by giving him political power through the primary; by protecting him against the cheats and swindles of trade; by curbing the privileges of unregulated corporate capital; by checking corrupt practices in politics and in commerce. These measures, which Wilson championed at Trenton, appealed keenly to the voters. When a governor was entrenched in power, it made him a hero to champion these measures; and if, as Wilson was, he was a man of tact and breeding, given to happy phrase and merry quip and common sense, the hero could go far in the politics of those days. So things came his way. He revived as a pundit; indeed, became a political pundit, with the magnificent trappings and background of his academic career. Again the smile came back—the seductive Irish smile that had won the boys of Princeton in his professorial days. Again the expansive manner returned. His wounded pride was healed by the balm of political success. Wilson, at Trenton, was only sixteen miles from Wilson, at Princeton, in the matter of solid space, but in the matter of temper and felicity he moved in another world. Success pampered him again. He was happy. He even learned to flip an occasional spiteful "damn" at his foes, for which he felt entitled to be called a good fellow, but not so good that anyone ever dared to caress him. Wilson never was embraced by the political hug with which small leaders like to fondle their idols publicly. No man ever got near enough to Wilson physically or emotionally to take him "by the right hand to kiss him" and therewith smite him "in the fifth rib and shed out his bowels to the ground." Wilson, in his gayest hours, in his times of greatest happiness, stood always aloof, distrusting men instinctively. It was this suspicion of men, founded upon ignorance of men, which led Wilson always to question the strong, to fraternize with the meek, and to break ruthlessly and irrevocably, without defense or explanation, any friendship which threatened his own prestige.

In New Jersey, Governor Wilson got his political education. A group of young Irish Liberals, out for a crusade and a lark after the Irish fashion, took Wilson in hand when he broke faith with the bosses who made him governor. These Irish lads spoke to something deeply submerged in Wilson, some Celtic sense of fairy adventure. They taught him the language of the political game. He learned quickly, on the whole profited by his mistakes, and after a manner succeeded; but succeeded only because he was riding the Liberal wave which was mounting a strong tide. Breasting the waves, Wilson surely would have failed.

Of course, there was geography in Wilson's success. As Governor of Nevada, or of Mississippi, doing something like the same job, Wilson would not have been available as a presidential candidate. The accident of geography was in his favor, but something more than geography made him loom large after two years as Governor of New Jersey. The Liberal movement was coming rapidly from flower to fruitage. The momentum of forty years of political agitation was behind Wilson when he began to rise on the horizon as a presidential candidate. It seems strange, when one considers Wilson as he was in 1912, to number him among those in the caravan of crusaders for Liberalism, whose bones have bleached the desert of failure in the past: Ben Butler, a sort of Falstaffian Murat; General James B. Weaver, of Iowa, grim, gray, deadly serious, the Greenback candidate for President in the eighties; Colonel Leonidas L. Polk, Jerry Simpson, Mary Elizabeth Lease, and Altgeld, the rabble-rousers of the early nineties in the Farmers' Alliance and Populism; Bryan, the pied-piper, who led the ragamuffins of Populism into the respectable mountain of democracy and lost them; La Follette, the implacable dervish of reform; Roosevelt, robust, dynamic, noisy, raucous in his joy, electric in his rage, deeply intuitive and highly emotionalized. Slowly, in the hands of these leaders through the generation, Liberalism had grown from a joke, through a menace, to a mass plea for justice. And here was Wilson, with his Irish heart, his Scotch dignity; well-tailored, silk-hatted, straight, erudite and aloof; the professor in the political bull-ring—none the less a hero, even if not the perfect toreador. How the old Grangers, the Greenbackers, and the Populists must have turned in their graves to see this man pulled out of Princeton by Wall Street.

turning his back on Wall Street with some show of perfidy in his righteous desertion, leading their cause, the cause of the common man, the cause of the old agrarians, facing their rulers in an industrial age. What a tableau this long procession of revolutionists must have made, from Ben Butler to Woodrow Wilson. But because he was an outstanding figure in his party, because he had won his New Jersey fight, and because he was unquestionably an intellectual leader in his party, Wilson assumed presidential size.

He accepted the new political dictum of the hour. To it he applied his mind and heart. He gave to Liberalism his best endeavors. From 1913 until the close of the Liberal epoch in America with our entrance to the World War, he became, by reason of his prestige and somewhat by reason of his intellectual capacity and greatly because of his charm and grace of personality, the leader of Liberalism in America.

### Our Hero Rises in Power and Glory

Fame came suddenly to Woodrow Wilson. In two years he moved from the academic circle where he was in the midst of intrigue and alarm, where he had paid no attention to politics, where he voted irregularly, where he never attended caucuses or primaries, where, indeed, he had only a book knowledge of the ways of our ruling classes, and found himself in the highest office in the gift of the world's most important Democracy. Fate has rarely played so gorgeous a game with a man apparently so unprepared for fate's caprices as she played with Woodrow Wilson when she led him off the campus of Princeton University into the White House.

Here it becomes necessary to consider the major influence in Wilson's life. For when he married Ellen Axson, in the beginning of his academic career in the mid-eighties, he attached a balance wheel to his temperamental nature. She was the type of wife who tried not to spoil her husband. She gave him what was good for him. She was a restraining influence. Being the daughter of a Presbyterian minister, she had a conscience and her emotional nature was well poised. Her advice was temperate and judicial. Her husband's greatness had come upon her so gradually that she was not awed by it. She had known him when he was less favored of fortune, and she knew what the wife of every man's youth knows—the limitations of his qualities and the danger points in his nature. She had seen those danger points threaten when he was a young instructor, when he was a professor, when he was president of Princeton, when he was Governor of New Jersey, and she did not ignore them when he was President of the United States. She knew the boy in him; the gentle, aloof, shy, sensitive, sometimes over-jealous, often over-suspicious boy, who stood apart from gangdom wistfully and found his place in the world only in the days of his adolescence. She shielded and mothered that boy, and so matured and strengthened the man.

She was not impressed by the spectacle of his power, and while she lived she tried to hold him in the ways of the meek. But the pressure of responsibility, the sense of power which comes to a President, must have inflamed his intellectual vanity in spite of himself; even in spite of Ellen Axson.

Yet he held a firm hand at the steering wheel of his life. Liberalism had advanced him; had given him his leadership, even though to be a Liberal leader he had to abandon his academic conservatism. So to the end he was a Liberal leader, and as nearly undefiled as men may be and live a practical life with practical men. The high gods were giving him his heart's desire, showering him with blessings, marking him for their choicest favors.

When Ellen Axson died, Woodrow Wilson was fifty-eight years old. He had been watched and tended for more than thirty years by a maternal wife. He took her body sadly to her former home in Georgia, and buried her in a narrow plot—too narrow for his own dust and ashes! After the funeral, and during the first few months of loneliness and grief, new duties came to him, new visions opened before him, and for the first time in his maturity he made his decisions with no one at his elbow to check him. Henry Watterson often said that there were two Grover Clevelands: one before his marriage, another afterward. Those who knew Woodrow Wilson best always felt that there were two

Woodrow Wilsons: one before the death of Ellen Axson, another afterward. No man who lives for thirty years in the relationship of marriage is the same man he was before he entered into that relationship, nor is he the same man after that relationship ends. It takes two to make one, and when either integer is changed the equation changes. It was inevitable that Woodrow Wilson would take another wife. He was essentially a woman's man, as Grover Cleveland was a man's man. Yet, no matter what his domestic qualities are, strong or weak, in domesticity a man takes the color of his domestic environment, of his wife's opinions, prejudices, desires, aspirations; in short, the color of her personality.

The year after Ellen Axson Wilson's death, President Wilson married Mrs. Galt, of Washington, and at sixty began a new experience. He was happy in his new relation, and in the new spiritual environment that he found; probably he looked at the new felicity as he had looked at his new fame, in wonder and in joy. Here he was with a youthful wife, the praise of a hundred million of his fellows, and a powerful place in the world.

Wilson's brand of Liberalism had come to differ from the Rooseveltian Liberalism in its attitude toward peace. As the war in Europe began to cast its menacing shadow over America in the midst of Wilson's first presidential term, the American attitude to that war and to war in general became an acute political issue. As early as 1914, the war, diverting men's minds from consideration of political and economic issues which had interested them for a dozen years, was one of the forces which demobilized the progressive party and left Roosevelt with a following of progressive captains and colonels, but with no progressive rank and file. The Germans began to fire on American vessels in their submarine warfare. The British violated United States ships searching for contraband. It became evident to the more intelligent of American statesmen that America's attitude toward the European conflict would have to be declared. It was inevitable that we should either join the Allies in the war or maintain what to many Americans seemed a shameful neutrality. When Roosevelt was counseling men to speak softly but carry a big stick,

Wilson still continued to plead for this neutrality. He coined the phrase "Too Proud to Fight," and the campaign slogan of his Democratic managers in 1916 was "He Kept Us Out of War"—but that slogan was only a part of Wilson's program of Liberalism. Roosevelt's attitude to the war became the major part of his program of Liberalism. He would have challenged those who were hectoring us. He would have put a fighting face on Uncle Sam. Wilson kept turning the other cheek. He was forced into a feint of preparedness only by the clamor of the Rooseveltians; and Woodrow Wilson, winning the election of 1916 as the Liberal leader, took Liberal leadership definitely from Roosevelt, who was at the moment interested in the Great War. To Roosevelt, the war seemed to threaten civilization. He had no patience with the Wilsonian neutrality.

Roosevelt, in 1917 and 1918, became no casual political opponent of Woodrow Wilson. In the campaign of 1912, it was the strategy of the Progressive party to attack Wilson, the Democratic candidate, and to let Taft, the Republican candidate, alone. Roosevelt, during the primary fight, had said all that was necessary to say about Taft and perhaps a word or two more. Anyway, Taft was clearly the weak candidate; Wilson, with the united Democracy behind him, was clearly the strong candidate. So Roosevelt, day after day, week after week, for three long months in 1912, hammered away at Woodrow Wilson, the presidential candidate of the Democratic party. The Roosevelt barrage was cruel. For the first time in his life Woodrow Wilson received blows publicly from an opponent of his own size. In New Jersey he had fought more or less with little state bosses, while he loomed as a national figure. In Princeton the details of the fight were for the most part under cover. But, in the campaign of 1912, Roosevelt lambasted Wilson right and left and laid to with a vigor of phrase which must have rankled the proud heart of the Southerner. So when Roosevelt espoused preparedness, and gathered General Wood into a military camp and practiced preparedness, Wilson, being human after the fashion that he was, refused to be stampeded by the clamor of the military party. He was convinced of his righteousness somewhat by the kind and character of his opponents, and again, being what he was, despised them bitterly. The knowledge that Wilson despised him was not soothing to Roosevelt. He glorified in antagonism, delighted in combat, even chuckled at another man's wrath; but he rankled under Wilson's contempt, and Wilson, fortified by presidential prestige, was able to triumph in his contempt; which was wormwood for Roosevelt.

As Wilson's first term drew to a close and the nation came further and further into the shadow of the war, the Liberal movement in American politics, which had fructified under Wilson, passed, a casualty of the World War. It was strange that a man of just his temperament—this arudite, complacent, bookish man from the cloisters—should be the instrument used by the Fates to write "Finis" to a national movement which he had championed less than half a decade. But with the eclipse of Roosevelt, Wilson became the instrument which, in so far as Liberalism ever was solidified into institutions and legislation, gave the cause its political direction at the close. It was the Roosevelt progressive platform and the La Follette measures which engaged the Democratic Congress, under President Wilson, from 1913 to 1917; the laws protecting American seamen, establishing the Federal Trade Commission, the Federal Tariff Commission, stabilizing credit and the currency, shortening the hours of labor and regulating the railroads, were enacted in those years. Wilson, with genuine enthusiasm, led Congress and the people into the adoption of those measures. He was at his best in those years; they were years of triumph, and hence years of his happy moods. By 1917 he was a convinced Liberal, who sensed in the approach of war the downfall of his cause. He knew, being a student of government, how reactionary war is, what entire denial of liberty it must be. But the hour had struck. Forces stronger than he were running across the hearts of men in Christendom and he could not check the debacle.

Probably humanity was not ready for further progress, men being what they were—lusty for blood and war. And the age-long struggle for equitable distribution of property, equalization of social and political opportunity, and for glorification of the

common man, came to an end because the common man had
gone as far as his light would lead him. Man must suffer in shame
and sorrow until, free of conceit, in all humility, he comes into a
larger wisdom which lights him further along the way into a
more abundant life. Some of these things, most of these things,
Wilson knew as he sat in the White House that night before his
great decision to lead his country to battle, and looked into the
abyss before him. Few statesmen have made war who knew so
well as he what it implied. Yet if he had seen the meaning of his
action less plainly he would not have visioned his work so well
when the war was done. Other statesmen have led their nations
to combat. But whatever high-sounding slogans other rulers may
have proclaimed, and however they may have protested the righteousness of their cause, actually and in truth, Wilson is the first
who ever led a united, disinterested nation into war for no reason
other than the hope of permanent world peace. Therein lies some
of his greatness.

Now, despite Wilson's contempt for him, Roosevelt, from
1914 to 1919, was, next to Wilson, the greatest figure in America.
But beyond America, in Germany, another figure was coming
into the circle of Wilson's detestation. Kaiser Wilhelm the Second
dramatized for the Allied world, and particularly for Wilson in
the White House, the barbarism of war, the savagery of physical
combat. The Allies, for one reason or another, were heroized in
America. The Central Powers carried the contumely of willing
the war. This contumely came, perhaps, because of the savagery
with which the Germans waged the war on the sea with submarines. Americans were killed. Wilson protested with a show of
more dignity than rage.

Let us remember that this Princeton teacher was standing
before kings. There must have been a certain balm to his pride
in the fact that he, who less than a decade before was putting
boys through their paces, was now lording it over Roosevelt,
America's popular idol, and wrestling before Christendom in a
great debate with the world's villain; the incarnate devil of
the Central Powers, Wilhelm the Second, King of Prussia and
Emperor of Germany. Cinderella in her golden coach knew no

finer thrill than Woodrow Wilson, who had been snatched from the ashes of a cloistered life, and transported to this high estate; discussing terms of war and peace with kings and potentates; happy with his newly married wife, who—as good wives will— admired his strength and ignored his frailties. Napoleon and Caesar had really less reason for their arrogance than this lean, solemn-faced figure who, to use a Rooseveltian phrase, "looked like an apothecary's clerk," and had to play Mercutio, and Romeo, and Richard of the Lion Heart all in one.

In early April, 1917, Wilson took America into the war. It was an hour of triumph, this world acclaim for him; that day when he stood before Congress, before the Supreme Court and before the diplomats of the nations—gaudy in their blazing emblems of power—and read the eloquent message to Congress which led America from neutrality to battle. It was a message worthy of the occasion. Wilson spoke well because he thought clearly and dramatized the issues of the hour as they were marshaled in his heart, with convincing language. In an age of physical miracles, we are sometimes blind to spiritual marvels; the marvels that move the human heart and mind. Wilson's speech, taking America into the war, was one of those cataclysms which transform human life and the courses of human destiny. For months before Wilson declared for war, the war party was growing stronger every day in America; but when Wilson joined it, America was well-nigh unanimous in its war spirit and the President suddenly became the most powerful man on earth. One hundred millions of his countrymen joined in his praise and, in praising him, surrendered their liberties to him. This surrender quickly expressed itself in legislation, and in many ways was implicit without legislation. By the very declaration of war, eloquent as it was, Wilson came into a power more absolute than that of Wilhelm the Kaiser, or Nicholas the Czar. It was a terrible thing to happen to a human being, and as well as a human being could, Wilson rose to it.

In his rise, his virtues were expanded, his vices magnified; and certainly his expanding virtues dominated his life. His virtues were of the mind, his vices of the heart.

It was as though the speech before Congress where he was

surrounded by all the pomp and panoply of power, had released a current that moved some vast lever which changed the direction of human life on the planet. Thereafter millions, hundreds of millions, all over the earth responded when he pressed buttons; gave their property, their lives, their heart's desire to him to have and hold and use. And he, feeling the impact of this overwhelming force, behaved under his responsibility as well as an ordinary mortal could.

Wilson's words melted even Roosevelt's rancor. Roosevelt was never a grudge-bearer. Magnanimity was one of his conspicuous virtues. The day after Wilson had sounded the war tocsin in his message, Roosevelt rode up the long curving pavement to the White House, where he had not been before for nearly a decade. Hat in hand, he knocked at the President's door. In token of his loyalty to Wilson and the war, he had come to congratulate Wilson, to offer his services to Wilson as liege lord, to let Wilson put his heel on his neck.

Wilson was busy! Roosevelt was turned away.

A few days later he appeared again, as a private citizen with no appointment. Again he knocked and stood hat in hand before the President's private door. It was opened. The two men faced each other; measured each other. Wilson was courteous. Roosevelt was punctilious. Roosevelt offered his services; would have raised a division, trained it and taken it to France. The President listened with smiling politeness, and with smiling civility—nothing more—shook hands with Roosevelt at parting. Each knew in his heart, when the door closed, that that episode was over. Roosevelt walked out of the White House, stopped a moment to gossip with the reporters and hurried down the broad steps. He rode away in his carriage, scorned and rejected—and he knew it. He was scorned and rejected in his most heroic hour. For he would have given his life to serve his country. But Wilson, being what he was, suspected Roosevelt's motives, and in his secret heart must have sucked some solace for his vanity out of the deep implications of the conventional scene. That day the gods were pouring for Wilson a heady wine. His cup ran over. The berserker rage of Roosevelt which followed when his rejection was made public, probably did not dull in Wilson's heart the thrill of triumph that he had power to humble his adversary. His counselors advised him in his course, as they would have advised another course had Wilson been generous. No one near him, except Colonel House, dared cross Wilson with a demand for a noble gesture in that scene. Possibly his habit of omnipotence was turning his head. He sent Elihu Root to Russia at the head of a fact-finding commission, and when Root returned Wilson imperiously refused to see him to get the commission's report because, forsooth, Root had talked to a reporter on his way home. Root waited about Washington a week and finally left, with no word from the President to explain his august retreat. So Wilson ever rationalized his conduct, squaring his prejudices with his righteousness, and drank the sweet poison of revenge while he walked his royal way. Then he turned to Kaiser Wilhelm, King and Emperor. There was a foe worthy even of Wilson.

What a man this American President was in those terrible days from April, 1917, until February, 1919! The world of democracy has never seen his like in power, in glory; but no chance caprice of fate brought him and held him on his throne of triumph. His own qualities, his own mind, his own eloquence, his own intellectual equipment—powers that for thirty years had been growing for that day—came to him, strengthened him, emboldened him, and ennobled him. He was indeed a looming figure—as great men are esteemed in this world; comparable with Napoleon and Alexander, save that his greatest work was not with arms, though there he was competent, but with words; winged, barbed, fiery, devastating words; words that were deeds and more than deeds. They were disembodied energies that rocked the world; words that conquered and scattered an army with banners.

The struggle between President Wilson and the German Kaiser, which began when the Central Powers used submarines with which they attacked American vessels along with the vessels of other neutrals, assumed international importance early in the naval phase of the war. The Kaiser was a world figure, possibly the world devil. He stood, at least in the Allied countries and somewhat in the neutral lands as well, as the embodiment of autocracy in government. He was pictured by the mythmakers as an arrogant, malicious, ruthless creature, who had gathered into himself as their embodiment the forces of evil in the world and was malignantly threatening democracy. The truth is, as they tell it who were near him in those years, that the Emperor came into the war after years of boredom on the throne, when nothing in particular was happening to stimulate his joy except a repetition of drills and parades and empty functions. As the war wore on and as the German military leaders realized that victory was not assured, their doubts obsessed the Kaiser. Behind the scenes he was irritable, mean, fitful, jealous of his prerogatives, which were slipping from him unconsciously. His hair was graying and his face breaking in wrinkles; a vastly different creature from the hell-god created by the Allies. But it was the hell-god that Wilson attacked. The notes from Germany to Wilson were merely signed by the Kaiser. They represented the German will to conquer, not the personal arrogance of the old flutter duck of Potsdam. This Wilson could not know. So, with his Presbyterian hate of devils, with the one weapon God gave him, his pen, Wilson rode out in front of the world and began charging the mask that was the German Emperor. Here Wilson was full panoplied. For he was essentially a crusader. Wilson came from a race of dragon-fighters, and the Kaiser—a fine pasteboard dragon—was a shining target for Wilson's wrath. Wilson managed quite unconsciously to dramatize himself as the world figure who should meet and vanquish the dragon. But the Kaiser was not entirely vanquished with arms. At the head of his army, Wilson was a minor figure in the war. No military group surrounded him. His Secretary of the Navy wore a soft sugar-loaf hat on shipboard. His Secretary of War was a philosophical pacifist, but a practical man at that. His Secretary of State, Mr. Bryan, was a grandmotherly Presbyterian elder with millennial illusions. After America came into the war, Secretary Lansing headed our State Department. He wrote a good Spencerian hand and took orders. The President's confidants were soft-spoken idealists—Colonel House, Bernard Baruch, Jesse Jones, of Texas, Edward M. Hurley of the shipping board —not a saber-rattler in the lot. He even had small use for Wall

Street. In the midst of the war, after much urging, Wilson went to New York to review a great civilian parade for the last Liberty Loan—or perhaps the Red Cross. Wall Street urged him to ride in the parade in a carriage surrounded by Wall Street notables in high hats, flanked by soldiers, guarded by major generals in glittering accoutrement. But Wilson said "No."

"No! I have never been tied up with that Wall Street crowd. They don't know me. I don't like them. No, I'll not be paraded down Fifth Avenue attached like a captive to the Wall Street chariot."

Instead of riding with Wall Street in pomp, Wilson headed the parade on foot, accompanied only by a little group of secret service men from the White House. He walked with his shoulders thrown back, his face aglow; a fine figure of a man in his early sixties under a shining tile. He was dressed in a dark afternoon coat with gray trousers, a dark purple necktie, and a suitable collar for his long neck. He had the easy swinging gait of young Tommy Wilson in Princeton, leading the parade across the campus when his glee club sang.

His battle with the dragon was going well. He had stated the terms of the Allies, the ideals of the Allies, and in a way had remotivated the war. He had made it seem to be a war for democracy; a war to end all war which came from the arrogance of aristocratic autocracy.

Then science put a new weapon in his hand. Woodrow Wilson was the first world leader to use wireless transmission for spreading his propaganda around the world. Because the device was new it seemed miraculous. So his words sang through the wireless spaces, and were heard in far-off lands. Germany heard them. The Kaiser heard them—the fretful, peevish, moody old gentleman in his gray cloak and his uniform splashed with gold braid and tinsel. The Kaiser heard Wilson's words, surrounded by a Cabinet jealous of his army and an army slowly undermining his own power. He heard Wilson's words, but they meant nothing to him. But his people listened to Wilson and were disturbed in their sorrow, puzzled as they hungered, harassed with a doubt of their own cause as they suffered. The German push of the spring of 1918 failed in the summer. American soldiers were before the

German trenches, and Wilson's eloquence, striking behind the lines, demoralized the German Government back of the trenches. As he walked so proudly down the Avenue that autumn day Wilson knew, in his heart, that he was the master of the world.

### The Man Who Would Be God

This knowledge should have ennobled him into godlike conduct. But Wilson's words were fairer than his deeds. General Leonard Wood, who defied the President in 1915 by talking preparedness and by setting up a training camp in the midst of peace, trained the Eighty-Ninth Division and came with it across the land to embark for France. On the eve of embarkation the general was stopped by the President, and sent back to Kansas to train another division. Wood was humiliated before the nation! The President explained afterward that certain army officers in France had asked him not to send General Wood to Europe. The army was wise, knowing Wilson. He got from France the excuse he needed. Roosevelt and Wood had their lesson. But the faith of the American people in their hero was for the moment shaken. Despite his consecration to a holy cause, and in the face of the inspired and rounded periods that carried the bolts of his dialectics, there lived in Wilson still a spoiled child. He had a lofty mind, an inspiring soul, and no particular heart. His capacity to rationalize great causes also enabled him to rationalize mean conduct. Man is that way sometimes.

As Wilson's discourses upon democracy electrified the world, doubts of the righteousness of their cause were heralded into German hearts by hunger and sorrow and shame. Slowly, during the spring of 1918, virtue—that curious power that follows the surrender which men make of their liberty to kings—left William II, Emperor of Germany and King of Prussia. One ally after another deserted the German standard. Inside his shell of power the little dried pea of a man rattled for nine months longer. At him Wilson aimed his shafts of eloquent logic, while one chancellor after another came and went, somewhat at the behest of the army, somewhat under the influence of the Reichstag.

When the tank attacks of the Allies succeeded in 1918, Wilson's

Secret Service Department told him of the crumbling morale behind the Rhine. He knew that Wilhelm's army was at the end of its rope. Wilson, before Wilhelm, knew that the unrest of the people was reflected in the signs of mutiny at the front. The Czar was gone. Bolshevism had come. Austria was in collapse. Autocracy all over Christendom was passing. Democracy, with America as the economic leader of the new order, was coming into power. It was this knowledge which threw Wilson's head back and called out of his inner heart young Tommy Wilson, who marched down Fifth Avenue so proudly that autumn day at the head of the big parade.

Finally, the Socialists captured the German Government. The commanders at the front were demanding an immediate armistice, fearing rout and anarchy. Between the lines of the German papers, whose contents were cabled to the White House every day, Wilson read this story, too. His thunderbolts had made at least the German world safe for democracy. That was in October, 1918. Disaster followed disaster as the days swirled by. Not armies, not navies, but the reasonableness of Wilson's eloquent plea for world peace, under democracy, had moved figures behind the iron line on the western front. Then, on November 9, Prince Max called the Emperor on the telephone. Imagine telephoning the All-Highest! Prince Max said he could no longer rely on the German troops, that red flags were flying all over Germany, which Wilson knew better even than Wilhelm; and, ultimately, Prince Max breathed into the Emperor's ear the stabbing truth that Wilhelm's abdication was all that would avert anarchy. Then the final picture.

In the White House it is the hour of triumph, of tense excitement; the hour whose every minute brings in its own trophy of victory. The President's long face is flecked with smiles, with complacent, mechanical smiles. But across the world the Emperor stands shivering before a wood fire, leaning against the mantelpiece, listening to Generals Groner and Pleseen, who are reporting upon the operations of the troops in the interior of Germany. The Emperor lifts his dull eyes and sighs:

"I desire to come home in peace at the head of my army."

Then General Groner stood up and spoke brutally:

"Under its leaders and generals the army will march quietly and steadily home, but not under the command of your Majesty; it is no longer behind you."

A little bluster—and that is over. Hindenburg added this drop to the poison of Wilhelm's agony: "There are no loyal troops left; would to God, your Majesty, it were otherwise!"

In Washington, smart young officers in shiny puttees are hurrying up the White House steps with news of the collapse of Germany and the steady retreat of the German troops. Newspaper reporters are buzzing like wasps in and out of the President's office. Congressmen, senators, Cabinet members, sleek dollar-a-year men clinking their millions, all are bustling through and out of the President's room, waving such kindly peacock feathers of flattery as he will take, all singing to him their hosannas of praise and glory. The great of the earth, through those electric currents which have abolished space, are huddling about Wilson in those last days of the lonely, shame-stricken old Emperor, warming Wilson's heart with their acclaim.

The Emperor, draining the cup of Hindenburg's poison, gloomily shook hands with his old commander and went out. Suddenly the royal train appeared outside the headquarters. The Emperor had not ordered it, no one could say how it came there. Wilhelm boarded it. He had no alternative. And before midnight the exulting group at the White House, surrounding Wilson, the world conqueror, had learned that the royal train was speeding to the Dutch frontier. In the dawn there, the next morning, an old man in a gray uniform and cloak, with a few soldiers about him, tried to pass the frontier guard. A mere civil officer stopped him. At that frontier, shorn of his glory, Herr Wilhelm Hohenzollern, late Emperor of Germany and King of Prussia, was just a man. The guard let him into a little iron cage, where he sat and waited while the telephone and telegraph bore his prayer to enter Holland to the Queen and her council. An hour he waited—the Emperor. Two hours—three! Another two, and still another long hour, he sat in the little iron cage alone, under the gray cloak that had been the symbol of power for thirty years. At last the message came. The iron gate clicked and creaked on it hinges and an old man—no longer an Emperor—trudged out to his motor car and sped away from the German border.

Woodrow Wilson had winged the gray eagle of the cliff. The world turned to its new hero and ruler with the fine fervor which that fickle courtesan, the mob, turns upon any new lover.

In that hour, when the world bowed before him, when humanity was warm with joy over the end of the war, when governments were forgotten and the popular heart was beating fast, Woodrow Wilson, by lightning-like insistence, possibly might have established his League of Nations by proclamation. For in that hour of the armistice, nationalism submerged. Christendom was almost Christian.

But the golden moment passed. Wilson could not know it passed. Perhaps the cynical ones knew. But out of the exaltation that followed the end of war—in a week, at least in a month—nationalism began to recast the new world on the old, old pattern. In those months after the armistice, Wilson's defects were revealed in cruel detail. He had no great vanity for personal glory, but all his life he had exalted his own mind. Just before the armistice, he wrote a letter asking for a Democratic Congress, thus transferring the war from a national to a party basis. And after the armistice he narrowed the peace into a personal proposal.

President Wilson had been working quietly with Colonel House and a group of European statesmen from 1915 to 1918, developing the idea of a League of Nations. It was characteristic of Wilson that he thought and worked in secret. For he feared criticism, never for himself, but always of his ideas until they were well born and established. He said nothing to the American people, nothing to the leaders of the country, of the League of Nations he had planned. He trusted to his intellectual prowess to force his ideas upon America. He was aflame with his vision—like Paul on the Damascus road. But he told no man except his household intimates. Because his heart held the Ark of the Covenant, he rose and took it to Europe. He decided to go to Europe —not, as his enemies thought, to receive the adulation of the multitude; probably he cared less for that than even his friends realized.

He went to Europe because he could not trust anyone else with his precious charge, the child of his intellectual loins. One faithful friend advised Wilson not to go to Europe. It was Colonel E. M. House, who had been his loyal messenger since he came to the White House. Colonel House felt that Wilson in America would be in a stronger position to enforce his will upon the Peace Conference than when sitting at the peace table with diplomats. With Wilson in America, his representatives in Paris could hold him up as the unreasonable but uncompromising absentee ruler; he would be master of the situation, and so bring Europe to terms. But with Wilson at the peace table, the European diplomats could trade him out of his eye teeth. Colonel House's plan provided a strong American delegation; not the sort that Wilson took.[1] Certainly he would not trust the wicked Republicans, as, for instance, Hughes, Root, and Taft, who had been leaders internationally, for nearly a decade, of an organized world peace movement. Yet their minds were as keen as his. "I have sucked his brains," said Wilson once of Root, meaning that he had got from Root all he was capable of giving; a vain, even puerile statement. But Wilson trusted only errand boys. So, surrounding himself with men of soft approach, and surrounding them with men of academic background and of no political training, of no sense of public opinion, Wilson was wafted to Europe and across the land, through an everlasting throng, from London to Rome and back to Paris, in a cloud of glory. Now he did not seek this glory. It came as a minor incident in his life. The glory followed his mad decision to pit himself, his prestige somewhat, but largely what he regarded as his god-like intellect, against the statesmen of Europe, because in his vast conceit he could not delegate his powers. In the gaudery of his intellection, like Satan, he fell. He would not be warned by the loss of Congress in November, just before the armistice, which followed one display of his precipitance. He would not be warned by an obviously growing hostil-

[1] The President's colleagues on the Peace Commission were honest, amiable gentlemen: Secretary Lansing, Colonel E. M. House, General Tasker Bliss, and Henry White; excepting Colonel House, entirely without American political influence.

ity to him in the Senate. Nor would he let his friends tell him of the danger which beset his European adventure. For his European glorification bred the jealousies of small men, "men of pigmy minds," if you will, who still had senatorial votes, and also— which was rather more important than the votes—had personal and political following. So, while Wilson preened across Europe, at home the forces of destruction organized against him that wayward wanton, public sentiment. If he had known less of political science, and more of practical politics, he might have avoided tragedy. But he sat down with men as wise and shrewd as he, who had no fine scruples. Clemenceau, Lloyd George, Sonnino, Balfour, Robert Cecil, found Wilson unguarded except by courtiers; and the Europeans, trading their national needs for his international aspirations, outplayed him at his own game. He went to Europe a god. He sat down at the green baize table in the Room of the Clocks at Versailles, a philosophical prig. He arose the incarnation of a tragedy. For old national aims came back and ancient national greeds were restored. The new Europe was revealed as the old Europe. And while Wilson was in Paris, the American jingoes joined the world jingoes, and took charge of things.

It was in these days of tension and excitement that Wilson broke with Colonel House. House, in running Wilson's errands, had learned the ropes of Europe, knew more than Wilson, and was not without glory in the capitals of Europe. When he advised Wilson against his will, Wilson distrusted him, and incontinently cut off and brushed aside a political friendship in which his obligations were deep and unmistakable. He banished House to England, and refused to see him in America—and indefensible gesture. House might have brought the Senate to Wilson's cause. But there, in Europe, Wilson was on his heaven-kissed throne. He who had burned with the ardor of his dreams for a League of Nations, who had crossed the ocean, who had stood before kings, who had thrown kisses at all the world, who had waved gay hands at multitudes and was the equal of potentates; even he —the schoolmaster, Wilson—who in his triumph was the spiritual ruler of Christendom, came back to America to find his own kingdom rotting beneath him. When he tried to make his vision reality, touching shoulders and elbows with men, they found that he was clay.

Wilson's emotional defects amounted to moral defects. And whatever failure came to his career at the end was moral failure, greedy vanity for the quality and caliber of his own mind. Too often in his career—at Princeton, at Trenton, at Washington—he had prided himself on his ability to separate himself, as a man, from his personal obligations; to follow what he regarded as a principle, irrespective of the cost. He was suspicious in his dearest friendships. He broke personally, time and again, with men to whom he owed moral obligations, when he thought these men were not loyal to his intellectual conclusions; which means bluntly that he could not get along with men who differed with him, however much he might owe to them in decent human gratitude. This quality, at the last, isolated him. This quality attracted sycophants; but in his great crisis, it repelled strong men. In all his courts, from Princeton to Washington, where Wilson set up his intellect as a graven image, always there was some Rasputin to grovel before it. Intriguing sapped his strength and undermined his power. Wilson's aspiring intellect gave the League of Nations to the world; Wilson's emotional defects withheld his gift from America. As a world visionary he walked and talked with the high gods. As an American politician, trying to realize his vision, he was possessed of a devil. But his vision lives. Perhaps some dumb, kindly man will one day bring the vision home to America and so put Wilson on his pedestal.

Humanity had come as far toward perfection as humanity could without a miracle. Wilson, his head in the clouds and his feet so prone to trample on the necks of his enemies, denied the world its miracle. Back in America he found his dream shattered, and in the end, even in the twinkling of an eye, his glory gone. Between December, 1918, and June, 1919, the Hero of the Armistice became, in the hearts of millions of Americans, the betrayer of the American birthright. They felt that in making them part of the United States of the World, he was making them less important as citizens of the United States of America. It was in the midst of this fight that Wilson received his death call—some sort of stroke, partially paralytic, fell upon him, affecting his brain, the organ of his pride. In that crisis he might have lost a leg, an eye, an ear, or an arm, and survived; but when disease touched his brain, Wilson fell. With calumny rampant around him, he tasted the ingratitude of his Republic—the statesman's ancient cup of hemlock. No wonder that, on the high and empty altar where the flame of his fame was quenched and the cold, charred ashes were strewn, he lay helpless while the high priests of the temple cut out his heart.

And so ends our hero tale that some day, when peace shall come to the earth, will be a folk tale. So ends the tragic story of a man who would be God.

# JOHN MAYNARD KEYNES

THIS is not the place to discuss John Maynard Keynes as a brilliant and influential economist, but no mention of him can omit reference to his chief works and no introduction to the following group portrait can pass silently over the career which made the portrait possible.

Mr. Keynes (pronounced "canes") was born at Cambridge, England, in 1883, and was educated at Eton and at King's College, Cambridge. Distinguished already at the University as President of the Cambridge Union Society in 1905, he entered the India Office the following year and the Treasury Department in 1915. At the Paris Peace Conference of 1919 he was the principal representative of the Treasury and the Deputy for the Chancellor of the Exchequer on the Supreme Economic Council. It is in this connection, of course, that he made the intimate observations of the "Council of Four" which went into the following sketch. The piece itself was written in 1919, but out of deference to his former chief the portrait of Lloyd George was withheld from his now famous book of that year, *The Economic Consequences of the Peace*, and not given out until 1933 in his *Essays in Biography*. His other works, several of them of the greatest importance as guides to national leaders and economists through the jungle of post-war affairs, include *A Treatise on Probability* (1921), *A Tract on Monetary Reform* (1925), *A Short View of Russia* (1925), *The End of Laissez-Faire* (1926), *A Treatise on Money* (1930), *Essays in Persuasion* (1933), and *The General Theory of Employment, Interest, and Money* (1936). Mr. Keynes and his wife, the former Russian dancer, Lydia Lopokova, are connected with the "Bloomsbury Group" of intellectuals (see the note on Virginia Woolf). Since 1912 he has been editor of *The Economic Journal*. He is also a Fellow and the Bursar of King's College.

Is "The Council of Four" a biography? Not, to be sure, in the sense of a full-rounded account of the characters and the careers of Wilson, Clémenceau, Lloyd George, and Orlando. Signor Orlando, in fact, is by a special touch of irony barely mentioned among the four. The reader is expected to possess, as a background, at least a general knowledge of the Paris Conference, its principal figures, and its results. These first-hand sketches are intended to fill in the foreground, and for this purpose they give the most intimate and subtle glimpses of the interaction of the minds and personalities of the statesmen who shaped so large a part of our modern destiny. Reference to the biographies by Mr. White and Miss Flanner and, beyond this book, to the memoirs of Lloyd George and Mrs. Woodrow Wilson, will enlarge the picture. Mr. Keynes will be found still indispensable for his sensitive and understanding close-ups. Within this scope few biographers have produced such telling portraiture.

## THE COUNCIL OF FOUR, PARIS, 1919

CLEMENCEAU was by far the most eminent member of the Council of Four, and he had taken the measure of his colleagues. He alone both had an idea and had considered it in all its consequences. His age, his character, his wit, and his appearance joined to give him objectivity and a defined outline in an environment of confusion. One could not despise Clemenceau or dislike him, but only take a different view as to the nature of civilised man, or indulge, at least, a different hope.

The figure and bearing of Clemenceau are universally familiar. At the Council of Four he wore a square-tailed coat of very good, thick black broadcloth, and on his hands, which were never uncovered, grey suède gloves; his boots were of thick black leather, very good, but of a country style, and sometimes fastened in front, curiously, by a buckle instead of laces. His seat in the room in the President's house, where the regular meetings of the Council of Four were held (as distinguished from their private and unattended conferences in a smaller chamber below), was on a square brocaded chair in the middle of the semicircle facing the fire-place, with Signor Orlando on his left, the President next by the fire-place, and the Prime Minister opposite on the other side of the fire-place on his right. He carried no papers and no portfolio, and was unattended by any personal secretary, though several French ministers and officials appropriate to the particular matter in hand would be present round him. His walk, his hand, and his voice were not lacking in vigour, but he bore, nevertheless, especially after the attempt upon him, the aspect of a very old man conserving his strength for important occasions. He spoke seldom, leaving the initial statement of the French case to his ministers or officials; he closed his eyes often and sat back in his chair with an impassive face of parchment, his grey-gloved hands clasped in front of him. A short sentence, decisive or cyni-

cal, was generally sufficient, a question, an unqualified abandonment of his ministers, whose face would not be saved, or a display
of obstinacy reinforced by a few words in a piquantly delivered
English.[1] But speech and passion were not lacking when they
were wanted, and the sudden outburst of words, often followed
by a fit of deep coughing from the chest, produced their impression rather by force and surprise than by persuasion.

Not infrequently, Mr. Lloyd George, after delivering a speech
in English, would, during the period of its interpretation into
French, cross the hearthrug to the President to reinforce his case
by some *ad hominem* argument in private conversation, or to
sound the ground for a compromise—and this would sometimes
be the signal for a general upheaval and disorder. The President's advisers would press round him, a moment later the British
experts would dribble across to learn the result or see that all was
well, and next the French would be there, a little suspicious lest
the others were arranging something behind them, until all the
room were on their feet and conversation was general in both
languages. My last and most vivid impression is of such a scene—
the President and the Prime Minister as the centre of a surging
mob and a babel of sound, a welter of eager, impromptu compromises and counter-compromises, all sound and fury signifying
nothing, on what was an unreal question anyhow, the great issues
of the morning's meeting forgotten and neglected; and Clemenceau, silent and aloof on the outskirts—for nothing which touched
the security of France was forward—throned, in his grey gloves,
on the brocade chair, dry in soul and empty of hope, very old
and tired, but surveying the scene with a cynical and almost impish air; and when at last silence was restored and the company
had returned to their places, it was to discover that he had
disappeared.

He felt about France what Pericles felt of Athens—unique value
in her, nothing else mattering; but his theory of politics was Bis-

---

[1] He alone amongst the Four could speak and understand both languages,
Orlando knowing only French and the Prime Minister and the President
only English; and it is of historical importance that Orlando and the President had no direct means of communication.

marck's. He had one illusion—France; and one disillusion—mankind, including Frenchmen and his colleagues not least. His principles for the Peace can be expressed simply. In the first place, he
was a foremost believer in the view of German psychology that
the German understands and can understand nothing but intimi-
dation, that he is without generosity or remorse in negotiation,
that there is no advantage he will not take of you, and no extent
to which he will not demean himself for profit, that he is without
honour, pride, or mercy. Therefore you must never negotiate
with a German or conciliate him; you must dictate to him. On no
other terms will he respect you, or will you prevent him from
cheating you. But it is doubtful how far he thought these characteristics peculiar to Germany, or whether his candid view of
some other nations was fundamentally different. His philosophy
had, therefore, no place for "sentimentality" in international relations. Nations are real things, of which you love one and feel
for the rest indifference—or hatred. The glory of the nation you
love is a desirable end—but generally to be obtained at your
neighbour's expense. The politics of power are inevitable, and
there is nothing very new to learn about this war or the end it
was fought for; England had destroyed, as in each preceding century, a trade rival; a mighty chapter had been closed in the secu-
lar struggle between the glories of Germany and of France.
Prudence required some measure of lip service to the "ideals" of
foolish Americans and hypocritical Englishmen; but it would be
stupid to believe that there is much room in the world, as it really
is, for such affairs as the League of Nations, or any sense in the
principle of self-determination except as an ingenious formula for
rearranging the balance of power in one's own interests.

These, however, are generalities. In tracing the practical details of the Peace which he thought necessary for the power
and the security of France, we must go back to the historical
causes which had operated during his lifetime. Before the Franco-
German war the populations of France and Germany were approximately equal; but the coal and iron and shipping of Germany were in their infancy and the wealth of France was greatly
superior. Even after the loss of Alsace-Lorraine there was no great

discrepancy between the real resources of the two countries. But in the intervening period the relative position had changed completely. By 1914 the population of Germany was nearly 70 per cent in excess of that of France; she had become one of the first manufacturing and trading nations of the world; her technical skill and her means for the production of future wealth were unequalled. France, on the other hand, had a stationary or declining population, and, relatively to others, had fallen seriously behind in wealth and in the power to produce it.

In spite, therefore, of France's victorious issue from the present struggle (with the aid, this time, of England and America), her future position remained precarious in the eyes of one who took the view that European civil war is to be regarded as a normal, or at least a recurrent, state of affairs for the future, and that the sort of conflicts between organised Great Powers which have occupied the past hundred years will also engage the next. According to this vision of the future, European history is to be a perpetual prize-fight, of which France has won this round, but of which this round is certainly not the last. From the belief that essentially the old order does not change, being based on human nature which is always the same, and from a consequent scepticism of all that class of doctrine which the League of Nations stands for, the policy of France and of Clemenceau followed logically. For a Peace of magnanimity or of fair and equal treatment, based on such "ideology" as the Fourteen Points of the President, could only have the effect of shortening the interval of Germany's recovery and hastening the day when she will once again hurl at France her greater numbers and her superior resources and technical skill. Hence the necessity of "guarantees"; and each guarantee that was taken, by increasing irritation and thus the probability of a subsequent *revanche* by Germany, made necessary yet further provisions to crush. Thus, as soon as this view of the world is adopted and the other discarded, a demand for a Carthaginian Peace is inevitable, to the full extent of the momentary power to impose it. For Clemenceau made no pretense of considering himself bound by the Fourteen Points, and left chiefly to others such concoctions as were necessary from time to time to save the scruples or the face of the President.

So far as possible, therefore, it was the policy of France to set the clock back and to undo what, since 1870, the progress of Germany had accomplished. By loss of territory and other measures her population was to be curtailed; but chiefly the economic system, upon which she depended for her new strength, the vast fabric built upon iron, coal, and transport, must be destroyed. If France could seize, even in part, what Germany was compelled to drop, the inequality of strength between the two rivals for European hegemony might be remedied for many generations. Hence sprang those cumulative provisions of the Treaty for the destruction of highly organised economic life.

This is the policy of an old man, whose most vivid impressions and most lively imagination are of the past and not of the future. He sees the issue in terms of France and Germany, not of humanity and of European civilisation struggling forwards to a new order. The war has bitten into his consciousness somewhat differently from ours, and he neither expects nor hopes that we are at the threshold of a new age.

It happens, however, that it is not only an ideal question that is at issue. The Carthaginian Peace is not *practically* right or possible. Although the school of thought from which it springs is aware of the economic factor, it overlooks, nevertheless, the deeper economic tendencies which are to govern the future. The clock cannot be set back. You cannot restore Central Europe to 1870 without setting up such strains in the European structure and letting loose such human and spiritual forces as, pushing beyond frontiers and races, will overwhelm not only you and your "guarantees," but your institutions, and the existing order of your Society.

By what legerdemain was this policy substituted for the Fourteen Points, and how did the President come to accept it? The answer to these questions is difficult and depends on elements of character and psychology and on the subtle influence of surroundings, which are hard to detect and harder still to describe. But, if ever the action of a single individual matters, the collapse of the President has been one of the decisive moral events of history; and I must make an attempt to explain it. What a place the President held in the hearts and hopes of the world when he sailed to us in the *George Washington!* What a great man came to Europe in those early days of our victory!

In November 1918 the armies of Foch and the words of Wilson had brought us sudden escape from what was swallowing up all we cared for. The conditions seemed favourable beyond any expectation. The victory was so complete that fear need play no part in the settlement. The enemy had laid down his arms in reliance on a solemn compact as to the general character of the Peace, the terms of which seemed to assure a settlement of justice and magnanimity and a fair hope for a restoration of the broken current of life. To make assurance certain the President was coming himself to set the seal on his work.

When President Wilson left Washington he enjoyed a prestige and a moral influence throughout the world unequalled in history. His bold and measured words carried to the peoples of Europe above and beyond the voices of their own politicians. The enemy peoples trusted him to carry out the compact he had made with them; and the allied peoples acknowledged him not as a victor only but almost as a prophet. In addition to this moral influence, the realities of power were in his hands. The American armies were at the height of their numbers, discipline, and equipment. Europe was in complete dependence on the food supplies of the United States; and financially she was even more absolutely at their mercy. Europe not only already owed the United States more than she could pay; but only a large measure of further assistance could save her from starvation and bankruptcy. Never had a philosopher held such weapons wherewith to bind the princes of this world. How the crowds of the European capitals pressed about the carriage of the President! With what curiosity, anxiety, and hope we sought a glimpse of the features and bearing of the man of destiny who, coming from the West, was to bring healing to the wounds of the ancient parent of his civilisation and lay for us the foundations of the future.

The disillusion was so complete that some of those who had trusted most hardly dared speak of it. Could it be true? they asked of those who returned from Paris. Was the Treaty really as bad as it seemed? What had happened to the President? What weakness or what misfortune had led to so extraordinary, so unlooked-for a betrayal?

Yet the causes were very ordinary and human. The President was not a hero or a prophet; he was not even a philosopher; but a generously intentioned man, with many of the weaknesses of other human beings, and lacking that dominating intellectual equipment which would have been necessary to cope with the subtle and dangerous spell-binders whom a tremendous clash of forces and personalities had brought to the top as triumphant masters in the swift game of give and take, face to face in Council—a game of which he had no experience at all.

We had indeed quite a wrong idea of the President. We knew him to be solitary and aloof, and believed him very strong-willed and obstinate. We did not figure him as a man of detail, but the clearness with which he had taken hold of certain main ideas would, we thought, in combination with his tenacity, enable him to sweep through cobwebs. Besides these qualities he would have the objectivity, the cultivation, and the wide knowledge of the student. The great distinction of language which had marked his famous Notes seemed to indicate a man of lofty and powerful imagination. His portraits indicated a fine presence and a commanding delivery. With all this he had attained and held with increasing authority the first position in a country where the arts of the politician are not neglected. All of which, without expecting the impossible, seemed a fine combination of qualities for the matter in hand.

The first impression of Mr. Wilson at close quarters was to impair some but not all of these illusions. His head and features were finely cut and exactly like his photographs, and the muscles of his neck and the carriage of his head were distinguished. But, like Odysseus, the President looked wiser when he was seated; and his hands, though capable and fairly strong, were wanting in sensitiveness and finesse. The first glance at the President suggested not only that, whatever else he might be, his temperament was not primarily that of the student or the scholar, but that he had not much even of that culture of the world which marks M. Clemenceau and Mr. Balfour as exquisitely cultivated gentlemen of their class and generation. But more serious than this, he was not only insensitive to his surroundings in the external sense, he was not sensitive to his environment at all. What chance could such a man have against Mr. Lloyd George's unerring, almost medium-like, sensibility to everyone immediately round him? To see the British Prime Minister watching the company, with six or seven senses not available to ordinary men, judging character, motive, and subconscious impulse, perceiving what each was thinking and even what each was going to say next, and compounding with telepathic instinct the argument or appeal best suited to the vanity, weakness, or self-interest of his immediate auditor, was to realise that the poor President would be playing blind-man's-buff in that party. Never could a man have stepped into the parlour a more perfect and predestined victim to the finished accomplishments of the Prime Minister. The Old World was tough in wickedness, anyhow; the Old World's heart of stone might blunt the sharpest blade of the bravest knight-errant. But this blind and deaf Don Quixote was entering a cavern where the swift and glittering blade was in the hands of the adversary.

But if the President was not the philosopher-king, what was he? After all, he was a man who had spent much of his life at a University. He was by no means a business man or an ordinary party politician, but a man of force, personality, and importance. What, then, was his temperament?

The clue, once found, was illuminating. The President was like a Nonconformist minister, perhaps a Presbyterian. His thought and his temperament were essentially theological, not intellectual, with all the strength and the weakness of that manner of thought, feeling, and expression. It is a type of which there are not now in England and Scotland such magnificent specimens as formerly; but this description, nevertheless, will give the ordinary Englishman the distinctest impression of the President.

With this picture of him in mind we can return to the actual course of events. The President's programme for the world, as set forth in his speeches and his Notes, had displayed a spirit and a purpose so admirable that the last desire of his sympathisers was to criticise details—the details, they felt, were quite rightly not filled in at present, but would be in due course. It was commonly believed at the commencement of the Paris Conference that the President had thought out, with the aid of a large body of advisers, a comprehensive scheme not only for the League of Nations but for the embodiment of the Fourteen Points in an actual Treaty of Peace. But in fact the President had thought out nothing; when it came to practice, his ideas were nebulous and incomplete. He had no plan, no scheme, no constructive ideas whatever for clothing with the flesh of life the commandments which he had thundered from the White House. He could have preached a sermon on any of them or have addressed a stately prayer to the Almighty for their fulfilment, but he could not frame their concrete application to the actual state of Europe.

He not only had no proposals in detail, but he was in many respects, perhaps inevitably, ill-informed as to European conditions. And not only was he ill-informed—that was true of Mr. Lloyd George also—but his mind was slow and unadaptable. The President's slowness amongst the Europeans was noteworthy. He could not, all in a minute, take in what the rest were saying, size up the situation with a glance, frame a reply, and meet the case by a slight change of ground; and he was liable, therefore, to defeat by the mere swiftness, apprehension, and agility of a Lloyd George. There can seldom have been a statesman of the first rank more incompetent than the President in the agilities of the council chamber. A moment often arrives when substantial victory is yours if by some slight appearance of a concession you can save the face of the opposition or conciliate them by a restatement of your proposal helpful to them and not injurious to anything essential to yourself. The President was not equipped with this simple and usual artfulness. His mind was too slow and unresourceful to be ready with *any* alternatives. The President was capable of digging his toes in and refusing to budge, as he did over Fiume. But he had no other mode of defence, and it needed as a rule but little manœuvring by his opponents to prevent matters from coming to such a head until it was too late. By pleasantness and an appearance of conciliation the President would be manœuvred off his ground, would miss the moment for digging his toes in, and, before he knew where he had been got to, it was too late. Besides, it is impossible month after month in intimate and ostensibly friendly converse between close associates to be digging the toes in all the time. Victory would only have been possible to one who had always a sufficiently lively apprehension of the position as a whole to reserve his fire and know for certain the rare exact moments for decisive action. And for that the President was far too slow-minded and bewildered.

He did not remedy these defects by seeking aid from the collective wisdom of his lieutenants. He had gathered round him for the economic chapters of the Treaty a very able group of business men; but they were inexperienced in public affairs and knew (with one or two exceptions) as little of Europe as he did, and they were only called in irregularly as he might need them for a particular purpose. Thus the aloofness which had been found effective in Washington was maintained, and the abnormal reserve of his nature did not allow near him anyone who aspired to moral equality or the continuous exercise of influence. His fellow-plenipotentiaries were dummies; and even the trusted Colonel House, with vastly more knowledge of men and of Europe than the President, from whose sensitiveness the President's dullness had gained so much, fell into the background as time went on. All this was encouraged by his colleagues on the Council of Four, who, by the break-up of the Council of Ten, completed the isolation which the President's own temperament had initiated. Thus day after day and week after week he allowed himself to be closeted, unsupported, unadvised, and alone, with men much sharper than himself, in situations of supreme difficulty, where he needed for success every description of resource, fertility, and knowledge. He allowed himself to be drugged by their atmosphere, to discuss on the basis of their plans and of their data, and to be led along their paths.

These and other various causes combined to produce the following situation. The reader must remember that the processes which are here compressed into a few pages took place slowly, gradually, insidiously, over a period of about five months.

As the President had thought nothing out, the Council was generally working on the basis of a French or British draft. He had to take up, therefore, a persistent attitude of obstruction, criticism, and negation if the draft was to become at all in line with his own ideas and purpose. If he was met on some points with apparent generosity (for there was always a safe margin of quite preposterous suggestions which no one took seriously), it was difficult for him not to yield on others. Compromise was inevitable, and never to compromise on the essential very difficult. Besides, he was soon made to appear to be taking the German part, and laid himself open to the suggestion (to which he was foolishly and unfortunately sensitive) of being "pro-German."

After a display of much principle and dignity in the early days of the Council of Ten, he discovered that there were certain very important points in the programme of his French, British, or Italian colleague, as the case might be, of which he was incapable of securing the surrender by the methods of secret diplomacy. What then was he to do in the last resort? He could let the Conference drag on an endless length by the exercise of sheer obstinacy. He could break it up and return to America in a rage with nothing settled. Or he could attempt an appeal to the world over the heads of the Conference. These were wretched alternatives, against each of which a great deal could be said. They were also very risky—especially for a politician. The President's mistaken policy over the Congressional election had weakened his personal position in his own country, and it was by no means certain that the American public would support him in a position of intransigency. It would mean a campaign in which the issues would be clouded by every sort of personal and party consideration, and who could say if right would triumph in a struggle which would certainly not be decided on its merits. Besides, any open rupture with his colleagues would certainly bring upon his head the blind passions of "anti-German" resentment with which the public of all allied countries were still inspired.

They would not listen to his arguments. They would not be cool enough to treat the issue as one of international morality or of the right governance of Europe. The cry would simply be that for various sinister and selfish reasons the President wished "to let the Hun off." The almost unanimous voice of the French and British Press could be anticipated. Thus, if he threw down the gauge publicly he might be defeated. And if he were defeated, would not the final Peace be far worse than if he were to retain his prestige and endeavour to make it as good as the limiting conditions of European politics would allow him? But above all, if he were defeated, would he not lose the League of Nations? And was not this, after all, by far the most important issue for the future happiness of the world? The Treaty would be altered and softened by time. Much in it which now seemed so vital would become trifling, and much which was impracticable would for that very reason never happen. But the League, even in an imperfect form, was permanent; it was the first commencement of a new principle in the government of the world; Truth and Justice in international relations could not be established in a few months—they must be born in due course by the slow gestation of the League. Clemenceau had been clever enough to let it be seen that he would swallow the League at a price.

At the crisis of his fortunes the President was a lonely man. Caught up in the toils of the Old World, he stood in great need of sympathy, of moral support, of the enthusiasm of masses. But buried in the Conference, stifled in the hot and poisoned atmosphere of Paris, no echo reached him from the outer world, and no throb of passion, sympathy, or encouragement from his silent constituents in all countries. He felt that the blaze of popularity which had greeted his arrival in Europe was already dimmed; the Paris Press jeered at him openly; his political opponents at home were taking advantage of his absence to create an atmosphere against him; England was cold, critical, and unresponsive. He had so formed his *entourage* that he did not receive through private channels the current of faith and enthusiasm of which the public sources seemed dammed up. He needed, but lacked, the added strength of collective faith. The German terror still overhung us, and even the sympathetic public was very cautious; the enemy must not be encouraged, our friends must be supported, this was not the time for discord or agitations, the President must be trusted to do his best. And in this drought the flower of the President's faith withered and dried up.

Thus it came to pass that the President countermanded the *George Washington*, which, in a moment of well-founded rage, he had ordered to be in readiness to carry him from the treacherous halls of Paris back to the seat of his authority, where he could have felt himself again. But as soon, alas, as he had taken the road of compromise the defects, already indicated, of his temperament and of his equipment were fatally apparent. He could take the high line; he could practice obstinacy; he could write Notes from Sinai or Olympus; he could remain unapproachable in the White House or even in the Council of Ten and be safe. But if he once stepped down to the intimate equality of the Four, the game was evidently up.

Now it was that what I have called his theological or Presbyterian temperament became dangerous. Having decided that some concessions were unavoidable, he might have sought by firmness and address and the use of the financial power of the United States to secure as much as he could of the substance, even at some sacrifice of the letter. But the President was not capable of so clear an understanding with himself as this implied. He was too conscientious. Although compromises were now necessary, he remained a man of principle and the Fourteen Points a contract absolutely binding upon him. He would do nothing that was not honourable; he would do nothing that was not just and right; he would do nothing that was contrary to his great profession of faith. Thus, without any abatement of the verbal inspiration of the Fourteen Points, they became a document for gloss and interpretation and for all the intellectual apparatus of self-deception, by which, I dare say, the President's forefathers had persuaded themselves that the course they thought it necessary to take was consistent with every syllable of the Pentateuch.

The President's attitude to his colleagues had now become: I want to meet you so far as I can; I see your difficulties and I should like to be able to agree to what you propose, but I can do nothing that is not just and right, and you must first of all show me that what you want does really fall within the words of the pronouncements which are binding on me. Then began the weaving of that web of sophistry and Jesuitical exegesis that was finally to clothe with insincerity the language and substance of the whole Treaty. The word was issued to the witches of all Paris:

> Fair is foul, and foul is fair,
> Hover through the fog and filthy air.

The subtlest sophisters and most hypocritical draftsmen were set to work, and produced many ingenious exercises which might have deceived for more than an hour a cleverer man than the President.

Thus instead of saying that German Austria is prohibited from uniting with Germany except by leave of France (which would be inconsistent with the principle of self-determination), the Treaty, with delicate draftsmanship, states that "Germany acknowledges and will respect strictly the independence of Austria, within the frontiers which may be fixed in a Treaty between that State and the Principal Allied and Associated Powers; she agrees that this independence shall be inalienable, except with the consent of the Council of the League of Nations," which sounds, but is not, quite different. And who knows but that the President forgot that another part of the Treaty provides that for this purpose the Council of the League must be *unanimous*.

Instead of giving Danzig to Poland, the Treaty establishes Danzig as a "Free" City, but includes this "Free" City within the Polish Customs frontier, entrusts to Poland the control of the river and railway system, and provides that "the Polish Government shall undertake the conduct of the foreign relations of the Free City of Danzig as well as the diplomatic protection of citizens of that city when abroad."

In placing the river system of Germany under foreign control, the Treaty speaks of declaring international those "river systems which naturally provide more than one State with access to the sea, with or without transhipment from one vessel to another."

Such instances could be multiplied. The honest and intelligible purpose of French policy, to limit the population of Germany and weaken her economic system, is clothed, for the President's sake, in the august language of freedom and international equality.

But perhaps the most decisive moment, in the disintegration of the President's moral position and the clouding of his mind, was when at last, to the dismay of his advisers, he allowed himself to be persuaded that the expenditure of the Allied Governments on pensions and separation allowances could be fairly regarded as "damage done to the civilian population of the Allied and Associated Powers by German aggression by land, by sea, and from the air," in a sense in which the other expenses of the war could not be so regarded. It was a long theological struggle in which, after the rejection of many different arguments, the President finally capitulated before a masterpiece of the sophist's art.[1]

At last the work was finished, and the President's conscience was still intact. In spite of everything, I believe that his temperament allowed him to leave Paris a really sincere man; and it is probable that to his death he was genuinely convinced that the Treaty contained practically nothing inconsistent with his former professions.

But the work was too complete, and to this was due the last tragic episode of the drama. The reply of Brockdorff-Rantzau naturally took the line that Germany had laid down her arms on the basis of certain assurances, and that the Treaty in many particulars was not consistent with these assurances. But this was exactly what the President could not admit; in the sweat of solitary contemplation and with prayers to God he had done *nothing* that was not just and right; for the President to admit that the German reply had force in it was to destroy his self-respect and to disrupt the inner equipoise of his soul, and every instinct of his stubborn nature rose in self-protection. In the language of medical psychology, to suggest to the President that the Treaty was an abandonment of his professions was to touch on the raw

[1] For the details of this piece of work *vide* the author's *A Revision of the Treaty*, chap. v.

a Freudian complex. It was a subject intolerable to discuss, and every subconscious instinct plotted to defeat its further exploration.

Thus it was that Clemenceau brought to success what had seemed to be, a few months before, the extraordinary and impossible proposal that the Germans should not be heard. If only the President had not been so conscientious, if only he had not concealed from himself what he had been doing, even at the last moment he was in a position to have recovered lost ground and to have achieved some very considerable successes. But the President was set. His arms and legs had been spliced by the surgeons to a certain posture, and they must be broken again before they could be altered. To his horror, Mr. Lloyd George, desiring at the last moment all the moderation he dared, discovered that he could not in five days persuade the President of error in what it had taken five months to prove to him to be just and right. After all, it was harder to de-bamboozle this old Presbyterian than it had been to bamboozle him, for the former involved his belief in and respect for himself.

Thus in the last act the President stood for stubbornness and a refusal of conciliations.

I should prefer to end this chapter here. But the reader may ask, What part in the result did the British Prime Minister play? What share had England in the final responsibility? The answer to the second question is not clear-cut. And as to the first, who shall paint the chameleon, who can tether a broomstick? The character of Lloyd George is not yet rendered, and I do not aspire to the task.

The selfish, or, if you like, the legitimate interests of England did not, as it happened, conflict with the Fourteen Points as vitally as did those of France. The destruction of the fleet, the expropriation of the marine, the surrender of the colonies, the suzerainty of Mesopotamia—there was not much here for the President to strain at, even in the light of his professions, especially as England, whose diplomatic moderation as always was not hampered by the logical intransigency of the French mind, was ready to concede in point of form whatever might be asked. England did not desire the German fleet for herself, and its destruction was a phase of Disarmament. The expropriation of the marine was a legitimate compensation, specifically provided for in the pre-Armistice conditions, for the lawless campaign of submarines which had been the express occasion of America's entering the war. Over the colonies and Mesopotamia England demanded no exclusive sovereignty, and they were covered by the Doctrine of Mandates under the League of Nations.

Thus when the British Delegation left for Paris there seemed no insuperable obstacles to an almost complete understanding between the British and the American negotiators. There were only two clouds on the horizon—the so-called Freedom of the Seas and the Prime Minister's election pledges on the Indemnity. The first, to the general surprise, was never raised by the President, a silence which, presumably, was the price he deemed it judicious to pay for British co-operation on other more vital issues; the second was more important.

The co-operation, which was thus rendered possible, was largely realised in practice. The individual members of the British and American delegations were united by bonds of fraternal feeling and mutual respect, and constantly worked together and stood together for a policy of honest dealing and broad-minded humanity. And the Prime Minister, too, soon established himself as the President's friend and powerful ally against the Latins' alleged rapacity or lack of international idealism. Why then did not the joint forces of these two powerful and enlightened autocrats give us the Good Peace?

The answer is to be sought more in those intimate workings of the heart and character which make the tragedies and comedies of the domestic hearthrug than in the supposed ambitions of empires or philosophies of statesmen. The President, the Tiger, and the Welsh witch were shut up in a room together for six months and the Treaty was what came out. Yes, the Welsh witch—for the British Prime Minister contributed the female element to this triangular intrigue. I have called Mr. Wilson a nonconformist clergyman. Let the reader figure Mr. Lloyd George as a *femme fatale*. An old man of the world, a *femme fatale*, and a nonconformist clergyman—these are the characters of our drama. Even though the lady was very religious at times, the Fourteen Commandments could hardly expect to emerge perfectly intact.

I must try to silhouette the broomstick as it sped through the twilit air of Paris.

Mr. Lloyd George's devotion to duty at the Paris Conference was an example to all servants of the public. He took no relaxation, enjoyed no pleasures, had no life and no occupation save that of Prime Minister and England's spokesman. His labour's were immense and he spent his vast stores of spirit and of energy without stint on the formidable task he had put his hand to. His advocacy of the League of Nations was sincere; his support of a fair application of the principle of Self-Determination to Germany's eastern frontiers was disinterested. He had no wish to impose a Carthaginian Peace; the crushing of Germany was no part of his purpose. His hatred of war is real, and the strain of pacifism and radical idealism, which governed him during the Boer War, is a genuine part of his composition. He would have defended a Good Peace before the House of Commons with more heart than he did that which he actually brought back to them.

But in such a test of character and method as Paris provided, the Prime Minister's naturally good instincts, his industry, his inexhaustible nervous vitality were not serviceable. In that furnace other qualities were called for—a policy deeply grounded in permanent principle, tenacity, fierce indignation, honesty, loyal leadership. If Mr. Lloyd George had no good qualities, no charms, no fascinations, he would not be dangerous. If he were not a siren, we need not fear the whirlpools.

But it is not appropriate to apply to him the ordinary standards. How can I convey to the reader, who does not know him, any just impression of this extraordinary figure of our time, this siren, this goat-footed bard, this half-human visitor to our age from the hag-ridden magic and enchanted woods of Celtic antiquity? One catches in his company that flavour of final purposelessness, inner irresponsibility, existence outside or away from our Saxon good and evil, mixed with cunning, remorselessness, love of power, that lend fascination, enthralment, and terror to the fair-seeming magicians of North European folklore. Prince Wilson sailing out from the West in his barque *George Washington* sets foot in the enchanted castle of Paris to free from chains and oppression and an ancient curse the maid Europe, of eternal youth and beauty, his mother and his bride in one. There in the castle is the King with yellow parchment face, a million years old, and with him an enchantress with a harp singing the Prince's own words to a magical tune. If only the Prince could cast off the paralysis which creeps on him and, crying to heaven, could make the Sign of the Cross, with a sound of thunder and crashing glass the castle would dissolve, the magicians vanish, and Europe leap to his arms. But in this fairy-tale the forces of the half-world win and the soul of Man is subordinated to the spirits of the earth.

Lloyd George is rooted in nothing; he is void and without content; he lives and feeds on his immediate surroundings; he is an instrument and a player at the same time which plays on the company and is played on by them too; he is a prism, as I have heard him described, which collects light and distorts it and is most brilliant if the light comes from many quarters at once; a vampire and a medium in one.

Whether by chance or by design, the principal British war aims (with the exception of the Indemnity, if this was one of them) were dealt with in the earliest stages of the Conference. Clemenceau was criticised at the time for his tardiness in securing the primary demands of France. But events proved him to be right in not forcing the pace. The French demands, as I have pointed out, were much more controversial than those of the British; and it was essential to get the British well embroiled in a Peace of selfish interests before putting the professions of the Conference to a severer test. The British demands afforded an excellent *hors-d'œuvre* to accustom the delicate palate of the President to the stronger flavours which were to come. This order of procedure laid the British Prime Minister open to the charge, whenever he seemed too critical of French demands, that, having first secured every conceivable thing that he wanted himself, he was now ready with characteristic treachery to abandon his undertakings to his French comrades. In the atmosphere of Paris this seemed a much more potent taunt than it really was. But it gained its real strength, in its influence on the Prime Minister, from three special attendant circumstances. In two respects the Prime Minister found himself unavoidably and inextricably on Clemenceau's side—in the matters of the Indemnity and of the Secret Treaties. If the President's morale was maintained intact, Mr. Lloyd George could not hope to get his way on these issues; he was, therefore, almost equally interested with Clemenceau in gradually breaking down this morale. But, besides, he had Lord Northcliffe and the British Jingoes on his heels, and complaints in the French Press were certain to find their echo in a certain section of the British also.

If, therefore, he were to take his stand firmly and effectively on the side of the President, there was needed an act of courage and faith which could only be based on fundamental beliefs and principles. But Mr. Lloyd George has none such, and political considerations pointed to a middle path.

Precisely, therefore, as the President had found himself pushed along the path of compromise, so also did the Prime Minister, though for very different reasons. But while the President failed because he was very bad at the game of compromise, the Prime Minister trod the way of ill-doing because he was far too good at it.

The reader will thus apprehend how Mr. Lloyd George came to occupy an ostensibly middle position, and how it became his rôle to explain the President to Clemenceau and Clemenceau to the President and to seduce everybody all round. He was only too well fitted for the task, but much better fitted for dealing with the President than with Clemenceau. Clemenceau was much too cynical, much too experienced, and much too well educated to be taken in, at his age, by the fascinations of the lady from Wales. But for the President it was a wonderful, almost delightful, experience to be taken in hand by such an expert. Mr. Lloyd George had soon established himself as the President's only real friend. The President's very masculine characteristics fell a complete victim to the feminine enticements, sharpness, quickness, sympathy of the Prime Minister.

We have Mr. Lloyd George, therefore, in his middle position, but exercising more sway over the President than over Clemenceau. Now let the reader's mind recur to the metaphors. Let him remember the Prime Minister's incurable love of a deal; his readiness to surrender the substance for the shadow; his intense desire, as the months dragged on, to get a conclusion and be back to England again. What wonder that in the eventual settlement the real victor was Clemenceau.

Even so, close observers never regarded it as impossible right up to the conclusion of the affair that the Prime Minister's better instincts and truer judgment might yet prevail—he knew in his heart that this Peace would disgrace him and that it might ruin Europe. But he had dug a pit for himself deeper than even he could leap out of; he was caught in his own toils, defeated by his own methods. Besides, it is a characteristic of his inner being, of his kinship with the trolls and the soulless simulacra of the earth, that at the great crises of his fortunes it is the lower instincts of the hour that conquer.

These were the personalities of Paris—I forbear to mention other nations or lesser men: Clemenceau, aesthetically the noblest; the President, morally the most admirable; Lloyd George, intellectually the subtlest. Out of their disparities and weaknesses the Treaty was born, child of the least worthy attributes of each of its parents, without nobility, without morality, without intellect.

# EMIL LUDWIG

"CHARACTER IS FATE" would be a fitting motto for *The Collected Works of Emil Ludwig*. For character, to Herr Ludwig, is clearly and overwhelmingly the determinant of every man's destiny—at least, since chance may affect outward events, of every man's spiritual and intellectual destiny. The modern biographer's first duty is to examine the consistency of his subject's character *per se*, "the personality almost devoid of temporal coördinates, considering the volume, intensity, and resistance of its vital forces, the restless fluid of its emotional configurations, and the balance between its impulse towards action and its repression through percept." This is R. W. Brown's concept of "dynamic tension" put into more scientific terms. Ludwig continues: "Whereas our fathers asked, 'How did the individual harmonize with his world?' our first question is, 'Does he harmonize with himself?' Questions of success and responsibility have been shifted from the environment back to the individual, so that analysis which was formerly expended upon the milieu now seeks to penetrate within." Yet the modern biographer is primarily not a scientist but an artist, not an historian but a portrait-painter and sometimes a dramatist. He can still draw upon science and history for needful corroboration, but with new tools and new methods he may excel his predecessors in the work of re-constructing human lives. How Herr Ludwig reached these interesting conclusions his own life shows.

The family name was Cohn; his grandfather was an important iron and steel man of Upper Silesia and his father, Professor Hermann Ludwig Cohn, a celebrated eye-specialist of Breslau. His father dropped the last name for his children at their birth to spare them needless anti-Semitic abuse. Young Emil, born in 1881, was intended for a legal career and, though not a very promising student at Breslau and Heidelberg, actually took his Doctorate of Jurisprudence, his thesis on "Emotional Murder" suggesting the psychology back of the sentences quoted above. For some time he studied social problems, but until the age of twenty-five he was for the most part uncongenially employed in a coal business.

He had become interested in drama when still a boy and, before thirty, composed a dozen plays (six of which were staged) about such typical figures as Napoleon, Tristan and Isolde, the Borgias, and other titans. By that time love, literary ambition, and an acquaintance with the dramatist Gerhart Hauptmann had determined him, once for all, to be a writer; a multitude of motives had made him a Swiss citizen; and the encouragement of the poet Richard Dehmel had confirmed him in the psychological

411

study of great men's characters and in the particular biographical *genre*
he has made his own as a notable pioneer and independent.

In 1911 his mind was stimulated by a table conversation between his
father and Prince Bismarck's personal physician and he at once set about
dramatizing the Iron Chancellor's life. He first examined carefully all the
portraits, busts, letters—especially the letters, which suggested a prose style
—until he came, as he says, by a purely optical sense to certain conclusions,
which he set forth in a preliminary working sketch. Later he read every
word he could find to gain a truer and deeper impression of the man.
Not until 1926 did his huge biography come out, followed the next year
by a trilogy of Bismarck plays. When at length all the scholarly research
was accomplished it was found to bear out exactly the author's original
intuitive characterization. There, without seeking it, lay a novel biographical procedure—"from intuitive prepossession to evidential conviction."
Meanwhile its first fruit (also perhaps the first long biography of the
modern school) was his masterly *Goethe: The History of a Man* (1920),
for which the poet-philosopher's voluminous works, minutely studied as
they are skillfully used, only reinforced Ludwig's initial ideas. The same
method has served, with varying success, in his full-length lives of
Napoleon, William II, Jesus, Lincoln, Schliemann, Hindenburg, Masaryk,
Cleopatra, and Franklin D. Roosevelt, not to mention his shorter portraits
of Michelangelo, Rembrandt, and Beethoven (*Three Titans,* 1930) and
his many current magazine profiles. Some of his trial sketches for longer
works, with a full discussion of his theory and approach, may be seen
in *Genius and Character* (1926). In the intervals between these biographical studies, amidst much travel and lecturing, have appeared books of
fiction, geography, history, journalism, a play or two, and his attractive
autobiography, *Gifts of Life* (1931)—all revealing in some measure his
extraordinary capacity for seeing and judging the "true inwardness" of
people and events. In short, Emil Ludwig has made a lifelong study of
man, of all sorts of men though especially of the great, and he has turned
all his experience into books. Even his journalism, in which he was trained
as a World War correspondent, has in later years fused more and more
with his writing of biography, repeated interviews and inspection of all
relevant newsreels helping him to establish and insure his understanding
of the living subject.

The following sketch of Signor Mussolini from *Nine Etched from Life*
(1934) is a product of such interviews with leaders of Europe. Mussolini,
himself one of the greatest journalists in the world before he deserted
words for action, talked with Ludwig every day for many weeks about
himself and his problems of government and power. The biographer's
task was to entice the Duce out of himself, to bring him into the light
and consider his personality from all sides, a task that required both skill

in questioning and reserve in answering. To these conversations, fully recorded in a separate book, Ludwig added his factual, first-hand knowledge of modern Europe and his special grasp of the ways of genius, producing a portrait which has satisfied both the subject and his critics by its fundamental truth.

Emil Ludwig, like the painter in oils or crayon, has always been more concerned with individuals than with what they are striving for. "What chiefly interests me," he says, "is the interaction between genius and character." And because the biographical portraitist of today, "who is first of all a psychologist, is much nearer to the biologist than to the historian," he finds his most valuable material in the facial type and build of his subject, in his voice, gait, and mannerisms, in photographs, private letters, conversations, anecdotes—in the very details that were formerly either ignored or else "inserted like bonbons for the reader's palate." For Ludwig, as for his master Plutarch, "the most trivial habit will often suggest the interpretation for some major trait of character." Obviously, the results of this approach cannot be seen to best advantage in a brief sketch. In a full-length work, such as his *Goethe* or *Napoleon*, the proofs of its validity are abundant. One of the salutary benefits he confers on his readers by its means is to show, without condescension or malice toward his subjects, "that great men are not gods, that they have been gripped by the same all-too-human passions, repressions, and encumbrances as afflict every other mortal, and that they have fought through, regardless, to their goal." This he can show even in a short view of an unfinished career.

# MUSSOLINI

## THE ITALIAN AUTOCRAT

A STATESMAN can be the subject of criticism more easily than an artist or a scientific inventor. These latter offer us their finished products, which we can take or leave according to our tastes and knowledge. But the statesman has assumed the right to direct our lives. He has placed himself above us. Even his personal opinions and prejudices may affect our daily existence. It is for this reason that criticism of a statesman, no matter how frivolous or foolish it may be, has a profound justification in the very nature of the relations between him and those over whom he rules. For every individual will defend his personal liberty so far as possible, and when he finds himself subjected to the will of another he will naturally turn the sting of his criticism on that other, just as the bee stings its captor.

In a democracy the statesman can to some extent defend himself against popular criticism. He can point to the fact that he has been chosen by the popular will and that he holds office subject to its sanction. He is only a sort of managing director whom the shareholders of the state can dismiss if they think he has muddled their public affairs. At one time the hereditary monarch could defend himself against the popular clamor by fostering a belief among his people that he held his position by divine right and choice. But those were days when the public was not quite so enlightened as it is now. Today the hereditary monarch is treated as a sort of decorative chairman, whose duty it is to receive distinguished visitors and, during the intervals of their business with ministers of state, to entertain them at luncheon or accompany them in his royal equipage to see a waterfall or a museum or witness a theatrical performance. The most difficult part is that which the dictator has to play. He can never dispense with Fear as his ally.

In the great circus which we call human society the elected president takes the part of the juggler who twirls six plates on the ends of two poles. In case the plates fall people merely laugh at the juggler. The king is like the fat old circus master who whips ten very tame horses round the ring, just as his father and his forefathers did before him with the same whip, making the whip crack, but never touching a hair of the animals, and applauded by the public merely because he is the chief representative of the whole menagerie. The dictator is like the lion tamer who stands in front of eight or ten growling beasts, constantly holding them in awe with scourge and revolver. They both hate him and obey him. At the tent door of the circus men stand ready with hydrants and rifles. Nevertheless, he forces the animals turn after turn to take their respective places on the wooden platform while at any moment one of them may make a single stroke with paw or tooth and stamp out the life of the tamer. It is not at all strange then that the lion tamer is rarely a favorite with the rest of the circus company. His chief admirers are the outside visitors who come to look on.

The history of the great dictators shows that when their rule had come to an end there was a general slacking off and even a relapse into a sort of coma after the extraordinary tension that had to be endured. And yet in spite of this it would be wrong to conclude that the dictatorships have done no creative work merely because a reaction follows. The case of Napoleon is in point here. After his banishment to St. Helena it was widely proclaimed in France, especially in democratic circles, that he left the country smaller in territorial extent than he had found it, that hundreds of thousands of his subjects had fallen in the wars, that the exchequer was empty and that huge numbers of Frenchmen had been banished from the country or otherwise persecuted. These are true statements so far as the facts are concerned. But in drawing conclusions from them two points must be taken into account: first, that on the soil of France itself he did constructive work of enduring value; second, that the example of personal achievement which he left to future generations of Frenchmen has been an invaluable asset to the French nation, especially as a source of inspirtion for the youth. Napoleon himself would probably never have made his mark in life had it not been for the fact that as a boy his imagination was set on fire by reading Plutarch's *Lives*. Just in the same way today every ambitious young Frenchman has the great example of Napoleon to inspire him. It is too often forgotten nowadays that this ambition is a creative urge or instinct and there is no reason whatsoever why the vision of domination over one's fellow men should necessarily be its goal.

Napoleon's contemporaries could not easily recognize his greatness. They were too near him. The revolutions of a planet can be observed only from another planet, except where the observers are expert astronomers and are in a position scientifically to calculate the revolutions of the planet on which they live. In a similar manner, the task of delineating the qualities of the outstanding men of our time must fall to those who can look upon them in a detached way and judge them in their proper historical perspective according to permanent standards of value.

## 2

When Mussolini assumed political power in Italy every act of him was looked upon with misgiving. He was a turncoat from socialism and had repudiated all international ideals. And we all feel today that only by the spirit of internationalism can that light be enkindled which will lead us out of the present wilderness. Mussolini's parentage and the conditions under which he lived as a youth made him antagonistic to the established social order and even a professed anarchist. "My real biography is to be found in the first fifteen years of my life," he once declared. He was the son of a revolutionary blacksmith in a tiny village. He used to sit in the evenings with his father on the hob of the smithy drinking hot spiced wine in the glow of the embers and reading publications that recorded the heroic deeds and sayings of the great socialists who were then in the van of the movement. He saw his father dragged off to prison because of the wild speeches he had made in their native Romagna, a province notorious at that time as a stronghold of the anarchists. The father died comparatively young. This was probably attributable to overwork and the nervous strain which his constant political activities entailed. Five thousand fellow workmen followed his remains to the grave. People were then wondering whether the son would take after him. Would he one day hurl a bomb at King Victor Emmanuel, as another anarchist had annihilated his predecessor and father, King Humbert? Or perhaps the young Benito would become a Member of Parliament and head a constitutional movement for the abolition of the monarchy.

But there was another side to Benito Mussolini's character. This was the side that he inherited from his mother. She was a schoolteacher by profession. In her nature she was reserved, thoughtful and gentle. If one makes a close study of Mussolini today at the age of fifty it is easy to detect that side of his nature which he inherited from his mother now coming into the foreground. He is becoming gradually less violent, less volcanic and less extreme. And he is correspondingly more pensive, slower to come to conclusions and far more careful about taking drastic decisions.

Yet while we watch this side of his temperament now becoming almost dominant we must not forget that up to his thirty-second year he was an out-and-out revolutionary. At the age of nineteen he threw up his job as a teacher, though it brought him in a livelihood, and went to Switzerland. Here he worked as bricklayer's assistant and is still proud of the fact that he knows how to build a round-arched window. He carried his hod of bricks up the scaffold to the second story a hundred twenty times a day. And he often slept under the arches of the bridges beside the lake in Geneva. One summer evening he was suddenly dismissed from his job and found himself without anything to eat. He saw a rich bourgeois family sitting around a well-laden table in their garden. The thought struck him to ask them for food. But as he approached the table a sense of self-loathing came over him, he told me. He ran away in terror of himself.

"I have turned my back on all my old memories and even my ideals," he wrote in a letter to a friend about that time. He did not have a cent in his pocket, only a metal medallion of Karl Marx. He was arrested and thrown into prison because he had been observed so often in the company of anarchists. During his sojourn in Switzerland he became acquainted with the insides of eleven different prisons. This experience made such a deep psychic impression on him that long afterwards in Milan when he used to wander alone in the evening through the public park he often shuddered when it came to closing time and he heard the gatekeeper's key turn the bolt.

"Hunger is a good trainer," he said to me once; "almost as good as the prison or a man's enemies. My mother was a school-mistress and earned fifty lire [about $10] per month at her job. My father was a blacksmith with an uncertain earning capacity. We lived in two rooms. We scarcely ever had any meat on the table. We used to have heated discussions and quarrels and then we would indulge together in the illusions of hope. Because he was a socialist agitator my father was imprisoned. When he died thousands of his comrades in the Socialist Party followed his remains to the grave. All this had the effect of creating a strong socialist bias in me. Had my father been different I might have turned out a different sort of person. But my character was definitely molded by these early experiences at home. Anyone who knew me intimately at that time when I was only sixteen years old would recognize that I am the same today as I then was, with all the light and shade. All the trump cards for life's game were put into my hands by the fact of my proletarian origin."

He spoke in a dark muffled tone that sounded like the ringing of a distant bell. I have heard that voice of his in two very different tone qualities. Sometimes when speaking in the open it has a military hardness that reminds me of Trotsky speaking to the crowd. On other occasions the tone is soft and gives one the impression that the speaker is definitely and consciously reserving his nervous resources. And he speaks in this quiet reserved way not merely indoors; for I have heard him speak thus also when addressing a group of twenty workmen who stood around him in a circle. This restraint is indicative of Mussolini's character. He nurses his energy generally so that he may be able to display it all the more forcefully in public when the occasion arises.

Two events in his life are responsible for detaching Mussolini from the dour nihilism of his early days. He became a soldier and he became a journalist. When he returned from Switzerland at the age of twenty he had to do his military service. This he accepted after the manner of a born fighter and utilized the course of military training as a school wherein to learn the technique of attack and defense.

"As a soldier I was really a model. And I never felt any conflict between military service and my socialist convictions. Why cannot a good soldier be also a protagonist in class warfare? Even today Italians are very critical in their attitude towards those who order them about. That is an excellent control signal. It is a constant warning that a man must learn to obey before he can command."

I suggested that it was difficult to discover any stage of his life at which he had learned to obey.

"As a soldier at any rate," he replied. But he could not discover any other occasion.

"And today, after the passing of fifteen years, do you still look upon war as a means of personal training, as if it were a duel?"

I noticed him scrutinizing me because I had put the question somewhat sharply. He turned a little on his chair and put his fingers together—a favorite gesture of his. Mussolini has well-shaped hands and I have noticed this same characteristic in other dictators.

"The school of war," he replied, "is undoubtedly a great experience. It brings a man up against naked realities. Each day and each hour of the day it is a question of whether he is to live or die."

He also became a journalist at an early age; but he used journalism only as a weapon of battle. He has sketched out some dramas on social questions but never finished them. He wrote a novel for a small paper and had to continue it in installments from day to day because the readers liked it. He also wrote a history of the Hussite revolt in Bohemia and some essays on French and German literature. But his real passion was for the daily editorial article in which he dealt with the growth of socialism, criticized and attacked it for its failings, as he criticized and attacked conditions in Italy and throughout the whole of Europe. In this way he gradually and steadily secured a numerous following among the reading public.

"For me," he said, "my newspaper was my weapon and my standard. It was my very soul. I have even called it the child of my heart."

"And today," I replied, "if you think journalism so important a school, why do you shackle the press?"

"Today things are no longer as they were before the war," he said decisively. "Most of the newspapers nowadays serve interests rather than ideas. How then can they be a means of moral training for those who read them? Today I read more newspapers than I ever did before and I sometimes think that the average ass's bray is better done. I have that feeling especially when I read newspaper attacks against somebody or other."

"And when you write an article today are you somewhat more moderate than in the old days?"

He looked at me mischievously and said:
"I can only write fiercely and without qualification."

### 3

Why do people sneer when they see a man who was a revolutionary in his early days turn out in later years to be a champion of the established order? Isn't the life of each individual an example of the same thing and isn't it quite natural? With a big NO the strong man starts on his road of life. He kicks traditional customs aside and in the strength of his youth he is always overdestructive. But when he reaches the middle thirties and brings up children and builds himself a home and changes his lawless and formless visions for a fixed plan of life, he then finds that the services he receives from the established order of society are for his benefit and he realizes that many of the things he wished to accomplish as a radical might easily turn out pernicious even to his own life. If he reaches forty years of age and then finds some share of public power placed in his hands, he suddenly feels that the assumption of power means the assumption of obligations and he knows that he must carefully consider the consequences of every step before he can take a decision. The rebel who began by being a party leader and later on becomes a statesman is like a river that takes its rise from a mountain spring and flows in an impetuous torrent downwards over rocks and cliffs, forming a hundred whirlpools and cascades, until it tires itself out and gradually settles down between fixed banks, flowing onwards quietly and majestically into a broad waterway which bears on its bosom big ships laden with men and merchandise, a servant and at the same time a master.

In Mussolini's character as a young man it is possible to detect those traits that eventually made him a champion of the established social order, just as you will find revolutionary features in the Mussolini of today. In 1911 he was brought before a law court on the charge of inciting the populace to revolt. In his defense he said to the jury: "There is such a thing as lawful and such a thing as unlawful sabotage. The destruction of telegraph wires may have a moral and political purpose. To derail a neutral

train is inhuman." This rather original classification of misde-
meanors against the state shows that at the age of twenty-eight
this man felt his responsibility to society. He was by no means
out for wholesale destruction. His concept of socialism was inspired by the same principle. He called it "the greatest drama
which mankind is enacting for the purpose of rising above its
animal nature and reaching a humanitarian level." He did not
judge socialist principles by ethical standards; for Mussolini is
essentially a constructive realist. In spite of all the opposition I
feel towards his system of government I believe that in his youth
Mussolini was not a mere revolutionary. He yearned, I think, for
the establishment of a definitely new order of things. And if he
sought power it was not for its own sake but rather that he
might help in building up this new order after which he yearned.

Even while he was a socialist he had distinct nationalist leanings which marked him off from the rest of his party. In him,
as in so many other socialists, there was a certain line along which
international principles were not pushed to their logical conclusions. In 1911 Mussolini was passionately anti-Austrian. He
threatened war to "redeem" the Italian Trentino and demanded
of the Austrian Government to allow the Italian language to be
spoken officially there. Yet in 1919 his concept of Parliament was
that it should be "an Italian department of the League of Nations." "Every nation," he said to me, "has a certain X which
characterizes its personality and distinguishes it from the great Y
of all that it has in common with other nations. At the present
time the emphasis of public feeling is on the X rather than on
the Y."

These contradictions were quite natural in a young man whose
sympathies were being tugged by two opposing forces, the sense
of class solidarity in the one direction and the national feeling in
the other. When the war broke out this confusion and contradiction expressed itself in Mussolini's declarations just as in those of
other socialist leaders. As a socialist he was against the war and
in August 1914 he wrote in his own paper: "Down with the
War. We remain neutral." But the idea that the Hapsburg Empire must be annihilated soon took hold of his mind, and there-

with the inherited antipathy of generations of Italians towards Austria and also the desire to liberate from the Hapsburg yoke those lands beyond the political borders of Italy which were populated by Italians but had for centuries been occupied by the Austrians. In the incalculable consequences that would result from the war he must have foreseen the possibility of a favorable opportunity for his own ambition. War has often been the prelude to revolution. We must remember also that Mussolini is a Latin through and through. At this historical crisis, therefore, when the neighboring Latin land of France was in danger, Mussolini's Latin nature asserted itself and in the late autumn of 1914 he cried out: "France, we have forgotten everything you contrived against our fleet two years ago. France, we love you." Mussolini's present misgiving about France is not inconsistent with the spirit in which that cry was uttered. We usually quarrel most with our brothers, but we will jump to their rescue at once if misfortune should befall them. If another war comes it will not find Italians and Frenchmen taking the field against each other.

And even his socialist sympathies must have urged him finally to take up arms against the Central Powers. The Hohenzollern régime in Germany and the Hapsburg régime in Austria had been consistently maltreating his socialist comrades for over forty years. Was it not natural then for him to believe, as so many other socialists in the Entente countries believed, that by making war on Hohenzollern Germany he was saving Germany from itself? Mussolini still upholds the Italian monarchy and quite recently he said to me, apropos of my book on Wilhelm II, "That kind of imperial rule is over for good. It must be relegated to the past."

When I questioned him about his change from the neutral attitude which he took up at the beginning of the war and asked why he did not remain so, he answered:

"Nobody likes a neutral. He is like a person who has to be forced to defend himself.

"But that dislike for the neutral attitude was only the first sentimental urge. More important was the consideration that no matter which side turned out victorious, we, as neutrals, should find ourselves faced by some coalition or other once the war was over. If Germany were victorious, we should never have been forgiven for having stood aside during the struggle. And if we had stood aside, then when the Entente met in Paris at the close of the war they would have treated us more contemptuously than they treated the other members of the old Triple Alliance. We had to reckon with the possibility that we might eventually have to fight against a combination of states, even though these would have been somewhat tired of war. The third motive that urged me from my neutral attitude was personal. I had hoped to see a national resurgence in Italy and I have lived to see that hope fulfilled. Indeed, I have borne a part in the fulfillment of it myself. There were three of us who held out that hope and worked towards its fulfillment: d'Annunzio, Corridoni and myself. When d'Annunzio wrote *Il Nave* [*The Ship*] some years previously he aroused a widespread enthusiasm for the fleet. He now spread the fire of militant nationalism throughout the universities and the Italian youth in general. Corridoni, who fell in the war, had organized the working masses in his syndicalist movement. And I transformed the Socialist Party."

"What was the purpose you had before your mind at that time? Was it to transform Italy in the mold of your own ideas?"

"It was," he admitted frankly. "I have never sought an alibi."

And so he broke with the party whose chief press organ he had hitherto conducted. When he was expelled from the party at the meeting which they subsequently held, he shouted from the platform: "You hate me because you love me."

## 4

That sentence was the cue for his new rôle. It was the dictum of a personality born to command. It expressed pride and contempt at the same time, like the outcry of a defiant woman who is turned out and proudly accepts her expulsion at the hands of a man she has long and passionately loved. From the moment of that cry and from that day onwards this young man, who was only just turned thirty, cut himself away not merely from his former ideas and his former companions but he defiantly committed himself to a new line of conduct for which there was no precedent. Whither it would finally lead him he did not know. It was now that he began to stand alone.

The road before his feet which led the way to the goal he had in view was by no means a safe or an easy one. He began to walk that road when he first organized the venturous spirits of young Italy in the new Fascist Party. Thousands followed him and enrolled in his movement. They had signs and gestures, banners and flags, and black shirts and caps which visibly marked out this young body of men from the rest of the nation. But their leader remained alone. "Live dangerously" is a Nietzschean motto which Mussolini likes to quote. Though he now acquired many new friends and thousands flocked after him and believed in him, he had no longer any trust in his fellow men. That is the penalty such natures have to pay when they take up an outstanding position in the public eye. "I haven't a friend," he said to me. "And I cannot have one. First because of my temperament, and secondly because of the opinion I hold of my fellow men. That is why I dispense with intimacies and conversation."

This contempt of his for mankind in general is the source of that self-approbation which seized him as a mastering passion even before the fate of the struggle in which he was engaged had turned in his favor. This feeling of having a mission to fulfill dominates every man who undertakes a life of action in the grand style. And the feeling for a mission in life is dominant in such men even before they have accomplished any part of their chief design. In the spring of 1922 Mussolini was only the leader of a party which was then in the early stages of its political growth. He was not a cabinet minister, nor did he hold any official political position. Yet at that juncture he said to a friend of mine in Berlin: "At the present time there are only two powers in Italy—I and the King." During three years of faction fighting (1919-1922) between Fascists and Socialists the whole country had become disorganized. The King and his ministers held council in Rome. The Parliament held its usual sittings. The army also seemed to be under constitutional control. In the meantime Mussolini had organized another army from his own followers. It was impossible to hold these troops in leash any longer; for they were mostly made up of young bloods who had nothing to lose.

During that period Mussolini displayed quite a good deal of forbearance which proved him in the circumstances to have the qualities of a statesman. Contrary to the exhortations of his closest followers, he waited for a whole year. It was only when he felt his organization strong enough and had appointed three generals of the regular army at the head of his volunteers that he gave the sign for the march on Rome. During the closing days of October 1922 he sat in his editorial office in Milan, just as a Commander-in-Chief in modern warfare conducts a battle through the telephone at a distance of some hundreds of miles from the actual fighting. The King signed the decree of martial law and at first decided to fight the Fascists. But later on he had to bow to the *force majeure* of circumstances. He withdrew his orders to the army and had Mussolini summoned to Rome by telegram for the purpose of forming a Government.

At that moment Mussolini showed himself the born journalist. When he received the news from Rome he ran into the composing room and called his brother. Instead of announcing that he had won he said: "Get out an extra edition right away."

"What's that you have there?"

"My appointment."

That night Mussolini left Milan where he had been a newspaper editor for ten years. He came to Rome, where he has now been ten years at the head of the Government. Thousands of problems were running through his head and he had no time, he told me, to indulge in any sentimental thoughts.

"I had already prepared my general plan but not the details. I was overwhelmed with a confused mass of things that had to be done. Within forty-eight hours I had to clear fifty-two thousand revolutionary troops out of the capital and prevent these excited young fellows from making any trouble. Within the first few days I had to make all the decisions about how the machinery of government was to be set in working order again.

And I had no experience or knowledge of the mechanism of public administration. Some of the high officials I dismissed immediately but I kept most of them on. Within the first few weeks of our régime the men whom you call *Geheimräte* [Right Honorable Privy Councilors] saw that we were not to be trifled with."

## 5

It was with mixed feelings that I paid my first visit to Mussolini, in the spring of 1929. He had already been in power for six years. He seemed definitely militarist. The murder of the Socialist leader, Matteotti, had seriously damaged Mussolini's prestige. Some of the outstanding leaders of European thought were strongly against him. Everybody knew that some of Mussolini's closest associates were mixed up in the Matteotti murder. Many of the ideals I had grown up with and had worked for since the close of the war were only half-heartedly subscribed to by him and many others were definitely banned from publication through the medium of the press censorship and the silencing of the Opposition. My friends and I thought at that time that if the ideas of this dictator were brought across the Alps into Germany they would there find a classic soil for their growth. For the Germans, and not the Italians, are the people who love Obedience. They are born with a bias towards it and they are educated to it. They are congenitally disposed to follow a leader in blind obedience rather than think out political problems for themselves. For a century of bourgeois rule in Germany, undisturbed by any revolutionary movements, Italy presents the spectacle of a chronically recurrent revolutionary challenge to the old feudal power of the bourgeoisie in the city-states and the principalities. And added to this there was the periodical upheaval of various contradictory elements in Italy against the temporal sway of the papacy. My friends and I were first attracted by the social features of Mussolini's revolution. I mean that part of his program which established an organization for the protection of the working classes. But of course we were opposed to the policy of shackling the press and prohibiting the free expression of opinion. When I first came to visit him I certainly felt more against him than for him.

The mental picture of Mussolini which is generally formed by the outside public is by no means true to life. As one enters the marvelous hall on which the master craftsmen of four centuries have lavished their artistic genius it appears at first to be quite empty. Soon a man stands up at a desk at the far end about twenty yards distant and approaches the center of the hall to greet his visitor. He is rather small and of stocky build. At first one is somewhat surprised to notice the delicate and almost feminine hands. But that feeling changes the moment he grasps the hand of the guest. It is a manly and firm shake. The deep black eyes and the large domed forehead are in striking contrast. And here you have an illustration of the basic contradiction that underlies Mussolini's whole nature. Like every man of creative genius, he is a combination of masculine and feminine qualities, the Act and the Dream.

I had long conversations with him, mostly on general problems. When we touched on questions of political science he was very keen and gave examples from his own career to illustrate theories which he sometimes sponsored and sometimes rejected. The first feature that struck me during these conversations was his perfect naturalness and absence of pose. But if one studies him while he is speaking to a crowd of twenty thousand from a balcony, then one realizes at once that he is consciously endeavoring to produce an effect. Great actors are generally simple and natural in private intercourse. But on the stage every great actor must calculate and adopt the means which will secure an effect with his audience. Otherwise he would not be an exponent of his art. The heroes in Homer had to play their rôle. And the kings of olden times had to parade as spectacular figures before the eyes of their people. But that was only one branch of their activities and by no means the most important one. The real work of the statesman is done in his office.

The gigantic size of the office in which Mussolini works is due to the Roman tradition and also to his liking for the antique. He has the Roman taste for massive external proportions and at the same time a gift for effective detail. He is like a painter who outlines an enormous fresco but paints in delicate arabesques with his own hand. "I don't like things to be *à peu près*," he told me. I heard the same from more than half a dozen political leaders and scientific inventors. The simplicity of the black suit, which he usually wears, suggests a striking contrast with the ribbons and medals that the public expects him to wear on special occasions. The public looks for signs and symbols but Mussolini has too much to do to be always acting.

His desk is almost clear of papers; for the complexity of the work he is engaged upon demands the exactness of the pedant. The greater the task a man has to fulfill the tidier his writing desk will be found. Only the bohemian who does not succeed in anything cultivates disorder among his papers and groans that he has no time to do this or that. The man who has much to do is the man who gets through his work effectively.

Because Mussolini has thought for a long time over the problems he discusses he is decisive in his answers. But if he has not an answer ready he looks silently into his interlocutor's face, a gesture which I prefer even to the best answer that could be hoped for. It gives the opportunity to make a sudden transition to another question along a different line. The look which he gives thus is not harsh when he has a stranger face to face. It might probably be otherwise if he were facing one of his forty million Italians. Meeting him alone it seems to be permissible only to strangers who want no favors of him to give expression to out-of-date ideas.

I once saw him decide an official question within a few minutes. I had brought him a request from an Italian peasant who had some complaints to make. His face changed when he took the letter in his hand. It became hard. He conned the lines studiously, stuck out his chin in the usual manner and put on the proud majestic look of a judge. I had brought the written request with me because I wished to study him for a few minutes when he would be engaged on something that had no relation to myself. My purpose was to get an idea of how he worked with his officials. He immediately addressed a letter to the prefect of the province wherein the peasant woman lived, so that an inquiry should be made. After a few weeks I heard the result of this investigation.

"Don't these things bring you pleasure?" I asked.

"Very much. I have dealt with more than a million of such individual cases within the past few years."

"And is not that a better claim to fame than whole colonies like Tripoli?"

There was a long interval of silence. He gave me the silent look and then he suddenly put me a question which led the conversation off in another direction.

Another time I asked him why he made such bellicose speeches in the spring of 1930.

"We had been irritated and I had to convince myself how far the nation would follow me in case of an emergency. When I had ascertained that it would follow me to a man in case of necessity I delivered a speech over the radio which gave assurances of peace in the opening of nineteen-thirty-one. And here again I was convinced that the feeling of the nation was with me. I have never urged people on to war. All constructive men need peace."

There are four reasons why I, as a convinced pacifist, consider Mussolini a guaranty of peace in Europe in spite of his bellicose utterances. The four reasons are as follows: First, he is a constructive statesman, desiring to lift his people to a higher standard of living and give them a more forward place among the nations. In doing this he has to take into account that, even in the event of a successful issue, any war in which the nation might engage would be bound to inflict injury from which it would take innumerable years to recover. In the second place, Mussolini is not a military man himself, and in case of war he would have to confide the destiny of the country to the hands of some general on whose capability he could not infallibly count. Here he is in quite a different position from that of Napoleon. During the last ten years he has taken all decisions on his own shoulders. In such circumstances, is it likely that he would knowingly walk into a situation wherin he would have to surrender his control?

On this dilemma he once spoke very dramatically to me. More-over, every dictator is conscious of the envy and ambition of his rivals and the big opportunities which a war might bring them. Finally, there is the character of the Italian people. Mus-solini knows these people and he knows how difficult it is to shake them out of their traditional ways, especially in the South. The sting of his appeal arouses these gay people to work, whereas the same goad might suddenly drive the Germans to war.

"But what happens," I asked, "if the national enthusiasm which you enkindle in the people should urge them eventually into war?"

"Are you a motorist? Good. So long as you feel the brake under your foot you can drive at a speed of sixty miles an hour without any danger."

"I read that on your first official journey, I think it was through Sicily, you always drove your car yourself. If the kings had driven their own horses long ago instead of shutting them-selves in closed carriages away from the eyes of the people, they might be sitting on their thrones today."

"Of course. It is well to let the peasant and the villages see that a responsible man can conduct the vehicle in which he travels. I thought of that myself as a boy when one of the big people from the outside world visited our village."

Thus he took his own experience as a guide in mending the mistakes made by former régimes and with that lead he strove to be a social force. Bernard Shaw, the ablest of all European Socialists, said to me once: "In spite of his dictatorship, Musso-lini practices more positive socialism than many of his adversaries whose names are inscribed in the party roll. People will keep on wondering where he is driving to."

### 6

Twenty thousand men filled the Piazza Venezia. A dozen bands crashed in mutual rivalry. Songs and slogans and hurrahs reverberated from the big walls on every side. It was a Fascist festival and they wanted to see the *Duce*. The palace, usually a tranquil building sunk in the dreams of the past, was accessible to me today only with the help of an officer. The staircases and corridors were thronged with men in uniform. In his great hall the Duce was alone, but in uniform. The King of Egypt once told me that the thoughts which filled his mind when he was clad in his uniform were different from those he had when in civilian dress. He meant that they were weaker. I myself have noticed that an officer alone among civilians feels dressed up and therefore uncomfortable, just as a civilian isolated among a hundred uniformed people thinks his position anomalous. Nor have I ever heard two officers in uniform talking philosophy to each other, any more than I have ever seen two philosophers sparring with their fists like a pair of boxers. Each of these anomalies would be possible, however. Though Mussolini looked quite strange to me in uniform, he was in the same frame of mind as always. The noise in the square made the continuance of our more philosophical discussions impossible. So I began to talk to him about Abyssinia. He continued walking to and fro in the room until an officer came to inquire whether the balcony windows were to be thrown open. He called for his cap, told me to watch from the adjoining window and asked me to return to him as soon as the demonstration came to an end. He had not a minute left in which to think over the speech that he was about to make. When he stepped out on the veranda in response to the reiterated shouts of the crowd, I studied his profile and noticed the firmness which he exhibits when he is speaking of constructive work. As he surveyed the throng beneath the balcony and remained for a moment silent, he reminded me of a playwright who comes into the theatre and finds the actors impatiently waiting for him to superintend the rehearsal.

Suddenly he gave a sign and the noise in the piazza ceased. His features became tense. He barked his opening words at the audience in a vigorous staccato. He had uttered no more than thirty sentences when the shouting reverberated again. As the balcony windows closed, rhythmical calls of "Duce! Duce!" came through the doors of the hall. He ordered the doors to be opened and then about sixty Fascists rushed into the room and gathered around his writing table. They were the secretaries of the party from all quarters of Italy. No ceremony or formality intruded on the friendly reception. In a soft, low-pitched voice, Mussolini began to address each of them, not by name, but by the name of the town from which he had come, pointing to the person concerned. Occasionally he hesitated and had to ask which was which. But most of them he recognized without any difficulty. They all looked up to him as to a father although some of them have been at least as old as himself. Finally they renewed their chanting and cheers and withdrew from the hall.

Mussolini went back towards the desk but stood for a few moments in front of the fireplace. Seeing on the floor an Order which one of the visitors had dropped, he picked it up and sat at his desk. He rang a bell and when the servant entered he called across the space of sixty feet to ask where I was. Whereupon I emerged from the deep window niche where I had been standing out of view. He smiled at me and the thought flashed across my mind that anybody hidden away as I had been might easily have assassinated him. It is not true to say that the Duce is watched like a Czar. Although his speech from the window and his reception of the secretaries had interrupted our talk, he resumed the conversation precisely where it had broken off half an hour earlier, as if nothing had happened.

Mussolini can be understood only if we realize that he is Latin. He is a pupil and admirer of Nietzsche, who always declared himself to be a man of the Mediterranean type. "I am an incorrigible Italian," he told me. "For me the noblest of all the arts is architecture, for it embraces all. Roman architecture, of course. To Greece I was attracted only by its philosophy."

"I will explain the development of my mind to you," he declared to me another time. "In my youth I believed in nothing. In vain I called on God that he might save my mother, but she died. Besides, anything mystic is foreign to my temperament, as were the colors and the sounds in the monastery in which I was educated. Just as Renan did, I admit that once in a million years perhaps a supernatural phenomenon may have taken place and that therefore Nature may be the work of God. But I have never witnessed a spiritual phenomenon. It may also happen that within another million years a similar supernatural phenomenon may happen. That might happen even within the ambit of the laws of nature, like gravity or death. As I grew older the belief became stronger that there might be a divine power ruling in the universe."

"A Christian power?"

"A divine power," he repeated with a gesture which did not answer my question. "Mankind can praise God in many ways. One must leave that to the individual."

"Granted," I said. "What way have you discovered out of the dilemma which the classic dramas dealt with? Why should man take any initiative at all if Fate leads him along a predestined way?"

Mussolini did not seem to see any problem here.

"Fatalism must be countered with the human will power. That is an interesting struggle. The will has to prepare the ground on which the laws of destiny will unfold themselves."

"And what place has the urge to glory or fame in this struggle?" I asked. "Is not fame the strongest motive force for any ruler, the only warrant against death? Has the vision of it not hovered before you since your boyhood days? And has it not inspired your whole work?"

Mussolini remained imperturbed. "Fame did not light my path in boyhood," he said, "and I do not hold with you that it is the strongest of motives. You are right in saying that it is a consolation to think that one will not wholly die. But my work has never been wholly inspired by the desire for fame. Immortality is the seal of fame. But that only comes afterwards." He made a sweeping gesture to indicate the impenetrable distance.

"Recently," I said, "I read in somebody's room here a proverb which made a strong impression on me. It ran *Oltre il Destino* (Beyond Destiny)."

"Was that a man who had already challenged Destiny?"

"Of course," I said, and mentioned the name of one of the great airmen.

"That is not my motto," said Mussolini. "Nobody may chal

lenge Destiny more than once. Anyhow, everybody meets the death that is in harmony with his character."

Naturally a dictator who governs in Rome must try to win the Pope to his side, just as the German Emperors did throughout a long thousand years, unless he is ready to rule as a vassal. So long as the Pope was a prisoner in the Vatican he was powerful. Mussolini's policy was to persuade this prisoner to come out and be free. When he finally succeeded, against the opposition of leading cardinals, nobody knew exactly who was victorious in this trial of wits. Even today you will get contradictory answers from men of quite independent views who are the most competent to give an opinion on the question. The King of Italy, with whom I spoke soon after the healing of the old breach with the Vatican, said, "I think it was fair on both sides." Anyhow it is a unique instance in history that negotiations between two independent rulers in the same city could be carried on for three years without either seeing the other. When Mussolini finally visited the Vatican he did not recognize the Pope as a spiritual ruler in the ceremonial way. When I asked him about this, he said: "Generally I abide by the rules of the country in which I am a guest. But before I went to the Vatican I had arranged that I should be dispensed from the duty of kneeling and kissing the Pope's hand." This action on Mussolini's part can be explained only by the spirit of resentment against the insatiable power of the papacy which is looked upon with misgiving by every statesman. As an accessory factor of leading importance there was also Mussolini's pride, which prevented him from bending the knee to God himself and therefore to His representative on earth.

This pride is one of the strongest traits in his character. Once as a young man in Switzerland an Italian made him a present of five lire. He took an Arabian knife from his pocket and gave it in return to the donor. That little act struck me as more eloquent than any other of his that I had heard of. At the age of nineteen he was arrested by the police in Zürich and treated as a major criminal. While still in their hands, he shouted. "Wait. The day of vengeance will come." A little while afterwards he was arrested in Austria and deported. When he was conducted to the frontier an official allowed him to go free on his own word of honor. Once in Lausanne his employer threw him his week's wages with the taunt that his work had not been satisfactory and that the taking of wages for it amounted to stealing the money. Mussolini immediately sprang at the man's throat.

We see the same trait of character uppermost at a trial of socialists which took place in Milan some time afterwards. Mussolini admitted seven points of the charge against him and opposed only one. This was to the effect that by destroying some telegraph wires he had imperiled the safety of a railway train. It was the same sort of pride that made him look upon the Peace of Versailles as the humiliation of a people rather than a wrong. He gave an example of the same pride when he attended the Conference of Cannes as a journalist in 1922. At the frontier they gave him five hundred francs in exchange for a thousand Italian lire. His pride boiled up and he swore that he would change that. When he came to power and was able to stabilize the lira at a higher level than the French franc his personal pride had to endure a certain amount of humiliation, because the financial authorities held it to be a false step. But the rulers of this earth do not always act wisely. The best of them are led astray by their visions.

This pride had developed a feeling of self-esteem in him long before he achieved any outer success. It has made him feel like a plastic artist. On this point he said to me once: "If I feel the masses in my hands as they think or if I mingle with them and become mobbed by them, then I feel a part of this mass of people. And yet I have a certain aversion to them, as the artist has towards the material he works on. Sometimes the sculptor will smash the marble in rage because it does not lend itself with sufficient pliancy to the shape he wishes to evoke from it. Here the material rebels against the will of the artist. The important thing is to rule the masses as an artist dominates his material." In his first manifesto to the workers, he wrote: "I shall set the example." And he has been giving that example since the first day he took over power. He avoids the Roman society that throngs around him and he spends about sixteen hours a day at work, just as did the great Russian leader whom the Fascist leader resembles in essentials.

Such a life, directed only by energy and pride, can maintain itself free of all skepticism only by faith in its own mission. For this reason Mussolini speaks sometimes of Destiny and of the stars which protected him as a soldier during the war and saved him when he was seriously wounded. In 1920 his motor car came into collision with a train, through a mistake made by the chauffeur, and several persons were killed. Of this incident Mussolini said: "I felt that the hatred of my enemies protected me as a talisman." When he was learning to fly and once fell from a height of one hundred fifty feet, his escape did not make him wonder in the least. Next day he carried on with his lessons as usual.

In the late hours of that night on which he journeyed by train from Milan to Rome to take over power he called to heaven for its aid, in his own way, and spoke of the invisible help his dead mother was giving him. To that extent he is definitely superstitious, as every man is who entrusts his whole life to a certain work and thus seeks to stand in well with the invisible powers. He often spoke to me of mascots and when I asked him why he ran gratuitous risks such as flying, he said: "Life has a prize and it must always be risked. Today I challenged it again."

On another occasion I mentioned the fact that the people and their leaders often speak of war as the work of Fate. He laughed and looked at me mischievously, saying: "It is only their mistakes that they attribute to Fate."

7

A stranger like myself, who has no party affiliations whatsoever and whose point of view is purely historical, must judge contemporary events as if they were a part of history. He must try to estimate them in their general bearing and not be led astray by the complaints of individuals. He must place the positive benefits which accrue to the nation above the personal losses of individual citizens. If I had been born a Frenchman under the Napoleonic régime, I know that I should have hated the Emperor and would probably have fled the country. But a hundred years later I look upon him with admiration as a marvelous historical phenomenon. When Italian friends complain of the coercion that exists under the Fascist régime, I believe all they say and thank my stars that for my own part I am free to write as I wish.

When Napoleon was at St. Helena he read in a newspaper a story to the effect that he had buried invaluable treasures somewhere or other. "What!" he cried out. "Have I buried my treasures? They are open to every man to see them in the light of day. The harbors of Antwerp and Flushing, the hydraulic works at Dunkirk, Le Hâvre and Nice, the great dock at Cherbourg, the harbor at Venice, the highway from Antwerp to Amsterdam, from Mainz to Metz, the passes over the Simplon and Mont Cenis. Then there are the bridges in Paris, the Tours and Lyons bridges. The establishment of new industries, the new Louvre, the Napoleon Museum, the millions which were spent on land reclamation and horse-breeding. These are the treasures which Napoleon amassed. They are worth billions and they will endure for centuries."

Mussolini might answer in much the same tone, except that the list of his works would have to be confined to Italy. Within the first eight years of his régime, that is to say, from 1922 to the end of 1930, twenty-five milliards of lire (roughly speaking, $1,300,000,000) were spent on public works. Of this sum 2.5 milliards were expended on the building of roads, 1.7 milliards for waterworks and aqueducts, 1 milliard for harbors, 1 milliard for reconstruction after earthquakes, 2 milliards for railways. I have not been able to compare these with the figures for the preceding eight years; but a glance at the annual budget is sufficient to show that the former expenditure cannot be compared with that of the Fascist decade. Anyone who lived in Italy for several years, as I did, and now goes through the country again,

cannot fail to be struck by the improvements which are everywhere visible and which sometimes bring a sigh into the soul
of those romantics who bewail the passing of the old easy-going
times. But the truth is that nothing has been lost. In the small
towns and villages the men of all ages still gather on the piazza
as they did before and at half past eleven wander around leisurely in the sun.

Naturally all these undertakings, the building of new roads
and railways and harbors everywhere, were initiated for an
internal political purpose and the widespread unemployment
made them more or less necessary. It is true, too, that Mussolini
did not think out the general plan of all this activity. He copied
much from the Russians. But the actual putting of the work in
hand was due to his ardent energy and his faculty for coming
to quick decisions and getting things done. Therefore he is entitled to call these works his own.

From north to south many roads have been reconstructed and
three new motor highways have been built. New canals have
been constructed and others have been widened. In the province
of Puglia a huge aqueduct has been erected across the Apen-
nines and a system of waterworks has been established which
will bring drinking water to every village in Italy. Seeing that
Italy has no coal, a huge system has been implanted for the
production of electricity by hydraulic power. New railways have
penetrated unknown quarters of the country. The old railways
have been improved and the trains speeded up. The harbors
have been enlarged and deepened and a new commercial harbor has been built at Venice. In the Pontine marshes gigantic
works have been completed which were dreamed of two thousand years ago by the Romans and vainly attempted by several
papal governments. Thousands of square miles of territory in
which it was impossible for human life to exist have now been
reclaimed and made fit for human dwelling. Within the next
decade hundreds of thousands will be able to build their homes
in a region that has hitherto been a deadly prey to malaria.
When I saw all this I quoted for Mussolini the concluding part
of *Faust* which runs thus:

Ein Sumpf zieht am Gebirge hin,
Verpestet alles schon Errungene;
Den faulen Pfuhl auch abzuziehn,
Das Letzte wär das Höchsterrungene.
Eröffn' ich Räume vielen Millionen,
Nicht sicher zwar, doch tätig frei zu wohnen.

A swamp extends towards the mountains,
It poisons all that has been up to now reclaimed
To abolish this cesspool
Would be a supreme achievement.
I open a dwelling space for many millions,
Not indeed to live there without risk, but in free activity.

Giant ships of 50,000 tons are now sailing under the Italian flag, carrying men and merchandise across the seas. An entirely new air fleet has been constructed. Three new universities have been founded, the old modernized, and in Perugia a university for foreigners has been established. The standard of all elementary schools has been raised by the dictator, who was first a schoolmaster himself. Attendance fees have been reduced or entirely abolished, and in the South illiteracy has been almost wiped out. In Rome, Ostia and Pompeii excavations have been carried out on a large scale and new archaeological treasures have been brought to light. With an energy that rivals the Russian example, the private interests of the worker, his wife and children, have been taken under the care of the state even to the extent of looking after their pleasures. At the same time the worker is insured against times of distress. "We take hold of the citizen when he is six years old and return him to his family when he is sixteen," Mussolini once told me. With this formula he copies the Russian practice, and admits it. We individualists turn with horror from the idea of nationalizing and standardizing human beings. And, while recognizing the dangers of both systems, we are and will remain individualists.

All that I have described could have come only from a man who is dominated by his imagination, but who at the same time directs the activity of that imagination. Mussolini told me that when he took over power he had no prepared plan, but that all these undertakings slowly developed from a resolute drive towards constructive action. The work a modern statesman has to perform is much more complex than it was in the days of Julius Caesar or even of Napoleon. I once said to Mussolini that many people think a leading man is at the peak of his genius from morning until night. He answered: "Inspiration comes to a man only twice a year at the most." All the rest is routine and detailed work. I heard the same words from Edison, but in a more ironical way: "Two per cent of inspiration," said he, "and ninety-eight per cent of perspiration." Everybody whose work is creative can verify this percentage by his own experience.

And yet Inspiration and Imagination are the wings on which the superior man is lifted so that he can view the whole scope of his activities from above. When he comes down to earth he has to work with his hands. This inspired vision may be discerned from studying a photograph of Mussolini when he was only nineteen years old. It is the vision of a poet. And it can be detected in the portraits taken of ll great men when they were young. In later life the head, and generally also the body, grows larger, not merely through eating and enjoyment but also through the expenditure of energy and hard work.

Mussolini's head has changed with the passing of time. One man, however, who does not know whether he ought to call Mussolini friend or enemy, declares that he has known him since 1915 and that he has not changed a whit since then. This observer, who is one of the outstanding figures in Italy, may have anticipated in the Mussolini of 1915 the man who took over supreme control of Italy in 1922. It was the unconscious forecast of his imagination. If I were a painter I should at the present moment be able to draw a portrait of Mussolini at the age of sixty.

But no man must forecast how the hand of Fate will work. If he have his own presentiments, he ought to remain silent.

# JOHN GUNTHER

TO people who through books, press, and radio keep abreast of current history the name of John Gunther can scarcely be unfamiliar. This fast-traveling foreign correspondent whom Harold J. Laski, British historian, calls "one of the best reporters now living," has interviewed almost every important head of state and observed nearly every war since the World War. Best known for his *Inside Europe,* a non-fiction best seller since 1936 which has been translated into twelve languages and suppressed in three countries, he is also author of other books and articles which X-ray the inner workings of modern history. The most recent volume is *Inside Asia* (1939), from which comes the following sketch.

Mr. Gunther was born in Chicago in 1901, educated at the University of Chicago, and given his first journalistic job in 1922 by *The Chicago Daily News,* becoming its assistant London correspondent in 1924. He was married in 1927, and has one son. From 1926 to 1935 he "worked" a territory which included Paris, Berlin, Rome, Scandinavia, the Near East, Geneva, Spain, Moscow, Vienna, and the Balkans. He was his paper's chief London correspondent from 1935 to 1936, when he resigned to give himself entirely to his own writing—not at first to the vein of fiction-writing which produced four novels between 1924 and 1928, but to his professional forte of political commentary. Recently he has turned to the writing of a long historical novel.

The following portrait of Chiang Kai-shek—and of his wife—should be considered for what it is, journalistic biography; that is, biography written because it is the best way of explaining complex circumstances and personalities, but written under both the stimulus and the pressure of immediate events, written perhaps in one sweep from cumulative notes and impressions, and cabled home to press. Writing done under such conditions and by one habituated to them is likely to differ somewhat in structure and pace from the more leisurely portraiture of a studio artist. What it loses and what it gains the reader is left to discover for himself. If he wishes to see how John Gunther writes when large masses of documentary material must be digested in a chapter or two, let him read the sections on Hitler, Mussolini, and Stalin in *Inside Europe.*

## GENERALISSIMO CHIANG KAI-SHEK

CHIANG KAI-SHEK, the son of a village merchant, who became China's generalissimo and political leader, is a psychological puzzle. He is a terrific disciplinarian; but the enemies he has forgiven—and given jobs to—are many. He has united China (with help from Japan!) more than any man in centuries of history—but he spent ten dreary years fighting civil wars against his own people. He is a popular leader of the stature of Stalin or Mussolini—but he is a bad politician.

He is a strong Chinese nationalist—but he got much of his education in Japan. He is an extremely typical Chinese—who nevertheless believes in Christianity and the Y.M.C.A.

Physically rather slight, wiry, with delicate features, Chiang carries himself with a curious elastic grace. He is quite tall—five feet ten—but is rather short-legged, and likes to be photographed sitting down, or wearing the broad black cloak that is his favorite costume. He weighs 141 pounds. His eyes are remarkable: a very dark grey, deep, both piercing and luminous, and never at rest.

He rises early—at dawn usually—and works hard till nightfall. He thinks that the time between dawn and breakfast is the best hour of the day. He likes to lie down, and does as much of his work as he can on a sofa. After lunch he takes a brief nap, usually falling asleep to the tune of a wheezy old gramophone. His favorite record is Schubert's *Ave Maria;* his friends in the next room know that he is asleep when the record stops. In the afternoon he has half an hour for prayer or meditation.

He is abstemious and methodical. He does not drink or smoke, he avoids even coffee and tea, and for many years has kept a very full diary. Chiang's diary, it might fairly be said, once saved his life. When he was kidnaped in December, 1936, by a group of Sian mutineers led by the sallow-faced Chang Hsueh-liang, young war lord who protested Nanking's passive policy toward Japan, Chiang's diary was carefully examined. After reading not only the diary but a number of letters to his wife, his kidnapers were impressed enough to change radically their attitude toward him.

The things he likes best are poetry, mountains, and his wife. His idea of a really good time, if he ever has time to have a good time, is to walk in hilly country on a sunny day, or to have a picnic lunch outdoors. When he walks he recites poetry. His family life is happy, and Madame Chiang is his indispensable and beloved associate, but he is definitely a lonely man, a person who admires solitude. His closest foreign friend is W. H. Donald, the Australian newspaper man who has been his unofficial "adviser" for some years. Another good friend is an American missionary, Dr. George Shepherd.

The Generalissimo is sensitive and sometimes stand-offish. He seldom sees people socially. When touring the provinces, he gives the proper official dinner to the local dignitaries, and then makes no further attempt to see them. When thousands of deliriously happy Chinese sought to celebrate a victory in March, 1938, by gathering outside his house and cheering, he wanted to send them home without a word; his advisers had to appeal to him not to clear the streets. He does not like people in the abstract—or even the particular.

But when the Generalissimo and Madame Chiang see a foreign visitor, they are conspicuously urbane. Madame Chiang interprets for him, since his only foreign language is Japanese; I had the feeling, however, that he knew more English than he admitted. Madame (everywhere in China she is known simply as "Madame") knows his mind so well that there are no pauses, no interruptions. The Generalissimo is not a time-waster. When I saw him, he first paid a pleasant compliment to my wife, then asked if I would explain the "European situation" in "one or two" sentences. I did my best. He receives journalists for official interviews only rarely.

On occasion the Generalissimo is closely guarded—for instance, he has a bullet-proof limousine with windows almost an inch thick—but at times he mixes freely with his people. My wife and I once saw him on the crowded Hankow Bund, walking along, apparently quite alone. He was so inconspicuous that few people in the crowd noticed him. Members of his bodyguard did accompany him, but about 200 feet away.

Chiang has no hobbies, no relaxations, except reading—especially the Chinese classics. His favorite passage from Confucius is:

In order to rule the country, one must first rule one's family;
In order to rule the family, one must first regulate one's body by moral training;
In order to regulate the body, one must first regulate one's mind;
In order to regulate the mind, one must first be sincere in one's intentions;
In order to be sincere in intentions, one must first increase one's knowledge.

Chiang was born in the village of Chikow, in the central coastal district of Fenghua, Chekiang province, in 1887. He was certainly not of a rich family, but he was never desperately poor. The family slaved to send him to school, where his record was not brilliant. He was a dutiful boy, however. In 1907 he cut off his queue—symbol that he intended to be "modern." He studied first at the Paoting Military Academy near Peking, then in Japan where he entered the Shinbo Gokyo, or Military Staff College. He actually served several years in the Japanese army.

In Japan he met Dr. Sun Yat-sen, father of the Chinese revolution. This was in 1909, when Chiang was 22. Dr. Sun was in exile. Promptly young Chiang became infected with Chinese nationalism. He stayed in Japan two more years, but he joined the Tungmenghui, a secret society of patriotic Chinese which was the forerunner of the Kuomintang. When, in 1911, the Manchu regime was overthrown in Peking and the Chinese republic was born, Chiang instantly set sail for China to join the revolution, though this meant technical desertion from the Japanese army. It is recorded that punctiliously he sent back his sword and uniform—by mail!

For five years, roughly from 1911 to 1916, Chiang fought in the variety of minor civil wars and insurrections that implemented the revolution. He was one of Sun's best subordinates, but in 1917 he quit the army suddenly to go into business. He knew that for a successful political career he had to have money—a lot of money. He set out to earn it. First he worked as a clerk in a brokerage house. His consequence as a human being must have been strongly marked, because he was successively "adopted" by two rich and influential men, who became his patrons and helped him win his fortune.

By 1921 Chiang was busy with military affairs and politics again—i.e., he was a revolutionist. In 1923 Sun Yat-sen sent him to Moscow, where he spent six months as a liaison officer. In Moscow he saw Trotsky, among others. By 1925 Chiang was chairman of the standing committee of the Kuomintang, and when Dr. Sun Yat-sen died he assumed office as commander-in-chief of the nationalist army.

In 1926 began Chiang's most amazing exploit. He set out on the gigantic, the illimitable, task of unifying China by military conquest. At this time the Kuomintang held power only in the extreme south; the Nationalists were considered in Shanghai to be little more than a gang of undisciplined reds; Chiang Kai-shek himself was called an obscure "Bolshevik." It is quite true that many forces helped Chiang in the campaigns that then electrified the world. The country was sagging with corruption and decay. Rival war lords were eliminating each other endlessly. Not much stiff resistance was encountered. Even so, his achievement was remarkable. He fought with arms; he fought with money. His armies (he himself was sometimes in the background) captured Wuchang in October, 1926; Hangchow in February, 1927; Shanghai and Nanking in March, 1927; Peking in July, 1928. This campaign is one of the seminal facts of modern history. Chiang made China, which was a continent, into a country—at least for the time being.

Then, having consolidated China into what might have been a permanent modern entity, he disrupted it! Ten weary years of civil war began. Why?

At this point we must inspect background. In 1921, Dr. Sun had announced his Three Principles, which in theory at least are still the determining motives of Chinese political action. They were (1) Nationalism, (2) Democracy, (3) People's Livelihood. By this the eminent doctor meant that China must, by abrogating the foreign concessions, achieve proper national unity; that the

country must be prepared for self-government through the establishment of democratic principles, with free elections to a national legislature; and that livelihood must be assured the starving
millions by social reform, economic advance, and the redistribu-
tion of wealth. The gigantic nature of Dr. Sun's task may be
gathered from the fact that, until he invented it, no *word* for
democracy existed in Chinese.

In 1921 Dr. Sun needed help—badly. The western powers
would have nothing to do with his struggling revolution, which
might end their own privileges. They didn't want China strong;
they didn't want China united. Dr. Sun turned to Soviet Russia.
He sent Chiang to Moscow.

Russian political advisers then came to Canton, like Michael
Borodin; Russian influence in the Kuomintang (National People's
Party) spread, though the Kuomintang, it is important to state,
never was a communist organization. When, in 1927, Chiang
captured Hankow, a government influenced by the communists
was established, though it was never a "communist" government.
But a Chinese variety of communism, which was largely a program of agricultural reform, surged like wildfire through the
left-wing of the Kuomintang, inflaming and irradiating the land-
less peasants. It was perhaps inevitable that the Kuomintang
should split. The right wing, thinking mostly of Dr. Sun's first
principle, nationalism, found itself more and more at variance
with the left wing, which emphasized the third principle, social
equality. The breach widened; the split became irremediable; and
civil war broke out. The leftist government in Hankow was overthrown (1927). Chiang overthrew it.

Chiang went to the right. His friends were dumbfounded. He
seemed to be destroying wantonly a large part of the program
of the revolution. He seemed to be betraying his pledges, his
friends, and the memory of Dr. Sun. Chiang, the revolutionist,
became a counter-revolutionary. His former associates and broth-
ers-in-arms, who joined the left, were ruthlessly hunted out and
extirpated. A white terror of unexampled ferocity struck China.
Chiang might have been a revolutionist; but he never was a

"radical." And he came to feel that the revolution was bound to be destroyed unless he could make it respectable—that is, get the support of the powerful business and foreign interests in Shanghai and the Yangtze Valley. He went to Shanghai, bowed to the bankers and international concessionnaires (whom he had promised to throw out) and became their man.

Later his anti-Red campaigns served several important corollary purposes. His long pursuit of the Reds gave him an excuse to put his national army in many Chinese provinces which otherwise he could not easily have invaded. Again, the Red heresy gave him something concrete to attack persistently: an item useful to a nationalist dictator.

Chiang's ten-year series of "pacification campaigns" were unsuccessful. He tried literally to bleed China "white"; he didn't quite do it. The communists never succumbed, and never surrendered. Finally came the kidnaping in Sian and, as a result, a volte-face as astonishing on Chiang Kai-shek's part as the first one. The communists had Chiang at their mercy, he who had murdered so many of their men; and they let him go. The reconciliation was as remarkable as the original split. Chiang made a United Front with these "enemies." After terrible dilemmas, terrible delays, a new chapter in Chinese history began.

The keynote to the Generalissimo's remarkable character is his stubbornness, his tenacity. This delicately featured soldier is a bull-dog. He has no tact. During the Sian kidnaping he dug himself in, emotionally, morally, and never budged—and kept begging his captors to kill him! His Sian diary gravely notes that Shao, the civil governor, advised him to be more "lenient" in his conversation with the Young Marshal, his captor! Chiang talked to the Young Marshal with complete confidence, and never glossed over his contempt for those who had captured him.

There is cruelty in his character, and the ruthlessness of his war against the communists is well known. He had thousands of people executed, many of them for no crime except that they disagreed with him. He is shrewd, suspicious, calculating, and not above the use of guile. On the other hand, both his physical and moral courage are indisputable. He has proved more than once that he has no fear of death.

He is so sure of himself that he is willing to wait until others see their errors, admit that he is right, and come to him repentant. Thus the extraordinary succession of war lords who, after revolts, have been pardoned, paid soundly, and sent abroad to "recuperate their health." Chiang in this way turns his late enemies into valuable supporters.

Another characteristic is his almost illimitable, dogged patience. Five years ago Chiang was submissively bowing to Japanese demands. He lost Manchuria; he lost Jehol; he saw Inner Mongolia threatened; yet for years he made no resistance, said nothing against the Japanese, and indeed punished Chinese who did. Several of his best officers, appalled at what they called his weakness, his pro-Japanese policy, flared up in civil wars. Still Chiang did nothing. Then the war of 1937, still raging, broke out. Chiang fought. But copies of secret lectures delivered in 1934 prove that even then he was passionately telling his best officers in confidence that eventually they must fight Japan; he implored them to prepare themselves for the war that was bound to come. Chiang probably knew, in the early 30's, that successful Chinese resistance was impossible; that at all costs the Chinese must buy off Japanese attack until the last minute, at which time they might have a chance to win.

Chiang makes shrewd use of money. Early in the war he invented a system of wound bounties unique in military annals; he paid bonuses for wounds. Every private soldier wounded in action in China gets $10 (Chinese) per wound which is more solid satisfaction to the realistic Chinese than a stripe on the sleeve. Officers get $30 to $50, and generals $100. The success of this system was immediate.

The Generalissimo's salary is $1,000 (Chinese dollars, worth roughly 25 cents in American money) per month. His private fortune is not believed to be great, though he made money freely in his early Shanghai days. The fortune of the Soong family, into which he married, is quite another matter. The Soongs are among the richest folk in China, and represent one of the most striking concentrations of power in the world; for the family includes not only the three Soong sisters, but Dr. H. H. Kung (the prime minister of China) and T. V. Soong, China's ablest financier.

The eldest Soong daughter is the present Madame Kung. The second daughter is the widow of Sun Yat-sen. Third is Mei-ling (often Anglicized into Mayling), Madame Chiang Kai-shek. All three daughters were brought up in a religious atmosphere; all went to missionary schools in China before completing their education in the United States, and all—most importantly—were associated from childhood with the Chinese revolution, for their father was Sun Yat-sen's trusted friend.

Madame Chiang, the youngest, is the most brilliant of the sisters. She is probably the second most important and powerful personage in China. Chiang makes his own decisions, but she is a competent adviser, a counselor, an indispensable agent for contact with foreigners and foreign opinion.

When he was 15, Chiang married the daughter of a neighbor, a Miss Mao of Fenghua. The marriage, arranged by his family, was terminated by divorce in 1921. This Madame Chiang is believed to be an old-style Chinese, with bound feet. The Generalissimo never sees her these days, though he continues to support her dutifully. She bore him one son, Ching-kuo, now about 30. Subsequently, he adopted another. After his divorce, the Generalissimo met Mei-ling Soong in Canton.

Madame is exceptionally good-looking and extremely *chic*. She went to Wellesley, and is perhaps a bit more Americanized than her sisters. She is alert, smoothly polished, full of graceful small talk, enormously competent.

Her courageous devotion to China and Chiang is beyond dispute. She goes everywhere; she does everything; she is like Mrs. Roosevelt. When an air raid comes, Madame Chiang drives up to the scene, sometimes in slacks or any costume, to superintend care of the wounded. She has been especially active in fostering rehabilitation work in rural areas, in encouraging development of simplified language instruction, and in the creation of the "New Life Movement," a popular program of self-help and betterment.

Her "last" message to Chiang at Sian, relayed by her brother, T. V. Soong, expressed a good deal of her character: "Should T. V. fail to return within three days, I will come to Shensi to live and die with you." (Chiang, reading this, records "My eyes got wet.") But Madame did not wait the stipulated three days; she arrived the next afternoon to make her husband's cause, his life, her own.

On October 23, 1930, Chiang Kai-shek was baptized into the Christian Church. All the Soongs are strong Christians, and when the Generalissimo was courting Madame, his suit was rejected at first because he was not a believer. Old Mme. Soong demanded that he adopt Christianity; the general, stubborn as always, said that she would think the less of him if he assumed a new religion merely to make marriage possible. She was impressed by this; then he promised that if the marriage took place, he would study Christianity seriously and become a convert if he came to believe in it.

Still his courtship met with disapproval, but Chiang was persistent. He interrupted the revolution; he rushed back and forth between Canton, Hankow and Shanghai; he was a man possessed. Finally, in 1927, Madame Kung, elder sister to Mei-ling, summoned a small group of newspaper men and, to their surprise, stated: "The general is going to marry my little sister." The marriage took place on December 1, 1927. Immediately after the ceremony Chiang said: "The work of the Revolution will now make greater progress, because henceforth I can bear my tremendous responsibility with peace at heart."

Subsequently he became a Christian, and is now a devout and even ardent believer. He chose "Why We Believe in Jesus" as the text for his most important radio address in 1938.

The Generalissimo is said to be as much in love with Madame today as in the days he courted her. His last message to her from Sian, when he thought he would die the next day, was, however, couched rather impersonally:

"As I have made up my mind to sacrifice my life, if necessary, for my country, please do not worry about me. I will never allow myself to do anything to make my wife ashamed of me or become unworthy of being a follower of Dr. Sun Yat-sen. Since I was born for the Revolution I will gladly die for the same cause."

Every Monday morning, wherever Chiang's government happens to be, a remarkable and significant ceremony occurs. About 600 men file briskly into a hall near his headquarters. The military band plays a march, and the audience comes to attention. Then everyone in the hall uncovers and bows three times to a portrait of Dr. Sun Yat-sen. One—two—three. The bows are made with precision and éclat. The Generalissimo then reads the testament of Dr. Sun Yat-sen, uttering it a sentence at a time, which the audience repeats. It is exactly like a prayer meeting and the reading of the gospels.

The Generalissimo asks silent meditation for three minutes and then delivers a lecture which lasts an hour or longer. He discusses the military situation, exhorts his officers and ministers to further efforts, scolds slackers, points out abuses, and issues moral injunctions. During the entire performance, the audience—which includes everyone of consequence in the government—must remain standing. When it is over, the General does not say thank you or *au revoir*, but simply a single abrupt word, "Completed!"

Chiang Kai-shek, after 30 years of revolution and civil war, has become the symbol of Chinese unity, the personification of Chinese resistance against Japan. The Japanese know this very well; they have announced that if they capture him he will be decapitated.

Probably Chiang is the strongest Chinese individual since the third century B.C. when the Great Wall was built. His friends say that he is happier now than they have ever known him, more poised, more confident. It is not hard to guess the reason. He himself is now trying to build another Great Wall—a wall to keep the Japanese out, to permit China an authentic national development, to allow China to belong to the Chinese. He is fighting a foreign invader, and not his own people.

# PHILIP GUEDALLA

LITERATURE is a house of many mansions, in the modern conservative wing of which Philip Guedalla dwells honorably among the historians for having written some of the best biographies of our time. "Historians" is said under advisement, since Mr. Guedalla sees biography as only an annex of history, "a branch of history devoted to the reconstruction of personal careers," instead of as an independent department of literature. In this he stands apart from Ludwig, Maurois, and most of the other moderns; but the distinction is not worth the pain of disagreement, since all readers of biography today have this gifted author to thank for many hours of sheer delight.

Philip Guedalla, born in 1889, was educated conventionally at Rugby and at Oxford (Balliol), where, besides being for a term president of the famous Oxford Union Society (1911), he further distinguished himself by publishing two pleasant volumes of prose and verse and by taking a First in Modern History and the degree of M.A. (1913). From the university he went directly to the Inner Temple, became a barrister, and began practicing law. Just before the World War broke out in 1914 he published his first historical work, *The Partition of Europe, 1715-1815*. During the War he was a legal adviser to the Contracts Department, the War Office, and the Ministry of Munitions, and organized and acted as secretary to the Flax Control Board (1917-20). In 1920 appeared the first of his books of short biographical sketches, *Supers and Supermen;* in 1921, *The Industrial Future;* and in 1922, *The Second Empire*, the brilliant study of Napoleon III with which his fame as a writer began. Thenceforth, retiring from legal practice, he divided his energy between letters and politics, standing several times for Parliament. Three more series of portraits came in rapid order: *Masters and Men* (1923), *A Gallery* (1924), and *Independence Day* (1926). It is from the last-named book, published in America as *Fathers of the Revolution*, that the following life of George III is taken. In 1926 Guedalla produced his second long biography, *Palmerston*, following it up two years later with a dual study, *Gladstone and Palmerston*. Again, after another series of delightful portraits, this time of real and imaginary Victorian ladies, in *Bonnet and Shawl: An Album* (1928), came another full-length life, *The Duke (Wellington,* 1931), and another "parallel" biography, *The Queen and Mr. Gladstone* (1933). These, taken with his recent books, *The Hundred Days* (1934), *The Hundred Years* (1936), and *The Hundredth Year* (1939), rank their author high as an historian of modern Europe.

Philip Guedalla, at his best, displays unusual biographical powers. Most valuable of these is his clear, graceful, expressive prose. This style, however, is only apparently simple; hardly a page is there that does not sparkle with wit, humor, irony, or satire inevitably suggestive of Lytton Strachey's —though not always so well under control. More individual is the romantic charm with which he can envelop the past by a wealth of pictorial imagery and literary allusion. Notable, too, is his craft in selecting and dramatizing the episodes of a long career like that of George III and framing the whole sequence in the solemn rites of pageantry. Above all, he is a master of the broad view. Opposite to Gamaliel Bradford, who seems to take the soul and let the body go, Guedalla never neglects the physical aspects of his characters, who usually appear in full-bodied participation in large events. With cinematographic multiplicity he delights in reconstructing the crowded scenes of battlefields and ballrooms. And while he has frequently been reproved for his habit of filling these panoramas with people and events contemporary with, but unrelated to, the main subject (as in the second paragraph below), most readers are grateful for the orientation supplied and flattered by the appeal to their erudition. One type of reader enjoys the pleasure of recognition; another type, the pleasure of discovery. The adept Mr. Guedalla thus wins both to his favor.

## THE STEPFATHER OF THE UNITED STATES

### PORTRAIT OF H.M. KING GEORGE III

IT WAS a cold February night in 1820; and from the black meadows by Eton they could see lights moving in the Castle. From the park, where the trumpeters stood in the darkness, the dismal note of horns rose on the night mist; and the Yeomen of the Guard, all in black, loomed "like black giants" through the half light of a room all hung with black. In a room beyond, the King of England lay dead; and anxious heralds were forming up a long procession of solemn gentlemen by candle-light. The King was dead; and in the darkness at Windsor they were burying the poor mad old man who, for nearly twenty years, had been King Lear without Goneril, without Regan, without Cordelia. The long round of imaginary ceremonials, of unreal reviews passed with royal dignity, of illusory Parliaments opened with royal affability, was over at last; and this strange replica of one of Blake's long-bearded allegories was still. The conqueror, the captor of Napoleon; the father of the Arts and Sciences; the royal person of whom the most sonorous of his subjects observed, after a conversation in the library at the Queen's House in St. James's Park, "Sir, they may talk of the King as they will; but he is the finest gentleman I have ever seen"; the master of Lord Chatham, of Lord North, of Mr. Pitt; the pupil of Lord Bute; the sovereign of Garrick and Siddons and Sir Joshua and Mr. Wesley and Mr. Burke; all this and more lay in the silent room beyond the tall Yeomen in their black. For on that winter night in 1820 they were burying the Eighteenth Century.

# I

It all seemed so far away. The sun shone in St. James's and Sir Robert Walpole was minister, when the Prince was born in a great house at the corner of the Square. Gin was the leading recreation and Captain Macheath the favourite character of the people of England; the sad, tinkling melodies of Miss Lockit and Miss Peachum were barely five years old, and the Italian singers had driven Handel into bankruptcy. Young Mr. Walpole was making the most of the Grand Tour, "very glad that I see Rome while it yet exists"; and little Mr. Pope was exasperating his contemporaries, whilst the outraged delicacy of Mr. Hogarth retorted in emphatic caricature. At Norfolk House the Princess of Wales lay beside a rather puny infant in the morning light. Anxious ladies scurried about the house; and her Frederick, unconscious of the impending tennis-ball, looked on with large, indifferent eyes. Someone rode off to the King with the news; and outside in the Square the tiny lake gleamed in the June sunshine of 1738.

With a kind provision for its soul's welfare and a sad feeling of its approaching end, they baptised the little creature before night. But it survived them all, survived the century, even survived itself. That hurried morning and that sudden baptism were the strange opening of George's eighty years. A bishop called the next day and gave him a string of royal names; the Poet Laureate, visited by his punctual Muse, improved the occasion in a smooth copy of heroic couplets, which contained a happy, though hardly an unexpected, allusion to Ascanius; and the infant in St. James's Square was fairly launched upon his long career of royalty.

The surroundings, it must be confessed, were not inspiring. A house in a London square without even a sentry at the door may be an apt school of simplicity. But for the other graces there was a sad dearth of instructors. The happy father, absorbed in the rather clumsy frolics to which the House of Hanover is lamentably apt in its deviations from propriety, was a rare visitor in the nursery; although he once took the child to a concert at the Foundling Hospital. Yet this dismal figure, whose heavy eyes stare aimlessly out of history, was strangely popular. Nothing endears their rulers to the people of England so much as the extremes of raffishness and respectability; and Frederick's claims upon the former count were singularly high. Alike by the scale of his debts and the range of his affections he stormed the popular heart. But possibly his absence from his son may be counted for a gain to George, since Frederick was unlikely to form the young mind; although he once composed an ode in French, and cherished an obscure ambition to become Chancellor of Cambridge University on the strength, perhaps, of a silver cup which he had offered to be rowed for in a boat race. But before the boy had turned thirteen, his father was removed. A fickle nation observed without discomposure that it was "only Fred"; and graduates of either University pursued him to the sky with dirges in all the learned languages. His royal grandfather was little beyond a distant vision of an alarming old gentleman with staring eyes and a large wig, who interrupted the child with boisterous noises at an investiture of the Garter and quite frightened out of his head the little speech which he had got by heart. Nothing remained for George to lean on but his mother. She was a patient lady, who had endured without complaint her introduction into a family which exhibited most of the filial imperfections of the Atreidae without their more pleasing features; and there was that "quiet sense" which she had brought with her from Saxe-Gotha to St. James's Square.

Two Earls, two bishops, and two gentlemen of mathematical attainments were enlisted to perfect the young intelligence, but with uneven success. The bishops did their work *à merveille* and produced a sound young Churchman. The Earls imparted whatever of peculiar attainment is in Earls. But the two scholars were a lamentable failure; and in his education George hardly reached the modest standard of a squire's son at a country grammar-school. His ignorance even became noticeable to himself in later years; and his tastes, in an age of taste, were non-existent. To this meagre curriculum his mother made two contributions, a distaste for society and the third Earl of Bute. Perhaps the first was almost natural in her. The poor lady had small cause to love the world; and she taught her son to avoid the bright and crowded assemblies, where he might, perhaps, have learnt by candle-light many lessons upon the management of men. So he remained always queer and a little lonely.

But Lord Bute was a more considerable ingredient in George's education. This accomplished person drifts into English history in a shower of rain, which stopped a cricket match near Richmond and drove the Prince's father to the dismal expedient of whist in a tent. Bute made a fourth at the card-table. His manners pleased; he called at Kew; and when he came to Court, he was attached to Frederick's Household. The Fates propelled the dreadful tennis-ball; and his master died, as he had lived, with bad French on his lips. But Bute remained beside the widow; and when her son was training to be King of England, she turned often to the graceful Scotchman. He was a man of taste; he had a leg, collected drawings, and patronised the Society of Scottish Antiquaries. His proximity to the bereaved Princess invited scandal; but he had the sense to face it. He was no fool, but merely (both by race and by conviction) a Tory. Slow to convince, the Scotch are still slower to abandon a conviction which they have once reached by the painful processes of logic; and having absorbed with difficulty the royal doctrines of the Seventeenth

Century, they still adhered to the creed in 1745. Perhaps the Prince's training owed a tinge of absolutism to Bute's direction. The comforting logic with which Jacobite writers excused the errors of the Stuarts could be adapted without undue strain to the House of Hanover; and it is not surprising that a startled bishop once came upon the boy reading a Jesuit's vindication of King James II. Such studies were unlikely to incline him to resign the throne in favour of Charles Edward (since even Princes are human); but they might prove a useful repertory of ideas, should he incline to revive the glories of the royal Prerogative. This tendency owed something also to his mother's guidance. Reared in a German Court where royalty had its due weight, she was pardonably shocked by the British system which confined the Lord's anointed to making stiff bows at a Levée, whilst the nation was administered by unconsecrated Whigs. This feeling, with a mother's pride, insisted that her son should "be a King"; and there can be small doubt that Bute showed the way. What else he taught the Prince is tolerably obscure. A tepid interest in medals, which Mr. Walpole once urged Sir Horace Mann to buy for him in Tuscany, and a total ignorance of law (imbibed from early study of Chief Justice Blackstone's *Commentaries* in manuscript) appear to be the only traces.

So the boy grew up; whilst the young men hunted Sir Robert Walpole out of office, and Mr. Pitt propelled his cheering countrymen through the great round of victories. He was a trifle solitary, "shut up in a room," playing at Comet (but for diminutive stakes) with the family, or living among his mother's plants at Kew. These mild pursuits exasperated his virile grandfather. The hero of Dettingen learned with disgust of a royal visit to a tapestry factory. "Damn," he exclaimed, "dat tapestry—I shall have de Princes made women of." A repetition of the offence evoked reprisals: he had "oder dings to show dem dan needles and dreads," and promptly took off a small Princess to a military review in Hyde Park. He was irked by the rather Methodist virtues of his heir, who seemed "good for nothing but to read the Bible to his mother." But when he proposed to the Prince of Wales a marriage of the usual pattern with a princess from

Brunswick, the mild young man refused; and Mr. Walpole was in transports over his reluctance to be "*bewolfenbuttled*, a word which I do not pretend to understand, as it is not in Mr. Johnson's new *Dictionary*." George's prejudice was personal rather than patriotic; since it appeared that he had no objection to the daughter of a German prince, upon whose territory "some frow," as Mr. Walpole said, "may have emptied her pail and drowned his dominions." For he boldly made application for the portrait of a rival beauty, who resided in the more favoured region of Saxe-Gotha. Perhaps his mother, who valued her own position as "the Lady Dowager Prudence," discouraged the Brunswick match. Perhaps (who knows?) he had a will of his own. No one could say, since the world knew little of him. And how little he knew of the world! His travels, in the age of the Grand Tour, took him no further than Cheltenham, with one wild excursion (in delicious *incognito*) to the south of Scotland. His studies kindled little beyond a mild taste for agriculture; though he betrayed that faint inclination towards mechanics which often haunts those whose livelihood is not dependent upon their skill. He once designed a watch of tiny proportions, "rather less than a silver twopence"; but the execution was wisely left in other hands, his own mechanical achievements being almost entirely confined to turning upon a lathe, with which he was positively believed to have made a button. As a little boy he had walked through the town at night with his father

> To look at garters black and white
> On legs of female rabble.

But in spite of this initiation he never figured in the raffish world, where it was the lofty ambition of young gentlemen

> To run a horse, to make a match,
> To revel deep, to roar a catch;
> To knock a tottering watchman down,
> To sweat a woman of the town.

Indeed, he was scarcely seen in those more elegant quarters where Mr. Selwyn paraded his wit and the hackney-chairs lined up outside assemblies. One catches a glimpse of him at Miss Chudleigh's party for his birthday, when she opened the dance with the Duke of York and the court was illuminated with "a battlement of lamps." There were "pyramids and troughs of strawberries and cherries" for supper, which covered all the sideboards and even filled the chairs, although the party from the Spanish Embassy supped off fish for their conscience' sake; and the gamblers played upstairs in a long room full of bookcases, "with the finest Indian pictures on different colours and with Chinese chairs of the same colours." But he was a rare visitor; and the world knew little of him.

Yet there was so little to know. If not to be a bad man is to be a good man, George was a good man. Indeed, the private virtues consist so largely of abstention that, on the private side, his negative equipment suffices to render him quite blameless. He was a dutiful son, a faithful husband, and a devoted parent, "revered," in the pleasant terms applied to another squire, "by his family, honoured by his tenants, and awful to his domestics." But such innocuous epitaphs rarely suffice for kings. Public figures are judged by more exacting tests; and in the sphere of politics George owed his failure (for he failed) to those more positive qualities which he did not possess.

## II

At twenty-two, this paragon of somewhat negative virtues became King of England. The season, in 1760, was singularly apt for his accession; and his subjects seemed to demand of him precisely what the mild young man could offer. Two revolutions and two elderly German kings had developed a new convention of the Constitution. The sovereign was no longer required to govern England. That anxious business had been transferred to a committee of his subjects, partly because, unlike the last two monarchs, they understood the English language, and partly because they were the political heirs of the men who had deposed James II and decapitated Charles I. This readjustment of responsibilities, which found a succession to the Protectorate of Oliver Cromwell in the virtual Premiership of Sir Robert Walpole and

Mr. Pitt, seemed to mark the end of effective monarchy in England. The Cabinet had replaced the throne; and the sovereign, at the death of George II, had become a costly (if not particularly decorative) dignitary with purely ceremonial functions. The Birthday, the Levée, the Drawing-room were his occasions; and he was expected to perform these exacting duties, moving with due solemnity through a respectful forest of white wands and gold sticks. He might even add a military touch from time to time with a review or so, or give a bright example of royal con-descension with an occasional act of charity in the more benevolent modern taste. But his main, his foremost duty was to smile and, at the appropriate moment, to incline his head. The King, in a word, had dwindled into royalty.

George was designed by Providence to play this amiable part. His physical equipment was sufficient, and the mental strain was not severe. His deportment satisfied the exacting standards of his age. He sat his throne, "graceful and genteel"; he read quite distinctly little speeches composed by other people; and in the Circle he "walks about and speaks to everybody" instead of standing, as a courtier wrote with a graceful reminiscence of his predecessor, "in one place, with his eyes fixed royally on the ground, and dropping bits of German news." The prevalent refinement seemed to have refined the coarse art of kingship into a sort of minuet. It was almost a dancing-master's business; and the formal movements, the royal airs and graces, and the ritual acts were well within George's range.

But some unhappy prompting set him a larger task. The middle years of the Eighteenth Century witnessed in almost every part of Europe a queer, belated revival of monarchy. Its inspiration came, perhaps, from the splendid pageant of autocracy through which the *Grand Monarque* had walked at Versailles. The gilt, the marble, the long perspective of respectful courtiers had stirred the envy of half the kings in Europe; and their emulation gave a sharp tilt to the falling scale of royal authority. The Seventeenth Century had been an age of great ministers; but the succeeding generations saw the kings assert themselves once more. They built great palaces and enamelled the ceilings with vast, impending goddesses; they ruled solemn vistas through the formal verdure of state gardens, with "pyramidal yews, *treillages,* and square cradle walks, with windows clipped in them"; and, stranger still, they resumed the government of their astonished countries. All Prussia was a rapier in the steady hand of Frederick; Austrian policy followed the changing moods of the Empress; and far to the north a stout, jewelled lady controlled the slow advance of Russia. Even in Spain there was a brisk revival of authority; and the scared Portuguese were bullied into progress by Pombal, as the new, glaring streets of Lisbon rose slowly in the sunshine from the dust of the earthquake. So George was in the mode when he resolved to be a King.

This project was almost the sole fruit of his meagre education. He had learned no law from Blackstone; but Lord Bute and the Jacobite pamphlets taught him a stranger lesson. George learned that he should be a King: it was his tragedy that no one taught him how to be one. His furtive study of high Stuart doctrine impressed the slow mind; ill-equipped persons are frequently consoled for their inadequacy by a belief in their sacred mission. If King James had been right (and his early reading taught George to think so), the Lord's anointed must surely be something more than a graceful gesture in a gilt chair, or an obliging signature on official sheepskins. And if, under the Whig dispensation, the royal function had almost come to that, then the Whigs must be wrong. So George, in his effort to be a King, turned Tory. There was, indeed, a Tory pattern of kingship ready to hand. The conduct of an ideal Tory on the throne had been foretold by the strange fancy of Bolingbroke; and George stumbled hopefully into the steps prescribed by that agile person for his *Patriot King.*

Defeated parties are frequently unanimous upon the impropriety of party government. Minorities are always apt to be stern critics of popular folly; and Tory thought, in the first years of Whig domination, harped on the vice of faction. But its main obsession was still the sanctity of kingship; and Bolingbroke, when he reeled back defeated from the hopeless task of imparting ideas to the exiled Stuarts and resumed the less exacting functions of a Tory oracle, blended the two notions into a strange amalgam. His friends were out of place; but he refreshed them with an odd vision of office. A new sort of monarch was to "espouse no party . . . but govern like the common father of his people." This chimera "must begin to govern as soon as he begins to reign"; and to achieve his purpose he will "call into the administration such men as he can assure himself will serve on the same principles on which he intends to govern." Such men, since the Whigs were unlikely bedfellows for an autocrat, must clearly be Tories; and in this happy dream, the dejected friends of Bolingbroke would march back into office behind the triumphant banner of "the most popular man in his country and a patriot king at the head of a united people." The bright vision faded; and in the grey light Sir Robert Walpole was ruling England for the Whig families and the German king, whom they had brought from Hanover. Even when Mr. Pitt controlled the nation, he preferred to lean on a Whig duke. So George, who wished to be King above all parties, found party in the ascendant on his coming in.

This queer young man, whom no one knew, set out to transform the government of his country; and, to a strange degree, he was successful. The odds were remarkable. The King's resources were his slender personal equipment, the vague prestige of a new reign, his mother's guidance, and the friendship of a Scotch Earl. With singular courage (and courage never failed him) he gathered these slight forces for an attack on the Whig system. A more intelligent man, one feels, would have discarded the attempt as hopeless. But George's nerve was unimpeded by sagacity; and he succeeded. The Whig façade in 1760 was impressive; Whiggery was entrenched in Parliament behind the serried rows of Newcastle's placemen; and its chosen minister, Mr. Pitt, was conquering half the world. "Two victories every week" formed an inspiring diet for civilians; and a cheering town responded with huzzas and fireworks, whilst the distant boom of the Park guns answered the salvos from the Tower. The world observed Lord Bute at the King's elbow and made little jokes about Pitt-coal, Newcastle-coal or (hateful alternative) Scotch-coal. The

King alarmed opinion with an announcement that he gloried "in the name of Briton," which sounds to posterity a brave denial of his German origins; but for contemporaries it had the more sinister ring of an admission that Scotland was in his thoughts. There was a Scotch Earl on the back stairs; and the town was not averse to little stories about "the Signora-Madre." Then, on the full tide of victory, Mr. Pitt was adroitly parted from the Whigs. His Olympian air prepared the way. That eye, that hooked, commanding nose, which awed the House of Commons, were merely intolerable in council. For almost six years he had monopolised the control of war and foreign affairs; and British armies followed British fleets to victory in three continents. But infallible pontiffs are rarely popular with their colleagues. An issue (upon which he was plainly right) was raised in Cabinet. The oracle spoke; but the priests refused to listen. He was exasperated into resignation; and when the Whigs lost Mr. Pitt, they forfeited their sole claim to popular esteem. The oracle retired to Bath; and as the priests sat on in the temple, the outer courts were slowly emptying.

The King had made his breach in the walls of the Whig system, and the Scotch Earl became his minister. Whiggery trailed sadly into Opposition or assumed the new livery. The King, like all opponents of the party system, recruited a new party briskly. Its principles were obscure; but its advantages, since the King's Friends were grouped conveniently round the fountain of honour, were obvious. The opinions of the House of Commons were governed through its appetite for places; and Masters of the Buckhounds followed Admirals of the Red into the lobby, whilst Comptrollers of the Green Cloth, Rangers of St. James's Park, and Verdurers of Whichwood Forest abandoned their absorbing duties in order to support Government in the congenial company of Lords of the Bedchamber and Governors of the Isle of Wight. For nine years the King worked steadily to impose his system. Sometimes he seemed to reach the goal, and his proud mother cried: "Now my son *is* King of England." Sometimes the dark forces of Whiggery returned upon him in the dreary form of George Grenville or the blameless incarnation of Lord Rockingham. Once there was a queer resurrection of Mr. Pitt; but he was hastily reburied under the dignity of Lord Chatham, and the patient King went on. It was a strange struggle; and it was waged against an even stranger background.

England, in the ten years between the accession of George III and the ministry of Lord North, was an odd blend of hysteria and decorum. The poets scanned; the magazines abounded in formal eloquence; and taverns echoed with the sonorous antiphonies of Johnson. The great world solemnly pursued the grave inanities of the Eighteenth Century. It dressed its hair; it played at ombre; it sat sedately through interminable plays. Mr. Walpole, up to the knees in shavings, fortified his home with gingerbread breastworks and asked the town to view the battlements, or pelted Sir Horace with commissions to buy up half the brocadella in Florence for his hangings. But beyond this decorous scene something was stirring. An odd ferment seemed to threaten the trim dignity of the age. Excited gentlemen defied propriety in hell-fire clubs; and less select assemblies grew strangely violent. There had been queer frenzies earlier in the century, when Sacheverell drove through the roaring streets, and later when half the world ran mad on stock-jobbing. But the crowds (even Mr. Walpole called it "the century of crowds") seemed madder than ever in the new reign. At first they stood to watch the little Queen come in, then stared at a Coronation, and mobbed the streets between-whiles to huzza for Pitt and Martinico or the Havannah. But their pleasant tumult dropped sharply to a deeper note as the town was swept by an odd fever; and astonished Liberty beheld the strange apostolate of Mr. Wilkes.

This indecorous, cross-eyed figure became an emblem of popular disorder upon one of those points of law by which the passionate interest of Englishmen is sometimes engaged. His private tastes lay in a simpler direction and had inspired him with an ambition to represent his country in the matrimonially congenial atmosphere of Constantinople. Failing of this, he declined in disappointment upon popular journalism and abused the Court with gusto. Involved in a welter of duels and litigation, his name became an excuse for unlimited mobbing. The tumult deepened;

and for a few years the London streets were a vulgar replica of Rome in the crowded, angry days of the dying Republic, when Milo's *bravi* fought with Clodius. Bute was scared out of public life, or effaced himself to save his master; but the King persisted. It was apparently no part of the duty of a *Patriot King* to be popular; and he faced the mobs without flinching. For he had always courage. Then, gradually, the tide of disorder ebbed. The voice of authority became faintly audible above the sound of breaking glass; and when it came, it spoke in the King's name. The Whigs were quite subdued now; and England was governed by George himself through a peering, pouting minister with "the air of a blind trumpeter." It was the year 1770, and Lord North was waiting sedately in the wings.

## III

Personal government depends for its success upon two factors, the person and the governed. When a rare conjunction unites administrative talent with a docile or a sympathetic people, the world is presented with the strange miracle of successful autocracy. But how rare such unions are. Capacity, infrequent among statesmen, is still less frequent among kings; and docility, west of the Vistula, has been extinct among subjects for almost three centuries. A national impulse rarely coincides with a monarch's wishes. The case, of course, is not unknown; the laborious versatility of Frederick might drive an obedient Prussia, and the universal competence of Napoleon found its true partner in the French energy released by a national revolution. But these are the rare triumphs of monarchy. More often, far more often, a distracted autocrat fumbles with his work; or a nation, disinclined to play its humble part, renders it impossible. If the ruler is unequal to his high position, autocracy fails. If his subjects withhold consent to his wide authority, it fails as gravely. The sole possibility of success for personal government lies in the combination of an adequate person with a consenting people; and its failures, for lack of that rare conjunction, are more numerous than its successes.

The King's experiment was sadly deficient in both elements. Viewed as a candidate for autocracy, George was singularly unimpressive; even Bolingbroke, one feels, would have been discouraged by the spectacle of his *Patriot King* in action. The patient, punctual creature minuting his correspondence with the hour of despatch; directing at "2 min. pt. 11 a.m." the march of some cavalry from Henley to Hounslow; consenting at "53 min. pt. 5 p.m." to the appointment of a Mr. Fountayne to the living of Worplesdon; complaining at "12 min. pt. 10 p.m." that if James Adam is appointed Surveyor-General to the Board of Works, he "shall certainly think it hard on Chambers, and shall in that case only think he must not be passed by"; insisting at "57 min. pt. 11 a.m." that the new prebendary of Durham must "continue to attend the young Chancellor"; this plodding figure, stooping over his green box in the candle-light and holding the papers close to his face before he traced the big G.R., seems so remote from the high dream of kingship. "The common father of his people . . ." and a light burning late in the Queen's House, where an angry man was writing little hints to the Common Council for unseating Mr. Alderman Wilkes. "The most popular man in his country . . ." noting gentlemen of the House of Commons to receive a frown at the Levée for an injudicious vote. "A patriot king at the head of a united people . . ." pelting a driven Minister with little punctual notes. How far they seem, those busy, irritable little figures, below that imagined monarch who was to sit enthroned above the clouds of party and bathed in the pure sunlight of autocracy. His teachers had urged him to be a King; and someone, it seemed, had taught him to be a passable Patronage Secretary. Clerks in his Treasury formed such habits; industrious merchants sought vainly to impart them to their sons; and his intellectual counterparts crouched on tall stools in counting-houses east of Temple Bar.

Yet he was not content to drug himself with the deadly narcotic of administrative detail. For he was King; and policy, as well as patronage, claimed the royal attention. Patronage was his forte, and it served well enough as a solvent of most domestic problems. He set about to govern England single-handed. Now, there was a House of Commons to be perpetually shielded from unwholesome influences, and George went in pursuit of political purity down unusual paths. The minor disorder of elections was cured with "gold pills"; and the tiresome scruples of elected persons yielded on most occasions to a gracious nod from the throne and a word behind Lord North's hand, followed after a becoming interval by a line in the *London Gazette* and a precious package from the Pay Office on quarter-day. The King, by this simple artifice, was his own First Minister and Chief Whip. His deputy sat dozing in the House of Commons, ran errands for his master, and stoutly maintained that the office of Prime Minister was unknown to the Constitution. The King had formed a party, led it, satisfied its simple needs, and maintained it in office. To that extent his experiment in personal government was verging towards success at home. The Whigs were helpless; since Parliament was for the King, and they professed to believe in government by Parliament. They roared in debate; they brought down votes "in flannels and blankets, till the floor of the House looked like the pool of Bethesda." But they were outvoted and retired to mutter in the deep libraries of country houses. Nothing seemed to remain in opposition except the City and the mob. But the Mansion House, strange temple of democracy, was a mere nest of preposterous Aldermen; and if the mob stirred, there were still the Guards.

George governed England with an odd blend of force and persuasion; and his subjects seemed curiously content to acquiesce. He had made peace; and great liberties are permitted to statesmen who make peace. He had unseated Mr. Pitt; but Mr. Pitt had made his name grotesque with a peerage. He challenged democracy; but democracy, in 1765, stood for little beyond the mob. Men had died for Hampden; but it would be fantastic to die for Mr. Wilkes. It almost seemed, at home, that it was possible to govern an empire with the arts of a Chief Whip. But one section of his people presented a queer, unyielding obstacle. Three thousand miles from the Levée, six weeks away from Lord North's significant smile, the Americans still persisted in their tedious debate. The ripe intelligence of Mr. Grenville had devised some taxes for them. Taxes, it seemed, were the common lot of victorious nations. So that imperial mind, which added the Isle of Man to the British Empire, sent stamps to Boston that inspired a strange repugnance. Mr. Grenville was frankly baffled. He had drawn the scheme (and he was at home in the schedule of a revenue Bill), because the neat device of stamps appealed irresistibly to that orderly mind. He had looked up the law (and he was a fair lawyer) and discovered the helpful precedent of the Channel Islands. Yet it was odd that mobs paraded in the clear American light and local orators abounded in deep-chested sentiments about liberty: perhaps the colour of the stamps was wrong. Then the grave leaders of the Whig groups faced the strange problem (and even Mr. Walpole began to notice that it was a "thorny point"). Mr. Grenville had thought of stamps; they thought of tea; few men in England thought of a larger issue. Then the Whigs subsided; and the King (with him, Lord North) resumed control of his bewildered empire. That he grasped the American issue is improbable. It was enough for that determined, angry man that the law of England had been defied on British territory. Wilkites in Southwark or Sons of Liberty in King Street, Boston, were the same to him; the troops must do their duty. Men who had ridden out the wild storm of the Middlesex election were not likely to parley with a mob; and at a distance of three thousand miles the solemn ratiocinations of a Boston town meeting were indistinguishable from the Brentford rabble. Even if he reflected, it was unlikely that the King would side with the colonists. Had he not learnt the sanctity of authority in a stiff Jacobite school? Passive obedience was the first duty of a loyal subject. Admirable in Great Britain, this virtue was yet more essential in America, since colonies (it was the lesson of his master Bolingbroke) were "like so many farms of the mother country." George was a farmer; and the strange claim of one of his farms to be consulted about its cultivation was clearly inadmissible.

The angry voices rose higher in the deepening tumult; and as the scattered shots rang out down the long road to Concord on a spring day in 1775, the argument drifted into civil war.

The King was firm. Indeed he had already fortified his resolution with the advice of the sagacious Gage. The conversation of military men upon political topics is a rare stimulant for civilians; and that warrior had persuaded his sovereign that the Americans "will be lyons whilst we are lambs; but, if we take the resolute part, they will undoubtedly prove very meek." In this hopeful mood he flogged the Boston Port Act through Parliament and hallooed Lord North to hunt the Opposition through the lobbies. He was still "well convinced they will soon submit," as Israel Putnam drove his sheep to Boston and Colonel Washington insisted warily that it was "a folly to attempt more than we can execute." The issue looked so simple in St. James's; and as the American tone hardened, the King could only ejaculate, "The dye is now cast, the colonies must either submit or triumph." But his mood was not one of blind repression. Like all Englishmen on the verge of a practical concession, he insisted firmly on his technical rights: "I do not wish to come to severer measures, but we must not retreat; by coolness and an unremitted pursuit of the measures that have been adopted I trust they will come to submit; I have no objection afterwards to their seeing that there is no inclination for the present to lay fresh taxes on them, but I am clear there must always be one tax to keep up the right, and as such I approve of the Tea Duty." So the student of Blackstone pressed his point of law, seeking little more than an admission which might cover his retreat. How many solicitors have been instructed to threaten proceedings in that confident tone. Unhappily he knew too little of men to measure the results of his threat. The lonely boy had become a lonely man; and his solitude was increased by the still lonelier elevation of a throne. He saw his fellow-creatures down the warped perspective of a king. But some instinct might have told him that Englishmen, in Boston or in Westminster Hall, willing enough to make all practical concessions, rarely give up a point of law. That, in essence, was his own attitude in the argument; and he lacked the wit to see that other men might feel the same. He knew so little of other men; and those incalculable creatures in America remained a mystery upon the far horizon of the world.

But when his challenge was accepted, when the expected lambs declined to play their part, he entered with gusto upon the detail of the war. Provisions for the army, the loan of infantry from Hanover, a purchase of recruits in Hesse-Cassel, sea strategy, dates of embarkation, biscuit and flour, the beating orders for enlisting Campbells, Gordons, and Macdonalds, plans of campaign, and news of privateers passed rapidly under the busy pen at Kew or the Queen's House. He watched the war like an eager parent, sailed the crowded troop-ships in imagination from Hamburgh to Sandy Hook, and followed his red-coats, as the winding line of bayonets vanished into the darkness of the great trees. Dimly he saw that personal government had met the fatal challenge of an unconsenting people. He seemed to feel that he was fighting for the throne of England; because if England thought with the unhappy rebels, "I should not esteem my situation in this country as a very dignified one, for the islands would soon cast off all obedience." It was (he saw the issue now) the decisive struggle of authority against all the dark forces which had ever opposed him, against the Whigs, against the mob, against the grinning mask of Wilkes and the sonorous tutorship of Chatham, against Mr. Burke and his heresies and the insidious logic of Dr. Franklin. George saw all his enemies gathered into the head of a single rebellion, and struck hard. The swelling strength of the Opposition alarmed Lord North; but the King's nerve was steady. "Whilst any ten men in the kingdom will stand by me, I will not give myself up into bondage. My dear Lord, I will rather risk my crown"—the sprawling hand wrote firmly on—"than do what I think personally disgraceful; and whilst I have no wish but for the good and prosperity of my country, it is impossible that the nation shall not stand by me; if they will not, they shall have another king, for I will never put my hand to what would make me miserable to the last hour of my life."

The French guns chimed in, as Versailles discovered a pleasing coincidence of romantic impulse with national interest; and for a moment he seemed almost to face the certainty of surrender in the revolted colonies. But "I will never consent that in any treaty that may be concluded a single word be mentioned concerning Canada, Nova Scotia, or the Floridas, which are colonies belonging to this country . . . for it is by them we are to keep a certain awe over the abandoned colonies." The issue had travelled far beyond taxation. In Europe it was now a war of existence with an ancient enemy; and in America it raised the vital problem of secession. That question was to haunt the continent for ninety years, and George stated it in terms which strangely anticipate the American echoes of a century later: "If Lord North can see with the same degree of enthusiasm I do the beauty, excellence, and perfection of the British constitution as by law established, and consider that, if any one branch of the empire is allowed to cast off its dependency, that the others will infallibly follow the example,"—how odd to find the thought of Lincoln in the mind of George III!—"that consequently, though an arduous struggle, that is worth going through any difficulty to preserve to latest posterity what the wisdom of our ancestors have carefully transmitted to us, he will not allow despondency to find a place in his breast, but resolve not merely out of duty to fill his post, but will resolve with vigour to meet every obstacle that may arise, he shall meet with most cordial support from me; but the times require vigour, or the state will be ruined." That cry, half strangled by the long, tortuous sentence, is not ignoble. The tenacious man, who stumbled into war in blind resentment of disorder, had a wider vision. The King could see the issue now; and, granted the fatal difference between autocracy and republic, he saw it almost with the eyes of 1861: "I own that, let any war be ever so successful, if persons will sit down and weigh the expenses, they will find, as in the last, that it has impoverished the state, enriched individuals, and perhaps raised the name only of the conquerors; but this is only weighing such events in the scale of a tradesman behind his counter; it is necessary for those in the station it has pleased Divine Providence to place me, to weigh whether expenses, though very great, are not sometimes necessary to prevent what might be more ruinous to a country than the loss of money. The present contest with America I cannot help seeing as the most serious in which any country was ever engaged; it contains such a train of consequences that they must be examined to feel its real weight. Whether the laying of a tax was deserving all the evils that have arisen from it, I should suppose no man could allege that without being more fit for Bedlam than a seat in the Senate; but step by step the demands of America have arisen; independence is their object; that certainly is one which every man not willing to sacrifice every object to a *momentary* and inglorious peace must concur with me in thinking that this country can never submit to: should America succeed in that, the West Indies must follow them . . . Ireland would soon follow the same plan and be a separate state; then this island would be reduced to itself, and soon would be a poor island indeed . . ."

The harassed man at Kew wrote on; and three thousand miles away the guns were booming in the summer sunshine of 1779. His courage held; he searched himself with "frequent and severe self-examination." When the news was good, he prepared to show America "that the parent's heart is still affectionate to the penitent child." When it was bad, he reflected that "in this world it is not right alone to view evils, but to consider whether they can be avoided, and what means are the most efficacious." In this sturdy temper he held on, defying the Opposition, heartening the pardonably despondent North. On a July day in 1781, he was still insisting that "this long contest will end as it ought, by the colonies returning to the mother country, and I confess I will never put my hand to any other conclusion of this business." But in those hot summer weeks a tired army was trailing about Virginia behind Cornwallis. At the fall of the year they stood behind a line of battered earthworks by the York River. The French lay off the coast; and in the sloping fields beyond the little town the parallels crept slowly nearer. There was a steady roll of musketry. Then the British guns fell silent; and the war was ended.

## IV

Four years later, on a dark winter afternoon Miss Burney was mildly startled by a visitor. They were playing Christmas games after dinner in Mrs. Delany's little drawing-room at Windsor, when the door opened quietly. It closed again behind "a large man in deep mourning," whom no one except Miss Burney seemed to notice. He said nothing; but as that sharp little eye travelled down the black suit, it encountered, heavens! the glitter of a star. Then one of the young ladies turned round on him, stifled a scream, and called out, "The King!—Aunt, the King!" The little company backed uneasily into the corners of the room; and presently there was a loud royal whisper of "Is that Miss Burney?" Her sovereign bowed politely; and the talk ran upon the whooping-cough, which prevailed in the royal nursery, and James's Powders, which Princess Elizabeth found so beneficial. Then he rained little questions on her; how she came to write *Evelina*, how to publish, how to print without a word to her father. Urged by the royal *What!* she said with a simper that she had "thought it would look very well in print." The awkward questioning went on, until a rap at the door announced the Queen, and someone slid out for candles to light the ugly little lady in.

Another day the royal mind was easier. The children were off to Kew for a change of air, and James's miraculous powders had done their work; so the talk ran on books. Voltaire was "a monster—I own it fairly." Rousseau was thought of "with more favour, though by no means with approbation." And Shake-speare—"was there ever such stuff as great part of Shakespeare? Only one must not say so! But what think you?—What?—Is there not sad stuff?—What?—what?" Miss Burney temporised. But her sovereign enjoyed his little heresy and laughed. "Oh! I know it is not to be said! but it's true. Only it's Shakespeare, and nobody dare abuse him." So the arch monarch developed his wicked theme and shocked the bookish lady—"but," as the coy iconoclast confessed, "one should be stoned for saying so!"

The "fatal day" had come, bringing an end to the strange experiment of personal government. At home he dwindled by slow degrees into an almost constitutional monarch; and overseas Mr. Jay read with some surprise that when Mr. Adams made his bow as ambassador, the King had stifled all resentment in a grace-ful confession—"I will be very frank with you. I was the last to conform to the separation; but the separation having been made, and having become inevitable, I have always said, as I say now, that I would be the first to meet the friendship of the United States as an independent power."

This pleasant, ageing, stoutish man, with his odd, jerky questions and his staring eyes, slowly became a ceremonial monarch of the standard Hanoverian pattern; displaying, on the appropriate occasions, a becoming versatility of martial and civilian accomplishments; strolling in the evening light on the Terrace at Windsor, surrounded by a family that was a Court in itself; admiring Miss Burney in the famous lilac tabby which the Queen gave her; pressing the remedial virtues of barley-water upon an exhausted colonel after a hard day in the hunting field; trotting, gnawed by the incurable inquisitiveness of royalty, into half the shops in Windsor; taking, after a more than usually incompetent attempt on his life, "his accustomed doze" at the theatre; peering, smiling, bowing. This amiable, domestic, elderly person, with his little jokes and the quick, questioning *What?—what?* forms a queer postscript to the high adventure of the young, friendless King, who set out to govern England and lost America. It all seemed so far away now. Mr. Wilkes had faded, Mr. Pitt had died in that theatrical way of his; Lord North was still living somewhere, but he was quite blind now. The King lived on, before all else a father and a husband, the Georgian head of an oddly Victorian court.

But he had still, had always his courage. It had not failed him on "Black Wednesday," when at the height of the war the mob ran wild for "No Popery" and Lord George Gordon. The streets were alight with the disordered worship of this singular idol, whose evangelical quest for a form of Christianity uncorrupted by Popish additions finally led him, by the fatal logic of a Scotsman or a lunatic, into a clear air where it was uncontaminated even by a Saviour. London passed sleepless nights and crept about behind its shutters. But the King informed his Council that, if the Riot Act was to be read before the troops could fire into the crowds, one magistrate at least would do his duty and then could take command of his Guards in person. The same even temper bore him up when a mad woman thrust a knife at him one afternoon outside the garden door at St. James's. He steadied the crowd, went in to hold his Levée, and then drove down to Windsor to show himself to the Queen. Three royal persons and two ladies in waiting mingled their tears. But the careful King enquired, "Has she cut my waistcoat? Look! for I have had no time to examine." His courage barely failed beneath the slow, dreadful gathering of a darker cloud, which hung above him. That he saw its coming is almost certain. Little doubt is left by his choking exclamation, "I wish to God I may die, for I am going to be mad." Then, staring with pitiable eyes at the ebbing tide of reason, he faded into insanity.

Once he returned; and for ten years he presided over the state where he had reigned. The Whigs were out; but England was ruled by a minister again, and Mr. Pitt—there was a new Mr. Pitt now, whose "damned long ugly face" was almost as trying as Chatham's eye—sat in his father's seat. The *Patriot King* had declined into dogeship, although there was a faint flicker of the old authority, when the minister roused his sovereign's Churchmanship with some nonsense about equality for Irish Papists. He rode; he played piquet; he bathed in the loyal waves of Weymouth. There was a pleasant jingle of Light Dragoons on the little Esplanade, and his troopers lounged in their sunny Capua beside the Wessex sea—

> When we lay where Budmouth Beach is,
>    O, the girls were fresh as peaches
> With their tall and tossing figures and their eyes of blue and brown!
>    And our hearts would ache with longing
>    As we paced from our sing-songing,
> With a smart *Clink! Clink!* up the Esplanade and down.

The bathing-women all wore "God save the King" on ample girdles round their waists; and as the royal person plunged, that pious invocation burst from the muffled fiddlers in a bathing-machine. He strolled again upon the Terrace at Windsor. But this time his airing was a martial exercise. For the French guns were speaking across Europe, and George called for the band to play, "Britons, strike home." So the old man (he was rising seventy now) confronted Buonaparte. He grasped, one feels, as little of the strange forces which opposed him as of the American tangle. He did little more than clench an English fist and shake it in the face of France.

But whilst he struggled to retain the last remains of sight, his watchful frigates kept the sea; his guns rang out where the Spanish hills dip to Trafalgar, and his red-coats stared at the cactus along the dusty roads of Portugal. Then, once again, a cloud swung over the sun and his sky darkened. The war went on; there was a steady thunder of guns in Europe, until at the last they stood smoking in the sodden fields by Waterloo. But the King sat muttering in a closed room at Windsor. He was far away in a pleasant world, where he gave interminable audiences to dead ministers. For hours, for days, for years he talked with them; and sometimes he made himself a little music on an old spinet, which had been silent since Queen Anne. Then he faded out of life; and on a winter night in 1820 Mr. Croker watched the mourners marshalling and heard the dismal note of horns from the Great Park.

# LYTTON STRACHEY

LYTTON STRACHEY did not invent the art of biography; he recaptured biography for art. In the now famous preface to *Eminent Victorians* he sounded the note of the new school—*brevity, freedom of spirit, dispassionate truth*—and then matched precept with example, setting the literary world by the ears. So extraordinary and diverse was the life-writing which poured forth in response to this declaration of independence from Victorian models that little note was taken of one fact: the manifesto was in reality a summons to raise again and higher the standards of Plutarch, Johnson, and Sainte-Beuve. This trail-blazer of the New Biography was an iconoclast, but an iconoclast who loved traditions.

By birth, education, and personal endowment Giles Lytton Strachey was well equipped to lead his generation to a new goal in letters. Born in 1880 into an intellectual and literary family—his father was a general and Indian administrator, his mother an author and brilliant aristocrat—he was, like Virginia Woolf, related to some of his most prominent countrymen, past and present. Educated mainly in France, he became "one of those rare Englishmen who know French from the inside." At Trinity College, Cambridge, he was known as a poet, and in his fourth year won the Chancellor's medal for English verse. He was unusually mature. Some of the essays and reviews from those years, as collected in his posthumous volume, *Characters and Commentaries* (1933), show him already perfecting at twenty-one the clear, compact prose and the swift, indelible portraiture that later won him fame. In person he struck people as "a sensitive, ungainly youth, awkward in his bearing, and presenting an appearance of great physical debility, as if he had recently risen from the bed of an invalid. His voice was faint and squeaky. The long red beard was a thing of the future. He was very silent, but uncannily quick and comprehending." Long before his thirty-second year, when he published his first book, *Landmarks of French Literature* (1912), he was a well-known figure in English social life of the more intellectual type.

Strachey did not serve in the World War, being both physically unfit and rationally opposed. But in February 1918, when the outcome was anything but certain, he managed to secure a publisher for a group of four short biographies; and after the conflict ended, the general revulsion against the old era and the universal eagerness for the new were found to be fittingly expressed in the pages of *Eminent Victorians*. Here, beginning with the very title, was an ironical revaluation of that age which had overstayed its welcome and whose claims to veneration had become intolerable to a war-stricken generation with a new world to build. Here were four of that age's most respectable great—Cardinal Manning, Miss Nightingale, Dr. Arnold, General Gordon—luminously restored to life, but minus their pedestals, their togas, their halos. Here dozens of related figures and events were fused into lively, flowing narratives as irresistible as any creations of fiction. Here were wit, style, erudition, logical vigor, and a point of view disarmingly sane. The book both shocked and captivated the public taste, inspiring a legion of imitators around the world.

Meanwhile, in the service of a greater task, Strachey plunged into other masses of nineteenth-century documents and in three years produced his masterpiece, *Queen Victoria* (1921). Here in three hundred pages was "not just a life of Victoria that happened to be a work of art, but a work of art that happened to be a life of Victoria." In style, treatment, construction, and creative purpose it was so far from the old "Life and Times" and "Life and Letters" that everybody, even Strachey's detractors, realized that a new "high" in literature had been reached. It was a triumphant demonstration of biography's principles. It was a triumph also of another sort, for long before the end of his work the author himself had yielded to the charm of his subject. *Queen Victoria* is the quintessence of "Stracheyism."

Except for *Books and Characters* (1922) with its brilliant essays on eighteenth-century figures and a sparkling lecture on Pope (1925), only two more volumes were to appear. Out of a recluse's admiration for men of action and his romantic fascination with the Renaissance he wrote *Elizabeth and Essex* (1928), swifter, more highly colored, more dramatic than anything he had yet done, a *tour de force* testing the limits of the biographer's freedom. Then he turned again to his favorite form and in the delightful *Portraits in Miniature* (1931) distilled into sprightly and mellow thumb-nail sketches a score of miscellaneous lives and much ripe comment on his own profession, illustrating his own advice given at the close of a two-thousand word portrait of the seventeenth-century biographer John Aubrey: "Let us have the pure essentials—a vivid image, on a page or two, without explanations, transitions, commentaries, or padding."

Master though he assuredly was of his art, Strachey was not invulnerable. He bore repeated attacks for his acerbity, for occasional distortions of fact, for verbal clichés and too regular purple patches. He has been blamed for the extravagances of the whole "debunking" school. Yet how few of those imitators who seized on the revolutionary liberties and caught the annihilating manner possessed either his compensatory poise and taste or his skill disciplined through a lifetime in the rigorous traditions of his craft! Though of small output and that by no means perfect, Lytton Strachey remains, for literature at least, the biographer's biographer.

He never married, but he enjoyed in the Bloomsbury Group the most congenial and stimulating friendships possible to a man who preferred the eighteenth century to his own yet led the vanguard of the twentieth in

English letters. There is significance in the fact that he dedicated his *Victoria* to his friend Virginia Woolf—who returned the honor in *The Common Reader*—and his *Portraits* to Max Beerbohm. Like theirs, his books have indeed been "few, but roses." Strachey died in February 1932.

To extract the fullest pleasure from "Florence Nightingale," the most sympathetic of the *Eminent Victorians,* one must know something of the sentimental legend it supplants and of the subject's own writings. The legend, mentioned in Strachey's opening paragraph and set forth in Long-fellow's poem, "The Lady with the Lamp," was simply the inevitable con-sequence of Miss Nightingale's heroic service in the Crimea followed by her almost total, permanent withdrawal from public view. That two-thirds of her active career was spent *after* her return, in strenuous and single-minded devotion to the more lasting work of organizing the medical and sanitary administration of the British army, went all but unnoticed while the saintly vision of the Angel of Mercy enveloped and hallowed her name. Strachey's emphasis on the nurse's demonic energy can be traced to the strong, terse, businesslike pointedness of her own *Notes on Nursing, Notes on Hospitals, Una and Her Lions,* of her own letters, diaries, and reported talk. His attitude results in her seeming more of a tigress than she was, yet who would now exchange this full-view portrait of the founder of nursing for the sugary cameo of Hollywood Victorianism?

Out of this famous piece of Stracheyan biography the observant reader can erect a number of indispensable criteria for judging the other "lives" in the present collection. Aside from that dispassionateness of which Strachey was a better exponent than exemplar—for he was neither impartial nor en-tirely unsympathetic—this piece displays the prime virtues of seeing a sub-ject whole and from a definite point of view, of preserving the correct scale in compressing a long career into a short account, of keeping just pro-portions also in emphasis, and of energizing the narrative by forward-push-ing paragraphs and clear, flowing sentences that insure total communication.

# FLORENCE NIGHTINGALE

EVERYONE knows the popular conception of Florence Night-ingale. The saintly, self-sacrificing woman, the delicate maiden of high degree who threw aside the pleasures of a life of ease to succour the afflicted, the Lady with the Lamp, glid-ing through the horrors of the hospital at Scutari, and consecrat-ing with the radiance of her goodness the dying soldier's couch—the vision is familiar to all. But the truth was different. The Miss Nightingale of fact was not as facile fancy painted her. She worked in another fashion, and towards another end; she moved under the stress of an impetus which finds no place in the popular imagination. A Demon possessed her. Now demons, whatever else they may be, are full of interest. And so it happens that in the real Miss Nightingale there was more that was interesting than in the legendary one; there was also less that was agreeable.

Her family was extremely well-to-do, and connected by marriage with a spreading circle of other well-to-do families. There was a large country house in Derbyshire; there was another in the New Forest; there were Mayfair rooms for the London season and all its finest parties; there were tours on the Continent with even more than the usual number of Italian operas and of glimpses at the celebrities of Paris. Brought up among such advantages, it was only natural to suppose that Florence would show a proper appreciation of them by doing her duty in that state of life unto which it had pleased God to call her—in other words, by marrying, after a fitting number of dances and dinner-parties, an eligible gentleman, and living happily ever afterwards. Her sister, her cousins, all the young ladies of her acquaintance, were either getting ready to do this or had already done it. It was inconceivable that Florence should dream of anything else; yet dream she did. Ah! To do her duty in that state of life unto which it had pleased God to call her! Assuredly she would not be behindhand in doing her duty; but unto what state of life *had* it pleased God to call her? That was the question. God's calls are many, and they are strange. Unto what state of life had it pleased Him to call Charlotte Corday, or Elizabeth of Hungary? What was that secret voice in her ear, if it was not a call? Why had she felt, from her earliest years, those mysterious promptings towards . . . she hardly knew what but certainly towards something very different from anything around her? Why, as a child in the nursery, when her sister had shown a healthy pleasure in tearing her dolls to pieces, had *she* shown an almost morbid one in sewing them up again? Why was she driven now to minister to the poor in their cottages, to watch by sick-beds, to put her dog's wounded paw into elaborate splints as if it was a human being? Why was her head filled with queer imaginations of the country house at Embley turned, by some enchantment, into a hospital, with herself as matron moving about among the beds? Why was even her vision of heaven itself filled with suffering patients to whom she was being useful? So she dreamed and wondered, and, taking out her diary, she poured into it the agitations of her soul. And then the bell rang, and it was time to go and dress for dinner.

As the years passed, a restlessness began to grow upon her. She was unhappy, and at last she knew it. Mrs. Nightingale, too, began to notice that there was something wrong. It was very odd; what could be the matter with dear Flo? Mr. Nightingale suggested that a husband might be advisable; but the curious thing was that she seemed to take no interest in husbands. And with her attractions, and her accomplishments, too! There was nothing in the world to prevent her making a really brilliant match. But no! She would think of nothing but how to satisfy that singular craving of hers to be *doing* something. As if there was not plenty to do in any case, in the ordinary way, at home. There was the china to look after, and there was her father to be read to after dinner. Mrs. Nightingale could not understand it; and then one day her perplexity was changed to consternation and alarm. Florence announced an extreme desire to go to Salisbury Hospital for several months as a nurse; and she confessed to some visionary plan of eventually setting up in a house of her own in a neighbouring village, and there founding "something like a Protestant Sisterhood, without vows, for women of educated feelings." The whole scheme was summarily brushed aside as preposterous; and Mrs. Nightingale, after the first shock of terror, was able to settle down again more or less comfortably to her embroidery. But Florence, who was now twenty-five and felt that the dream of her life had been shattered, came near to desperation.

And, indeed, the difficulties in her path were great. For not only was it an almost unimaginable thing in those days for a woman of means to make her own way in the world and to live in independence, but the particular profession for which Florence was clearly marked out both by her instincts and her capacities was at that time a peculiarly disreputable one. A "nurse" meant then a coarse old woman, always ignorant, usually dirty, often brutal, a Mrs. Gamp, in bunched-up sordid garments, tippling at the brandy-bottle or indulging in worse irregularities. The nurses in the hospitals were especially notorious for immoral conduct; sobriety almost unknown among them; and they could hardly be trusted to carry out the simplest medical duties. Certainly, things have changed since those days; and that they *have* changed is due, far more than to any other human being, to Miss Nightingale herself. It is not to be wondered at that her parents should have shuddered at the notion of their daughter devoting her life to such an occupation. "It was as if," she herself said afterwards, "I had wanted to be a kitchen-maid." Yet the want, absurd, impracticable as it was, not only remained fixed immovably in her heart, but grew in intensity day by day. Her wretchedness deepened into a morbid melancholy. Everything about her was vile, and she herself, it was clear, to have deserved such misery, was even viler than her surroundings. Yes, she had sinned—"standing before God's judgment seat." "No one," she declared, "has so grieved the Holy Spirit"; of that she was quite certain. It was in vain that she prayed to be delivered from vanity and hypocrisy, and she could not bear to smile or to be gay, "because she hated God to hear her laugh, as if she had not repented of her sin."

A weaker spirit would have been overwhelmed by the load of such distresses—would have yielded or snapped. But this extraordinary young woman held firm, and fought her way to victory. With an amazing persistency, during the eight years that followed her rebuff over Salisbury Hospital, she struggled and worked and planned. While superficially she was carrying on the life of a brilliant girl in high society, while internally she was a prey to the tortures of regret and of remorse, she yet possessed the energy to collect the knowledge and to undergo the experience which alone could enable her to do what she had determined she would do in the end. In secret she devoured the reports of medical commissions, the pamphlets of sanitary authorities, the histories of hospitals and homes. She spent the intervals of the London season in ragged schools and workhouses. When she went abroad with her family, she used her spare time so well that there was hardly a great hospital in Europe with which she was not acquainted, hardly a great city whose slums she had not passed through. She managed to spend some days in a convent school in Rome, and some weeks as a "Sœur de Charité" in Paris. Then, while her mother and sister were taking the waters at Carlsbad, she succeeded in slipping off to a nursing institution at Kaiserswerth, where she remained for more than three months. This was the critical event of her life. The experience which she gained as a nurse at Kaiserswerth formed the foundation of all her future action and finally fixed her in her career.

But one other trial awaited her. The allurements of the world she had brushed aside with disdain and loathing; she had resisted the subtler temptation which, in her weariness, had sometimes come upon her, of devoting her baffled energies to art or literature; the last ordeal appeared in the shape of a desirable young man. Hitherto, her lovers had been nothing to her but an added burden and a mockery; but now— For a moment, she wavered. A new feeling swept over her—a feeling which she had never known before, which she was never to know again. The most powerful and the profoundest of all the instincts of humanity laid claim upon her. But it rose before her, that instinct, arrayed—how could it be otherwise?—in the inevitable habiliments of a Victorian marriage; and she had the strength to stamp it underfoot.

I have an intellectual nature which requires satisfaction [she noted], and that would find it in him. I have a passional nature which requires satisfaction, and that would find it in him. I have a moral, an active nature which requires satisfaction, and that would not find it in his life. Sometimes I think that I will satisfy my passional nature at all events. . . .

But no, she knew in her heart that it could not be. "To be nailed to a continuation and exaggeration of my present life . . . to put it out of my power ever to be able to seize the chance of forming for myself a true and rich life"—that would be a suicide. She made her choice, and refused what was at least a certain happiness for a visionary good which might never come to her at all. And so she returned to her old life of waiting and bitterness.

The thoughts and feelings that I have now [she wrote] I can remember since I was six years old. A profession, a trade, a necessary occupation, something to fill and employ all my faculties, I have always felt essential to me, I have always longed for. The first thought I can remember, and the last, was nursing work; and in the absence of this, education work, but more the education of the bad than of the young. . . . Everything has been tried, foreign travel, kind friends, everything. My God! What is to become of me?

A desirable young man? Dust and ashes! What was there desirable in such a thing as that? "In my thirty-first year," she noted in her diary, "I see nothing desirable but death."

Three more years passed, and then at last the pressure of time told; her family seemed to realise that she was old enough and strong enough to have her way; and she became the superintendent of a charitable nursing home in Harley Street. She had gained her independence, though it was in a meagre sphere enough; and her mother was still not quite resigned: surely Florence might at least spend the summer in the country. At times, indeed, among her intimates, Mrs. Nightingale almost wept. "We are ducks," she said with tears in her eyes, "who have hatched a wild swan." But the poor lady was wrong; it was not a swan that they had hatched; it was an eagle.

## II

Miss Nightingale had been a year in her nursing-home in Harley Street, when Fate knocked at the door. The Crimean War broke out; the battle of the Alma was fought; and the terrible condition of our military hospitals at Scutari began to be known in England. It sometimes happens that the plans of Providence are a little difficult to follow, but on this occasion all was plain; there was a perfect co-ordination of events. For years Miss Nightingale had been getting ready; at last she was prepared—experienced, free, mature, yet still young—she was thirty-four—desirous to serve, accustomed to command: at that precise moment the desperate need of a great nation came, and she was there to satisfy it. If the war had fallen a few years earlier, she would have lacked the knowledge, perhaps even the power, for such a work; a few years later and she would, no doubt, have been fixed in the routine of some absorbing task, and moreover, she would have been growing old. Nor was it only the coincidence of Time that was remarkable. It so fell out that Sidney Herbert was at the War Office and in the Cabinet; and Sidney Herbert was an intimate friend of Miss Nightingale's, convinced, from personal experience in charitable work, of her supreme capacity. After such premises, it seems hardly more than a matter of course that her letter, in which she offered her services for the East, and Sidney Herbert's letter, in which he asked for them, should actually have crossed in the post. Thus it all happened, without a hitch. The appointment was made, and even Mrs. Nightingale, overawed by the magnitude of the venture, could only approve. A pair of faithful friends offered themselves as personal attendants; thirty-eight nurses were collected; and within a week of the crossing of the letters Miss Nightingale, amid a great burst of popular enthusiasm, left for Constantinople.

Among the numerous letters which she received on her departure was one from Dr. Manning, who at that time was working in comparative obscurity as a Catholic priest in Bayswater. "God will keep you," he wrote, "and my prayer for you will be that your one object of Worship, Pattern of Imitation, and source of consolation and strength may be the Sacred Heart of our Divine Lord."

To what extent Dr. Manning's prayer was answered must remain a matter of doubt; but this much is certain, that, if ever a prayer was needed, it was needed then for Florence Nightingale. For dark as had been the picture of the state of affairs at Scutari, revealed to the English public in the despatches of the *Times* correspondent and in a multitude of private letters, yet the reality turned out to be darker still. What had occurred was, in brief, the complete break-down of our medical arrangements at the seat of war. The origins of this awful failure were complex and manifold; they stretched back through long years of peace and carelessness in England; they could be traced through endless ramifications of administrative incapacity—from the inherent faults of confused systems to the petty bunglings of minor officials, from the inevitable ignorance of Cabinet Ministers to the fatal exactitudes of narrow routine. In the inquiries which followed it was clearly shown that the evil was in reality that worst of all evils—one which has been caused by nothing in particular and for which no one in particular is to blame. The whole organisation of the war machine was incompetent and out of date. The old Duke had sat for a generation at the Horse Guards repressing innovations with an iron hand. There was an extraordinary overlapping of authorities, an almost incredible shifting of responsibilities to and fro. As for such a notion as the creation and the maintenance of a really adequate medical service for the army—in that atmosphere of aged chaos, how could it have entered anybody's head? Before the war, the easy-going officials at Westminster were naturally persuaded that all was well—or at least as well as could be expected; when someone, for instance, actually had the temerity to suggest the formation of a corps of army nurses, he was at once laughed out of court. When the war had begun, the gallant British officers in control of affairs had other things to think about than the petty details of medical organisation. Who had bothered with such trifles in the Peninsula? And surely, on that occasion, we had done pretty well. Thus the most obvious precautions were neglected, the most necessary preparations put off from day to day. The principal medical officer of the army, Dr. Hall, was summoned from India at a moment's notice, and was unable to visit England before taking up his duties at the front. And it was not until after the battle of the Alma, when we had been at war for many months, that we acquired hospital accommodation at Scutari for more than a thousand men. Errors, follies, and vices on the part of individuals there doubtless were; but, in the general reckoning, they were of small account—insignificant symptoms of the deep disease of the body politic—the enormous calamity of administrative collapse.

Miss Nightingale arrived at Scutari—a suburb of Constantinople, on the Asiatic side of the Bosphorus—on November 4th, 1854; it was ten days after the battle of Balaclava, and the day before the battle of Inkerman. The organisation of the hospitals, which had already given way under the stress of the battle of the Alma, was now to be subjected to the further pressure which these

two desperate and bloody engagements implied. Great detach-
ments of wounded were already beginning to pour in. The men,
after receiving such summary treatment as could be given them at
the smaller hospitals in the Crimea itself, were forthwith shipped
in batches of two hundred across the Black Sea to Scutari. This
voyage was in normal times one of four days and a half; but the
times were no longer normal, and now the transit often lasted
for a fortnight or three weeks. It received, not without reason,
the name of "the middle passage." Between, and sometimes on the
decks, the wounded, the sick, and the dying were crowded—men
who had just undergone the amputation of limbs, men in the
clutches of fever or of frostbite, men in the last stages of dysen-
tery and cholera—without beds, sometimes without blankets,
often hardly clothed. The one or two surgeons on board did
what they could; but medical stores were lacking, and the only
form of nursing available was that provided by a handful of invalid soldiers, who were usually themselves prostrate by the end
of the voyage. There was no other food beside the ordinary salt
rations of ship diet; and even the water was sometimes so stored
that it was out of reach of the weak. For many months, the
average of deaths during these voyages was seventy-four in the
thousand; the corpses were shot out into the waters; and who
shall say that they were the most unfortunate? At Scutari, the
landing-stage, constructed with all the perverseness of Oriental
ingenuity, could only be approached with great difficulty, and,
in rough weather, not at all. When it was reached, what remained
of the men in the ships had first to be disembarked, and then conveyed up a steep slope of a quarter of a mile to the nearest of the
hospitals. The most serious cases might be put upon stretchers—
for there were far too few for all; the rest were carried or
dragged up the hill by such convalescent soldiers as could be got
together, who were not too obviously infirm for the work. At
last the journey was accomplished; slowly, one by one, living or
dying, the wounded were carried up into the hospital. And in the
hospital what did they find?

*Lasciate ogni speranza, voi ch'entrate:* the delusive doors bore
no such inscription; and yet behind them Hell yawned. Want,

neglect, confusion, misery—in every shape and in every degree of intensity—filled the endless corridors and the vast apartments of the gigantic barrack-house, which, without forethought or preparation, had been hurriedly set aside as the chief shelter for the victims of the war. The very building itself was radically defective. Huge sewers underlay it, and cess-pools loaded with filth wafted their poison into the upper rooms. The floors were in so rotten a condition that many of them could not be scrubbed; the walls were thick with dirt; incredible multitudes of vermin swarmed everywhere. And, enormous as the building was, it was yet too small. It contained four miles of beds, crushed together so close that there was but just room to pass between them. Under such conditions, the most elaborate system of ventilation might well have been at fault; but here there was no ventilation. The stench was indescribable. "I have been well acquainted," said Miss Nightingale, "with the dwellings of the worst parts of most of the great cities in Europe, but have never been in any atmosphere which I could compare with that of the Barrack Hospital at night." The structural defects were equalled by the deficiencies in the commonest objects of hospital use. There were not enough bedsteads; the sheets were of canvas, and so coarse that the wounded men recoiled from them, begging to be left in their blankets; there was no bedroom furniture of any kind, and empty beer-bottles were used for candlesticks. There were no basins, no towels, no soap, no brooms, no mops, no trays, no plates; there were neither slippers nor scissors, neither shoebrushes nor blacking; there were no knives or forks or spoons. The supply of fuel was constantly deficient. The cooking arrangements were preposterously inadequate, and the laundry was a farce. As for purely medical materials, the tale was no better. Stretchers, splints, bandages—all were lacking; and so were the most ordinary drugs.

To replace such wants, to struggle against such difficulties, there was a handful of men overburdened by the strain of ceaseless work, bound down by the traditions of official routine, and enfeebled either by old age or inexperience or sheer incompetence. They had proved utterly unequal to their task. The principal doctor was lost in the imbecilities of a senile optimism. The wretched official whose business it was to provide for the wants of the hospital was tied fast hand and foot by red tape. A few of the younger doctors struggled valiantly, but what could they do? Unprepared, disorganised, with such help only as they could find among the miserable band of convalescent soldiers drafted off to tend their sick comrades, they were faced with disease, mutilation, and death in all their most appalling forms, crowded multitudinously about them in an ever increasing mass. They were like men in a shipwreck, fighting, not for safety, but for the next moment's bare existence—to gain, by yet another frenzied effort, some brief respite from the waters of destruction.

In these surroundings, those who had been long inured to scenes of human suffering—surgeons with a world-wide knowledge of agonies, soldiers familiar with fields of carnage, missionaries with remembrances of famine and of plague—yet found a depth of horror which they had never known before. There were moments, there were places, in the Barrack Hospital at Scutari, where the strongest hand was struck with trembling, and the boldest eye would turn away its gaze.

Miss Nightingale came, and she, at any rate, in that Inferno, did not abandon hope. For one thing, she brought material succour. Before she left London she had consulted Dr. Andrew Smith, the head of the Army Medical Board, as to whether it would be useful to take out stores of any kind to Scutari; and Dr. Andrew Smith had told her that "nothing was needed." Even Sidney Herbert had given her similar assurances; possibly, owing to an oversight, there might have been some delay in the delivery of the medical stores, which, he said, had been sent out from England "in profusion," but "four days would have remedied this." She preferred to trust her own instincts, and at Marseilles purchased a large quantity of miscellaneous provisions, which were of the utmost use at Scutari. She came, too, amply provided with money—in all, during her stay in the East, about £7,000 reached her from private sources; and, in addition, she was able to avail herself of another valuable means of help. At the same time as herself, Mr. Macdonald, of the *Times*, had arrived at Scutari, charged with the duty of administering the large sums of money collected through the agency of that newspaper in aid of the sick and wounded; and Mr. Macdonald had the sense to see that the best use he could make of the *Times* Fund was to put it at the disposal of Miss Nightingale.

I cannot conceive [wrote an eye-witness], as I now calmly look back on the first three weeks after the arrival of the wounded from Inkerman, how it could have been possible to have avoided a state of things too disastrous to contemplate, had not Miss Nightingale been there, with the means placed at her disposal by Mr. Macdonald.

But the official view was different. What! Was the public service to admit, by accepting outside charity, that it was unable to discharge its own duties without the assistance of private and irregular benevolence? Never! And accordingly when Lord Stratford de Redcliffe, our Ambassador at Constantinople, was asked by Mr. Macdonald to indicate how the *Times* Fund could best be employed, he answered that there was indeed one object to which it might very well be devoted—the building of an English Protestant Church at Pera.

Mr. Macdonald did not waste further time with Lord Stratford, and immediately joined forces with Miss Nightingale. But, with such a frame of mind in the highest quarters, it is easy to imagine the kind of disgust and alarm with which the sudden intrusion of a band of amateurs and females must have filled the minds of the ordinary officer and the ordinary military surgeon. They could not understand it; what had women to do with war? Honest Colonels relieved their spleen by the cracking of heavy jokes about "the Bird"; while poor Dr. Hall, a rough terrier of a man, who had worried his way to the top of his profession, was struck speechless with astonishment, and at last observed that Miss Nightingale's appointment was extremely droll.

Her position was, indeed, an official one, but it was hardly the easier for that. In the hospitals it was her duty to provide the services of herself and her nurses when they were asked for by the doctors, and not until then. At first some of the surgeons would have nothing to say to her, and, though she was welcomed by others, the majority were hostile and suspicious. But gradually she gained ground. Her good will could not be denied, and her capacity could not be disregarded. With consummate tact, with all the gentleness of supreme strength, she managed at last to impose her personality upon the susceptible, overwrought, discouraged, and helpless group of men in authority who surrounded her. She stood firm; she was a rock in the angry ocean; with her alone was safety, comfort, life. And so it was that hope dawned at Scutari. The reign of chaos and old night began to dwindle; order came upon the scene, and common sense, and forethought, and decision, radiating out from the little room off the great gallery in the Barrack Hospital where day and night the Lady Superintendent was at her task. Progress might be slow, but it was sure. The first sign of a great change came with the appearance of some of those necessary objects with which the hospitals had been unprovided for months. The sick men began to enjoy the use of towels and soap, knives and forks, combs and tooth-brushes. Dr. Hall might snort when he heard of it, asking, with a growl, what a soldier wanted with a tooth-brush; but the good work went on. Eventually the whole business of purveying to the hospitals was, in effect, carried out by Miss Nightingale. She alone, it seemed, whatever the contingency, knew where to lay her hands on what was wanted; she alone could dispense her stores with readiness; above all she alone possessed the art of circumventing the pernicious influences of official etiquette. This was her greatest enemy, and sometimes even she was baffled by it. On one occasion 27,000 shirts sent out at her instance by the Home Government, arrived, were landed, and were only waiting to be unpacked. But the official "Purveyor" intervened; "he could not unpack them," he said, "without a board." Miss Nightingale pleaded in vain; the sick and wounded lay half-naked shivering for want of clothing; and three weeks elapsed before the Board released the shirts. A little later, however, on a similar occasion, Miss Nightingale felt that she could assert her own authority. She ordered a Government consignment to be forcibly opened, while the miserable "Purveyor" stood by, wringing his hands in departmental agony.

Vast quantities of valuable stores sent from England lay, she found, engulfed in the bottomless abyss of the Turkish Customs

House. Other ship-loads, buried beneath munitions of war destined for Balaclava, passed Scutari without a sign, and thus hospital materials were sometimes carried to and fro three times
over the Black Sea, before they reached their destination. The
whole system was clearly at fault, and Miss Nightingale suggested to the home authorities that a Government Store House
should be instituted at Scutari for the reception and distribution
of the consignments. Six months after her arrival this was done.

In the meantime she had reorganised the kitchens and the laun-
dries in the hospitals. The ill-cooked hunks of meat, vilely served
at irregular intervals, which had hitherto been the only diet for
the sick men were replaced by punctual meals, well-prepared and
appetising, while strengthening extra foods—soups and wines, and
jellies ("preposterous luxuries," snarled Dr. Hall)—were distributed to those who needed them. One thing, however, she could
not effect. The separation of the bones from the meat was no
part of official cookery: the rule was that the food must be divided into equal portions, and if some of the portions were all
bone—well, every man must take his chance. The rule, perhaps,
was not a very good one; but there it was. "It would require a
new Regulation of the Service," she was told, "to bone the meat."
As for the washing arrangements, they were revolutionised. Up
to the time of Miss Nightingale's arrival the number of shirts
which the authorities had succeeded in washing was seven. The
hospital bedding, she found, was "washed" in cold water. She
took a Turkish house, had boilers installed, and employed soldiers' wives to do the laundry work. The expenses were defrayed
from her own funds and that of the *Times;* and henceforward the
sick and wounded had the comfort of clean linen.

Then she turned her attention to their clothing. Owing to military exigencies the greater number of the men had abandoned
their kit; their knapsacks were lost for ever; they possessed nothing but what was on their persons, and that was usually only fit
for speedy destruction. The "Purveyor," of course, pointed out
that, according to the regulations, all soldiers should bring with
them into hospital an adequate supply of clothing, and he declared that it was no business of his to make good their defi-

ciencies. Apparently, it was the business of Miss Nightingale. She procured socks, boots, and shirts in enormous quantities; she had trousers made; she rigged up dressing-gowns. "The fact is," she told Sidney Herbert, "I am now clothing the British Army."

All at once, word came from the Crimea that a great new contingent of sick and wounded might shortly be expected. Where were they to go? Every available inch in the wards was occupied; the affair was serious and pressing, and the authorities stood aghast. There were some dilapidated rooms in the Barrack Hospital, unfit for human habitation, but Miss Nightingale believed that if measures were promptly taken they might be made capable of accommodating several hundred beds. One of the doctors agreed with her; the rest of the officials were irresolute: it would be a very expensive job, they said; it would involve building; and who could take the responsibility? The proper course was that a representation should be made to the Director-General of the Army Medical Department in London; then the Director-General would apply to the Horse Guards, the Horse Guards would move the Ordnance, the Ordnance would lay the matter before the Treasury, and, if the Treasury gave its consent, the work might be correctly carried through, several months after the necessity for it had disappeared. Miss Nightingale, however, had made up her mind, and she persuaded Lord Stratford—or thought she had persuaded him—to give his sanction to the required expenditure. A hundred and twenty-five workmen were immediately engaged, and the work was begun. The workmen struck; whereupon Lord Stratford washed his hands of the whole business. Miss Nightingale engaged two hundred other workmen on her own authority, and paid the bill out of her own resources. The wards were ready by the required date; five hundred sick men were received in them; and all the utensils, including knives, forks, spoons, cans and towels, were supplied by Miss Nightingale.

This remarkable woman was in truth performing the function of an administrative chief. How had this come about? Was she not in reality merely a nurse? Was it not her duty simply to tend to the sick? And indeed, was it not as a ministering angel, a gentle "lady with a lamp" that she actually impressed the minds of her contemporaries? No doubt that was so; and yet it is no less certain that, as she herself said, the specific business of nursing was "the least important of the functions into which she had been forced." It was clear that in the state of disorganisation into which the hospitals at Scutari had fallen the most pressing, the really vital, need was for something more than nursing; it was for the necessary elements of civilised life—the commonest material objects, the most ordinary cleanliness, the rudimentary habits of order and authority. "Oh, dear Miss Nightingale," said one of her party as they were approaching Constantinople, "when we land, let there be no delays, let us get straight to nursing the poor fellows!" "The strongest will be wanted at the wash-tub," was Miss Nightingale's answer. And it was upon the wash-tub, and all that the wash-tub stood for, that she expended her greatest energies. Yet to say that is perhaps to say too much. For to those who watched her at work among the sick, moving day and night from bed to bed, with that unflinching courage, with that indefatigable vigilance, it seemed as if the concentrated force of an undivided and unparalleled devotion could hardly suffice for that portion of her task alone. Wherever, in those vast wards, suffering was at its worst and the need for help was greatest, there, as if by magic, was Miss Nightingale. Her superhuman equanimity would, at the moment of some ghastly operation, nerve the victim to endure and almost to hope. Her sympathy would assuage the pangs of dying and bring back to those still living something of the forgotten charm of life. Over and over again her untiring efforts rescued those whom the surgeons had abandoned as beyond the possibility of cure. Her mere presence brought with it a strange influence. A passionate idolatry spread among the men: they kissed her shadow as it passed. They did more. "Before she came," said a soldier, "there was cussin' and swearin', but after that it was as 'oly as a church." The most cherished privilege of the fighting man was abandoned for the sake of Miss Nightingale. In those "lowest sinks of human misery," as she herself put it, she never heard the use of one expression "which could distress a gentlewoman."

She was heroic; and these were the humble tributes paid by

those of grosser mould to that high quality. Certainly, she was heroic. Yet her heroism was not of that simple sort so dear to the readers of novels and the compilers of hagiologies—the romantic sentimental heroism with which mankind loves to invest its chosen darlings: it was made of sterner stuff. To the wounded soldier on his couch of agony she might well appear in the guise of a gracious angel of mercy; but the military surgeons, and the orderlies, and her own nurses, and the "Purveyor," and Dr. Hall, and even Lord Stratford himself could tell a different story. It was not by gentle sweetness and womanly self-abnegation that she had brought order out of chaos in the Scutari Hospitals, that, from her own resources, she had clothed the British Army, that she had spread her dominion over the serried and reluctant powers of the official world; it was by strict method, by stern discipline, by rigid attention to detail, by ceaseless labour, by the fixed determination of an indomitable will. Beneath her cool and calm demeanour lurked fierce and passionate fires. As she passed through the wards in her plain dress, so quiet, so unassuming, she struck the casual observer simply as the pattern of a perfect lady; but the keener eye perceived something more than that—the serenity of high deliberation in the scope of the capacious brow, the sign of power in the dominating curve of the thin nose, and the traces of a harsh and dangerous temper—something peevish, something mocking, and yet something precise—in the small and delicate mouth. There was humour in the face; but the curious watcher might wonder whether it was humour of a very pleasant kind; might ask himself, even as he heard the laughter and marked the jokes with which she cheered the spirits of her patients, what sort of sardonic merriment this same lady might not give vent to, in the privacy of her chamber. As for her voice, it was true of it, even more than of her countenance, that it "had that in it one must fain call master." Those clear tones were in no need of emphasis: "I never heard her raise her voice," said one of her companions. Only, when she had spoken, it seemed as if nothing could follow but obedience. Once, when she had given some direction, a doctor ventured to remark that the thing could not be done. "But it must be done," said Miss Nightingale. A chance bystander,

who heard the words, never forgot through all his life the irresistible authority of them. And they were spoken quietly—very
quietly indeed.

Late at night, when the long miles of beds lay wrapped in
darkness, Miss Nightingale would sit at work in her little room,
over her correspondence. It was one of the most formidable of
all her duties. There were hundreds of letters to be written to the
friends and relations of soldiers; there was the enormous mass of
official documents to be dealt with; there were her own private
letters to be answered; and, most important of all, there was the
composition of her long and confidential reports to Sidney Herbert. These were by no means official communications. Her soul,
pent up all day in the restraint and reserve of a vast responsibility,
now at last poured itself out in these letters with all its natural
vehemence, like a swollen torrent through an open sluice. Here,
at least, she did not mince matters. Here she painted in her dark-
est colours the hideous scenes which surrounded her; here she
tore away remorselessly the last veils still shrouding the abominable truth. Then she would fill the pages with recommendations
and suggestions, with criticisms of the minutest details of organisation, with elaborate calculations of contingencies, with exhaustive analyses and statistical statements piled up in breathless eagerness one on the top of the other. And then her pen, in the viru-
lence of its volubility, would rush on to the discussion of individuals, to the denunciation of an incompetent surgeon or the
ridicule of a self-sufficient nurse. Her sarcasm searched the ranks
of the officials with the deadly and unsparing precision of a
machine-gun. Her nicknames were terrible. She respected no
one: Lord Stratford, Lord Raglan, Lady Stratford, Dr. Andrew
Smith, Dr. Hall, the Commissary-General, the Purveyor—she ful-
minated against them all. The intolerable futility of mankind obsessed her like a nightmare, and she gnashed her teeth against it.
"I do well to be angry," was the burden of her cry. How many
just men were there at Scutari? How many who cared at all for
the sick, or had done anything for their relief? Were there ten?
Were there five? Was there even one? She could not be sure.

At one time, during several weeks, her vituperations descended upon the head of Sidney Herbert himself. He had misinterpreted her wishes, he had traversed her positive instructions, and it was not until he had admitted his error and apologised in abject terms that he was allowed again into favour. While this misunderstanding was at its height an aristocratic young gentleman arrived at Scutari with a recommendation from the Minister. He had come out from England filled with a romantic desire to render homage to the angelic heroine of his dreams. He had, he said, cast aside his life of ease and luxury; he would devote his days and nights to the service of that gentle lady; he would perform the most menial offices, he would "fag" for her, he would be her footman—and feel requited by a single smile. A single smile, indeed, he had, but it was of an unexpected kind. Miss Nightingale at first refused to see him, and then, when she consented, believing that he was an emissary sent by Sidney Herbert to put her in the wrong over their dispute, she took notes of her conversation with him, and insisted on his signing them at the end of it. The young gentleman returned to England by the next ship.

This quarrel with Sidney Herbert was, however, an exceptional incident. Alike by him, and by Lord Panmure, his successor at the War Office, she was firmly supported; and the fact that during the whole of her stay at Scutari she had the Home Government at her back, was her trump card in her dealings with the hospital authorities. Nor was it only the Government that was behind her: public opinion in England early recognised the high importance of her mission, and its enthusiastic appreciation of her work soon reached an extraordinary height. The Queen herself was deeply moved. She made repeated inquiries as to the welfare of Miss Nightingale; she asked to see her accounts of the wounded, and made her the intermediary between the throne and the troops.

Let Mrs. Herbert know [she wrote to the War Minister] that I wish Miss Nightingale and the ladies would tell these poor noble, wounded, and sick men that *no one* takes a warmer interest or feels *more* for their sufferings or admires their courage and heroism *more* than their Queen. Day and night she thinks of her beloved troops. So does the Prince. Beg Mrs. Herbert to communicate these my words to those ladies, as I know that *our* sympathy is much valued by these noble fellows.

The letter was read aloud in the wards by the Chaplain. "It is a very feeling letter," said the men.

And so the months passed, and that fell winter which had begun with Inkerman and had dragged itself out through the long agony of the investment of Sebastopol, at last was over. In May, 1855, after six months of labour, Miss Nightingale could look with something like satisfaction at the condition of the Scutari hospitals. Had they done nothing more than survive the terrible strain which had been put upon them, it would have been a matter for congratulation; but they had done much more than that; they had marvellously improved. The confusion and the pressure in the wards had come to an end; order reigned in them, and cleanliness; the supplies were bountiful and prompt; important sanitary works had been carried out. One simple comparison of figures was enough to reveal the extraordinary change: the rate of mortality among the cases treated had fallen from 42 per cent. to 22 per thousand. But still the indefatigable lady was not satisfied. The main problem had been solved—the physical needs of the men had been provided for; their mental and spiritual needs remained. She set up and furnished reading-rooms and recreation-rooms. She started classes and lectures. Officers were amazed to see her treating their men as if they were human beings, and assured her that she would only end by "spoiling the brutes." But that was not Miss Nightingale's opinion, and she was justified. The private soldier began to drink less, and even—though that seemed impossible—to save his pay. Miss Nightingale became a banker for the army, receiving and sending home large sums of money every month. At last, reluctantly, the Government followed suit, and established machinery of its own for the remission of money. Lord Panmure, however, remained sceptical; "it will do no good," he pronounced; "the British soldier is not a remitting animal." But, in fact, during the next six months, £71,000 was sent home.

Amid all these activities, Miss Nightingale took up the further task of inspecting the hospitals in the Crimea itself. The labour was extreme, and the conditions of life were almost intolerable. She spent whole days in the saddle, or was driven over those bleak and rocky heights in a baggage cart. Sometimes she stood for hours in the heavily falling snow, and would only reach her hut at dead of night after walking for miles through perilous ravines. Her powers of resistance seemed incredible, but at last they were exhausted. She was attacked by fever, and for a moment came very near to death. Yet she worked on; if she could not move, she could at least write; and write she did until her mind had left her; and after it had left her, in what seemed the delirious trance of death itself, she still wrote. When, after many weeks, she was strong enough to travel, she was to return to England, but she utterly refused. She would not go back, she said, before the last of the soldiers had left Scutari.

This happy moment had almost arrived, when suddenly the smouldering hostilities of the medical authorities burst out into a flame. Dr. Hall's labours had been rewarded by a K.C.B.—letters which, as Miss Nightingale told Sidney Herbert, she could only suppose to mean "Knight of the Crimean Burial-grounds"—and the honour had turned his head. He was Sir John, and he would be thwarted no longer. Disputes had lately arisen between Miss Nightingale and some of the nurses in the Crimean hospitals. The situation had been embittered by rumours of religious dissensions, for, while the Crimean nurses were Roman Catholics, many of those at Scutari were suspected of a regrettable propensity towards the tenets of Dr. Pusey. Miss Nightingale was by no means disturbed by these sectarian differences, but any suggestion that her supreme authority over all the nurses with the Army was in doubt was enough to rouse her to fury; and it appeared that Mrs. Bridgeman, the Reverend Mother in the Crimeas, had ventured to call that authority in question. Sir John Hall thought that his opportunity had come, and strongly supported Mrs. Bridgeman—or, as Miss Nightingale preferred to call her, the "Reverend Brickbat." There was a violent struggle; Miss Nightingale's rage was terrible. Dr. Hall, she declared, was doing his best to "root her out of the Crimea." She would bear it no longer; the War Office was playing her false; there was only one thing to be done —Sidney Herbert must move for the production of papers in the House of Commons, so that the public might be able to judge between her and her enemies. Sidney Herbert with great difficulty calmed her down. Orders were immediately dispatched putting her supremacy beyond doubt, and the Reverend Brickbat withdrew from the scene. Sir John, however, was more tenacious. A few weeks later, Miss Nightingale and her nurses visited the Crimea for the last time, and the brilliant idea occurred to him that he could crush her by a very simple expedient—he would starve her into submission; and he actually ordered that no rations of any kind should be supplied to her. He had already tried this plan with great effect upon an unfortunate medical man whose presence in the Crimea he had considered an intrusion; but he was now to learn that such tricks were thrown away upon Miss Nightingale. With extraordinary foresight, she had brought with her a great supply of food; she succeeded in obtaining more at her own expense and by her own exertions; and thus for ten days, in that inhospitable country, she was able to feed herself and twenty-four nurses. Eventually the military authorities intervened in her favour, and Sir John had to confess that he was beaten.

It was not until July, 1856—four months after the Declaration of Peace—that Miss Nightingale left Scutari for England. Her reputation was now enormous, and the enthusiasm of the public was unbounded. The Royal approbation was expressed by the gift of a brooch, accompanied by a private letter.

You are, I know, well aware [wrote Her Majesty] of the high sense I entertain of the Christian devotion which you have displayed during this great and bloody war, and I need hardly repeat to you how warm my admiration is for your services, which are fully equal to those of my dear and brave soldiers, whose sufferings you have had the *privilege* of alleviating is so merciful a manner. I am, however, anxious of marking my feelings in a manner which I trust will be agreeable to you, and therefore send you with this letter a brooch, the form and emblems of which commemorate your great and blessed work, and which I hope you will wear as a mark of the high approbation of your Sovereign!

"It will be a very great satisfaction to me," Her Majesty added, "to make the acquaintance of one who has set so bright an example to our sex."

The brooch, which was designed by the Prince Consort, bore a St. George's cross in red enamel, and the Royal cypher surmounted by diamonds. The whole was encircled by the inscription, "Blessed are the Merciful."

## III

The name of Florence Nightingale lives in the memory of the world by virtue of the lurid and heroic adventure of the Crimea. Had she died—as she nearly did—upon her return to England, her reputation would hardly have been different; her legend would have come down to us almost as we know it today—that gentle vision of female virtue which first took shape before the adoring eyes of the sick soldiers at Scutari. Yet, as a matter of fact, she lived for more than half a century after the Crimean War; and during the greater part of that long period all the energy and all the devotion of her extraordinary nature were working at their highest pitch. What she accomplished in those years of unknown labour could, indeed, hardly have been more glorious than her Crimean triumphs; but it was certainly more important. The true history was far stranger even than the myth. In Miss Nightingale's own eyes the adventure of the Crimea was a mere incident—scarcely more than a useful stepping-stone in her career. It was the fulcrum with which she hoped to move the world; but it was only the fulcrum. For more than a generation she was to sit in secret, working her lever: and her real life began at the very moment when, in the popular imagination, it had ended.

She arrived in England in a shattered state of health. The hardships and the ceaseless effort of the last two years had undermined her nervous system; her heart was pronounced to be affected; she suffered constantly from fainting-fits and terrible attacks of utter physical prostration. The doctors declared that one thing alone would save her—a complete and prolonged rest. But that was also the one thing with which she would have nothing to do. She had never been in the habit of resting; why should she begin now? Now, when her opportunity had come at last; now, when the iron was hot, and it was time to strike? No; she had work to do; and, come what might, she would do it. The doctors protested in vain; in vain her family lamented and entreated, in vain her friends pointed out to her the madness of such a course. Madness? Mad—possessed—perhaps she was. A demoniac frenzy had seized upon her. As she lay upon her sofa, gasping, she devoured blue-books, dictated letters, and, in the intervals of her palpitations, cracked her febrile jokes. For months at a stretch she never left her bed. For years she was in daily expectation of Death. But she would not rest. At this rate, the doctors assured her, even if she did not die, she would become an invalid for life. She could not help that; there was the work to be done; and, as for rest, very likely she might rest . . . when she had done it.

Wherever she went, in London or in the country, in the hills of Derbyshire, or among the rhododendrons at Embley, she was haunted by a ghost. It was the spectre of Scutari—the hideous vision of the organisation of a military hospital. She would lay that phantom, or she would perish. The whole system of the Army Medical Department, the education of the Medical Officer, the regulations of hospital procedure . . . *rest?* How could she rest while these things were as they were, while, if the like necessity were to arise again, the like results would follow? And, even in peace and at home, what was the sanitary condition of the Army? The mortality in the barracks was, she found, nearly double the mortality in civil life. "You might as well take 1,100 men every year out upon Salisbury Plain and shoot them," she said. After inspecting the hospitals at Chatham, she smiled grimly. "Yes, this is one more symptom of the system which, in the Crimea, put to death 16,000 men." Scutari had given her knowledge; and it had given her power too: her enormous reputation was at her back—an incalculable force. Other work, other duties, might lie before her; but the most urgent, the most obvious of all was to look to the health of the Army.

One of her very first steps was to take advantage of the invitation which Queen Victoria had sent her to the Crimea, together with the commemorative brooch. Within a few weeks of her return, she visited Balmoral, and had several interviews both with the Queen and the Prince Consort. "She put before us," wrote the

Prince in his diary, "all the defects of our present military hospital system and the reforms that are needed." She related the
whole story of her experiences in the East; and, in addition, she
managed to have some long and confidential talks with His Royal
Highness on metaphysics and religion. The impression which she
created was excellent. "Sie gefällt uns sehr," noted the Prince, "ist
sehr bescheiden." Her Majesty's comment was different—"Such a
*head!* I wish we had her at the War Office."

But Miss Nightingale was not at the War Office, and for a
very simple reason: she was a woman. Lord Panmure, however,
*was* (though indeed the reason for that was not quite so simple);
and it was upon Lord Panmure that the issue of Miss Nightingale's efforts for reform must primarily depend. That burly Scottish nobleman had not, in spite of his most earnest endeavours,
had a very easy time of it as Secretary of State for War. He had
come into office in the middle of the Sebastopol campaign, and
had felt himself very well fitted for the position, since he had acquired in former days an inside knowledge of the Army—as a
Captain of Hussars. It was this inside knowledge which had enabled him to inform Miss Nightingale with such authority that
"the British soldier is not a remitting animal." And perhaps it was
this same consciousness of a command of his subject which had
impelled him to write a dispatch to Lord Raglan, blandly informing the Commander-in-Chief in the Field just how he was neg-
lecting his duties, and pointing out to him that if he would only
try he really might do a little better next time. Lord Raglan's
reply, calculated as it was to make its recipient sink into the earth,
did not quite have that effect upon Lord Panmure, who, whatever might have been his faults, had never been accused of being
supersensitive. However, he allowed the matter to drop; and a
little later Lord Raglan died—worn out, some people said, by
work and anxiety. He was succeeded by an excellent red-nosed
old gentleman, General Simpson, whom nobody has ever heard
of, and who took Sebastopol. But Lord Panmure's relations with
him were hardly more satisfactory than his relations with Lord
Raglan; for, while Lord Raglan had been too independent, poor
General Simpson erred in the opposite direction, perpetually

asked advice, suffered from lumbago, doubted, his nose growing daily redder and redder, whether he was fit for his post, and, by alternate mails, sent in and withdrew his resignation. Then, too, both the General and the Minister suffered acutely from that distressingly useful new invention, the electric telegraph. On one occasion General Simpson felt obliged actually to expostulate.

I think, my Lord [he wrote], that some telegraphic messages reach us that cannot be sent under due authority, and are perhaps unknown to you, although under the protection of your Lordship's name. For instance, I was called up last night, a dragoon having come express with a telegraphic message in these words, "Lord Panmure to General Simpson—Captain Jarvis has been bitten by a centipede. How is he now?"

General Simpson might have put up with this, though to be sure it did seem "rather too trifling an affair to call for a dragoon to ride a couple of miles in the dark that he may knock up the Commander of the Army out of the very small allowance of sleep permitted him"; but what was really more than he could bear was to find "upon sending in the morning another mounted dragoon to inquire after Captain Jarvis, four miles off, that he never has been bitten at all, but has had a boil, from which he is fast recovering." But Lord Panmure had troubles of his own. His favourite nephew, Captain Dowbiggin, was at the front, and to one of his telegrams to the Commander-in-Chief the Minister had taken occasion to append the following carefully qualified sentence—"I recommend Dowbiggin to your notice, should you have a vacancy, and if he is fit." Unfortunately, in those early days, it was left to the discretion of the telegraphist to compress the messages which passed through his hands; so that the result was that Lord Panmure's delicate appeal reached its destination in the laconic form of "Look after Dowb." The Headquarters Staff were at first extremely puzzled; they were at last extremely amused. The story spread; and "Look after Dowb" remained for many years the familiar formula for describing official hints in favour of deserving nephews.

And now that all this was over, now that Sebastopol had been, somehow or another, taken, now that peace was, somehow or another, made, now that the troubles of office might surely be ex-

pected to be at an end at last—here was Miss Nightingale breaking in upon the scene, with her talk about the state of the hospitals and the necessity for sanitary reform. It was most irksome;
and Lord Panmure almost began to wish that he was engaged
upon some more congenial occupation—discussing, perhaps, the
constitution of the Free Church of Scotland—a question in which
he was profoundly interested. But no; duty was paramount; and
he set himself, with a sigh of resignation, to the task of doing
as little of it as he possibly could.

"The Bison" his friends called him; and the name fitted both
his physical demeanour and his habit of mind. That large low
head seemed to have been created for butting rather than for anything else. There he stood, four-square and menacing, in the
doorway of reform; and it remained to be seen whether the bulky
mass, upon whose solid hide even the barbed arrows of Lord Raglan's scorn had made no mark, would prove amenable to the pressure of Miss Nightingale. Nor was he alone in the doorway.
There loomed behind him the whole phalanx of professional conservatism, the stubborn supporters of the out-of-date, the worshippers and the victims of War Office routine. Among these it
was only natural that Dr. Andrew Smith, the head of the Army
Medical Department, should have been pre-eminent—Dr. Andrew
Smith, who had assured Miss Nightingale before she left England
that "nothing was wanted at Scutari." Such were her opponents;
but she too was not without allies. She had gained the ear of Royalty—which was something; at any moment that she pleased she
could gain the ear of the public—which was a great deal. She had a
host of admirers and friends; and—to say nothing of her personal
qualities—her knowledge, her tenacity, her tact—she possessed,
too, one advantage which then, far more even than now, carried
an immense weight—she belonged to the highest circle of society.
She moved naturally among Peers and Cabinet Ministers—she
was one of their own set; and in those days their set was a very
narrow one. What kind of attention would such persons have
paid to some middle-class woman with whom they were not
acquainted, who possessed great experience of army nursing and
had decided views upon hospital reform? They would have po-

litely ignored her; but it was impossible to ignore Flo Nightingale. When she spoke, they were obliged to listen; and, when
they had once begun to do that—what might not follow? She
knew her power, and she used it. She supported her weightiest
minutes with familiar witty little notes. The Bison began to look
grave. It might be difficult—it might be damned difficult—to put
down one's head against the white hand of a lady.

Of Miss Nightingale's friends, the most important was Sidney
Herbert. He was a man upon whom the good fairies seemed to
have showered, as he lay in his cradle, all their most enviable
gifts. Well born, handsome, rich, the master of Wilton—one of
those great country-houses, clothed with the glamour of a his-
toric past, which are the peculiar glory of England—he possessed,
besides all these advantages, so charming, so lively, so gentle a
disposition that no one who had once come near him could ever
be his enemy. He was, in fact, a man of whom it was difficult not
to say that he was a perfect English gentleman. For his virtues
were equal even to his good fortune. He was religious—deeply
religious: "I am more and more convinced every day," he wrote,
when he had been for some years a Cabinet Minister, "that in
politics, as in everything else, nothing can be right which is not
in accordance with the spirit of the Gospel." No one was more
unselfish; he was charitable and benevolent to a remarkable degree; and he devoted the whole of his life with an unwavering
conscientiousness to the public service. With such a character,
with such opportunities, what high hopes must have danced before him, what radiant visions of accomplished duties, of ever-
increasing usefulness, of beneficent power, of the consciousness
of disinterested success! Some of those hopes and visions were,
indeed, realised; but, in the end, the career of Sidney Herbert
seemed to show that, with all their generosity, there was some
gift or other—what was it?—some essential gift—which the good
fairies had withheld, and that even the qualities of a perfect English gentleman may be no safeguard against anguish, humiliation,
and defeat.

That career would certainly have been very different if he had
never known Miss Nightingale. The alliance between them, which

had begun with her appointment to Scutari, which had grown closer and closer while the war lasted, developed, after her return, into one of the most extraordinary of friendships. It was the friendship of a man and a woman intimately bound together by their devotion to a public cause; mutual affection, of course, played a part in it, but it was an incidental part; the whole soul of the relationship was a community of work. Perhaps out of England such an intimacy could hardly have existed—an intimacy so utterly untinctured not only by passion itself but by the suspicion of it. For years Sidney Herbert saw Miss Nightingale almost daily, for long hours together, corresponding with her incessantly when they were apart; and the tongue of scandal was silent; and one of the most devoted of her admirers was his wife. But what made the connection still more remarkable was the way in which the parts that were played in it were divided between the two. The man who acts, decides, and achieves; the woman who encourages, applauds, and—from a distance—inspires:—the combination is common enough; but Miss Nightingale was neither an Aspasia nor an Egeria. In her case it is almost true to say that the rôles were reversed; the qualities of pliancy and sympathy fell to the man, those of command and initiative to the woman. There was one thing only which Miss Nightingale lacked in her equipment for public life; she had not—she never could have—the public power and authority which belong to the successful politician. That power and authority Sidney Herbert possessed; the fact was obvious, and the conclusion no less so: it was through the man that the woman must work her will. She took hold of him, taught him, shaped him, absorbed him, dominated him through and through. He did not resist—he did not wish to resist; his natural inclination lay along the same path as hers; only that terrific personality swept him forward at her own fierce pace and with her own relentless stride. Swept him—where to? Ah! Why had he ever known Miss Nightingale? If Lord Panmure was a bison, Sidney Herbert, no doubt, was a stag—a comely, gallant creature springing through the forest; but the forest is a dangerous place. One has the image of those wide eyes fascinated suddenly by something feline, something strong; there is a pause; and then the tigress has her claws in the quivering haunches; and then—!

Besides Sidney Herbert, she had other friends who, in a more restricted sphere, were hardly less essential to her. If, in her condition of bodily collapse, she were to accomplish what she was determined that she should accomplish, the attentions and the services of others would be absolutely indispensable. Helpers and servers she must have; and accordingly there was soon formed about her a little group of devoted disciples upon whose affections and energies she could implicitly rely. Devoted, indeed, these disciples were, in no ordinary sense of the term; for certainly she was no light task-mistress, and he who set out to be of use to Miss Nightingale was apt to find, before he had gone very far, that he was in truth being made use of in good earnest—to the very limit of his endurance and his capacity. Perhaps, even beyond those limits; why not? Was she asking of others more than she was giving herself? Let them look at her lying there pale and breathless on the couch; could it be said that she spared herself? Why, then, should she spare others? And it was not for her own sake that she made these claims. For her own sake, indeed! No! They all knew it! it was for the sake of the work. And so the little band, bound body and soul in that strange servitude, laboured on ungrudgingly. Among the most faithful was her "Aunt Mai," her father's sister, who from the earliest days had stood beside her, who had helped her to escape from the thraldom of family life, who had been with her at Scutari, and who now acted almost the part of a mother to her, watching over her with infinite care in all the movements and uncertainties which her state of health involved. Another constant attendant was her brother-in-law, Sir Harry Verney, whom she found particularly valuable in parliamentary affairs. Arthur Clough, the poet, also a connection by marriage, she used in other ways. Ever since he had lost his faith at the time of the Oxford Movement, Clough had passed his life in a condition of considerable uneasiness, which was increased rather than diminished by the practice of poetry. Unable to decide upon the purpose of an existence whose savour had fled together with his belief in the Resurrection, his spirits lowered still further by ill-health, and his income not all that it should be, he had determined to seek the solution of his difficulties in the United States of America. But, even there, the solution was not forthcoming; and when, a little later, he was offered a post in a government department at home, he accepted it, came to live in London, and immediately fell under the influence of Miss Nightingale. Though the purpose of existence might be still uncertain and its nature still unsavoury, here, at any rate, under the eye of this inspired woman, was something real, something earnest: his only doubt was—could he be of any use? Certainly he could. There were a great number of miscellaneous little jobs which there was nobody handy to do. For instance, when Miss Nightingale was travelling, there were the railway-tickets to be taken; and there were proof-sheets to be corrected; and then there were parcels to be done up in brown paper, and carried to the post. Certainly he could be useful. And so, upon such occupations as these, Arthur Clough was set to work. "This that I see, is not all," he comforted himself by reflecting, "and this that I do is but little; nevertheless it is good, though there is better than it."

As time went on, her "Cabinet," as she called it, grew larger. Officials with whom her work brought her into touch and who sympathised with her objects, were pressed into her service; and old friends of the Crimean days gathered round her when they returned to England. Among these the most indefatigable was Dr. Sutherland, a sanitary expert, who for more than thirty years acted as her confidential private secretary, and surrendered to her purposes literally the whole of his life. Thus sustained and assisted, thus slaved for and adored, she prepared to beard the Bison.

Two facts soon emerged, and all that followed turned upon them. It became clear, in the first place, that that imposing mass was not immovable, and, in the second, that its movement, when it did move, would be exceedingly slow. The Bison was no match for the Lady. It was in vain that he put down his head and planted his feet in the earth; he could not withstand her; the white hand forced him back. But the process was an extraordinarily gradual one. Dr. Andrew Smith and all his War Office phalanx stood behind, blocking the way; the poor Bison groaned inwardly, and cast a wistful eye towards the happy pastures of the Free Church of Scotland; then slowly, with infinite reluctance, step by step, he retreated, disputing every inch of the ground.

The first great measure, which, supported as it was by the Queen, the Cabinet, and the united opinion of the country, it was impossible to resist, was the appointment of a Royal Commission to report upon the health of the Army. The question of the composition of the Commission then immediately arose; and it was over this matter that the first hand-to-hand encounter between Lord Panmure and Miss Nightingale took place. They met, and Miss Nightingale was victorious; Sidney Herbert was appointed Chairman; and, in the end the only member of the Commission opposed to her views was Dr. Andrew Smith. During the interview, Miss Nightingale made an important discovery: she found that "the Bison was bullyable"—the hide was the hide of a Mexican buffalo, but the spirit was the spirit of an Alderney calf. And there was one thing above all others which the huge creature dreaded—an appeal to public opinion. The faintest hint of such a terrible eventuality made his heart dissolve within him; he would agree to anything—he would cut short his grouse-shooting—he would make a speech in the House of Lords—he would even overrule Dr. Andrew Smith—rather than that. Miss Nightingale held the fearful threat in reserve—she would speak out what she knew; she would publish the truth to the whole world, and let the whole world judge between them. With supreme skill, she kept this sword of Damocles poised above the Bison's head, and more than once she was actually on the point of really dropping it. For his recalcitrancy grew and grew. The *personnel* of the Commission once determined upon, there was a struggle, which lasted for six months, over the nature of its powers. Was it to be an efficient body, armed with the right of full inquiry and wide examination, or was it to be a polite official contrivance for exonerating Dr. Andrew Smith? The War Office phalanx closed its ranks, and fought tooth and nail; but it was defeated: the Bison was bullyable.

Three months from this day [Miss Nightingale had written at last] I publish my experience of the Crimean Campaign, and my suggestions for improvement, unless there has been a fair and tangible pledge by that time for
reform.

Who could face that?

And, if the need came, she meant to be as good as her word.
For she had now determined, whatever might be the fate of the
Commission, to draw up her own report upon the questions at
issue. The labour involved was enormous; her health was almost
desperate; but she did not flinch, and after six months of incredible industry she had put together and written with her own hand
her "Notes affecting the Health, Efficiency, and Hospital Administration of the British Army." This extraordinary composition,
filling more than eight hundred closely printed pages, laying
down vast principles of far-reaching reform, discussing the minutest details of a multitude of controversial subjects, containing
an enormous mass of information of the most varied kinds—military, statistical, sanitary, architectural—was never given to the
public, for the need never came; but it formed the basis of the
Report of the Royal Commission; and it remains to this day the
leading authority on the medical administration of armies.

Before it had been completed the struggle over the powers of
the Commission had been brought to a victorious close. Lord
Panmure had given way once more; he had immediately hurried
to the Queen to obtain her consent; and only then, when her
Majesty's initials had been irrevocably affixed to the fatal document, did he dare to tell Dr. Andrew Smith what he had done.
The Commission met, and another immense load fell upon Miss
Nightingale's shoulders. Today she would, of course, have been
one of the Commission herself; but at that time the idea of a
woman appearing in such a capacity was unheard of; and no one
even suggested the possibility of Miss Nightingale's doing so.
The result was that she was obliged to remain behind the scenes
throughout, to coach Sidney Herbert in private at every important juncture, and to convey to him and to her other friends
upon the Commission the vast funds of her expert knowledge—

so essential in the examination of witnesses—by means of innumerable consultations, letters, and memoranda. It was even doubtful whether the proprieties would admit of her giving evidence; and at last, as a compromise, her modesty only allowed her to do so in the form of written answers to written questions. At length the grand affair was finished. The Commission's Report, embodying almost word for word the suggestions of Miss Nightingale, was drawn up by Sidney Herbert. Only one question remained to be answered—would anything, after all, be done? Or would the Royal Commission, like so many other Royal Commissions before and since, turn out to have achieved nothing but the concoction of a very fat blue-book on a very high shelf?

And so the last and the deadliest struggle with the Bison began. Six months had been spent in coercing him into granting the Commission effective powers; six more months were occupied by the work of the Commission; and now yet another six were to pass in extorting from him the means whereby the recommendations of the Commission might be actually carried out. But, in the end, the thing was done. Miss Nightingale seemed indeed, during these months, to be upon the very brink of death. Accompanied by the faithful Aunt Mai, she moved from place to place—to Hampstead, to Highgate, to Derbyshire, to Malvern—in what appeared to be a last desperate effort to find health somewhere; but she carried that with her which made health impossible. Her desire for work could now scarcely be distinguished from mania. At one moment she was writing a "last letter" to Sidney Herbert; at the next she was offering to go out to India to nurse the sufferers in the Mutiny. When Dr. Sutherland wrote, imploring her to take a holiday, she raved. Rest!—

I am lying without my head, without my claws, and you all peck at me. It is *de rigueur, d'obligation*, like the saying something to one's hat, when one goes into church, to say to me all that has been said to me 110 times a day during the last three months. It is the *obbligato* on the violin, and the twelve violins all practise it together, like the clocks striking 12 o'clock at night all over London, till I say like Xavier de Maistre, *Assez, je le sais, je ne le sais que trop.* I am not a penitent; but you are like the R. C. confessor, who says what is *de rigueur.* . . .

Her wits began to turn, and there was no holding her. She worked like a slave in a mine. She began to believe, as she had begun to believe at Scutari, that none of her fellow-workers had their hearts in the business; if they had, why did they not work as she did? She could only see slackness and stupidity around her. Dr. Sutherland, of course, was grotesquely muddle-headed; and Arthur Clough incurably lazy. Even Sidney Herbert . . . oh, yes, he had simplicity and candour and quickness of perception, no doubt; but he was an eclectic; and what could one hope for from a man who went away to fish in Ireland just when the Bison most needed bullying? As for the Bison himself he had fled to Scotland, where he remained buried for many months. The fate of the vital recommendation in the Commission's Report—the appointment of four Sub-Commissions charged with the duty of determining upon the details of the proposed reforms and of putting them into execution—still hung in the balance. The Bison consented to everything; and then, on a flying visit to London, withdrew his consent and hastily returned to Scotland. Then for many weeks all business was suspended; he had gout—gout in the hands, so that he could not write. "His gout was always handy," remarked Miss Nightingale. But eventually it was clear even to the Bison that the game was up, and the inevitable surrender came.

There was, however, one point in which he triumphed over Miss Nightingale. The building of Netley Hospital had been begun, under his orders, before her return to England. Soon after her arrival she examined the plans, and found that they reproduced all the worst faults of an out-of-date and mischievous system of hospital construction. She therefore urged that the matter should be reconsidered, and in the meantime building stopped. But the Bison was obdurate; it would be very expensive, and in any case it was too late. Unable to make any impression on him, and convinced of the extreme importance of the question, she determined to appeal to a higher authority. Lord Palmerston was Prime Minister; she had known him from her childhood; he was a near neighbour of her father's in the New Forest. She went down to the New Forest, armed with the plans of the proposed

hospital and all the relevant information, stayed the night at Lord
Palmerston's house, and convinced him of the necessity of re-
building Netley.

It seems to me [Lord Palmerston wrote to Lord Panmure] that at Netley
all consideration of what would best tend to the comfort and recovery of
the patients has been sacrificed to the vanity of the architect, whose sole
object has been to make a building which should cut a dash when looked
at from the Southampton river. . . . Pray, therefore, stop all further progress in the work until the matter can be duly considered.

But the Bison was not to be moved by one peremptory letter,
even if it was from the Prime Minister. He put forth all his
powers of procrastination, Lord Palmerston lost interest in the
subject, and so the chief military hospital in England was triumphantly completed on unsanitary principles, with unventi-
lated rooms, and with all the patients' windows facing northeast.

But now the time had come when the Bison was to trouble and
to be troubled no more. A vote in the House of Commons
brought about the fall of Lord Palmerston's Government, and
Lord Panmure found himself at liberty to devote the rest of his
life to the Free Church of Scotland. After a brief interval, Sidney
Herbert became Secretary of State for War. Great was the jubila-
tion in the Nightingale Cabinet; the day of achievement had
dawned at last. The next two and a half years (1859-61) saw the
introduction of the whole system of reforms for which Miss
Nightingale had been struggling so fiercely—reforms which make
Sidney Herbert's tenure of power at the War Office an important epoch in the history of the British Army. The four Sub-
Commissions, firmly established under the immediate control of
the Minister, and urged forward by the relentless perseverance of
Miss Nightingale, set to work with a will. The barracks and the
hospitals were remodelled; they were properly ventilated and
warmed and lighted for the first time; they were given a water
supply which actually supplied water, and kitchens where,
strange to say, it was possible to cook. Then the great question
of the Purveyor—that portentous functionary whose powers and
whose lack of powers had weighed like a nightmare upon Scutari
—was taken in hand, and new regulations were laid down, ac-

curately defining his responsibilities and his duties. One Sub-Commission reorganised the medical statistics of the Army. Another established—in spite of the last convulsive efforts of the Department—an Army Medical School. Finally the Army Medical Department itself was completely reorganised; an administrative code was drawn up; and the great and novel principle was established that it was as much a part of the duty of the authorities to look after the soldier's health as to look after his sickness. Besides this, it was at last officially admitted that he had a moral and intellectual side. Coffee-rooms and reading-rooms, gymnasiums and workshops were instituted. A new era did in truth appear to have begun. Already by 1861 the mortality in the army had decreased by one half since the days of the Crimea. It was no wonder that even vaster possibilities began now to open out before Miss Nightingale. One thing was still needed to complete and to assure her triumphs. The Army Medical Department was indeed reorganised; but the great central machine was still untouched. The War Office itself—!—If she could remould *that* nearer to her heart's desire—there indeed would be a victory! And until that final act was accomplished, how could she be certain that all the rest of her achievements might not, by some capricious turn of Fortune's wheel—a change of Ministry, perhaps, replacing Sidney Herbert by some puppet of the permanent official gang—be swept to limbo in a moment?

Meanwhile, still ravenous for more and yet more work, her activities had branched out into new directions. The army in India claimed her attention. A Sanitary Commission, appointed at her suggestion, and working under her auspices, did for our troops there what the four Sub-Commissions were doing for those at home. At the same time, these very years which saw her laying the foundations of the whole modern system of medical work in the army, saw her also beginning to bring her knowledge, her influence, and her activity into the service of the country at large. Her *Notes on Hospitals* (1859) revolutionised the theory of hospital construction and hospital management. She was immediately recognised as the leading expert upon all the questions involved; her advice flowed unceasingly and in all directions, so that there is no great hospital today which does not bear upon it the impress of her mind. Nor was this all. With the opening of the Nightingale Training School for Nurses at St. Thomas's Hospital (1860), she became the founder of modern nursing.

But a terrible crisis was now fast approaching. Sidney Herbert had consented to undertake the root and branch reform of the War Office. He had sallied forth into that tropical jungle of festooned obstructiveness, of intertwisted irresponsibilities, of crouching prejudices, of abuses grown stiff and rigid with antiquity, which for so many years to come was destined to lure reforming ministers to their doom.

The War Office [said Miss Nightingale] is a very slow office, an enormously expensive office, and one in which the Minister's intentions can be entirely negatived by all his sub-departments, and those of each of the sub-departments by every other.

It was true; and, of course, at the first rumour of a change, the old phalanx of reaction was bristling with its accustomed spears. At its head stood no longer Dr. Andrew Smith, who, some time since, had followed the Bison into outer darkness, but a yet more formidable figure, the permanent Under-Secretary himself, Sir Benjamin Hawes—Ben Hawes the Nightingale Cabinet irreverently dubbed him—a man remarkable even among civil servants for adroitness in baffling inconvenient inquiries, resource in raising false issues, and, in short, a consummate command of all the arts of officially sticking in the mud. "Our scheme will probably result in Ben Hawes's resignation," Miss Nightingale said; "and that is another of its advantages." Ben Hawes himself, however, did not quite see it in that light. He set himself to resist the wishes of the Minister by every means in his power. The struggle was long and desperate; and, as it proceeded, it gradually became evident to Miss Nightingale that something was the matter with Sidney Herbert. What was it? His health, never very strong, was, he said, in danger of collapsing under the strain of his work. But, after all, what is illness, when there is a War Office to be reorganised? Then he began to talk of retiring altogether from public life. The doctors were consulted, and declared that, above all things, what was necessary was rest. Rest! She grew seriously alarmed. Was it possible that, at the last moment, the crowning wreath of victory was to be snatched from her grasp? She was not to be put aside by doctors; they were talking nonsense; the necessary thing was not rest but the reform of the War Office; and, besides, she knew very well from her own case what one could do even when one was on the point of death. She expostulated vehemently, passionately: the goal was so near, so very near; he could not turn back now! At any rate, he could not resist Miss Nightingale. A compromise was arranged. Very reluctantly, he exchanged the turmoil of the House of Commons for the dignity of the House of Lords, and he remained at the War Office. She was delighted. "One fight more, the best and the last," she said.

For several more months the fight did indeed go on. But the strain upon him was greater even than she perhaps could realise. Besides the intestine war in his office, he had to face a constant battle in the Cabinet with Mr. Gladstone—a more redoubtable antagonist even than Ben Hawes—over the estimates. His health grew worse and worse. He was attacked by fainting-fits; and there were some days when he could only just keep himself going by gulps of brandy. Miss Nightingale spurred him forward with her encouragements and her admonitions, her zeal and her example. But at last his spirit began to sink as well as his body. He could no longer hope; he could no longer desire; it was useless, all useless; it was utterly impossible. He had failed. The dreadful moment came when the truth was forced upon him: he would never be able to reform the War Office. But a yet more dreadful moment lay behind; he must go to Miss Nightingale and tell her that he was a failure, a beaten man.

Blessed are the merciful! What strange ironic prescience had led Prince Albert, in the simplicity of his heart, to choose that motto for the Crimean brooch? The words hold a double lesson; and, alas! when she brought herself to realise at length what was indeed the fact and what there was no helping, it was not in mercy that she turned upon her old friend.

Beaten! [she exclaimed]. Can't you see that you've simply thrown away the game? And with all the winning cards in your hands! And so noble a game! Sidney Herbert beaten! And beaten by Ben Hawes! It is a worse disgrace . . . [her full rage burst out at last] . . . a worse disgrace than the hospitals at Scutari.

He dragged himself away from her, dragged himself to Spa, hoping vainly for a return of health, and then, despairing, back again to England, to Wilton, to the majestic house standing there resplendent in the summer sunshine, among the great cedars which had lent their shade to Sir Philip Sidney, and all those familiar, darling haunts of beauty which he loved, each one of them, "as if they were persons"; and at Wilton he died. After having received the Eucharist he had become perfectly calm; then, almost unconscious, his lips were seen to be moving. Those about him bent down. "Poor Florence! Poor Florence!" they just caught. ". . . Our joint work . . . unfinished . . . tried to do . . ." and they could hear no more.

When the onward rush of a powerful spirit sweeps a weaker one to its destruction, the commonplaces of the moral judgment are better left unmade. If Miss Nightingale had been less ruthless, Sidney Herbert would not have perished; but then, she would not have been Miss Nightingale. The force that created was the force that destroyed. It was her Demon that was responsible. When the fatal news reached her, she was overcome by agony. In the revulsion of her feelings, she made a worship of the dead man's memory; and the facile instrument which had broken in her hand she spoke of for ever after as her "Master." Then, almost at the same moment, another blow fell upon her. Arthur Clough, worn out by labours very different from those of Sidney Herbert, died too: never more would he tie up her parcels. And yet a third disaster followed. The faithful Aunt Mai did not, to be sure, die; no, she did something almost worse: she left Miss Nightingale. She was growing old, and she felt that she had closer and more imperative duties with her own family. Her niece could hardly forgive her. She poured out, in one of her enormous letters, a passionate diatribe upon the faithlessness, the lack of sympathy, the stupidity, the ineptitude of women. Her doctrines had taken no hold among them; she had never known one who had *appris à apprendre;* she could not even get a woman secretary; "they don't know the names of the Cabinet Ministers— they don't know which of the Churches has Bishops and which not." As for the spirit of self-sacrifice, well—Sidney Herbert and Arthur Clough were men, and they indeed had shown their devotion; but women—! She would mount three widow's caps "for a sign." The first two would be for Clough and for her Master; but the third, "the biggest widow's cap of all"—would be for Aunt Mai. She did well to be angry; she was deserted in her hour of need; and, after all, could she be sure that even the male sex was so impeccable? There was Dr. Sutherland, bungling as usual. Perhaps even he intended to go off, one of these days, too? She gave him a look, and he shivered in his shoes. No!—she grinned sardonically; she would always have Dr. Sutherland. And then she reflected that there was one thing more that she would always have—her work.

## IV

Sidney Herbert's death finally put an end to Miss Nightingale's dream of a reformed War Office. For a moment, indeed, in the first agony of her disappointment, she had wildly clutched at a straw; she had written to Mr. Gladstone to beg him to take up the burden of Sidney Herbert's work. And Mr. Gladstone had replied with a sympathetic account of the funeral.

Succeeding Secretaries of State managed between them to undo a good deal of what had been accomplished, but they could not undo it all; and for ten years more (1862-72) Miss Nightingale remained a potent influence at the War Office. After that, her direct connection with the army came to an end, and her energies began to turn more and more completely towards more general objects. Her work upon hospital reform assumed enormous pro-portions; she was able to improve the conditions in infirmaries and workhouses; and one of her most remarkable papers forestalls the recommendations of the Poor Law Commission of 1909. Her training school for nurses, with all that it involved in initiative, control, responsibility, and combat, would have been enough in itself to have absorbed the whole efforts of at least two lives of ordinary vigour. And at the same time her work in connection with India, which had begun with the Sanitary Commission on the Indian Army, spread and ramified in a multitude of directions. Her tentacles reached the India Office and succeeded in establishing a hold even upon those slippery high places. For many years it was *de rigueur* for the newly appointed Viceroy, before he left England, to pay a visit to Miss Nightingale.

After much hesitation, she had settled down in a small house in South Street, where she remained for the rest of her life. That life was a very long one; the dying woman reached her ninety-first year. Her ill-health gradually diminished; the crises of extreme danger became less frequent, and at last, altogether ceased; she remained an invalid, but an invalid of a curious character— an invalid who was too weak to walk downstairs and who worked far harder than most Cabinet Ministers. Her illness, whatever it may have been, was certainly not inconvenient. It involved seclusion; and an extraordinary, an unparalleled seclusion was, it might almost have been said, the mainspring of Miss Nightingale's life. Lying on her sofa in the little upper room in South Street, she combined the intense vitality of a dominating woman of the world with the mysterious and romantic quality of a myth. She was a legend in her lifetime, and she knew it. She tasted the joys of power, like those Eastern Emperors whose autocratic rule was based upon invisibility, with the mingled satisfactions of obscurity and fame. And she found the machinery of illness hardly less effective as a barrier against the eyes of men than the ceremonial of a palace. Great statesmen and renowned generals were obliged to beg for audiences; admiring princesses from foreign countries found that they must see her at her own time, or not at all; and the ordinary mortal had no hope of ever getting beyond the downstairs sitting-room and Dr. Sutherland. For that indefatigable disciple did, indeed, never desert her. He might be impatient, he might be restless, but he remained. His "incurable looseness of thought," for so she termed it, continued at her service to the end. Once, it is true, he had actually ventured to take a holiday; but he was recalled, and he did not repeat the experiment. He was wanted downstairs. There he sat, transacting business, answering correspondence, interviewing callers, and exchanging innumerable notes with the unseen power above. Sometimes word came down that Miss Nightingale was just well enough to see one of her visitors. The fortunate man was led up, was ushered, trembling, into the shaded chamber, and, of course, could never afterwards forget the interview. Very rarely, indeed, once or twice a year, perhaps, but nobody could be quite certain, in deadly secrecy, Miss Nightingale went out for a drive in the Park. Unrecognised, the living legend flitted for a moment before the common gaze. And the precaution was necessary; for there were times when, at some public function, the rumour of her presence was spread abroad; and ladies, mistaken by the crowd for Miss Nightingale, were followed, pressed upon, and vehemently supplicated—"Let me touch your shawl,"—"Let me stroke your arm"; such was the strange adoration in the hearts of the people. That vast reserve of force lay there behind her; she could use it, if she would. But she preferred never to use it. On occasions, she might hint or threaten; she might balance the sword of Damocles over the head of the Bison; she might, by a word, by a glance, remind some refractory minister, some unpersuadable viceroy, sitting in audience with her in the little upper room, that she was something more than a mere sick woman, that she had only, so to speak, to go to the window and wave her handkerchief, for . . . dreadful things to follow. But that was enough; they understood; the myth was there—obvious, portentous, impalpable; and so it remained to the last.

With statesmen and governors at her beck and call, with her hands on a hundred strings, with mighty provinces at her feet, with foreign governments agog for her counsel, building hospitals, training nurses—she still felt that she had not enough to do. She sighed for more worlds to conquer—more, and yet more. She looked about her—what was there left? Of course! Philosophy! After the world of action, the world of thought. Having set right the health of the British Army, she would now do the same good service for the religious convictions of mankind. She had long noticed—with regret—the growing tendency towards free-thinking among artisans. With regret, but not altogether with surprise: the current teaching of Christianity was sadly to seek; nay, Christianity itself was not without its defects. She would rectify these errors. She would correct the mistakes of the Churches; she would point out just where Christianity was wrong; and she would explain to the artisans what the facts of the case really were. Before her departure for the Crimea, she had begun this work; and now, in the intervals of her other labours, she completed it. Her *Suggestions for Thought to the Searchers after Truth among the Artisans of England* (1860), unravels, in the course of three portly volumes, the difficulties—hitherto, curiously enough, unsolved—connected with such matters as Belief in God, the Plan of Creation, the Origin of Evil, the Future Life, Necessity and Free Will, Law, and the Nature of Morality. The Origin of Evil, in particular, held no perplexities for Miss Nightingale. "We cannot conceive," she remarks, "that Omnipotent Righteousness would find satisfaction in *solitary existence*." This being so, the only question remaining to be asked is, "What beings should we then conceive that God would create?" Now, He cannot create perfect beings, "since, essentially, perfection is one"; if He did so, He would only be adding to Himself. Thus the conclusion is obvious: He *must* create *im*perfect ones. Omnipotent Righteousness, faced by the intolerable *impasse* of a solitary existence, finds itself bound, by the very nature of the case, to create the hospitals at Scutari. Whether this argument would have satisfied the artisans was never discovered, for only a very few copies of the book were printed for private circulation. One copy was sent to Mr. Mill, who acknowledged it in an extremely polite letter. He felt himself obliged, however, to confess that he had not been altogether convinced by Miss Nightingale's proof of the existence of God. Miss Nightingale was surprised and mortified; she had thought better of Mr. Mill; for surely her proof of the existence of God could hardly be improved upon. "A law," she had pointed out, "implies a lawgiver." Now the Universe is full of laws—the law of gravitation, the law of the excluded middle, and many others; hence it follows that the

Universe has a lawgiver—and what would Mr. Mill be satisfied with, if he was not satisfied with that?

Perhaps Mr. Mill might have asked why the argument had not been pushed to its logical conclusion. Clearly, if we are to trust the analogy of human institutions, we must remember that laws are, as a matter of fact, not dispensed by lawgivers, but passed by Act of Parliament. Miss Nightingale, however, with all her experience of public life, never stopped to consider the question whether God might not be a Limited Monarchy.

Yet her conception of God was certainly not orthodox. She felt towards Him as she might have felt towards a glorified sanitary engineer; and in some of her speculations she seems hardly to distinguish between the Deity and the Drains. As one turns over these singular pages, one has the impression that Miss Nightingale has got the Almighty too into her clutches, and that, if He is not careful, she will kill Him with overwork.

Then, suddenly, in the very midst of the ramifying generalities of her metaphysical disquisitions there is an unexpected turn, and the reader is plunged all at once into something particular, something personal, something impregnated with intense experience— a virulent invective upon the position of women in the upper ranks of society. Forgetful alike of her high argument and of the artisans, the bitter creature rails through a hundred pages of close print at the falsities of family life, the ineptitudes of marriage, the emptinesses of convention, in the spirit of an Ibsen or a Samuel Butler. Her fierce pen, shaking with intimate anger, depicts in biting sentences the fearful fate of an unmarried girl in a wealthy household. It is a *cri du cœur;* and then, as suddenly, she returns once more to instruct the artisans upon the nature of Omnipotent Righteousness.

Her mind was, indeed, better qualified to dissect the concrete and distasteful fruits of actual life than to construct a coherent system of abstract philosophy. In spite of her respect for Law, she was never at home with a generalisation. Thus, though the great achievement of her life lay in the immense impetus which she gave to the scientific treatment of sickness, a true comprehension of the scientific method itself was alien to her spirit. Like most great men of action—perhaps like all—she was simply an empiricist. She believed in what she saw, and she acted accordingly; beyond that she would not go. She had found in Scutari that fresh air and light played an effective part in the prevention of the maladies with which she had to deal; and that was enough for her; she would not inquire further; what were the general principles underlying that fact—or even whether there were any—she refused to consider. Years after the discoveries of Pasteur and Lister, she laughed at what she called the "germ-fetish." There was no such thing as "infection"; she had never seen it, therefore it did not exist. But she *had* seen the good effects of fresh air; therefore there could be no doubt about them; and therefore it was essential that the bedrooms of patients should be well ventilated. Such was her doctrine; and in those days of hermetically sealed windows it was a very valuable one. But it was a purely empirical doctrine, and thus it led to some unfortunate results. When, for instance, her influence in India was at its height, she issued orders that all hospital windows should be invariably kept open. The authorities, who knew what an open window in the hot weather meant, protested, but in vain; Miss Nightingale was incredulous. She knew nothing of the hot weather, but she did know the value of fresh air—from personal experience; the authorities were talking nonsense and the windows must be kept open all the year round. There was a great outcry from all the doctors in India, but she was firm; and for a moment it seemed possible that her terrible commands would have to be put into execution. Lord Lawrence, however, was Viceroy, and he was able to intimate to Miss Nightingale, with sufficient authority, that he himself had decided upon the question, and that his decision must stand, even against her own. Upon that, she gave way, but reluctantly and quite unconvinced; she was only puzzled by the unexpected weakness of Lord Lawrence. No doubt, if she had lived today, and if her experience had lain, not among cholera cases at Scutari but among yellow-fever cases in Panama, she would have declared fresh air a fetish, and would have maintained to her dying day that the only really effective way of dealing with disease was by the destruction of mosquitoes.

Yet her mind, so positive, so realistic, so ultra-practical, had its singular revulsions, its mysterious moods of mysticism and of doubt. At times, lying sleepless in the early hours, she fell into long strange agonised meditations, and then, seizing a pencil, she would commit to paper the confessions of her soul. The morbid longings of her pre-Crimean days came over her once more; she filled page after page with self-examination, self-criticism, self-surrender. "O Father," she wrote, "I submit, I resign myself, I accept with all my heart this stretching out of Thy hand to save me. . . . O how vain it is, the vanity of vanities, to live in men's thoughts instead of God's!" She was lonely, she was miserable. "Thou knowest that through all these horrible twenty years, I have been supported by the belief that I was working with Thee who wert bringing everyone, even our poor nurses, to perfection,"—and yet, after all, what was the result? Had not even she been an unprofitable servant? One night, waking suddenly, she saw, in the dim light of the night-lamp, tenebrous shapes upon the wall. The past rushed back upon her. "Am I she who once stood on that Crimean height?" she wildly asked—" 'The Lady with a lamp shall stand. . . .' The lamp shows me only my utter shipwreck."

She sought consolation in the writings of the Mystics and in a correspondence with Mr. Jowett. For many years the Master of Balliol acted as her spiritual adviser. He discussed with her in a series of enormous letters the problems of religion and philosophy; he criticised her writings on those subjects with the tactful sympathy of a cleric who was also a man of the world; and he even ventured to attempt at times to instil into her rebellious nature some of his own peculiar suavity. "I sometimes think," he told her, "that you ought seriously to consider how your work may be carried on, not with less energy, but in a calmer spirit. I am not blaming the past. . . . But I want the peace of God to settle on the future." He recommended her to spend her time no longer in "conflicts with Government offices," and to take up some literary work. He urged her to "work out her notion of Divine Perfection," in a series of essays for *Frazer's Magazine*. She did so; and the result was submitted to Mr. Froude, who pronounced the second essay to be "even more pregnant than the first. I cannot tell," he said, "how sanitary, with disordered intellects, the effects of such papers will be." Mr. Carlyle, indeed, used different language, and some remarks of his about a lost lamb bleating on the mountains having been unfortunately repeated to Miss Nightingale, all Mr. Jowett's suavity was required to keep the peace. In a letter of fourteen sheets, he turned her attention from this painful topic towards a discussion of Quietism. "I don't see why," said the Master of Balliol, "active life might not become a sort of passive life too." And then, he added, "I sometimes fancy there are possibilities of human character much greater than have been realised." She found such sentiments helpful, underlining them in blue pencil; and, in return, she assisted her friend with a long series of elaborate comments upon the Dialogues of Plato, most of which he embodied in the second edition of his translation. Gradually her interest became more personal; she told him never to work again after midnight, and he obeyed her. Then she helped him to draw up a special form of daily service for the College Chapel, with selections from the Psalms, under the heads of "God the Lord, God the Judge, God the Father, and God the Friend,"—though, indeed, this project was never realised; for the Bishop of Oxford disallowed the alterations, exercising his legal powers, on the advice of Sir Travers Twiss.

Their relations became intimate. "The spirit of the twenty-third psalm and the spirit of the nineteenth psalm should be united in our lives," Mr. Jowett said. Eventually, she asked him to do her a singular favour. Would he, knowing what he did of her religious views, come to London and administer to her the Holy Sacrament? He did not hesitate, and afterwards declared that he would always regard the occasion as a solemn event in his life. He was devoted to her; though the precise nature of his feelings towards her never quite transpired. Her feelings towards him were more mixed. At first, he was "that great and good man,"—"that true saint, Mr. Jowett"; but, as time went on, some gall was mingled with the balm; the acrimony of her nature asserted itself. She felt that she gave more sympathy than she

eceived; she was exhausted, she was annoyed, by his conversa-
ion. Her tongue, one day, could not refrain from shooting out
at him. "He comes to me, and he talks to me," she said, "as if I
were someone else."

## V

At one time she had almost decided to end her life in retirement, as a patient at St. Thomas's Hospital. But partly owing to
the persuasions of Mr. Jowett, she changed her mind; for forty-
five years she remained in South Street; and in South Street she
died. As old age approached, though her influence with the official world gradually diminished, her activities seemed to remain
as intense and widespread as before. When hospitals were to be
built, when schemes of sanitary reform were in agitation, when
wars broke out, she was still the adviser of all Europe. Still, with
a characteristic self-assurance, she watched from her Mayfair bedroom over the welfare of India. Still, with an indefatigable enthusiasm, she pushed forward the work, which, perhaps, was
nearer to her heart, more completely her own, than all the rest—
the training of nurses. In her moments of deepest depression,
when her greatest achievements seemed to lose their lustre, she
thought of her nurses, and was comforted. The ways of God,
she found, were strange indeed. "How inefficient I was in the
Crimea," she noted. "Yet He has raised up from it trained
nursing."

At other times she was better satisfied. Looking back, she was
amazed by the enormous change which, since her early days,
had come over the whole treatment of illness, the whole conception of public and domestic health—a change in which, she
knew, she had played her part. One of her Indian admirers, the
Aga Khan, came to visit her. She expatiated on the marvellous
advances she had lived to see in the management of hospitals, in
drainage, in ventilation, in sanitary work of every kind. There
was a pause; and then, "Do you think you are improving?" asked
the Aga Khan. She was a little taken aback, and said, "What do
you mean by 'improving'?" He replied, "Believing more in God."
She saw that he had a view of God which was different from

hers. "A most interesting man," she noted after the interview, "but you could never teach him sanitation."

When old age actually came, something curious happened. Destiny, having waited very patiently, played a queer trick on Miss Nightingale. The benevolence and public spirit of that long life had only been equalled by its acerbity. Her virtue had dwelt in hardness, and she had poured forth her unstinted usefulness with a bitter smile upon her lips. And now the sarcastic years brought the proud woman her punishment. She was not to die as she had lived. The sting was to be taken out of her: she was to be made soft; she was to be reduced to compliance and complacency. The change came gradually, but at last it was unmistakable. The terrible commander who had driven Sidney Herbert to his death, to whom Mr. Jowett had applied the words of Homer, ἄμοτον μεμαυῖα—raging insatiably—now accepted small compliments with gratitude, and indulged in sentimental friendships with young girls. The author of "Notes on Nursing"— that classical compendium of the besetting sins of the sisterhood, drawn up with the detailed acrimony, the vindictive relish, of a Swift—now spent long hours in composing sympathetic Addresses to Probationers, whom she petted and wept over in turn. And, at the same time, there appeared a corresponding alteration in her physical mould. The thin, angular woman, with her haughty eye and her acrid mouth had vanished; and in her place was the rounded bulky form of a fat old lady, smiling all day long. Then something else became visible. The brain which had been steeled at Scutari was indeed, literally, growing soft. Senility—an ever more and more amiable senility—descended. Towards the end, consciousness itself grew lost in a roseate haze, and melted into nothingness. It was just then, three years before her death, when she was eighty-seven years old (1907), that those in authority bethought them that the opportune moment had come for bestowing a public honour on Florence Nightingale. She was offered the Order of Merit. That Order, whose roll contains, among other distinguished names, those of Sir Laurence Alma Tadema and Sir Edward Elgar, is remarkable chiefly for the fact that, as its title indicates, it is bestowed because its recipient deserves it, and for no other reason. Miss Nightingale's representatives accepted the honour, and her name, after a lapse of many years, once more appeared in the Press. Congratulations from all sides came pouring in. There was a universal burst of enthusiasm—a final revivification of the ancient myth. Among her other admirers, the German Emperor took this opportunity of expressing his feelings towards her. "His Majesty," wrote the German Ambassador, "having just brought to a close a most enjoyable stay in the beautiful neighbourhood of your old home near Romsey, has commanded me to present you with some flowers as a token of his esteem." Then, by Royal command, the Order of Merit was brought to South Street, and there was a little ceremony of presentation. Sir Douglas Dawson, after a short speech, stepped forward, and handed the insignia of the Order to Miss Nightingale. Propped up by pillows, she dimly recognised that some compliment was being paid her. "Too kind —too kind," she murmured; and she was not ironical.

# VIRGINIA WOOLF

OF all the authors represented in this volume, none except James Joyce equals Virginia Woolf in sheer virtuosity. Her remarkable novels—*The Voyage Out* (1915), *Jacob's Room* (1922), *Mrs. Dalloway* (1925), *To the Lighthouse* (1927), *A Room of One's Own* (1929), *The Waves* (1931), *The Years* (1937)—enchant the sensitive reader while they defy classification. *Orlando, A Biography*, founded though it be on the character of her friend V. Sackville-West, sweeps its subject through a breathless, two-sexed career from the Age of Queen Elizabeth to 1928. Her other "biography," *Flush* (1932), is the story of the familiar cocker spaniel of Elizabeth Barrett Browning. Her two series of prose pieces entitled *The Common Reader* (1925 and 1932)—and it is rather the *un*common reader, one fears, who is agile enough to catch all her bright shafts and follow her swift mental twistings—are usually called, for want of a preciser term, essays. Yet, sharing the same high intelligence, the same word-mastery, the same subtlety of comprehension as her novels, they give us a variety of original and complex effects that amaze while delighting—as "Miss Ormerod" proves.

Mrs. Woolf, born in London in 1882, was the third of four children of the distinguished nineteenth-century critic, philosopher, and biographer, Leslie (later Sir Leslie) Stephen, by his second marriage. Through his first marriage to the younger daughter of W. M. Thackeray, the family was related to the Macaulays, Trevelyans, Darwins, Maitlands, Symondses, Stracheys, and other scholarly Englishmen; and many of these ties were strengthened by friendship. The Stephen home, where Mrs. Woolf obtained her education, was a gathering place of the most eminent writers of the day; and after their parents' death, when the two sons and two daughters moved to a small house in the Bloomsbury quarter of London, they became the nucleus of a no less brilliant company of their contemporaries. Among this Bloomsbury Group were Clive Bell, vigorous leader of contemporary art, whom the elder sister, Vanessa, married; and Leonard Woolf, editor, publisher, and political economist, whom Virginia Stephen married in 1912. Also there were the novelist, Edward Morgan Forster; John Maynard Keynes, economist and politician, and his wife, Lydia Lopokova, the celebrated dancer; the painters, Duncan Grant and Roger Fry; and, most influential of all in literature, Giles Lytton Strachey. It was quite the liveliest band of intellectuals in contemporary England, each member of which was a notable pioneer in his respective field. Their unifying spirit has been sympathetically set forth as "a belief in Reason, and a conviction that the pursuit of Truth and a contemplation of Beauty are the most important of human activities"; their chief distinction, that "they have acted upon it to an extraordinary extent. No subject of conversation has been taboo, no tradition accepted without examination, and no conclusion evaded. In a hypercritical society, they have been indecent; in a conservative society, curious; in a gentlemanly society, ruthless; and in a fighting society, pacifist. They have been passionate in their devotion to what they thought good, brutal in their rejection of what they thought second-rate, resolute in their refusal to compromise." At the center of this group was Mrs. Woolf, who, in addition to authorship, has given her efforts to fine printing, beginning with a small handpress and ending with the publishing house, the Hogarth Press.

The modern reader could not fail to recognize "Miss Ormerod" as the work of Virginia Woolf, but he would search in vain for its model or parallel. Here is an intelligent, rather masculine, Victorian woman with an independent mind and a bold scientific purpose belying both her sex and her time—"pioneer of purity even more than of Paris Green"—whom the author, herself independent and bold and intelligent, must have found most congenial to describe. Moreover, Eleanor A. Ormerod (1828-1901) was prominent enough as an entomologist to merit a full-length biography, yet obscure enough to "the common reader" to give him the delight of a fresh discovery and Mrs. Woolf, who relishes out-of-the-way figures, the challenge that seems always to evoke her subtlest powers. She reveals her subject's career with sympathy and vivid concreteness in a sequence of brief, fragmentary episodes, beginning with a childhood scene and ending with an impersonal announcement of her death. Like the blobs and splashes of color in a pointillist painting, these seeming scraps of narrative and description are all found, when at last the mind has the time and perspective to take them in, to fit together by an invisible joinery like the sharp-cut and well-polished mosaics they really are. Like all novel expression in art, it is hard to grasp the first time at the customary rate of reading. Technically, too, this is not a method to be imitated wantonly; but its minute study will well repay the effort.

## MISS ORMEROD[1]

THE TREES stood massively in all their summer foliage spotted and grouped upon a meadow which sloped gently down from the big white house. There were unmistakable signs of the year 1835 both in the trees and in the sky, for modern trees are not nearly so voluminous as these ones, and the sky of those days had a kind of pale diffusion in its texture which was different from the more concentrated tone of the skies we know.

Mr. George Ormerod stepped from the drawing-room window of Sedbury House, Gloucestershire, wearing a tall furry hat and white trousers strapped under his instep; he was closely, though deferentially, followed by a lady wearing a yellow-spotted dress over a crinoline, and behind her, singly and arm in arm, came nine children in nankeen jackets and long white drawers. They were going to see the water let out of a pond.

The youngest child, Eleanor, a little girl with a pale face, rather elongated features, and black hair, was left by herself in the drawing-room, a large sallow apartment with pillars, two chandeliers, for some reason enclosed in holland bags, and several octagonal tables, some of inlaid wood and others of greenish malachite. At one of these little Eleanor Ormerod was seated in a high chair.

"Now, Eleanor," said her mother, as the party assembled for the expedition to the pond, "here are some pretty beetles. Don't touch the glass. Don't get down from your chair, and when we come back little George will tell you all about it."

So saying, Mrs. Ormerod placed a tumbler of water containing about half a dozen great water grubs in the middle of the malachite table, at a safe distance from the child, and followed her husband down the slope of old-fashioned turf towards a cluster of extremely old-fashioned sheep; opening, directly she stepped on to the terrace, a tiny parasol of bottle green silk with a bottle green fringe, though the sky was like nothing so much as a flock bed covered with a counterpane of white dimity.

[1] Founded upon *The Life of Eleanor Ormerod*, by Robert Wallace Murray. 1904.

The plump pale grubs gyrated slowly round and round in the tumbler. So simple an entertainment must surely soon have ceased to satisfy. Surely Eleanor would shake the tumbler, upset the grubs, and scramble down from her chair. Why, even a grown person can hardly watch those grubs crawling down the glass wall, then floating to the surface, without a sense of boredom not untinged with disgust. But the child sat perfectly still. Was it her custom, then, to be entertained by the gyrations of grubs? Her eyes were reflective, even critical. But they shone with increasing excitement. She beat one hand upon the edge of the table. What was the reason? One of the grubs had ceased to float: he lay at the bottom; the rest, descending, proceeded to tear him to pieces.

"And how has little Eleanor enjoyed herself?" asked Mr. Ormerod, in rather a deep voice, stepping into the room and with a slight air of heat and of fatigue upon his face.

"Papa," said Eleanor, almost interrupting her father in her eagerness to impart her observation, "I saw one of the grubs fall down and the rest came and ate him!"

"Nonsense, Eleanor," said Mr. Ormerod. "You are not telling the truth." He looked severely at the tumbler in which the beetles were still gyrating as before.

"Papa, it was true!"

"Eleanor, little girls are not allowed to contradict their fathers," said Mrs. Ormerod, coming in through the window, and closing her green parasol with a snap.

"Let this be a lesson," Mr. Ormerod began, signing to the other children to approach, when the door opened, and the servant announced,

"Captain Fenton."

Captain Fenton "was at times thought to be tedious in his recurrence to the charge of the Scots Greys in which he had served at the battle of Waterloo."

But what is this crowd gathered round the door of the George Hotel in Chepstow? A faint cheer rises from the bottom of the hill. Up comes the mail coach, horses steaming, panels mud-splashed. "Make way! Make way!" cries the ostler and the vehicle dashes into the courtyard, pulls up sharp before the door. Down jumps the coachman, the horses are led off, and a fine team of spanking greys is harnessed with incredible speed in their stead. Upon all this—coachman, horses, coach, and passengers— the crowd looked with gaping admiration every Wednesday all through the year. But today, the twelfth of March, 1852, as the coachman settled his rug, and stretched his hands for the reins, he observed that instead of being fixed upon him, the eyes of the people of Chepstow darted this way and that. Heads were jerked. Arms flung out. Here a hat swooped in a semi-circle. Off drove the coach almost unnoticed. As it turned the corner all the out-side passengers craned their necks, and one gentleman rose to his feet and shouted, "There! there! there!" before he was bowled into eternity. It was an insect—a red-winged insect. Out the people of Chepstow poured into the high road; down the hill they ran; always the insect flew in front of them; at length by Chepstow Bridge a young man, throwing his bandanna over the blade of an oar, captured it alive and presented it to a highly respectable elderly gentleman who now came puffing upon the scene—Samuel Budge, doctor, of Chepstow. By Samuel Budge it was presented to Miss Ormerod; by her sent to a professor at Oxford. And he, declaring it "a fine specimen of the rose under-winged locust," added the gratifying information that it "was the first of the kind to be captured so far west."

And so, at the age of twenty-four Miss Eleanor Ormerod was thought the proper person to receive the gift of a locust.

When Eleanor Ormerod appeared at archery meetings and cro-quet tournaments young men pulled their whiskers and young la-dies looked grave. It was so difficult to make friends with a girl who could talk of nothing but black beetles and earwigs—"Yes, that's what she likes, isn't it queer?—Why, the other day Ellen, Mama's maid, heard from Jane, who's under-kitchenmaid at Sed-bury House, that Eleanor tried to boil a beetle in the kitchen saucepan and he wouldn't die, and swam round and round, and she got into a terrible state and sent the groom all the way to Gloucester to fetch chloroform—all for an insect, my dear!—and she gives the cottagers shillings to collect beetles for her—and she spends hours in her bedroom cutting them up—and she climbs trees like a boy to find wasps' nests—oh, you can't think what they don't say about her in the village—for she does look so odd, dressed anyhow, with that great big nose and those bright little eyes, so like a caterpillar herself, I always think—but of course she's wonderfully clever and very good, too, both of them. Georgiana has a lending library for the cottagers, and Eleanor never misses a service—but there she is—that short pale girl in the large bonnet. Do go and talk to her, for I'm sure I'm too stupid, but you'll find plenty to say—" But neither Fred nor Arthur, Henry nor William found anything to say—

". . . probably the lecturer would have been equally well pleased had none of her own sex put in an appearance."

This comment upon a lecture delivered in the year 1889 throws some light, perhaps, upon archery meetings in the 'fifties.

It being nine o'clock on a February night some time about 1862, all the Ormerods were in the library; Mr. Ormerod making architectural designs at a table; Mrs. Ormerod lying on a sofa making pencil drawings upon grey paper; Eleanor making a model of a snake to serve as a paper weight; Georgiana making a copy of the font in Tidenham Church; some of the others examining books with beautiful illustrations; while at intervals someone rose, unlocked the wire book case, took down a volume for instruction or entertainment, and perused it beneath the chandelier.

Mr. Ormerod required complete silence for his studies. His word was law, even to the dogs, who, in the absence of their master, instinctively obeyed the eldest male person in the room. Some whispered colloquy there might be between Mrs. Ormerod and her daughters—

"The draught under the pew was really worse than ever this morning, Mama—"

"And we could only unfasten the latch of the chancel because Eleanor happened to have her ruler with her—"

"—hm-m-m. Dr. Armstrong— Hm-m-m—"

"—Anyhow things aren't as bad with us as they are at King-hampton. They say Mrs. Briscoe's Newfoundland dog follows her right up to the chancel rails when she takes the sacrament—"

"And the turkey is still sitting on its eggs in the pulpit."

—"The period of incubation for a turkey is between three and four weeks"—said Eleanor, thoughtfully looking up from her cast of the snake and forgetting, in the interest of her subject, to speak in a whisper.

"Am I to be allowed no peace in my own house?" Mr. Ormerod exclaimed angrily, rapping with his ruler on the table, upon which Mrs. Ormerod half shut one eye and squeezed a little blob of Chinese white on to her high light, and they remained silent until the servants came in, when everyone, with the exception of Mrs. Ormerod, fell on their knees. For she, poor lady, suffered from a chronic complaint and left the family forever a year or two later, when the green sofa was moved into the corner, and the drawings given to her nieces in memory of her. But Mr. Ormerod went on making architectural drawings at nine p.m. every night (save on Sundays when he read a sermon) until he too lay upon the green sofa, which had not been used since Mrs. Ormerod lay there, but still looked much the same. "We deeply felt the happiness of ministering to his welfare," Miss Ormerod wrote, "for he would not hear of our leaving him for even twenty-four hours and he objected to visits from my brothers excepting occasionally for a short time. They, not being used to the gentle ways necessary for an aged invalid, worried him . . . the Thursday following, the 9th October, 1873, he passed gently away at the mature age of eighty-seven years." Oh, graves in country churchyards—respectable burials—mature old gentlemen —D.C.L., LL.D., F.R.S., F.S.A.—lots of letters come after your names, but lots of women are buried with you!

There remained the Hessian Fly and the Bot—mysterious insects! Not, one would have thought, among God's most triumphant creations, and yet—if you see them under a microscope! —the Bot, obese, globular, obscene; the Hessian, booted, spurred, whiskered, cadaverous. Next slip under the glass an innocent grain; behold it pock-marked and livid; or take this strip of hide, and note those pollulating lumps—well, what does the landscape look like then?

The only palatable object for the eye to rest on in acres of England is a lump of Paris Green. But English people won't use microscopes; you can't make them use Paris Green either—or if they do, they let it drip. Dr. Ritzema Bos is a great stand-by. For they won't take a woman's word. And indeed, though for the sake of the Ox Warble one must stretch a point, there are matters, questions of stock infestation, things one has to go into—things a lady doesn't even like to see, much less discuss, in print—"these, I say, I intend to leave entirely to the Veterinary surgeons. My brother—oh, he's dead now—a very good man—for whom I collected wasps' nests—lived at Brighton and wrote about wasps—he, I say, wouldn't let me learn anatomy, never liked me to do more than take sections of teeth."

Ah, but Eleanor, the Bot and the Hessian have more power over you than Mr. Edward Ormerod himself. Under the microscope you clearly perceive that these insects have organs, orifices, excrement; they do, most emphatically, copulate. Escorted on the one side by the Bot or Warble, on the other by the Hessian Fly, Miss Ormerod advanced statelily, if slowly, into the open. Never did her features show more sublime than when lit up by the candour of her avowal. "This is excrement; these, though Ritzema Bos is positive to the contrary, are the generative organs of the male. I've proved it." Upon her head the hood of Edinburgh most fitly descended; pioneer of purity even more than of Paris Green.

"If you're sure I'm not in your way," said Miss Lipscomb, unstrapping her paint box and planting her tripod firmly in the path, "—I'll try to get a picture of these lovely hydrangeas against the sky— What flowers you have in Penzance!"

The market gardener crossed his hands on his hoe, slowly twined a piece of bass round his finger, looked at the sky, said something about the sun, also about the prevalence of lady artists, and then, with a nod of his head, observed sententiously that it was to a lady that he owed everything he had.

"Ah?" said Miss Lipscomb, flattered, but already much occupied with her composition.

"A lady with a queer-sounding name," said Mr. Pascoe, "but that's the lady I've called my little girl after— I don't think there's such another in Christendom."

Of course it was Miss Ormerod, equally of course Miss Lipscomb was the sister of Miss Ormerod's family doctor; and so she did no sketching that morning, but left with a handsome bunch of grapes instead—for every flower had drooped, ruin had stared him in the face—he had written, not believing one bit what they told him—to the lady with the queer name, back there came a book, *In-ju-ri-ous In-sects*, with the page turned down, perhaps by her very hand, also a letter which he kept at home under the clock, but he knew every word by heart, since it was due to what she said there that he wasn't a ruined man—and the tears ran down his face and Miss Lipscomb, clearing a space on the lodging-house table, wrote the whole story to her brother.

"The prejudice against Paris Green certainly seems to be dying down," said Miss Ormerod when she read it.—"But now," she sighed rather heavily, being no longer young and much afflicted with the gout, "now it's the sparrows."

One might have thought that *they* would have left her alone—innocent dirt-grey birds, taking more than their share of the breakfast crumbs, otherwise inoffensive. But once you look through a microscope—once you see the Hessian and the Bot as they really are—there's no peace for an elderly lady pacing her terrace on a fine May morning. For example, why, when there are crumbs enough for all, do only the sparrows get them? Why not swallows or martins? Why—oh, here come the servants for prayers—

"Forgive us our trespasses as we forgive them that trespass against us. . . . For thine is the Kingdom and the power and the glory, for ever and ever. Amen—"

"*The Times*, ma'am—"

"Thank you, Dixon. . . . The Queen's birthday! We must

drink her Majesty's health in the old white port, Dixon. Home Rule—tut—tut—tut. All that madman Gladstone. My father would have thought the world was coming to an end, and I'm not at all sure that it isn't. I must talk to Dr. Lipscomb—"

Yet all the time in the tail of her eye she saw myriads of sparrows, and retiring to the study proclaimed in a pamphlet of which 36,000 copies were gratuitously distributed that the sparrow is a pest.

"When he eats an insect," she said to her sister Georgiana, "which isn't often, it's one of the few insects that one wants to keep—one of the very few," she added with a touch of acidity natural to one whose investigations have all tended to the discredit of the insect race.

"But there'll be some very unpleasant consequences to face," she concluded—"Very unpleasant indeed."

Happily the port was now brought in, the servants assembled; and Miss Ormerod, rising to her feet, gave the toast "Her Blessed Majesty." She was extremely loyal, and moreover she liked nothing better than a glass of her father's old white port. She kept his pigtail, too, in a box.

Such being her disposition it went hard with her to analyse the sparrow's crop, for the sparrow, she felt, symbolises something of the homely virtue of English domestic life, and to proclaim it stuffed with deceit was disloyal to much that she, and her fathers before her, held dear. Sure enough the clergy—the Rev. J. E. Walker—denounced her for her brutality; "God Save the Sparrow!" exclaimed the Animal's Friend; and Miss Carrington, of the Humanitarian League, replied in a leaflet described by Miss Ormerod as "spirity, discourteous, and inaccurate."

"Well," said Miss Ormerod to her sister, "it did me no harm before to be threatened to be shot at, also hanged in effigy, and other little attentions."

"Still it was very disagreeable, Eleanor—more disagreeable, I believe, to me than to you," said Georgiana. Soon Georgiana died. She had however finished the beautiful series of insect diagrams at which she worked every morning in the dining-room and they were presented to Edinburgh University. But Eleanor was never the same woman after that.

Dear forest fly—flour moths—weevils—grouse and cheese flies—beetles—foreign correspondents—eel worms—ladybirds—wheat midges—resignation from the Royal Agricultural Society—gall mites—boot beetles—announcement of honorary degree to be conferred—feelings of appreciation and anxiety—paper on wasps—last annual report—warnings of serious illness—proposed pension—gradual loss of strength—finally Death.

That is life, so they say.

"It does no good to keep people waiting for an answer," sighed Miss Ormerod, "though I don't feel as able as I did since that unlucky accident at Waterloo. And no one realises what the strain of the work is—often I'm the only lady in the room, and the gentlemen so learned, though I've always found them most helpful, most generous in every way. But I'm growing old, Miss Hartwell, that's what it is. That's what led me to be thinking of this difficult matter of flour infestation in the middle of the road so that I didn't see the horse until he had poked his nose into my ear. . . . Then there's this nonsense about a pension. What could possess Mr. Barron to think of such a thing? I should feel inexpressibly lowered if I accepted a pension. Why, I don't altogether like writing LL.D. after my name, though Georgie would have liked it. All I ask is to be let go on in my own quiet way. Now where is Messrs. Langridge's sample? We must take that first. 'Gentlemen, I have examined your sample and find . . .'"

"If anyone deserves a thorough rest it's you, Miss Ormerod," said Dr. Lipscomb, who had grown a little white over the ears. "I should say the farmers of England ought to set up a statue to you, bring offerings of corn and wine—make you a kind of Goddess, eh—what was her name?"

"Not a very shapely figure for a Goddess," said Miss Ormerod with a little laugh. "I should enjoy the wine though. You're not going to cut me off my one glass of port surely?"

"You must remember," said Dr. Lipscomb, shaking his head, "how much your life means to others."

"Well, I don't know about that," said Miss Ormerod, pondering a little. "To be sure, I've chosen my epitaph. 'She introduced Paris Green into England,' and there might be a word or two about the Hessian Fly—that, I do believe, was a good piece of work."

"No need to think about epitaphs yet," said Dr. Lipscomb.

"Our lives are in the hands of the Lord," said Miss Ormerod simply.

Dr. Lipscomb bent his head and looked out of the window. Miss Ormerod remained silent.

"English entomologists care little or nothing for objects of practical importance," she exclaimed suddenly. "Take this question of flour infestation—I can't say how many grey hairs that has grown me."

"Figuratively speaking, Miss Ormerod," said Dr. Lipscomb, for her hair was still raven black.

"Well, I do believe all good work is done in concert," Miss Ormerod continued. "It is often a great comfort to me to think that."

"It's beginning to rain," said Dr. Lipscomb. "How will your enemies like that, Miss Ormerod?"

"Hot or cold, wet or dry, insects always flourish!" cried Miss Ormerod energetically sitting up in bed.

"Old Miss Ormerod is dead," said Mr. Drummond, opening *The Times* on Saturday, July 20th, 1901.

"Old Miss Ormerod?" asked Mrs. Drummond.

# ANDRÉ MAUROIS

"A BEAUTIFUL portrait is at once a portrait resembling its subject and an artistic transference of reality." This characteristic utterance of André Maurois may be set with another, quoting Bacon: "'Art is essentially man added to nature'; that is, facts ordered by the human mind." From the kernel of truth expressed in these sentences has sprung the modern conception of biography as a work of art, of which M. Maurois is both the clearest exponent and the happiest practitioner. As a Frenchman he is heir to that nation's great classical tradition of clarity, form, and restraint; as a modern intellectual he falls in congenially with the new scientific and literary ideals of certain Anglo-Saxon contemporaries, especially the Bloomsbury Group; as an artist he combines with a racial romanticism the acutest gifts of perception and expression and a remarkable creative imagination.

He was born Émile Herzog in 1885 in the small manufacturing town of Elbeuf, a dozen miles above Rouen on the Seine, where his family owned and operated textile mills. At the Lycée of Rouen he mastered English, distinguished himself for his French prose, and came under the direct influence of the philosopher "Alain," to whom he pays the high homage of saying, "À Chartier, professeur de philosophie, je dois tout." After his formal education he married and returned to the Elbeuf mills, writing in spare hours. He was freed from this distasteful work by the World War, in which his knowledge of languages soon made him valuable as a liaison officer to a Scottish regiment and later at the British G.H.Q. There in the officers' mess he noted down the refreshing manifestations of the Anglo-Saxon mind and, toward the end of the War, composed these jottings into a small narrative called *Les Silences du Colonel Bramble* (1918) and a companion volume, *Les Discours du Docteur O'Grady* (1920). The immense success of these books confirmed his will to write. An experimental novel based on the life of Shelley, *Ni Ange ni Bête* (1919), he reinforced and entirely recast as *Ariel* (1923), which was at once taken up enthusiastically in Europe and America and established its author in the first rank of modern biographers. The success was repeated in *Disraeli* (1927). But the "biographie romancée" found also plenty of detractors among the skeptics reluctant to accept as authentic a life that read like a novel, dissociated the man from his works, and lacked the reassurance of footnotes and bibliography. Maurois, who of course used secondary as well as primary sources, was publicly attacked as a plagiarist and romancer, but gave a conclusive answer by a full defense of his working methods, by evidence of his exhaustive research, and especially by his long biography, *Byron* (1930), in which the same vivid narrative style is strengthened by generous illustrations from the subject's writings and further substantiated by detailed documentation at the end. His *Edward VII* (1933) and *Chateaubriand* (1938) are works of similar magnitude. Meanwhile he produced a succession of shorter biographies, *Lyautey*, *Tourgeniev* (1931), *Voltaire* (1932), *Dickens* (1934); novels, including the autobiographical *Bernard Quesnay* (1926); biographical sketches, *Meïpe, ou la Délivrance* (1926), and *Prophets and Poets* (1936); critical works, notably *Aspects of Biography* (1929); as well as a history of England and numerous writings ranging from fantasy to politics and manners. Nearly all his books and articles are available to his vast English-speaking public. He has made many lecture-visits to America and even taught for a most successful term at Princeton. In Great Britain, where M. Maurois is an even more familiar figure, he was knighted by George VI. His election in 1938 to the French Academy officially crowned at fifty-three his rare literary genius, which happily shows no signs of lessening productiveness.

Whoever would understand M. Maurois's biographical aims and methods, and to a great extent those of the whole modern school, should read his Cambridge University lectures, *Aspects of Biography*, and contrast one of his three early biographies (of Shelley, Disraeli, and Byron) with the corresponding Victorian work. But in a smaller scope the reader may see the same principles applied in the following selection from *Meïpe*, translated as *Mape: The World of Illusion*. To M. Maurois, biography is not only an art and a science, but a personal means of expression as well, the subject chosen "in order to respond to a secret need in [the author's] own nature." Thus after purging himself of certain feelings in his lives of Shelley and Disraeli, M. Maurois wished to study, "in a third manifestation, the reconciliation of an incurable romanticism of youth with the perfect serenity of a purified philosophy [of old age]." For this somewhat homeopathic treatment no character seemed more fitting than Goethe, who "begins his life with Werther, that is, in the full tide of romantic enthusiasm, and towards the end of it attains an equilibrium." Hence "The Sorrows of the Young Werther," in which the creator of an illusory world is finally reconciled to the actual one in a conclusion superbly ironical.

But the fact that the author sees himself in the character and that the character is real and historical need not prevent the resulting study from being a work of art. For the character has been selected partly because his career has a natural symmetry of its own. Like the painter in oils, then, the biographer eschews the photograph, which tells everything without color, shading, or "values," and by a skillful selection of details, by the use, not of invention, but of a re-creative imagination, and above all by a singularly limpid style (in the original), he paints his portrait of the individual as he sees him. The details in this portrait of Goethe are all veracious and most of them may be found in G. H. Lewes's full-length biography. The picture, like Goethe's own far freer adaptation of life in *Werthers Leiden*, must be accredited to the artist who made it. Under a significant text from one creative genius the formative life of another gives a third, Maurois, the occasion for a testament of the universal artist.

# THE SORROWS OF THE YOUNG
## WERTHER[1]

> *He is said to have been so given over to Love that, as soon as he met a woman he liked, he tried to win her favours. If he failed, he painted her portrait, and thus extinguished his desire.*—LIFE OF FRA FILIPPO LIPPI.

### STRASBOURG

THE FRANKFURT coach stopped at the Geist; a German student set down his luggage, astonished the inn-keeper by refusing dinner, and rushed wildly off to the Cathedral. The vergers, as they watched him climb the tower, looked at each other with some misgiving.

The gabled roofs surged in waves against the hard, pure lines of the Castle of the Rohans. The plains of Alsace sparkled under the midday sun, dotted with villages, forests, and vineyards. At this very hour, in every one of those villages, girls and women would be dreaming. As he looked at this virgin canvas on which his desire had begun to sketch out so many and so various delights, he felt all the vague delightful charm of amorous expectancy. He came again many times. The platform at the top overhung the adjacent parts of the building so that he could imagine himself surrounded by the open sky. At first he felt giddy. Long illnesses in his childhood had left him morbidly sensitive and afraid of empty space, noise, and the dark. But he wanted to cure himself of these weaknesses.

Gradually the vast plain, a chart upon which his heart had written nothing, became enriched with names and recollections.

Alsace had become "my beloved Alsace." He could now distinguish Saverne, where Weyland had taken him; Drusenheim, whence a lovely meadow path leads to Sesenheim. There in a rustic parsonage, surrounded by gardens and embowered in jasmine, lived the charming Frédérique Brion. In the far distance, beyond the hills and castle towers, dark clouds were gathering. The student's thoughts turned to the little moving human figures who were hurrying about the narrow streets three hundred feet below. How much he would have liked to enter into those lives, remote as they seemed from one another and yet united by all manner of mysterious bonds; to lift up the roofs of the houses, to be present unseen at all those secret and surprising actions through which alone we can understand our fellows. On the previous evening, at the Marionette Theatre, he had seen a performance of the legend of Doctor Faust.

As he looked up and watched the clouds sail past the spire he felt as though it had suddenly taken flight and was carrying him away. "Supposing the Devil offered me power, possessions, women in return for the bond of Faust; should I sign?" After a short but honest examination of his conscience, he said to himself, "I would not sign it to be master of the world; but for knowledge—yes. Ah, you are too inquisitive, my fine friend."

Rain began to fall and he made his way down the narrow twisting stairway. "One might write a Faust. There are a good many already. . . . But Spiess, and poor old Widmann—that is second-rate stuff. Their Faust is a vulgar rascal who is damned by his own baseness. The devil was cheated: he would have got him anyhow. . . . Mine? Mine would be a greater character—a kind of Prometheus. Defeated by the gods if you like, but at least because he tried to snatch their secret from them."

Below, in the Cathedral, a dark velvety light poured through the stained windows. A few kneeling women were praying in the gloom. The organs were murmuring vaguely as though under the touch of gentle fingers. Goethe looked long at the vaulting of the roof. When he saw a beautiful tree, he often had the sensation of losing himself in its growth and penetrating its perfect scheme. His thought rose like sap, spread into the branches, and expanded into leaves, flowers, and fruits. The immense converging arches of the nave recalled the same manifold and splendid design.

"Here, as in the works of Nature, everything has its purpose, everything is proportioned to the whole. . . . Oh, to write books that should be like cathedrals! If only you could express what you feel! If you could only put on to paper the fire that runs through your veins! . . ."

As soon as he withdrew into himself like this he came upon a whole world of his own. He had just discovered Shakespeare, and he admired him as a man does who takes the measure of a rival. Why not be the German Shakespeare? He had the power; he knew it. But how could he lay hold on it? What form should he impose upon this living force? He longed to see his emotion, a prisoner at last, rigid like those mighty vaultings. Perhaps the architect himself had once hesitated and despaired in the presence of the dream-cathedrals that had preceded the Cathedral.

There were plenty of subjects. The story of Sir Götz . . . Faust . . . idylls of the German countryside, in the manner of a modern Theocritus. A Mahomet perhaps, or a Prometheus. Any hero would do through whom he could fling a challenge to the world. He would model his heroes from himself, but on gigantic scale, and then breathe his own life into them. A Caesar perhaps? His span of life would not be long enough for so many projects. "A bird-like nature full of vain excitement," his master Herder had said of him. But to fill these wonderful empty frames he needed ideas and feelings: he had to live and live a thousand lives. "Not the being," he said to himself again and again, "but the becoming everything."

"Being nothing? Not even the husband of the charming Frédérique? No, not even that." He pictured to himself Frédérique's grief. Had he really the right to leave her, when his entire behaviour had let her believe that he would marry her, when Pastor Brion had welcomed him as a son? "The right? Are there any rights in love? After all, the adventure was as pleasant for her as for me. Had not Frédérique understood all along that the son of Councillor Goethe of Frankfurt would not marry a pretty country girl? Would my father ever have consented?

Would she have been happy in a world so different from her own?"

"Sophisms! If you must be false, at least be frank. The son of Councillor Goethe is of no greater importance than the daughter of the Pastor. My mother was poorer than Frédérique. And as for the world so different from her own, was she not delightful this winter when she danced on the waxed floors of the great drawing-rooms of Strasbourg?"

"You are right, but what am I to do? I cannot . . . no, I cannot . . . I should be in bondage if I did. The first duty is to develop all that one has, all that one can become. I shall always be Goethe. When I use my name I mean all it stands for. My qualities and my faults—all are good, all are part of my nature. I was right to love Frédérique because I felt so at the time. If one day I feel I must go away from her to recover myself, I shall still be Goethe when I go and all will be as it should."

At this moment he imagined Frédérique in tears by the roadside and himself riding away, his head bent, not daring to look back. "What a scene for a *Faust*," he thought.

## II

A parchment with a red seal turned the student into a lawyer. The deserted Frédérique wept, Doctor Goethe's horse trotted towards Frankfurt. Skating and philosophy proved effectual remedies against some tolerably sharp attacks of remorse. In the spring a course at the Imperial Chamber at Wetzlar seemed to Councillor Goethe an indispensable adjunct to his son's legal studies.

For a century the Holy Empire had been sinking into the sands of oblivion, and only three mutilated arches of the vast edifice which had for so long sheltered the land of Germany could still be observed: the Aulic Council at Vienna, the Diet at Ratisbon, and the Imperial Chamber at Wetzlar. This latter, the supreme tribunal for all the kings, dukes, archdukes, palatines, bishops, and margraves who had divided the authority of the Emperor between them, should have been maintained by contributions from the various States; but, as often happens in the case of collective institutions, each of the participants, in order to make sure that he should not be the only one to pay, had fallen into the habit of paying nothing. The customary financial expedients were under discussion: some proposed a special stamp, others a lottery or a tax upon the Jews. In the meantime, as some means of subsistence had to be found, the judges obtained their salaries from the litigants.

The principal sovereigns of Germany maintained legations in attendance on this grandiose and sordid shadow of a great judicial institution, and thus created an agreeable and leisured little circle in this provincial town. When Goethe arrived at the Kronprinz Inn he found a noisy table of young attachés and secretaries. He was at once invited to join it, and from the moment of his first conversation realized that he was in familiar spiritual surroundings.

Europe was going through one of its crises of intellectual unrest. For nine years its kings had lived in peace; within their States worn-out constitutions had managed to preserve enough vigour to make revolutions seem impossible. The contrast between the ardour of youth and the stagnation of society gave birth to a feeling of impatience and disgust, a melancholy peculiar to periods of transition and peace, which was then called, as it always will be, the malady of the age. The young attachés at Wetzlar were afflicted like all their contemporaries. They were great readers: they sought for emotional inspiration in Rousseau and Herder; and when in doubt, and while they were waiting to find it, they drank a great deal of wine.

They were delighted with Doctor Goethe, who was one of their own kind and yet their superior. He, like them, repeated at the turn of each phrase: "Nature . . . respect Nature . . . live in Nature." For Nature was the key-word of that time, as Reason had been for the preceding generation, and as Liberty, then Sincerity, then Violence and then Justice were later to become. But for Goethe Nature was much more than a word. He lived in her, became part of her and accepted her with a kind of gay abandonment. While his new friends, diplomats and literary amateurs, shut themselves up in their offices in order at least to make a pretence of work, Goethe, boldly displaying his contempt of the Imperial Court and his own determination to learn public law out of Homer and Pindar only, set out every morning with a book under his arm into the lovely country that surrounded Wetzlar. The spring was exquisite. The trees in the fields and meadows looked like great white and pink bouquets. Lying among the tall grasses, near the bank of a stream, Goethe lost himself in the contemplation of all the myriad little plants and insects, and the blue sky. After the tortures of Strasbourg, the doubts and the remorse of Frankfurt, came a strange serenity, and an amazing activity of mind.

He opened his Homer, and the modern, human aspect of the story delighted him. Those young girls at the fountain were Nausicaa and her companions. The green peas and roast meat which a woman was preparing in yonder great inn kitchen was the banquet of the suitors and the kitchen of Penelope. Men do not change; heroes are not statues of white marble; their skin is hairy and cracked, their hands swollen and restless. Like the divine Ulysses we sail upon the open sea, in a little vessel suspended above an abyss, and in the hands of the mighty Gods. A fearful yet a beautiful thought when one is lying on one's back among soft grasses, gazing at the vault of heaven.

In the evening, at the Kronprinz Inn, the great delight now of the Round Table was to listen to Doctor Goethe relating his discoveries of the day. A verse of Pindar, or a rustic church that he had drawn as well as he could; some lovely lime trees in a village square, children, or a beautiful farm girl. He had the gift of charging his stories with an almost naïve enthusiasm which made the most trifling things interesting. As soon as he came in, the movement of life seemed to grow quicker. Among the young men who listened to him, some had talent, but none had genius. "Ah, Goethe," said one of them to him, "how can one help loving you?"

All Wetzlar soon sought his acquaintance. Two of the secretaries, although unmarried, lived on the outskirts of the Round Table. One of them, young Jerusalem, of the Brunswick Legation, was a very handsome youth with soft, melancholy blue eyes.

He kept himself at a distance, people said, because of an unhappy passion for the wife of one of his colleagues. He came once or twice to see Goethe, who was interested in his pessimism. But Jerusalem was too reserved to allow of the establishment of a real friendship.

The other hermit was Kestner of the Hanover Legation. When his comrades spoke of him they always called him the "Fiancé." He was, in fact, understood to be engaged to a girl in the town. He was extremely serious-minded, and his chief, who had a great respect for him, left him, in spite of his youth, a great deal of responsibility. It was for this reason that he had not time to come and dine at the Kronprinz. At the outset, the praises which the choicer spirits bestowed on the new arrival had put Kestner against him. But one day, when he was taking a walk in the country with a friend, they came upon Goethe under the trees. The conversation at once became deep and earnest, and after two or three meetings, Kestner, too, made up his mind, with the solemn deliberation that was characteristic of him, that he had undoubtedly met a very remarkable man.

Admired by his circle, free from all worldly or academic restraint, enraptured by the beauty of that springtime, Goethe was completely happy. Sometimes a transitory feeling clouded his enthusiasm as a light ripple stirs the calm surface of a lake. . . . Frédérique? No, it was not her recollection that passed across the steady glow of his thought. Once more it was like an uneasy expectation. He looked down upon Wetzlar as in days gone by he had looked down upon Alsace from the Cathedral.

"Shall I one day feel a delightful shiver as I open one of those doors? . . . Shall I be unable to read a stanza without my thoughts flying to a beloved face? . . . When I leave a lady, in the evening by moonlight, shall I already find the night too long and the morning too far off? Yes, all this is coming; I feel it. . . . And yet, Frédérique . . ."

He noted down a recollection. "When I was a little boy I happened to plant a cherry tree, and I loved to watch it grow. The spring frosts destroyed the buds and I had to wait another year before I could see ripe cherries on my tree. Then the birds ate

hem, then the caterpillars, and then a greedy neighbour. . . .
And yet if I ever have another garden I shall plant another cherry
ree."

Thus Doctor Goethe took his walks beneath the blossoming
rees, afire with his new passion. He knew all about it, except the
1ame of his beloved.

## III

When the fine weather came the young men of the Legations
used to organize dances in the country. A village inn was appointed as rendezvous. Some came on horseback, others brought
their partners from Wetzlar in carriages. When Goethe was invited for the first time to one of these little fêtes it was agreed
that he should go with two of the girls to fetch Fräulein Charlotte Buff, whom everyone called Lotte.

She was the daughter of old Herr Buff, the steward of the Teutonic Order, and she lived in the house of the Order, a pleasant
white mansion. Goethe got out of the carriage, crossed quite an
imposing courtyard, and, as he saw no one, went into the house.

A young girl was standing in the middle of a group of children
to whom she was handing out bread-and-butter. She was a
blonde with blue eyes and a slightly turned-up nose; her features
were not regular and a severe critic might perhaps have thought
her scarcely pretty. But she busied herself with the children with
so much charm and simplicity, she seemed so joyous, so unaf-
fected, the whole scene was so happy a picture of one of those
Germanic idylls that haunted Goethe's mind, that he was delighted with it.

A man pursues all his life among the race of women the type
which, for some mysterious reason, is the only one that can arouse
his feelings. In Goethe's eyes the bread-and-butter and the children formed part of this typical picture. It was a rustic grace, a
delicate touch in homely matters that moved him. Frédérique of
Strasbourg had already figured as a Muse of the countryside.
Nausicaa, a king's daughter washing her linen, had perhaps given
birth, in his mind, to this race of pure and homely maidens. In

any case Charlotte Buff's slices of bread-and-butter seemed to him a perfect theme for a domestic symphony.

The girl's conversation during the journey, her childlike pleasure, the good-humoured determination which she showed in amusing her friends with little games during a storm, finished her conquest of the Doctor. In the completeness of his delight he realized beyond all question that he had found the woman with whom he had been in love for a fortnight.

Lotte herself was also well aware that she had found favour. It must be admitted that she was pleased. Goethe was handsome and agreeable; for a month past all Lotte's friends had talked of nothing but this marvellous intellect. She was a coquette, and a dangerous one, as only virtuous women can be.

Later in the evening Kestner, who had been, as he always was, kept later than the others by his work (he was a meticulous person—he made a rough copy of every letter and never sent off the despatches to Hanover without having read everything before signing it), rode out to join the little party, and from his attitude and that of the young girl, Goethe understood that Lotte Buff was the famous fiancée. This discovery took him aback, but he controlled himself, and without any sign of discomposure went on dancing, and amusing and entertaining the company. They did not break up till dawn. Goethe escorted his three companions back through the misty woods and the fields refreshed by the storm. Charlotte and he were the only ones who did not fall asleep.

"Please, please," said she, "do not trouble about me."

"As long as I see those eyes of yours still open," he answered, looking at her, "I cannot shut mine."

From that moment they did not speak another word.

When Goethe moved he lightly brushed the young girl's warm knees, and this imperceptible contact gave him one of the keenest pleasures he had ever known. The beauty of the morning light, the slightly ludicrous slumbers of their companions, the astonishing happiness that they shared made them feel like confederates in some delightful plot.

"I am in love with her," thought Goethe. "I am sure of that.

ut how is it possible? At this moment at Sesenheim . . . Ah, ell . . . one love fades and another blooms. This is Nature's ay. . . . But she is engaged to Kestner, to the good and loyal estner. What can I hope for? Need I hope? It will be enough to e her, watch her living among the children, in her house, talk her and listen to her laughter. What will come of all this? Vho knows, and why try to foresee the end of anything? One ould live like a running brook."

When the carriage at last stopped at the Teutonic House, which vas still sleeping in the grey morning light, he felt quite dazed vith happiness.

## IV

On the following day he came to ask after Nausicaa and made he acquaintance of Alcinoüs. Old Herr Buff had lost his wife a ear before; he had eleven children over whom Lotte reigned vith benevolent despotism. Goethe, at his very first visit, as might ave been expected, immediately won the hearts of the old gen-leman and his children. He told some excellent stories and in-ented some new games. In everything that he said or did there vas something youthful and captivating that was quite irresistible.

When he took his departure all the little company begged him o come back soon. A smile from Lotte confirmed the children's nvitation. Goethe reappeared on the following day. He had no ousiness to keep him away; he found no happiness except in _otte's company, and he was not the man to deny himself a hap-oiness that was within his reach. He came in the morning and in he evening, and in a few days he was an established visitor to he house.

Charlotte's life was indeed delightful to watch. Goethe found once more in her what he had so much loved in Frédérique: an activity practical in its purpose but poetic, too, from a certain deli-cate ease in the performance. She worked from morning till night. She washed the small children, dressed them, played with them, while at the same time superintending the studies of the older ones with a great deal of good sense and modesty. She took Goethe out to pick fruit in the orchard and occupied him in shell-

ing peas or stringing beans. When it grew dark the whole famil
assembled in the drawing-room and at the request of Charlott
who did not like leaving a friend without useful employmen
Goethe tuned the harpsichord. Lotte was not sentimental. Sh
was sensitive, but she was too much occupied to have the leisu
or the wish to make play with her feelings. Her conversatior
with Goethe were instructive and serious. He talked about h
life, his religious beliefs, and sometimes, too, about Homer an
Shakespeare. She was intelligent enough to appreciate the rar
qualities of the companion who was becoming a part of he
daily life. She was conscious of emotion and perhaps love i
all he said, and she was pleased without being disturbed. She knev
that her own heart was untouched and that she remained Kest
ner's faithful and immaculate fiancée.

On his part the Fiancé was a little melancholy. His devotion t
his diplomatic duties kept him away from her nearly all day
When he reached Lotte's house he saw Goethe sitting on the ter
race at the girl's feet, holding a skein of wool, or found them i
a corner of the garden choosing flowers for a bouquet. They wel
comed him warmly and at once carried on with him the con
versation that they had begun, so that his arrival never gave ris
to an embarrassed silence. Nevertheless Kestner guessed tha
Goethe was not very pleased to see him. He would himself hav
sooner been alone with Charlotte, and Goethe, on the strengt
of his standing invitation, was in no hurry to take his leave. A
they were both men of education and breeding, they did not ir
any way betray these somewhat painful feelings, but both o
them were on their guard. Kestner was all the more alarmed because he was extremely modest. He greatly admired his rival; he
thought him handsome and clever. What was worse, Goethe wa
unoccupied, and one who is always at hand to unburden the restless and unsatisfied souls of those eternal hermits of the home
gains great power over them.

The Fiancé would have been more reassured if he had been
able to read the more intimate thoughts of his rival. From the
very first day the latter had understood that Lotte would not fall
in love with him. A woman of her character does not give up a

Kestner for a Goethe. He was sure she liked him, and that was a good deal. Besides, what could he have asked for? To marry her? That would certainly ensure his happiness. But that was a happiness that did not tempt him. No, he was satisfied as he was. To sit at Charlotte's feet, watch her play with her young brothers, wait for a smile when he had done her a service or said something that she liked, receive a little tap, light as a caress, when he had ventured too direct a compliment—in this monotonous and narrow life he found an infinite contentment.

The spring was warm and they passed the days in the garden. All the incidents of this tranquil, pure affection figured in Goethe's journal like little scenes out of an idyll. He began to create. Not indeed his mighty edifice, not the Cathedral, but charming little Greek temples in a lovely countryside. What was to come of all this? He would not think about it. He began to accept his actions more and more as natural phenomena.

The evenings grew ever more delightful. When Kestner arrived the three friends went and sat together on the terrace and talked very late into the night. Sometimes they went for a walk by moonlight in the meadows and orchards. They had achieved that quality of perfect confidence which gives so much charm to conversation. No subject seemed absurd, and they had for one another that affection and mutual regard which alone make possible a true simplicity of intercourse.

For the most part it was Goethe who talked; Kestner and Lotte delighted in the amazing brilliance of his intellect. He described his Frankfurt friends, Fräulein von Klettenberg, Doctor Merck, strange creature of evil eye and insinuating talk, who looked for cures in books on mysticism. He told them how he had read the alchemists in his company and populated the universe with sylphs, Undines, and salamanders. For a long while he had been devoted to the pietists. They seemed to him more sensitive than others to personal religion, less attached to empty practices. Then he had grown tired of them. "They are people of commonplace intelligence who imagine there is nothing outside religion because they are ignorant of all the rest. They are intolerant; they want to mould other people's noses to the shape of their own."

Goethe himself believed that the truth could not lie in th
idea of a God external to man. "It must be so very inconvenien
to believe in the perpetual presence of God at one's side. I thin
I should feel as if I had the Great Elector always at my elbow
I believe in the presence of God within me."

Religion, next to love, is women's favourite topic. Lotte fol
lowed their conversation with the liveliest interest.

After having escorted their friend home, Goethe and Kestne
would often go on wandering about for a long while in the de
serted streets of Wetzlar. The edges of the shadows were sharply
cut by the moonlight. About two in the morning, Goethe woul
sit on the top of a wall and declaim the wildest poetry. Sometimes they heard a noise of footsteps, and after a moment saw
young Jerusalem pass by, walking by himself with measured step
and bent head.

"Ah," said Goethe, "the Lover!"

And he burst out laughing.

## V

Spring gave way to summer and affection to desire. Lotte was
too kind and Goethe too young. Sometimes as they were walking
along the narrow paths of the garden their bodies brushed against
each other for one instant; sometimes as they were disentangling
a skein of wool or picking a flower their hands met. The recollection of such moments kept Goethe awake for entire nights. He
found it very difficult to wait for the morning, when he could see
Charlotte once more. He recaptured even to their slightest shades
the powerful and exquisite emotions that he had experienced with
Frédérique, and this return of the seasons in his heart put him out
of humour.

"When love comes back it destroys its own quality, which is
the expression of the Eternal, the Infinite." Since this, too, was to
repeat itself, human life was a mortally monotonous performance.

With the heavy August days, which cut short their little common tasks and left him long hours to spend at Charlotte's feet,

Goethe became more enterprising. One day he kissed her. Unimpeachable fiancée as she was, she told Kestner.

It was a difficult position for the grave and tender secretary. An unguarded remark, a reflection on the unconscious coquetry of Lotte and all would have been lost. But Kestner, no doubt because he was deeply in love with her, had the secret of a gift which, in a lover, is called delicacy. He contented himself by assuring Charlotte of his confidence in her and, as she asked him to do, left it to her to bring Goethe back to the ways of propriety. In the evening she asked the Doctor to stay after Kestner had gone, and told him that he must not make any mistake about her feelings: that she was and always had been in love with her betrothed and that she would never fall in love with any other man. Kestner watched Goethe come up with him, his head bent and looking rather sad, and he at once felt incomparably happy, kind, and sympathetic.

The three friends then became united in an odd and charming conspiracy. Following the example of Goethe, who concealed nothing, Kestner and Charlotte fell into the habit of revealing their feelings with the greatest freedom. Of an evening on the terrace Goethe's love for Lotte was the subject of long and delightful conversations. They talked of it as of a natural phenomenon, at once dangerous and interesting. Goethe's birthday was the same as Kestner's. They exchanged presents. Kestner's to Goethe was a little pocket Homer; Lotte's was the pink ribbon she had worn in her bosom on the day of their first meeting. Kestner had thought of sacrificing himself. He did not tell the others, but he noted down his misgivings in his private diary. Goethe was younger, handsomer, and more brilliant than he was. Perhaps he would make Lotte happier. But Lotte herself had reassured him: she had said she liked him best, and that Goethe with all his striking qualities was hardly made for a husband. And then no doubt Kestner's courage would have failed him, for he was deeply smitten.

Goethe, himself, under a gay and natural exterior, was suffering. Lotte's firm decision and her quite definite choice wounded his self-respect. The continual temptation of their life in common

increased his desires. He had attacks of violent passion durin
which, in the presence of the indulgent and sympathetic Kestne
he seized Charlotte's hands and wept and he kissed them.

But in the worst moments of despair he knew that underneat
this layer of genuine sadness there lay dormant a deep serenit
in which he could one day find refuge. Just as a man out in
storm knows that the sun is bright above the clouds and pos
sesses some means of reaching that untroubled space, so Goeth
in his torment knew that he would soon escape his sorrow an
would perhaps find something like a bitter and gloomy pleasure i
describing it.

The evenings became shorter and cooler. The September rose
began to fall. Goethe's satanic friend, the brilliant Merck, came t
Wetzlar; he met Charlotte and found her charming, but he di
not tell Goethe so. With a grimace of indifference he counselle
flight to other loves. The Doctor, somewhat out of humour
thought that the time had come to tear himself away from a vai
delight that was nearing its exhaustion. The man still found th
same pleasure in living in Charlotte's shadow, in feeling the rustl
of her dress against him in the darkness, in winning from he
infinitesimal and precious proofs of her affection, snatched from
the silent watchfulness of Kestner; the artist was satiated with
these monotonous emotions. He had increased his spiritual resources by his stay in the place; he had made a collection of beautiful landscapes saturated in romance; the vein was worked out,
the harvest gathered, and he must go.

"Must I really go? My soul is turning like the weather-vane on
the top of a steeple. The world is so beautiful, and he is fortunate
who can take pleasure in it without thinking overmuch. I am
often annoyed because I cannot do this, and preach myself sermons on the art of enjoying the present."

But the world was calling him, the world with its infinite
promises. "Not to be anything, but to become everything," that
must be his aim. He had his work to do, his cathedral to build.
What would it be like? That was still a mystery, hidden in the
mists of the future. Yet it was to this dim prospect that he was

ing to sacrifice joys that would be secure. He forced himself to
ttle the day of his departure, and thenceforward, sure in his
termination, he could plunge into the pleasing frenzy of his
ssion.

He had arranged to meet his friends in the garden after dinner,
d he was waiting for them under the chestnut trees on the ter-
ce. They would come, full of friendliness and gaiety; they
ould treat this evening just like any other. But this was the last
ening. The Master of Events, Doctor Goethe, had decided it;
thing could alter his decree. Departure was painful, but it was
t unpleasant to find oneself so inflexible.

He had inherited from his mother such a lively horror of scenes
at he could not endure the idea of formal farewells. He wanted
pass this last evening with his friends in a serene and sad enjoy-
ent. He felt in advance the pathos of this conversation, in which
vo of the participants, in their ignorance of the true position,
ere unconsciously to wound the third, who, because he alone
as aware of it, would be the only one to be hurt.

He had indulged himself for some time with the agreeable tor-
ent of these reflections when he heard the footsteps of Char-
tte and Kestner on the sandy path. He ran to meet them and
pturously kissed Lotte's hand. They walked to a dark leafy
rbour at the end of the avenue and sat down. The garden was so
vely under the pale moonlight that they stayed a long while
silence. Then Charlotte said:

"I never walk in the moonlight without thinking of death. . . .
believe we shall be born again. . . . But shall we meet again,
;oethe? . . . Shall we recognize each other? . . . What do you
iink? . . ."

"What are you saying, Charlotte?" he asked, completely over-
ome. "We shall meet again. In this life or the next we shall meet
gain."

"Do the friends that we have lost," she went on, "know any-
hing about us? Do they feel all that is in our minds when we
hink of them? The image of my mother is always before my
yes when I am sitting quietly in the evening among her children,

among our children, when they cluster round as they did rour her."

She talked thus for a long time in a voice as soft and tender the night itself. Goethe wondered if this unwonted melanchol were due to some strange presentiment. For himself, he felt h eyes fill with tears, and the emotion that he had wished to avo was gaining possession of him. In spite of Kestner's presence, l took Charlotte's hand. It was the last day. What did it matter

"We must go in," she said gently: "it is time."

She attempted to withdraw her hand, but he held it forcibl

"Let us agree," said Kestner gaily, "let us agree that the first c us who dies shall give the two survivors some information abou the other world."

"We shall meet again," said Goethe: "under whatever form may be, we shall meet again. Good-bye, Charlotte. Good-by Kestner; we shall see each other again."

"Tomorrow, I think," said she, smiling. She got up and wer with her fiancé towards the house. Goethe saw her white dres still gleaming for a few seconds in the shadow of the lime tree and then everything disappeared.

After Kestner had gone, the Doctor wandered alone for a whil in the lane from which the front of the house was visible. He sav a window lit up: it was Lotte's room. A little later the window grew dark. Charlotte slept. She knew nothing. The novelist wa satisfied.

The next day when Kestner came home he found a letter fron Goethe.

"He is gone, Kestner. When you receive this letter, he wil have gone. Give Lotte the enclosed note. I had made up my mind but your conversation yesterday has shattered me. I cannot say anything at the moment. If I had stayed with you an instan longer I could not have held out. Now I am alone and tomorrow I go. Oh, my poor head!

"Lotte, I hope I shall indeed come back, but God knows when Lotte, what were the feelings of my heart when you were talk ing, knowing that I was seeing you for the last time? . . . He i gone. What spirit made you choose such a subject? . . . I am now alone and I can weep. I shall see you again, but 'tomorrow' never comes. Tell my young ruffians he has gone. . . . I cannot go on."

Kestner took the letter to Lotte early in the afternoon. All the children of the house echoed sadly, "Doctor Goethe has gone."

Lotte was sad, and while she was reading the letter the tears came into her eyes. "It was better for him to go," she said.

Kestner and she could talk of nothing else. Visitors came; they were amazed at Goethe's precipitate departure and found fault with his want of courtesy. Kestner defended him with much warmth.

## VI

While his friends, much affected, read and re-read his letters, pitied him and pictured to themselves with feelings of anxious sympathy what his solitude would be like, Goethe was walking quickly down the lovely valley of the Lahn. He was going to Coblenz, where Merck was to meet him at the house of Frau de la Roche.

In the distance a hazy chain of mountains, above him the white summits of the rocks, at his feet, in the depths of a gloomy gorge, a river flowing under a curved roof of willows—all this composed a pleasantly melancholy landscape.

The pride of having broken the enchantment of Wetzlar tempered the melancholy of his still lively recollection. At times when he thought over the adventure he had just lived through, he said to himself, "Could not an elegy be made out of it? . . . or perhaps an idyll?" Or again he would ask himself if he were not better fitted to draw and paint landscapes like the one he was then passing through. "Come," said he, "I will throw my fine pocket-knife into the river. If I see it fall into the water, I will become a painter; if the willows hide it from my sight as it drops, I will give up the idea for ever."

He did not see the knife plunge into the stream, but caught sight of the splash, and the oracle seemed ambiguous. He postponed his decision. He walked as far as Ems, then went down the

Rhine in a boat and arrived at Frau de la Roche's house. He received the most delightful welcome. Councillor de la Roche was a man of the world, a great reader of Voltaire, a sceptic and a cynic. His wife was accordingly a woman of feeling. She had published a novel, she was interested in literary men and had turned her house, in spite of her husband and perhaps in protest, into a meeting-place for the Apostles of the Heart.

Goethe was more particularly interested in the dark eyes of Maxmiliane de la Roche, a beautiful girl of sixteen, intelligent and precocious. He took long walks with her in the country, talked about God and the Devil, Nature and the Heart, Rousseau and Goldsmith, and indeed spread himself superbly just as if Lotte had never existed. And the recollection of Lotte even gave a zest to this new friendship. "It is a very pleasant sensation," he noted, "to listen to the first accents of a dawning affection murmuring in one's heart before the echo of the last sigh of an extinct affection is altogether lost in the void. Thus when we turn our eyes from the setting sun we like to see the moon rising on the opposite horizon."

But he had soon to return to Frankfurt.

A return to the paternal house, after a reverse, brings a double feeling of relief and of discouragement. The bird has tried to fly away but has had to fold his wings once more. While he keeps to the nest he pines for the free air for which his wings had not proved strong enough. The child escapes from the difficulties of a hard and hostile world; he is absorbed once more in the familiar round, which is naturally less opposed than any other to the habits he has formed. There he discovers again the monotony of sensations grown too familiar, the affectionate slavery of the family.

His travels have been teaching him a sense of proportion, and he is surprised to find his own people still engaged upon their old foolish disputes. Goethe once more heard at home the very phrases that had so exasperated his childhood. His sister Cornelia complained of her father, his mother complained of Cornelia, and Councillor Goethe, whose temper was not accommodating, wished to send back to the study of lawyers' files a son whose head was full of half-created characters and who had no notion of the world of reality.

Goethe had a positive dread of melancholy, and realizing that it was mastering him, decided that his only chance of salvation lay in at once undertaking an important literary work. He was still thinking of a Faust, perhaps of a Prometheus, and perhaps, too, of a Caesar. But after having sketched out several plans, written a few verses, crossed them out and torn them up, he recognized that he was doing no good. Between them and his work came the image of Lotte.

His lips retained the savour of the only kiss that he had ever had from her, his hands the touch of her firm soft hand, and his ears the sound of that vivid, lively voice of hers. Now that he was far away from her, he found out that she was everything to him. As soon as he sat down at the table his mind went off into sad and fruitless reveries. He tried, as one always does, to reconstruct the past as he would like it to have been. If Lotte had not been engaged. . . . If Kestner had been less estimable and less kind. . . . If he himself had been less conscientious. . . . If he had had the courage to stay . . . or the courage to disappear altogether and force his mind to destroy the images that tormented him. He had hung above his bed a silhouette of Lotte cut in black paper by a gipsy artist, and he looked at this picture with a sort of frenzied devotion. Every evening before he went to bed he kissed it and said, "Good-night, Lotte." When he wanted a pin he took one of those that fastened the portrait to the wall and said, "Lotte, will you let me take one of your pins?" As evening fell he would often sit down and carry on long conversations in an undertone with his lost friend. These acts, which were natural and spontaneous on the first occasion, had in a few days become empty and melancholy rites, but he found in their accomplishment a certain relief to his distress of mind. He looked upon the commonplace, even absurd silhouette as a kind of altar.

He wrote to Kestner nearly every day and gave him affectionate messages for Charlotte. When speaking of his love he still kept up the half-jesting, half-tragic tone that he had assumed at

Wetzlar, because it was the only one that made it possible for him to express the feelings that troubled him without offending Kestner.

"We have spoken," he wrote, "of what may possibly take place beyond the clouds. I do not know; but what I do know is that the Lord our God must be a very cold-blooded person to leave you Lotte."

Another time: "So Lotte has not dreamed about me? I take this very ill, and I insist on her dreaming about me this very night and telling you nothing about it."

Sometimes he gave way to spitefulness and pride. "I shall not write again until I can tell Lotte that I am loved, and deeply loved, by another."

After a few attempts he was forced to realize that it would be impossible for him to get to work again on the subjects that had interested him in the past until he had rid his mind of this obsession. The only task of which he felt capable was to write about Lotte, to write a work of which Lotte should be the heroine.

But though he had considerable material—his diary, his recollections, even his feelings, which were still vivid—he was faced with great difficulties. The subject was very thin: a young man arrives in a town, he falls in love with a woman who is not free and draws back before the difficulties of the situation. Would this make a book? And why did the hero go away? His female readers would not like this at all. If he had been truly in love he would have stayed. In the adventure as it really happened Goethe had gone away because the call of his art, the will to create, had been stronger than his love. The more he thought about it the more commonplace and inadequate the subject seemed, the more incapable he felt of working it out, the more his weariness and disgust with all literary labours increased.

In the middle of November Kestner made known to him a surprising piece of news. Young Jerusalem, the handsome, melancholy youth who took so many walks in the moonlight wearing a blue frock-coat and yellow waistcoat, and who had been called in jest "The Lover," had lately shot himself.

"Unhappy Jerusalem!" Goethe wrote in reply. "Your news

was shocking and quite unexpected. . . . The people who know not joy because their hearts have been hardened by vanity and the worship of illusions are responsible for this and for all our misfortunes. For them there is no forgiveness, my friends! Poor young fellow! When I came back from a walk and met him in the moonlight, I said, 'He is in love,' and Lotte will remember that I laughed. I spoke with him very little. When I left I brought away with me one of his books, which I shall preserve, with his memory, as long as I live."

Events in another's life always aroused sincere emotion in Goethe when they represented possible and unrealized fragments of his own existence. He studied Jerusalem's story with an almost morbid curiosity. He was quite aware that if he himself had been slightly different, if certain elements had been lacking in the composition of his intellect, he might have gone the same way. But he was especially interested in it because his first thought had been, when he heard the news: "Here is my *dénouement*." Yes, the hero of his unlucky idyll might, indeed he ought to, commit suicide. Death, and death only, supplied the element of tragic grandeur that had been lacking in his adventure.

He asked Kestner to send him a complete account of all that he could learn about the affair, and Kestner did so, not without ability.

## VII

The memories of Wetzlar and the account of Jerusalem's death certainly provided Goethe with the beginning and the end of a notable book. It would be a work of the truest and most vivid passion. The part played by the imagination would be, as was always Goethe's aim, reduced to a minimum. He had confidence in himself and he liked his subject. And yet he could not get to work and was still absorbed in his dreams.

He had always needed, before he could start writing, a brief illumination in which, as in a flash of lightning, he had a sudden view of the work as a whole without having time to distinguish the details. But this time he could get no such view of it. His love affair with Lotte and the death of his friend were two episodes

taken from two different series of Destiny's successions and did
not fit in together.

There was nothing in the characters of the people in the diary
that suggested the drama of the *dénouement*. Kestner's kindness
and freedom from jealousy, Lotte's wholesome simplicity and
lightness of heart, Goethe's unassailable happiness and curiosity—
such qualities made the hero's suicide improbable. He tried in vain
to picture to himself what the scene between Frau Herd and
Jerusalem could have been like, and Jerusalem's final reflections.
He must remodel the characters and weave another chain of
events. But events are strangely linked together. As soon as one
is touched the whole edifice is shaken. It seems that the truth
must be one, and that if it is touched up a little, even with the
most delicate and careful strokes, the mind is torn between an
infinity of possibilities.

Once more Goethe was unable to find peace. A fantastic population of plans and projects ranged over his weary brain. Sometimes he thought he could distinguish shadowy and lovely forms,
but they vanished forthwith. Like a pregnant woman who cannot find relief, he sought in vain for a position in which he could
be at rest. The hour of his delivery seemed far off.

He travelled to Wetzlar to get details of the drama. He saw the
house in which the young man had killed himself, the pistols,
armchair, and bed. He spent a few hours with Charlotte. The happiness of the engaged pair seemed complete. The very recollection of their evenings of old seemed to have passed out of their
calm and well-ordered life. Goethe felt very unhappy and very
lonely. His love revived. As he sat upon the sofa in the Teutonic
House looking at the cool and peaceful Lotte, who continued to
manage the household with her graceful competence, he said to
himself, "Jerusalem was right. Even I myself could perhaps . . ."
But Goethe remained Goethe and he returned quietly to Frankfurt.

The house seemed more melancholy than ever. The time of
Kestner's marriage drew near. In the evening, alone in his room,
"in his barren bed," Goethe pictured Charlotte in the nuptial
chamber, in a blue striped dressing-jacket, her hair arranged for

the night, chaste and charming. Desire and jealousy kept him painfully awake. In order to live, a man needs to look forward to some shining point, the goal of his journey. But what was there left for him to hope for? He saw himself condemned to live, as a humble lawyer or official, in this town whose commonplace middle-class would always dislike him for his intellectual gifts. His mind, which he knew to be capable of creation, would be worn out in drawing up reports or stupid statements for the courts. He thought, without modesty, but not without reason, "I shall live here like a giant chained by dwarfs."

He saw himself buried alive. All the companions of his youth left him one after another. His sister Cornelia was going to be married. His friend Merck was soon leaving for Berlin. Charlotte and her husband would in their turn go away from Wetzlar. "And I am alone. If I do not marry or hang myself, you may say that I like life very much"; thus he wrote to Kestner, and a little later: "I am wandering in waterless deserts."

He came to think that the cause of suicides must often be the need felt by a man leading a monotonous and melancholy life to astonish himself and, one might almost say, to divert his mind by an unusual action. "The love of life," he thought, "depends on the interest we take in the regular alternation of day and of night, of the seasons, and in the pleasure that these alternations offer us. When this interest comes to an end, life is simply a tedious burden. An Englishman hanged himself so as not to be forced to dress and undress every day. I heard a gardener exclaim wearily: 'Must I always be looking at those gloomy clouds passing from west to east?' These are symptoms of a disgust with life which, in thoughtful people, is commoner than is believed. As for myself, if I think about the matter coldly, what has life still to give me? Another Frédérique whom I shall desert? Another Lotte who will forget me? The foolish career of a lawyer at Frankfurt? Truly it would be a natural and courageous act to renounce such splendid prospects of one's own free will.

"And yet when we think of the various ways of suicide, we recognize that to diminish the number of the living is so contrary to human nature that in order to achieve the result man has recourse to mechanical aids. Though Ajax transfixes himself with his sword, it is the weight of his body that renders him this last service; when we turn a pistol on ourselves, it is the backward movement of the trigger that really kills us. The only authentic suicide is that of the Emperor Otho, who himself drove a dagger into his heart."

For several evenings when he went to bed he laid a dagger beside him. Before he put out the light he tried to drive the point into his chest. But he did not succeed in inflicting even the slightest of wounds. The body betrayed the spirit. "Ah, well," he thought, "at the bottom of my heart I must want to live."

When he looked into his heart sincerely, trying to rid himself of commonplaces, those insubstantial phantoms that hover above genuine thought, and sought for the reasons which, in spite of everything, made him wish to live, he discovered first of all his pleasure, which for him was perennial, in the marvellous spectacle of the world, that god-sent curiosity of his; then the sad sweet certainty of the approaching birth of a fresh affection; and lastly the more obscure but irresistible instinct to watch over the work that was, he felt, forming within him with an implacable deliberation.

"Don't worry," he wrote to his friends at Wetzlar. "I am almost as happy as two people who are in love, like you. I have in me as much hope as lovers have."

When the time of Charlotte's marriage drew near he asked the favour of being allowed to buy the wedding-ring. He found something of a strange pleasure in irritating this sore. Determined to portray his own sad state, he insisted that it should be hopeless. Goethe was his own model and he posed to perfection.

On the morning of the marriage, Kestner, the perfect friend, wrote him an affectionate letter. As Goethe had requested, the bride's nosegay was sent to him; he put it in his hat for his Sunday walk. He decided to take down the silhouette of Lotte on Good Friday, make a grave in the garden, and solemnly bury it. When the day came, the ceremony seemed to him a little ridiculous and he gave up the idea. The black-and-white silhouette now watched over untroubled slumbers. The Kestners had left for Hanover. Knowing nothing of their life in this new world, Goethe could not imagine it. In his case pain as well as love needed images to make it last. Had he not already let go the favourable moment for recording such fragile feelings as these?

## VIII

He was still in correspondence with the charming Maximiliane de la Roche, whose black eyes had so helped him to console himself after Wetzlar. One day he learnt that she was going to marry a wholesale grocer of Frankfurt, Peter Anton Brentano, a widower with five children, and fifteen years older than herself. "Admirable!" wrote Goethe to Kestner, "dear Max de la Roche is going to marry a prominent shopkeeper!" Doubtless the sceptical Herr de la Roche had considered a large fortune and a numerous family preferable to a youthful heart.

Goethe expressed great pity for poor Max, who, for a gloomy house in Frankfurt, was going to abandon one of the most delightful places in the world and exchange her mother's cultivated and charming circle for the society of opulent tradesmen. Still he was overjoyed to think that so charming a creature was to be within reach.

As soon as he heard of her arrival at Frankfurt, he rushed to the house, used all his powers of conquest to captivate the widower's five children, and naturally succeeded in a quarter of an hour in making himself indispensable for ever. When Goethe wished to be agreeable, no one could resist him. Brentano was flattered by the presence in his house of the Burgomaster's grandson who was said to be a bright youth, so he gave Goethe a warm welcome.

Goethe immediately recovered his ardour and flung himself into a passionate friendship with his customary impetuosity. Soon his sole purpose in life was to keep Max company, to console her for the smell of cheese and for her husband's manners, to distract her mind by taking her for walks and reading to her. Once more all work was given up. And why should he write? Is there anything that is worth the smile, the sweet expression of contentment and gratitude, that for one fleeting instant flashes on a lovely face?

Max was not a little unhappy among the jars of oil and the barrels of herrings. She did not like Frankfurt. She tried to love her husband, but it was a difficult undertaking. Goethe became her confidant. Less practical than Charlotte Buff, she did not employ him to peel vegetables nor to pick fruit, but she spent the days with him playing duets for violoncello and piano and reading the latest French novels.

They often went out skating together. Goethe borrowed his mother's red velvet mantle and threw it round his shoulders like a cape. He skated perfectly, and as he glided along with sovereign ease, the wind behind him swelling out his royal train, he looked like a young god. Such at least was the opinion of his mother, the Councillor's wife, and of pretty Frau Brentano, for whose benefit the performance was given.

"Everything is going very well for me," he wrote. "The three last weeks have been nothing but pleasure, and we are now just as contented and happy as it is possible to be. I say we, for since January 15th there is not a single occupation in which I have been alone; and fate, that I have so often cursed, I am now well ready to flatter and call kindly and wise, for since my sister went away this is the only gift that could be called a compensation.

"Max is still the same angel whose simple and delightful qualities appeal to every heart, and my feelings for her are the joy of my existence."

But, alas! perfect pleasure cannot last and Brentano was soon to upset this unduly agreeable situation. At the outset he had found this young fellow who took his wife for walks extremely convenient; his own time was entirely taken up by the wares of his business and no one could take his place. On several occasions he had chosen Goethe to arbitrate between his wife and himself. It seemed to him that on certain questions the good sense of all the males of the species must be in agreement. Unfortunately Goethe was an artist and, in so far, a traitor to his sex. A husband always becomes, as the comic poets have remarked, most agreeably attached to any right-thinking man, one who, in other words, is of his own way of thinking; but a lover who undermines marital authority must be deservedly odious.

Brentano, noticing that his wife was not settling down at Frankfurt, that she criticized the mode of life of an ancient and respectable family, always talked about music, literature, and other unhealthy subjects, concluded, not without reason, that some evil counsellor must be making suggestions contrary to conjugal good order, and that the enemy was Goethe.

As soon as he had come to this conclusion, he treated Goethe with such insulting coldness that the latter's position in the house became extremely difficult. If he retaliated furiously, as he would have liked to do, he would sentence himself to exile; to endure the affronts in silence was to invite their multiplication. Soon Max herself, who was tired by disputes that spoilt all her pleasure, begged him to be careful and come less often. "I ask you for my own peace and quiet," she said to him. "Things cannot go on like this, they positively cannot."

He fell to walking up and down the room with long strides, repeating between his teeth, "It cannot go on like this." Max, who noticed his violent condition, tried to calm him. "I beg you," she said to him, "I beg you to control yourself. Your intellect, your knowledge, your talents promise you every happiness; be a man. Why must it be I? I who belong to someone else, I and no other?"

He went home, having promised that he would not come back again, but he was in a state of despair, distraught and talking to himself. So he was always to come upon the pitiful laws of society on the path of happiness. He could only find peace of mind, joy, and self-forgetfulness in the constant and affectionate society of a woman, and to obtain the right to this happiness he had either to surrender his liberty or condemn the woman he loved to become "guilty." Never had the conflict between the desires of the individual and the rules of society appeared to him so intolerable. Charlotte . . . ? Charlotte was after all in love with Kestner. But Max could not love her oil merchant and did not even pretend to love him. And he had to give way. "Your talents, your knowledge will bring you happiness." How ludicrous! Knowledge is grey and the tree of life is green. Besides, knowledge also is limited by human imperfection. What do the greatest scientists really know? Nothing about the true nature of things. What is man? His strength fails him just when he needs it most. In his joy, as in his sorrow, is he not limited, always confronted by the melancholy feeling of his own littleness just when he is hoping to lose himself in the infinite?

Quite suddenly, without knowing how the transformation had been worked, he felt once more at peace, master of himself, soaring far above these melancholy thoughts, as if they had belonged to another. "Why, of course," he thought, "that is how Jerusalem must have argued with himself; and no doubt it happened after a scene like the one I have just had with Max."

Thereupon he suddenly saw, with amazing lucidity, how his last unhappy adventure could be worked into the account of Jerusalem's death. Max and her husband, Charlotte and Kestner, Goethe and Jerusalem, seemed to melt, dissolve, and disappear, while their constituent elements, moving with incredible rapidity over the vast plains of the mind, combined harmoniously and in due proportions. The artist was awake at last, and Goethe was completely happy.

Then three new characters were born: Werther, Charlotte, and Albert. Werther was Goethe if he had not been an artist. Albert was a slightly meaner Kestner, endowed with Brentano's jealousy and with Goethe's own intellectual powers. Charlotte was Lotte, but brought up by Frau de la Roche, and a reader of Rousseau and Klopstock.

On the following day he shut himself up to work, and in four weeks the book was written.

## IX

When Goethe had finished *The Sorrows of the Young Werther* he felt as free and happy as after a general confession. Dreams, doubts, remorse, desires—all had found their eternal and inevitable place. The Cathedral was built. The last of his workmen-thoughts had already left the yard, and in the silence that had fallen on the place the Architect waited for the earliest worshippers. His past life was no longer in him, but before his eyes. It was beautiful, and as he contemplated it from the outside with a triumphant lassitude he thought vaguely of the new life that he now had the right to begin.

The book was not to be on sale until the Leipzig Fair, but the author could not wait so long before sending it to Charlotte at least. He often tried to imagine when and how she would read it. Perhaps she would begin *Werther* one evening, in bed, her firm breasts outlined under the delicate linen; or perhaps sitting in an armchair opposite Kestner, who would be a little jealous and try to find out without being observed what his wife was feeling. She would know for the first time what Goethe's love had been. She would doubtless blush when she came to the passionate scenes at the end, to the furious kisses which he had never given her and which, by an almost magical art, he could now force her to receive. . . . And dear Max Brentano? She, too, would doubtless fall to dreaming.

As soon as he had received the first volumes from the printer, he packed up two copies, one for Charlotte and one for Kestner, and wrote to Lotte: "You will realize when you read this book how dear it is to me; and this copy above all I value as much as if it were the only one in the world. It is for you, Lotte. I have kissed it a hundred times, and I kept it shut up so that no one might touch it. Oh, Lotte, I want each of you to read it by yourselves and separately. You by yourself and Kestner by himself, and then I want each of you to write me a line. Lotte—good-bye, Lotte."

Kestner and his wife smiled and hastened to obey. They each took one of the little volumes and opened it with affectionate eagerness.

Charlotte was a little uneasy. She knew Goethe's ardent nature, his refusal to restrain the violence of his feelings, to accept the useful conventions of the world. In real life, the fear of committing himself, of missing opportunities, had nearly always in the end confined this torrent of lava to a channel. But what would Goethe be like when let loose?

As soon as she had read the first pages she realized that her husband would be severely tried. The scene at the ball, so natural in her recollection, had here, she knew not how, taken on a passionate sensuality. "To hold the most charming of creatures in my arms! Fly with her like the storm! See everything about one pass and fade! To feel! . . . It was then I vowed that a woman I loved should waltz with none but me though I died for it! You will understand me."

Charlotte sat pensive. To be quite frank with herself, she had understood from the first day that Goethe loved her in this way. It was an idea that had slipped into the recesses of her consciousness; she had kept it carefully shut up there and had long since succeeded in forgetting this discreet and disturbing presence. Yet the recollection was there, for as she read the burning sentences, Charlotte felt the sweet uneasy impression of a reminiscence.

When she came to the passage: "What fire runs through all my veins when my finger happens to touch hers, when our feet come together under the table. I start away as from a flame, but a secret force draws me back once more. I am seized with giddiness and my senses are in a whirl. Ah! her innocence, the purity of her soul prevent her from realizing how the slightest familiarities put me to the torture. When she puts her hand on mine, as she talks to me . . ." Charlotte put the book down and reflected for some time. Had she not, in moments like those of which she had just read the description, nearly always guessed Gothe's agitation, and found it not at all displeasing? Even now to read the account of it made her, she had to admit, surprisingly happy. She reproached herself for her coquetry. She looked at her husband sitting opposite her. He was rapidly turning over the pages of the little volume with a gloomy and worried expression.

After a short interval he raised his eyes in his turn and asked her what she was thinking about. He seemed angry and ill at ease. "It is a disgraceful act," he said warmly. "Goethe describes people who at the outset are like ourselves and then he changes them in some way into false and romantic characters. . . . What sort of creature is this sentimental Lotte who weeps unceasingly over Werther's hand? . . . Did you ever say, 'Oh, Klopstock!' and look up at the sky, especially to a young man whom you had only just met? I find it difficult to picture you in such a part. . . . Ah! I can now see clearly that Goethe has never understood what gives you your charm. It is I alone, Charlotte, I alone who understand that. What is so attractive in you is just your perfect simplicity that is never out of place, that joyous and natural self-possession of yours that banishes all evil thoughts. But he has even spoilt his own portrait. The real Goethe behaved much better than Werther. There was something fine and generous about our relations during those four months which he has not been able to express. . . . As for myself, whom he has described as so destitute of sensibility, I whose heart 'does not beat sympathetically at the reading of a favourite book,' am I so cold as all that? Oh, I know very well that if I had had to lose you, Lotte, it is I who would have been Werther."

At this instant husband and wife drew near to each other, and there followed a little scene of conjugal affection which would not, perhaps, have been exactly in accordance with the author's wishes. They finished the book together, side by side and hand in hand. At the end of it Kestner, at any rate, was in a state of acute anger. The transformation of their innocent simple story into a tragic adventure seemed to him really abominable. He was indeed a monster—this two-headed individual who was both Goethe and Jerusalem. And no doubt Kestner did not fail to notice that the account of the last interview between Werther and his beloved was taken entirely from the letter that he had himself written to Goethe about the death of Jerusalem. But when he was confronted with a heroine whose name was Lotte, and who at the beginning of the book had been described with all Lotte's characteristics, he was as hurt as if some coarse-minded painter had taken the face and person of his wife for the subject of an obscene picture.

Charlotte herself was more moved than displeased, but she could imagine and sympathize with her husband's feelings, and in order to soothe him she said she thought he was right. Besides, she shared his apprehensions. What would be said about them in their own circle? All their friends in Wetzlar and even in Hanover could not fail to recognize them. How would it be possible to explain which parts of the book faithfully presented them and which were alien additions? How could they escape all the malicious and quite natural gossip? If they had been less sensitive they would have realized that society is, in general, profoundly indifferent and forgetful, and what seemed now so very important would be quite forgotten in six months. But Wisdom and Pain seldom keep house together. They felt that their happy retired life had been wrecked by their friend's indiscretion.

## X

On the following day Kestner wrote to Goethe in terms of severe displeasure. "It is true that you have interwoven some alien elements into each character and that you have blended several persons into one. Well and good. But if in these processes of interweaving and blending you had consulted your heart, the real people whose characteristics you have borrowed would not have been prostituted in this way. You wished to draw from nature in order to give verisimilitude to your picture, and you have brought together so many contradictory elements that you have failed in your purpose. The real Lotte would indeed be a poor creature if she were like your Lotte. And Lotte's husband—you called him your friend, and God knows whether he was so—is in like case.

"What a wretched object Albert is! If he had to be commonplace, was it necessary to make him such an utter idiot for you to be able to dominate him so haughtily and say: 'See what a fine fellow I am'?"

Goethe had for several days waited very impatiently for Kestner's and Lotte's opinions. He hoped for two long and enthusiastic letters, a list of passages that had more especially struck them, some quotations perhaps, a reminder of incidents that he had forgotten or missed out. He broke the seal with a cheerful sense of curiosity and was dumbfounded to come upon this bitter criticism. Was it possible that an intelligent man could so little understand the nature of a book? Why should he want Werther to be Goethe? "No doubt there are elements of Werther in me. But I was suddenly rescued from all that by something that is called Will. Take this away from Goethe and Werther will be left. Take away his imagination and we shall find Albert. Why does he say that Albert is a wretched creature? Why should I have made Albert commonplace? The beauty of my subject is that though Albert and Werther are opposed to each other, they fight on equal terms. Besides, what makes Kestner think that he is Albert? Does he believe that I am incapable of discovering a reasonable being in myself?"

The more he thought it over, the more he re-read Kestner's letter, the less he understood it and the more astonished he was. Yet it was distressing to him to think that he was giving his friends pain. He tried for a long time to find a means of pacifying them. But what was he to do? Not publish his novel? He had not the courage for that sacrifice.

"I must write at once and unburden my soul to you, my dear angry friends. The thing is done, the book is out; forgive me if you can. I will not listen to anything until events have proved how exaggerated are your fears, until you come to see in the book itself the harmless mingling of fact and fiction that it contains. . . . And now, my dears, when you feel anger rising within you, think, only think, that your old friend Goethe is always, always, and now more than ever, yours."

The publication of the book involved the Kestners, as they had anticipated, in requests for explanations and expressions of sympathy. Lotte's brother, Hans Buff, sent them the impression of the Teutonic House. There, at least, everyone knew Goethe, and young Werther's sufferings had had an uproarious success.

"By the way," wrote Hans, "have you read *Werther*? What do you think of it? The situation here is singular. There are only two copies in the whole town, and as everyone wants to read the book, everyone steals them as best he can. Yesterday evening, Papa, Caroline, Lele, Wilhelm, and I were all of us reading a single copy whose cover we had torn off. Each page passed through five hands. . . . Poor Werther! We laughed a great deal when we read it. Did he laugh too when he wrote it?"

Kestner had to assure his officious friends who sent their condolences, that his home life was happy, that his wife had always loved him, that Goethe had never thought of committing suicide, and that a novel was only a novel. Finally, Charlotte induced him to write Goethe a letter granting him absolution.

But there was little question of forgiveness. The young author was completely carried away. All Germany was now shedding tears over Werther's fate. The young men wore his blue frock-coat and yellow waistcoat and his brown-topped boots. The young women copied Charlotte's dresses, and above all the white dress with pink bows that she had worn at her first meeting with her friend. In every garden romantic hearts raised little monuments to Werther's memory. Climbing plants twined themselves about Wertherian urns. Songs and poems were written about Werther. The French themselves, so often contemptuous, welcomed this disciple of Rousseau with enthusiasm. Europe had not been so roused by a work of the imagination since *La Nouvelle Héloïse*.

Goethe answered in a tone which was scarcely that of a penitent. "O ye of little faith! If you could feel the thousandth part of what Werther stands for in a thousand hearts you would not even stop to think of the sacrifice that you have made for him. I would not, to save my own life, see Werther suppressed. Kestner, believe me, believe in me; your fears and your uneasiness will vanish away like the phantoms of a night. If you are generous, and if you do not worry me, I will send you letters, tears, sighs over Werther; and if you have faith, believe me, all will go well and gossip does not matter. Lotte, good-bye. Kestner, love me and do not bother me any more."

After this date his correspondence with the Kestners became extremely desultory.

Thenceforward, embalmed and enshrined in his sentences, they had lost for him the greater part of their reality. Once a year, over a long period, he wrote them letters which began "My

Dear Children," to ask for news of a continually increasing family. Then the excellent Kestner died.

In 1816 Frau Sekretärin Kestner, a widow of fifty-nine, plain but pleasantly good-humoured, came to visit His Excellency the Minister of State von Goethe at Weimar. She hoped that the great man might be useful to her sons August and Theodore, especially to Theodore, who wished to devote himself to the study of natural science.

She found a cultivated but worn-out old gentleman in whose features she looked in vain for the face of the wild youth of Wetzlar, whom no one could help loving. Conversation was difficult. Goethe, who did not know what to say, showed her prints and dried plants. Each of them read in the other's eyes astonishment and disillusion.

The Minister finally offered the old lady his own box at the theatre, excusing himself for not being able to join her there later. She thought, as she went out, "If I had met him by accident and without knowing his name, he would have made no impression on me."

The truth is that Doctor Goethe had long been dead; dead too was Fräulein Lotte Buff, who had so loved dancing and walks by moonlight. Of all the characters in this story one only was still alive, and that was the unhappy Werther.

# FOR FURTHER READING

## IN THE MODERN SHORT BIOGRAPHY

NOTE: The following list does not include books by the authors represented in the present collection, whose biographical works are enumerated in the separate notes. Furthermore, the list makes no claim to completeness, but offers a wide range of reading in all varieties of this literary type as cultivated during the past twenty years. Exhaustive lists will be found in *The Essay and General Literature Index, 1900-33;* Hefling and Dyde's *Index to Contemporary Biography and Criticism,* 1934; Logasa's *Biography in Collections,* 1937; and Edward H. O'Neill's *Biography by Americans, 1658-1936,* 1939.

Inasmuch as many of the separate short biographies in these collections made their first appearance in periodicals, and others are appearing continually, the reader desiring to keep up with the trends of this genre is advised to consult recent and current numbers of *The American Scholar, The Atlantic Monthly, Current History, Fortune, Forum, Harper's Magazine, Life, The New Yorker, The North American Review, Scribner's Magazine, The Yale Review,* and others.

Abbott, Lawrence F., *Twelve Great Modernists,* New York, Doubleday, 1927.

Abbott, Wilbur C., *Adventures in Reputation,* 1935; *Conflicts with Oblivion,* 2nd ed., 1935, Cambridge, Harvard University Press.

Agar, Herbert, *The People's Choice,* Boston, Houghton Mifflin, 1933.

Balch, Marston, ed., *Modern Short Biographies,* 1st ed., New York, Harcourt, Brace, 1935.

Beckdolt, F. R., *Giants of the Old West,* New York, Century, 1930.

Beerbohm, Max, *And Even Now,* New York, Dutton, 1921.

Beers, Henry A., *Four Americans,* New Haven, Yale University Press, 1929.

Belloc, Hilaire, *Characters of the Reformation,* New York, Sheed and Ward, 1936.

Best, Mary Agnes, *Rebel Saints,* New York, Harcourt, Brace, 1925.

Bishop, Morris, *A Gallery of Eccentrics,* New York, Minton, Balch, 1928.

Blunt, Hugh F., *Great Magdalens,* 1928; *Great Penitents,* 1936, New York, Macmillan.

Bolitho, Hector, *Twelve Jews,* Toronto, Ryerson, 1934.

Bolitho, William, *Twelve Against the Gods,* New York, Simon and Schuster, 1929.

Bowen, Marjorie, *Sundry Great Gentlemen,* New York, Dodd, Mead, 1928.

Boyd, Ernest, *Portraits: Real and Imaginary,* New York, Doran, 1924.

Boyle, Sir Edward, *Biographical Essays, 1790-1890,* London, Oxford University Press, 1936.

Brandes, Georg, *Creative Spirits of the Nineteenth Century,* New York, Crowell, 1923. Translated from the Danish.

Britt, Albert, *Great Indian Chiefs*, New York, Whittlesey, 1938.

Brown, Charles R., *They Were Giants*, New York, Macmillan, 1934.

Bruce, Philip A., *The Virginia Plutarch*, 2 vols., Chapel Hill, University of North Carolina Press, 1929.

Bryant, Arthur, *Man and the Hour*, London, P. Allan, 1934; *The American Ideal*, New York, Longmans, Green, 1936.

Buchan, John, *Men and Deeds*, London, Davies, 1935.

Burrows, Millar, *Founders of Great Religions*, New York, Scribner, 1931.

Busch, Niven, Jr., *Twenty-One Americans*, New York, Doubleday, 1930.

Butchart, Isabel, *Other People's Fires*, London, Sidgwick and Jackson, 1924.

Canby, H. S., *Classic Americans*, New York, Harcourt, Brace, 1931.

Charlesworth, M. P., *Five Men*, Cambridge, Harvard University Press, 1936.

Churchill, Winston, *Great Contemporaries*, New York, Putnam, 1937.

Clark, Barrett H., ed., *Great Short Biographies of the World*, 2 vols., New York, Boni, 1928.

Cournos, John, *A Modern Plutarch*, Indianapolis, Bobbs-Merrill, 1928.

Courtney, Janet E., *Freethinkers of the Nineteenth Century*, New York, Dutton, 1920; *Oxford Portrait Gallery*, London, Chapman, 1931; *The Adventurous Thirties*, London, Oxford University Press, 1934.

Craven, Thomas, *Men of Art*, New York, Simon and Schuster, 1931.

Dark, Sidney, *Twelve Bad Men*, 1929; *Twelve Royal Ladies*, 1929; *Twelve More Ladies: Good, Bad, and Indifferent*, 1932, New York, Crowell.

De Kruif, Paul, *Microbe Hunters*, 1926; *Hunger Fighters*, 1928; *Seven Iron Men*, 1929; *Men Against Death*, 1932, New York, Harcourt, Brace.

Dobrée, Bonamy, *Essays in Biography, 1680-1726*, London, Oxford University Press, 1925; *As Their Friends Saw Them*, New York, H. Smith, 1934.

Durant, Will, *Adventures in Genius*, New York, Simon and Schuster, 1931.

Eastman, Fred, *Men of Power*, Nashville, Cokesbury, 1938, 1939, etc.

Eddy, Sherwood, and Page, Kirby, *Makers of Freedom*, New York, Doran, 1926.

Eshleman, Lloyd W., *Moulders of Destiny*, New York, Covici-Friede, 1938.

Faris, John T., *The Romance of Forgotten Men*, New York, Harper, 1928.

Feiling, Keith, *Sketches in Nineteenth-Century Biography*, New York, Longmans, Green, 1935.

Flexner, James T., *America's Old Masters*, New York, Viking, 1939.

Ford, Ford Madox, *Portraits from Life*, Boston, Houghton Mifflin, 1937.

Frank, Waldo D., *Time Exposures*, New York, Boni and Liveright, 1926.

Frothingham, Paul R., *All These*, Cambridge, Harvard University Press, 1927.

Fulford, Roger, *The Wicked Uncles: The Father of Queen Victoria and His Six Brothers*, New York, Putnam, 1933.

Garvin, Katharine, ed., *Great Tudors*, New York, Dutton, 1935.

Griggs, E. H., *American Statesmen*, Croton (N. Y.), Orchard Hill, 1927.

Hagberg, Knut, *Kings, Churchills, and Statesmen*, New York, Dodd, Mead, 1929; *Personalities and Powers*, London, Lane, 1930. Translated from the Swedish.

Hall, Josef W., *Eminent Asians*, New York, Appleton, 1929.

Hansen, Harry, *Midwest Portraits*, New York, Harcourt, Brace, 1923.

Harris, Frank, *Contemporary Portraits* (five series, various publishers),1915-27.

Henderson, Archibald, *Contemporary Immortals*, New York, Appleton, 1930.

Howe, Mark A. DeWolfe, *Causes and Their Champions*, 1926; *Classic Shades: Five Leaders of Learning*, 1928, Boston, Little, Brown.

Jaeger, Muriel, *Adventures in Living: From Cato to George Sand*, New York, Morrow, 1932.

Jaffe, Bernard, *Crucibles: The Great Chemists*, New York, Simon and Schuster, 1930.

Josephson, Matthew, *The Robber Barons*, New York, Harcourt, Brace, 1934.

Krutch, J. W., *Five Masters*, New York, H. Smith, 1930.

Law, Frederick H., *Modern Great Americans*, New York, Century, 1926.

Lenard, Philipp, *Great Men of Science*, New York, Macmillan, 1933. Translated from the German.

Leonard, Jonathan N., *Crusaders of Chemistry*, New York, Doubleday, 1930.

Leslie, Shane, *Men Were Different*, Toronto, Saunders, 1937.

Lockhart, John Gilbert, *The Peacemakers (1814-1815)*, New York, Putnam, 1934.

Long, Orrie W., *Literary Pioneers*, Cambridge, Harvard University Press, 1936.

Lucas, F. L., *Studies French and English*, London, Cassell, 1934.

MacCarthy, Desmond, *Portraits, I*, New York, Putnam, 1931.

McGovern, John T., *Diogenes Discovers Us*, New York, Dial, 1933.

MacLaurin, Charles, *Post Mortem of Mere Mortals*, New York, Doubleday, 1930.

Madelin, Louis, *Figures of the Revolution*, New York, Macaulay, 1929. Translated from the French.

Massingham, H. J. and Hugh, eds., *The Great Victorians*, New York, Doubleday, 1932.

Minnigerode, Meade, *Lives and Times*, 1925; *Some American Ladies*, 1926; *Certain Rich Men*, 1927, New York, Putnam.

Mitchell, J. Leslie, *Earth Conquerors*, New York, Simon and Schuster, 1934.

Moran, Thomas F., *American Presidents*, New York, Crowell, 1933.

Morison, Samuel E., *Builders of the Bay Colony*, Boston, Houghton Mifflin, 1930.

Murdock, Kenneth B., *The Sun at Noon*, New York, Macmillan, 1939.

Nathan, G. J., *The Intimate Notebooks of George Jean Nathan*, New York, Knopf, 1932.

Neumann, Robert, *Passion: Six Literary Marriages*, New York, Harcourt, Brace, 1932. Translated from the German.

Newbolt, Henry, *The Book of the Long Trail*, New York, Longmans, Green, 1930.

Nomad, Max, *Rebels and Renegades*, New York, Macmillan, 1932.

Notestein, Wallace, *English Folk*, New York, Harcourt, Brace, 1938.

O'Higgins, Harvey, and Reede, E. J., *The American Mind in Action*, New York, Harper, 1924.

Parrington, Vernon L., *Main Currents in American Thought*, New York, Harcourt, Brace, 1927-30; 3 vols. in one, 1939.

Paston, George, and Quennel, Peter, *"To Lord Byron": Feminine Profiles Based on Unpublished Letters*, London, Murray, 1939.

Pearson, Drew, and Allen, R. S., *The Nine Old Men*, New York, Doubleday, 1937.

Ponsonby, Arthur and Dorothea, *Rebels and Reformers*, New York, Holt, 1919.

*The Post Victorians*, London, Nicholson and Watson, 1933. By various authors.

Pound, Arthur, *Native Stock*, New York, Macmillan, 1931.

Powys, Llewelyn, *Thirteen Worthies*, New York, American Library Service, 1923.

Pringle, Henry F., *Industrial Explorers*, New York, Harper, 1928.

*Profiles from The New Yorker*, New York, Knopf, 1938. By various authors.

Quiller-Couch, Arthur, *Victors of Peace: Florence Nightingale, Pasteur, Father Damien*, New York, Nelson, 1937.

Read, Conyers, *The Tudors*, London, Oxford University Press, 1936.

Roeder, Ralph, *The Man of the Renaissance*, New York, Viking, 1933.

Rogers, Cameron, *Gallant Ladies*, New York, Harcourt, Brace, 1928.

Rourke, Constance M., *Trumpets of Jubilee*, New York, Harcourt, 1927.

Sabatini, Rafael, *Heroic Lives*, Boston, Houghton Mifflin, 1933.

Seitz, Don C., *Uncommon Americans*, 1925; *The "Also Rans": Great Men Who Missed Making the Presidential Goal*, 1928, Indianapolis, Bobbs-Merrill.

Sergeant, Elizabeth S., *Fire Under the Andes*, New York, Knopf, 1927.

Sitwell, Edith, *The English Eccentrics*, Boston, Houghton Mifflin, 1933.

Slocombe, George, *Rebels of Art: Manet to Matisse*, New York, McBride, 1939.

Stowe, Lyman Beecher, *Saints, Sinners, and Beechers*, Indianapolis, Bobbs-Merrill, 1934.

Sutro, Alfred, *Celebrities and Simple Souls*, London, Duckworth, 1933.

Taylor, G. R. Stirling, *Seven Nineteenth Century Statesmen*, London, Cape, 1929.

Tucker, B. R., *The Gift of Genius*, New York, Stratford, 1930.

Ulmann, Albert, *New Yorkers*, New York, Chaucer Head, 1928.

Umbreit, K. B., *Our Eleven Chief Justices*, New York, Harper, 1938.

Undset, Sigrid, *Men, Women, and Places*, New York, Knopf, 1939.

VanBuskirk, William R., *Saviors of Mankind*, New York, Macmillan, 1929.

Wiegler, Paul, *Genius in Love and Death*, New York, Boni, 1929. Translated from the German.

Winkler, J. K., and Bromberg, Walter, *Mind Explorers*, New York, Reynal and Hitchcock, 1939.

Wolfe, Humbert, *Portraits by Inference*, London, Methuen, 1934.

Woolf, S. J., *Drawn from Life*, New York, Whittlesey, 1932.

Wortham, H. E., *Three Women*, Boston, Little, Brown, 1930.

Wright, Richardson, *Forgotten Ladies*, Philadelphia, Lippincott, 1928.

Young, G. F., *The Medici*, New York, Boni, 1930.

Zweig, Stefan, *Master Builders: A Typology of the Spirit* (includes *Three Masters*, *Adepts in Self-Portraiture*, and *The Struggle With the Daimon*), New York, Viking, 1939. Translated from the German.

## ON BIOGRAPHY

NOTE: The following list will direct the special student to most of the available books and articles on modern biography, but to only a few on the individual biographers. Additional articles may be found by consulting the *Reader's Guide to Periodical Literature*, the *International Index*, and the *New York Times Index*.

Adams, James T., "New Modes in Biography" and "Biography as an Art" in *The Tempo of Modern Life*, New York, Boni, 1931.

Balch, Marston, Introduction to *Modern Short Biographies*, 1st ed., 1935; "The Appreciation and Enjoyment of Biography" in *The College Omnibus*, 1936, and *The Revised College Omnibus*, 1939, ed. by James Dow McCallum, New York, Harcourt, Brace.

Barzun, Jacques, "Truth in Biography: Berlioz," *University Review*, Summer 1939.

Benson, A. C., "The Art of the Biographer," Royal Society of Literature Transactions, New Series, VI, London, Milford, 1926.

Boas, Guy, "Lytton Strachey," English Association Pamphlet No. 93, London, Oxford University Press, 1935.

Bowerman, G. F., "The New Biography" in *Censorship and the Public Library and Other Papers*, New York, H. W. Wilson, 1931.

Bower-Shore, Clifford, *Lytton Strachey: An Essay*, London, Fenland, 1933.

Boyd, Ernest, "Sex in Biography," *Harper's Magazine*, November 1932.

Bradford, Gamaliel, "Psychography" in *A Naturalist of Souls*, Boston, Houghton Mifflin, 1917; "The Art of Psychography," *Literary Review*, April 28, 1923; "The Art of Biography," *Saturday Review of Literature*, May 23, 1925; "Confessions of a Biographer" in *Wives*, New York, Harper, 1926; "Sainte-Beuve and Biography," *Saturday Review of Literature*, July 11, 1931; "Biography and the Human Heart" in *Biography and the Human Heart*, Boston, Houghton Mifflin, 1932.

Britt, Albert, *The Great Biographers*, New York, Whittlesey, 1936.

Bruce, Harold L., "Biography" in *Essays in Criticism* by Members of the Department of English, University of California, Berkeley, 1929.

Bryant, Arthur, "The Art of Biography," *London Mercury*, July 1934.

Burdett, Osbert, "Experiment in Biography" in *Tradition and Experiment in Present-Day Literature*, New York, Oxford, 1929.

Canby, H. S., "Biography and Truth," *Current Literature*, April 6, 1931.

Carlyle, Thomas, "Biography" in *Critical and Miscellaneous Essays*, II (1832).

Carter, John, "The Rewrite School of Biography," *Independent*, April 9, 1927.

Cecil, Lord David, Introduction to *An Anthology of Modern Biography*, New York, Nelson, 1936.

Chamberlain, John, "Walking the Tightrope: An Inquiry into the Art of Political Biography," *Modern Monthly*, March 1933. (An answer in part to Bernard DeVoto, *q.v.*)

Chesterton, G. K., "About Historians" in *As I Was Saying*, New York, Dodd, Mead, 1936.

Collins, Joseph, *The Doctor Looks at Biography*, New York, Doran, 1925.

Colton, Arthur, "Modern Biography," *Saturday Review of Literature*, January 18, 1930.

Cross, Wilbur L., *An Outline of Biography: From Plutarch to Strachey*, New York, Holt, 1924.

Crothers, S. M., "Satan Among the Biographers" in *The Cheerful Giver*, Boston, Houghton Mifflin, 1923.

Dangerfield, George, "The Insistent Past," *North American Review*, March 1937; "Lytton Strachey," *Saturday Review of Literature*, July 23, 1938.

DeVoto, Bernard, "The Skeptical Biographer," *Harper's Magazine*, January 1933, and in *Forays and Rebuttals*, Boston, Little, Brown, 1936.

Dobrée, Bonamy, "Modern Biography," *National Review*, July 1932; "Lytton Strachey" in *The Post Victorians*, London, Nicholson and Watson, 1933.

Drew, Elizabeth A., "Biography" in *The Enjoyment of Literature*, New York, Norton, 1935.

Dunn, Waldo, *English Biography*, New York, Dutton, 1916.

Ellis, Havelock, "An Open Letter to Biographers" in *Views and Reviews*, Boston, Houghton Mifflin, 1932.

Erskine, Stuart R. J., "History and Personality" in *King Edward VII and Some Other Figures*, London, Dent, 1936.

Fadiman, Clifton, Preface to *Profiles from The New Yorker*, New York, Knopf, 1938.

Field, Louise M., "Biography Boom," October 1930; "Biographical New Dealing," December 1934, *North American Review*.

Freeman, Douglas S., "Biography as a Pastime," *Saturday Review of Literature*, May 11, 1935.

Fuess, Claude M., "The Biographer and His Victims," January 1932; "Debunkery and Biography," March 1933, *Atlantic Monthly*.

Gelber, Lionel M., "History and the New Biography," *Queen's Quarterly* (Toronto), Winter 1930.

Gilman, Charlotte P., "A Psalm of 'Lives,'" *Saturday Review of Literature*, November 26, 1927.

Gosse, Sir Edmund, "Biography" in *The Encyclopaedia Britannica; Tallemant des Réaux, or The Art of Miniature Biography* (Zaharoff Lecture), London, Milford, 1925.

Guedalla, Philip, "The Missing Muse" in *The Missing Muse and Other Essays*, New York, Harper, 1930.

Harris, Frank, "The Art of Biography" in *Confessional*, New York, Panurge, 1930.

Hart, Liddell, "Neo-Georgian Biography," *Cornhill Magazine*, February 1934.

Henderson, Archibald, "Biographies—for Better, for Worse," *Virginia Quarterly Review*, October 1929.

Hergesheimer, Joseph, *Biography and Biographers* (10 pp.), New York, privately printed, 1932.

Howe, Mark A. DeWolfe, "Biography Drifts Toward the Novel," *Independent*, April 9, 1927.

Hughes, Rupert, "Pitfalls of the Biographer," *Pacific Historical Review*, March 1933.

Hyde, Marietta A., "Background for Reading Biography" in *Modern Biography*, New York, Harcourt, Brace, 1926, 1934.

Johnson, Edgar, *One Mighty Torrent: The Drama of Biography*, New York, Stackpole, 1937; "American Biography and the Modern World," *North American Review*, June 1938.

Johnston, George A., "The New Biography: Ludwig, Maurois, and Strachey," *Atlantic Monthly*, March 1929.

Johnston, James C., *Biography: The Literature of Personality*, New York, Century, 1927.

Jones, George J., and Sleman, E. F., *History in Biography*, Boston, Heath, 1939.

Jones, Howard Mumford, "Methods in Contemporary Biography," *English Journal*, January-February 1932.

King, H. R., "Biography and Curiosity," *Life and Letters*, August 1934.

Larg, David G., *André Maurois*, London, Shaylor, 1931.

Lee, Sir Sidney, *Principles of Biography*, New York, Macmillan, 1911.

Lehman, B. H., "The Art of Lytton Strachey" in *Essays in Criticism* by Members of the Department of English, University of California, Berkeley, 1929.

Lockitt, Charles H., ed., *Biography of Today*, New York, Longmans, 1938.

Longaker, Mark, *English Biography in the Eighteenth Century*, 1931; *Contemporary Biography*, 1934, Philadelphia, University of Pennsylvania Press.

Loveman, Amy, "The Art of Biography," *Saturday Review of Literature*, March 17, 1934.

Ludwig, Emil, Introduction to *Genius and Character*, New York, Harcourt, Brace, 1927; *Gifts of Life: A Retrospect*, Boston, Little, Brown, 1931. Translated from the German.

MacCarthy, Desmond, "Modern Biography," *Life and Letters*, July 1, 1928; "Lytton Strachey as a Biographer," *Life and Letters*, March 1932.

Mackenzie, Compton, "Modern Biography" in *Literature in My Time*, Toronto, Ryerson, 1936.

Macy, John, "The New Biography," *English Journal*, May 1928.

Malone, Dumas, "The Intellectual Melting Pot," *American Scholar*, Autumn 1935.

Maurois, André, *Aspects of Biography*, New York, Appleton, 1929; "The Modern Biographer," *Yale Review*, January 1928; "The Tales Dead Men Tell: A Biographer's Difficulties in Weighing Historical Evidence," *Bookman* (New York), June 1929.

Mayer, Frederick P., "The Biographical Mania," *Virginia Quarterly Review*, April 1929.

Merrill, D. K., *The Development of American Biography*, Portland (Maine), Southworth, 1932.

Metcalf, John C., ed., *The Stream of English Biography*, New York, Century, 1930.

Mumford, Lewis, "Biographies," front matter of *Atlantic Monthly*, December 1929; "The Task of Modern Biography," *English Journal*, January 1934.

Myers, Clara L., ed., *Readings in Biography*, New York, Macmillan, 1931.

Nicolson, Harold, *The Development of English Biography*, New York, Harcourt, Brace, 1928; "How I Write Biography," *Saturday Review of Literature*, May 26, 1934; "Biographies Old and New," *Living Age*, May 1937.

Notestein, Wallace, "History and the Biographer," *Yale Review*, March 1933.

O'Neill, Edward H., *A History of American Biography, 1800-1935*, Philadelphia, University of Pennsylvania Press, 1935; "Modern American Biography," *North American Review*, December 1935.

Pearson, Hesketh, *Ventilations: Being Biographical Asides*, Philadelphia, Lippincott, 1930.

Ponsonby, Arthur, "Biographies" in *Casual Observations*, London, Allen and Unwin, 1930.

*Revaluations: Studies in Biography*, Oxford, Oxford University Press, 1931. By various authors.

Saintsbury, George, "Biography: Modern Developments" in *The Encyclopaedia Britannica*.

Schindler, Margaret C., "Fictitious Biography," *American Historical Review*, July 1937.

Sitwell, Osbert, "On the Belittlement of the Great" in *Penny Foolish*, New York, Macmillan, 1935.

Smith, Robert M., ed., *The Book of Biography*, New York, Doubleday, 1930.

Smyth, Charles, "A Note on Historical Biography and Mr. Strachey," *Criterion*, July 1929.

Squire, J. C., "Biography" in *Flowers of Speech*, London, Allen, 1935.

Stauffer, Donald A., *English Biography Before 1700*, Cambridge, Harvard University Press, 1930.

Stephen, Leslie, "On Biography," *National Review*, August 1933.

Stillman, Clara G., "English Biography," *Hound and Horn*, Winter 1934.

Strachey, Lytton, Preface to *Eminent Victorians*, Garden City, 1918.

Stuart, Duane R., *Epochs of Greek and Roman Biography*, Berkeley, California, 1928.

Symonds, A. J. A., "Tradition in Biography" in *Tradition and Experiment in Present-Day Literature*, New York, Oxford, 1929.

Thayer, W. R., *The Art of Biography*, New York, Scribner, 1920.

Tozzer, A. M., "Biography and Biology," *American Anthropologist*, July 1933.

Trueblood, C. K., "Biography," *Dial*, August 1927.

Wallis, N. Hardy, "Biography, Its Use and Abuse" in *The Ethics of Criticism and Other Essays*, London, Chapman and Hall, 1924.

Ward, A. C., "Biography" in *Foundations of English Prose*, London, Bell, 1931.

Ward, Wilfrid P., "Candour in Biography" in *Problems and Persons*, New York, Longmans, 1903.

Werner, M. R., "The Biography Rush," *Nation*, February 28, 1934.

Williams, O., "The Subject of Present-Day Biography," *National Review*, May 1933.

Woolf, Virginia, "The Art of Biography," *Atlantic Monthly*, April 1939.
Wyatt, E. C., "The Drama of Biography," *Catholic World*, October 1938.


## ON AUTOBIOGRAPHY

Baird, Theodore, ed., *The First Years*, New York, Farrar and Rinehart, 1935. Revised ed.
Bates, E. Stuart, *Inside Out: An Introduction to Autobiography*, New York, Sheridan House, 1937.
Belloc, Hilaire, "Autobiography" in *Conversations with a Cat*, New York, Harper, 1931.
Birrell, Augustine, "A Few Warning Words to Would-Be Autobiographers" in *Et Cetera*, Toronto, Musson, 1930.
*Book of Great Autobiographies*, New York, Doubleday, 1934.
Bradford, Gamaliel, "Biography by Mirror" in *Biography and the Human Heart*, Boston, Houghton Mifflin, 1932.
Burr, Anna Robeson, *The Autobiography: A Critical and Comparative Study*, Boston, Houghton Mifflin, 1909.
Cantwell, Robert, "Autobiographers: American Intellectuals," *New Republic*, April 27, 1938.
Chesterton, G. K., "About Widows" in *As I Was Saying*, New York, Dodd, Mead, 1936.
Clark, Arthur M., *Autobiography: Its Genesis and Phases*, Edinburgh, Oliver and Boyd, 1935.
Colum, Mary M., "Personality and Autobiography," *Forum*, February 1935.
*Greatest Autobiographies of All Times*, New York, Tudor, c. 1936.
Holt, E., "The New Autobiography," *Bookman* (London), October 1931.
Jha, Aramantha, *Some Autobiographies*, London, Oxford University Press, 1937.
Jones, P. M., "A Paradox of Literary Introspection," *London Mercury*, September 1935.
McDowell, Arthur S., "Autobiography as an Art" in *Ruminations*, Boston, Houghton Mifflin, 1925.
Murchison, C. A., ed., *The History of Psychology in Autobiography*, Worcester (Mass.), Clark University Press, 1930-36.
Repplier, Agnes, "The Happiness of Writing an Autobiography" in *Under Dispute*, Boston, Houghton Mifflin, 1924.
Squire, J. C., "New Style of Memoir" in *Essays at Large*, New York, Doran, 1922.
Taft, Henry W., "Formal Autobiographies and Informal Exploitations" in *Opinions, Literary and Otherwise*, New York, Macmillan, 1934.
Tickner, F. W., ed., *An Anthology of Modern Memoirs*, Toronto, Nelson, 1936.
Wilkinson, C., "Confessional," *London Mercury*, October 1931.